THE SAGE HANDBOOK
of
HEALTH PSYCHOLOGY

Advisory Board

THE SAGE HANDBOOK
of
HEALTH PSYCHOLOGY

Edited by
STEPHEN SUTTON, ANDREW BAUM
and MARIE JOHNSTON

SAGE Publications
London • Thousand Oaks • New Delhi

Editorial Arrangement and Editors' Preface
  © Stephen Sutton, Andrew Baum and
  Marie Johnston 2005
Chapter 1 © Edward P. Sarafino 2005
Chapter 2 © Reiner Rugulies, Birgit Aust and
  S. Leonard Syme 2005
Chapter 3 © Brent N. Henderson and
  Andrew Baum 2005
Chapter 4 © Stephen Sutton 2005
Chapter 5 © Keith J. Petrie and James W.
  Pennebaker 2005
Chapter 6 © Richard J. Contrada and
  Tanya M. Goyal 2005
Chapter 7 © Andrew Steptoe and
  Susan Ayers 2005

Chapter 8 © Howard Leventhal, Ethan Halm,
  Carol Horowitz, Elaine A. Leventhal and
  Gozde Ozakinci 2005
Chapter 9 © Simon Murphy and
  Paul Bennett 2005
Chapter 10 © Theresa M. Marteau and
  John Weinman 2005
Chapter 11 © Stan Maes and Sandra N.
  Boersma 2005
Chapter 12 © David P. French, Lucy Yardley
  and Stephen Sutton 2005
Chapter 13 © Marie Johnston, David P. French,
  Debbie Bonetti and Derek W. Johnston 2005
Chapter 14 © Cynthia D. Belar and
  Teresa McIntyre 2005

First published 2004

SAGE Publications Ltd
1 Oliver's Yard
55 City Road
London EC1Y 1SP

SAGE Publications Inc.
2455 Teller Road
Thousand Oaks, California 91320

SAGE Publications India Pvt Ltd
B-42, Panchsheel Enclave
Post Box 4109
New Delhi 110 017

British Library Cataloguing in Publication data

A catalogue record for this book is available from
the British Library

ISBN 0-7619-6849-0

Library of Congress Control Number available

Typeset by C&M Digitals (P) Ltd., Chennai, India
Printed in Great Britain by Cromwell Press, Trowbridge, Wiltshire

Contents

List of Contributors

Birgit Aust is Senior Researcher at the National Institute of Occupational Health in Copenhagen, Denmark. She got her Diploma in Sociology from the Free University of Berlin and her DrPH from the University of Bielefeld, Germany, and was a postdoctoral research fellow at the University of California, Berkeley. Her main research interests are workplace intervention studies to promote health and reduce the risk of illness. Further research interests include the evaluation of patient satisfaction and medical guidelines. She is the author of a monograph on worksite health promotion and a handbook on promoting health and preventing diseases in bus drivers, and author and co-author of several articles and book chapters on psychosocial factors and health.

Susan Ayers is a senior lecturer in health psychology at the University of Sussex and previously worked as a lecturer at St George's Hospital Medical School, University of London. She primarily teaches medical students about health psychology and communication skills. Her research interests include stress and coping in healthcare settings, particularly anxiety and stress disorders following health events. She is also interested in psychological factors in obstetrics and gynaecology.

Andrew Baum is Professor of Psychiatry and Psychology at the University of Pittsburgh and Deputy Director for Cancer Control and Population Sciences at the University of Pittsburgh Cancer Institute, and is primarily responsible for oversight and coordination of cancer control and prevention research activities. As such, he has fostered projects to better understand the basis of individual susceptibility to cancer; the conditions that promote cancer development; and the social and behavioral barriers to effective prevention, early detection, and treatment of cancer. His current research interests include the biobehavioral aspects of cancer and chronic illness, chronic stress and illness, and psychoneuroimmunology. Dr. Baum was awarded his PhD in Psychology from the State University of New York at Stony Brook in 1974. Dr. Baum has authored or co-authored more than 150 scientific articles, chapters, and books, and is editor of the *Journal of Applied Social Psychology* and *Journal of Applied BioBehavioral Research*.

Cynthia D. Belar received her PhD in psychology from Ohio University in 1974 after an internship at Duke University Medical Center. She is currently the Executive Director of the Education Directorate of the American Psychological Association (APA) and Professor in the Department of Clinical and Health Psychology at the University of Florida Health Science Center. She has published numerous articles and chapters on competencies in professional practice, including those with a focus on clinical psychology, clinical health psychology, managed health care, primary care, and scientist-practitioner models of education and training.

Paul Bennett has worked both as an academic and clinical health psychologist in the Universities of Cardiff and Bristol and their health care Trusts. He presently holds a chair in clinical psychology at the University of Wales, Swansea. He has over 100 publications, among them four books, including *An Introduction to Clinical Health Psychology* and *Psychology and Health Promotion* (with Simon Murphy).

Sandra N. Boersma, PhD, is affiliated to the section of Medical and Health Psychology at Leiden University, The Netherlands, where she also carried out her doctoral research. She has experience with various types of interventions for chronic patients. Her current research focuses on determinants of quality of life in various patient groups from a self-regulation perspective.

Debbie Bonetti is a research fellow at the University of Aberdeen. She received her BA from the University of Sydney and her PhD from the University of St Andrews in 2000. Her publications reflect her main area of interest, which is the application of health psychology models in health service research. She is particularly interested in developing and evaluating interventions to enhance health outcomes and developing measures using theoretical frameworks for use in practical situations. Her current work is conducted with research groups in the Universities of Aberdeen, Dundee, Newcastle, and Ottawa.

Richard J. Contrada is Professor of Psychology at Rutgers University. He has been on the Rutgers faculty since 1986, when he completed a postdoctoral fellowship in Medical Psychology at the Uniformed Services University of the Health Sciences. His major area of interest is cardiovascular health psychology and he has contributed several dozen articles on this topic. Other research interests include health effects of personality, religious involvement, and physiologic responses to stress. He is co-editor of *Self, social identity, and physical health: Interdisciplinary explorations.*

David P. French joined the School of Sport and Exercise Science at the University of Birmingham in 2003, upon completion of a Wellcome Trust Fellowship at the University of Cambridge. He received his PhD from the Guy's, King's and St Thomas's School of Medicine, University of London, in 1999. His current research concerns risk communication, assessment of beliefs, and the use of psycho-logical theories to predict and influence health behaviour. A theme that cuts across much of this work is the extent to which psychological phenomena are products of the research methods employed.

Tanya M. Goyal is a clinical associate in the Division of Medical Psychology at Duke University Medical Center. She completed her graduate education in Clinical

Psychology at Rutgers University (PhD, 2003). Her current research focuses on the impact of depression and other psychosocial factors on cardiovascular disease outcomes.

Ethan A. Halm, MD, MPH, is an Associate Professor in the Departments of Medicine and Health Policy at the Mount Sinai School of Medicine in New York City. He is a practicing general internist, clinical epidemiologist and health services researcher whose research focuses on measuring overuse, underuse and misuse in health care, and developing strategies for changing physician, patient and organizational behavior. He is actively involved in examining self-regulation beliefs and self-management behaviors and their relation to outcomes among inner city adults with asthma. Dr Halm received his medical degree from the Yale School of Medicine. He received a master's degree in public health from Harvard University. He completed an internal medicine residency at the University of California, San Francisco, and a general medicine/clinical epidemiology fellowship at the Massachusetts General Hospital.

Brent N. Henderson is an Assistant Professor in the Behavioral Medicine and Oncology Program at the University of Pittsburgh. He received his PhD from the University of Texas Southwestern Medical Center in 1998. His research and clinical work is centered on uncovering and intervening in biobehavioral processes related to cancer onset or progression. He also studies the usefulness of psychological strategies to promote adjustment to cancer among cancer patients and their families.

Carol R. Horowitz is an Assistant Professor in the Departments of Health Policy and Medicine at Mount Sinai School of Medicine in New York City. She has an MD from Cornell University and an MPH from the University of Washington, where she was a Robert Wood Johnson Foundation Clinical Scholar. She currently practices and teaches primary care internal medicine. She conducts multimethod (qualitative and quantitative) research projects to understand the reasons for and to address health disparities among persons of color with common chronic conditions, such as diabetes, hypertension and heart failure. She uses community-based participatory research methods to allow for the persons in communities being studied to partner in the research, and to receive immediate benefits from its results.

Derek W. Johnston is Professor of Psychology in the University of Aberdeen. He is a graduate of Aberdeen who obtained his PhD from the University of Hull and subsequently worked in the Universities of Oxford, London and St Andrews before returning to Aberdeen in 2003. He conducts research on the psychology and psychobiology of cardiovascular disease and psychological interventions to improve health. He has written over 120 papers and chapters, and co-written or edited two books. He is currently Chair elect of the Division of Health Psychology of the British Psychological Society.

Marie Johnston joined the University of Aberdeen in 2003 as Professor in Health Psychology in the School of Psychology and the Institute of Applied Health

Sciences. She is a graduate of the Universities of Aberdeen (BSc) and Hull (PhD) and previously held appointments in the Universities of St Andrews, London and Oxford. Her research focuses in two areas: behavioural factors in disability in chronic diseases such as stroke and arthritis; and the behaviour of health professionals in delivering evidence-base clinical care. She is a previous President of the European Health Psychology Society.

Elaine A. Leventhal is Professor of Medicine, Department of Medicine, Robert Wood Johnson School of Medicine, and Director of the Gerontological Institute at Robert Wood Johnson Medical School, funded by the Robert Wood Johnson Foundation. She holds a PhD from Yale University in Developmental Genetics and is a graduate of the University of Wisconsin School of Medicine, completing her Internal Medicine training at UW, Mt Sinai Medical Center, Milwaukee and her Geriatric Fellowship training at the William S. Middleton Memorial Veterans Medical Center, Madison, Wisconsin. She is a fellow of the American College of Physicians, and the Gerontological Society of America. She is a past President of the Academy of Behavioral Medicine Research and currently a member of their executive board. Her research interests include defining risks for frailty in the ambulatory elderly, exploring the role of immune competency in health and chronic illness, and studying health and illness behaviors that affect health care utilization. She has also looked at elder-specific treatment for substance abuse and the identification and treatment of geriatric depression in the primary care setting.

Howard Leventhal is Board of Governors Professor of Health Psychology at Rutgers University and a member of the Institute of Medicine of the National Academy of Sciences. His work spans topics including the 'role of affect in health and illness behavior', 'illness cognition' or common-sense models of illnesses, and treatments for chronic illnesses such as hypertension, congestive heart failure, asthma, and diabetes; the effects of self-appraisals and self-management strategies on health outcomes; and expertise in identifying and sharing implicit illness models. Most recently he co-edited *Self regulation of health and illness* with Linda Cameron.

Stan Maes, PhD, is Professor of Health Psychology at Leiden University, The Netherlands. He was Co-founder and first President of the European Health Psychology Society (1986–1992), President of the Health Psychology Division of the International Association of Applied Psychology (1990–1994), and President of the International Society of Health Psychology Research (1998–2002). He has over 250 scientific publications including five books concerning health promotion and interventions in patients with chronic diseases. His current work focuses on the development of a new model for the prediction of health behaviour (the health behaviour goal model) and an extension of traditional stress-coping models applied to chronic illnesses from a self-regulation perspective.

Theresa M. Marteau, PhD, CPsychol, is Professor of Health Psychology and Director of the Psychology and Genetics Research Group at King's College,

London. Over the past 15 years she has been conducting research on psychological aspects of health risk assessment. The work has covered genetic testing in pregnancy, adulthood and childhood, as well as population-based screening programmes. The conditions studied include heart disease, cervical, breast and bowel cancer, and cystic fibrosis. The aim of this research is to understand responses as a first step towards evaluating different methods of communicating information to promote understanding, reduce emotional distress and enhance health promoting behaviours. She has published over 150 peer-reviewed articles in this and related areas and is co-editor of *The troubled helix* (1996, paperback 1999), a book reviewing the psychological implications of the new human genetics. This research is funded by research grants from The Wellcome Trust, The Medical Research Council, the National Health Service Research and Development Programme, and the European Union.

Teresa Mendonça McIntyre, PhD is Professor of Health Psychology at the University of Minho, Portugal, where she co-ordinates the graduate program in Health Psychology and the psychology curricula at the Minho Medical School. She was a Fulbright student in the US where she received her PhD in Clinical Psychology (Georgia State University) and was an advanced fellow in Behavioral Medicine (Harvard Medical School) before returning to Portugal in 1991. Her research interests include gender and cultural issues in health and illness, occupational stress in health professionals, psychological trauma and health, health promotion at the school level and outcome evaluation. She is the President of the European Health Psychology Society, is Book Review Editor for the journal *Psychology and Health* and is on the editorial board of *The European Psychologist*. She has edited and co-edited several clinical and health psychology books, such as *Health Psychology* and *The Psychological Impact of War Trauma on Civilians*, and has published internationally in this domain both in Europe and the United States.

Simon Murphy, PhD, CPsychol, is a senior research fellow at Cardiff University, Institute of Society, Health and Ethics. His main research interests are understanding and predicting health related behaviours, the evaluation of theoretically driven health promotion interventions, health inequalities and public health. He completed his PhD at the University of East London on psychological approaches to curriculum based HIV education. He then spent a number of years working as a senior researcher for the health service, examining health needs and public health initiatives and as a Principal Lecturer in Health Psychology at UWE, Bristol. He has published extensively on health promotion and is co-author of a text in this area.

Gozde Ozakinci is a doctoral candidate at Rutgers – The State University of New Jersey. She holds an MSc from University College London in Health Psychology and is a graduate of Bogazici University, Turkey. Her research interests include the role of affect in health and illness behavior; psychological reactions to predictive genetic testing; effects of self-appraisals and self-management strategies on health outcomes; understanding Gulf War related physical and psychological reactions; and predictors of STD/AIDS preventive behaviours in Turkey.

James W. Pennebaker is Professor of Psychology at the University of Texas at Austin, where he received his PhD in 1977. He has been on the faculty at the University of Virginia, Southern Methodist University, and since 1997 at The University of Texas. He and his students are exploring the links between traumatic experiences, disclosure, and health. His studies find that physician use, medical costs, and biological markers of stress can be reduced by simple writing exercises. His most recent research focuses on the role that language plays in reflecting and changing social, personality, and biological processes. Author or editor of eight books and over 150 articles, Pennebaker has received numerous awards and honors.

Keith J. Petrie is an Associate Professor at the University of Auckland in New Zealand. He initially trained and worked as a clinical psychologist before moving into health psychology, which has now become his primary research and clinical area. His research interests are primarily in how patients' perceptions of their illness and symptoms influence their adjustment and coping with disease and injury. He also does research work in psychoneuroimmunology and fatigue in international airline pilots. He is co-editor of the book *Perceptions of health and illness* and currently co-editor of the journal *Psychology and Health.*

Reiner Rugulies is Senior Researcher at the National Institute of Occupational Health in Copenhagen, Denmark. He got his Diploma in Psychology and his PhD from the University of Bielefeld, Germany, and his Master of Public Health from the University of California, Berkeley, where he was also a postdoctoral research fellow. His main research interests are psychological and social determinants of health and illness, especially at the workplace, and pathways that link the social environment, psychological processes and physiological changes. He is the author of a monograph on the psychosocial dimension of coronary heart disease and the author and co-author of several articles and book chapters on psychosocial factors and health.

Edward P. Sarafino received his PhD from the University of Colorado and has been a faculty member with the Department of Psychology at The College of New Jersey for more than 30 years. His areas of scholarship have combined health, developmental, and behavioral psychology, particularly with respect to the study of asthma. In addition to publishing dozens of research articles and chapters, he is the author of six books, including the text *Health psychology: Biopsychosocial interactions,* which is currently in its fourth edition.

Andrew Steptoe is British Heart Foundation Professor of Psychology in the Department of Epidemiology and Public Health at University College London, UK. He graduated from the University of Cambridge in 1972, and completed his doctorate at Oxford University in 1975. He then worked in the Department of Psychology at St. George's Hospital Medical School in the University of London until 2000, becoming Professor in 1988. He was President of the Society for Psychosomatic Research (UK) from 1983–1985, and of the International Society of

Behavioral Medicine (1994–1996). He was founding Editor (with Jane Wardle) of the *British Journal of Health Psychology*, and has been an associate editor of *Psychophysiology*, the *Annals of Behavioral Medicine*, the *British Journal of Clinical Psychology*, and the *Journal of Psychosomatic Research*. He is the author/editor of 14 books including *Psychological Factors in Cardiovascular Disorders*, *Health Care and Human Behaviour*, *Psychosocial Processes and Health* and *Genius and the Mind*.

Stephen Sutton is Professor of Behavioural Science at the University of Cambridge and Visiting Professor of Psychology at the University of Bergen, Norway. He studied social psychology at the London School of Economics and computer science at City University. He received his PhD from the University of London in 1981 for research on the effects of fear appeals. Before moving to Cambridge, he held posts at the Institute of Psychiatry and University College London. His current research programme focuses on risk communication and behaviour change. He has a particular interest in the methodological issues surrounding the specification and testing of theories of health behaviour, and is a consultant to the US National Cancer Institute's 'Improving Theories' project.

S. Leonard Syme is Emeritus Professor of Epidemiology at the School of Public Health at the University of California in Berkeley. He has studied the social determinants of health and disease for many years and is now heavily involved in developing community interventions to prevent disease and promote health. His most recent publication on this topic is an Institute of Medicine volume on *Promoting health: Intervention strategies from social and behavioral research*.

John Weinman is Professor of Psychology as applied to Medicine at the Guy's, King's and St Thomas's School of Medicine in the University of London. He is a Fellow of the British Psychological Society and has played a major role in the development of academic and professional health psychology in the UK. His main research areas are cognition and health, communication and decision-making in health care, and self-regulation and self-management in chronic illness. He was the founding editor of *Psychology and Health: An International Journal* and has edited and written a large number of books, chapters and research papers in the field of health psychology.

Lucy Yardley is Professor of Health Psychology at the University of Southampton. Her current research focuses on chronic illness (especially dizziness and falling) and attitudes and adherence to treatment and rehabilitation, with an emphasis on empowering people in the community to take control over their illness and treatment. She has expertise in using and combining a wide range of both quantitative and qualitative methods, and has championed the use of qualitative approaches in psychology as editor of *Material discourses in health and illness* (1997) and co-editor of *Qualitative research in psychology* (2003).

Editors' Preface

Health psychology is still a relatively young discipline, but interest and activity in the field are expanding rapidly, as indicated, for example, by the number of specialist journals, master's level courses, introductory texts and, indeed, handbooks of health psychology. So why produce another handbook? Both Sage as publishers, and we as editors, felt that there was a pressing need for a higher-level text providing comprehensive and in-depth treatment of the field and aimed at final year undergraduate psychology students, master's students, and specialist researchers, teachers and practitioners in the field. The *Sage Handbook of Health Psychology* therefore aims to provide a comprehensive, authoritative, detailed, state-of the-art picture of health psychology at the beginning of the twenty-first century. We wanted to do this in a single self-contained volume that would be affordable to individuals rather than a multi-volume handbook aimed at the library market. We were particularly keen to organize the *Handbook* on *psychological* lines rather than by diseases and conditions. However, we struggled to find a logical way of carving up the field. The nature of the subject matter is such that it does not naturally fall into discrete subtopics: everything is related to everything else. We devised a number of organizational schemes, but they all seemed unsatisfactory and arbitrary. Then one of us (MJ) came up with the idea of basing the *Handbook* on the British Psychological Society's core curriculum or 'knowledge base'. Although no less arbitrary than other schemes, this had the advantage of grounding the content and organization of the *Handbook* in the reality of how the subject is taught.

The result is 14 substantial chapters by 31 contributors, amounting to over a quarter of a million words. We did minimal content editing of the chapters, following the principle that if you ask leading experts to write about their pet topics, they are bound to produce something good, and we tolerated departures from the recommended chapter length. We are delighted with the final product.

We would like to thank Naomi Meredith and Michael Carmichael of Sage for their encouragement and patience, members of the International Editorial Advisory Board for their advice and help, particularly in the early stages of the project, the contributors for producing such fine chapters, and Karen Hinkins for her painstaking work in editing the chapters for style and consistency.

Stephen Sutton, Andrew Baum, Marie Johnston
December 2003

1

Context and Perspectives in Health Psychology

EDWARD P. SARAFINO

INTRODUCTION

Health psychology is a young discipline, and its knowledge is growing rapidly. In the opening chapter, we will examine the context and perspectives of this field by dividing the material into five sections. In the following order, these sections will:

1 discuss the concepts of health and illness and how patterns of illness vary around the world and across time
2 consider how people across history have viewed the roles of the body and the mind in the development of disease and some evidence that psychosocial processes are involved
3 describe several areas of research and application in health psychology, along with a sampling of associated theories and approaches used in the discipline
4 examine the relationships of health psychology to other disciplines
5 discuss the impact of sociocultural, gender, and developmental factors in health and illness.

THE CHANGING FACE OF HEALTH AND ILLNESS

People commonly think about health in terms of an absence of (1) subjective symptoms of disease or injury, such as pain or nausea, or (2) objective signs that the body is not functioning properly, such as measured high blood pressure (Birren & Zarit, 1985; Thoresen, 1984). But illness and wellness are not entirely separate concepts: they overlap, with increasing degrees of wellness and of illness varying along a continuum with a neutral status in the middle. At the opposite ends are optimal wellness and death (Sarafino, 2002). Thus, the term *health* refers to a range of positive states of physical, mental, and social wellbeing – not just the absence of injury or disease – characterized by variations in healthful signs and lifestyles. In states of illness or injury, destructive processes produce characteristic signs, symptoms, or disabilities.

People in developed, industrialized nations today live longer, on the average, than in the past, and they suffer from a different pattern of illnesses. For example, during the seventeenth, eighteenth, and nineteenth centuries, people in North America suffered and died mainly from dietary and infectious diseases (Grob, 1983). By the end of the nineteenth century, deaths from infectious diseases had decreased sharply. For instance, in a 25-year period around the turn of the century in the United States, the death rate from tuberculosis declined by about 60 per cent. Although medical advances were responsible for some of these changes, the decreases occurred long before the introduction of effective vaccines and medications (Grob, 1983; Leventhal, Prohaska & Hirschman, 1985). The main cause of these changes was probably preventive measures such as improved personal hygiene, better nutrition, and public health innovations, such as in water purification and sewage treatment. Fewer deaths occurred from dietary and infectious diseases in the United States and other developed nations because fewer people contracted them. But preventive measures have not been adopted as widely in less advanced societies. As a result, infectious diseases continue to be the main causes of death in most of the world today (World Health Organization, 1999).

The patterns of illness that afflict people have continued to change during the twentieth century, particularly in developed nations, and the average life expectancy has increased dramatically (World Health Organization, 1999). For instance, at the turn of the century in the United States, babies' life expectancy at birth was about 48 years (US Department of Health and Human Services, 1987); today it is 76 years (US Bureau of the Census, 1999). Much of the poor life expectancy at birth many years ago resulted from the very high death rate among children then. Those who survived to the age of 20 years could expect to live to nearly 63 years of age. The death rate for American children is much lower today, and only a small difference exists between the expected life spans of newborns and 20-year-olds.

In developed countries today, the main health problems and causes of death are *chronic diseases*, that is, degenerative illnesses that develop or persist over a long period of time. Three chronic diseases – heart disease, cancer,

and stroke – account for about two-thirds of all deaths in developed nations (World Health Organization, 1999). These are diseases that tend to afflict elderly people. Before the twentieth century, these diseases caused a much smaller proportion of deaths partly because fewer people lived to an age when they would be at high risk for contracting chronic diseases (US Department of Health and Human Services, 1982). The causes of death differ greatly at different points in the life span. In the United States, for example, the leading cause of death in children and adolescents is not an illness; it is accidental injury (US Bureau of the Census, 1999). The next two most frequent causes of death in childhood are diseases, but in adolescence they are homicide and suicide.

HISTORICAL VIEWPOINTS: MIND AND BODY IN DISEASE PROCESSES

The best educated people thousands of years ago probably believed that mystical forces, such as evil spirits, caused physical and mental illness (Stone, 1979). Because there are no written records from those times, researchers have inferred this conclusion from indirect evidence, such as the discovery of ancient skulls in several areas of the world with coin-size circular holes in them that could not have been battle wounds. These holes were probably made for superstitious reasons in a procedure called trephination, to allow illness-causing demons to leave the head, for instance. In many cultures around the world today, large numbers of people still believe that mystical forces have a major impact on health and illness.

The Mind–Body Problem

Philosophers of ancient Greece between 500 and 300 BC produced the earliest written ideas about physiology, disease processes, and the mind. Many leading philosophers believed that the mind and body were separate entities (Marx & Hillix, 1963; Schneider & Tarshis, 1975). The body – one's physical being, including the skin, muscles, bones, heart, and brain – was thought to function independently from the mind. Although it is possible to distinguish between the mind and the body conceptually, an important question is whether they actually function independently. The issue of their relationship is called the mind–body problem.

Hippocrates, often called 'the Father of Medicine', proposed that people get sick when the mixture of four body fluids called humors (in biology, the term 'humor' refers to plant or animal fluid) is faulty (Stone, 1979). When the mixture of these humors is balanced or harmonious, people are in a state of health. The mind was considered to have little or no relationship to the body and its state of health. According to Hippocrates, people could achieve humoral balance by eating a good diet and avoiding excesses. Galen was a highly respected physician and writer of the second century AD who was born in Greece, practiced in Rome, and believed generally in the role of humors in health and the mind–body split. By dissecting animals of many species and examining their brains and other internal organs, he discovered that illnesses can involve pathology in specific parts of the body and different diseases have different effects (Stone, 1979).

Following the fall of the Roman Empire in the fifth century AD, knowledge and culture advanced slowly in Europe throughout the Middle Ages, which lasted about a thousand years. Galen's views on physiology and disease processes were favored for most of this time. The influence of the Church in slowing the advancement of medical knowledge during the Middle Ages was enormous, particularly through its prohibition against dissection of human and animal cadavers (Marx & Hillix, 1963). Religious ideas shaped views about the cause of illness, and the belief in demons became strong again (Sarason & Sarason, 1984). Sickness was seen as God's punishment for evil acts. As a result, the Church came to control medical practice, often with priests treating the ill by torturing the body to drive out evil spirits. In the thirteenth century, new ideas about the mind–body problem emerged. St Thomas Aquinas rejected the view that the mind and body are separate, and his

position renewed interest in the issue and influenced later philosophers (Leahey, 1987).

During the Renaissance of the fourteenth and fifteenth centuries, Europe saw a rebirth of inquiry, culture, and politics. Scholars began to focus less on religious doctrine and more on logic and empirical issues and methods in their search for truth (Leahey, 1987). They proposed that differing perspectives can lead to different views of truth. These ideas brought about important changes in philosophy once the scientific revolution began after 1600. The seventeenth-century philosopher and mathematician René Descartes probably had the greatest influence on scientific thought of any philosopher in history (Schneider & Tarshis, 1975). Like the Greeks, he thought the mind and body were separate entities, but he proposed that the mind and body could communicate through the pineal gland in the brain (Leahey, 1987). His belief that animals have no soul and that the soul in humans leaves the body at death was eventually accepted by the Church, which meant that dissection could be used again (Engel, 1977; Marx & Hillix, 1963)

Knowledge in science and medicine grew quickly in the eighteenth and nineteenth centuries in Europe and North America. The advent of the microscope and the use of dissection in autopsies enabled scientists to learn how the body functioned and to discover that microorganisms cause certain diseases. With this knowledge, they were able to reject the humoral theory of illness and propose new theories (Stone, 1979). The development of antiseptics and anesthesia in the mid nineteenth century improved medical treatment, which enhanced the reputation of physicians and hospitals and people's trust in the ability of doctors to heal. These changes and the belief that the mind and body are separate gave rise to a new way to conceptualize health and disease processes. This approach – called the *biomedical model* – proposes that all physical disorders can be explained by disturbances in physiological processes, which result from injury, biochemical imbalances, bacterial or viral infection, and the like (Engel, 1977; Leventhal et al., 1985). The biomedical model assumes that disease is an affliction of the body; psychological and social processes are of little relevance. This viewpoint became widely accepted during the nineteenth and twentieth centuries and still represents the dominant view in Western medicine today.

Psychosocial Processes in Health and Illness

Using the biomedical model as a guide, researchers have made enormous medical advances, such as in developing vaccines, antibiotics, and other effective medical procedures. But there are two reasons to view the model as incomplete (Sarafino, 2002). First, people can act to prevent or detect in early stages the development of illness, and psychosocial processes govern these actions. The need to find ways to improve the practice of these measures is clearly shown by the escalating costs of medical care worldwide. Although chronic diseases are a principal cause of death and disability around the world, particularly in developed nations, they can be prevented or delayed. Many individuals now are more aware of signs and symptoms of illness, more motivated to take care of their health, and better able to afford visits to physicians than in the past. Second, there is now considerable evidence that personality processes play a role in health and illness. The role of people's health habits and personality differences in illness is not included in the biomedical model (Engel, 1977, 1980).

Health habits and illness

Earlier we saw that the occurrence of infectious diseases declined sharply in the late nineteenth century chiefly because of preventive measures, such as improving nutrition and personal hygiene. These measures involved changes in people's *health habits* – their usual health-related behaviors, such as the types of foods they consume – which become part of their lifestyles, or everyday patterns of behavior. People's lives often contain many risk factors for illness and injury. Characteristics or conditions that are associated with the development of a disease or injury are called *risk*

factors for that health problem. Some risk factors are biological, such as having inherited certain genes. Others are behavioral: for example, people who smoke cigarettes are at higher risk than nonsmokers for the two leading causes of death in the United States, cancer and heart disease, and other illnesses. Other risk factors for cancer and heart disease include eating diets high in saturated fat (behavioral) and having a family history of the disease (biological). Behavioral risk factors for the fifth leading cause of death, accidents (including motor vehicle), are alcohol or drug use, driving vehicles too fast, and not using seat belts (McGinnis, 1994; US Bureau of the Census, 1999). Although risk factors are associated with a health problem, they do not necessarily cause it. For example, being poor is a risk factor for cancer (Levy, 1985), but it does not cause the disease – at least, not directly.

People live longer if they practice *health behaviors*, that is, activities to maintain or improve their current good health, obtain a diagnosis or remedy when feeling ill, or carry out a program to recover from an illness or injury. Belloc and Breslow (1972) studied the impact of personal lifestyles on future health, surveying nearly 7,000 adults about their patterns of sleep, eating breakfast, eating between meals, maintaining an appropriate weight, smoking cigarettes, drinking alcohol, and getting physical activity. A follow-up 9½ years later revealed that the greater the number of health behaviors practiced, the lower the percentage of these people who had died, and the impact of these lifestyle differences increased as individuals got older after middle age.

Personality and illness

The term *personality* refers to a person's cognitive, affective, or behavioral tendencies that are fairly stable across time and situations. Researchers have found that personality traits are linked to health. For example, low levels of conscientiousness in childhood and poor mental health in adulthood are related to dying at earlier ages from diseases, such as heart disease and cancer (Friedman et al., 1995). And individuals whose personalities include high levels of anxiety, depression, anger/hostility, or pessimism appear to be at risk of developing heart disease and several other illnesses (Everson et al., 1996; Friedman & Booth-Kewley, 1987; Scheier & Bridges, 1995). These four emotions are reactions that often occur when people experience stress, such as when they have more work to do than they think they can finish or suffer a tragedy. Not only are optimistic individuals less likely to become sick than people with less positive personalities, but when they are ill, they tend to recover more quickly (Reker & Wong, 1985; Scheier & Carver, 2001).

The connection between personality and illness is not a one-way street: illness can affect one's personality, too (Cohen & Rodriguez, 1995). Individuals who suffer from serious illness and disability often experience high levels of anxiety, depression, anger, and hopelessness. And as Sarason and Sarason (1984) have pointed out, even minor health problems, such as the flu or a backache, produce temporary negative thoughts and feelings. Medical patients who overcome their negative thoughts and feelings can speed their recovery.

Current Perspectives on Health and Illness

Combining psychosocial processes with the biomedical model produces a different and broader picture of how health and illness come about. This new perspective, called the *biopsychosocial model*, expands the biomedical view by adding to biological factors the role of psychological and social factors (Engel, 1977, 1980; Schwartz, 1982). This new model proposes that all three factors affect and are affected by the person's health. Engel (1980) has proposed that we can conceptualize these influences by applying the concept of 'systems'. A *system* is a dynamic entity with constituents that continuously interrelate, such as by exchanging energy, substances, and information (Bertalanffy, 1968). Thus, one's body qualifies as a system – and it includes the circulatory and nervous systems, which consist of tissues and cells. One's family is a system, too, and so are the community and society.

As an example of the biopsychosocial perspective, we can consider how a person might become severely overweight, which is a risk factor for several illnesses, including diabetes and heart disease. The body is a complex physical system that contains organs, bones, and nerves, and these are composed of tissues, which in turn consist of cells, molecules, and atoms. The body's efficient, effective, and healthful functioning depends on the way these components operate and interact with each other. Biological factors include genetic materials and processes that affect the structure and operation of these components. Inheritance is a biological factor that is known to influence weight (Allison, Heshka, Neale, Lykken & Heymsfield, 1994; Stunkard, Foch & Hrubec, 1986), perhaps through its influence on metabolism and taste sensation (Logue, 1991). Psychological factors can include cognition, emotion, and motivation. For instance, people report that they eat more when they are anxious or upset, and evidence supports the view that stress can induce eating (Arnow, Kenardy & Agras, 1992; Logue, 1991). And food-related cues, such as a waiter's description or display of a dessert, are more likely to persuade an obese person than a nonobese person to order the food (Herman, Olmstead & Polivy, 1983). Social factors include the modeling and consequences other people provide for behavior. One's social world includes family members, friends, classmates and coworkers, and people in the mass media. The role of social factors on weight can be seen in the finding that parents give more encouragement for eating and offer food more frequently to heavier children than to slimmer ones (Baranowski & Nader, 1985). Other research has found that children of overweight parents are more likely to become overweight than children of normal weight parents (Whitaker, Wright, Pepe, Seidel & Dietz, 1997), which may support the role of either genetic or social factors. The combination of biological, psychological, and social factors determines the person's likelihood of becoming overweight, and as individuals gain weight, their biological, psychological, and social processes change. In similar ways, these factors can influence whether a person will develop an illness, such as cancer or heart disease, through their effects on disease processes directly or on behaviors that increase the risk of these diseases.

Development of Professional Organizations and Functions

The view that medicine and psychology are related has a long history, dating back at least to ancient Greece. Early in the twentieth century, it became somewhat more formalized in the work of Freud, who noticed that some patients showed symptoms of physical illness, such as blindness or the loss of sensation in part of the body, without any organic disorder. He proposed that these symptoms were 'converted' from unconscious emotional conflicts and called this condition conversion hysteria (Alexander, 1950; Davison & Neale, 1998).

The need to understand conditions such as conversion hysteria led professionals to develop the first field dedicated to studying the interplay between emotional life and bodily processes. The field called *psychosomatic medicine* was formed in the 1930s in association with the National Research Council, which then published the journal *Psychosomatic Medicine* (Alexander, 1950). Its founders were mainly trained in medicine and psychoanalysis. Four years later the field organized a society that is now called the American Psychosomatic Society. For the next 30 years or so, research in psychosomatic medicine emphasized psychoanalytic interpretations for specific, real health problems, including asthma, high blood pressure, ulcers, migraine headaches, and rheumatoid arthritis. In the 1960s, psychosomatic medicine began to adopt new approaches and theories (Totman, 1982). It is a broader field today, concerned with the relationships among psychosocial factors, biological and physiological functions, and the development and course of illness (Lipowski, 1986).

Two new fields emerged in the 1970s to study the role of psychology in illness. One of these fields, *behavioral medicine*, began in association with the National Academy of Sciences. The *Journal of Behavioral Medicine* and the Society of Behavioral Medicine were then founded. The society's members come from a variety of fields, including psychology and various areas of medicine (Gentry, 1984). The field grew out of the behavioral perspective in psychology, focusing on the role of classical (or respondent) and operant conditioning in behavior. Operant and classical conditioning therapy methods had shown considerable success in helping people modify problem behaviors, such as overeating, and emotions, such as anxiety and fear (Sarafino, 2001). By the 1970s, physiological psychologists had shown that psychological events, particularly emotions, influence body functions, such as blood pressure. They had also demonstrated that people can learn to control physiological systems through biofeedback, a technique that provides information as to what a system is doing (Miller, 1978). Behavior modification approaches now include *behavioral methods* (techniques based on operant and classical conditioning) and *cognitive methods*, which are geared toward changing people's feelings and thought processes (Sarafino, 2001).

The behavioral perspective also served as an important foundation for the field of *health psychology*, which is within the discipline of psychology and was formally established as a division of the American Psychological Association in 1978 (Wallston, 1993). The official journal of this division, *Health Psychology*, began publication 4 years later. Matarazzo (1982), the first president of the division, outlined four goals of health psychology: to promote and maintain health, to prevent and treat illness, to identify the causes and diagnostic correlates of health, illness, and related dysfunction, and to analyze and improve health care systems and health policy. International organizations have also developed: for example, the European Health Psychology Society (2001) was formed in 1986 and currently has representation from most European nations. Psychologists around the world work to achieve the goals of health psychology in a variety of ways.

The functions of health psychology professionals are expanding as the field matures. Most health psychologists work in hospitals, clinics, and academic departments of colleges and universities where they can provide direct and indirect help to patients. The direct help they provide generally relates to the individual's psychological adjustment to and management of health problems. Health psychologists with clinical training provide therapy for adjustment problems that being ill or disabled can produce – for example, in reducing the patient's feelings of depression. They also teach patients psychological methods to help them manage health problems; patients can learn biofeedback to control certain pain conditions, for instance. Health psychologists provide indirect help to patients through research on lifestyle and personality factors in illness and injury, by designing programs to help people lead more healthful lifestyles, and by educating health care workers to understand more fully the psychosocial needs of patients.

The qualifications for becoming a health psychologist include completion of a doctoral degree in psychology (Belar, 1997). More study may be called for if the doctoral program contained little training in health psychology. *Clinical health psychology* is an accredited specialty of the American Psychological Association. To practice clinical techniques, state licensing is required in the United States, and board certification is available (Deardorff, 1996).

Psychosomatic medicine, behavioral medicine, and health psychology have very similar goals, study similar topics, and share the same knowledge. These fields are separate mainly in an organizational sense, and many professionals are members of all three. Although the fields have slightly different perspectives, they share the position that health and illness result from the interplay of biological, psychological, and social forces. As this suggests, these fields use knowledge from a wide variety of disciplines and work together to enhance wellness and reduce illness.

AREAS OF STUDY AND APPLICATION

The field of health psychology has made enormous advances since the 1970s, generating new knowledge and designing and implementing programs and techniques to supplement medical efforts in promoting health. This section describes a sample of the many areas of study and application in which health psychologists have made important contributions.

Stress, Coping, and Health

Researchers have examined stress in three ways (Baum, 1990; Hobfoll, 1989). One approach focuses on physically or psychologically challenging events or circumstances called *stressors*. Another approach centers on the psychological and physiological responses to a stressor, which are called *strain*. The third approach treats stress as a process involving continuous interactions and adjustments, called *transactions*, between the person and the environment (Lazarus & Folkman, 1984). Transactions generally involve cognitive appraisal processes in which individuals assess the meaning or demands of a stressor and the resources available to cope with or manage it. In effect, transactions allow the person to affect a stressor's impact through cognitive processes, aided by behavioral and emotional coping strategies, such as taking direct action to eliminate the stressor or expressing distress.

Consistent with all three approaches, we can define *stress* as the condition that results when transactions lead the person to appraise a discrepancy between the demands of a stressor and the resources of his or her biological, psychological, and social systems. Strain occurs when stress exists and can involve psychological distress and physiological reactions, called *reactivity*, that include heightened blood pressure, heart rate, and serum levels of two classes of hormones: catecholamines (e.g., epinephrine) and corticosteroids (e.g., cortisol). People who experience chronic stress show high reactivity when a stressor occurs, and their arousal takes more time to return to its baseline, or 'resting', level (Gump & Matthews, 1999). This and other research findings support Selye's (1956, 1976) *general adaptation syndrome*. Selye proposed that the effects of long-term, intense stress advance through three stages: the alarm reaction with very high arousal, the stage of resistance in which arousal declines somewhat but remains above normal as the body tries to adapt, and the stage of exhaustion when the body's defenses weaken.

Stress can have a variety of sources (Sarafino, 2002). Within the person, for instance, it can arise from disability or pain in illness or from decisional conflicts, such as whether to change jobs or which treatment approach to get when sick. A person's family can create stressors through the birth of a baby, especially one with a difficult temperament; divorce; or a member's illness, disability, or death. And one's community can generate stressors through problems in the environment, such as noise or hazardous pollution, and on the job or at school through work demands, supervisors' evaluations, or interpersonal conflicts. Common measures of stress involve assessing physiological arousal – using a polygraph or biochemical analyses – and self-reports of the person's experiences (Sarafino, 2002). These experiences can be major life events, such as losing a job or a loved one, or daily hassles, such as misplacing something or hearing a loud party when trying to sleep.

Psychosocial factors can modify the impact of stressors on individuals. One of these factors is *social support* – the perceived help, comfort, caring, or esteem one receives from other people (Cobb, 1976; Wallston, Alagna, DeVellis & DeVellis, 1983; Wills, 1984). High levels of social support appear to reduce stress. Another psychosocial modifier of stress is the person's sense of *personal control*, the feeling of being able to make decisions and take effective action to avoid undesirable outcomes and produce desirable ones (Miller, 1979; Rodin, 1986; Thompson, 1981). People's sense of personal control can involve two beliefs: (1) that they can influence events in their lives, that is, they are high in internal locus of control (Rotter, 1966); and (2) that they can succeed at specific activities, that is, they have a high degree of self-efficacy (Bandura, 1977, 1986). A strong sense of personal control appears to reduce stress. People with a weak sense of personal control who experience chronic high levels of stress tend to feel helpless. Another psychosocial modifier of stress is the *type A behavior pattern*, which is marked by a competitive achievement orientation, time urgency, and anger or hostility (Chesney, Frautschi & Rosenman, 1985; Friedman & Rosenman, 1974).

Compared with people with the more easygoing type B pattern, type A individuals respond more quickly and strongly to stressors, with overt behaviors and physiological reactivity, and are more likely to develop coronary heart disease and hypertension (Booth-Kewley & Friedman, 1987; Carver, Diamond & Humphries, 1985; Diamond, 1982; Glass, 1977; Matthews, 1988).

Research has demonstrated clear links between illness and people's degree of reactivity in their cardiovascular, endocrine, and immune systems when stressed. For example, people's high cardiovascular reactivity to laboratory stressors in early adulthood is associated with later development of atherosclerosis (the buildup of fatty plaques on artery walls) and hypertension (Matthews et al., 1998; Menkes et al., 1989). Chronically high levels of catecholamines and corticosteroids (endocrine hormones) appear to increase atherosclerosis (Lundberg, 1999). Some of these hormones are also associated with impaired immune function, which seems to be important in the development and progression of infectious diseases and cancer (Kiecolt-Glaser & Glaser, 1995; Vedhara et al., 1999). Evidence on the connections between psychosocial and physiological processes led researchers to form a new field of study, *psychoneuroimmunology*, which focuses on the interplay between psychosocial factors and the nervous, endocrine, and immune systems (Ader & Cohen, 1985; Dunn, 1995). It is now known that negative emotions, such as depression and stress from major and minor events, are related to impaired immune function (Biondi & Pancheri, 1995; Dunn, 1995; Leonard, 1995). In contrast, positive emotions seem to enhance immune function (Stone et al., 1994).

The impact of stress is also clear in the symptoms and development of various illnesses, and we will consider four. First, evidence indicates that stress can trigger asthma episodes (Sarafino & Goldfedder, 1995; Wright, Rodriguez & Cohen, 1998). Second, studies have found that stress, particularly from everyday hassles, is among the most common triggers of migraine and tension-type headaches (Robbins, 1994; Wittrock & Myers, 1998). Third, stress and blood pressure are also linked. For example, Cobb and Rose (1973) compared the medical records of thousands of traffic controllers at airports with high and low traffic density. They found that the prevalence rates of hypertension were higher among subjects at high-density sites than at low-density sites. Last, because of the connections between reactivity and both atherosclerosis and hypertension, one would expect that stress would be related to coronary heart disease, and it is. High levels of stress at work or from life events are associated with high incidence rates of heart disease and recurrence of heart attack (Cottington & House, 1987; Theorell & Rahe, 1975).

Stress management techniques are available to help people who have trouble coping. One behavioral method is progressive muscle relaxation, in which individuals focus their attention on specific muscle groups while alternately tensing and relaxing these muscles (Sarafino, 2001). Another is biofeedback, which can help reduce physiological reactivity to stressors. Other approaches use cognitive methods to help people modify their thoughts when they encounter stressors. Some of these methods use cognitive restructuring strategies: the person learns to replace stress-provoking beliefs or thoughts with more constructive or realistic ones. These methods assume that stress appraisals are frequently based on misperceptions, a lack of information, or irrational ideas. Ellis's (1962, 1977) rational-emotive therapy and Beck's (1976) cognitive therapy are prominent examples of the cognitive restructuring approach. Other cognitive methods focus on teaching skills to help the person cope with or avoid stressful situations, as stress-inoculation training (Meichenbaum & Cameron, 1983) and problem-solving training (D'Zurilla, 1988; Nezu, Nezu & Perri, 1989) do. Stress management techniques are also effective in treating hypertension (Linden & Chambers, 1994) and reducing type A behavior (Roskies, 1983). Furthermore, research has shown that cardiac patients who receive stress management training to decrease type A behavior have much lower rates of heart problems and death in the next several years than patients who do not get training (Powell & Friedman, 1986).

Health Habits and Health Promotion

People's lifestyles typically include many health habits that are risk factors for illness or injury. They may smoke cigarettes, drink excessively, use drugs, eat high-fat or high-cholesterol diets, eat too much and become overweight, get too little physical activity, and behave in unsafe ways, such as by not using seat belts in automobiles or condoms when having sex with a new partner. Practicing health behaviors prevents illness, and this is an important area of interest in health psychology.

Although people tend to think of prevention as occurring before an illness develops, there are actually three levels of prevention – primary, secondary, and tertiary – that differ on the basis of the health status of the person (Runyan, 1985; Sanson-Fisher, 1993). Each level of prevention can include efforts of oneself, one's family or community, and professionals who work to promote health. Primary prevention involves activities to avoid illness or injury, such as getting a flu inoculation or eating a low-fat diet and exercising to avoid heart disease. These activities might be initiated by oneself or at the suggestion and encouragement of one's family, physician, or employer. Secondary prevention refers to actions taken to identify and treat an illness or injury early with the goal of curbing or reversing the problem. Receiving a dental examination or a mammogram would be examples. Tertiary prevention occurs after a health problem has progressed beyond the early stages and includes actions to rehabilitate the patient and to avoid lasting or irreversible damage, disability, and recurrence. Health psychologists study factors that determine the health-related behaviors people practice and try to promote the adoption of health behaviors.

Factors that influence health habits

Biological, psychological, and social factors can influence the likelihood that individuals will engage in specific health-related behaviors. The role of biological processes in health habits can be seen in people's excessive alcohol use: heredity has an influence (Ciraulo & Renner, 1991; Prescott & Kendler, 1999; Schuckit, 1985). Twin studies have generally found that if one member of a same-sex twin pair is alcoholic, the likelihood that the other member is alcoholic is twice as great if the twins are monozygotic (identical) rather than dizygotic (fraternal). But these links are complex, and developmental processes may moderate them. For instance, genetic factors appear to play a stronger role when alcohol abuse begins before age 25 than after that age (Kranzler & Anton, 1994).

Psychological processes also affect the development of health habits. Learning plays a major role, particularly through operant conditioning in which behavior is changed by its consequences, either reinforcement or punishment (Sarafino, 2001). Reinforcement causes an increase and punishment causes a decrease in performance of the behavior on which the consequence is contingent. A child who has a good deal of success and receives praise for athletic pursuits is more likely to be physically active in the future than a child who experiences failure and derision for those behaviors. If the reinforcing consequences are discontinued at some point, the behavior tends to weaken through the process of extinction. Operant behavior generally occurs following or in the presence of antecedents – that is, cues that precede and set the occasion for an action. Another important learning process is classical (respondent) conditioning in which a stimulus (the conditioned stimulus) gains the ability to elicit a response through repeated association with a stimulus (the unconditioned stimulus) that already elicits that response (Sarafino, 2001). One way classical conditioning affects health habits is by establishing cues that serve as antecedents to the behavior. For example, people who smoke cigarettes, drink alcohol, or use other substances learn antecedents that set the occasion for use, often with feelings of craving. Some behaviors that are prompted by cues may become habitual, or automatic, often occurring without awareness of the behavior or the cues that initiated it, as when a smoker absentmindedly reaches for and lights a cigarette.

Cognition plays an important role in the performance of health-related behaviors. People are more likely to start and continue a health behavior if they have correct knowledge about relevant health issues and the ability to solve problems that arise when trying to practice the behavior, such as how to eat a healthful diet when other family members dislike nutritious foods. One of the most influential theories of people's practicing healthful behaviors is the *health belief model*, which proposes a series of cognitive activities that leads to the likelihood of taking preventive action (Becker, 1979; Becker & Rosenstock, 1984; Rosenstock, 1966). A person's likelihood of preventive action depends directly on two assessments: the perceived threat of illness or injury and the sum of the benefits and barriers of taking the action. These assessments depend on the person's perceptions, such as of the seriousness of and susceptibility to the illness or injury, and modifying factors, such as the person's age, sex, and knowledge about the health issue. Research has generally supported the theory (Becker, 1979; Becker & Rosenstock, 1984; Curry & Emmons, 1994; Kirscht, 1983). For instance, comparisons have been made of people who do and do not regularly get breast and cervical cancer tests, have dental visits, or engage in exercise. These studies have found that people who do these health behaviors are more likely to believe that they are susceptible to the related health problem, that the health problem would have serious effects, and that the benefits outweigh the barriers of preventive action.

The *stages of change model* attempts to account for people's likelihood of changing unhealthful habits by focusing on their cognitive and behavioral 'readiness' to change (Prochaska & DiClemente, 1984; Prochaska, DiClemente & Norcross, 1992). The model outlines five stages of intention to change, ranging from not considering changing at all, to being ready to start soon, to having succeeded and maintained the change for at least several months. According to the stages of change model, people advance from one stage to the next in the process of changing, their psychosocial characteristics at each stage differ, and it is possible to match intervention strategies with these characteristics to help people advance to the next stage. Research has confirmed that people at higher stages are more likely to adopt relevant health behaviors, such as using safer sex practices and quitting smoking (Bowen & Trotter, 1995; DiClemente et al., 1991). But tests of the utility of matching strategies to help people advance to higher stages have yielded some inconsistent results (see e.g., Quinlan & McCaul, 2000; Velicer, Prochaska, Fava, LaForge & Rossi, 1999).

Most theories focusing on the role of cognition in practicing health habits assume that the processes are mainly rational. But three lines of evidence indicate that nonrational processes also play a role. First, people tend to be overly optimistic about their health, believing that the chances of getting serious illnesses are lower for themselves than for other people who are much like them (Weinstein, 1987). Second, studies have found that people's desires and preferences influence the judgments they make of the validity and utility of new information – a process called motivated reasoning (Kunda, 1990). For instance, people who prefer to reach a particular conclusion about the hazards of eating certain foods will search for reasons to accept supportive information and discount opposing information. And the tendency to use biased reasoning processes appears to be fairly stable and consistent across a variety of situations (Sarafino, 1999). Third, stress and other emotional factors can affect the cognitive processes people use in making decisions, particularly decisions relating to health, because of conflicts about the best course of action (Janis, 1984).

Social factors influence people's health habits through modeling processes and social consequences, such as praise. In modeling, people learn by observing the behavior of another person, especially if the model is similar to themselves and has high status, such as a popular classmate or a movie star or athlete (Bandura, 1969, 1986). Modeling also involves imitation: when drinking socially, for example, people tend to adjust their drinking rates to match those of their companions (McCarty, 1985). Friends and family promote health behavior by reinforcing it with praise and conveying a value for good health, and they discourage health behavior by punishing it, such as by complaining about how the behavior interferes with other activities (Burg & Seeman, 1994; Weiss, Larsen & Baker, 1996).

Substance use and abuse

Using certain substances repeatedly can produce addiction, the condition of being physically and psychologically dependent on a substance. In *physical dependence*, the body adjusts to the substance and incorporates it into its usual functioning, as reflected in the phenomena of tolerance (requiring increasing doses to achieve the same effect) and withdrawal (symptoms when substance use is sharply reduced). *Psychological dependence* involves feeling compelled to use the substance for its pleasant effect. Health psychologists study factors relating to people's use of various substances; we will focus on tobacco and alcohol. Cigarette smoking is a risk factor for several illnesses, particularly lung cancer and heart disease (American Cancer Society, 2000; American Heart Association, 2000). Heavy alcohol use is related to a variety of health problems, including fetal alcohol syndrome in babies of drinking mothers, injury from automobile accidents, and cirrhosis of the liver (National Institute on Alcohol Abuse and Alcoholism, 1993).

About 1.1 billion people in the world smoke cigarettes (World Health Organization, 1998). Biopsychosocial factors influence people's beginning and continuing to smoke. The role of biological factors is clear: heredity affects whether people will begin and continue to smoke (Hughes, 1986), and people with a specific gene pattern are less likely to become smokers and more able to quit after starting (Lerman et al., 1999). The nicotine in cigarettes is an addictive substance that produces physiological effects quickly by leading to the release of chemicals, including acetylcholine and norepinephrine, that have desirable effects. For example, they increase alertness and decrease symptoms of withdrawal, feelings of anxiety, and pain. One prominent explanation of continued smoking is the *nicotine regulation model*, which proposes that people continue to smoke to avoid withdrawal symptoms. Although research has supported this model (Schachter et al., 1977), it appears to provide only part of the reasons for continued use. For instance, some smokers don't show the tolerance and withdrawal characteristics of addiction, and most people who quit smoking still crave it long after no nicotine remains in their bodies (Leventhal & Cleary, 1980; Shiffman, Paty, Gnys, Kassel & Elash, 1995).

Psychosocial factors are also involved and may account for some phenomena that the nicotine regulation model cannot explain. For one thing, nicotine appears to have reinforcing effects (Shadel, Shiffman, Niaura, Nichter & Abrams, 2000). A theory called the *biobehavioral model* proposes that because nicotine decreases anxiety and increases alertness, smokers come to depend on it to regulate their cognitive and emotional states, thereby helping them cope better (Pomerleau & Pomerleau, 1989). Second, other psychosocial factors have been linked with smoking. For example, adolescents who start and continue to smoke tend to have peer and adult models of smoking, experience peer pressure to smoke, and believe that smoking can enhance their image (Conrad, Flay & Hill, 1992; Killen et al., 1997; Robinson & Klesges, 1997). It seems clear that a complete explanation of smoking behavior involves the interplay of biological, psychological, and social factors.

Biopsychosocial processes are also involved in the development of heavy alcohol use. In the United States alone, 20 per cent of the men and 8 per cent of the women have abused alcohol at some time in their lives (Davison & Neale, 1998). As mentioned earlier, heredity influences the likelihood of people's excessive alcohol use (Ciraulo & Renner, 1991; Prescott & Kendler, 1999; Schuckit, 1985). Psychosocial processes also play a role. Children and adolescents learn from watching people around them and on TV to expect positive effects of drinking alcohol (Adesso, 1985; Dunn & Goldman, 1998; Scheier & Botvin, 1997). People continue or increase their drinking partly as a result of

positive and negative reinforcement in operant conditioning (Adesso, 1985; Cunningham, 1998; National Institute on Alcohol Abuse and Alcoholism, 1993). With positive reinforcement, people may drink for the taste or the feeling they get from it; with negative reinforcement, they may drink because it reduces unpleasant feelings, such as stress or anxiety, at least in the short run.

Health psychologists have participated in designing and applying interventions to prevent and help people quit smoking and drinking. Programs introduced before adolescence to prevent smoking and drinking can successfully reduce the number of individuals who begin these behaviors, but the effects appear to last only 2 or 3 years and need to be refreshed with booster sessions to maintain the success (Botvin & Epstein, 1999; Klepp, Kelder & Perry, 1995; National Institute on Alcohol Abuse and Alcoholism, 1993). Treatment approaches to help people quit smoking are most effective if they include behavioral methods, the nicotine patch, and advice by a physician to quit (Cinciripini, Cinciripini, Wallfisch, Haque & Van Vunakis, 1996; Fiore, Jorenby & Baker, 1997). For quitting drinking, effective approaches include Alcoholics Anonymous (Ouimette, Finney & Moos, 1997) and programs that use behavioral and cognitive methods (Miller & Hester, 1980; Monti et al., 1993).

Nutrition and exercise

Eating high-cholesterol, low-fiber diets and getting little physical activity are associated with the development of illnesses, including hypertension, heart disease, and some forms of cancer (American Cancer Society, 2000; American Heart Association, 2000). Biopsychosocial factors are involved in the diets people consume and the level of physical activity they get.

Inborn factors influence aspects of an individual's diet. Most people around the world appear to like sweet tastes and dislike bitter ones, right from birth (Rozin, 1989). Furthermore, research findings indicate that brain chemicals influence people's tendency to eat fatty foods (Azar, 1994). Psychosocial factors in people's diets can be seen in the role of individual and social experiences (Hearn et al., 1998; Rozin, 1989; Schutz & Diaz-Knauf, 1989). For instance, some foods are more available than others at home, work, or school, and exposing individuals to a specific food can increase their liking of it. Modeling is also important, allowing people to develop an attraction to a food if they see that other individuals eat it and like it. Interventions that include nutrition education and other approaches, such as behavioral methods, to change diets that place people at risk for cardiovascular problems appear to reduce serum cholesterol levels and blood pressure (Brunner et al., 1997).

People's age and gender affect their getting physical exercise, and these differences may be partly the result of actual and expected physical capabilities. In the United States, men engage more in exercise in early adulthood and old age than at ages in between, but women exercise relatively little throughout the adult years (US Bureau of the Census, 1999). Older men and women tend to underestimate their ability to perform vigorous exercise and exaggerate the health risks of exercising (Vertinsky & Auman, 1988; Woods & Birren, 1984). Whether people exercise depends also on psychosocial influences, such as modeling, encouragement, and reinforcement by peers and family (Dishman, Sallis & Orenstein, 1985). Interventions can successfully promote exercise behavior, especially if they include behavioral methods (Sallis & Owen, 1999).

Receiving Medical Care

When people experience clear health symptoms, some use medical services right away, some delay getting care, and some don't seek care at all. The health belief model explains part of these differences (Becker & Rosenstock, 1984; Langlie, 1977). For individuals who do get treatment, their *compliance* with, or *adherence* to, the medical regimen and their adjustment to a hospital stay have been of particular interest to health psychologists.

Estimates indicate that about 40 per cent of patients fail to adhere reasonably closely to the treatment regimen their physician recommends (DiMatteo, 1985; Rand & Weeks, 1998). Low compliance is common if the regimen has a very long duration, is complex, and requires them to change long-standing habits (Burke, Dunbar-Jacob & Hill, 1997; Haynes, 1976; Parrish, 1986). Patients also show poor adherence if the physician does not explain the regimen carefully and they feel a poor relationship with the physician (DiMatteo, 1985). Health psychologists have helped to design and implement successful interventions to improve physicians' communication skills (Roter & Hall, 1989) and patients' compliance motivation through behavioral methods (Burke et al., 1997; Roter et al., 1998).

Being hospitalized with a serious illness or injury produces a great deal of stress and anxiety, which impairs medical recovery. Health psychologists can help by providing psychological counseling and information to enhance patients' understanding and sense of personal control over some of the difficult circumstances they will experience. Providing such help reduces patients' anxiety, recovery time, post-surgical complications, and medication use (Anderson, 1987; Gruen, 1975).

Managing and Adjusting to Pain Conditions

Pain involves the interplay between physiological and psychosocial processes (Bakal, 1979). Most pains are *acute*, and the experiences disappear in hours or weeks; others are *chronic* and last for more than a few months, often becoming worse over time (Turk, Meichenbaum & Genest, 1983). Pain sensations generally arise when injured tissues release chemicals called algogenic substances that activate nerve endings called nociceptors to send pain signals through the spinal cord to the brain (Chapman, 1984; Tortora & Grabowski, 2000). Evidence of the role of psychosocial processes led Melzack and Wall (1965, 1982) to propose the *gate control theory*, which describes a physiological mechanism by which psychological factors can affect people's experience of pain. Psychological factors that increase pain sensations include anxiety, tension, depression, and focusing attention on the pain. The results of most studies that have tested this theory have supported it (Melzack & Wall, 1982; Winters, 1985).

Chronic, disabling pain has psychosocial effects, often in the form of a syndrome called the *neurotic triad* (Cox, Chapman & Black, 1978; Rosen, Grubman, Bevins & Frymoyer, 1987). The neurotic triad involves extremely high levels of *depression, hypochondriasis* (preoccupation with physical symptoms and health), and *hysteria* (tendency to cope with problems by developing physical symptoms and using avoidance coping methods), as measured with the Minnesota Multiphasic Personality Inventory (MMPI). Health psychologists apply a variety of approaches to reduce patients' pain, drug consumption, and disability. In treating migraine and tension-type headache, for example, relaxation and biofeedback methods yield substantial and durable relief (Blanchard, Appelbaum, Guarnieri, Morrill & Dentinger, 1987; Holroyd & Penzien, 1990). Cognitive methods, such as distracting one's attention and using mental imagery of scenes, effectively reduce acute pain (Fernandez & Turk, 1989; Manne, Bakeman, Jacobsen, Gorfinkle & Redd, 1994). For chronic pain, such as from arthritis or headache, programs combining cognitive and behavioral methods are particularly helpful in reducing pain (Compas, Haaga, Keefe, Leitenberg & Williams, 1998; Morley, Eccleston & Williams, 1999). Hypnosis can relieve pain in patients who can be hypnotized easily and deeply (DeBenedittis, Panerai & Villamira, 1989).

Managing and Adjusting to Disabling and Life-Threatening Conditions

We have seen that chronic diseases are the main health problems in industrialized countries today, where they account for the large majority of deaths. Some chronic illnesses can lead to disability, and some have high rates of death. For people who develop a chronic illness, health psychologists can contribute to tertiary prevention efforts by helping patients manage their health condition and adjust to it psychosocially.

When people develop illnesses that do not pose a very high risk of death, the chief concern in tertiary prevention is helping them manage the illness to reduce symptoms and disability and to prevent a worsening of the condition. We will consider a few psychological techniques that can help these patients, concentrating for our purposes on two illnesses: asthma and diabetes. For asthma, biofeedback and relaxation techniques have had success (Sarafino, 1997). With biofeedback, an asthmatic breathes through an apparatus that measures the flow of air and learns to control the diameter of bronchial airways by receiving periodic feedback regarding airflow. Progressive muscle relaxation is used to help the patient reduce the role of stress in initiating an asthma attack or in making it worse when one occurs. For diabetes, an important concern is fostering compliance with difficult self-management regimens of monitoring serum glucose levels and controlling diet and exercise. Studies with child and adolescent diabetics have found that programs using behavioral methods, such as providing prompts and reinforcers for performing tasks, improve self-management actions and serum glucose levels (Goodall & Halford, 1991).

For people with life-threatening diseases, two common needs involve promoting their adherence to the medical regimen and adjusting to their disability and possibility of dying. In considering some psychological approaches for these patients, we will focus on promoting psychosocial adjustment in heart disease. Initial elevations of anxiety and depression after a heart attack continue in many patients beyond a few months. The poor adjustment these emotions reflect has been linked to decreased regimen adherence and physical condition and increased risk of subsequent heart problems and death (Carney, Freedland, Rich & Jaffe, 1995; Carney et al., 1988; Frasure-Smith, Lespérance, Juneau, Talajic & Bourassa, 1999). Studies with 1- and 2-year follow-up periods have found that interventions with regimen training and psychosocial counseling reduce the risk of heart problems and death (Dusseldorp, van Elderen, Maes, Meulman & Kraaij, 1999; Linden, Stossel & Maurice, 1996).

RELATING HEALTH PSYCHOLOGY TO OTHER DISCIPLINES

Knowledge in health psychology is enriched by information from many other disciplines, including disciplines within *psychology*, such as the clinical and social areas; *medicine*, including psychiatry and pediatrics; and *allied fields*, such as nursing, nutrition, pharmacology, and social work. We will look at some of the fields that provide information and a context for health psychology.

Understanding health psychology fully requires knowledge of the context in which health and illness exist. Part of the context comes from the field of *epidemiology* – the scientific study of the frequency and distribution of disease and injury. Epidemiologists determine the occurrence of illness in a given population and organize these data by relevant variables, such as when the disease or injury occurred, where, and to which age, gender, and racial or cultural groups. Then they conduct research to discover why specific illnesses are distributed as they are. The mass media often report the results of epidemiologists' work – for example, areas of the United States where Lyme disease occurs at high levels and where cancer is linked to high levels of toxic substances in the environment. Five terms epidemiologists use in describing aspects of their findings are: *mortality*, i.e., death, generally on a large scale; *morbidity*, i.e., illness, injury, or disability; *prevalence*, i.e., the number of cases, such as of a disease or of persons infected or at risk, including continuing (previously reported) and new cases at a given moment in time; *incidence*, i.e., the number of new cases; and epidemic, i.e., the situation in which the incidence has increased rapidly (Gerace & Vorp, 1985; Runyan, 1985). Adding the word *rate* conveys relativity to the meaning, as in describing a mortality rate of 6 babies per 1,000 births dying in their first year of life.

Another important discipline for health psychology is *public health*, the field concerned with protecting and improving health through organized effort in the community. Public health workers do research and set up programs to improve health education, immunizations, sanitation, and community health services (Runyan, 1985). This field considers health and illness in the context of the community as a social system. Many health psychologists study the success of public health programs and the way individuals react to them.

Two other related fields are sociology and anthropology (Adler & Stone, 1979). *Sociology* focuses on human social life in groups or communities and evaluates the impact of social factors, such as the mass media, population growth, and institutions. *Medical sociology* is a subfield that examines, for instance, the impact of social relationships on the distribution of illness, socioeconomic factors of health care use, and the way hospital services and medical practices are organized. *Anthropology* includes the study of human cultures; its subfield, *medical anthropology*, focuses on differences in health and health care across cultures. Medical anthropologists study how different cultures structure health care systems and react to and treat disease and injury. Knowledge from sociology and anthropology enables health psychologists to have a broad social and cultural view of medical issues and to consider different ways to interpret and treat illness.

A variety of professionals work together with physicians and nurses as a team to provide care for patients who are suffering from a chronic illness, serious injury, or disability. Professionals in each of the four allied fields we will consider have specific training for a special role in a patient's treatment or rehabilitation process, and most of them have some education in psychology. *Dietitians* work in hospitals, clinics, nursing homes, colleges, and schools to study and apply knowledge about food and its effect on the body (American Dietetic Association, 2000). Many dietitians work directly with patients to assess nutritional needs, implement and evaluate dietary plans, and instruct patients and their families on ways to adhere to needed diets after hospital discharge. Some dietitians work for social service agencies, counseling people on nutritional practices to help maintain health and speed recovery when they are ill. *Physical therapists* plan and apply techniques to help patients restore functional movement to parts of their body, relieve pain, and prevent or limit permanent disability (American Physical Therapy Association, 2000). The most common technique used in physical therapy involves exercise, which generally begins by requiring little effort and becomes more and more challenging. Another technique uses electrical stimulation to move paralyzed muscles or to reduce pain. Physical therapists also give instructions for carrying out everyday tasks, such as cooking meals or tying shoelaces, and using adaptive devices, such as crutches or a prosthesis, if needed. *Occupational therapists* help physically, mentally, and emotionally disabled individuals gain skills needed for daily activities at home, in a work setting or school, and in the community (American Occupational Therapy Association, 2000). Their patients often had these skills at one time, but lost them because of a spinal cord injury or a disease, such as muscular dystrophy. *Medical social workers* provide services in hospitals, nursing homes, rehabilitation centers, and public health programs to help patients and their families make psychological and social adjustments to an illness and obtain needed community services, including income maintenance and occupational therapy (National Association of Social Workers, 2000).

SOCIOCULTURAL, GENDER, AND DEVELOPMENTAL FACTORS IN HEALTH

Health and illness vary across the history and cultures of the world. Comparisons of mortality data in Europe and North America in 1900 and in developing nations of the world today reveal very similar infant mortality rates and causes: diarrheal diseases, malnutrition, respiratory infections, and whooping cough (UNICEF, cited in Skolnick, 1986). Looking only at health patterns today, we see that substantial variations occur across ethnic groups and social classes, between males and females, and across the life span. What variations occur now, and why do they exist?

Sociocultural Differences and Health

The term *sociocultural* means involving or relating to social and cultural factors, such as ethnic and income variations within and across nations. Epidemiological studies of sociocultural differences in health have found, for instance, that stomach cancer has a far higher prevalence rate in Japan than in the United States today, but the opposite is true for breast (in females) and prostate (in males) cancers (Williams, 1990). Moreover, large sociocultural differences exist in the prevalence of specific cancers within the same country (Williams & Rucker, 1996). In the United States, for example, Chinese Americans have much higher rates of liver cancer than Caucasians do. The differences found in the illness patterns of countries, regions, or ethnic groups result from variations in people's heredity, environmental pollution, economic barriers to health care, diets, health-related beliefs, and values (Flack et al., 1995; Johnson et al., 1995). Although people in all parts of the world value good health, people differ in the importance they place on maintaining health. The more people value their health, the more likely they are to take care of it.

Research has revealed wide variations in the health habits of individuals around the world. A survey examined improvements in health behaviors over a 2-year period in three countries (Retchin, Wells, Valleron & Albrecht, 1992). It found that the highest percentage of individuals reporting that they had increased exercising and decreased their consumption of alcohol and red meat was in the United States; England had a much lower percentage, followed by France. Other research has shown that people consume far more animal fat in Denmark than in the United States; people in Israel and Japan consume very little (Criqui & Ringel, 1994). Cigarette smoking shows large variations across and within countries (World Health Organization, 1998). Almost three-fourths of the world's smokers reside in underdeveloped nations, where 48 per cent of the men and 7 per cent of the women smoke. Smoking decreased in the 1990s in industrialized countries, but 42 per cent of men and 24 per cent of women in these nations continue to smoke. In the United States, 27 per cent of men and 23 per cent of women smoke, and the percentage of individuals under age 25 who smoke is much greater for whites than blacks (National Center for Health Statistics, 2000). Alcohol use also varies widely: for instance, Norwegians drink very little, but French and Italian people drink much more, mainly as wine with meals (Criqui & Ringel, 1994). People in Central and Eastern Europe have high levels of smoking and drinking (Little, 1998).

Research conducted in the United States has shown that minority group background and low social class – or *socioeconomic status*, as measured by income, occupational prestige, and education – are often risk factors for poor health (Myers, Kagawa-Singer, Kumanyika, Lex & Markides, 1995; Ostrove, Feldman & Adler, 1999; Williams & Rucker, 1996). For example, compared with Caucasians, African Americans have higher rates of morbidity and mortality from chronic diseases and greater vulnerability to HIV infection and injury or death from violence. Also, people from the lower classes tend to have poorer health habits – for instance, smoking more and exercising less – than people from higher social classes.

Differences across history and culture can be seen in people's ideas about the causes of illness. Recall that people in the Middle Ages generally believed that evil spirits caused illness. Although educated people in technological societies today typically reject such ideas, less sophisticated people in the same societies and in underdeveloped countries often do not. This is important to recognize because the large majority of people in the world live in underdeveloped societies. And immigrants to industrialized countries carry with them health ideas and customs from their former countries. For example, many Chinese immigrants have entered the United States with the belief that imbalances of two opposing forces, *yin* and *yang*, within the body cause illness: too much yin causes colds and gastric disorders, for example, and too much yang causes dehydration and fever (Campbell & Chang, 1981). Practitioners of traditional Chinese medicine treat illnesses with acupuncture and special herbs and foods to correct the balance of yin and yang. Immigrants and others with these beliefs who are sick will often use these methods instead of or as a supplement to treatment by an American physician, and pressure family members to do this too. As an example, a pregnant registered nurse of Chinese background followed her obstetrician's advice, but also ate special herbs and foods under pressure from her mother and mother-in-law to insure the health of her baby (Campbell & Chang, 1981).

Many religious doctrines relate to health and illness. For instance, Jehovah's Witnesses reject the use of blood and blood products in medical treatment (Sacks & Koppes, 1986). Christian Scientists reject the use of medicine entirely and believe that only mental processes in the sick person can cure the illness, which is promoted through prayer and counsel (Henderson & Primeaux, 1981). These beliefs are controversial and have led to legal conflicts in the United States, particularly when parents' religious beliefs lead them to reject medical treatments for life-threatening illnesses for their children. In such cases, medical authorities can move quickly to seek an immediate judicial decision (Sacks & Koppes, 1986). Some religions include specific beliefs that promote healthful lifestyles. For example, Seventh-Day Adventists believe in taking care of their bodies because the body is the 'temple of the Holy Spirit'. As a result, they encourage exercise and healthful eating and abstain from using tobacco, alcohol, and illicit drugs (Henderson & Primeaux, 1981). Although it is clear that cultural factors influence health, our knowledge about this influence is sparse and needs to be expanded through more research.

Gender and Health

Worldwide, the average life expectancy at birth is about 4 years longer for females than males, and in developed nations the gap in expected longevity is nearly twice as great (World Health Organization, 1999). Although the reasons for these differences are not entirely clear, some possibilities can be described (National Center for Health Statistics, 2000; Reddy, Fleming & Adesso, 1992). First, males have far higher rates of accidental injury and death, such as in drowning and automobile mishaps.

Second, men smoke and drink more than women do and are more likely to be overweight. Third, men show higher physiological reactivity, such as blood pressure and serum catecholamine elevations, when under stress, making them more vulnerable to heart disease and stroke. Paradoxically, even though women have longer lives than men, they appear to have more health problems, having higher rates of acute illnesses, such as respiratory and digestive illnesses, and nonfatal chronic diseases, such as arthritis and headache (National Center for Health Statistics, 2000; Reddy et al., 1992).

Development and Health

People change as they develop, and each portion of the life span is affected by happenings in earlier years and affects the happenings in future years. Because people's health, illness, and biopsychosocial systems change throughout life, the life-span perspective in health psychology considers characteristics of a person with respect to their prior development, current level, and likely development in the future. Because of these changes, the kinds of illnesses people have tend to change with age. Children are far less likely than older people to suffer from chronic diseases (US Bureau of the Census, 1999). Childhood illnesses tend to be short-term infectious diseases, such as colds or the flu. In contrast, prevalence rates for heart disease, cancer, and stroke are high in late adulthood and old age.

People's biopsychosocial systems change in many ways as they develop. The size, strength, and efficiency of virtually all biological systems increase throughout childhood and decline in old age. The decline can be seen in the decrease older people notice in their physical stamina because their muscles are weaker and the heart and lungs function less efficiently (Tortora & Grabowski, 2000). They also recover more slowly from illness and injury. Over the life span, people's psychological systems change, too. For example, children's cognitive abilities are limited during the preschool years but grow rapidly during later childhood. As children get older and their cognitive skills

improve, they become better able to assume responsibility for their health and understand how their behavior can affect it (Maddux, Roberts, Sledden & Wright, 1986). Social relationships and social systems also change with development. As people develop, they progress through levels of education and employment, family life, and retirement. Changes in social relationships also relate to health and illness. In adolescence, teenagers take on more and more responsibilities for their own health, but their social links with age-mates and strong need to be accepted by peers sometimes lead teens toward unhealthful or unsafe behavior. For example, an adolescent who has a chronic illness that can be controlled – as diabetes can – may neglect his or her medical care to avoid looking and feeling different from age-mates (La Greca & Stone, 1985). Adolescence is also the time in the life span when individuals are most likely to start to smoke, drink, use drugs, and have sexual relations.

Health psychology research and health promotion efforts in the future must address and be sensitive to the needs of diverse populations that differ in sociocultural background, gender, and developmental level.

SUMMARY

Health and illness are overlapping concepts that exist along a continuum, with optimal wellness at one end and major disability and death at the other end. Historically, compared with time periods before the twentieth century, people today die at later ages and from different causes. Infectious diseases are no longer the principal cause of death in technological societies around the world. Chronic illnesses constitute the main health problem in developed nations now.

Ideas about physiology, disease processes, and the mind have changed since the early cultures thousands of years ago, when people apparently believed that illness was caused by evil spirits and the like. Ancient Greek philosophers proposed that the mind and body are separate entities. After the Middle Ages, philosophers and scientists from the seventeenth to the twentieth centuries provided the foundation for the biomedical model as a way to conceptualize health and illness. This model has enabled researchers to make great advances in medicine. But many researchers today believe people's social relationships, lifestyles, personalities, mental processes, and biological processes must be included in a full conceptualization of health and illness. As a result, the biopsychosocial model has emerged, proposing that health status results from and produces a constant interplay of biological, psychological, and social systems.

Health psychologists study factors that affect people's health and apply psychosocial methods to reduce stress, enhance the practice of healthful behavior, reduce illness symptoms and disability, and prevent a worsening of patients' condition or, perhaps, death. The knowledge health psychologists use draws from other subfields in psychology and several nonpsychology fields, such as medicine, biology, social work, epidemiology, public health, sociology, and anthropology. Variations in health and health behaviors can be seen across sociocultural, gender, and developmental groups.

REFERENCES

Ader, R., & Cohen, N. (1985). CNS–immune system interactions: Conditioning phenomena. *Behavioral and Brain Sciences, 8*, 379–395.

Adesso, V. J. (1985). Cognitive factors in alcohol and drug use. In M. Galizio & S. A. Maisto (Eds.), *Determinants of substance abuse: Biological, psychological, and environmental factors* (pp. 179–208). New York: Plenum.

Adler, N. E., & Stone, G. C. (1979). Social science perspectives on the health system. In G. C. Stone, F. Cohen & N. E. Adler (Eds.), *Health psychology: A handbook* (pp. 19–46). San Francisco: Jossey-Bass.

Alexander, F. (1950). *Psychosomatic medicine: Its principles and applications*. New York: Norton.

Allison, D. B., Heshka, S., Neale, M. C., Lykken, D. T., & Heymsfield, S. B. (1994). A genetic analysis of relative weight among 4,020 twin pairs, with an emphasis on sex effects. *Health Psychology, 13*, 362–365.

American Cancer Society (2000). *Cancer facts and figures – 1999*. Retrieved (7 March 2000) from http://www.cancer.org.

American Dietetic Association (2000). *Becoming a registered dietitian*. Retrieved (3 March 2000) from http://www.eatright.org.

American Heart Association (2000). *Heart and stroke A–Z guide*. Retrieved (7 March 2000) from http://www. americanheart.org.

American Occupational Therapy Association (2000). *About us*. Retrieved (4 March 2000) from http://www. aota.org.

American Physical Therapy Association (2000). *APTA background sheet 1999*. Retrieved (4 March 2000) from http://www.apta.org.

Anderson, E. A. (1987). Preoperative preparation for cardiac surgery facilitates recovery, reduces psychological distress, and reduces the incidence of acute postoperative hypertension. *Journal of Consulting and Clinical Psychology, 55*, 513–520.

Arnow, B., Kenardy, J., & Agras, W. S. (1992). Binge eating among the obese. *Journal of Behavioral Medicine, 15*, 155–170.

Azar, B. (1994). Eating fat: Why does the brain say, 'Ahhh'? *American Psychological Association Monitor*, November, p. 20.

Bakal, D. A. (1979). *Psychology and medicine: Psychological dimensions of health and illness*. New York: Springer.

Bandura, A. (1969). *Principles of behavior modification*. New York: Holt, Rinehart & Winston.

Bandura, A. (1977). Self-efficacy: Toward a unifying theory of behavioral change. *Psychological Review, 84*, 191–215.

Bandura, A. (1986). *Social foundations of thought and action: A social cognitive theory*. Englewood Cliffs, NJ: Prentice-Hall.

Baranowski, T., & Nader, P. R. (1985). Family health behavior. In D. C. Turk & R. D. Kerns (Eds.), *Health, illness, and families: A life-span perspective* (pp. 51–80). New York: Wiley.

Baum, A. (1990). Stress, intrusive imagery, and chronic distress. *Health Psychology, 9*, 653–675.

Beck, A. T. (1976). *Cognitive therapy and the emotional disorders*. New York: International Universities Press.

Becker, M. H. (1979). Understanding patient compliance: The contributions of attitudes and other psychosocial factors. In S. J. Cohen (Ed.), *New directions in patient compliance* (pp. 1–31). Lexington, MA: Heath.

Becker, M. H., & Rosenstock, I. M. (1984). Compliance with medical advice. In A. Steptoe & A. Mathews (Eds.), *Health care and human behaviour* (pp. 175–208). London: Academic.

Belar, C. D. (1997). Clinical health psychology: A specialty for the 21st century. *Health Psychology, 16*, 411–416.

Belloc, N. B., & Breslow, L. (1972). Relationship of physical health status and health practices. *Preventive Medicine, 1*, 409–421.

Bertalanffy, L. von (1968). *General systems theory.* New York: Braziller.

Biondi, M., & Pancheri, P. (1995). Clinical research strategies in psychoimmunology: A review of 46 human research studies (1972–1992). In B. Leonard & K. Miller (Eds.), *Stress, the immune system and psychiatry* (pp. 85–111). New York: Wiley.

Birren, J. E., & Zarit, J. M. (1985). Concepts of health, behavior, and aging. In J. E. Birren & J. Livingston (Eds.), *Cognition, stress, and aging.* Englewood Cliffs, NJ: Prentice-Hall.

Blanchard, E. B., Appelbaum, K. A., Guarnieri, P., Morrill, B., & Dentinger, M. P. (1987). Five year prospective follow-up on the treatment of chronic headache with biofeedback and/or relaxation. *Headache, 27*, 580–583.

Booth-Kewley, S., & Friedman, H. S. (1987). Psychological predictors of heart disease: A quantitative review. *Psychological Bulletin, 101*, 343–362.

Botvin, G. J., & Epstein, J. A. (1999). Preventing cigarette smoking among children and adolescents. In D. F. Seidman & L. S. Covey (Eds.), *Helping the hard-core smoker: A clinician's guide* (pp. 51–71). Mahwah, NJ: Erlbaum.

Bowen, A. M., & Trotter, R. (1995). HIV risk in intravenous drug users and crack cocaine smokers: Predicting stage of change for condom use. *Journal of Consulting and Clinical Psychology, 63*, 238–248.

Brunner, E., White, I., Thorogood, M., Bristow, A., Curle, D., & Marmot, M. (1997). Can dietary interventions change diet and cardiovascular risk factors? A meta-analysis of randomized controlled trials. *American Journal of Public Health, 87*, 1415–1422.

Burg, M. M., & Seeman, T. E. (1994). Families and health: The negative side of social ties. *Annals of Behavioral Medicine, 16*, 109–115.

Burke, L. E., Dunbar-Jacob, J. M., & Hill, M. N. (1997). Compliance with cardiovascular disease prevention strategies: A review of the research. *Annals of Behavioral Medicine, 19*, 239–263.

Campbell, T., & Chang, B. (1981). Health care of the Chinese in America. In G. Henderson & M. Primeaux (Eds.), *Transcultural health care* (pp. 163–172). Menlo Park, CA: Addison-Wesley.

Carney, R. M., Freedland, K. E., Rich, M. W., & Jaffe, A. S. (1995). Depression as a risk factor for cardiac events in established coronary heart disease: A review of possible mechanisms. *Annals of Behavioral Medicine, 17*, 142–149.

Carney, R. M., Rich, M. W., Freedland, K. E., Saini, J., teVelde, A., Simeone, C., & Clark, K. (1988). Major depressive disorder predicts cardiac events in patients with coronary artery disease. *Psychosomatic Medicine, 50*, 627–633.

Carver, C. S., Diamond, E. L., & Humphries, C. (1985). Coronary prone behavior. In N. Schneiderman & J. T. Tapp (Eds.), *Behavioral medicine: The biopsychosocial approach* (pp. 437–465). Hillsdale, NJ: Erlbaum.

Chapman, C. R. (1984). New directions in the understanding and management of pain. *Social Science and Medicine, 19*, 1261–1277.

Chesney, M. A., Frautschi, N. M., & Rosenman, R. H. (1985). Modifying type A behavior. In J. C. Rosen & L. J. Solomon (Eds.), *Prevention in health psychology* (pp. 130–142). Hanover, NH: University Press of New England.

Cinciripini, P. M., Cinciripini, L. G., Wallfisch, A., Haque, W., & Van Vunakis, H. (1996). Behavior therapy and the transdermal nicotine patch: Effects on cessation outcome, affect, and coping. *Journal of Consulting and Clinical Psychology, 64*, 314–323.

Ciraulo, D. A., & Renner, J. A. (1991). Alcoholism. In D. A. Ciraulo & R. I. Shader (Eds.), *Clinical manual of chemical dependence* (pp. 1–93). Washington, DC: American Psychiatric Press.

Cobb, S. (1976). Social support as a moderator of stress. *Psychosomatic Medicine, 38*, 300–314.

Cobb, S., & Rose, R. M. (1973). Hypertension, peptic ulcer, and diabetes in air traffic controllers. *Journal of the American Medical Association, 224*, 489–492.

Cohen, S., & Rodriguez, M. S. (1995). Pathways linking affective disturbances and physical disorders. *Health Psychology, 14*, 374–380.

Compas, B. E., Haaga, D. A. F., Keefe, F. J., Leitenberg, H., & Williams, D. A. (1998). Sampling of empirically supported psychological treatments from health psychology: Smoking, chronic pain, cancer, and bulimia nervosa. *Journal of Consulting and Clinical Psychology, 66*, 89–112.

Conrad, K. M., Flay, B. R., & Hill, D. (1992). Why children start smoking cigarettes: Predictors of onset. *British Journal of Addiction, 87*, 1711–1724.

Cottington, E. M., & House, J. S. (1987). Occupational stress and health: A multivariate relationship. In A. Baum & J. E. Singer (Eds.), *Handbook of psychology and health* (Vol. 5, pp. 41–62). Hillsdale, NJ: Erlbaum.

Cox, G. B., Chapman, C. R., & Black, R. G. (1978). The MMPI and chronic pain: The diagnosis of psychogenic pain. *Journal of Behavioral Medicine*, *1*, 437–443.

Criqui, M. H., & Ringel, B. L. (1994). Does diet or alcohol explain the French paradox? *Lancet, 344*, 1719–1723.

Cunningham, C. L. (1998). Drug conditioning and drug-seeking behavior. In W. O'Donahue (Ed.), *Learning and behavior therapy* (pp. 518–544). Boston: Allyn & Bacon.

Curry, S. J., & Emmons, K. M. (1994). Theoretical models for predicting and improving compliance with breast cancer screening. *Annals of Behavioral Medicine, 16*, 302–316.

Davison, G. C., & Neale, J. M. (1998). *Abnormal psychology* (7th edn.). New York: Wiley.

Deardorff, W. W. (1996). Board certification: What do you mean you're not board certified? *Health Psychologist, 18*, 10–11.

DeBenedittis, G., Panerai, A. A., & Villamira, M. A. (1989). Effects of hypnotic analgesia and hypnotizability on experimental ischemic pain. *International Journal of Clinical and Experimental Hypnosis, 35*, 55–69.

Diamond, E. L. (1982). The role of anger and hostility in essential hypertension and coronary heart disease. *Psychological Bulletin, 92*, 410–433.

DiClemente, C. C., Prochaska, J. O., Fairhurst, S. K., Velicer, W. F., Velasquez, M. M., & Rossi, J. S. (1991). The process of smoking cessation: An analysis of precontemplation, contemplation, and preparation stages of change. *Journal of Consulting and Clinical Psychology, 59*, 295–304.

DiMatteo, M. R. (1985). Physician–patient communication: Promoting a positive health care setting. In J. C. Rosen & L. J. Solomon (Eds.), *Prevention in health psychology* (pp. 328–365). Hanover, NH: University Press of New England.

Dishman, R. K., Sallis, J. F., & Orenstein, D. R. (1985). The determinants of physical activity and exercise. *Public Health Reports, 100*, 158–171.

Dunn, A. J. (1995). Psychoneuroimmunology: Introduction and general perspectives. In B. Leonard & K. Miller (Eds.), *Stress, the immune system and psychiatry* (pp. 1–16). New York: Wiley.

Dunn, M. E., & Goldman, M. S. (1998). Age and drinking-related differences in the memory organization of alcohol expectancies in 3rd-, 6th-, 9th, and 12th-grade children. *Journal of Consulting and Clinical Psychology, 66*, 579–585.

Dusseldorp, E., van Elderen, T., Maes, S., Meulman, J., & Kraaij, V. (1999). A meta-analysis of psycho-educational programs for coronary heart disease patients. *Health Psychology, 18*, 506–519.

D'Zurilla, T. J. (1988). Problem-solving therapies. In K. S. Dobson (Ed.), *Handbook of cognitive-behavioral therapies* (pp. 85–135). New York: Guilford.

Ellis, A. (1962). *Reason and emotion in psychotherapy*. New York: Lyle Stuart.

Ellis, A. (1977). The basic clinical theory of rational-emotive therapy. In A. Ellis & R. Grieger (Eds.), *Handbook of rational-emotive therapy* (pp. 3–34). New York: Springer.

Engel, G. L. (1977). The need for a new medical model: A challenge for biomedicine. *Science, 196*, 129–136.

Engel, G. L. (1980). The clinical application of the biopsychosocial model. *American Journal of Psychiatry, 137*, 535–544.

European Health Psychology Society (2001). *Aims and scope: EHPS national delegates*. Retrieved (7 August 2001) from www.ehps.net.

Everson, S. A., Goldberg, D. E., Kaplan, G. A., Cohen, R. D., Pukkala, E., Tuomilehto, J., & Salonen, J. T. (1996). Hopelessness and risk of mortality and incidence of myocardial infarction and cancer. *Psychosomatic Medicine, 58*, 113–121.

Fernandez, E., & Turk, D. C. (1989). The utility of cognitive coping strategies for altering pain perception: A meta-analysis. *Pain, 38*, 123–135.

Fiore, M. C., Jorenby, D. E., & Baker, T. B. (1997). Smoking cessation: Principles and practice based upon the AHCPR guideline, 1996. *Annals of Behavioral Medicine, 19*, 213–219.

Flack, J. M., Amaro, H., Jenkins, W., Kunitz, S., Levy, J., Mixon, M., & Yu, E. (1995). Panel I: Epidemiology of minority health. *Health Psychology, 14*, 592–600.

Frasure-Smith, N., Lespérance, F., Juneau, M., Talajic, M., & Bourassa, M. G. (1999). Gender, depression, and one-year prognosis after myocardial infarction. *Psychosomatic Medicine, 61*, 26–37.

Friedman, H. S., & Booth-Kewley, S. (1987). The 'disease-prone' personality. *American Psychologist, 42*, 539–555.

Friedman, H. S., Tucker, J. S., Schwartz, J. E., Tomlinson-Keasey, C., Wingard, D. L., & Criqui, M. H. (1995). Psychosocial and behavioral predictors of longevity: The aging and death of the 'Termites'. *American Psychologist, 50*, 69–78.

Friedman, M., & Rosenman, R. H. (1974). *Type A behavior and your heart*. New York: Knopf.

Gentry, W. D. (1984). Behavioral medicine: A new research paradigm. In W. D. Gentry (Ed.), *Handbook of behavioral medicine* (pp. 1–12). New York: Guilford.

Gerace, R. A., & Vorp, R. (1985). Epidemiology and behavior. In N. Schneiderman & J. T. Tapp (Eds.),

Behavioral medicine: The biopsychosocial approach (pp. 25–44). Hillsdale, NJ: Erlbaum.

Glass, D. C. (1977). *Behavior patterns, stress, and coronary heart disease*. Hillsdale, NJ: Erlbaum.

Goodall, T. A., & Halford, W. K. (1991). Self-management of diabetes mellitus: A critical review. *Health Psychology, 10*, 1–8.

Grob, G. N. (1983). Disease and environment in American history. In D. Mechanic (Ed.), *Handbook of health, health care, and the health professions* (pp. 3–22). New York: Free Press.

Gruen, W. (1975). Effects of brief psychotherapy during the hospitalization period on the recovery process in heart attacks. *Journal of Consulting and Clinical Psychology, 43*, 223–232.

Gump, B. B., & Matthews, K. A. (1999). Do background stressors influence reactivity to and recovery from acute stressors? *Journal of Applied Social Psychology, 29*, 469–494.

Haynes, R. B. (1976). A critical review of the 'determinants' of patient compliance with therapeutic regimens. In D. L. Sackett & R. B. Haynes (Eds.), *Compliance with therapeutic regimens* (pp. 26–40). Baltimore: Johns Hopkins University Press.

Hearn, M. D., Baranowski, T., Baranowski, J., Doyle, C., Smith, M., Lin, L. S., & Resnicow, K. (1998). Environmental influences on dietary behavior among children: Availability and accessibility of fruits and vegetables enable consumption. *Journal of Health Education, 29*, 26–32.

Henderson, G., & Primeaux, M. (1981). Religious beliefs and healing. In G. Henderson & M. Primeaux (Eds.), *Transcultural health care* (pp. 185–195). Menlo Park, CA: Addison-Wesley.

Herman, C. P., Olmstead, M. P., & Polivy, J. (1983). Obesity, externality, and susceptibility to social influence: An integrated analysis. *Journal of Personality and Social Psychology, 45*, 926–934.

Hobfoll, S. E. (1989). Conservation of resources: A new attempt at conceptualizing stress. *American Psychologist, 44*, 513–524.

Holroyd, K. A., & Penzien, D. B. (1990). Pharmacological versus non-pharmacological prophylaxis of recurrent migraine headache: A meta-analytic review of clinical trials. *Pain, 42*, 1–13.

Hughes, J. R. (1986). Genetics of smoking: A brief review. *Behavior Therapy, 17*, 335–345.

Janis, I. L. (1984). The patient as decision maker. In W. D. Gentry (Ed.), *Handbook of behavioral medicine* (pp. 326–368). New York: Guilford.

Johnson, K., Anderson, N. B., Bastida, E., Kramer, B. J., Williams, D., & Wong, M. (1995). Panel II:

Macrosocial and environmental influences on minority health. *Health Psychology, 14*, 601–612.

Kiecolt-Glaser, J. K., & Glaser, R. (1995). Psychoneuroimmunology and health consequences: Data and shared mechanisms. *Psychosomatic Medicine, 57*, 269–274.

Killen, J. D., Robinson, T. N., Haydel, K. F., Hayward, C., Wilson, D. M., Hammer, L. D., Litt, I. F., & Taylor, C. B. (1997). Prospective study of risk factors for the initiation of cigarette smoking. *Journal of Consulting and Clinical Psychology, 65*, 1011–1016.

Kirscht, J. P. (1983). Preventive health behavior: A review of research and issues. *Health Psychology, 2*, 277–301.

Klepp, K.-I., Kelder, S. H., & Perry, C. L. (1995). Alcohol and marijuana use among adolescents: Long-term outcomes of the Class of 1989 Study. *Annals of Behavioral Medicine, 17*, 19–24.

Kranzler, H. R., & Anton, R. F. (1994). Implications of recent neuropsychopharmacologic research for understanding the etiology and development of alcoholism. *Journal of Consulting and Clinical Psychology, 62*, 1116–1126.

Kunda, Z. (1990). The case for motivated reasoning. *Psychological Bulletin, 108*, 480–498.

La Greca, A. M., & Stone, W. L. (1985). Behavioral pediatrics. In N. Schneiderman & J. T. Tapp (Eds.), *Behavioral medicine: The biopsychosocial approach* (pp. 255–291). Hillsdale, NJ: Erlbaum.

Langlie, J. K. (1977). Social networks, health beliefs, and preventive health behavior. *Journal of Health and Social Behavior, 18*, 244–260.

Lazarus, R. S., & Folkman, S. (1984). *Stress, appraisal, and coping*. New York: Springer.

Leahey, T. H. (1987). *A history of psychology: Main currents in psychological thought* (2nd edn.). Englewood Cliffs, NJ: Prentice-Hall.

Leonard, B. E. (1995). Stress and the immune system: Immunological aspects of depressive illness. In B. E. Leonard & K. Miller (Eds.), *Stress, the immune system and psychiatry* (pp. 113–136). New York: Wiley.

Lerman, C., Caporaso, N. E., Audrain, J., Main, D., Bowman, E. D., Lockshin, B., Boyd, N. R., & Shields, P. G. (1999). Evidence suggesting the role of specific genetic factors in cigarette smoking. *Health Psychology, 18*, 14–20.

Leventhal, H., & Cleary, P. D. (1980). The smoking problem: A review of research and theory in behavioral risk modification. *Psychological Bulletin, 88*, 370–405.

Leventhal, H., Prohaska, T. R., & Hirschman, R. S. (1985). Preventive health behavior across the life span. In J. C. Rosen & L. J. Solomon (Eds.), *Prevention in health psychology* (pp. 191–235). Hanover, NH: University Press of New England.

Levy, S. M. (1985). *Behavior and cancer.* San Francisco: Jossey-Bass.

Linden, W., & Chambers, L. (1994). Clinical effectiveness of non-drug treatment for hypertension: A meta-analysis. *Annals of Behavioral Medicine, 16,* 35–45.

Linden, W., Stossel, C., & Maurice, J. (1996). Psychosocial interventions for patients with coronary artery disease. *Archives of Internal Medicine, 156,* 745–752.

Lipowski, Z. J. (1986). What does the word 'psychosomatic' really mean? A historical and semantic inquiry. In M. J. Christie & P. G. Mellett (Eds.), *The psychosomatic approach: Contemporary practice and whole-person care* (pp. 17–38). New York: Wiley.

Little, R. E. (1998). Public health in Central and Eastern Europe and the role of environmental pollution. *Annual Review of Public Health, 19,* 153–172.

Logue, A. W. (1991). *The psychology of eating and drinking: An introduction* (2nd edn.). New York: Freeman.

Lundberg, U. (1999). Coping with stress: Neuroendocrine reactions and implications for health. *Noise and Health, 4,* 67–74.

Maddux, J. E., Roberts, M. C., Sledden, E. A., & Wright, L. (1986). Developmental issues in child health psychology. *American Psychologist, 41,* 25–34.

Manne, S. L., Bakeman, R., Jacobsen, P. B., Gorfinkle, K., & Redd, W. H. (1994). An analysis of a behavioral intervention for children undergoing venipuncture. *Health Psychology, 13,* 556–566.

Marx, M. H., & Hillix, W. A. (1963). *Systems and theories in psychology.* New York: McGraw-Hill.

Matarazzo, J. D. (1982). Behavioral health's challenge to academic, scientific, and professional psychology. *American Psychologist, 37,* 1–14.

Matthews, K. A. (1988). Coronary heart disease and type A behaviors: Update on and alternative to the Booth-Kewley and Friedman (1987) quantitative review. *Psychological Bulletin, 104,* 373–380.

Matthews, K. A., Owens, J. F., Kuller, L. H., Sutton-Tyrrell, K., Lassila, H. C., & Wolfson, S. K. (1998). Stress-induced pulse pressure change predicts women's carotid atherosclerosis. *Stroke, 29,* 1525–1530.

McCarty, D. (1985). Environmental factors in substance abuse: The microsetting. In M. Galizio &

S. A. Maisto (Eds.), *Determinants of substance abuse: Biological, psychological, and environmental factors* (pp. 247–281). New York: Plenum.

McGinnis, J. M. (1994). The role of behavioral research in national health policy. In J. A. Blumenthal, K. Matthews & S. M. Weiss (Eds.), *New frontiers in behavioral medicine: Proceedings of the national conference* (pp. 217–222). Washington, DC: National Institutes of Health.

Meichenbaum, D., & Cameron, R. (1983). Stress inoculation training: Toward a general paradigm for training coping skills. In D. Meichenbaum & M. E. Jaremko (Eds.), *Stress reduction and prevention* (pp. 115–154). New York: Plenum.

Melzack, R., & Wall, P. D. (1965). Pain mechanisms: A new theory. *Science, 150,* 971–979.

Melzack, R., & Wall, P. D. (1982). *The challenge of pain.* New York: Basic.

Menkes, M. S., Matthews, K. A., Krantz, D. S., Lundberg, U., Mead, L. A., Qaqish, B., & Liang, K.-Y. (1989). Cardiovascular reactivity to the cold pressor test as a predictor of hypertension. *Hypertension, 14,* 524–530.

Miller, N. E. (1978). Biofeedback and visceral learning. *Annual Review of Psychology, 29,* 373–404.

Miller, S. M. (1979). Controllability and human stress: Method, evidence and theory. *Behaviour Research and Therapy, 17,* 287–304.

Miller, W. R., & Hester, R. K. (1980). Treating the problem drinker: Modern approaches. In W. R. Miller (Ed.), *The addictive behaviors: Treatment of alcoholism, drug abuse, smoking, and obesity.* New York: Pergamon.

Monti, P. M., Rohsenow, D. J., Rubonis, A. V., Naiura, R. S., Sirota, A. D., Colby, S. M., Goddard, P., & Abrams, D. B. (1993). Cue exposure with coping skills treatment for male alcoholics: A preliminary investigation. *Journal of Consulting and Clinical Psychology, 61,* 1011–1019.

Morley, S., Eccleston, C., & Williams, A. (1999). Systematic review and meta-analysis of randomized controlled trials of cognitive behaviour therapy and behaviour therapy for chronic pain in adults, excluding headache. *Pain, 80,* 1–13.

Myers, H. F., Kagawa-Singer, M., Kumanyika, S. K., Lex, B. W., & Markides, K. S. (1995). Panel III: Behavioral risk factors related to chronic diseases in ethnic minorities. *Health Psychology, 14,* 613–621.

National Association of Social Workers (2000). *Social work careers.* Retrieved (4 March 2000) from http://www.naswdc.org.

National Center for Health Statistics (2000). *Health, United States, 1999.* Retrieved (21 March 2000) from http://www.cdc.gov/nchs.

National Institute on Alcohol Abuse and Alcoholism (1993). *Alcohol and health* (8th Special Report to the US Congress; Publication no. 94-3699). Washington, DC: US Government Printing Office.

Nezu, A. M., Nezu, C. M., & Perri, M. G. (1989). *Problem-solving therapy for depression: Theory, research, and clinical guidelines.* New York: Wiley.

Ostrove, J. M., Feldman, P., & Adler, N. E. (1999). Relations among socioeconomic status indicators and health for African-Americans and whites. *Journal of Health Psychology, 4,* 451–463.

Ouimette, P. C., Finney, J. W., & Moos, R. H. (1997). Twelve-step and cognitive-behavioral treatment for substance abuse: A comparison of treatment effectiveness. *Journal of Consulting and Clinical Psychology, 65,* 230–240.

Parrish, J. M. (1986). Parent compliance with medical and behavioral recommendations. In N. A. Krasnegor, J. D. Arasteh & M. F. Cataldo (Eds.), *Child health behavior: A behavioral pediatrics perspective* (pp. 453–501). New York: Wiley.

Pomerleau, O. F., & Pomerleau, C. S. (1989). A biobehavioral perspective on smoking. In T. Ney & A. Gale (Eds.), *Smoking and human behavior* (pp. 69–90). New York: Wiley.

Powell, L. H., & Friedman, M. (1986). Alteration of type A behaviour in coronary patients. In M. J. Christie & P. G. Mellett (Eds.), *The psychosomatic approach: Contemporary practice of whole-person care* (pp. 191–214). New York: Wiley.

Prescott, C. A., & Kendler, K. S. (1999). Genetic and environmental contributions to alcohol abuse and dependence in a population-based sample of male twins. *American Journal of Psychiatry, 156,* 34–40.

Prochaska, J. O., & DiClemente, C. C. (1984). *The transtheoretical approach: Crossing traditional boundaries of therapy.* Homewood, IL: Dow Jones/Irwin.

Prochaska, J. O., DiClemente, C. C., & Norcross, J. C. (1992). In search of how people change: Applications to addictive behaviors. *American Psychologist, 47,* 1102–1114.

Quinlan, K. B., & McCaul, K. D. (2000). Matched and mismatched interventions with young adult smokers: Testing a stage theory. *Health Psychology, 19,* 165–171.

Rand, C. S., & Weeks, K. (1998). Measuring adherence with medication regimens in clinical care research. In S. A. Shumaker, E. B. Schron, J. L. Ockene & W. L. McBee (Eds.), *The handbook of health behavior change* (2nd edn., pp. 114–132). New York: Springer.

Reddy, D. M., Fleming, R., & Adesso, V. J. (1992). Gender and health. In S. Maes, H. Leventhal, &

M. Johnston (Eds.), *International review of health psychology* (Vol. 1, pp. 3–32). New York: Wiley.

Reker, G. T., & Wong, P. T. P. (1985). Personal optimism, physical and mental health. In J. E. Birren & J. Livingston (Eds.), *Cognition, stress, and aging.* Englewood Cliffs, NJ: Prentice-Hall.

Retchin, S. M., Wells, J. A., Valleron, A.-J., & Albrecht, G. L. (1992). Health behavior changes in the United States, the United Kingdom, and France. *Journal of General Internal Medicine, 7,* 615–622.

Robbins, L. (1994). Precipitating factors in migraine: A retrospective review of 494 patients. *Headache, 34,* 214–216.

Robinson, L. A., & Klesges, R. C. (1997). Ethnic and gender differences in risk factors for smoking onset. *Health Psychology, 16,* 499–505.

Rodin, J. (1986). Health, control, and aging. In M. M. Baltes & P. B. Baltes (Eds.), *The psychology of control and aging* (pp. 139–165). Hillsdale, NJ: Erlbaum.

Rosen, J. C., Grubman, J. A., Bevins, T., & Frymoyer, J. W. (1987). Musculoskeletal status and disability of MMPI profile subgroups among patients with low back pain. *Health Psychology, 6,* 581–598.

Rosenstock, I. M. (1966). Why people use health services. *Milbank Memorial Fund Quarterly, 44,* 94–127.

Roskies, E. (1983). Stress management for type A individuals. In D. Meichenbaum & M. E. Jaremko (Eds.), *Stress reduction and prevention* (pp. 261–288). New York: Plenum.

Roter, D. L., & Hall, J. A. (1989). Studies of doctor–patient interaction. *Annual Review of Public Health, 10,* 163–180.

Roter, D. L., Hall, J. A., Mersica, R., Nordstrom, B., Cretin, D., & Svarstad, B. (1998). Effectiveness of interventions to improve patient compliance: A meta-analysis. *Medical Care, 36,* 1138–1161.

Rotter, J. B. (1966). Generalized expectancies for the internal versus external control of reinforcement. *Psychological Monographs, 90,* 1–28.

Rozin, P. (1989). The role of learning in the acquisition of food preferences by humans. In R. Shepherd (Ed.), *Handbook of the psychophysiology of human eating* (pp. 205–227). Chichester: Wiley.

Runyan, C. W. (1985). Health assessment and public policy within a public health framework. In P. Karoly (Ed.), *Measurement strategies in health psychology* (pp. 601–627). New York: Wiley.

Sacks, D. A., & Koppes, R. H. (1986). Blood transfusion and Jehovah's Witnesses: Medical and legal issues in obstetrics and gynecology. *American Journal of Obstetrics and Gynecology, 154,* 483–486.

Sallis, J. F., & Owen, N. (1999). *Physical activity and behavioral medicine.* Thousand Oaks, CA: Sage.

Sanson-Fisher, R. (1993). Primary and secondary prevention of cancer: Opportunities for behavioural scientists. In S. Maes, H. Leventhal & M. Johnston (Eds.), *International review of health psychology* (Vol. 2, pp. 117–146). New York: Wiley.

Sarafino, E. P. (1997). *Behavioral treatments for asthma: Biofeedback-, respondent-, and relaxation-based approaches.* Lewiston, NY: Mellon.

Sarafino, E. P. (1999). *Health psychology: An overview and focus on nonrational processes in decisions about health.* Paper presented at the Iowa Psychological Association Convention in Pella, Iowa, October.

Sarafino, E. P. (2001). *Behavior modification: Principles of behavior change* (2nd edn.). Mountain View, CA: Mayfield.

Sarafino, E. P. (2002). *Health psychology: Biopsychosocial interactions* (4th edn.). New York: Wiley.

Sarafino, E. P., & Goldfedder, J. (1995). Genetic factors in the presence, severity, and triggers of asthma. *Archives of Disease in Childhood, 73,* 112–116.

Sarason, I. G., & Sarason, B. R. (1984). *Abnormal psychology* (4th edn.). Englewood Cliffs, NJ: Prentice-Hall.

Schachter, S., Silverstein, B., Kozlowski, L. T., Perlick, D., Herman, C. P., & Liebling, B. (1977). Studies of the interaction of psychological and pharmacological determinants of smoking. *Journal of Experimental Psychology: General, 106,* 3–40.

Scheier, L. M., & Botvin, G. J. (1997). Expectancies as mediators of the effects of social influences and alcohol knowledge on adolescent alcohol use: A prospective analysis. *Psychology of Addictive Behaviors, 11,* 48–64.

Scheier, M. F., & Bridges, M. W. (1995). Person variables and health: Personality predispositions and acute psychological states as shared determinants for disease. *Psychosomatic Medicine, 57,* 255–268.

Scheier, M. F., & Carver, C. S. (2001). Adapting to cancer: The importance of hope and purpose. In A. Baum & B. L. Anderson (Eds.), *Psychosocial interventions for cancer* (pp. 15–36). Washington, DC: American Psychological Association.

Schneider, A. M., & Tarshis, B. (1975). *An introduction to physiological psychology.* New York: Random House.

Schuckit, M. A. (1985). Genetics and the risk for alcoholism. *Journal of the American Medical Association, 254,* 2614–2617.

Schutz, H. G., & Diaz-Knauf, K. V. (1989). The role of the mass media in influencing eating. In R. Shepherd (Ed.), *Handbook of the psychophysiology of human eating* (pp. 141–154). Chichester: Wiley.

Schwartz, G. E. (1982). Testing the biopsychosocial model: The ultimate challenge facing behavioral medicine? *Journal of Consulting and Clinical Psychology, 50,* 1040–1053.

Selye, H. (1956). *The stress of life.* New York: McGraw-Hill.

Selye, H. (1976). *Stress in health and disease.* Reading, MA: Butterworth.

Shadel, W. G., Shiffman, S., Niaura, R., Nichter, M., & Abrams, D. B. (2000). Current models of nicotine dependence: What is known and what is needed to advance understanding of tobacco etiology among youth. *Drug and Alcohol Dependence, 59* (Supp.), S9–S22.

Shiffman, S., Paty, J. A., Gnys, M., Kassel, J. D., & Elash, C. (1995). Nicotine withdrawal in chippers and regular smokers: Subjective and cognitive effects. *Health Psychology, 14,* 301–309.

Skolnick, A. S. (1986). *The psychology of human development.* San Diego: Harcourt Brace Jovanovich.

Stone, A. A., Neale, J. M., Cox, D. S., Napoli, A., Valdimarsdottir, H., & Kennedy-Moore, E. (1994). Daily events are associated with a secretory immune response to an oral antigen in men. *Health Psychology, 13,* 440–446.

Stone, G. C. (1979). Health and the health system: A historical overview and conceptual framework. In G. C. Stone, F. Cohen & N. E. Adler (Eds.), *Health psychology: A handbook* (pp. 1–17). San Francisco: Jossey-Bass.

Stunkard, A. J., Foch, T. T., & Hrubec, Z. (1986). A twin study of human obesity. *Journal of the American Medical Association, 256,* 51–54.

Theorell, T., & Rahe, R. H. (1975). Life change events, ballistocardiography, and coronary death. *Journal of Human Stress, 1,* 18–24.

Thompson, S. C. (1981). Will it hurt less if I can control it? A complex answer to a simple question. *Psychological Bulletin, 90,* 89–101.

Thoresen, C. E. (1984). Overview. In J. D. Matarazzo, S. M. Weiss, J. A. Herd, N. E. Miller, & S. M. Weiss (Eds.), *Behavioral health: A handbook of health enhancement and disease prevention* (pp. 297–307). New York: Wiley.

Tortora, G. J., & Grabowski, S. R. (2000). *Principles of anatomy and physiology* (9th edn.). New York: Wiley.

Totman, R. (1982). Psychosomatic theories. In J. R. Eiser (Ed.), *Social psychology and behavioral medicine* (pp. 143–175). New York: Wiley.

Turk, D. C., Meichenbaum, D., & Genest, M. (1983). *Pain and behavioral medicine: A cognitive-behavioral perspective.* New York: Guilford.

US Bureau of the Census (1999). *Statistical abstracts of the United States: 1998* (118th edn.). Retrieved (28 February 2000) from http://www.census.gov.

US Department of Health and Human Services (1982). *Changes in mortality among the elderly: United States, 1940–78* (Publication no. PHS 82–1406). Washington, DC: US Government Printing Office.

US Department of Health and Human Services (1987). *Vital statistics of the United States, 1984: Life tables* (Publication no. PHS 87–1104). Washington, DC: US Government Printing Office.

Vedhara, K., Cox, N. K. M., Wilcock, G. K., Perks, P., Hunt, M., Anderson, S., Lightman, S. L., & Shanks, N. M. (1999). Chronic stress in elderly carers of dementia patients and antibody response to influenza vaccination. *Lancet, 353,* 627–631.

Velicer, W. F., Prochaska, J. O., Fava, J. L., LaForge, R. G., & Rossi, J. S. (1999). Interactive versus noninteractive interventions and dose–response relationships for stage-matched smoking cessation programs in a managed care setting. *Health Psychology, 18,* 21–28.

Vertinsky, P., & Auman, J. T. (1988). Elderly women's barriers to exercise, Part I: Perceived risks. *Health Values, 12,* 13–19.

Wallston, B. S., Alagna, S. W., DeVellis, B. M., & DeVellis, R. F. (1983). Social support and physical illness. *Health Psychology, 2,* 367–391.

Wallston, K. A. (1993). Health psychology in the USA. In S. Maes, H. Leventhal & M. Johnston (Eds.), *International review of health psychology* (Vol. 2, pp. 215–228). Chichester: Wiley.

Weinstein, N. D. (1987). Unrealistic optimism about susceptibility to health problems: Conclusions from a community-wide sample. *Journal of Behavioral Medicine, 10,* 481–500.

Weiss, G. L., Larsen, D. L., & Baker, W. K. (1996). The development of health protective behaviors among college students. *Journal of Behavioral Medicine, 19,* 143–161.

Whitaker, R. C., Wright, J. A., Pepe, M. S., Seidel, K. D., & Dietz, W. H. (1997). Predicting obesity in young adulthood from childhood and parental obesity. *New England Journal of Medicine, 337,* 869–873.

Williams, C. J. (1990). *Cancer biology and management: An introduction.* New York: Wiley.

Williams, D. R., & Rucker, T. (1996). Socioeconomic status and the health of racial minority populations. In P. M. Kato & T. Mann (Eds.), *Handbook of diversity issues in health psychology* (pp. 407–423). New York: Plenum.

Wills, T. A. (1984). Supportive functions of interpersonal relationships. In S. Cohen & L. Syme (Eds.), *Social support and health* (pp. 61–82). New York: Academic.

Winters, R. (1985). Behavioral approaches to pain. In N. Schneiderman & J. T. Tapp (Eds.), *Behavioral medicine: The biopsychosocial approach* (pp. 565–587). Hillsdale, NJ: Erlbaum.

Wittrock, D. A., & Myers, T. C. (1998). The comparison of individuals with recurrent tension-type headache and headache-free controls in physiological response, appraisal, and coping with stressors: A review of the literature. *Annals of Behavioral Medicine, 20,* 118–134.

Woods, A. M., & Birren, J. E. (1984). Late adulthood and aging. In J. D. Matarazzo, S. M. Weiss, J. A. Herd, N. E. Miller & S. M. Weiss (Eds.), *Behavioral health: A handbook of health enhancement and disease prevention* (pp. 91–100). New York: Wiley.

World Health Organization (1998). *Tobacco epidemic: Health dimensions.* Retrieved (28 February 2000) from http://www.who.org.

World Health Organization (1999). *World health report.* Retrieved (28 February 2000) from http://www.who. org.

Wright, R. J., Rodriguez, M., & Cohen, S. (1998). Review of psychosocial stress and asthma: An integrated biopsychosocial approach. *Thorax, 53,* 1066–1074.

2

Epidemiology of Health and Illness: A Socio-Psycho-Physiological Perspective

REINER RUGULIES, BIRGIT AUST
AND S. LEONARD SYME

> The primary determinants of disease are mainly economic and social, and therefore its remedies must also be economic and social.
>
> (Geoffrey Rose, 1992: 129)

INTRODUCTION

When we were invited to write this chapter, one of the editors sent us an e-mail stating that 'this chapter is supposed to include everything that a health psychologist needs to know about the epidemiology of health and illness, so it will be quite a challenge'. We agree that this is a challenge, both for us and for the reader, but we think that it is a challenge worth taking.

So, what does a health psychologist need to know about epidemiology? We will start with a definition. Epidemiology can be defined as the study of the distribution and determinants of health and illness in populations and of the action that is necessary to prevent disease and promote health. Based on this definition, epidemiology can be differentiated into three dimensions: in *descriptive epidemiology*, studies show how health and illness are distributed; in *analytic epidemiology*, research investigates the determinants of health and illness; and in *intervention epidemiology*, strategies are studied to prevent disease and promote health. We will address all three dimensions in this chapter.

Following this introduction, we will give an overview of the distribution of health and illness, that is, life expectancy in different parts of the world, its changes over time and the identification of the diseases that present the greatest burden today. We will then discuss historical and theoretical considerations of epidemiologic research on the determinants of health and illness, and we will introduce a conceptual model for an interdisciplinary, socio-psycho-physiological perspective on this issue. After this, we will present recent and classical findings from analytic and intervention epidemiology studies, and will discuss several important controversies. The chapter ends with some final thoughts on the importance of an interdisciplinary and 'upstream' perspective.

Table 2.1   *Life expectancy (years) at birth in WHO member states,*
estimates for 2000

	Men		Women	
1	Japan	77.5	Japan	84.7
2	Sweden	77.3	Monaco	84.4
3	Andorra	77.2	Andorra	83.8
4	Iceland	77.1	San Marino	83.8
5	Monaco	76.8	France	83.1
6	Switzerland	76.7	Switzerland	82.5
7	Australia	76.6	Italy	82.4
8	Israel	76.6	Spain	82.3
9	San Marino	76.1	Australia	82.1
10	Canada	76.0	Sweden	82.0
11	Italy	76.0	Iceland	81.8
12	New Zealand	75.9	Canada	81.5
13	Norway	75.7	Norway	81.4
14	Greece	75.4	Austria	81.4
15	Malta	75.4	Netherlands	81.0
16	Netherlands	75.4	New Zealand	80.9
17	Singapore	75.4	Belgium	80.9
18	Spain	75.4	Finland	80.9
19	France	75.2	Greece	80.8
20	Austria	74.9	Luxembourg	80.8
21	Cyprus	74.8	Malta	80.7
22	United Kingdom	74.8	Israel	80.6
23	Belgium	74.6	Germany	80.6
24	Germany	74.3	Singapore	80.2
25	Denmark	74.2	United Kingdom	79.9
26	Kuwait	74.2	Ireland	79.7
27	Ireland	74.1	USA	79.5
28	Luxembourg	73.9	Chile	79.5
29	USA	73.9	Slovenia	79.4
30	Cuba	73.7	Portugal	79.3
188	Burkina Faso	42.6	Burkina Faso	43.6
189	Lesotho	42.0	Namibia	42.6
190	Central African Rep.	41.6	Central African Rep.	42.5
191	Democratic Rep. Congo	41.6	Lesotho	42.2
192	Burundi	40.6	Burundi	41.3
193	Zambia	39.2	Rwanda	40.5
194	Rwanda	38.5	Zambia	39.5
195	Mozambique	37.9	Mozambique	39.5
196	Malawi	37.1	Sierra Leone	38.8
197	Sierra Leone	37.0	Malawi	37.8

Data source: WHO (2001). *The world health report 2001. Mental health: New understanding,*
new hope. Statistical annex, Table 1. Geneva: World Health Organization. Also available at:
http://www.who.int/whr/2001/main/pdf/whr2001.en.pdf (accessed 16 June 2002).

DISTRIBUTION OF HEALTH AND ILLNESS

An excellent source of information on the distribution of health and illness is the World Health Organization of the United Nations (WHO) and its epidemiologic databank system WHOSIS (World Health Organization Statistical Information System). It is freely accessible through the World Wide Web (http://www.who.int/whosis). Among other things, WHOSIS provides information on life expectancy, cause of death and burden of disease in the WHO member states.

Life Expectancy

Table 2.1 shows life expectancy at birth for the 30 countries with the highest and the 10

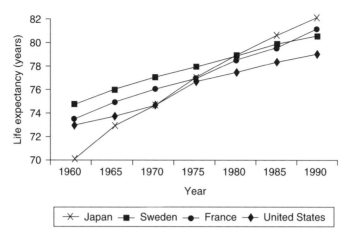

Figure 2.1   *Changes in female life expectancy between 1960 and 1990 in selected countries [Data source: Schieber, G. J., Poullier, J. P., & Greenwald, L. M. (1992). U.S. health expediture performance: An international comparison and data update. Health Care Financing Review, 13, 1–87]*

countries with the lowest life expectancy. The differences are enormous. A newborn boy in Japan can expect to live 40 years longer than his counterpart in Sierra Leone, while a newborn girl in Japan has an advantage of 47 years over a girl born in Malawi (World Health Organization, 2001). It is obvious from the table that life expectancy is not randomly distributed around the globe, but follows a distinct pattern. Almost all of the countries at the top of the list are highly industrialized, wealthy countries, with a high gross domestic product per capita (GDPpC), such as Japan, Australia, New Zealand, Singapore, Canada and numerous countries of the European Union. The 10 countries at the bottom of the list are all non-industrialized countries in sub-Saharan Africa with very low GDPpC. However, while the wealth of a country is in general an excellent predictor of life expectancy, there are some remarkable exceptions. The United States, which has one of the highest GDPpC in the world, is ranked only 29th and 27th (males and females respectively) with a male life expectancy comparable to Cuba and a female life expectancy comparable to Chile.

Changes in Life Expectancy

One of the most fascinating findings in research on life expectancy is that it can exhibit

relatively rapid change over time. Figure 2.1 shows changes in female life expectancy between 1960 and 1990 in Japan, Sweden, France, and the United States (Evans, 1994; Schieber, Poullier & Greenwald, 1992). Among these four countries, Japan had the lowest life expectancy in 1960, approximately 70 years, which was 3 years less than the United States and 5 years less than Sweden. In only 30 years, Japanese women gained almost 12 years of life expectancy, surpassing all other countries, which gained only 5 to 7 years during this period. Male life expectancy showed a similar pattern of change during this time period (for details, see Evans, 1994; Schieber et al., 1992).

The reason for the impressive increase in Japanese longevity is not clear. Certainly, genetics cannot be responsible for an increase in such a short time. Japan does not spend more money on health services and does not have more rigorous standards for protecting the environment from pollution than other industrialized countries (Evans, 1994; Marmot & Davey Smith, 1989). Unique features of Japanese diet (e.g., low in meat, high in fish) and social relationships (e.g., less individualistic, more group oriented) have been discussed as possible explanations. However, these diet and social relationships have not changed much during the years in which Japan saw this substantial improvement in life expectancy. Evans has pointed out that the only thing that certainly changed was 'the hierarchical position of Japanese society as a whole, relative to the rest of the world. These observations demonstrate the extremely large influence of "macroenvironmental" factors, both social and physical, on illness patterns. They also show that disease patterns and health status can change rapidly, and by a large amount, when these external factors change' (1994: 18).

A recent powerful example of how sensitive life expectancy is to changes in the macro-environment can be found in Eastern Europe where countries rapidly transformed from socialist planned economies to capitalistic market economies during the 1990s. The most dramatic changes were observed for the region that constitutes Russia today, which was a part of the Soviet Union until 1991. After the breakup of the Soviet Union, Russia underwent drastic social and economic changes. Numerous factories were closed, a large number of people became unemployed, and the government was no longer able to pay salaries to civil servants and pensions to retirees on time. The average income per capita decreased by almost two-thirds, while the number of families living in poverty rose from 2 per cent to 38 per cent. In addition, public services, including law enforcement and health services, were no longer functioning efficiently (Notzon et al., 1998). The health consequences of these social and economic changes were dramatic. In the 5-year period between 1990 and 1994, life expectancy at birth declined for men from 63.8 to 57.7 years, and for women from 74.4 to 71.2 years. The mortality rate for men between the ages of 35 and 44 increased by almost 100 per cent. Analyses showed that more than half of the decline in life expectancy was due to either cardiovascular disease or fatal injuries, including road traffic accidents, suicides and homicides (Notzon et al., 1998).

While life expectancy in Russia and in the whole Soviet Union was already considerably lower than in Western Europe before 1990 (it actually slowly declined for men and stagnated for women from the mid 1960s to the mid 1980s), the decrease of 6.1 years and 3.2 years

for men and women respectively between 1990 and 1994 was unprecedented for an industrialized country in the twentieth century. Several possible explanations have been discussed in the literature. Among them are the crumbling of the health care system, and a deterioration in health behaviors, especially increases in excessive alcohol consumption, but also the impact of heightened psychosocial stress, in particular the experience of loss of control and a rise in depression and hopelessness (Marmot & Bobak, 2000; Notzon et al., 1998). These factors are not mutually exclusive and are probably connected to each other (e.g., hopelessness may contribute to binge drinking). A detailed debate about possible pathways for the declining life expectancy in Russia and other Eastern European countries can be found in the special issue of the journal *Social Science and Medicine* on 'The health crisis in Russia and Eastern Europe' (*Social Science and Medicine*, 1 November 2000, Volume 51, Issue 9).

Cause-Specific Mortality and Burden of Disease

In addition to life expectancy, statistics on cause of mortality are important for understanding the distribution of health and illness. Table 2.2 shows data from WHOSIS on causes of death in Europe and Africa. The two leading causes of death in Europe are ischemic heart disease (also called coronary heart disease) and cerebrovascular disease, followed by cancers of the respiratory system. In Africa, infectious diseases are the most dominant cause of death, especially HIV and AIDS, but also included are other infectious or infectious-related diseases like lower respiratory infections, malaria, diarrhea (often caused by infections with cholera and other waterborne pathogens), measles, and tuberculosis.

Statistics on cause-specific mortality provide important information to compare the health status in specific regions and also to analyze changes over time. However, the usefulness of these data in understanding the burden of disease is restricted in two ways. First, these statistics do not take into account that diseases often occur at different ages in life. Measles, for

Table 2.2   *Leading causes of death in the WHO regions of Europe and Africa,*
estimates for 2000

Rank	European region	% total deaths	African region	% total deaths
1	Ischemic heart disease	24.3%	HIV/AIDS	22.6%
2	Cerebrovascular disease	15.4%	Lower respiratory infections	10.1%
3	Trachea, bronchus, lung cancers	3.9%	Malaria	9.1%
4	Lower respiratory infections	3.0%	Diarrheal diseases	6.7%
5	Chronic obstructive pulmonary disease	2.8%	Perinatal conditions	5.5%
6	Colon and rectum cancers	2.5%	Measles	4.3%
7	Self-inflicted injuries	1.9%	Tuberculosis	3.6%
8	Stomach cancer	1.9%	Ischemic heart disease	3.1%
9	Cirrhosis of the liver	1.8%	Cerebrovascular disease	2.9%
10	Hypertensive heart disease	1.6%	Road traffic accidents	1.6%

Data source: Murray, C. J. L., Lopez, A. D., Mathers, C. D., & Stein, C. (2002). The Global Burden of
Disease 2000 Project: Aims, methods and data sources. Paper 36. Available at: http://www3.who.int/whosis/menu.
cfm?path=whosis,burden,burden_gbd2000&language=english (accessed 14 June 2002).

Table 2.3   *Leading causes of disability-adjusted life years (DALYs) in the WHO regions of*
Europe and Africa, estimates for 2000

Rank	European region	% total DALYs	African region	% total DALYs
1	Ischemic heart disease	10.1%	HIV/AIDS	20.6%
2	Cerebrovascular disease	6.8%	Malaria	10.1%
3	Unipolar depressive disorders	6.0%	Lower respiratory infections	8.6%
4	Alcohol use disorders	3.4%	Perinatal conditions	6.3%
5	Alzheimer and other dementias	3.0%	Diarrheal diseases	6.1%
6	Self-inflicted injuries	2.6%	Measles	4.5%
7	Road traffic accidents	2.5%	Tuberculosis	2.8%
8	Lower respiratory infections	2.4%	Whooping cough	1.8%
9	Hearing loss, adult onset	2.3%	Road traffic accidents	1.6%
10	Trachea, bronchus, lung cancers	2.2%	Protein-energy malnutrition	1.6%

Data source: Murray, C. J. L., Lopez, A. D., Mathers, C. D., & Stein, C. (2002). The Global Burden of Disease 2000 Project:
Aims, methods and data sources. Paper 36. Available at: http://www3.who.int/whosis/menu.cfm?path=whosis,
burden,burden_gbd2000&language=english (accessed 14 June 2002).

example, usually occurs in children, while cardiovascular diseases occur in people of middle or older age. Therefore, even if more people in the entire population die of cardiovascular diseases than of measles, the health impact in terms of years of lost life might be greater for measles, because this disease kills people at much younger ages. A second limitation is that mortality data do not take into account the suffering and the reduced quality of life from diseases that are not fatal.

A way to create a more sensitive measure of burden of disease is to measure health in units of a 'disability-adjusted life year' (DALY). This measure takes account of the severity of each disease and considers both years of life lost and years lost to disability (Murray, Salomon &

Mathers, 2000). DALY is defined as 'a health gap measure, which combines information on the impact of premature death and of disability and other non-fatal health outcomes. One DALY can be thought of as one lost year of "healthy" life and the burden of disease as a measurement of the gap between current health status and an ideal situation where everyone lives into old age free of disease and disability' (Murray, Lopez, Mathers & Stein, 2002: 2).

Table 2.3 shows the leading causes of DALYs for Europe and Africa. In Europe ischemic heart disease, the leading cause of death, is also the greatest burden of disease in this region. However, the relative contribution of ischemic heart disease to the total burden of disease is

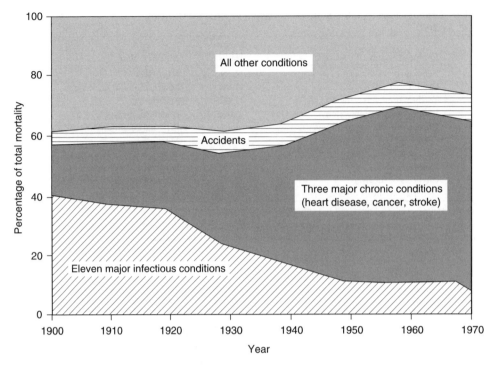

Figure 2.2   *The changing contribution of chronic and infectious conditions to US total mortality [Adapted from McKinlay, J. B., McKinlay, S. M., & Beaglehole, R. (1989) A review of the evidence concerning the impact of medical measures on recent mortality and morbidity in the United States. International Journal of Health Services, 19, 181–208. © Baywood Publishing Company, with permission]*

smaller (10.1 per cent, see Table 2.3) than its contribution to total mortality (24.3 per cent, see Table 2.2). We can also see that unipolar depressive disorders, which do not play an important role for mortality, rank third in burden of disease in Europe. In Africa, on the other hand, the leading causes of death have a similar strong impact on the total burden of disease. In addition to infectious diseases that have been known in Africa and other places for a long time like malaria, measles and tuberculosis, in recent years AIDS has taken a huge toll in Africa. Especially in the sub-Saharan countries AIDS has a devastating effect. Decades of slow progress in life expectancy have been erased by this epidemic. A recent United Nation Report estimates that the average life expectancy in sub-Saharan Africa which is currently 47 years would have been 62 years without AIDS (UNAIDS, 2002).

Changes in Cause-Specific Mortality over Time

The construct of disability-adjusted life years is a fairly recent innovation and cannot therefore be used to analyze changes in health during the last century. To do this, one has to rely on datasets dealing with cause-specific mortality. Figure 2.2 shows how the causes of death have changed in the United States between 1900 and 1970 (McKinlay, McKinlay & Beaglehole, 1989). In 1900, around 40 per cent of all deaths were due to the 11 major infectious diseases (tuberculosis, measles, whooping cough, pneumonia, typhoid, smallpox, scarlet fever, diphtheria, influenza, poliomyelitis, and acute digestive infections). During the century their contribution decreased to 10 per cent, while at the same time the mortality from the three major chronic diseases (heart disease, cancer, and stroke) rose from 20 to 60 per cent of all causes of death. This clear trend from infectious to chronic diseases, which was also seen in the other industrialized countries in the twentieth century, is called the 'epidemiologic transition'. Interestingly, medical treatment and vaccination played only a limited role in the epidemiologic transition, which indicates that medicine is only one of several factors that influence the health of a population (McKinlay et al., 1989).

DETERMINANTS OF HEALTH AND ILLNESS: HISTORICAL AND THEORETICAL CONSIDERATIONS

In this section we will give a brief overview and critique of past and contemporary analytic and intervention epidemiology by contrasting a population with an individual perspective. After this, we will present an interdisciplinary *socio-psycho-physiological framework* that shows how societal, psychological, and physiological factors interact as determinants of health and illness.

The Population and the Individual Perspective in Epidemiology

In a seminal article, Geoffrey Rose pointed out that the determinants of health and illness are very different, depending on whether one takes an individual or a population perspective (Rose, 1985). The individual perspective asks why some individuals contract a specific disease, whereas the population perspective inquires why certain health conditions are more frequent in one population than in another. Rose explained the difference between the two approaches by using the example of systolic blood pressure in middle-aged men in Kenyan nomads and London civil servants. In both populations, blood pressure is more or less normally distributed, so most people are clustered around the mean, while only a few per cent have very high or very low blood pressure. However, the mean is very different in the two populations: it is around 120 mmHg among Kenyan nomads but around 130 mmHg among London civil servants.

A blood pressure of 140 mmHg, which is relatively close to the mean in the London population, would be considered very high in the Kenyan population. While research on the individual determinants of high blood pressure might reveal the same individual factors in both populations (e.g., genetics or health behaviors), these individual factors would not explain why blood pressure in general is so much higher among the London civil servants. This can be understood only by studying differences in the environment of these populations.

The population perspective in epidemiology from the eighteenth to the early twentieth century

The question of how the environment impacts on the health of populations was the main focus of epidemiology when it began to establish itself as an empirical research discipline during the time of the Enlightenment and industrialization in the Europe of the eighteenth and nineteenth centuries. Among the first scholars in this field were Johann Peter Frank (1745–1821), author of the voluminous *A system of complete medical police* (Frank, 1786/1976); Rudolf Virchow (1821–1902), who reported on the social causes of the typhus epidemic in Upper Silesia (Taylor & Rieger, 1985; Virchow, 1849/1968); and Friedrich Engels (1820–1895), who described the 'condition of the working class in England' and its effect on health (Engels, 1845/1987). An important institution in early epidemiologic research was the British Registrar General of Births, Deaths, and Marriages that started under the leadership of the great pioneering statistician and epidemiologist William Farr (1807–1883) to collect and analyze statistical information on mortality in the 1830s (Hamlin, 1995; Susser & Adelstein, 1975).

One of the most famous epidemiologic findings in the nineteenth century was the discovery by the British physician John Snow (1813–1858) that cholera is transmitted through polluted water. Based on careful record-taking and meticulous field research during the cholera epidemics in London in the early 1850s, he discovered that deaths from cholera occurred substantially more often in houses that obtained their water from the Southwark and Vauxhall Company as opposed to the Lambeth Company. Since Southwark and Vauxhall drew their water from parts of the Thames river that was heavily polluted with sewage, Snow concluded that polluted drinking water was the cause of the cholera epidemic (Snow, 1855). He came to this conclusion during a time when the germ theory was still controversial and 30 years before Robert Koch discovered *Vibrio cholerae*, the bacterium that causes the disease.

While early epidemiologic research mainly focused on the effects of material living conditions and sanitation, there was also research on the health effects of the psychosocial environment. A landmark study in this regard was Émile Durkheim's (1858–1917) investigation on suicide in France in the 1890s (Durkheim, 1897/1951). At this time, suicide rates were higher for Protestants than for Catholics, higher for the unmarried than for the married, and higher in times of economic instability (either recession or prosperity) than in times of economic stability. Durkheim argued that while individuals have many different reasons for committing suicide, the differences among the social groups have to be explained by social factors. He reasoned that if different groups have different suicide rates, there must be something about the social organization of the groups that encourages or deters individuals to take their life. Durkheim's research led him to conclude that the major factor affecting suicide rates was the degree of social integration of groups. He suggested that the extent to which the individual was integrated into group life determined whether he or she would be motivated to commit suicide. His research and writings contributed substantially to the development of sociology as an empirical science.

The population perspective in epidemiology in the eighteenth and nineteenth centuries was crucial for the understanding of how infectious diseases are transmitted and led to important public health reforms and improvements in living conditions. As a result, morbidity and mortality from infectious diseases declined

sharply in industrialized countries, as we have seen in Figure 2.2. Contrary to a still widely held belief, medicine (that is primarily vaccination and treatment) played only a limited role in the decline of infectious diseases. While vaccination was very important for the containment of smallpox or poliomyelitis, it had less impact on the decline of several other diseases. This was impressively shown by Thomas McKeown in his famous book *The role of medicine: Dream, mirage, or nemesis?* (1979). Tuberculosis, the major cause of death in the eighteenth century, declined long before the tubercle bacillus was discovered and any vaccination or treatment was available (Figure 2.3). McKeown stressed that improvements in general living conditions and especially in nutrition were the major factors explaining the decline. It has also been argued that due to socioeconomic changes fertility had declined, which resulted in increased spacing between births and reduced infection rates (Frank, 1995a; Reves, 1985). Others have pointed out that public health interventions, such as improvements in water sanitation, contributed to the decrease in tuberculosis deaths, because people were less infected with other pathogens and became more resistant against the tubercle bacillus (Szreter, 1988). Regardless of this discussion on the relative contribution of general living conditions and specific public health interventions, it is clear that vaccination and medical treatment were not important factors in the decline in tuberculosis since 1840 (Figure 2.3). Similar patterns can be seen for several other important infectious diseases, such as measles, pneumonia, and whooping cough (McKeown, 1979; McKinlay et al., 1989).

The individual perspective in risk factor epidemiology in the second part of the twentieth century

While infectious diseases declined, chronic diseases like coronary heart disease, cerebrovascular disease and cancer became an increasing public health concern in wealthy, industrialized countries during the twentieth century. Epidemiologic research naturally followed this change. The focus in epidemiology shifted from

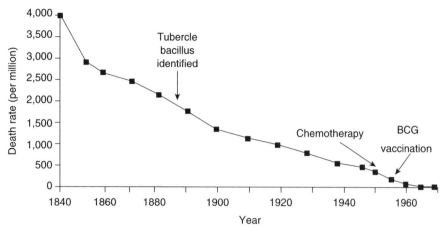

Figure 2.3   *Changes in mean annual death rates for respiratory tuberculosis in England and Wales between 1840 and 1970 [Adapted from McKeown, T. (1979). The role of medicine: Dream, mirage, or nemesis? (2nd edn., p. 92). Oxford: Blackwell. © Basil Blackwell, with permission]*

environmental determinants of population health to individual factors that increase the risk of chronic disease. As a result, 'risk factor epidemiology' became the dominant paradigm.

A risk factor is usually defined as 'an aspect of personal behavior or life-style, an environmental exposure, or an inborn or inherited characteristic, which on the basis of epidemiologic evidence is known to be associated with health-related condition(s) considered important to prevent' (Last, 1995: 48). The word 'associated' indicates that the relationship between a risk factor and a health condition is of a statistical nature. A factor is regarded as a risk factor if its presence increases the probability of the incidence of the health condition and if this association holds after other potential biasing factors (so-called 'confounders') are controlled for. It is important to note that a risk factor is not a cause in the classical philosophical and epistemological sense. A risk factor is not a necessary factor, because the health-related condition could appear even without its presence. And it is also not a sufficient factor, because even if the risk factor is present, the health problem might not occur. Rather, people who are exposed to a risk factor have a higher probability, called 'relative risk', of developing a health-related condition than people who are not exposed.

To investigate risk factors, epidemiologists usually use observational, that is non-experimental, studies. The three main types of observational studies are: (1) *cross-sectional studies*, which assess risk factors and health outcomes at the same time in a sample; (2) *case-control studies*, which compare the frequency of risk factors in individuals with the disease to individuals without the disease; and (3) *prospective studies*, also called longitudinal or cohort studies, which measure the presence or absence of a risk factor in a healthy sample and follow the participants for some time until some of them have developed the health outcome of interest. Among observational studies, prospective studies are the most powerful for investigating the causal relationship between a risk factor and an outcome because, by design, the presence of the risk factor is established before the incidence of the disease. However, prospective studies usually require large resources and are often difficult to conduct, especially if the disease under study is relatively rare.

Calculating measures of association

Table 2.4 gives an example of how relative risks and other measures of association are

Table 2.4   *Smoking and coronary death: calculation of measures of association*

		Coronary death		
		Yes	No	Total
Cigarette smoker	Yes	270	39,730	40,000
	No	250	59,750	60,000
	Total	520	99,480	100,000

Relative risk:

$$\frac{\text{incidence exposed}}{\text{incidence unexposed}} = \frac{(270/40{,}000)}{(250/60{,}000)} = 1.62$$

Attributable risk fraction:

$$\frac{\text{incidence exposed} - \text{incidence unexposed}}{\text{incidence exposed}} = \frac{(270/40{,}000) - (250/60{,}000)}{(270/40{,}000)} = 0.38 \text{ or } 38\%$$

Population attributable risk fraction:

$$\frac{\text{total incidence} - \text{incidence unexposed}}{\text{total incidence}} = \frac{(520/100{,}000) - (250/60{,}000)}{(520/100{,}000)} = 0.20 \text{ or } 20\%$$

Data adapted and modified from: Doll, R., & Peto, R. (1976). Mortality in relation to smoking: 20 years' observations on male British doctors. *British Medical Journal, 2*(6051), 1525–1536.

calculated in a prospective study. The data used in this example are based on the classical study by Richard Doll and A. Bradford Hill on causes of death from smoking (Doll & Hill, 1956; Doll & Peto, 1976); however, for clarification and simplification, the data have been somewhat modified.

In the example, the smoking status in a cohort of 100,000 people is assessed, revealing that 40 per cent are cigarette smokers while the other 60 per cent are non-smokers. After a 1-year observation period, it is established that 520 subjects have died because of coronary heart disease, 270 among the 40,000 smokers (incidence rate = 0.00675) and 250 among the 60,000 non-smokers (incidence rate = 0.00417). The ratio between the incidence rates of smokers and non-smokers is 1.62, which indicates that smokers have a 1.62-fold higher risk of dying from coronary heart disease than non-smokers. To determine if this difference is substantial or just caused by chance, a confidence interval is calculated which, by convention, is based on a 95 per cent confidence level. The confidence interval gives the range in which we can expect the true value. In the example, the 95 per cent confidence interval is 1.36 to 1.92, which means that if this study was

repeated, 95 times out of 100 the relative risk would be between these lower and upper boundaries (see Hennekens & Buring, 1987: 254–256, for formulas to calculate confidence intervals). Since the confidence interval in this example does not include values smaller than 1, we assume that the higher risk of coronary death among smokers is not due to chance.

The two other measures of association presented in Table 2.4 are the attributable risk fraction and the population attributable risk fraction. The first indicates the percentage of cases that could be prevented *among the exposed*, if they were not exposed. In our example, 38 per cent of coronary deaths among smokers would not have occurred if the smokers did not smoke. The population attributable risk fraction gives the percentage of cases that could be prevented *among the whole population* if no one in the population was exposed. We can conclude from the data in Table 2.4 that 20 per cent of all coronary deaths would have been avoided if no one in the population smoked.

The relative risks or rate ratios in Table 2.4 are only one of several ways to calculate risks in exposed groups. Other measures of relative risks are incidence density ratios, which take person time into account; odds ratios, which are used in case-control studies; and hazard rate ratios, which are based on the Cox proportional hazards model. For description and discussions of these and other methodological aspects of epidemiology, see the textbook *Epidemiology in medicine* by Hennekens and Buring (1987). For more in-depth information on methodological features see *Epidemiologic research: Principles and quantitative methods* by Kleinbaum, Kupper and Morgenstern (1982) or *Modern epidemiology* by Rothman and Greenland (1998b).

A crucial issue in the interpretation of any effect size is how much of the association between risk factor and outcome is biased by confounding. A confounder is a factor that is associated with the risk factor and independently affects the likelihood of the outcome. For example, suppose one finds an increased risk of myocardial infarction among people who drink coffee compared to coffee abstainers. Suppose also that coffee drinkers are more likely to be smokers than are non-coffee drinkers. In this case, it is not clear if the higher risk of myocardial infarction is due to coffee consumption or to the higher smoking rates among coffee drinkers.

The problem of confounding is usually addressed by multivariate analysis, which allows us to adjust for possible confounding effects and to calculate a relative risk that is independent of the confounder. Multivariate analysis is a powerful tool for controlling confounders and is a standard procedure in epidemiology today. However, there are two major limitations. First, one can obviously only control for variables that have been measured in the study. Second, one has to conceptually clarify whether a variable is a confounder or a step in the causal pathway. For example, studies that investigate the impact of psychosocial stressors at the workplace on the risk of myocardial infarction usually control for high blood pressure. This is the correct procedure if one wants to isolate the independent effects of psychosocial stressors. However, there is evidence that psychosocial stressors at the workplace are a cause of high blood pressure, which then subsequently increases the risk of myocardial infarction (Schnall, Belkić, Landsbergis & Baker, 2000; Schnall, Schwartz,

Landsbergis, Warren & Pickering, 1998). In this case, blood pressure is not a confounder, but an intermediate step in the causal pathway between psychosocial workplace stressors and myocardial infarction. Adjusting for blood pressure in multivariate analyses would therefore lead to an underestimation of the effects of psychosocial workplace stressors on myocardial infarction.

The limitations of risk factor epidemiology

Risk factor epidemiology has discovered some important determinants of health in the twentieth century. Probably the greatest success was the investigation of the causal association between smoking and lung cancer. Epidemiologists were able to show that smokers have a 14- to 20-fold higher risk of lung cancer than non-smokers, that there is a dose–response relationship between the number of cigarettes smoked per day and lung cancer risk, and that smoking is responsible for more than 90 per cent of all lung cancer cases in the general population (Doll & Hill, 1956; Doll & Peto, 1976).

Unfortunately, the success epidemiologists had in linking smoking to lung cancer is the exception not the rule. Consider, for example, the case of coronary heart disease, the leading cause of death in North America and Europe. Beginning with the famous Framingham Study that started in 1948 (Dawber, 1980), numerous prospective studies have been conducted to identify the risk factors that cause this disease, especially in middle adulthood before the age of 65. While hundreds of factors have been discussed as possible causes of coronary heart disease, the four factors virtually everyone agrees on are smoking, hypertension, diabetes and elevated serum cholesterol, also called 'conventional risk factors'. The predictive validity of these factors is limited, however. Each of these factors is usually associated with a 1.5- to 3-fold increased relative risk, depending on the cut-off points for the reference group and the group at highest risk (Keil & Spelsberg, 1995; Schnohr, Jensen, Scharling & Nordestgaard, 2002). This is not trivial, but compared to the 14- to 20-fold increase of lung cancer for smokers, the strength of association is moderate at best. Each single risk factor also explains only a relatively small amount of the total variation in coronary heart disease, and it is still debated how large is the contribution of the combination of these risk factors to CHD incidence (Braunwald, 1997; Canto & Iskandrian, 2003; Hennekens, 1998; Marmot & Winkelstein, 1975; Stamler, 1981). Moreover, it is widely agreed that the four conventional risk factors are widespread in industrialized countries and that it remains unclear why some people with these risk factors develop coronary heart disease and others do not.

The failure of intervention programs to modify behavioral risk factors

The dominance of the risk factor model gave rise to several large-scale intervention studies that were aimed at reducing smoking, improving diets, and increasing physical activity. One of the largest and most ambitious of such intervention studies was the Multiple Risk Factor Intervention Trial (MRFIT), which was primarily conducted to reduce the risk of coronary heart disease. This study involved almost 13,000 middle-aged men with a distinct coronary risk factor profile (men who smoked, who had elevated cholesterol levels and who had high blood pressure), but who had no signs of manifest coronary heart disease. These men were randomized to either a usual care group or a special intervention program designed to promote health behaviors (smoking cessation, dietary changes, blood pressure control). Given the intensity of this behavioral modification program and the substantial resources invested, the outcome was disappointing. The evaluation of the program after 7 years of follow-up showed only modest behavior changes in the intervention group and revealed that the intervention did not reduce either total mortality or mortality from coronary heart disease (Multiple Risk Factor Intervention Trial Research Group, 1981, 1982).

The disappointing results of the MRFIT study and other one-to-one behavior change programs led to the development of community intervention trials in which entire communities were encouraged to change their health behaviors. The aim was to raise public awareness of risk factors mainly for coronary heart disease and to change risk-related behaviors through public education, education of health professionals, and environmental change programs (Altman, 1995; Sorensen, Emmons, Hunt & Johnston, 1998). In these trials the focus was shifted from individual to population risk. Instead of trying to achieve large changes in the health behavior of a few high-risk individuals, the aim of these studies was to achieve small changes in behavior across an entire population.

While a Finnish community intervention trial, the North Karelia Project (Puska et al., 1983), showed a substantial reduction in smoking rates, serum cholesterol levels, and blood pressure, other studies like the Stanford Five City Project (Farquhar et al., 1990), the Minnesota Heart Health Program (Luepker et al., 1994), the Pawtucket Heart Health Program (Carleton, Lasater, Assaf, Feldman & McKinlay, 1995) and the Göteborg Primary Prevention Trial (Wilhelmsen et al., 1986) found only small changes or found that participants in both the intervention and the control group had changed their behavior in a similar way. Moreover, when further analyses on the subsequent manifestation of cardiovascular disease were conducted in Pawtucket (Luepker et al., 1996) and Göteborg (Wilhelmsen et al., 1986), no differences in incidence rates between intervention and control groups were found (for a review of these and other studies, see Sorensen et al., 1998).

Several reasons have been discussed for these disappointing results of behavioral modification programs. It has been pointed out that these programs 'decontextualize' health behaviors, that is, they overlook how behavior is culturally and structurally maintained. It has been shown that in low-income neighborhoods smoking is less regulated, nutritious food is more expensive and difficult to get, recreational areas are more sparse and less safe, environmental toxins are more present, and preventive and curative services are harder to access (Kaplan, Everson & Lynch, 2000; Morland, Wing, Diez Roux & Poole, 2002; Sooman, Macintyre & Anderson,

1993). In addition, researchers have pointed out that for people of low socioeconomic position, smoking is often a rational way of coping with exposure to economic hardships and psychosocial stressors because it is of low cost and easily accessible (Emmons, 2000). A qualitative study on socioeconomic position and smoking in Britain concluded that low-income women who also had to care for children or other family members had exhausted the adaptive capacity needed to quit smoking (Graham, 1994). It has also been pointed out that for people of lower socioeconomic position, smoking often offers a way to spend time with friends and therefore increases social support (Emmons, 2000).

Obviously, behavior modification programs do not address the structural determinants of behavior. And since the underlying forces in society that contribute to problematic health behaviors are not addressed, these programs fail to prevent new people (e.g., children or young adults) from entering the at-risk population. Furthermore, behavior modification programs do not take into account that chronic diseases are multifactorial and that health behaviors are only one of several factors that determine health and illness.

A Socio-Psycho-Physiological Framework of Health and Illness

The failure of intervention programs to improve health through behavioral modification, the substantial variation of coronary heart disease that remains unexplained despite 50 years of intense research, and the fact that we know even less about the determinants of other widespread chronic health conditions, like most cancers, cerebrovascular disease, diabetes, hypertension, musculoskeletal disorders or psychological disorders, are becoming more and more recognized. As a result, risk factor epidemiology, and especially its reductionist perspective and its focus on individual biological (e.g., genetics, cholesterol) and behavioral factors (e.g., smoking, lack of exercise), has come under increasing criticism (Krieger, 1994; Pearce, 1996; Shy, 1997; Susser & Susser, 1996a, 1996b). It has been pointed out that in order to

further enhance the understanding of the causes of disease and develop effective interventions, an interdisciplinary perspective that integrates social, psychological, and biological factors is needed (Frank, 1995a, 1995b). While individual risk factors are important, they have to be included in a broader framework and be connected with a population perspective – the perspective epidemiology had in its early history. Or, as Neal Pearce (1996) put it, epidemiology has to 'go back to the future'.

Figure 2.4 shows a conceptual model for an interdisciplinary understanding of health and illness. Similar models have been suggested by distinguished scholars like Aaron Antonovsky (1979), George Engel (1977), Robert Evans and Gregory Stoddart (1990), Clyde Hertzman (1999), George Kaplan (1999), and Michael Marmot (1996).

We call the conceptual model in Figure 2.4 a *socio-psycho-physiological framework*, because in our view this term better expresses the hierarchical relationship between the social structure, psychological states and processes, and physiological reactions than the more common term *biopsychosocial* (Engel, 1977). On the very top of this hierarchy, one finds the social and economic structure of a society, in particular its wealth and how this wealth is distributed. The ownership and control of the means of production, the balance of power between capital and labor, and the ability of a society to regulate and restrict market forces and to invest in public goods are important issues at this level.

The next level shows the material and psychosocial environment of individuals, which is the direct result of the social and economic structure of the society. Here, one can find the concrete living conditions of the individuals in their communities, at their workplaces and in their social relationships. These living conditions affect health and illness through three pathways.

Pathway A directly connects the living conditions, and especially the material environment, with health and illness. From a global perspective this is probably the pathway with the strongest impact. As we have discussed above, poverty is one of the most important

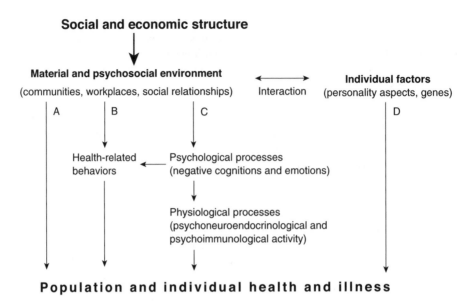

Figure 2.4   *A hierarchical socio-psycho-physiological framework of health and illness*

determinants of health. According to recent data from the World Bank, 1.2 billion people live on less than 1 US dollar and 2.8 billion live on less than 2 US dollars a day (World Bank, 2002). People living in this extreme poverty often do not have access to basic resources (e.g., nutritious food, clean drinking water, adequate shelter) that are crucial for maintaining health. The fact that children in Western Europe today usually are unharmed when exposed to measles infections, whereas in Africa more than 440,000 children died from this disease in the year 2000 (WHOSIS, 2002), has little to do with the virus, and much to do with the malnutrition, the general poor living conditions and the lack of health care for children in Africa. But also in wealthy countries, material living conditions are an important determinant of health (Shaw, Dorling & Davey Smith, 1999). In the United States, for example, 44 million people do not have health insurance and subsequently face higher risks for suffering and dying from numerous diseases (Lurie, 2001).

Pathway B shows how the environment contributes to health and illness through health-related behaviors of individuals. Research has shown that smoking, excessive alcohol consumption, lack of leisure time physical activity, and diets high in fat and low in vegetables and fruits are important contributors to many diseases (McGinnis & Foege, 1993). These health behaviors are not simply individual choices, but are influenced by the social and economic structure and encouraged or discouraged by forces in the environment. People of low socioeconomic position, for example, are more likely to smoke and less likely to eat fruits and to be engaged in leisure time physical activity (Emmons, 2000). The causes for this are multifactorial, including differences between socioeconomic groups in health norms, the value and conceptual understanding of health, and the perceived amount of control over one's health, as well as the presence or absence of health-damaging and health-enhancing agents and resources in the areas in which people of different socioeconomic positions live (Emmons, 2000; Frohlich, Potvin, Chabot & Corin, 2002; Frohlich, Potvin, Gauvin & Chabot, 2002; Kaplan et al., 2000; Lynch, Kaplan & Salonen, 1997; Macintyre, MacIver & Sooman, 1993; Morland et al., 2002; Sooman et al., 1993).

Pathway C explains how the environment affects health and illness through psychological and physiological processes, also called stress reactions. This is probably the most controversial pathway. Here, it is assumed that adverse psychosocial and material living conditions (chronic stressors), like the daily struggle to make ends meet, low job security, or the continuous experience of lack of control over important aspects of one's life, increase the probability of chronic negative cognitions and emotions like depressive mood, hopelessness, or hostility. These negative cognitions and emotions influence health in two ways. First, they increase the likelihood of problematic health behaviors. For example, it has been found that both hostility and depression are associated with higher smoking rates and less physical activity (Allgöwer, Wardle & Steptoe, 2001; Scherwitz & Rugulies, 1992). It has also been shown that psychosocial working conditions can influence smoking rates (Albertsen, Hannerz, Borg & Burr, 2004). Second, psychological states and processes seem to be associated with an increase in psychoneuroendocrinological and psychoimmunological activity, especially dysregulations of the autonomic nervous system and the hypothalamic–pituitary–adrenal axis (Carney & Freedland, 2000; Henry & Stephens, 1977; Kaplan, Manuck, Adams, Weingand & Clarkson, 1987; Musselman, Evans & Nemeroff, 1998; Weiner, 1992). These dysregulations have been found to be associated with hemodynamic changes (Christensen & Smith, 1993), diminished heart rate variability (Stein et al., 2000), metabolic changes (Schneiderman & Skyler, 1996), and decreased functioning of the immune system (Cohen, Tyrrell & Smith, 1991).

In addition to these three main pathways that have their origins in the social and economic structure of society, we have added a fourth pathway (D) to Figure 2.4 that takes individual factors into account. In our definition, individual factors include both genes and personality factors. Genetic defects can directly and independently cause diseases, for example Down syndrome, which is caused by trisomy-21. However, at the current stage of knowledge, it seems that purely genetically determined diseases are rare. Instead, many scientists assume today that diseases are often caused by an interaction between genetics and the environment. A classic example of this is phenylketonuria.

This disease is caused by a genetic defect that disables the body in converting the amino acid phenylalanine to tyrosine, which usually leads to severe mental retardation. However, if newborns with this genetic defect are fed a special diet free of phenylalanine, they live normal healthy lives. This is an example of how a disease can be both 100 per cent genetic and 100 per cent environmental (Rothman & Greenland, 1998a). Without the genetic defect, the disease would not occur, but it would also not occur in a phenylalanine-free environment. In fact, in such an environment, the inability to process phenylalanine would not even be considered a defect. The genetic composition makes the individual vulnerable, but this vulnerability has health consequences only under certain environmental conditions. It is possible that this kind of interaction is true for many diseases for which we today know neither the genetic nor the environmental causes, let alone how they interact.

Another aspect of the interaction between individual factors and environment has been shown by the research of Boyce and his group (Boyce, Chesney, Alkon & Tschann, 1995; Boyce, Chesterman, Martin & Folkman, 1993; Liang & Boyce, 1993). In their work, they have found that some young children show a substantially higher physiological reactivity to environmental stimuli than other children. This high reactivity could be a product of an interaction between genetics and very early, perhaps even prenatal, life experiences (Liang & Boyce, 1993). Whatever the cause, once it is established, the high-reactivity pattern seems to be a stable trait of these children. Interestingly, Boyce and colleagues found that children with high reactivity are more likely to sustain injuries (Liang & Boyce, 1993) and respiratory infections (Boyce et al., 1993) when exposed to high-stress situations in childcare. However, in low-stress situations, these children have lower injury and infection rates than children with more average physiological reactivity, an impressive example of how the interaction of individual and environmental factors influences health (Liang & Boyce, 1993).

Like most conceptual models, the framework presented in Figure 2.4 is oversimplified. One could argue that most arrows could also go in the opposite direction, because people who are sick might be prone to negative emotions which could affect their material and psychosocial environment (e.g. job loss, withdrawal from friends). We acknowledge that such a reverse causation exists to a certain extent. However, over the last two decades for most diseases epidemiological research has convincingly shown that the causal direction does indeed go from the social structure to the disease and not the other way around (Blane, Davey Smith & Bartley, 1993; Macintyre, 1997).

While the conceptual model is oversimplified, it is on the other hand too complex to be tested in a single empirical study. Instead, the model should serve as a framework for more specific empirical research projects. In the following sections, we will discuss how findings from major epidemiological research studies fit into this framework.

THE IMPACT OF THE SOCIAL AND ECONOMIC STRUCTURE ON HEALTH AND ILLNESS

The analysis of societal structures is a core research subject in sociology, but it is also an important theme in philosophy and economics. Obviously, it is beyond the scope of this chapter to discuss even peripherally the very complex and controversial debates within these disciplines. However, with oversimplification, we think that it can be cautiously said that contemporary discussions about the structure of society are still strongly influenced by two schools of thought from the middle of the nineteenth century. The first school of thought is based on the political-economic analysis of Karl Marx (1818–1883), with its central focus on the class structure of society. According to Marx, modern societies are divided between the few who own and control the means of production and the vast majority of people who do not. Ownership of the means of production gives the individual power, control, dominance and the ability to exploit other members of the society. Exploitation defines the relationship of the two classes, which is therefore necessarily antagonistic and

confrontational. The individuals themselves, their inner structure, their thinking, feelings and actions are shaped by their position in the production process, by their general position as an exploiter or an exploited, and also by their more specific position as a factory worker, a clerk, a factory owner, a stockholder, a petit bourgeois, a researcher and so on (Johnson & Hall, 1995; Marx, 1867/1981).

The second major school of thought in understanding the structure of society is based on the work of Max Weber (1864–1920). In this view, social class is defined not by ownership of the means of production, but by common characteristics of individuals, like education, assets, or values, that determine their 'life chances' and their success in the market place (Abel, 1991; Lynch & Kaplan, 2000; Weber, 1922/1968). The Weberian tradition is more descriptive than the Marxian; it focuses less on the origins of social differences between individuals and more on the consequences of these differences. However, it is important to note one major agreement: both approaches view societies as hierarchically organized structures, in which some groups are privileged.

As a positivistic science, epidemiology usually follows the Weberian approach and investigates the health status of different social groups in the societal hierarchy, while interest in the origins of the social structure is less prevalent (for notable exceptions, see Johnson & Hall, 1995; Muntaner, Lynch & Oates, 1999; Navarro, 1990). The construction of social groups is mostly conducted by relatively simple and quantifiable characteristics such as years and highest degree of education, amount of income or type of occupation. Different terms are used by researchers for the resulting social hierarchy, like social classes, social strata, socioeconomic statuses or socioeconomic positions. Sometimes these terms are interchangeable, while sometimes a specific conceptual or historical reference is intended. In this chapter, we use the term *socioeconomic positions*, in accordance with the definition by Lynch and Kaplan that social and economic factors 'influence what position(s) individuals and groups hold within the structure of society'

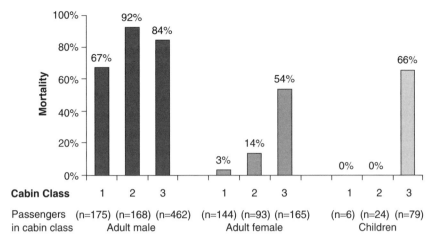

Figure 2.5   *Distribution of mortality by cabin class for passengers of the Titanic*
[Data source: Dawson, R. J. M. (1995). The 'unusual episode' data revisited.
Journal of Statistics Education, 3. Electronic journal article, available at:
http://www.amstat.org./publications/jse/v3n3/datasets.dawson.html. Accessed 14 June 2002]

and are therefore indicators 'of location in the social structure that may have influences on health' (2000: 14).

Socioeconomic Position and Health

Following the Weberian school of thought, epidemiologists have hypothesized that people at higher positions have better chances of good health. Those who had only a few years of education, have low income or are manual workers are thought to be more likely to be exposed to health hazards and less likely to have access to health-protecting or health-enhancing resources than their counterparts at higher positions (Lynch & Kaplan, 2000).

A dramatic example of the impact of socioeconomic position on life chances is the sinking of the *Titanic*. When on 14 April 1912 the *Titanic* rammed an iceberg on her maiden voyage from Southampton to New York, 817 of the 1,316 passengers and 673 of the 885 crew members died, according to the official record (Dawson, 1995). Survival was exclusively determined by access to the limited number of lifeboats, since the icy temperature of the Atlantic made it impossible to stay alive in the water until the rescue ship arrived. Figure 2.5 shows the probability of dying for passengers according to cabin class, stratified for men,

women and children. Men were much more likely to die, which is explained by the belief that women and children should have priority access to lifeboats. However, there was also a strong effect of socioeconomic position. A third of the men traveling in the first cabin class survived the tragedy, while among passengers in second and third cabin class, the proportion of survival was only 8 and 16 per cent respectively. Compared to women traveling in the first class, women in the second class had a 5-fold higher and women in the third class a strikingly 19-fold higher risk of dying. No child died in the first or second class, while two-thirds of the third class children did not survive, a death toll comparable to men in the first class (Dawson, 1995).

While socioeconomic position defined by cabin class was a crucial determinant of access to life-saving resources on the *Titanic*, one might wonder if socioeconomic position defined by such simple measures as education, income or occupation is of importance for health and illness. It is. In a brilliant review, Antonovsky (1967) showed that anecdotal evidence of a shorter life expectancy for people of lower socioeconomic position can be tracked back to as early as the twelfth century. A major breakthrough for the statistical analysis of social inequalities in health was the decision by

Table 2.5   *Death rates for men and women (age 15 to 64) by occupational class per 100,000 population in England and Wales, 1971*

Occupational class		Men	Women
I	Professional (e.g., lawyers)	398	215
II	Intermediate (e.g., schoolteachers)	554	285
IIIN	Skilled non-manual (e.g., shop assistants)	580	276
IIIM	Skilled manual (e.g., butchers)	608	341
IV	Partly skilled (e.g., agricultural workers)	796	427
V	Unskilled (e.g., dock workers)	988	531

Data source: Townsend, P., & Davidson, N. (Eds.). (1982). *Inequalities in health: The Black Report* (p. 57). Harmondsworth: Penguin.

the British Registrar General of Births, Deaths, and Marriages to record type of occupation on death certificates in the 1850s (Macintyre, 1997). In the 1911 to 1921 census the Registrar General's Social Classes system was developed which classified occupations in six groups: classes I (highest), II, III non-manual, III manual, IV, and V (lowest) (see Table 2.5). This simple classification scheme is still in place and laid the foundation for one of the most famous modern-day research projects on socioeconomic position and health, the Black Report (Department of Health and Social Security, 1980; Townsend & Davidson, 1982).

The Black Report, which was named after the chair of the research commission, Sir Douglas Black, showed strikingly higher morbidity and mortality rates for people of lower socioeconomic positions (class V) in the Britain of the 1970s (Table 2.5). It concluded that 'class differences in mortality are a constant feature of the entire human life-span. They are found at birth, during the first year of life, in childhood, adolescence and adult life. At *any* age people in occupational class V have a higher rate of death than their better-off counterparts' (Townsend & Davidson, 1982: 51, italics in original). This was a shocking finding, since these health inequalities were not supposed to happen in a highly industrialized country in the second half of the twentieth century, where food was plentiful, sanitation was adequate, infectious diseases had been successfully contained, and everyone had free access to health care. However, the Black Report showed that while mortality rates dropped substantially in all occupational classes during the twentieth century, the differences between the classes had not been eliminated.

The Black Report provoked a highly controversial political debate, especially since the research commission was appointed by a secretary of state from the Labour Party, but finished its work under the newly elected Conservative government, which obviously did not welcome the findings. The government produced only 260 copies of the report and released them during the week of the August Bank Holiday, while in the foreword the Secretary of State for Social Services, Patrick Jenkin, frankly expressed his disappointment and rejected the recommendations of the research group (Townsend & Davidson, 1982).

In most parts of the British and international scientific community, however, the reception of the report was very positive, stimulating discussions and research projects on the causes of social inequalities in health. In 1990, on its 10th anniversary, both the *Lancet* and the *British Medical Journal* published special articles praising the report and its contribution to epidemiologic research (Davey Smith, Bartley & Blane, 1990; Morris, 1990). For more details of the content, reception, and consequences of the Black Report, see the excellent article by Sally Macintyre, 'The Black Report and beyond: What are the issues?' (1997).

Since the publication of the Black Report, research on social inequalities in health has increased exponentially both in Western Europe and in North America (Kaplan & Lynch, 1997). The findings from these research activities show conclusively that marked social inequalities in health exist not only in Britain, but also in virtually all other nations. Whether the indicator is education, income or occupational status, men, women and children of lower socioeconomic position are always at a substantially higher risk of developing illnesses, becoming disabled, and dying prematurely (European Science Foundation, 2000; Lynch & Kaplan, 2000; Mackenbach et al., 1997; Syme & Balfour, 1998). Higher mortality rates for people of lower socioeconomic position have been found not only for total mortality, but also for cause-specific mortality, including lung cancer, all other cancers combined, cardiovascular disease, respiratory disease, gastrointestinal causes, and external causes (Adler et al., 1994; Kunst et al., 1998; Syme & Balfour, 1998). There are only very few diseases where the association is absent or even reversed. The most notable exception is breast cancer, which is found more often in women of higher socioeconomic positions. It has been speculated that this is caused by the later average age of first full-term pregnancy by women with higher education and income (Kelsey & Bernstein, 1996).

The Challenge of the Gradient

One of the most fascinating epidemiologic findings is the discovery of a gradient relationship between socioeconomic position and health (Adler et al., 1994; Evans, Barer & Marmor, 1994; Marmot, 1994; McDonough, Duncan, Williams & House, 1997; Syme, 1996). Health inequalities are not simply limited to dichotomous comparisons of the very poor versus the very rich, or unskilled manual workers versus professionals. Instead, there is a steady decrease in health with declining socioeconomic position. The association is not strictly linear, but curvilinear: that is, people at the very lowest position, who are living in poverty, have an especially high risk, while for the rest of the population, ill-health decreases continuously with increasing socioeconomic position (Wolfson, Kaplan, Lynch, Ross & Backlund, 1999). Some have suggested that the gradient might be explained by social selection processes. Social selection addresses the possibility of reverse causation: people who become sick drift to lower socioeconomic positions because of their health status. It has been shown, however, that the drift hypothesis has only a marginal impact on the gradient, and it

is now widely accepted that the direction of causality goes from the socioeconomic position to the health outcome and not vice versa (Blane et al., 1993; Macintyre, 1997).

Among the most important research projects for a better understanding of the social gradients in health are the British Whitehall Studies. These prospective studies on 17,530 male (Whitehall I, completed in the 1980s), and 10,308 male and female civil servants in London (Whitehall II, ongoing) have measured not only socioeconomic positions and health outcomes but also potential mediating factors. Figure 2.6 shows results from Whitehall I for death due to coronary heart disease. The first graph illustrates the age-adjusted mortality rates in relation to occupational class (Marmot, Shipley & Rose, 1984). There is a clear gradient, with the lowest mortality rate in the highest occupational class and the highest mortality rate in the lowest class. The second graph shows what happens if the results are controlled for the coronary risk factors of smoking, blood pressure, cholesterol, blood sugar, and height (as a proxy measure for deprivation in childhood). The gradient becomes somewhat smaller, indicating that these risk factors indeed explain a part of the association between socioeconomic position and coronary death. However, while reduced, the gradient is still visible and very clear, so there must be other powerful, yet unknown factors that contribute to the higher coronary heart disease risk in lower socioeconomic positions. Findings from the ongoing Whitehall II Study suggest that adverse psychosocial conditions at the workplace, especially lack of control over work tasks, might play an important role. The lower people are in an occupational hierarchy, the less control they usually have over how to cope with their daily workload, which could result in higher levels of psychophysiological stress reactions that might affect health (Marmot, Bosma, Hemingway, Brunner & Stansfeld, 1997). Other researchers, however, have suggested that a psychosocial interpretation for the gradient is premature and that subtle material differences between people of different socioeconomic positions should be more closely investigated

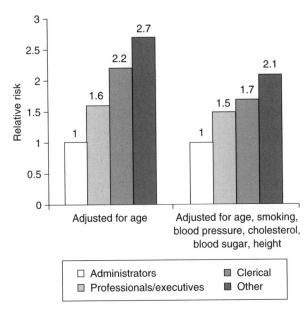

Figure 2.6   *Relative risk of death due to coronary heart disease in British civil servants [Adapted from Marmot, M. G., Shipley, N., & Rose, G. (1984). Inequalities in death: Specific explanation of a general pattern? Lancet, i (8384), 1003–1006.* © The Lancet Ltd, with permission]

(Davey Smith, 1997; Lynch, Davey Smith, Kaplan & House, 2000; Macleod et al., 2002).

Area Deprivation, Income Inequality and Health

Research on the health impact of the social and economic structure has mostly focused on the association between socioeconomic position of the individual and health outcomes. However, there is an increasing body of research showing that the socioeconomic status of the area in which people live has an independent relationship with mortality, over and above individual socioeconomic positions. Using data from the Alameda County Study, a longitudinal population-based research project that started in 1965, Yen and Kaplan (1999a) showed that people who live in poor, deprived neighborhoods have a 1.6-fold higher risk of dying than their counterparts in better-off neighborhoods, independently of their own income, education, age, sex, race/ethnicity, health behaviors, and perceived health. In other words, living in neighborhoods of low

socioeconomic status increases the mortality risk, even for those of higher individual socio-economic position. Further analysis from the Alameda County Study showed similar patterns for worsening of depressive symptoms (Yen & Kaplan, 1999b), self-reported health (Yen & Kaplan, 1999b), physical activity (Yen & Kaplan, 1998), and physical functioning (Balfour & Kaplan, 2002).

Another approach to studying social characteristics of the environment is research on income inequality and health. The leading scholar in this field is the British economist Richard Wilkinson, who published a comprehensive summary of his research findings in the book *Unhealthy societies: The afflictions of wealth* (1996). He showed that life expectancy is substantially higher in countries that redistribute wealth through high taxation and social transfer payments, like Sweden and Norway, than in countries in which wealth is less equally distributed, like the United States and Britain.

Wilkinson's work was received with great interest, especially in the United States. In 1996, two research teams from the University of

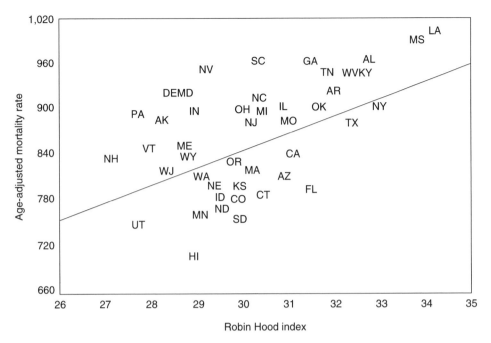

Figure 2.7   *Income inequality and age-adjusted mortality rates in the United States*
[Adapted from Kennedy, B. P., Kawachi, I., & Prothrow-Stith, D. (1996). Income distribution
and mortality: Cross sectional ecological study of the Robin Hood index
in the United States. British Medical Journal, 312, 1004–1007. © BMJ Publishing Group,
with permission]

Michigan (Kaplan, Pamuk, Lynch, Cohen & Balfour, 1996) and from Harvard University (Kennedy, Kawachi & Prothrow-Stith, 1996) independently published findings on the association between income inequality and mortality in the 50 US states. While they used different measures to assess income inequality, both studies produced the same spectacular result: a strong dose–response relationship between level of inequality and age-standardized mortality rate. Figure 2.7 shows the results from the Harvard group. Mortality rates are presented on the *y*-axis, while income inequality is defined by the Robin Hood index on the *x*-axis. The Robin Hood index gives the percentage of the wealth that has to be transferred from the rich households (those above the median) to the poor households (those below the median) to achieve total equality in wealth. States with relatively low inequality, like Utah (UT) or New Hampshire (NH), had substantially lower mortality rates than states with relatively high inequality, like Mississippi (MS) or Louisiana

(LA). The correlation coefficient over all 50 states was 0.54. The analyses showed further that for every 1 per cent increase in the Robin Hood index, there were 22 additional deaths per 100,000 people (Kennedy et al., 1996).

The findings from Kennedy and colleagues are impressive, but recent analyses have shown that the association between income inequality and life expectancy among countries is more complex. While it is true that Sweden has a higher life expectancy than Britain and the United States, other countries do not fit into this picture quite as well. Denmark, for example, which is a relatively egalitarian country, has one of the lowest life expectancies in the European Union, while people in France show one of the highest longevities, despite the relative large income inequalities in this country (Lynch et al., 2001).

While the empirical evidence for the income inequality hypothesis is disputed, an even more fierce and controversial discussion has arisen about the interpretation of the possible association between income inequality and health. In his writings, Wilkinson (1996) has suggested that inequality affects health mainly through psychosocial processes. With some over-simplification, it can be said that Wilkinson argues that societies with high income inequalities and distinct social hierarchies produce high levels of distrust and low social cohesion among their members. Distrust and low social cohesion, which is often described as 'lack of social capital', leads to negative emotions like shame, anger, and hostility, which harm health through behavioral (e.g., smoking, violence) and psychophysiological pathways (e.g., release of stress hormones). Recently, researchers have indeed shown a correlation between income inequality and distrust and an association between distrust and mortality rates in the United States (Kawachi, Kennedy, Lochner & Prothrow-Stith, 1997).

In opposition to Wilkinson, other researchers have argued that income inequality affects health not through psychosocial but through material pathways (Lynch, 2000; Muntaner & Lynch, 1999; Muntaner et al., 1999). They point out that societies with high income inequality, like the United States, underinvest in public resources. Examples are unavailability or severe restrictions of health, disability and unemployment insurance, lack of regulation to protect people from air pollution, lack of recreational areas, poor public transportation and so on. From a material perspective, the failure to provide these public resources, and not the lack of trust or social cohesion, is responsible for the higher mortality rates in areas with marked income inequality.

The discussion on income inequality and health has produced a large body of literature. Examples are the debates between Lynch and colleagues (2000) and Marmot and Wilkinson (2001) in the *British Medical Journal* and between Muntaner and colleagues (Muntaner & Lynch, 1999; Muntaner et al., 1999) and Wilkinson (1999) in the *International Journal of Health Services*.

Summary of the Importance of the Social and Economic Structure

In summary, there is overwhelming evidence for a strong impact of the social and economic structure on health and illness. Both the socioeconomic position of individuals, and the socioeconomic characteristics of the places in which they live, are strong and consistent predictors of morbidity and mortality. It is less clear, however, through which pathways the socioeconomic structure influences health. A certain part of the variance can be explained by health behaviors, especially smoking, but a substantial part remains unexplained, and the relative contribution of psychosocial versus material factors is currently subject to intense discussions. There is certainly a need to improve research methods on this issue. One of the most promising new approaches is the so-called *life-course perspective*. This approach tries to analyze the specific influences of the social and economic structure during the different stages of life, from the prenatal phase, through childhood, adolescence, and adulthood, to old age (Amick et al., 2002; Hertzman, 1999; Kuh & Ben-Shlomo, 1997; Lynch, Everson, Kaplan, Salonen & Salonen, 1998; Wamala, Lynch & Kaplan, 2001). This is an ambitious goal, which requires sophisticated measurements over a very long observation period, but it has great potential to improve our understanding of the specific pathways through which the social and economic structure gets 'under the skin' and affects the health of individuals and populations.

Social inequalities in health have become a major research topic in both the United States and Europe. This issue has been recognized, funded and supported by political organizations, social activist groups and governments (Auerbach & Krimgold, 2001; European Science Foundation, 2000; Smedley & Syme, 2000). On the other hand, data from intervention studies are sparse. This is not surprising, since interventions that target aspects of the socioeconomic structure are necessarily complex and therefore difficult to evaluate. One of the few exceptions is a randomized research project in Boston which showed that children of mothers who received housing subsidies that enabled them to move to more wealthy neighborhoods had a significantly lower prevalence of injuries, asthma attacks and personal victimization than children in the control group (Sampson & Morenoff, 2000). However, the design of innovative intervention projects on improving the socioeconomic conditions of communities, like the Tenderloin Study in San Francisco (Minkler, 1992) or the WHO Healthy Cities Project (Hancock, 1993), usually does not allow a quantitative epidemiologic evaluation of the health effects.

Since intervention studies on social inequalities are so difficult to conduct and evaluate, analysis of natural experiments and comparison of different societies can be an important alternative. In an interesting analysis, Ross and colleagues (2000) compared the effects of income inequality on health in the United States and Canada. As was shown in Figure 2.7, there are different levels of income inequality across the 50 states of the United States, and Ross and colleagues found that there are also differences in income inequality across the Canadian provinces. However, there were two major differences between the two countries. First, income inequality was in general much lower in Canada than in the United States; and second, while there was a clear correlation between income inequality and mortality in the United States (see Figure 2.7), no statistically significant association could be found between these two variables in Canada. The authors point out that in contrast to the United States, the Canadian government runs large-scale interventions to mute the effects of social inequalities (e.g., providing universal access to health care and higher education), but also invests in public goods like parks and libraries in low-income areas. The strong correlation between income inequality and mortality in the United States and the absence of such an association in Canada suggest that these interventions on the policy level are very effective in influencing health and illness.

THE IMPACT OF THE WORKPLACE ON HEALTH AND ILLNESS

The workplace is an important source of health and illness. For most people, work is the primary source of income, and involuntary exclusion from the labor market usually results in severe financial setbacks and might even lead to health-threatening material deprivation. At the workplace people are exposed to physical hazards, like toxins, noise, or ergonomic misfits, as well as to psychosocial hazards, like the experience of loss of control, humiliation, failure, or unfair treatment. The workplace, however, also provides the opportunity for positive experiences, like being able to make an impact and to be creative, doing something meaningful, being successful, or being connected to other people.

Work and Health Research in a Changing Economy

One of the early pioneers in the field of work and health was the Italian researcher Bernardino Ramazzini (1633–1714). He was a famous and highly respected scholar who taught medicine at the Universities of Modena and Padua. His book *De morbis artificium* (*Diseases of workers*), a comprehensive investigation on how working conditions cause disease for a wide range of occupations, can be regarded as the founding work of occupational safety and health.

While until recently occupational safety and health research has been primarily concerned with injury prevention and physical hazards at the workplace, the focus here will be on psychosocial workplace conditions. We are doing this not only because the readers of this chapter will mostly come from a psychological background, but also because of the increasing importance of psychosocial factors in a changing economy. Whereas exposure to physical hazards is still a cause of death and disability in North America and Europe, workers in these countries are better protected today than a few decades ago. This has been achieved by regulations and better equipment, but also by transferring physically hazardous jobs to poor countries in the southern hemisphere (Mergler, 1999), which shoulder today a great burden of industrialized hazardous work (Benach, Amable, Muntaner & Benavides, 2002; La Botz, 2001). Employees in North America and Europe are facing today fewer physical and more psychosocial hazards. A recent study among 21,500 European employees showed that most employees work at very high speed or under tight deadlines for more than 50 per cent of the time (Merllié & Paoli, 2000). New economic developments, like downsizing and outsourcing, have led to intensified work and to the broad recognition in societies that 'stress levels' at the workplace are constantly increasing (Geurts & Gründemann, 1999; Landsbergis, Cahill & Schnall, 1999).

Psychosocial Stress and Stressors at the Workplace

While the term 'stress' is widely used, in research as well as among the public, it is a poorly defined construct with many different meanings. It is therefore important to clarify the definition used in this section.

A psychosocial *stressor* at the workplace is a factor or a constellation in the psychosocial work environment that – alone or in combination with other factors – has potentially negative effects for the worker. This could be unrealistic workload, time pressure, high emotional demands, lack of job security and so on. Especially if these factors are difficult to control and if exposure is chronic, individuals are likely to show *stress reactions*, which are manifested on the cognitive (e.g., cynicism), emotional (e.g., anger, fear, hopelessness), behavioral (e.g., substance abuse), and physiological level (e.g., dysregulations of the autonomic nervous system and the hypothalamic–pituitary– adrenal axis). It is thought that these stress reactions have the potential to create severe psychological and physical health problems.

Theoretical Models of Workplace Stressors and Health

Currently, psychosocial work and health research is dominated by two theoretical models: the *demand–control–support* model developed by Karasek, and the *effort–reward imbalance* model developed by Siegrist. In the demand– control–support model it is assumed that 'job

strain' (a combination of high psychological demands, such as time pressure, and low decision latitude) increases the risk of psycho-physiological stress reactions and subsequent ill-health, especially cardiovascular disease (Karasek, 1979; Theorell & Karasek, 1996). If an individual is also exposed to low social support from coworkers and supervisors, a three-way health-hazardous interaction of high demands, low decision latitude and low support is assumed, which is called iso-strain (Johnson & Hall, 1988; Theorell & Karasek, 1996). In the effort–reward imbalance model, a mismatch between high efforts and low rewards (in terms of wages/salaries, respect, promotion prospects, and job security) is thought to increase the likelihood of stress reactions and disease. In addition, the model includes a variable called work-related overcommitment, which is thought to be a personality aspect that makes certain individuals more vulnerable to experiencing psychosocial stress reactions (Siegrist, 1996; Siegrist et al., 2004). For both models, standardized self-administered questionnaires with acceptable psychometric properties are available (Landsbergis, Theorell, Schwartz, Greiner & Krause, 2000).

The models have been tested in several prospective studies, mainly for the incidence of cardiovascular disease, but also for musculoskeletal and psychological disorders (for reviews, see Belkić, Landsbergis, Schnall & Baker, 2004; Karasek & Theorell, 1990; Rugulies & Siegrist, 2002; Schnall et al., 2000; Siegrist, 1996; Theorell & Karasek, 1996). While several studies have shown that exposure to job strain, iso-strain and effort–reward imbalance could result in a 2- or 3-fold increased risk of ill-health (especially of coronary heart disease), the results are not conclusive. For job strain, there is a growing number of findings indicating that the subcomponent of low decision latitude is of relevance, but not job strain itself (Kristensen, 1999; Rugulies & Siegrist, 2002). Effort–reward imbalance has shown more consistent findings, but some of the studies used proxy measures instead of the original questionnaire, and it therefore seems advisable to wait for further results from ongoing studies.

Challenges for Future Research on Psychosocial Workplace Conditions

Recently, it has been suggested that some psychosocial working conditions that are especially important in the growing service industry, like emotional demands, conflicts with clients, or meaningfulness of work, are not covered by either the demand–control–support model or the effort–reward imbalance model (de Jonge, Mulder & Nijhuis, 1999; Söderfeldt, 1997). This might explain some of the null findings, and calls for an expansion of both the theoretical conceptualization and the empirical assessment of workplace stressors. Instruments like the National Institute of Occupational Safety and Health Generic Job Stress Questionnaire (Hurrell & McLaney, 1988) or the recently developed Copenhagen Psychosocial Questionnaire (Kristensen, 2001) strive to get a more comprehensive perspective of potential health-hazardous psychosocial workplace conditions.

In addition to improvements of current questionnaires, more direct workplace observations would be desirable. Whereas responses to self-administered questionnaires can be biased by perceptions and psychological dispositions of the workers, workplace observations should give a more objective assessment of the psychosocial workplace conditions. See Frese and Zapf (1988) and Greiner and colleagues (Greiner, Krause, Ragland & Fisher, 1998; Greiner & Leitner, 1989; Greiner, Ragland, Krause, Syme & Fisher, 1997) for a more detailed discussion of this method.

Workplace observations would also help to address one of the most crucial problems in psychosocial research: bias due to common method variance when both predictor and outcome rely on self-report. For example, some individuals might have a relatively stable psychological disposition for a generally negative view of the world, including their work environment and their health. It is likely that these individuals report more psychosocial stressors at baseline as well as more health problems at the end of the study. If this is true, the association between stressors and health problems would have been driven by the biased perspective of the individuals and not by a causal relation between stressors and health. Common method variance can be avoided if the outcome is assessed objectively (e.g., death, myocardial infarction, stroke, cancer etc.) or can be reduced if the focus is on changes over time (e.g., psychosocial stressors at baseline predict decline in self-rated health during the follow-up). However, for several important health outcomes, like incidence of low back pain, self-report of the outcome is unavoidable, so more research using objective assessments of the predictor variables would be desirable.

Another important issue for future research is the fact that workplace conditions can change over time and that people are more and more likely to work in many different workplaces throughout their occupational career. The life-course perspective, which has gained increasing interest in epidemiology (Hertzman, 1999; Kuh & Ben-Shlomo, 1997; Lynch et al., 1998; Wamala et al., 2001), needs to be applied to research on work and health. Interestingly, two recent studies have investigated the impact of psychosocial stressors over the life course. While these studies did not assess stressors at the individual level, but used job titles as proxy measures for presence or absence of adverse psychosocial workplace conditions, they found that lifetime exposure to low decision latitude predicted all-cause mortality (Amick et al., 2002) and cardiovascular mortality (Johnson, Stewart, Hall, Fredlund & Theorell, 1996) respectively.

Workplace Interventions

It has become customary to distinguish three levels of workplace intervention: the individual level (e.g., health education, using personal protective equipment), the individual/group interface level (e.g., cooperation with others, social support) and the organizational or structural level (e.g., improvement of working conditions and circumstances). While interventions on all three levels can contribute to improvements in employee health, interventions on the structural or organizational level usually have the greatest impact, because they target the problems at their source and reach most employees (Aust & Ducki, 2004; Kristensen, 2000). However, since often a complex mix of physical and psychosocial working conditions as well as individual behavior affects workers' health, multilevel interventions are frequently recommended (Kompier, Geurts, Gründemann, Vink & Smulders, 1998; McLeroy, Bibeau, Steckler & Glanz, 1988; Rütten et al., 2000). For example, workplace intervention programs that attempt to improve employee health behaviors (e.g., to eat less fat, to do more exercise, to better cope with psychosocial stress) through health education programs should also address the corresponding factors in the work environment (e.g., more low-fat food choices in the cafeteria, limiting excessive overtime so employees have time to exercise, reducing exposure to psychosocial stressors). Unfortunately, most of the so-called worksite health promotion programs, which are a dominant concept especially in the United States, are restricted to behavior modification through health education. This narrow approach has been criticized for a long time, and it is now widely agreed that a broader approach is needed (Donaldson, Gooler & Weiss, 1998; Heaney & van Ryn, 1990; Minkler, 1989; Rosenbrock & Müller, 1998). We will therefore focus on comprehensive workplace interventions, which mainly address working conditions as a means to improve employee health.

Comprehensive worksite health promotion

Comprehensive workplace interventions present a challenge for researchers and practitioners. Organizational interventions are time consuming, expensive and difficult to design, control and evaluate. In addition, a number of barriers have to be overcome, since these interventions might be viewed as interfering with existing hierarchies and responsibilities within a company (Kristensen, 2000).

In order to overcome these obstacles, comprehensive interventions need to be carefully planned and implemented. Several factors have been identified as crucial for a successful

intervention: support from top management as well as from all other relevant actors within the company (unions, employees, health and safety experts etc.); a clear determination of aims, tasks, responsibilities, planning and financial resources; a detailed problem analysis in order to choose and plan the right intervention; a strong focus on organizational changes complemented by person-directed measures; a participative approach (that is, worker involvement during problem analysis and development of appropriate solutions); and a long-term perspective that allows continuous improvement of the intervention measures (Aust, 1999, 2001; Kompier et al., 1998; Kristensen, 2000).

Evaluation of Workplace Interventions

Due to the nature of organizational interventions, which take place in a constantly changing work environment, experimental studies can seldom be conducted (Griffiths, 1999). For example, most comprehensive workplace interventions are based on the active support of employees and employers, so random assignment to intervention and control groups is rarely possible. Instead alternative research strategies have been proposed, like multiple case studies and natural experiments, where researchers approach workplaces as soon as they become aware of imminent relevant changes, in order to collect data before and after the intervention (Kompier & Kristensen, 2001). While these strategies use less rigorous scientific methods, they are often the only way to evaluate the health impact of an intervention. However, because of their complexity, comprehensive workplace interventions also need to be evaluated by a wider spectrum of scientific methods and approaches. In particular, a detailed process evaluation as well as an analysis of context conditions is crucial. This information, often assessed through qualitative methods, is necessary for an accurate interpretation of the results from outcome evaluations (Goldenhar & Schulte, 1996; Griffiths, 1999; Mergler, 1999).

Although evaluating comprehensive workplace intervention studies is a challenging task, several studies have investigated the feasibility and effectiveness of these interventions and more large-scale evaluation studies are on their way (Nielsen, Kristensen & Smith-Hansen, 2002). There are some especially good examples from comprehensive interventions that have been conducted in transportation companies to improve the health and well-being of inner-city bus drivers, an occupational group that has a high risk of myocardial infarction, hypertension, and musculoskeletal disorders (Aust, 1999; Tüchsen & Endahl, 1999; Winkleby, Ragland, Fisher & Syme, 1988). It is thought that this increased risk is caused by high exposure both to physical hazards, like constant vibration and poor ergonomics, and to psychosocial stressors like time pressure due to unrealistic schedules, the requirement of constant high concentration to steer a bus through traffic, shift work, and frequent conflicts with passengers (Aust, 1999; Evans & Johansson, 1998; Krause, Ragland, Fisher & Syme, 1998). Workplace intervention programs have tried to address these problems by reducing driving hours, introducing self-governing groups and giving drivers more input in choosing their shifts. Recent evaluations have shown positive effects of these programs, such as reductions in sickness absence and improvements in self-rated health (Aust, 1999, 2001; Kompier, Aust, van den Berg & Siegrist, 2000).

In Germany, so-called health circles represent an interesting and innovative approach to workplace health interventions. Health circles are employee discussion groups, formed at the workplace, to develop change options for the improvement of potentially harmful working conditions (Westermayer & Bähr, 1994). Inspired by other employee problem solving groups, like the quality circles, health circles use the expertise of employees about their workplaces. A health circle usually starts with a careful problem analysis to assess health-related factors within the work environment, and to identify a department with a high level of adverse working conditions and/or increased levels of health problems. After this assessment, usually five to eight employees of the problematic department are invited to participate in the health circle. Further participants can include supervisors, safety officers,

union work council members, the company physician or safety engineers. In six to 10 meetings, held during paid working time, participants discuss and develop solutions to the various health problems and complaints. If possible, suggestions are implemented immediately. In the last health circle meeting, all participants evaluate the accomplishments. Sometimes an additional evaluation meeting is held about 6 months after the last circle meeting, in order to review what has been done in the meantime (Schröer & Sochert, 2000).

The majority of the hundreds of health circles that have been conducted in recent years have not been accompanied by careful scientific evaluation studies. However, for some health circles, enough data have been collected to perform at least some kind of evaluation. Aust and Ducki (2004) recently reviewed 11 studies that described the results of 81 health circles conducted in 30 different companies. The findings indicate that the health circles had a positive effect on workers' health and on their satisfaction and motivation. Further, the health circles seem to be able to contribute to a more efficient work process through improved workflow and better communication.

Another innovative intervention research strategy is participatory action research (PAR), which was developed in the United States (Israel, Baker, Goldenhar, Heaney & Schurman, 1996; Israel, Schurman & Hugentobler, 1992). PAR strongly emphasizes the participation of employees and refers to a broad framework of circumstances that affect workers' health. In an attempt to bridge the gap between researchers and practitioners, PAR is based on the collaboration of outside experts and organization members (Schurman, 1996). Following principles of system development, continuous learning and co-learning processes in a participative and democratic environment, the goal is to solve practical problems while striving to contribute to theoretical advances in intervention research. With its commitment to worker participation and the involvement of researchers through the entire intervention process, PAR represents a strong contrast to the traditional methodological canon. Intervention projects that used the PAR method suggest that this approach has positive

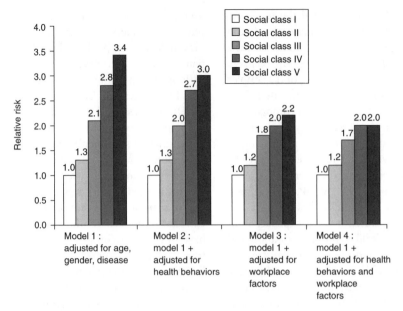

Figure 2.8   *Social gradient in deterioration of self-rated health after adjusting for health behaviors and physical and psychosocial workplace factors [Adapted from Borg, V., & Kristensen, T. S. (2000). Social class and self-rated health: Can the gradient be explained by differences in life style or work environment? Social Science and Medicine, 51, 1019–1030. © Elsevier Science, with permission]*

effects on both work organization and employee's health (Schurman, 1996). While it has also been pointed out that PAR still needs to overcome several obstacles in order to achieve recognition as both good science and good intervention practice (Schurman, 1996), it certainly represents one of the innovative approaches needed in order to develop intervention and research strategies capable of dealing with the complex workplace conditions that affect employees' health.

Integrating Psychosocial Workplace Conditions in a Broader Framework

With regard to the conceptual model in Figure 2.4, we have argued that the higher risk of ill-health in people of lower socioeconomic position is at least partly mediated by material and psychosocial workplace conditions and therefore that the workplace is an important link in the causal relationship between the social and economic structure and individual and population health. If this assumption is correct, one would expect that

adjusting for psychosocial workplace stressors in a multivariate analysis would diminish the association between socioeconomic position and ill-health. Borg and Kristensen (2000) found in a representative cohort of the Danish working population a clear social gradient in deterioration of self-rated health over a 5-year follow-up period. As can be seen in Figure 2.8, the gradient decreased only slightly after adjusting for smoking and body mass index, but was reduced substantially when the analysis was adjusted for physical and psychosocial workplace factors. Further analysis revealed that the largest reduction of the gradient was caused by two physical (ergonomic and climatic exposures) and three psychosocial job factors (repetitive work, low level of skill discretion, job insecurity) and that these five factors explained 59 per cent of the gradient. In the British Whitehall II Study, Marmot and colleagues (1997) showed that adjustment for psychosocial workplace conditions, especially lack of job control, reduces the social gradient for coronary heart disease.

While the studies from Denmark and Britain support the idea of the mediating effect of psychosocial workplace factors for the social health gradient, other research indicates that the relationship between socioeconomic position, psychosocial workplace stressors and health outcomes is more complex. In a recent Swedish case-control study on women who had suffered a myocardial infarction, the social gradient was only marginally affected by job strain and its subcomponents (Wamala, Mittleman, Horsten, Schenck-Gustafsson & Orth-Gomer, 2000). In addition, some researchers have started to question the association of socioeconomic position and specific psychosocial workplace factors, namely low job control, on a theoretical level and have asked if low job control might be just another marker for low socioeconomic position (Davey Smith, 1997; Macleod et al., 2002). This is an important criticism and indicates that more empirical research as well as more theoretical reflections are needed on this issue.

THE IMPACT OF PSYCHOLOGICAL TRAITS, STATES, AND PROCESSES ON HEALTH AND ILLNESS

Epidemiologists investigate not only how environmental factors can cause disease but also how psychological traits, states, and processes contribute to health and illness. Since these psychological aspects will be addressed in much greater detail in several other chapters in this book, we will restrict this section to a few general discussions and some selected findings.

Psychological research can contribute to epidemiology in at least two ways. First, psychological experiments and laboratory research help us to understand how cognitions and emotions are linked to physiological changes. For example, psychologists have shown that when subjects are exposed to respiratory viruses in a controlled clinical experiment, those with current high levels of stress reactions are significantly more vulnerable than low-stress subjects to developing a cold (Cohen et al., 1991). It has also been demonstrated that subjects with high scores on hostility and depression scales are

more prone to show behaviors (e.g., smoking) and physiological reactions (e.g., high blood pressure reactivity, decreased heart rate variability) that are potentially harmful for health (Allgöwer et al., 2001; Christensen & Smith, 1993; Scherwitz & Rugulies, 1992). Psychologists have also developed several theoretical models, like *health locus of control* (Wallston, Wallston, Kaplan & Maides, 1976), *self-efficacy* (Bandura, 1995) and the *theory of planned behavior* (Ajzen & Madden, 1986), that help in understanding the psychological mechanisms that influence health-enhancing or health-damaging behaviors.

In addition to this research, which is mainly based on laboratory experiments and cross-sectional studies, psychological factors have also been tested directly as predictors in prospective epidemiologic studies. One of the most interesting stories in this field is the search for psychological factors that increase the risk of coronary heart disease. For most of the time since research on this issue started in the 1950s, investigators have looked into psychological aspects that are associated with the tendency of individuals to wear themselves down. The most widely known construct from this research tradition is the 'type A behavior pattern', a conglomerate of a hostile and hard-driving behavior, including competitiveness, and chronic feelings of time urgency (Friedman & Rosenman, 1959; Rosenman & Chesney, 1980). A large-cohort study, published in 1975, showed a 2-fold increased risk of coronary heart disease for type A subjects, even after controlling for biomedical risk factors (Rosenman et al., 1975), and the construct was subsequently accepted by the United States National Heart, Lung, and Blood Institute as an independent predictor of coronary heart disease (Review Panel on Coronary-Prone Behavior and Coronary Heart Disease, 1981). However, later research projects either were not able to replicate this finding (Case, Heller, Case & Moss, 1985; Shekelle et al., 1985) or even reported contradictory results (Ragland & Brand, 1988). Today type A behavior is no longer viewed as an important risk factor for coronary disease. Further research on one type A component, hostility, produced an immense body of psychological and psychophysiological

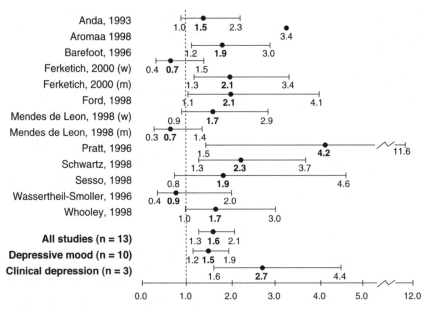

Figure 2.9   *Meta-analysis on depression as a predictor for myocardial infarction and coronary death [Adapted from Rugulies, R. (2002). Depression as a predictor for coronary heart disease: A review and meta-analysis. American Journal of Preventive Medicine, 23, 51–61. © Elsevier Science, with permission]*

literature (for a review, see Smith, 1992). While the evidence is somewhat better than for type A behavior, prospective epidemiological studies on hostility and coronary heart disease have shown inconsistent results (Miller, Smith, Turner, Guijarro & Hallet, 1996; Myrtek, 2000).

Whereas the 1970s and the 1980s were dominated by the type A behavior and the hostility constructs respectively, current research is focusing more on depression and anxiety as predictors of coronary heart disease. A recent meta-analysis of prospective studies showed that among people without any sign of coronary heart disease at baseline, those with depressive mood had a 1.5-fold higher risk of myocardial infarction and coronary death at follow-up (Rugulies, 2002). People with clinical depression had an even more impressive 2.7-fold increased risk (Figure 2.9). Since the meta-analysis was restricted to objective outcomes and excluded angina pectoris, the findings cannot be explained by response bias. In addition, the studies in the meta-analysis had in general a high methodological standard and most had adjusted for numerous risk factors.

Findings on depression and coronary death are even more impressive for people who have already been diagnosed with coronary heart disease. Several studies have shown that in coronary patients who have just survived a myocardial infarction, depression was associated with a 4- to 6-fold higher risk of cardiac death in the following 6 to 18 months (Frasure-Smith, Lespérance & Talajic, 1995; Hermann-Lingen & Buss, 2002; Ladwig, Kieser, Konig, Breithardt & Borggrefe, 1991). There are also some findings that support an association between anxiety and cardiovascular disease, especially sudden cardiac death. However, until now, only a few prospective studies have been conducted on this construct (Kubzansky, Kawachi, Weiss & Sparrow, 1998).

Intervention Studies to Change Psychological Factors

A recent large-scale randomized intervention program, the ENRICHD study (ENhancing Recovery in Coronary Heart Disease patients), was designed to see if cognitive behavioral therapy applied to patients who had survived a myocardial infarction can reduce depression, increase social support and subsequently reduce mortality (ENRICHD Study Group, 2001). While there was a decrease in depression scores in the intervention group, the program did not succeed in reducing mortality, which was similar in the intervention and control group at 29 months of follow-up (Berkman et al., 2003). On the other hand, two older intervention studies on reducing type A behavior showed positive effects on mortality and incidence of clinical events in the intervention groups (Burell, 1996; Friedman et al., 1986). This is somewhat ironic, since type A behavior is no longer regarded as a predictor for coronary heart disease.

Integrating Epidemiologic Findings on Psychological Predictors in a Broader Framework

The inconsistent findings on type A behavior and hostility and the change of the research focus to depression and anxiety over the last decades indicate that psychological factors might be important for physical diseases but that the mechanisms are not well understood. We think that, in a similar way to research on work and health, findings on psychological factors need to be integrated into a broader theoretical framework and that psychological research is crucial to help us in understanding how an adverse environment gets under the skin (Rugulies, 1998; Taylor, Repetti & Seeman, 1997). It is of great interest to note that there is a clear social gradient for hostility, with people of lower socioeconomic position showing the highest hostility scores (Barefoot, Peterson, Dahlstrom & Siegler, 1991; Marmot et al., 1991; Scherwitz, Perkins, Chesney & Hughes, 1991). Unfortunately, psychological research on hostility has ignored the socioeconomic dimension of the construct for a long time and has viewed hostility as a personality trait of unknown origin (Smith, 1992). Only recently have researchers begun to investigate the development of hostility in a socioeconomic context (Harper et al., 2002).

For depression research, the situation is similar. There is some epidemiologic evidence for a social gradient of depressive mood (Griffin, Fuhrer, Stansfeld & Marmot, 2002), and there are also studies showing that exposure to psychosocial stressors, both at the workplace (Stansfeld, Fuhrer, Shipley & Marmot, 1999) and outside the workplace (Kaplan, Roberts, Camacho & Coyne, 1987), increases the risk of clinical depression. However, the majority of studies investigating the epidemiologic association between depression and coronary heart disease did not integrate their findings in a socioeconomic context.

FINAL THOUGHTS

After having presented several theoretical concepts and numerous empirical findings within the field of epidemiology, we would like to close this chapter with a parable, well known to many public health students in the United States, which nicely illustrates our main arguments. Suppose a group of people is standing on the banks of a river. Suddenly, they see that someone is drowning in the water. Some go into the river, bring the person to land and attempt resuscitation. While they are doing this, more and more people are flowing down the river, crying for help. Some of them are strong enough to reach the banks, but many drown. A few rescuers decide to enter a couple of boats and to try to prevent the people from drowning. One group throws life-belts in the water, another group gives swimming lessons, and a third group tries to talk to the people in the river, to reduce their panic and to motivate them to fight against the currents. To a certain extent, this has an effect and helps some people to reach the banks on their own strength. However, it also keeps everyone busy and prevents the rescue workers from going upstream to find out why all these people are in the river in the first place. If they were to do this, they would discover that there is an old run-down bridge, with rotten planks and missing guard rails, and it would occur to them that fixing the structure of the bridge would greatly reduce the number of drowning people.

The work that is done downstream is important. It is important to understand the physical and psychological characteristics of the people who are not able to swim to the banks on their own, and it is important to help people to fight against the currents, to give them life-belts and to attempt resuscitation. But if the activities downstream prevent one from inquiring what is going on upstream, one will not get a comprehensive, interdisciplinary perspective of the problem and will miss a crucial opportunity to save many lives.

To follow an interdisciplinary perspective and to look upstream is not easy. It requires a high degree of open-mindedness, mental flexibility, hard work, and courage. Interdisciplinary research means not only being willing to work with researchers from other disciplines but also becoming interested in and gaining insight into these other fields. For health psychologists this means, in addition to acquiring knowledge in biomedicine, also learning the theoretical and methodological basics of epidemiology, sociology, and economics. This will not only broaden one's own perspective, but also enable health psychologists to more efficiently communicate their much needed psychological knowledge to other health researchers. Interdisciplinary research is a great intellectual challenge, but since psychologists are coming from a field that is rooted in both natural and social sciences, they might be better prepared for this challenge than researchers from most other disciplines.

Whereas interdisciplinary research is not easy, to maintain an upstream perspective is even more difficult. In general, major societal forces reward downstream and discourage upstream approaches. Only a tiny fraction of the overall spending in the health sector goes to prevention, and of this fraction, most is spent on prevention that lies downstream (e.g., pharmaceuticals that target biomedical risk factors). Prevention efforts that are located further upstream, like regulation at the workplace, improvements in the infrastructure of communities and redistribution of wealth in societies, face a great deal of resistance. This is both irrational and rational. It is irrational, because one can reasonably assume that

upstream interventions would be the more effective type of prevention and would even reduce the overall societal costs for disease in the long run. But the resistance is also rational, at least for those groups who are profiting from the current situation and therefore have something to lose. To take away even a tiny part of their profits and power will not happen without a constant struggle. In fact, as the continuous demands for workplace deregulation and assaults on the welfare systems by major societal forces show, just to defend the status quo requires great efforts.

However, to end this chapter on an optimistic note, we want to point out some recent positive developments. In the United States, the National Institutes of Health have now launched several funding initiatives on social health inequalities, and organizations like the MacArthur Foundation and the Robert Wood Johnson Foundation are also committing major resources to this work (MacArthur Network on SES and Health, 2002; Robert Wood Johnson Foundation, 2002). In Canada, the government has created the Canadian Institutes of Health Research, which includes several institutes that are committed to a comprehensive understanding of health and illness (Canadian Institutes of Health Research, 2002). In Europe, the European Science Foundation has founded a major research initiative on social variations in health (European Science Foundation, 2000). These are welcome developments and we hope this will encourage many readers of this book to go upstream and to look at health and illness from an interdisciplinary perspective.

ACKNOWLEDGEMENT

We wish to thank all scholars who participated in the weekly seminars of the Behavioral Risk Factors Training Program at the University of California at Berkeley between 1999 and 2002. The stimulating discussions in this group contributed greatly to this chapter. Our special thanks go to Dr John Frank, Scientific Director of the Institute of Population and Public Health at the Canadian Institutes of Health Research, for his tremendous insight and inspiration.

REFERENCES

Abel, T. (1991). Measuring health lifestyles in a comparative analysis: Theoretical issues and empirical findings. *Social Science and Medicine, 32,* 899–908.

Adler, N. E., Boyce, T., Chesney, M. A., Cohen, S., Folkman, S., Kahn, R. L., & Syme, S. L. (1994). Socioeconomic status and health: The challenge of the gradient. *American Psychologist, 49,* 15–24.

Ajzen, I., & Madden, T. J. (1986). Prediction of goal-directed behavior: Attitudes, intentions, and perceived behavioral control. *Journal of Experimental Social Psychology, 22,* 453–474.

Albertsen, K., Hannerz, H., Borg, V., & Burr, H. (2004). Work environment and smoking cessation over a five-year period. *Scandinavian Journal of Public Health, 32,* 164–171.

Allgöwer, A., Wardle, J., & Steptoe, A. (2001). Depressive symptoms, social support, and personal health behaviors in young men and women. *Health Psychology, 20,* 223–227.

Altman, D. G. (1995). Strategies for community health intervention: Promises, paradoxes, pitfalls. *Psychosomatic Medicine, 57,* 226–233.

Amick, B. C. 3rd, McDonough, P., Chang, H., Rogers, W. H., Pieper, C. F., & Duncan, G. (2002). Relationship between all-cause mortality and cumulative working life course psychosocial and physical exposures in the United States labor market from 1968 to 1992. *Psychosomatic Medicine, 64,* 370–381.

Anda, R., Williamson, D., Jones, D., Macera, C., Eaker, E., Glassman, A., & Marks, J. (1993). Depressed affect, hopelessness, and the risk of ischemic heart disease in a cohort of U. S. adults. *Epidemiology, 4,* 285–294.

Antonovsky, A. (1967). Social class, life expectancy and overall mortality. *Milbank Memorial Fund Quarterly, 45,* 31–73.

Antonovsky, A. (1979). *Health, stress, and coping.* San Francisco, CA: Jossey-Bass.

Aromaa, A., Raitasalo, R., Reunanen, A., Impivaara, O., Heliovaara, M., Knekt, P., Lehtinen, V., Joukamaa, M., & Maatela, J. (1994). Depression and cardiovascular diseases. *Acta Psychiatrica Scandinavica (Supplement), 377,* 77–82.

Auerbach, J. A., & Krimgold, B. K. (Eds.) (2001). *Income, socioeconomic status, and health.* Washington, DC: National Policy Association.

Aust, B. (1999). *Gesundheitsförderung in der Arbeitswelt: Umsetzung streßtheoretischer Erkenntnisse in eine Intervention bei Busfahrern* [Worksite health promotion: Application of knowledge from stress research into an intervention study with bus drivers]. Münster: LIT.

Aust, B. (2001). *Gesundheitsförderung in Verkehrsunternehmen: Betrieb- und mitarbeiterbezogene Maßnahmen im Fahrdienst* [Health promotion in public transportation companies: Company and individual oriented approaches to health promotion for transit operators]. Hamburg: BG Bahnen.

Aust, B., & Ducki, A. (2004). Comprehensive health promotion interventions at the workplace: Experiences with health circles from Germany. *Journal of Occupational Health Psychology, 9,* 258–270.

Balfour, J. L., & Kaplan, G. A. (2002). Neighborhood environment and loss of physical function in older adults: Evidence from the Alameda County Study. *American Journal of Epidemiology, 155,* 507–515.

Bandura, A. (1995). *Self-efficacy: The exercise of control.* New York: Freeman.

Barefoot, J. C., Peterson, B. L., Dahlstrom, W. G., & Siegler, I. C. (1991). Hostility patterns and health implications: Correlates of Cook–Medley Hostility Scale scores in a national survey. *Health Psychology, 10,* 18–24.

Barefoot, J. C., & Schroll, M. (1996). Symptoms of depression, acute myocardial infarction, and total mortality in a community sample. *Circulation, 93,* 1976–1980.

Belkić, K. L., Landsbergis, P. A., Schnall, P. L., & Baker, D. (2004). Is job strain a major source of cardiovascular disease risk? *Scandinavian Journal of Work, Environment and Health, 30,* 85–128.

Benach, J., Amable, M., Muntaner, C., & Benavides, F. G. (2002). The consequences of flexible work for health: Are we looking at the right place? *Journal of Epidemiology and Community Health, 56,* 405–406.

Berkman, L. F., Blumenthal, J., Burg, M., Carney, R. M., Catellier, D., Cowan, M. J., Czajkowski, S. M., DeBusk, R., Hosking, J., Jaffe, A., Kaufmann, P. G., Mitchell, P., Norman, J., Powell, L. H., Raczynski, J. M., & Schneiderman, N. (2003). Effects of treating depression and low perceived social support on clinical events after myocardial infarction: the Enhancing Recovery in Coronary Heart Disease Patients (ENRICHD) Randomized Trial. *Journal of the American Medical Association, 289,* 3106–3116.

Blane, D., Davey Smith, G., & Bartley, M. (1993). Social selection: What does it contribute to social class differences in health? *Sociology of Health and Illness, 15,* 2–15.

Borg, V., & Kristensen, T. S. (2000). Social class and self-rated health: Can the gradient be explained by differences in life style or work environment? *Social Science and Medicine, 51,* 1019–1030.

Boyce, W. T., Chesney, M., Alkon, A., & Tschann, J. M. (1995). Psychobiologic reactivity to stress and childhood respiratory illnesses: Results of two prospective studies. *Psychosomatic Medicine, 57,* 411–422.

Boyce, W. T., Chesterman, E. A., Martin, N., & Folkman, S. (1993). Immunologic changes occurring at kindergarten entry predict respiratory illnesses after the Loma Prieta earthquake. *Journal of Developmental and Behavioral Pediatrics, 14,* 296–303.

Braunwald, E. (1997). Shattuck lecture. Cardiovascular medicine at the turn of the millennium: Triumphs, concerns, and opportunities. *New England Journal of Medicine, 337,* 1360–1369.

Burell, G. (1996). Group psychotherapy in Project New Life: Treatment of coronary-prone behaviors for patients who have had coronary artery bypass graft surgery. In R. Allan & S. S. Scheidt (Eds.), *Heart and mind: The practice of cardiac psychology* (pp. 291–310). Washington, DC: American Psychological Association.

Canadian Institutes of Health Research. (2002). Homepage of the Canadian Institutes of Health Research. Retrieved (31 July 2002) from http://www. cihr-irsc.gc.ca.

Canto, J. G., & Iskandrian, A. E. (2003). Major risk factors for cardiovascular disease: Debunking the 'only 50%' myth. *Journal of the American Medical Association, 290,* 947–949.

Carleton, R. A., Lasater, T. M., Assaf, A. R., Feldman, H. A., & McKinlay, S. (1995). The Pawtucket Heart Health Program: Community changes in cardiovascular risk factors and projected disease risk. *American Journal of Public Health, 85,* 777–785.

Carney, R. M., & Freedland, K. E. (2000). Depression and medical illness. In L. F. Berkman & I. Kawachi (Eds.), *Social epidemiology* (pp. 191–212). New York: Oxford University Press.

Case, R. B., Heller, S. S., Case, N. B., & Moss, A. J. (1985). Type A behavior and survival after acute myocardial infarction. *New England Journal of Medicine, 312,* 737–741.

Christensen, A. J., & Smith, T. W. (1993). Cynical hostility and cardiovascular reactivity during self-disclosure. *Psychosomatic Medicine, 55,* 193–202.

Cohen, S., Tyrrell, D. A., & Smith, A. P. (1991). Psychological stress and susceptibility to the common cold. *New England Journal of Medicine, 325,* 606–612.

Davey Smith, G. (1997). Is control at work the key to socioeconomic gradients in mortality? (letter). *Lancet, 350,* 1369.

Davey Smith, G., Bartley, M., & Blane, D. (1990). The Black Report on socioeconomic inequalities in health 10 years on. *British Medical Journal, 301,* 373–377.

Dawber, T. R. (1980). *The Framingham Study: The epidemiology of atherosclerotic disease.* Cambridge, MA: Harvard University Press.

Dawson, R. J. M. (1995). The 'unusual episode' data revisited. *Journal of Statistics Education, 3,* Electronic Journal. Retrieved (10 May 2002) from www.amstat.org./publications/jse/v3n/datasets. dawson.html.

de Jonge, J., Mulder, M. J., & Nijhuis, F. J. (1999). The incorporation of different demand concepts in the job demand–control model: Effects on health care professionals. *Social Science and Medicine, 48,* 1149–1160.

Department of Health and Social Security (1980). *Inequalities in health: Report of a working group chaired by Sir Douglas Black.* London: DHSS.

Doll, R., & Hill, N. E. (1956). Lung cancer and other causes of death in relation to smoking: A second report on the mortality of British doctors. *British Medical Journal, 2,* 1071–1081.

Doll, R., & Peto, R. (1976). Mortality in relation to smoking: 20 years' observations on male British doctors. *British Medical Journal, 2,* 1525–1536.

Donaldson, S., Gooler, L., & Weiss, R. (1998). Promoting health and well-being through work: Science and practice. In X. Arriaga & S. Oskamp (Eds.), *Addressing community problems: Psychological research and intervention* (pp. 160–194) Thousand Oaks, CA: Sage.

Durkheim, É. (1897/1951). *Suicide: A study in sociology.* Glencoe, IL: Free Press.

Emmons, K. M. (2000). Health behaviors in a social context. In L. F. Berkman & I. Kawachi (Eds.), *Social epidemiology* (pp. 242–266). New York: Oxford University Press.

Engel, G. L. (1977). The need for a new medical model: A challenge for biomedicine. *Science, 196,* 129–136.

Engels, F. (1845/1987). *The condition of the working class in England.* Harmondsworth: Penguin.

ENRICHD Study Group (2001). Enhancing Recovery in Coronary Heart Disease (ENRICHD) study intervention: Rationale and design. *Psychosomatic Medicine, 63,* 747–755.

European Science Foundation (2000). Social variations in health expectancy in Europe. Retrieved (9 June 2002) from http://www.uni-duesseldorf.de/health.

Evans, G. W., & Johansson, G. (1998). Urban bus driving: An international arena for the study of occupational health psychology. *Journal of Occupational Health Psychology, 3*, 99–108.

Evans, R. G. (1994). Introduction. In R. G. Evans, M. L. Barer & T. R. Marmor (Eds.), *Why are some people healthy and others not? The determinants of health of populations* (pp. 161–188). New York: de Gruyter.

Evans, R. G., Barer, M. L., & Marmor, T. R. (Eds.) (1994). *Why are some people healthy and others not? The determinants of health of populations.* New York: de Gruyter.

Evans, R. G., & Stoddart, G. L. (1990). Producing health, consuming health care. *Social Science and Medicine, 31*, 1347–1363.

Farquhar, J. W., Fortmann, S. P., Flora, J. A., Taylor, C. B., Haskell, W. L., Williams, P. T., Maccoby, N., & Wood, P. D. (1990). Effects of communitywide education on cardiovascular disease risk factors: The Stanford Five-City Project. *Journal of the American Medical Association, 264*, 359–365.

Ferketich, A. K., Schwartzbaum, J. A., Frid, D. J., & Moeschberger, M. L. (2000). Depression as an antecedent to heart disease among women and men in the NHANES I study. National Health and Nutrition Examination Survey. *Archives of Internal Medicine, 160*, 1261–1268.

Ford, D. E., Mead, L. A., Chang, P. P., Cooper-Patrick, L., Wang, N. Y., & Klag, M. J. (1998). Depression is a risk factor for coronary artery disease in men: the precursors study. *Archives of Internal Medicine, 158*, 1422–1426.

Frank, J. P. (1786/1976). *A system of complete medical police: Selections from Johann Peter Frank.* Baltimore: Johns Hopkins University Press.

Frank, J. W. (1995a). The determinants of health: A new synthesis. *Current Issues in Public Health, 1*, 233–240.

Frank, J. W. (1995b). Why 'population health'? *Canadian Journal of Public Health – Revue Canadienne de Santé Publique, 86*, 162–164.

Frasure-Smith, N., Lespérance, F., & Talajic, M. (1995). Depression and 18-month prognosis after myocardial infarction. *Circulation, 91*, 999–1005.

Frese, M., & Zapf, D. (1988). Methodological issues in the study of work stress: Objective vs subjective measurement of work stress and the question of longitudinal studies. In C. L. Cooper & R. Payne (Eds.), *Causes, coping and consequences of stress at work* (pp. 375–411). Chichester: Wiley.

Friedman, M., & Rosenman, R. (1959). Association of specific overt behavior pattern with blood and cardiovascular findings. *Journal of the American Medical Association, 169*, 1286–1296.

Friedman, M., Thoresen, C. E., Gill, J. J., Ulmer, D., Powell, L. H., Price, V. A., Brown, B., Thompson, L., Rabin, D. D., Breall, W. S., Bourg, E., Levy, R., & Dixon, T. (1986). Alteration of type A behavior and its effect on cardiac recurrences in post myocardial infarction patients: Summary results of the recurrent coronary prevention project. *American Heart Journal, 112*, 653–665.

Frohlich, K. L., Potvin, L., Chabot, P., & Corin, E. (2002). A theoretical and empirical analysis of context: Neighbourhoods, smoking and youth. *Social Science and Medicine, 54*, 1401–1417.

Frohlich, K. L., Potvin, L., Gauvin, L., & Chabot, P. (2002). Youth smoking initiation: Disentangling context from composition. *Health and Place, 8*, 155–166.

Geurts, S., & Gründemann, R. (1999). Workplace stress and stress prevention in Europe. In M. Kompier & C. Cooper (Eds.), *Preventing stress, improving productivity: European case studies in the workplace* (pp. 9–32). London: Routledge.

Goldenhar, L. M., & Schulte, P. A. (1996). Methodological issues for intervention research in occupational health and safety. *American Journal of Industrial Medicine, 29*, 289–294.

Graham, H. (1994). *When life's a drag.* London: HMSO.

Greiner, B. A., Krause, N., Ragland, D. R., & Fisher, J. M. (1998). Objective stress factors, accidents, and absenteeism in transit operators: A theoretical framework and empirical evidence. *Journal of Occupational Health Psychology, 3*, 130–146.

Greiner, B. A., & Leitner, K. (1989). Assessment of job stress: The RHIA instrument. In K. Landau & W. Rohmert (Eds.), *Recent development in work analysis* (pp. 53–66). Philadelphia, PA: Taylor & Francis.

Greiner, B. A., Ragland, D. R., Krause, N., Syme, S. L., & Fisher, J. M. (1997). Objective measurement of occupational stress factors: An example with San Francisco urban transit operators. *Journal of Occupational Health Psychology, 2*, 325–342.

Griffin, J. M., Fuhrer, R., Stansfeld, S. A., & Marmot, M. (2002). The importance of low control at work and home on depression and anxiety: Do these effects vary by gender and social class? *Social Science and Medicine, 54*, 783–798.

Griffiths, A. (1999). Organizational interventions: Facing the limits of the natural science paradigm. *Scandinavian Journal of Work, Environment and Health, 25*, 589–596.

Hamlin, C. (1995). Could you starve to death in England in 1839? The Chadwick–Farr controversy and the loss of the 'social' in public health. *American Journal of Public Health, 85*, 856–866.

Hancock, T. (1993). The evolution, impact and significance of the healthy cities/healthy communities movement. *Journal of Public Health Policy, 14,* 5–18.

Harper, S., Lynch, J., Hsu, W. L., Everson, S. A., Hillemeier, M. M., Raghunathan, T. E., Salonen, J. T., & Kaplan, G. A. (2002). Life course socioeconomic conditions and adult psychosocial functioning. *International Journal of Epidemiology, 31,* 395–403.

Heaney, C. A., & van Ryn, M. (1990). Broadening the scope of worksite stress programs: A guiding framework. *American Journal of Health Promotion, 4,* 413–420.

Hennekens, C. H. (1998). Increasing burden of cardiovascular disease: Current knowledge and future directions for research on risk factors. *Circulation, 97,* 1095–1102.

Hennekens, C., & Buring, J. (1987). *Epidemiology in medicine.* Boston: Little, Brown.

Henry, J. P., & Stephens, P. M. (1977). *Stress, health, and the social environment.* New York: Springer.

Hermann-Lingen, C., & Buss, U. (2002). *Angst und Depressivität im Verlauf der koronaren Herzkrankheit [Depression and anxiety during the course of coronary heart disease].* Frankfurt a.M.: Akademischer Schriften.

Hertzman, C. (1999). The biological embedding of early experience and its effects on health in adulthood. *Annals of the New York Academy of Sciences, 896,* 85–95.

Hurrell, J. J. Jr., & McLaney, M. A. (1988). Exposure to job stress: A new psychometric instrument. *Scandinavian Journal of Work, Environment and Health, 14* (Supp. 1), 27–28.

Israel, B. A., Baker, E. A., Goldenhar, L. M., Heaney, C. A., & Schurman, S. J. (1996). Occupational stress, safety, and health: Conceptual framework and principles for effective prevention interventions. *Journal of Occupational Health Psychology, 1,* 261–286.

Israel, B. A., Schurman, S. J., & Hugentobler, M. K. (1992). Conducting action research: Relationships between organization members and researchers. *Journal of Applied Behavioral Science, 28,* 74–101.

Johnson, J. V., & Hall, E. M. (1988). Job strain, workplace social support, and cardiovascular disease: A cross-sectional study of a random sample of the Swedish working population. *American Journal of Public Health, 78,* 1336–1342.

Johnson, J. V., & Hall, E. M. (1995). Class, work, and health. In B. Amick, S. Levine, A. Tarlov & D. Chapman Walsh (Eds.), *Society and health* (pp. 247–271). New York/ London: Oxford University Press.

Johnson, J. V., Stewart, W., Hall, E. M., Fredlund, P., & Theorell, T. (1996). Long-term psychosocial work environment and cardiovascular mortality among Swedish men. *American Journal of Public Health, 86,* 324–331.

Kaplan, G. A. (1999). What is the role of the social environment in understanding inequalities in health? *Annals of the New York Academy of Sciences, 896,* 116–119.

Kaplan, G. A., Everson, S. A., & Lynch, J. W. (2000). The contribution of social and behavioral research to an understanding of the distribution of disease: A multilevel approach. In B. D. Smedley & S. L. Syme (Eds.), *Promoting health: Intervention strategies from social and behavioral research* (pp. 37–80). Washington, DC: National Academy Press.

Kaplan, G. A., & Lynch, J. W. (1997). Whither studies on the socioeconomic foundations of population health? *American Journal of Public Health, 87,* 1409–1411.

Kaplan, G. A., Pamuk, E. R., Lynch, J. W., Cohen, R. D., & Balfour, J. L. (1996). Inequality in income and mortality in the United States: Analysis of mortality and potential pathways. *British Medical Journal, 312,* 999–1003.

Kaplan, G. A., Roberts, R. E., Camacho, T. C., & Coyne, J. C. (1987). Psychosocial predictors of depression: Prospective evidence from the human population laboratory studies. *American Journal of Epidemiology, 125,* 206–220.

Kaplan, J. R., Manuck, S. B., Adams, M. R., Weingand, K. W., & Clarkson, T. B. (1987). Inhibition of coronary atherosclerosis by propranolol in behaviorally predisposed monkeys fed an atherogenic diet. *Circulation, 76,* 1364–1372.

Karasek, R. (1979). Job demands, job decision latitude, and mental strain: Implications for job redesign. *Administration Science Quarterly, 24,* 285–307.

Karasek, R., & Theorell, T. (1990). *Healthy work: Stress, productivity, and the reconstruction of working life.* New York: Basic.

Kawachi, I., Kennedy, B. P., Lochner, K., & Prothrow-Stith, D. (1997). Social capital, income inequality, and mortality. *American Journal of Public Health, 87,* 1491–1498.

Keil, U., & Spelsberg, A. (1995). Epidemiologie der Atheroskleroserisiken [Epidemiology of risk for atherosclerosis]. In P. Schwandt & W. O. Richter

(Eds.), *Handbuch der Fettstoffwechselstörungen* (pp. 65–83). Stuttgart: Schattauer.

Kelsey, J. L., & Bernstein, L. (1996). Epidemiology and prevention of breast cancer. *Annual Review of Public Health, 17,* 47–67.

Kennedy, B. P., Kawachi, I., & Prothrow-Stith, D. (1996). Income distribution and mortality: Cross sectional ecological study of the Robin Hood index in the United States. *British Medical Journal, 312,* 1004–1007.

Kleinbaum, D. G., Kupper, L., & Morgenstern, H. (Eds.) (1982). *Epidemiologic research: Principles and quantitative methods.* New York: Van Nostrand Reinhold.

Kompier, M. A. J., Aust, B., van den Berg, A.-M., & Siegrist, J. (2000). Stress prevention in bus drivers: Evaluation of 13 natural experiments. *Journal of Occupational Health Psychology, 5,* 11–31.

Kompier, M. A. J., Geurts, S. A. E., Gründemann, R. W. M., Vink, P., & Smulders, P. G. W. (1998). Cases in stress prevention: The success of a participative and stepwise approach. *Stress Medicine, 14,* 155–168.

Kompier, M. A. J., & Kristensen, T. S. (2001). Organizational work stress interventions in a theoretical, methodological and practical context. In J. Dunham (Ed.), *Stress in the workplace: Past, present and future* (pp. 164–190). London: Whurr.

Krause, N., Ragland, D. R., Fisher, J. M., & Syme, S. L. (1998). Psychosocial job factors, physical workload, and incidence of work-related spinal injury: A 5-year prospective study of urban transit operators. *Spine, 23,* 2507–2516.

Krieger, N. (1994). Epidemiology and the web of causation: Has anyone seen the spider? *Social Science and Medicine, 39,* 887–903.

Kristensen, T. S. (1999). Challenges for research and prevention in relation to work and cardiovascular diseases. *Scandinavian Journal of Work, Environment and Health, 25,* 550–557.

Kristensen, T. S. (2000). Workplace intervention studies. *Occupational Medicine, 15,* 293–305.

Kristensen, T. S. (2001). A new tool for assessing psychosocial factors at work: Copenhagen Psychosocial Questionnaire (COPSOQ). Paper presented at the European Academy of Occupational Health Psychology, Barcelona, Spain, 24–27 October 2001. Retrieved (31 July 2002) from http://www.ami.dk/presentations/Barcelona_oct_24to27_2001.pdf.

Kubzansky, L. D., Kawachi, I., Weiss, S. T., & Sparrow, D. (1998). Anxiety and coronary heart disease: A synthesis of epidemiological, psychological, and experimental evidence. *Annals of Behavioral Medicine, 20,* 47–58.

Kuh, D., & Ben-Shlomo, Y. (Eds.) (1997). *A life course approach to chronic disease epidemiology: Tracing the origins of ill-health from early to adult life.* Oxford: Oxford University Press.

Kunst, A. E., Groenhof, F., Mackenbach, J. P., & The EU Working Group on Socioeconomic Inequalities in Health (1998). Occupational class and cause specific mortality in middle aged men in 11 European countries: Comparison of population based studies. EU Working Group on Socioeconomic Inequalities in Health. *British Medical Journal, 316,* 1636–1642.

La Botz, D. (2001). *Made in Indonesia: Indonesian workers since Suharto.* Cambridge, MA: South End Press.

Ladwig, K. H., Kieser, M., Konig, J., Breithardt, G., & Borggrefe, M. (1991). Affective disorders and survival after acute myocardial infarction: Results from the post-infarction late potential study. *European Heart Journal, 12,* 959–964.

Landsbergis, P. A., Cahill, J., & Schnall, P. (1999). The impact of lean production and related new systems of work organization on worker health. *Journal of Occupational Health Psychology, 4,* 108–130.

Landsbergis, P. A., Theorell, T., Schwartz, J., Greiner, B. A., & Krause, N. (2000). Measurement of psychosocial workplace exposure variables. *Occupational Medicine, 15,* 163–188.

Last, J. M. (1995). *A dictionary of epidemiology.* Oxford: Oxford University Press.

Liang, S. W., & Boyce, W. T. (1993). The psychobiology of childhood stress. *Current Opinion in Pediatrics, 5,* 545–551.

Luepker, R. V., Murray, D. M., Jacobs, D. R. Jr., Mittelmark, M. B., Bracht, N., Carlaw, R., Crow, R., Elmer, P., Finnegan, J., Folsom, A. R., Grimm, R., Hannan, P. J., Jeffrey, R., Lando, H., McGovern, P., Mullis, R., Perry, C. L., Pechacek, T., Pirie, P., Sprafka, J. M., Weisbrod, R., & Blackburn, H. (1994). Community education for cardiovascular disease prevention: Risk factor changes in the Minnesota Heart Health Program. *American Journal of Public Health, 84,* 1383–1393.

Luepker, R. V., Rastam, L., Hannan, P. J., Murray, D. M., Gray, C., Baker, W. L., Crow, R., Jacobs, D. R. Jr., Pirie, P. L., Mascioli, S. R., Mittelmark, M. B., & Blackburn, H. (1996). Community education for cardiovascular disease prevention: Morbidity and mortality results from the Minnesota Heart Health Program. *American Journal of Epidemiology, 144,* 351–362.

Lurie, N. (2001). Eliminating inequalities in the U.S. health care system: Efforts of the U.S. Department of Health and Human Services. In

J. A. Auerbach & B. K. Krimgold (Eds.), *Income, socioeconomic status, and health* (pp. 91–100). Washington, DC: National Policy Association.

Lynch, J. W. (2000). Income inequality and health: Expanding the debate. *Social Science and Medicine, 51*, 1001–1005.

Lynch, J. W., Davey Smith, G., Hillemeier, M., Shaw, M., Raghunathan, T., & Kaplan, G. A. (2001). Income inequality, the psychosocial environment, and health: Comparisons of wealthy nations. *Lancet, 358*, 194–200.

Lynch, J. W., Davey Smith, G., Kaplan, G. A., & House, J. S. (2000). Income inequality and mortality: Importance to health of individual income, psychosocial environment, or material conditions. *British Medical Journal, 320*, 1200–1204.

Lynch, J. W., Everson, S. A., Kaplan, G. A., Salonen, R., & Salonen, J. T. (1998). Does low socioeconomic status potentiate the effects of heightened cardiovascular responses to stress on the progression of carotid atherosclerosis? *American Journal of Public Health, 88*, 389–394.

Lynch, J. W., & Kaplan, G. A. (2000). Socioeconomic position. In L. F. Berkman & I. Kawachi (Eds.), *Social epidemiology* (pp. 13–35). New York: Oxford University Press.

Lynch, J. W., Kaplan, G. A., & Salonen, J. T. (1997). Why do poor people behave poorly? Variation in adult health behaviours and psychosocial characteristics by stages of the socioeconomic lifecourse. *Social Science and Medicine, 44*, 809–819.

MacArthur Network on SES and Health (2002). Homepage of the MacArthur Network on SES and Health. Retrieved (31 July 2002) from http://www. macfdn.org.

Macintyre, S. (1997). The Black Report and beyond: What are the issues? *Social Science and Medicine, 44*, 723–745.

Macintyre, S., MacIver, S., & Sooman, A. (1993). Area, class and health: Should we be focusing on places or people? *Journal of Social Policies, 22*, 213–234.

Mackenbach, J. P., Kunst, A. E., Cavelaars, A. E., Groenhof, F., Geurts, J. J., & The EU Working Group on Socioeconomic Inequalities in Health (1997). Socioeconomic inequalities in morbidity and mortality in western Europe. *Lancet, 349*, 1655–1659.

Macleod, J., Davey Smith, G., Heslop, P., Metcalfe, C., Carroll, D., & Hart, C. (2002). Psychological stress and cardiovascular disease: Empirical demonstration of bias in a prospective observational study of Scottish men. *British Medical Journal, 324*, 1247.

Marmot, M. G. (1994). Social differentials in health within and between populations. *Daedalus, 123*, 197–216.

Marmot, M. G. (1996). The social pattern of health and illness. In D. Blane, E. Brunner & R. Wilkinson (Eds.), *Health and social organization: Towards a health policy in the twenty-first century* (pp. 42–67). London: Routledge.

Marmot, M., & Bobak, M. (2000). International comparators and poverty and health in Europe. *British Medical Journal, 321*, 1124–1128.

Marmot, M., Bosma, H., Hemingway, H., Brunner, E., & Stansfeld, S. (1997). Contribution of job control and other risk factors to social variations in coronary heart disease incidence. *Lancet, 350*, 235–239.

Marmot, M. G., & Davey Smith, G. (1989). Why are the Japanese living longer? *British Medical Journal, 299*, 1547–1551.

Marmot, M. G., Davey Smith, G., Stansfeld, S., Patel, C., North, F., Head, J., White, I., Brunner, E., & Feeney, A. (1991). Health inequalities among British civil servants: The Whitehall II Study. *Lancet, 337*, 1387–1393.

Marmot, M. G., Shipley, M., & Rose, G. (1984). Inequalities in death: Specific explanation of a general pattern? *Lancet*, i (8384), 1003–1006.

Marmot, M., & Wilkinson, R. G. (2001). Psychosocial and material pathways in the relation between income and health: A response to Lynch et al. *British Medical Journal, 322*, 1233–1236.

Marmot, M., & Winkelstein, W. Jr. (1975). Epidemiologic observations on intervention trials for prevention of coronary heart disease. *American Journal of Epidemiology, 101*, 177–181.

Marx, K. (1867/1981). *Capital: A critique of political economy*. Harmondsworth: Penguin.

McDonough, P., Duncan, G. J., Williams, D., & House, J. (1997). Income dynamics and adult mortality in the United States, 1972 through 1989. *American Journal of Public Health, 87*, 1476–1483.

McGinnis, J. M., & Foege, W. H. (1993). Actual cause of death in the United States. *Journal of the American Medical Association, 270*, 2207–2212.

McKeown, T. (1979). *The role of medicine: Dream, mirage, or nemesis?* (2nd edn.). Oxford: Blackwell.

McKinlay, J. B., McKinlay, S. M., & Beaglehole, R. (1989). A review of the evidence concerning the impact of medical measures on recent mortality and morbidity in the United States. *International Journal of Health Services, 19*, 181–208.

McLeroy, K. R., Bibeau, D., Steckler, A., & Glanz, K. (1988). An ecological perspective on health promotion programs. *Health Education Quarterly*, *15*, 351–377.

Mendes de Leon, C. F., Krumholz, H. M., Seeman, T. S., Vaccarino, V., Williams, C. S., Kasl, S. V., & Berkman, L. F. (1998). Depression and risk of coronary heart disease in elderly men and women: New Haven EPESE, 1982–1991. Established Populations for the Epidemiologic Studies of the Elderly. *Archives of Internal Medicine*, *158*, 2341–2348.

Mergler, D. (1999). Combining quantitative and qualitative approaches in occupational health for a better understanding of the impact of work-related disorders. *Scandinavian Journal of Work, Environment and Health*, *25*(Supp. 4), 54–60.

Merllié, D., & Paoli, P. (2000). *Ten years of working conditions in the European Union*. Dublin: European Foundation for the Improvement of Living and Working Conditions.

Miller, T. Q., Smith, T. W., Turner, C. W., Guijarro, M. L., & Hallet, A. J. (1996). A meta-analytic review of research on hostility and physical health. *Psychological Bulletin*, *119*, 322–348.

Minkler, M. (1989). Health education, health promotion and the open society: An historical perspective. *Health Education Quarterly*, *16*, 17–30.

Minkler, M. (1992). Community organizing among the elderly poor in the United States: A case study. *International Journal of Health Services*, *22*, 303–316.

Morland, K., Wing, S., Diez Roux, A., & Poole, C. (2002). Neighborhood characteristics associated with the location of food stores and food service places. *American Journal of Preventive Medicine*, *22*, 23–29.

Morris, J. N. (1990). Inequalities in health: Ten years and little further on. *Lancet*, *336*, 491–493.

Multiple Risk Factor Intervention Trial Research Group (1981). The multiple risk factor intervention trial (MRFIT): The methods and impact of intervention over four years. *Preventive Medicine*, *10*, 387–553.

Multiple Risk Factor Intervention Trial Research Group (1982). Multiple risk factor intervention trial: Risk factor changes and mortality results. *Journal of the American Medical Association*, *248*, 1465–1477.

Muntaner, C., & Lynch, J. (1999). Income inequality, social cohesion, and class relations: A critique of Wilkinson's neo-Durkheimian research program. *International Journal of Health Services*, *29*, 59–81.

Muntaner, C., Lynch, J., & Oates, G. L. (1999). The social class determinants of income inequality and social cohesion. *International Journal of Health Services*, *29*, 699–732.

Murray, C. J. L., Lopez, A. D., Mathers, C. D., & Stein, C. (2002). The Global Burden of Disease 2000 Project: Aims, methods and data sources. Paper 36. Retrieved (14 June 2002) from http://www3.who.int/whosis/menu.cfm?path=whosis,burden,burden_gbd2000&language=english.

Murray, C. J., Salomon, J. A., & Mathers, C. (2000). A critical examination of summary measures of population health. *Bulletin of the World Health Organization*, *78*, 981–994.

Musselman, D. L., Evans, D. L., & Nemeroff, C. B. (1998). The relationship of depression to cardiovascular disease: Epidemiology, biology, and treatment. *Archives of General Psychiatry*, *55*, 580–592.

Myrtek, M. (2000). *Das Typ-A-Verhaltensmuster und Hostility als eigenständige Risikofaktoren der koronaren Herzkrankheit [Type-A behavior pattern and hostility as independent risk factors for coronary heart disease]*. Frankfurt a.M.: Akademischer Schriften.

Navarro, V. (1990). Race or class versus race and class: Mortality differentials in the United States. *Lancet*, *336*, 1238–1240.

Nielsen, M. L., Kristensen, T. S., & Smith-Hansen, L. (2002). The Intervention Project on Absence and Well-being (IPAW): Design and results from the baseline of a 5-year study. *Work & Stress*, *16*, 191–206.

Notzon, F. C., Komarov, Y. M., Ermakov, S. P., Sempos, C. T., Marks, J. S., & Sempos, E. V. (1998). Causes of declining life expectancy in Russia. *Journal of the American Medical Association*, *279*, 793–800.

Pearce, N. (1996). Traditional epidemiology, modern epidemiology, and public health. *American Journal of Public Health*, *86*, 678–683.

Pratt, L. A., Ford, D. E., Crum, R. M., Armenian, H. K., Gallo, J. J., & Eaton, W. W. (1996). Depression, psychotropic medication, and risk of myocardial infarction. Prospective data from the Baltimore ECA follow-up. *Circulation*, *94*, 3123–3129.

Puska, P., Salonen, J. T., Nissinen, A., Tuomilehto, J., Vartiainen, E., Korhonen, H., Tanskanen, A., Ronnqvist, P., Koskela, K., & Huttunen, J. (1983). Change in risk factors for coronary heart disease during 10 years of a community intervention programme (North Karelia Project). *British Medical Journal (Clinical Research Ed.)*, *287*, 1840–1844.

Ragland, D. R., & Brand, R. J. (1988). Type A behavior and mortality from coronary heart disease. *New England Journal of Medicine*, *318*, 65–69.

Reves, R. (1985). Declining fertility in England and Wales as a major cause of the twentieth century decline in mortality: The role of changing family size and age structure in infectious disease mortality in infancy. *American Journal of Epidemiology, 122,* 112–126.

Review Panel on Coronary-Prone Behavior and Coronary Heart Disease (1981). Coronary-prone behavior and coronary heart disease: A critical review. *Circulation, 63,* 1199–1215.

Robert Wood Johnson Foundation (2002). Homepage of the Robert Wood Johnson Foundation. Retrieved (31 July 2002) from http://www.rwjf.org/index.jsp.

Rose, G. (1985). Sick individuals and sick populations. *International Journal of Epidemiology, 14,* 32–38.

Rose, G. (1992). *The strategy of preventive medicine.* Oxford: Oxford University Press.

Rosenbrock, R., & Müller, R. (1998). Prävention arbeitsbedingter Gesundheitsgefahren und Erkrankungen: Perspektiven für den Arbeitsschutz [Prevention of occupational health risks and diseases: Perspectives for occupational health]. In R. Müller & R. Rosenbrock (Eds.), *Betriebliches Gesundheitsmanagement, Arbeitsschutz und Gesundheitsförderung* (pp. 10–32). Sankt Augustin: Asgard.

Rosenman, R. H., Brand, R. J., Jenkins, D., Friedman, M., Straus, R., & Wurm, M. (1975). Coronary heart disease in Western Collaborative Group Study: Final follow-up experience of 8½ years. *Journal of the American Medical Association, 233,* 872–877.

Rosenman, R. H., & Chesney, M. A. (1980). The relationship of type A behavior pattern to coronary heart disease. *Activitas Nervosa Superior, 22,* 1–45.

Ross, N. A., Wolfson, M. C., Dunn, J. R., Berthelot, J. M., Kaplan, G. A., & Lynch, J. W. (2000). Relation between income inequality and mortality in Canada and in the United States: Cross sectional assessment using census data and vital statistics. *British Medical Journal, 320,* 898–902.

Rothman, K., & Greenland, S. (1998a). Causation and causal inference. In K. Rothman & S. Greenland (Eds.), *Modern epidemiology* (2nd edn., pp. 7–28). Philadelphia, PA: Lippincott Williams & Wilkins.

Rothman, K., & Greenland, S. (Eds.) (1998b). *Modern epidemiology* (2nd edn.). Philadelphia, PA: Lippincott Williams & Wilkins.

Rugulies, R. (1998). *Die psychosoziale Dimension der koronaren Herzkrankheit und die Chancen multiprofessioneller Intervention* [*The psychosocial dimension of coronary heart disease and the chances of multiprofessional intervention*]. Lengerich: Pabst.

Rugulies, R. (2002). Depression as a predictor for coronary heart disease: A review and meta-analysis. *American Journal of Preventive Medicine, 23,* 51–61.

Rugulies, R., & Siegrist, J. (2002). *Soziologische Aspekte der Entstehung und des Verlaufs der koronaren Herzkrankheit: Soziale Ungleichverteilung der Erkrankung und chronische Distress-Erfahrungen im Erwerbsleben* [*Sociological aspects of the development and course of coronary heart disease: Social inequality and chronic emotional stress at the workplace*]. Frankfurt a.M.: Akademischer Schriften.

Rütten, A., von Lengerke, T., Abel, T., Kannas, L., Lüschen, G., Diaz, J. A. R., Vinck, J., & van der Zee, J. (2000). Policy, competence and participation: Empirical evidence for a multilevel health promotion model. *Health Promotion International, 15,* 35–47.

Sampson, R., & Morenoff, J. (2000). Public health and safety in context: Lessons from community-level theory on social capital. In B. D. Smedley & S. L. Syme (Eds.), *Promoting health: Intervention strategies from social and behavioral research* (pp. 366–389). Washington, DC: National Academy Press.

Scherwitz, L., Perkins, L., Chesney, M., & Hughes, G. (1991). Cook–Medley Hostility Scale and subsets: Relationship to demographic and psychosocial characteristics in young adults in the CARDIA study. *Psychosomatic Medicine, 53,* 36–49.

Scherwitz, L., & Rugulies, R. (1992). Lifestyle and hostility. In H. S. Friedman (Ed.), *Hostility, coping, and health* (pp. 77–98). Washington, DC: American Psychological Association.

Schieber, G. J., Poullier, J. P., & Greenwald, L. M. (1992). U.S. health expenditure performance: An international comparison and data update. *Health Care Financing Review, 13,* 1–87.

Schnall, P. L., Belkić, K., Landsbergis, P., & Baker, D. (2000). The workplace and cardiovascular disease. *Occupational Medicine: State of the Art Reviews, 15,* 1–322.

Schnall, P. L., Schwartz, J. E., Landsbergis, P. A., Warren, K., & Pickering, T. G. (1998). A longitudinal study of job strain and ambulatory blood pressure: Results from a three-year follow-up. *Psychosomatic Medicine, 60,* 697–706.

Schneiderman, N., & Skyler, J. (1996). Insulin metabolism, sympathetic nervous system regulation and coronary heart disease. In K. Orth-Gomér & N. Schneiderman (Eds.), *Behavioral medicine approaches to cardiovascular disease prevention* (pp. 105–33). Mahwah, NJ: Erlbaum.

Schnohr, P., Jensen, J. S., Scharling, H., & Nordestgaard, B. G. (2002). Coronary heart disease risk factors ranked by importance for the individual and community: A 21 year follow-up of 12,000 men and women from the Copenhagen City Heart Study. *European Heart Journal*, 23, 620–626.

Schröer, A., & Sochert, M. (2000). *Health promotion circles at the workplace*. Essen: BKK Bundesverband.

Schurman, S. J. (1996). Making the 'new American workplace' safe and healthy: A joint labor–management– researcher approach. *American Journal of Industrial Medicine*, 29, 373–377.

Schwartz, S. W., Cornoni-Huntley, J., Cole, S. R., Hays, J. C., Blazer, D. G., & Schocken, D. D. (1998). Are sleep complaints an independent risk factor for myocardial infarction? *Annals of Epidemiology*, 8, 384–392.

Sesso, H. D., Kawachi, I., Vokonas, P. S., & Sparrow, D. (1998). Depression and the risk of coronary heart disease in the Normative Aging Study. *American Journal of Cardiology*, 82, 851–856.

Shaw, M., Dorling, D., & Davey Smith, G. (1999). Poverty, social exclusion, and minorities. In M. Marmot & R. G. Wilkinson (Eds.), *Social determinants of health* (pp. 209–239). New York: Oxford University Press.

Shekelle, R. B., Hulley, S. B., Neaton, J. D., Billings, J. H., Borhani, N. O., Gerace, T. A., Jacobs, D. R., Lasser, N. L., Mittlemark, M. B., & Stamler, J. (1985). The MRFIT behavior pattern study: II. Type A behavior and incidence of coronary heart disease. *American Journal of Epidemiology*, 122, 559–570.

Shy, C. M. (1997). The failure of academic epidemiology: Witness for the prosecution. *American Journal of Epidemiology*, 145, 479–484; discussion 485–487.

Siegrist, J. (1996). Adverse health effects of high-effort/low-reward conditions. *Journal of Occupational Health Psychology*, 1, 27–41.

Siegrist, J., Starke, D., Chandola, T., Godin. I., Marmot, M., Niedhammer, I., & Peter, R. (2004). The measurement of effort–reward imbalance at work: European comparisons. *Social Science and Medicine*, 58, 1483–1499.

Smedley, B. D., & Syme, S. L. (Eds.) (2000). *Promoting health: Intervention strategies from social and behavioral research*. Washington, DC: National Academy Press.

Smith, T. W. (1992). Hostility and health: Current status of a psychosomatic hypothesis. *Health Psychology*, 11, 139–150.

Snow, J. (1855). *On the mode of communication of cholera*. London: Churchill.

Söderfeldt, M. (1997). *Burnout?* Unpublished PhD thesis, Lund University, Sweden.

Sooman, A., Macintyre, S., & Anderson, A. (1993). Scotland's health: A more difficult challenge for some? The price and availability of healthy foods in socially contrasting localities in the west of Scotland. *Health Bulletin*, 51, 276–284.

Sorensen, G., Emmons, K., Hunt, M. K., & Johnston, D. (1998). Implications of the results of community intervention trials. *Annual Review of Public Health*, 19, 379–416.

Stamler, J. (1981). Primary prevention of coronary heart disease: The last 20 years. *American Journal of Cardiology*, 47, 722–735.

Stansfeld, S. A., Fuhrer, R., Shipley, M. J., & Marmot, M. G. (1999). Work characteristics predict psychiatric disorder: Prospective results from the Whitehall II Study. *Occupational and Environmental Medicine*, 56, 302–307.

Stein, P. K., Carney, R. M., Freedland, K. E., Skala, J. A., Jaffe, A. S., Kleiger, R. E., & Rottman, J. N. (2000). Severe depression is associated with markedly reduced heart rate variability in patients with stable coronary heart disease. *Journal of Psychosomatic Research*, 48, 493–500.

Susser, M., & Adelstein, A. (1975). An introduction to the work of William Farr. *American Journal of Epidemiology*, 101, 469–476.

Susser, M., & Susser, E. (1996a). Choosing a future for epidemiology: I. Eras and paradigms. *American Journal of Public Health*, 86, 668–673.

Susser, M., & Susser, E. (1996b). Choosing a future for epidemiology: II. From black box to Chinese boxes and eco-epidemiology. *American Journal of Public Health*, 86, 674–677.

Syme, S. L. (1996). Rethinking disease: Where do we go from here? *Annals of Epidemiology*, 6, 463–468.

Syme, S. L., & Balfour, J. L. (1998). Social determinants of disease. In R. B. Wallace (Ed.) *Maxcy–Rosenau–Last public health & preventive medicine* (14th edn., pp. 795–810). Stamford, CT: Appelton & Lange.

Szreter, R. (1988). The importance of social intervention in Britain's mortality decline c. 1850–1914: A re-interpretation of the role of public health. *Society of the Social History of Medicine*, 1, 1–37.

Taylor, S. E., Repetti, R. L., & Seeman, T. (1997). Health psychology: What is an unhealthy environment and how does it get under the skin? *Annual Review of Psychology*, 48, 411–447.

Taylor, R., & Rieger, A. (1985). Medicine as social science: Rudolf Virchow on the typhus epidemic in Upper Silesia. *International Journal of Health Services*, 15, 547–559.

Theorell, T., & Karasek, R. (1996). Current issues relating to psychological job strain and cardiovascular disease research. *Journal of Occupational Health Psychology, 1*, 9–26.

Townsend, P., & Davidson, N. (Eds.) (1982). *Inequalities in health: The Black Report.* Harmondsworth: Penguin.

Tüchsen, F., & Endahl, L. A. (1999). Increasing inequality in ischaemic heart disease morbidity among employed men in Denmark 1981–1993: The need for a new preventive policy. *International Journal of Epidemiology, 28*, 640–644.

UNAIDS (2002). The report on the global HIV/AIDS epidemic, 'The Barcelona Report'. Retrieved (12 August 2002) from http://www. unaids.org/barcelona/presskit/report.html.

Virchow, R. (1849/1968). *Mitteilungen über die in Oberschlesien herrschende Typhusepidemie [Report on the typhus epidemic prevailing in Upper Silesia].* Darmstadt: Wissenschaftliche Buchgesellschaft.

Wallston, B. S., Wallston, K. A., Kaplan, G. D., & Maides, S. A. (1976). Development and validation of the Health Locus of Control (HLC) Scale. *Journal of Consulting and Clinical Psychology, 4*, 580–585.

Wamala, S. P., Lynch, J., & Kaplan, G. A. (2001). Women's exposure to early and later life socio-economic disadvantage and coronary heart disease risk: The Stockholm Female Coronary Risk Study. *International Journal of Epidemiology, 30*, 275–284.

Wamala, S. P., Mittleman, M. A., Horsten, M., Schenck-Gustafsson, K., & Orth-Gomer, K. (2000). Job stress and the occupational gradient in coronary heart disease risk in women: The Stockholm Female Coronary Risk Study. *Social Science and Medicine, 51*, 481–489.

Wassertheil-Smoller, S., Applegate, W. B., Berge, K., Chang, C. J., Davis, B. R., Grimm, R. Jr., Kostis, J., Pressel, S., & Schron, E. (1996). Change in depression as a precursor of cardiovascular events. *Archives of Internal Medicine, 156*, 553–561.

Weber, M. (1922/1968). *Economy and society.* New York: Bedminster.

Weiner, H. (1992). *Perturbing the organism: The biology of stressful experience.* Chicago: The University of Chicago Press.

Westermayer, G., & Bähr, B. (1994). *Betriebliche Gesundheitszirkel [Workplace health circles].* Göttingen: Verlag für Angewandte Psychologie.

Whooley, M. A., & Browner, W. S. (1998). Association between depressive symptoms and

mortality in older women. Study of Osteoporotic Fractures Research Group. *Archives of Internal Medicine, 158*, 2129–2135.

WHOSIS (2002). Burden of disease. GBD 2000 Version 1 estimates by region: Mortality. Retrieved (8 June 2002) from http://www3.who.int/whosis/menu.cfm?path=whosis,burden,burden_gbd2000, burden_gbd2000_region&language=english.

Wilhelmsen, L., Berglund, G., Elmfeldt, D., Tibblin, G., Wedel, H., Pennert, K., Vedin, A., Wilhelmsson, C., & Werko, L. (1986). The multifactor primary prevention trial in Göteborg, Sweden. *European Heart Journal, 7*, 279–288.

Wilkinson, R. G. (1996). *Unhealthy societies: The afflictions of inequality.* London: Routledge.

Wilkinson, R. G. (1999). Income inequality, social cohesion, and health: Clarifying the theory – a reply to Muntaner and Lynch. *International Journal of Health Services, 29*, 525–543.

Winkleby, M. A., Ragland, D. R., Fisher, J. M., & Syme, S. L. (1988). Excess risk of sickness and disease in bus drivers: A review and synthesis of epidemiological studies. *International Journal of Epidemiology, 17*, 255–262.

Wolfson, M., Kaplan, G., Lynch, J., Ross, N., & Backlund, E. (1999). Relation between income inequality and mortality: Empirical demonstration. *British Medical Journal, 319*, 953–955.

World Bank (2002). Income poverty: The latest global numbers. Retrieved (16 April 2002) from http://www.worldbank.org/poverty/data/trends/income.htm.

World Health Organization (2001). The world health report 2001. Mental health: New understanding, new hope. Geneva: World Health Organization.

Yen, I. H., & Kaplan, G. A. (1998). Poverty area residence and changes in physical activity level: Evidence from the Alameda County Study. *American Journal of Public Health, 88*, 1709–1712.

Yen, I. H., & Kaplan, G. A. (1999a). Neighborhood social environment and risk of death: Multilevel evidence from the Alameda County Study. *American Journal of Epidemiology, 149*, 898–907.

Yen, I. H., & Kaplan, G. A. (1999b). Poverty area residence and changes in depression and perceived health status: Evidence from the Alameda County Study. *International Journal of Epidemiology, 28*, 90–94.

3

Biological Mechanisms of Health and Disease

BRENT N. HENDERSON AND ANDREW BAUM

INTRODUCTION

The emergence and success of behavioral medicine and health psychology have been due in part to the changing nature of health and disease over the past 100 years. This is evident in several aspects of modern medicine. The nature of health threats has changed, from infectious diseases like influenza to chronic illness and cancer. Life expectancy has increased substantially and gains of 50 per cent or more have been attributed to the elimination of polio, tuberculosis, influenza, and smallpox (Matarazzo, 1984). A 1979 Surgeon General's Report in the US estimated that, in 1900, for every 100,000 people there were about 480 deaths per year due to influenza, diphtheria, pneumonia, tuberculosis, and other infectious illnesses (Califano, 1979). In 2000, this figure dropped to only 30 deaths per 100,000 people. However, this dramatic decline in infectious illness was matched by a steep climb in more chronic diseases that have substantial behavioral causes. Cancer deaths have more than tripled, and heart disease, cancer, and AIDS have become prominent causes of death and disability. These diseases have no cure, no vaccine to prevent them, but are caused in part by lifestyle and behavior, which can be modified. Diet, tobacco

use, drug use, stress, and exercise are intertwined with people's lifestyles, and modification of these processes should help us control and manage these diseases. Health psychology offers unique insight and promise in controlling these modern 'epidemics'.

Health psychology is a biobehavioral discipline, focusing on behavioral and biological mechanisms by which environmental or social experiences are translated into physiological changes and changes in one's health. Interest in biobehavioral interactions is not new, but its most recent emergence in health-related areas has been both catalytic and controversial. The extent to which health and wellness are biological versus psychological states remains a point of debate and contention despite the recognition that biological events are immediate, 'proximate' causes while psychological or behavioral variables promote or impair health by influencing these biological events. Disease is essentially a biological event; it typically involves dysfunction or damage to bodily tissue, organs or systems, and whether it has behavioral causes or not it remains a biological process. For example, tobacco use certainly affects health and is a cause of cancers, heart disease and other illnesses. However, it affects these outcomes by causing biological damage, such as making cells in the lungs more susceptible to mutations and malignancies or by promoting atherosclerosis in the circulatory system. Stress also has a range of effects on disease etiology or progression, but it conveys these effects by affecting changes in the immune, endocrine, cardiovascular, gastrointestinal, and other bodily systems' activity. 'Disease-bearing variables' or behavioral pathogens (Matarazzo, 1984) must be translated into biological changes in order to contribute to physical disease. Biobehavioral pathways or mechanisms, then, are sets of related behavioral and biological processes that can modify one another and provide ways to explain and transmit behavioral influences on health and illness. Research in health psychology is focused on the pathways by which behavioral effects are conveyed, amplified, and/or modified, and herein lies the promise of health psychology for understanding and controlling disease.

This chapter is about these biobehavioral mechanisms, with an emphasis on how various bodily systems are altered by behavioral variables and how these changes contribute to pathophysiology. There are several ways to categorize and cluster these systems. One such taxonomy centers on function: systems can be *regulatory systems* (e.g., nervous system, endocrine system), *transport systems* (e.g., cardiovascular system, lymph system), *resource systems* (e.g., respiratory system, gastrointestinal systems), and *effector or defense systems* (e.g., immune system, DNA repair system). Such a classification permits evaluation of different levels of behavioral influences; effects on regulatory systems, for example, are likely to reverberate in other systems since they exert some control over these other systems. It also permits generation of testable hypotheses about channels or pathways through which behavioral effects are transmitted. It should be noted that our coverage of biological systems includes most but not all bodily systems; readers are referred elsewhere for a comprehensive and more thorough review of biological systems or divisions relevant for health and disease (West, 1991).

There are three main ways in which behavioral variables influence health-related outcomes. First, some of these variables or conditions exert direct effects on the functioning of a system or systems. These direct effects are considered to be primary outcomes of a set of conditions. For example, stress is thought to exert direct effects on most systems of the body, many of which can be pathogenic. In addition, behavioral or social variables may affect other behaviors that in turn have direct consequences for health. These indirect pathways would include, for example, any variables or conditions that influenced smoking or other tobacco use (smoking and tobacco have direct effects on several pathogenic processes), diet, exercise, sleep, and so on. A third set of pathways includes behavioral variables or conditions that affect treatment once one is ill. Access to care, adherence, lifestyle change, and other factors influencing access, compliance, and maintenance of appropriate treatments/changes are representative of these pathways. Both chronic burdens and acute stressors would be expected to exert effects in these ways, suggesting generally that behavioral and social variables can create vulnerabilities as well as exacerbate or 'realize' pre-existing vulnerabilities.

BODILY SYSTEMS AND BEHAVIOR

In describing these systems, we provide a brief overview of how each functions and where behavioral influences are most likely to be manifest, review representative research linking behavioral and biological changes to one another and to health outcomes, and describe some potential ameliorative strategies for minimizing health impairing effects.

Regulatory Systems

Regulatory systems, primarily the nervous and endocrine systems, serve communication and integration functions by stimulating or inhibiting the activity of other systems. These activities are typically in the service of maintenance of homeostasis or balance, or of coping or adaptation in response to environmental inputs signaling threats or opportunities. They include detection and interpretation of external and internal events as well as direction of responses to these events and evaluation of the efficacy of these responses. Changes in external or internal environments are detected by sensory systems that relay information to the brain, a central processing unit that interprets the information sent to it and sends general and specific directions back out to the periphery that determine how the organism copes or reacts. These incoming signals, called afferents, constitute a major determinant of how events are appraised or resolved. They evoke both novel and well-established appraisals of responses, influenced by past experience and severity of threat or demand, and send action directives to other regulatory centers and specific organs. These instructions for coping and adaptation are called efferents and typically terminate in action by target systems.

The hypothalamus plays a primary regulatory role for the nervous system. Among its many important functions is its control of the sympathetic nervous system (SNS) and parasympathetic nervous system (PNS), which are coordinated to regulate arousal and reduction of arousal in response to change or threat. The SNS and PNS interface with nearly every organ or organ system in the body and help to control such diverse activity as respiration, digestion, heart rate, and energy storage or release. Given these broad connections, it is not surprising that changes in activity in the nervous system have been linked to various disease states and processes.

Of some interest is the close interaction between the two major regulatory systems in the body, the nervous and endocrine systems. The central nervous system (CNS) consists of the brain and spinal cord and serves an integration function. The peripheral nervous system includes all ganglia, neurons, and synapses that detect and relay information to the spinal cord and brain. Excitation of a pathway stimulates activity that eventually sends regulatory messages to effector organs such as skeletal muscles. Afferent excitation sends these messages to the CNS; efferent excitation involves information from the CNS going to the periphery.

The endocrine system is closely connected to the nervous system and often works in concert with it to achieve desired objectives. For example, neurally mediated activation of the sympathetic nervous system lasts a relatively short time and needs to occur periodically to maintain an aroused state. However, endocrine activity can augment sympathetic activity and is reliably associated with the same modulation of organ systems activity as nervous system activation. The chief difference is that endocrine-mediated arousal has the potential to last longer and most cases of simultaneous activation of nervous system and endocrine pathways appear to be designed to intensify and extend arousal.

These regulatory systems are organized in ways that allow them to play key gatekeeper and regulatory roles in orchestrating response to nearly any stimulus or set of conditions. Most incoming information from external sensors (e.g., eyes, ears, touch) is transmitted to the brain through the spinal cord, permitting immediate local activity or reflexive responses as well as more reflective, cognitively mediated responses. The efferents that emanate from the CNS in turn lead to both neural and endocrine changes that inhibit activity in some systems and stimulate activity in others. Control of blood pressure, for example, is responsive to external and internal events and often involves both local, non-CNS-mediated regulation as well as CNS-derived messages that inhibit some cardiovascular activity and increase other activity. This complex orchestration of responses is but one example of the extraordinarily adaptive nature of the body.

Stress and regulatory systems

A good example of how these systems work together is stress, a complex, biobehavioral process that heightens adaptive capacity and motivates action that will eliminate or accommodate threats or demands. Stress involves nearly every organ system in the body, is clearly mediated by the CNS, and is an often-cited pathway by which environmental events may affect health. It is also a useful exemplar of many of the biobehavioral mechanisms discussed in this chapter. For our purposes, we focus on the nature of regulatory signals in stress. Popular theory suggests that stress is appraised and experienced as a function of detection and interpretation of environmental changes or conditions. External events, ranging from disasters, weather, noise, crowding, and job stress or loss, to interpersonal conflicts and social stressors, pose threats to people, require some form of adaptation, and motivate and support coping that will reduce arousal and perceived danger. These events or changes are detected and relayed to the CNS where they are interpreted and responses formulated. Such appraisals trigger neural- and endocrine-mediated SNS activation, which can be relatively long-lasting and generalized. Many of the health effects linked to stress are associated with SNS activity mediated primarily by the endocrine system, which interfaces with nervous system activity at various points.

The cascade of biological changes associated with stress is accomplished primarily through two major endocrine systems: the sympathetic–adrenomedullary (SAM) and the hypothalamic–pituitary–adrenocortical (HPA) axes. The SAM is activated when sympathetic innervation stimulates the adrenal medulla and causes the release of epinephrine. Some norepinephrine is also released from the adrenal medulla but most norepinephrine is released by sympathetic nerve endings concentrated in several areas of the body. These hormones, also known as catecholamines, enter the bloodstream and, as described, can have wide-ranging and relatively long-lasting effects, augmenting and supporting direct SNS effects on cardiovascular and respiratory function, digestion, metabolism, skeletal muscle tone, and other activities. The HPA axis is not a component of sympathetic activation, representing a separate system that has effects on metabolism, inflammation and immune system activity. The system is activated by release of corticotropin-releasing factor (CRF) from the hypothalamus, which stimulates release of adrenocorticotropin hormone (ACTH) from the pituitary gland, which in turn travels to the adrenal cortex and stimulates the release of corticosteroids such as cortisol from the adrenal cortex. Neurons in the hypothalamus monitor the rate of change of cortisol in the blood, and when this

monitoring indicates that circulating levels of cortisol are sufficiently high, exert inhibitory effects on further release of CRF from the hypothalamus. Receptors that mediate this negative feedback loop are also present in pituitary tissue, permitting control over ACTH release.

Secreted glucocorticoids facilitate the conversion of fats and carbohydrates to immediately usable forms of energy and other steroids help to govern mineral balance in several systems. Changes in glucocorticoids appear coordinated to mobilize or liberate stored energy in preparation for behavioral response to threat. They are also anti-inflammatory agents and appear to help regulate some immune system activities. It should be noted that the functioning of major neuroendocrine systems is more complex than described here. Although we have presented them as relatively autonomous, they overlap considerably, have some redundant functions, and regulate one another in a variety of ways. For example, CRH also influences activity associated with SNS such as epinephrine and norepinephrine release, and HPA products affect the synthesis and activity of other SNS components (Griffin & Ojeda, 1992).

Stress, regulatory systems, and disease

Stress-related changes in nervous and endocrine system activity are believed to be adaptive in the sense that they can facilitate survival during acute stress, particularly when alertness, strength, or speed is critical. However, this benefit does not come without a cost. When activation of these systems is chronic or excessive, damage can occur. Chronic or excessive activation of nervous or endocrine systems may occur as a result of dispositional hyperresponsivity or as a result of 'normal' response systems operating under conditions of unusually frequent or intense stress. Stress can also affect endocrine activity by disrupting negative feedback loops involved in HPA regulation, as when chronically high levels of cortisol affect these feedback mechanisms (e.g., Sapolsky, Krey & McEwen, 1984). Stress can also affect endocrine activity by altering gene expression.

For example, the release of catecholamines during SNS activity can lead to an increase in the expression of genes that encode enzymes involved in the production of more catecholamines (Sabban & Kvetnansk, 2001). Because stress effects occur in systems that are actively influencing other systems, they may reverberate and directly or indirectly cause dysfunction in other systems. The damage stemming from chronic or excessive activation can contribute to pathophysiology as well as to the progression or exacerbation of existing disease conditions.

One example is cardiovascular disease. High levels of sympathetic or HPA activity can influence the development of cardiovascular disease as well as trigger coronary events among patients with pre-existing coronary artery disease (e.g., Rozanski et al., 1988). Evidence suggests that direct effects of sympathetic activation may be involved in arterial wall damage, that stress may increase platelet aggregation and clotting and may even precipitate ischemia or myocardial infarction (Smith & Ruiz, 2002). The mechanisms underlying these influences are described below (see section 'Stress, cardiovascular function, and cardiovascular disease').

Diabetes is another useful example of the clinical importance of stress-related endocrine changes. Diabetes mellitus can be divided into two forms, type I (insulin dependent) and type II (insulin independent). Both disorders are characterized by a buildup of glucose levels in the blood as a consequence of the absence or dysfunction of a hormone called insulin. Short-term symptoms can include increased thirst and urination, fatigue, and blurred vision, while diabetes can eventually cause severe damage to the retina, kidneys, and other tissues, potentially leading to loss of sight, kidney failure, leg and foot ulcers or gangrene, or diabetic coma (Guyton, 1991).

Glucose is a primary fuel that cells use to function. Its production is a major task of the digestive system as glucose is extracted or derived from foods that have been eaten. Glucose is taken up into cells through the action of insulin. In type I diabetes, pancreatic cells fail to produce enough insulin for glucose to be properly taken up and used in cells throughout the body; in type II diabetes, bodily cells gradually become resistant to the effects of insulin, causing similar problems with glucose uptake. As discussed, HPA activity facilitates the conversion of stored energy into available energy, which results in increased release of glucose into the bloodstream. Glucocorticoids can also inhibit insulin production. These effects present obvious problems for diabetic individuals who are already compromised in their ability to take glucose from the bloodstream into cells. By increasing blood glucose levels, or reducing insulin levels, stress-related HPA activity can affect symptom expression or onset as well as disease course and management in both type I and type II diabetes (Surwit & Schneider, 1983; Surwit & Williams, 1996).

Elevated glucocorticoids can also exert inhibitory effects on various metabolic processes, including protein and triglyceride synthesis and glucose and calcium transport. These processes can lead to loss of bone and muscle mass (Griffin & Ojeda, 1992). Excessive HPA activity can also have deleterious CNS effects. High levels of cortisol or other corticosteroids can damage the hippocampus, a critical brain area for memory storage, and have been associated with some cognitive deficits (e.g., Davis et al., 1986; Ling, Perry & Tsuang, 1981; Starkman, Giordani, Berent, Schork & Schteingart, 2001). Finally, recent evidence has also shown a positive association between cortisol and disease progression in HIV disease (Leserman et al., 2002).

As noted, excessive or pathogenic endocrine responses can result from 'normal' systems operating under extreme conditions, or from 'normal' conditions operating on hyperresponsive systems. While the former has been the focus of considerable research into links between endocrine functioning and types of stressful experiences or other environmental risk factors, dispositional differences are the focus of efforts to identify genetic or biological risk factors. Genetic or biologically based differences in patterns of endocrine responses between people of different genders, ages or ethnicities have been suggested to account for some differences in disease risk observed in these groups (Schooler & Baum, 2000).

Implications for adaptation

Most descriptions of the functional utility of regulatory systems converge on a single theme: preparing and enabling the body to respond to challenges or threats in ways that will increase the likelihood of surviving this threat. From an evolutionary perspective, this speaks to the concept of adaptive value or reproductive fitness and may help explain why these survival-enhancing systems evolved. At the same time, an evolutionary perspective can provide insight into why biobehavioral processes contribute to disease vulnerabilities. In considering the evolutionary significance of biological and biobehavioral systems, it is a mistake to assume that the products of evolution by natural selection have been perfected over time for optimal health. Current biological or biobehavioral systems do not represent a pinnacle of evolutionary processes or a finished product. Natural selection does not result in perfectly designed solutions to adaptive challenges, but rather proceeds by selecting among randomly generated and often suboptimal alternatives that are bound by various forms of constraints. Furthermore, what is being selected for is not the maintenance of health *per se*, but rather reproductive success. Although health is obviously important for reproducing and leaving viable descendants, natural selection can and does at times favor biological or biobehavioral features or processes that have the potential to impair health. Examples include adaptive features or processes that have health-impairing costs or byproducts, those that provide immediate fitness benefits at the expense of health consequences that emerge after reproductive consequences have diminished or ceased, those that result from dysregulation or chronic activation of otherwise adaptive processes, or those that may have been adaptive in the past but compromise health when they operate in the context of a modern, evolutionarily novel environment.

These considerations can offer insight into why the physiological machinery underlying many biobehavioral processes is imperfectly designed with respect to human health, helping to explain the presence of biobehaviorally mediated disease vulnerabilities. They also suggest that the effects of these vulnerabilities may be modifiable and can be identified and isolated. To the extent that these vulnerabilities are species-wide, controlling disease risk will involve identification and management of behavioral or psychosocial correlates that may shift these vulnerabilities in one direction or another or cause clinical manifestations of these vulnerabilities to occur in the first place. For example, the flexible and modifiable nature of cognitive appraisal processes offers opportunities to lessen the health-impairing effects of some pathogenic biobehavioral processes, as illustrated by the use of cognitively based intervention strategies to successfully modify perceptions and effects of stress among at-risk individuals (e.g., Antoni et al., 2000).

Defense Systems

The immune system serves a primary defense role for the human body against foreign materials, or antigens, such as invading bacteria and viruses or more difficult to detect altered or irregular host cells such as malignancies. It is a complex system consisting of natural barriers such as skin and mucous membranes as well as an array of immune organs and cells. As described, lymphatic nodes and vessels also play a complementary role for the immune system. Immune cells are white blood cells or leukocytes, and include lymphocytes (T cells, B cells, and natural killer cells), monocytes (which become macrophages), and granulocytes (neutrophils, basophils, and eosinophils). These cells have effector actions and participate in the production of intercellular messengers called cytokines. Together, these barriers, cells, and cell products attack pathogens, keep them out, or alter the bodily environment to make it inhospitable.

Deficient immune function is thought to create susceptibility to disease, much as any weak defense structure is vulnerable to infiltration. These deficiencies can occur at any point in the process of bodily defense. A cut provides a path into the body through the skin, a primary immune system barrier. Weakness in local or initial systemic defenses can allow infections to develop, and weakened cellular activity can result in persistence and spread of that infection. Immune function clearly influences susceptibility to and control of infectious diseases. There is also evidence that it may be involved in the etiology or course of cardiovascular disease (by affecting relevant inflammatory processes) and cancer (by affecting host immunosurveillance). Growing evidence of behavioral and psychosocial influences on immune function has led to the emergence of psychoneuroimmunology and given it prominence in health psychology research.

The immune system consists of at least two kinds of agents, those associated with the innate immune system and those associated with acquired immunity. Natural killer (NK) cells, macrophages, monocytes and neutrophils, which comprise innate or non-specific immunity, need no prior exposure in order to target antigens. These cells represent a first line of defense against pathogens. Other immune cells, including T cells and B cells, require prior exposure to antigens before they can recognize them as targets. This represents what is known as specific or acquired immunity. After an initial exposure to an antigen, T cells are able to retain a specific memory of the antigen and mount a powerful defense against the same antigens in future encounters.

One important function of innate immunity is to mediate inflammation. Inflammation is a local response to tissue damage or the presence of microbial invasion or infection. An adaptive benefit of inflammation is that it can limit the extent of damage at the site of injury, either by promoting destruction and elimination of invading pathogens or by initiating tissue repair processes. In this way, these processes represent a first line of defense against various invasive agents. However, under some circumstances these same inflammatory mechanisms can contribute to rather than protect against disease.

Immune cells originate in bone marrow from pluripotent stem cells. Some of these cells migrate to the thymus where they develop into T cells, and are agents of cell-mediated immunity. These cells then circulate through the blood or lymph and reside in other immune organs such as the spleen or lymph nodes. B cells mature elsewhere and become agents of humoral immunity, which provides defense by producing antibodies. For the purposes of this chapter, it will suffice to say that cell-mediated and humoral immunity are sophisticated systems that require complex coordination and interaction between various types of cells. What will be emphasized here is the growing recognition of the relevance of behavior and emotion for the functioning of these defense systems.

Considerable research with both humans and animals demonstrates that the immune system shares bidirectional relationships with the central nervous system, through direct sympathetic innervation as well as endocrine system pathways (Ader, Felten & Cohen, 1991). Sympathetic connections communicate with a variety of immune organs including spleen, thymus, bone marrow and lymph nodes, representing direct physical links between the CNS and immune system. Indirect connections are suggested by evidence showing that immune cells, including T and B cells, contain receptors for several hormones and neuropeptides including corticosteroids, catecholamines, and opioid peptides (Plaut, 1987). At the same time, some immune system changes have corresponding effects on how people feel or how well they perform; increases in some cytokines, for example, are associated with feeling ill, increased inflammation, and general malaise (e.g., Watkins, Maier & Goehler, 1995). Nervous and endocrine system influences on some aspects of immune function have been confirmed by several areas of research (e.g., Irwin, Hauger, Jones, Provencio & Britton, 1990). Injections of epinephrine that in some ways mimic sympathetic arousal have been found to cause changes in the proportions of lymphocyte subsets in peripheral blood (Crary et al., 1983). This is consistent with evidence that high SNS reactors show the largest stress-related immune changes (Zakowski, McAllister, Deal & Baum, 1992) and with a number of studies suggesting that sympathetic stimulation causes increased migration of some immune cells from storage in lymphoid tissue into the bloodstream (e.g., Delahanty et al., 1996; Manuck, Rabin, Muldoon & Bachen, 1991). In addition, when medications are administered that block adrenergic receptors, stress-related immune effects are reduced or eliminated (e.g., Bachen et al., 1995). Biological bases for an interface between regulatory systems and the immune system have thus been demonstrated.

Stress and immune system activity

Assessing the effects of stress or other psychosocial influences on immune function and the measurement of immune competence in general are complicated by the complexity of the immune system and the related difficulty involved in selecting and interpreting samples. Quantitative and functional assessments of immune parameters can be performed in the laboratory, and several *in vivo* parameters can also be assessed. But it can be difficult to generalize or draw conclusions about the clinical or even biological significance of observed changes or fluctuations in these measures. Moreover, there are significant differences in the magnitude of immune changes following stress from one individual to the next, although there is some evidence that these responses are stable across time and stressor type for any given individual (Marsland, Henderson, Chambers & Baum, 2002; Marsland, Manuck, Fazzari, Stewart & Rabin, 1995). Nevertheless, research has begun to identify the types of psychosocial conditions that can elicit nervous- and endocrine-mediated immune changes, as well as those that may be associated with clinically relevant outcomes such as disease risk (Kiecolt-Glaser & Glaser, 1995).

Loneliness, poor social support, negative mood, disruption of marital relationships, bereavement, natural disasters and other forms of stress have been associated with changes in various aspects of immune function (reviewed in Cohen & Herbert, 1996). For the most part, these naturalistic stressors have been associated with suppression of both functional and quantitative parameters, particularly when the stressor is severe and sustained (e.g.,

McKinnon, Weisse, Reynolds, Bowles & Baum, 1989). On the other hand, acute laboratory stressors often precipitate immediate and short-lived increases in the numbers of circulating T cells and NK cells (e.g., Wang, Delahanty, Dougall & Baum, 1998) as well as transient increases in NK cell activity (Naliboff et al., 1991). Stress-related changes in some immune parameters may occur in a biphasic fashion, exhibiting temporary increases during or immediately following stress, followed by a more sustained post-stressor drop below baseline levels (Cohen, Delahanty, Schmitz, Jenkins & Baum, 1993). At least two studies have prospectively documented this pattern within a single sample, finding increased NK cell activity during acute stress and subsequent below-baseline reductions within 1 hour after stressor termination (Breznitz et al., 1998; Schedlowski et al., 1993). Stress-related suppression of NK cell activity may be especially relevant because natural killer cells can spontaneously destroy cancer cells (e.g., Herberman & Orlando, 1981) and may play an important role in defense against the progression of some cancers (Tajima, Kawatani, Endo & Kawasaki, 1996; Whiteside & Herberman, 1995).

Stress, immune activity, and disease

The relationship between stress and disease risk has been more difficult to establish than have simple stress effects on immune function. Not all biological manifestations of stress will necessarily translate into clinically observable effects. Nevertheless, there is considerable support for the likelihood that stress increases risk of upper respiratory infections such as colds (e.g., Cohen et al., 1998; Cohen, Tyrell & Smith, 1991) and some research supporting the possibility that stress or other psychosocial factors increase the risk or progression of cancer or other illnesses (Cole, Kemeny, Taylor & Visscher, 1996; Ramirez et al., 1989). Studies that have intervened to reduce stress among cancer patients have found a variety of benefits associated with stress reduction, including some evidence of slowed disease course (Baum & Andersen, 2001; Fawzy et al., 1993; Spiegel, Bloom, Kraemer &

Gottheil, 1989). Although the immune system is considered a likely mediator of these observed relationships, verification of immune mediation of stress-related health effects has been elusive (e.g., Cohen et al., 1998), and clinical relevance of stress-related immune changes has not been empirically established for any diseases. Researchers are still attempting to confirm the possibility that stress-related immune changes affect the incidence or progression of colds and influenzas (e.g., Cohen et al., 1991), HIV disease (e.g., Leserman et al., 1997), and cancer (e.g., Andersen, Kiecolt-Glaser & Glaser, 1994). In addition, asthma, arthritis, irritable bowel syndrome, and psoriasis may be influenced through similar psychoimmune mechanisms. Stress-related changes in immune function remain an unconfirmed but plausible biobehavioral pathway through which psychosocial factors influence disease etiology or progression.

Given the plausibility of this pathway, substantial research has been directed towards evaluating the extent to which the psychosocial milieu or psychological interventions can favorably modulate immune function. Although it may not be possible or even desirable to enhance immune function beyond normal or baseline levels, preventing or buffering stress-related immune decrements is considered beneficial. Research suggests that some psychosocial influences are influential in this regard. High levels of reported social support have been positively associated with functional immune parameters in a number of populations at risk for stress-related immune suppression, including cancer patients (Levy et al., 1990), spouses of cancer patients (Baron, Cutrona, Hicklin, Russell & Lubaroff, 1990), and individuals reporting high levels of general stress (Schlesinger & Yodfat, 1991). These effects have been attributed to the ability of a strong social support network to minimize or buffer stress-related decreases in immune function, perhaps by modulating stress effects on biological activities like endocrine function or effects on behaviors such as sleep or diet.

Such findings have stimulated a number of attempts to deliver beneficial psychosocial interventions to populations who are at risk for immune suppression in order to evaluate whether similar immune benefits might be generated. There have been some promising results. For example, among a sample of newly diagnosed malignant melanoma patients, a structured psychiatric intervention was associated with increased interferon-augmented NK cell activity at 6-month follow-up (Fawzy et al., 1990). Increased NK cell activity was also observed in geriatric subjects who underwent a psychosocial intervention (Kiecolt-Glaser, Glaser et al., 1985). In addition, a stress-management intervention attenuated the reduction in immunocompetence associated with notifying people of their HIV seropositive status (Antoni et al., 1991). These studies provide evidence that psychosocial interventions have the potential to buffer the immunosuppressive effects of stress. However a recent meta-analysis of the effects of psychological interventions on immune function indicated that these effects are modest, with intervention strategies emphasizing hypnosis and conditioning showing the strongest immune effects (Miller & Cohen, 2001). Although evidence for the effects of stress on immune function is well established, evidence for the clinical relevance of these effects and for the ability to modulate these effects is considerably less compelling.

Subcellular defense systems

The immune system may represent a primary mode of biological defense, but there are subcellular levels of defense that are also relevant. Cells periodically sustain damage from external agents or random events. This damage is ordinarily repaired and DNA restored to its prior state. These molecular defense systems act upstream of immune surveillance and serve to protect DNA by preventing and repairing damage that could lead to deleterious changes in cell structure or function. Changes in cellular structure or function are particularly relevant for the development of cancer, although they may also contribute to other forms of illness or disability. DNA damage can result from a variety of external insults as well as from biochemical interactions with endogenous chemicals, and may contribute to tumor initiation and progression (Jackson & Loeb, 2001). Autonomous DNA repair systems operate through a variety of pathways to maintain genomic stability by fixing this damage before it gives rise to somatic mutations (Wood, Mitchell, Sgouros & Lindahl, 2001). Failure to repair DNA damage potentially allows the propagation of mutations in future generations of cells leading eventually to clinical disease. Immune-mediated processes and apoptosis become the major defense against continued replication of altered cells once these mutations have occurred. Apoptosis is the process of programmed cell death, signaled by the nuclei in normally functioning cells. It is a process that requires metabolic activity and results in disintegration of cells into membrane-bound particles that are later eliminated by the body. In some ways apoptosis reflects a 'failsafe' system that is needed when basic defenses against propagation of mutations fall short and potentially dangerous mutations are poised to replicate and in some cases become malignant. Ironically, however, one of the characteristic features of cancer cells is their ability to avoid apoptosis; cancer cells appear to be resistant to these processes.

Research suggests that DNA repair systems and/or the extent of DNA damage may be moderated by stress. Various forms of stress have been associated with altered repair of damaged DNA in both human and animal studies (Cohen, Marshall, Cheng, Agarwal & Wei, 2000; Forlenza, Latimer & Baum, 2000; Glaser, Thorn, Tarr, Kiecolt-Glaser & D'Ambrosio, 1985; Kiecolt-Glaser, Stephens, Lipetz, Speicher & Glaser, 1985). These studies suggest additional pathways through which stress or other psychosocial factors may influence carcinogenesis beyond immune surveillance (Forlenza & Baum, 2000). In addition to processes like stress and mood states, overt behaviors such as tobacco use, alcohol use and sun exposure are also known to affect this defense system (Nakajima, Takeuchi, Takeshita & Morimoto, 1996; van Zeeland, de Groot, Hall & Donato, 1999). Exposure to ultraviolet radiation in sunlight inflicts genetic damage and is considered to be responsible for the majority of skin cancers (International Agency for Research on Cancer, 1992). Alcohol consumption has been found to inhibit endogenous DNA repair processes (Brooks, 1997). Tobacco smoke is also known to contain a variety of substances that initiate genetic damage, and may indirectly promote carcinogenesis through affecting activation and detoxification of xenobiotic compounds and the generation of oxidative damage from free radicals in cigarette smoke (Pryor, 1993).

Transport Systems

Several systems can be considered in this category because they are wholly or partly involved in movement of nutrients, waste products, chemical messengers, and other elements of normal bodily function. The cardiovascular system consists of the heart, arteries, capillaries, and veins. It falls under the rubric of a transport system because it carries a variety of substances to places in the body that need them and transports waste products to places where they can be removed. The heart functions as a central pumping and collection unit, moving blood through blood vessels. This system transports nutrients absorbed through digestion, oxygen absorbed through respiration, and regulatory hormones and peptides released during endocrine activity. These substances are often destined for distant organs and tissues, and the pervasiveness and reach of this system is critical for timely and targeted delivery. The system reaches every region of the body and has some regulatory function, typically due to innervation or hormone receptors of the nervous and endocrine system.

There are four chambers in the heart: the right atrium, left atrium, right ventricle, and left ventricle. Once blood is oxygenated in lung tissue, it travels into the left atrium and left ventricle. The heart pumps blood from the left ventricle into the arteries, where it is dispersed throughout the body, where oxygen and nutrients are delivered and waste products are taken up. Venules and veins then return the oxygen-depleted blood to the right atrium and right ventricle, where it is pumped into the pulmonary region, and carbon dioxide in the blood is taken up prior to being exhaled. Heart valves ensure the continuous forward movement of this system.

Breakdown or dysfunction of the cardiovascular system can threaten the viability of cells, organs, and ultimately the organism. Some of the conditions that cause dysfunction have increased over the past 100 years, and cardiovascular disease has been the most common cause of death among people living in industrialized countries during the past century. This suggests that stress, diet, exercise, and a few other biobehavioral variables are major sources of risk for heart disease. There are several syndromes and kinds of cardiovascular disease that differ in dynamics and locus. Coronary heart disease (CHD), which involves arteries that provide nutrients to the heart muscle itself, and the narrowing of arteries in the brain or other areas of circulatory activity both involve the accumulation of plaque on the inner lining of arteries, a process known as atherosclerosis. Atherosclerosis typically develops insidiously over the course of many years, as blood flow to the heart is increasingly restricted. When coronary arteries are sufficiently restricted they are not able to deliver oxygen to the heart, causing ischemia, and this previously asymptomatic condition can result in clinical manifestations of CHD including chest pain, heart attack and sudden cardiac death. Other diseases and disorders involve blood clotting, hemorrhage, or other dynamics that can cause stroke, irregular heart rate, and other syndromes.

Stress, cardiovascular function, and cardiovascular disease

The pathogenesis of CHD is complex, involving various biochemical, inflammatory, and hemodynamic processes (Black & Garbutt, 2002; Ross, 1999). Likewise, biobehavioral mechanisms in the etiology or course of CHD may intersect with CHD pathophysiology at multiple levels. As noted, nervous and endocrine systems interface with the heart, causing changes that are ostensibly adaptive in the short term when faced with acute stress. However, increases in the frequency of exposure to glucocorticoids or catecholamines or other stress-related changes can precipitate a number of hemodynamic and immune/inflammatory changes that can be pathogenic over the long run.

Stress-related hemodynamic changes may contribute to CHD processes by influencing heart rate, cardiac output, blood pressure, and clotting processes including coronary vasoconstriction and platelet aggregation (Smith & Ruiz, 2002). Increases in heart rate and blood pressure increase the force and pressure within vessels and arteries, which can contribute to shear stress that may damage the endothelium (Traub & Berk, 1998). Once the interior lining of the blood vessel has been damaged, the resulting lesions may constitute vulnerabilities for subsequent buildup of atherosclerotic plaque at these sites. In addition to causing hemodynamic changes that can damage arteries and coronary vessels, stress-related endocrine effects may be pathogenic by promoting the formation of blood clots or altering neural transmissions to the heart (e.g., Kamarck & Jennings, 1991). Stress-related SNS or HPA activity may also contribute by mediating immune and inflammatory processes, and growing evidence suggests that these processes are centrally involved in CHD. For example, products of HPA and SNS activity such as corticosteroids and cytokines can mediate inflammatory processes at sites of endothelial damage, promoting the adhesion of immune cells to the arterial wall (Black & Garbutt, 2002). This, then, contributes to narrowing of the interior of the vessel.

Behavioral and psychosocial variables have been clearly linked to CHD risk and progression in a variety of epidemiological and animal studies (Smith & Ruiz, 2002). Men who are especially impatient, hostile, and antagonistic or have recently endured stressful life events appear to have an increased risk for CHD (e.g., Helmer, Ragland & Syme, 1991; Mittleman et al., 1995). These individuals have been shown to have higher circulating levels of epinephrine and less favorable cholesterol profiles, and respond to stress with greater SNS and HPA activity (e.g., Williams, Suarez, Kuhn, Zimmerman & Schanberg, 1991). Experimental studies with non-human primates suggest that disruption of the social environment, heightened cardiovascular reactivity, and behavioral dominance increase CHD risk (Manuck, Marsland, Kaplan & Williams, 1995). The use of medications that block endocrine signals confirms that neuroendocrine pathways play a mediating role between psychosocial conditions and CHD processes (Manuck et al., 1995).

Identification of behavioral and emotional correlates of cardiovascular disease outcomes or processes, such as anger and hostility, has led to efforts to manage or reduce these processes and associated disease risk. The fact that behavioral risk is largely modifiable is encouraging because it permits a possible pathway to reduce overall risk for disease and disability. A variety of behavioral and cognitive strategies have been used among cardiac patients or those at risk, including relaxation training, cognitive behavioral stress management, meditation, group emotional support, and cognitive therapy (reviewed in Linden, Stossel & Maurice, 1996; Schneiderman, Antoni, Saab & Ironson, 2001). Despite some reports that such approaches can indeed reduce psychological and biological risk factors as well as the incidence of recurrent myocardial infarctions (e.g., Friedman et al., 1986; Linden et al., 1996), negative or inconsistent findings have also been reported (Rozanski, Blumenthal & Kaplan, 1999). While stress and some of its physiological consequences have clearly been linked to the etiology of CHD, the ability to successfully reduce CHD-associated morbidity or mortality by modifying these processes, while promising, is less certain.

Other transport systems

A second transport system is the lymphatic system, a network of nodes connected by low-pressure vessels that carry a fluid called lymph to and from bodily tissues and back into circulation again. As an alternative circulatory system, it conveys immune cells, growth factors, and the like, and removes spent immune cells and debris from invading pathogens. Lymph contains lymphocytes (immune cells) along with protein and fats. Approximately 3 liters of lymph seep from blood vessels into body tissues every day before being carried by lymphatic vessels, passing through lymph nodes, and being delivered back into the bloodstream.

The lymphatic system comprises lymphoid organs, which include the spleen, tonsils, Peyer's patches, thymus, and lymph nodes. Lymph nodes contain a mesh of tissue in which lymphocytes and macrophages are housed. These nodes are a staging area for immune cells, are involved in the production of antibodies, and serve to filter, attack, and destroy antigens such as cancer cells, bacteria, and viruses. Lymph nodes are spread throughout the body, clustering where lymphatic vessels branch off such as in the armpits, neck, and groin. Although this is a transport system, it plays a crucial supporting role in bodily defense, representing another example of the overlapping and complementary nature of many of these systems. The development of new lymphatic vessels is also centrally involved in tissue repair and inflammatory reactions throughout the body, as healing of damaged bodily tissue requires the successful regrowth and reconnections of lymphatic vasculature (Oliver & Detmar, 2002).

As noted, acute stress can cause rapid changes in concentrations of immune cells in circulation, reflecting stimulation of nodes and lymphoid organs to release immune cells. There is also some animal research showing increases in flow of lymph fluid and immune cell output from lymphatic nodes following administration of acute pain or adrenaline injections, suggesting that lymphocytes in regional tissues can be mobilized in response to acute stress (Shannon, Quin & Jones, 1976). Additional research is needed to better understand the clinical implications of stress-related alterations in lymphatic system activity and how this interfaces with the well-documented stress-related changes in various immune parameters.

Resource Systems

The digestive or gastrointestinal (GI) system transforms consumed food into usable resources. It includes the mouth, salivary glands, esophagus, stomach, and intestines. Digestion takes place in stages, beginning in the mouth where food is broken down through chewing and the action of salivary enzymes. After food is swallowed, it is pushed to the stomach by contractions called peristalsis, where gastric acids and enzymes further break down the food. Breakdown is completed as food then passes through the small and large intestines, where secretions from the pancreas, liver, and gallbladder aid in the process of absorption through the lining of the intestines and into the bloodstream.

The respiratory system is a second resource system. It works closely with the cardiovascular system to remove carbon dioxide from the blood and replenish it with oxygen. These processes occur in the lungs, the primary organ in the respiratory system. The lungs are large organs that contain about 1000 square feet (100 m^2) of surface area. A normal breath brings in approximately 0.5 liter of gas, while maximum adult capacity is between 5 and 6 liters. The nose, mouth, pharynx, trachea, diaphragm and abdominal muscles also play supporting roles in respiration.

Air is inhaled through the nose or mouth with the help of the pharynx, a muscular organ at the back of the throat, and the diaphragm, a muscle at the bottom of the rib cage. The activity of the diaphragm causes the rib cage to raise, increasing lung volume and causing a low-pressure area. This pressure brings air into the lungs through the trachea or windpipe, which branches into bronchial tubes and then smaller bronchioles, terminating in small air sacs called alveoli that have permeable membranes allowing the exchange of oxygen and carbon dioxide. The exchange of these gases is carried out through diffusion. The diffusion gradient is maintained by inhalation, which renews air in the alveoli with an oxygen concentration near levels of atmospheric air, and alveolar capillaries, which supply blood from circulation with a low oxygen concentration and high carbon dioxide concentration.

The respiratory system is controlled by both voluntary and involuntary mechanisms, overlapping to some extent with regulatory systems that function to promote optimal levels of blood gases. Part of the brain known as the medulla monitors carbon dioxide levels in the blood in order to maintain respiration at this optimal rate, and can independently initiate respiration if necessary.

The leading respiratory disease is chronic obstructive pulmonary disease (COPD). COPD is a progressive, largely irreversible disorder marked by airflow limitation associated with inflammatory responses in the lungs to noxious substances (National Institutes of Health, 2001). These disorders include or involve emphysema, small airway inflammation and fibrosis, chronic bronchitis, and mucus gland hyperplasia. Cigarette smoking is the primary risk factor for COPD, lung cancer and other respiratory disorders (National Institutes of Health, 2001). Despite clear evidence that there is a causal relationship between this preventable behavior and illness and death, efforts to get people to quit smoking have largely been discouraging. The best current approaches to cessation among healthy individuals, which combine pharmacological and behavioral strategies, result in modest 1-year cigarette abstinence rates of 20–25 per cent (Centers for Disease Control, 2000). The effectiveness of these interventions is likely hampered by the strong reinforcing and addictive properties of nicotine (e.g., Gamberino & Gold, 1999), and by psychosocial and behavioral factors that play a role in maintaining smoking behavior (e.g., Hiatt & Rimer, 1999). For most individuals who smoke, the possibility of remote health benefits may not be sufficient to outweigh the immediate reward and alleviation of withdrawal symptoms associated with continued use of tobacco products.

Stress, resources system activity, and disease

In addition to smoking, stress and other psychosocial or behavioral influences such as negative emotional states can affect the activity of these resource systems, often at multiple levels or stages. For example, these influences can alter choice of food intake, disrupt digestion by inhibiting saliva production, slow the flow of food into the stomach, alter the concentration of digestive acids or enzymes, alter blood flow to the stomach, slow nutrient absorption through the intestinal lining, and alter contractile or other digestive activities in the intestines (Astertita, 1985). These changes can contribute to disease or disease processes throughout the digestive tract, including an increased risk of developing ulcers, ulcerative colitis, and other GI problems (Sapolsky, 1998).

MODELS OF BIOBEHAVIORAL INFLUENCE

As described, ambient or stable environmental conditions and chronic conditions such as stress affect a number of aspects of normal human functioning. Temperature, weather, social conditions such as support or interpersonal conflict, socioeconomic status, ethnicity and minority status, gender, age, and conditions characterizing work or home can affect mood, behavior, and biological processes. Different models order these elements differently, so one theory might argue that these conditions produce negative emotional states or cognitive appraisals that then affect biological and behavioral responses, while others would suggest that negative affective states occur in part because of experienced arousal of biological systems and serve a motivational function. Behavior change is ordinarily due to efforts to adapt to these conditions, either through direct action and manipulation, flight, or accommodation to them, but may also occur as a 'byproduct' of other dynamics.

General Biobehavioral Model

Biological changes in a stress model would be more central to the process and would trace back to detection and appraisal processes in the CNS. This central processing would be a source of the negative affective states and peripheral biological activation that often appear to emerge simultaneously. Placed in this context, biological changes would also be modified by personal attributes of people acting in a particular setting, either by modulation of biological systems themselves (as in, for example, genetic modulation of defense or transport system strengths or weaknesses) or by altering the ways in which environmental or social conditions are appraised or experienced (see Figure 3.1).

There are several important implications of viewing biobehavioral influences in this way. First, the importance of considering personal attributes in these equations cannot be overstated. Basic genetic predispositions are key elements of tendencies to experience particular moods, to behave in specific ways, and to have predispositions for vulnerability or 'immunity' to certain illnesses. Ethnic genetic variability is known; some diseases, such as sickle cell anemia among African Americans or Tay Sachs disease in European Jews, are far more prominent in susceptible groups. Age affects both biological responses (e.g., response systems may become inelastic, or total response may be diminished as in immunosenescence); gender also influences these systems. Clearly, behavioral and affective differences are important as well, and, together with well-known differences in disease vulnerabilities, biological reactivity, and response to treatment, contribute to disparities in the burden of chronic diseases. African Americans generally experience more cancer morbidity and mortality as well as greater risk of hypertension than do white people in the US (Jemal, Thomas, Murray & Thun, 2002). Men have greater risks for most diseases and exhibit larger regulatory and transport system changes when provoked than do women (e.g., Canto et al., 2000). Age increases the likelihood of mutations in cells that can produce malignancies, and is associated with declines in immune defenses that may heighten vulnerability to infectious illness. These kinds of deficits are correlated with systemic wear and tear that can eventually produce dysfunction.

Another source of personal influence includes habitual behavior patterns or personality variables, including hostility, optimism, and emotional expressiveness. To some extent these styles probably reflect genetic variability

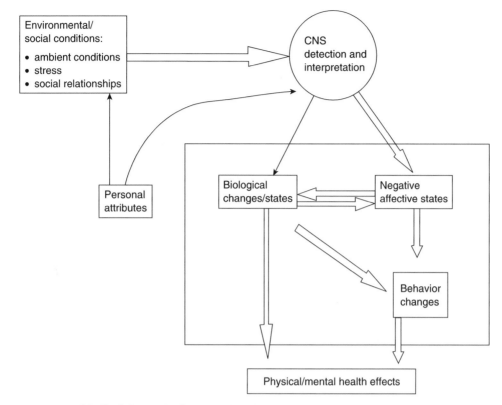

Figure 3.1 *Model of biobehavioral influences on health*

but to some degree they appear to be learned as well. Hostility can be conceptualized as a set of cynical attitudes that increase proneness to anger (Smith, 1992), and is commonly assessed with the Cook–Medley Hostility Inventory (Cook & Medley, 1954). Hostility has been clearly linked to differences in cardiovascular reactivity and to risk for cardiovascular disease (Smith & Ruiz, 2002). Early studies demonstrated that these effects are independent of hypertension or other cardiovascular risk factors (e.g., Barefoot, Dahlstrohm & Williams, 1983; Barefoot, Dodge, Peterson, Dahlstrom & Williams, 1989).

Optimism is another dispositional variable that has received considerable research attention in studies of coping and illness. Most of this research has used the Life Orientation Test (LOT: Scheier & Carver, 1985) to measure optimism. The LOT is an instrument that assesses the extent to which people expect or believe that things will work out for the best.

These studies generally show that optimism is associated with better physical and psychological wellbeing (Scheier & Carver, 1992). The mechanisms through which optimism influences health have not been established. There is some evidence that differences in stress responses or cognitive styles may be involved (Carver et al., 1993; MacLeod, Williams & Bekerian, 1991). Optimistic individuals demonstrate a bias towards control and efficacy, variables that appear to sustain favorable expectations in the face of ambiguity, as well as use action-oriented problem solving strategies.

Some evidence also suggests a link between styles of emotional expression and disease risk. For example, women with a repressive coping style who fail to express strong negative emotions such as anger appear to be at moderately increased risk for cancer (Greer & Morris, 1975; McKenna, Zevon, Corn & Rounds, 1999). Other forms of behavioral or emotional inhibition have also been associated with unfavorable health outcomes (e.g., Cole et al., 1996). Haynes and colleagues found relationships between suppressed hostility and coronary heart disease in analyses of Framingham Study data (Haynes, Feinleib & Kannel, 1980). Conversely, interventions aimed at eliciting written expression of emotionally upsetting events have shown some health benefits (Smyth, 1998). Additional research is necessary to establish the extent to which disposition or personality influences disease and the biological mechanisms that mediate these possible effects.

Joint determination of behaviors that are beneficial or harmful for health is also important in this context. Behavioral responses to environmental change, for example, are motivated by the negative affective states that are associated with threatening, harmful, or dangerous events. These affective states are a joint function of negative cognitions and physical discomfort associated with arousal or activation of key regulatory systems. Because the organism 'feels bad', it is motivated to cope, either by attacking the problem or by fleeing from it. At the same time these responses are shaped and supported by biological sequelae of threatening or harmful appraisal. Coping, whether adaptive or maladaptive (or simply ineffective), can contribute to pathophysiology as byproducts of coping or as poor fit between coping repertoires and stressors; to the extent that coping is unsuccessful, that the readying responses associated with stress are not helpful or are harmful to adaptation to a given set of conditions, or that systems are hyperengaged for long periods of time, specific damage and non-specific wear and tear that can precipitate or contribute to illness are likely.

These models also generate a number of testable hypotheses and offer multiple pathways for intervention and moderation of risk. However, there are other useful models and/or perspectives in the general health and behavior field that provide key insights into mind–body interactions and health and that feature specific influential biobehavioral interactions as central pathways.

Diet and Disease

Diet is a behavior that intersects with a number of biological systems, with important implications for health and disease. The amount and type of resources taken into the body can obviously affect the ability of resource and transport systems to process and deliver critical substances or optimal levels of these substances to places in the body that need them. Food intake plays a particularly strong role in cardiovascular and cerebrovascular disease (e.g., Huijbregts et al., 1997), diabetes (e.g., Feskens, 1992) and certain cancers (e.g., Willett, 1996). The importance of diet in disease and mortality is suggested by the estimate that diet accounts for 35 per cent of all cancer deaths (Doll, 1992). Although the pathways through which diet affects disease risk are still being uncovered, general dietary effects on disease risk can be categorized as: (1) overconsumption of foods that can be health impairing when consumed beyond certain levels; (2) underconsumption of potentially health promoting or protective foods; and (3) the balance between amount of calories consumed and expended.

Consumption of specific foods is one key dietary behavior. Saturated fat and trans-fatty acids clearly increase cardiovascular and cerebrovascular disease risk (e.g., Hu et al., 1999). A high ratio of omega 6 to omega 3 fatty acids may also contribute to these diseases (Simopoulos, 1999). Specific types of dietary fat may also influence risk of non-insulin-dependent diabetes (Feskens, 1992) and certain cancers (Guthrie & Carroll, 1999), although these relationships are less clear. Similarly, sodium intake is known to increase the risk of hypertension, which is a risk factor for cardiovascular disease, stroke, and renovascular disease (He & Whelton, 1999). Members of remote rural populations, such as the Xingu Indians of Brazil, who do not add salt to food, have lower blood pressure, reduced lifetime incidence of hypertension, and increased stability of blood pressure over the lifespan compared to controls (Carvalho et al., 1989). Sodium intake may also be associated with risk for some cancers (Joossens et al., 1996).

Diets high in plant foods appear to reduce the risk of a number of diseases, including cancer (Kelloff et al., 1996; Potter & Steinmetz, 1996) and cardiovascular disease (Ness & Powles, 1997). However, many individuals do not consume these foods at optimal levels for protective benefits, and suffer disease risk as a result (e.g., American Institute for Cancer Research, 1997). In some Western societies, plant foods are consumed at less than one-third the level estimated among recent human ancestors (Peters & O'Brien, 1981).

Overweight and obesity promote a variety of chronic diseases and disease processes (reviewed in Must et al., 1999; Pi-Sunyer, 1998), contributing to approximately 300,000 deaths in the United States annually (Allison, Fontaine, Manson, Stevens & Van Itallie, 1999). Diet can contribute to overweight and obesity by leading to excess energy intake relative to expenditure, or a positive energy balance. A positive energy balance may promote cardiovascular and cerebrovascular disease by contributing to high levels of circulating free-fatty acids, excess fat stores, which increase hyperlipidemia and hyperglycemia and promote oxidation and glycoselation processes, and elevated LDL cholesterol. A positive energy balance appears to promote the development of type II diabetes through contributing to insulin resistance. Muscle is more efficient at taking up glucose in response to insulin than is adipose tissue (DeFronzo, 1997). In genetically susceptible individuals, high levels of adiposity and low levels of lean muscle mass therefore contribute to the failure of insulin secretion to restore glucose homeostasis, leading to insulin resistance, glucose intolerance, and clinical type II diabetes (Eaton, Eaton & Cordain, 2002). Although more research is needed to clarify the relationship between energy balance and cancer risk, a positive energy balance may promote breast carcinogenesis due to the effects of adipose tissue on epithelial cell growth (Guthrie & Carroll, 1999), or on the production of estrogen among postmenopausal women (Mezzetti et al., 1998). A positive energy balance has also been associated with an increased risk of colon, endometrial, gall bladder, pancreatic, and other forms of cancer (Ford, 1999; Pi-Sunyer, 1998; Wolk et al., 2001).

Exercise or physical activity appears to reduce disease risk by helping to restore a balance between energy intake and expenditure. Additional ways in which exercise may be beneficial may include immediate reduction of stress (Scully, Kremer, Meade, Graham & Dudgeon, 1998), reduction of subsequent physiological reactivity to stress (Hinde, Moraska, Gaykema & Fleshner, 1999), reduction of LDL cholesterol or increases in HDL cholesterol (Williams, 1998), reduction of blood pressure (Williams, 1998), increases in endogenous free radical scavengers (Ji, 1999), alteration of hormonal levels (Thune, Brenn, Lund & Gaard, 1997) or alteration of aspects of innate immune system functioning (Woods, Davis, Smith & Nieman, 1999). The clinical relevance of these effects is suggested by studies that link physical activity to reduced risk of cardiovascular disease (Bijnen et al., 1998) and diabetes (Baan, Stolk, Grobbee, Witteman & Feskens, 1999) after controlling for body mass. Exercise may have independent protective effects for certain cancers as well (Longnecker, Gerhardsson le Verdier, Frumkin & Carpenter, 1995; Thune et al., 1997).

A cluster of conditions referred to as 'metabolic syndrome X' (Hansen, 1999) may represent another biological mechanism through which behavior or lifestyle contributes to disease risk. As typically characterized, this syndrome includes glucose intolerance (including type II diabetes), hyperinsulinemia/insulin resistance, abdominal or visceral obesity, dyslipidemia, and hypertension (Hansen, 1999). There is still some debate about whether this syndrome actually represents one distinct risk factor or process, what its core pathogenic elements are, and the relative contribution of genetic and environmental influences on its development (e.g., Matsuzawa, Funahashi & Nakamura, 1999; Zimmet, Boyko, Collier & de Courten, 1999). Nevertheless, there is evidence that this syndrome or its representative conditions play an etiological role in cardiovascular disease and contribute to neuropathy and liver and kidney damage or dysfunction (Hansen, 1999; Lempiäinen, Mykkänen, Pyörälä, Laakso & Kuusisto, 1999). As reviewed, exercise, diet, and other behaviors can influence important components of this syndrome such as blood lipid profiles and obesity, suggesting that the disease mechanisms involved in metabolic syndrome X may transmit some behavioral influences on disease risk.

Evolutionary and Genetic Considerations

Biological systems typically operate in the service of homeostasis and survival, but they can also represent pathways to disease and disability, and biobehavioral influences can contribute substantially to these outcomes. The mechanisms by which biobehavioral processes exert these effects, as well as the reasons why some individuals are more at risk than others, are being uncovered by research in fields like health psychology, developmental biology, and molecular and behavioral genetics. The reason why human biological systems appear universally vulnerable to pathogenic biobehavioral processes is a different sort of question, and one that is likely to require a better understanding of the development and interaction of these systems over evolutionary time. Of particular interest is the process by which regulatory systems became interconnected with other biological systems, since these networks seem to constitute disease vulnerabilities as well as adaptive capabilities. While the overlapping of different biological systems is beneficial in that it allows for networks with extensive and sophisticated communication and regulation capacities, this engineering scheme seems less optimal when disease processes are initiated as a consequence of system design or inelasticity.

The fact that many of these overlapping systems are layered on top of one another belies a fundamental reality of natural selection that may help explain the presence of these vulnerabilities: meaningful increases in phylogenetic complexity proceed by building on top of or adding to existing structures. That is, species cannot scrap their existing design and start

again when environmental change calls for new modes of responding or when individual members begin to wish for improved health and longevity or other outcomes that natural selection has not optimized. Existing design can impose significant constraints on the subsequent structure and adaptability of organisms and the systems that comprise them. It remains to be determined whether biobehaviorally mediated disease vulnerabilities ultimately reflect design constraints imposed during the course of our evolutionary heritage, costs or byproducts of adaptive processes, effects of evolutionarily novel inputs, or other manifestations of the imprecision of evolutionary processes. It can be argued that stress responses and some behavioral motivational systems can simply operate at cross-purposes with health and longevity, reflecting natural selection pressures that do not place premiums on these outcomes. Many physiological consequences of stress appear adaptive in response to acute threats, but carry costs that are especially evident when this activation is prolonged or severe. Inflammation and related immune processes are adaptive and health protective in many instances of acute injury or microbial threat, but can promote cardiovascular disease when operating in response to coronary vessel lesions or in conjunction with evolutionarily novel blood triglyceride or cholesterol levels. Appetites for sugary, salty, and fatty foods may promote sustenance in environments of scarcity, but can contribute to disease in evolutionarily novel environments that provide an abundance of these foods. These accounts comprise considerations of species-typical vulnerabilities or ultimate (evolutionary) causes that complement and inform descriptions of proximate relationships. Proximate explanations, which center on mechanism and development, and evolutionary explanations, which center on function and phylogeny, are complementary but independently necessary components of thorough explanatory models (Nesse, 1999).

The selective pressures faced by our human ancestors are reflected in the modern genome, which transmits evolutionarily shaped vulnerabilities. In this sense, current human genes place fundamental constraints on the health and longevity of all people, including those imposed by apoptosis and other normal cellular processes involved in ageing or senescence (Wick, Jansen-Durr, Berger, Blasko & Grubeck-Loebenstein, 2000). Many forms of disability and disease that manifest late in life are related to these cellular processes and are considered consequences of normal but suboptimal somatic mutation or repair capabilities.

Another way that genes are relevant for health and disease is by contributing to genetic differences between individuals. These individual differences can shift disease vulnerabilities in one direction or another, and clearly contribute to disease risk for a range of diseases including diabetes, myocardial infarction, Alzheimer's disease, Parkinson's disease, and asthma (Ruse & Parker, 2001). These influences are the subject matter of molecular genetics and epidemiology, which can identify genetic variants through biochemical and cellular studies, linkage and positional cloning, candidate gene studies, or genome-wide studies (Day, Gu, Ganderton, Spanakis & Ye, 2001). Genetic differences between individuals also define the parameters within which biobehavioral systems function (Nesse & Berridge, 1997). For example, genetic differences appear to contribute to individual differences in cardiovascular responses to stress (Hewitt & Turner, 1995), diet and activity patterns (Faith, Johnson & Allison, 1997; Reed, Bachmanov, Beauchamp, Tordoff & Price, 1997), resting energy expenditure and substrate utilization (Goran, 1997) and substance use (Blum et al., 1996; Heath & Madden, 1995). As such, genetic differences between individuals can influence risk for biobehaviorally mediated disease vulnerabilities.

The range of genetic variation that exists among modern humans may reflect a variety of processes, including variation in selective pressures exerted over differing evolutionary environments or passive maintenance of variation that has had little or inconsistent fitness consequences. In addition, the presence of clinically meaningful genetic differences in biobehavioral systems may reflect a number of processes at work during human evolution, such as ecological imperatives for substantial

physical activity, constraints on availability of health-impairing foods or substances of abuse, or earlier death by unrelated causes. Such factors may have masked potentially deleterious gene effects, contributing to the maintenance of genes that may have otherwise been selected out.

CONCLUSIONS

This chapter has broadly described some biological mechanisms underlying health and behavior relationships. We have emphasized biobehavioral interactions for several reasons, most related to the complexity of the relationships that are being modeled. The explanatory power of these interactions, particularly when unpacking the layers of influence in the human body and the array of determinants of behavior, lies in careful consideration of the multiple, partially overlapping effects of biobehavioral interactions on outcomes such as health and wellbeing or disease and disability. It is clear that the interaction of biobehavioral processes with biological systems can affect pathophysiology in many instances, and efforts to control or undermine these disease pathways, while promising, have generally achieved modest success. Understanding ultimate as well as proximate causes of these processes requires a broader perspective than is typically applied in health psychology, but a more thorough understanding of causality may provide novel ways of thinking about solutions, and looking for ways to subvert evolutionarily shaped vulnerabilities should complement efforts to control empirically based psychosocial or biobehavioral antecedents of disease.

REFERENCES

Ader, R., Felten, D., & Cohen, N. (1991). *Psychoneuroimmunology* (2nd edn). New York: Academic.

Allison, D., Fontaine, K., Manson, J., Stevens, J., & Van Itallie, T. (1999). Annual deaths attributable to obesity in the United States. *Journal of the American Medical Association, 282*, 1530–1538.

American Institute for Cancer Research (1997). *Food, nutrition, and the prevention of cancer: A global perspective.* Washington, DC.

Andersen, B., Kiecolt-Glaser, J., & Glaser, R. (1994). A biobehavioral model of cancer stress and disease course. *American Psychologist, 49,* 389–404.

Antoni, M., Baggett, L., Ironson, G., LaPerriere, A., August, S., Klimas, N., Schneiderman, N., & Fletcher, M. (1991). Cognitive-behavioral stress management intervention buffers distress responses and immunologic changes following notification of HIV-1 seropositivity. *Journal of Consulting and Clinical Psychology, 59,* 906–915.

Antoni, M. H., Cruess, S., Cruess, D. G., Kumar, M., Lutgendorf, S., Ironson, G., Dettmer, E., Williams, J., Klimas, N., Fletcher, M. A., & Schneiderman, N. (2000). Cognitive-behavioral stress management reduces distress and 24-hour urinary free cortisol output among symptomatic HIV-infected gay men. *Annals of Behavioral Medicine, 22,* 29–37.

Astertita, M. F. (1985). *The physiology of stress.* New York: Human Sciences Press.

Baan, C., Stolk, R., Grobbee, D., Witteman, J., & Feskens, E. (1999). Physical activity in elderly subjects with impaired glucose intolerance and newly diagnosed diabetes mellitus. *American Journal of Epidemiology, 149,* 219–227.

Bachen, E. A., Manuck, S. B., Cohen, S., Muldoon, M. F., Raible, R., Herbert, T. B., & Rabin, B. (1995). Adrenergic blockade ameliorates cellular immune responses to mental stress in humans. *Psychosomatic Medicine, 57,* 366–372.

Barefoot, J. C., Dahlstrom, W. C., & Williams, R. B. (1983). Hostility, CHD incidence, and total mortality: A 25 year follow-up study of 255 physicians. *Psychosomatic Medicine, 45,* 59–63.

Barefoot, J. C., Dodge, K. A., Peterson, B. L., Dahlstrom, W. G., & Williams., R. B. Jr. (1989). The Cook–Medley Hostility Scale: Item content and ability to predict survival. *Psychosomatic Medicine, 51,* 46–57.

Baron, R., Cutrona, C., Hicklin, D., Russell, D., & Lubaroff, D. (1990). Social support and immune function among spouses of cancer patients. *Journal of Personality and Social Psychology, 59,* 344–352.

Baum, A., & Andersen, B. L. (Eds.) (2001). Psychosocial interventions for cancer. Washington, DC: American Psychological Association.

Bijnen, F., Caspersen, C., Feskens, E., Saris, W., Mosterd, W., & Kromhout, D. (1998). Physical activity and 10-year mortality from cardiovascular disease and all causes: The Zutphen Elderly Study. *Archives of Internal Medicine, 158,* 1499–1505.

Black, P. H., & Garbutt, L. D. (2002). Stress, inflammation, and cardiovascular disease. *Journal of Psychosomatic Research, 52,* 1–23.

Blum, K., Sheridan, P. J., Wood, R. C., Braverman, E. R., Chen, T. J., Cull, J. G., & Comings, D. E. (1996). The D2 dopamine receptor gene as a determinant of reward deficiency syndrome. *Journal of the Royal Society of Medicine, 89,* 396–400.

Breznitz, S., Ben-Zur, H., Berzon, Y., Weiss, D., Levitan, G., Tarcic, N., Lischinsky, S., Greenburg, A., Levi, N., & Zinder, O. (1998). Experimental induction and termination of acute psychological stress in human volunteers: Effects on immunological, neuroendocrine, cardiovascular, and psychological parameters. *Brain Behavior and Immunity, 12,* 34–52.

Brooks. P. J. (1997). DNA damage, DNA repair, and alcohol toxicity: A review. *Alcoholism, Clinical and Experimental Research, 21,* 1073–1082.

Califano, J. A. (1979). *Healthy people: The Surgeon General's report on health promotion and disease prevention.* Washington, DC: Government Printing Office.

Canto, J. G., Shlipak, M. G., Rogers, W. J., Malmgren, J. A., Frederick, P. D., Lambrew, C. T., Ornato, J. P., Barron, H. V., & Kiefe, C. I. (2000). Prevalence, clinical characteristics, and mortality among patients with myocardial infarction presenting without chest pain. *Journal of the American Medical Association, 283,* 3223–3229.

Carvalho, J., Baruzzi, R., Howard, P., Poulter, N., Alpers, M., Franco, L., Marcopito, L., Spooner, V., Dyer, A., Elliott, P., Stamler, J., & Stamler, R. (1989). Blood pressure in four remote populations in the Intersalt Study. *Hypertension, 14,* 238–246.

Carver, C. S., Pozo, C., Harris, S. D., Noriega, V., Scheier, M. F., Robinson, D. S., Ketcham, A. S., Moffat, F. L. Jr., & Clark, K. C. (1993). How coping mediates the effects of optimism on distress: A study of women with early stage breast cancer. *Journal of Personality and Social Psychology, 65,* 375–390.

Centers for Disease Control (2000). Publication of Surgeon General's Report on Smoking and Health. *Morbidity and Mortality Weekly Report, 49,* 718–727.

Cohen, L., Delahanty, D., Schmitz, J., Jenkins, F., & Baum, A. (1993). The effects of stress on natural killer cell activity in healthy men. *Journal of Applied Biobehavioral Research, 1,* 120–132.

Cohen, L., Marshall, G. D., Cheng, L., Agarwal, S. K., & Wei, Q. (2000). DNA repair capacity in healthy medical students during and after exam stress. *Journal of Behavioral Medicine, 23*, 531–544.

Cohen, S., Doyle, W. J., Skoner, D. P., Frank, E., Rabin, B. S., & Gwaltney, J. M. Jr. (1998). Types of stressors that increase susceptibility to common cold in healthy adults. *Health Psychology, 17*, 214–223.

Cohen, S., & Herbert, T. (1996). Health psychology: Psychological factors and physical disease from the perspective of human psychoneuroimmunology. *Annual Review of Psychology, 47*, 113–142.

Cohen, S., Tyrell, D., & Smith, A. (1991). Psychological stress and susceptibility to the common cold. *New England Journal of Medicine, 325*, 606–612.

Cole, S., Kemeny, M., Taylor, S., & Visscher, B. (1996). Elevated physical health risk among gay men who conceal their homosexual identity. *Health Psychology, 15*, 243–251.

Cook, W. W., & Medley, D. M. (1954). Proposed hostility and pharisaic virtue scales for the MMPI. *Journal of Applied Psychology, 38*, 414–418.

Crary, B., Hauser, S. L., Borysenko, M., Kutz, I., Hoban, C., Ault, K. A., Weiner, H. L., & Benson, H. (1983). Epinephrine-induced changes in the distribution of lymphocyte subsets in peripheral blood of humans. *Journal of Immunology, 131*, 1178–1181.

Davis, K. L., Davis, B. M., Greenwald, B. S., Mohs, R., Mathe, A. A., Johns, C. A., & Horvath, T. B. (1986). Cortisol and Alzheimer's disease: I. Basal studies. *American Journal of Psychiatry, 143*, 300–305.

Day, I., Gu, D., Ganderton, R. H., Spanakis, E., & Ye, S. (2001). Epidemiology and the genetic basis of disease. *International Journal of Epidemiology, 30*, 661–667.

DeFronzo, R. (1997). Pathogenesis of type 2 diabetes: Metabolic and molecular implications for identifying diabetes genes. *Diabetes Review, 5*, 177–269.

Delahanty, D. L., Dougall, A. L., Hawken, L., Trakowski, J. H., Schmitz, J. B., Jenkins, F. J. & Baum, A. (1996). Time course of natural killer cell activity and lymphocyte proliferation in response to two acute stressors. *Health Psychology, 15*, 48–55.

Doll, R. (1992). The lessons of life: Keynote address to the nutrition and cancer conference. *Cancer Research, 52*, 2024S–2029S.

Eaton, S. B., Eaton, S. B. III, & Cordain, L. (2002). Evolution, diet and health. In P. S. Ungar & M. F. Teaford (Eds.), *Human diet: Its origin and evolution* (pp. 7–18). Westport, CT: Greenwood, Bergin & Garvey.

Faith, M. S., Johnson, S. L., & Allison, D. B. (1997). Putting the behavior into the behavior genetics of obesity. *Behavior Genetics, 27*, 423–439.

Fawzy, F., Fawzy, N. W., Hyun, C. S., Elashoff, R., Guthrie, D., Fahey, J. L., & Morton, D. L. (1993). Malignant melanoma: Effects of an early structured psychiatric intervention, coping, and affective state on recurrence and survival 6 years later. *Archives of General Psychiatry, 50*, 681–689.

Fawzy, F., Kemeny, M. E., Fawzy, N. W., Elasoff, R., Morton, D. L., Cousins, N., & Fahey, J. L. (1990). A structured psychiatric intervention for cancer patients: Changes over time in immunological measures. *Archives of General Psychiatry, 47*, 729–735.

Feskens, E. (1992). Nutritional factors and the etiology of non-insulin diabetes mellitus: An epidemiological overview. *World Review of Nutrition & Dietetics, 69*, 1–39.

Ford, E. (1999). Body mass index and colon cancer in a national sample of adult US men and women. *American Journal of Epidemiology, 150*, 390–398.

Forlenza, M. J., & Baum, A. (2000). Psychosocial influences on cancer progression: Alternative cellular and molecular mechanisms. *Current Opinion in Psychiatry, 13*, 639–645.

Forlenza, M. J., Latimer, J. J., & Baum, A. (2000). The effects of stress on DNA repair. *Psychology and Health, 15*, 881–891.

Friedman, M., Thoresen, C. E., Gill, J. J., Ulmer, D., Powell, L. H., Price, V. A., Brown, B., Thompson, L., Rabin, D. D., & Breall, W. S. (1986). Alteration of type A behavior and its effect on cardiac reoccurrence in post myocardial infarction patients: Summary results of the recurrent coronary prevention project. *American Heart Journal, 112*, 653–665.

Gamberino, W., & Gold, M. (1999). Neurobiology of tobacco smoking and other addictive disorders. *Psychiatric Clinics of North America, 22*, 301–312.

Glaser, R., Thorn, B. E., Tarr, K. L., Kiecolt-Glaser, J. K., & D'Ambrosio, S. M. (1985). Effects of stress on methyltransferase synthesis: An important DNA repair enzyme. *Health Psychology, 4*, 403–412.

Goran, M. (1997). Genetic influences on human energy expenditure and substrate utilization. *Behavior Genetics, 27*, 389–399.

Greer, S., & Morris, T. (1975). Psychological attributes of women who develop breast cancer: A controlled study. *Journal of Psychosomatic Research, 19*, 147–153.

Griffin, J. E., & Ojeda, S. R. (1992). *Textbook of endocrine physiology*. New York: Oxford University Press.

Guthrie, N., & Carroll, K. (1999). Specific versus non-specific effects of dietary fat on carcinogenesis. *Progress in Lipid Research*, *38*, 261–271.

Guyton, A. C. (1991). *Textbook of medical physiology* (8th edn.). Philadelphia, PA: Saunders.

Hansen, B. C. (1999). The metabolic syndrome X. *Annals of the New York Academy of Sciences*, *892*, 1–24.

Haynes, S. G., Feinleib, M., & Kannel, W. B. (1980). The relationship of psychosocial factors in coronary heart disease in the Framingham Study III: Eight year incidence of coronary heart disease. *American Journal of Epidemiology*, *111*, 37–58.

He, J., & Whelton, P. (1999). What is the role of dietary sodium and potassium in hypertension and target organ injury? *American Journal of Medical Science*, *317*, 152–159.

Heath, A., & Madden, P. (1995). Genetic influences on smoking behavior. In J. R. Turner, L. R. Cardon & J. K. Hewitt (Eds.), *Behavior genetic approaches in behavioral medicine* (pp. 45–66). New York: Plenum.

Helmer, D. C., Ragland, D. R., & Syme, S. L. (1991). Hostility and coronary artery disease. *American Journal of Epidemiology*, *133*, 112–122.

Herberman, R., & Orlando, J. (1981). Natural killer cells, their role in defense against disease. *Science*, *214*, 24–30.

Hewitt, J., & Turner, J. (1995). Behavior genetic studies of cardiovascular responses to stress. In J. R. Turner, L. R. Cardon & J. K. Hewitt (Eds.), *Behavior genetic approaches in behavioral medicine* (pp. 87–103). New York: Plenum.

Hiatt R. A., & Rimer, B. K. (1999). A new strategy for cancer control research. *Cancer Epidemiology, Biomarkers & Prevention*, *8*, 957–964.

Hinde, J. L., Moraska, A., Gaykema, R. P. A., & Fleshner, M. (1999). Physical activity modulates the stress reactive neurocircuitry as measured by Fos. *Neuroimmunomodulation*, *6*, 225.

Hu, F., Stampfer, M., Rimm, E., Ascherio, A., Rosner, B., Spiegelman, D., & Willett, W. (1999). Dietary fat and coronary heart disease: A comparison of approaches for adjusting for total energy intake and modeling repeated dietary measurements. *American Journal of Epidemiology*, *149*, 531–540.

Huijbregts, P., Feskens, E., Rasanen, L., Fidanza, F., Nissinen, A., Menotti, A., & Kromhout, D. (1997). Dietary pattern and 20 year mortality in elderly men in Finland, Italy, and the Netherlands: Longitudinal cohort study. *British Medical Journal*, *315*, 13–17.

International Agency for Research on Cancer (1992). *Monographs on the evaluation of carcinogenic risks to humans. Volume 55: Solar and ultraviolet radiation.* Lyon: International Agency for Research on Cancer.

Irwin, M., Hauger, R. L., Jones, L., Provencio, M., & Britton, K. T. (1990). Sympathetic nervous system mediates central corticotropin-releasing factor induced suppression of natural killer cytotoxicity. *Journal of Pharmacology and Experimental Therapeutics*, *255*, 101–107.

Jackson, A. L., & Loeb, L. A. (2001). The contribution of endogenous sources of DNA damage to the multiple mutations in cancer. *Mutation Research*, *477*, 7–21.

Jemal, A., Thomas, A., Murray, T., & Thun, M. (2002). Cancer statistics. *CA: A Cancer Journal for Clinicians*, *52*, 23–47.

Ji, L. L. (1999). Antioxidants and oxidative stress in exercise. *Proceedings of the Society for Experimental Biology and Medicine*, *222*, 283–292.

Joossens, J., Hill, M., Elliot, P., Stamler, R., Lesaffre, E., Dyer, A., Nichols, R., & Kesteloot, H. (1996). Dietary salt, nitrate and stomach cancer mortality in 24 countries: European Cancer Prevention (ECP) and the INTERSALT Cooperative Research Group. *International Journal of Epidemiology*, *25*, 494–504.

Kamarck, T., & Jennings, J. R. (1999). Biobehavioral factors in sudden death. *Psychological Bulletin*, *109*, 42–75.

Kelloff, G., Boone, C., Steele, V., Crowell, J., Lubet, R., Greenwald, P., Hawk, E., Fay, J., & Sigman, C. (1996). Mechanistic considerations in the evaluation of chemopreventive data. In B. W. Stewart et al. (Eds.), *Principles of chemoprevention* (pp. 203–219). Lyon: International Agency for Research on Cancer.

Kiecolt-Glaser, J. K., & Glaser, R. (1995). Psychoneuroimmunology and health consequences: Data and shared mechanisms. *Psychosomatic Medicine*, *57*, 269–274.

Kiecolt-Glaser, J. K., Glaser, R., Williger, D., Stout, J., Messick, G., Sheppard, S., Ricker, D., Romisher, S., Briner, W., Bonnell, G., & Donnerberg, R. (1985). Psychosocial enhancement of immunocompetence in a geriatric population. *Health Psychology*, *4*, 25–41.

Kiecolt-Glaser, J. K., Stephens, R. E., Lipetz, P. D., Speicher, C. E., & Glaser, R. (1985). Distress and DNA repair in human lymphocytes. *Journal of Behavioral Medicine*, *8*, 311–320.

Lempiäinen, P., Mykkänen, L., Pyörälä, K., Laakso, M., & Kuusisto, J. (1999). Insulin resistance syndrome predicts coronary heart disease events in elderly nondiabetic men. *Circulation*, *100*, 123–128.

Leserman, J., Petitto, J., Perkins, D., Folds, J., Golden, R., & Evans, D. (1997). Severe stress, depressive symptoms, and changes in lymphocyte subsets in human immunodeficiency virus-infected men: A 2-year follow-up study. *Archives of General Psychiatry, 54,* 279–285.

Leserman, J., Petitto, J. M., Gu, H., Gaynes, B. N., Barroso, J., Golden, R. N., Perkins, D. O., Folds, J. D., & Evans, D. L. (2002). Progression to AIDS, a clinical AIDS condition and mortality: Psychosocial and physiological predictors. *Psychological Medicine, 32,* 1059–1073.

Levy, S., Hermerban, R., Whiteside, T., Sanzo, K., Lee, J., & Kirkwood, J. (1990). Perceived social support and tumor estrogen/progesterone receptor status as predictors of natural killer cell activity in breast cancer patients. *Psychosomatic Medicine, 52,* 73–85.

Linden, W., Stossel, C., & Maurice. J. (1996). Psychological interventions for patients with coronary artery disease. *Archives of Internal Medicine, 156,* 745–752.

Ling, M., Perry, P., & Tsuang, M. (1981). Side effects of corticosteroid therapy. *Archives of General Psychiatry, 38,* 471–477.

Longnecker, M., Gerhardsson le Verdier, M., Frumkin, H., & Carpenter, C. (1995). A case-control study of physical activity in relation to risk of cancer of the right colon and rectum in men. *International Journal of Epidemiology, 24,* 42–50.

MacLeod, A. K., Williams, J. M., & Bekerian, D. A. (1991). Worry is reasonable: The role of explanations in pessimism about future personal events. *Journal of Abnormal Psychology, 100,* 478–486.

Manuck, S., Marsland, A., Kaplan, J., & Williams, J. (1995). The pathogenicity of behavior and its neuroendocrine mediation: An example from coronary artery disease. *Psychosomatic Medicine, 57,* 275–283.

Manuck, S. B., Rabin, B. S., Muldoon, M. F., & Bachen, E. A. (1991). Individual differences in cellular immune response to stress. *Psychological Science, 2,* 111–115.

Marsland, A., Henderson, B. N., Chambers, W., & Baum, A. (2002). Stability of immune reactivity during acute psychological stress. *Psychophysiology, 39,* 865–868.

Marsland, A., Manuck, S. B., Fazzari, T. V., Stewart, C. J., & Rabin, B. S. (1995). Stability of individual differences in cellular immune responses to acute psychological stress. *Psychosomatic Medicine, 57,* 295–298.

Matarazzo, J. D. (1984). *Behavioral health: A handbook of health enhancement and disease prevention.* New York: Wiley.

Matsuzawa, Y., Funahashi, T., & Nakamura T. (1999). Molecular mechanism of metabolic syndrome X: Contribution of adipocytokines adipocyte-derived bioactive substances. *Annals of the New York Academy of Sciences, 892,* 146–154.

McKenna, M. C., Zevon, M. A., Corn, B., & Rounds, J. (1999). Psychosocial factors and the development of breast cancer: A meta-analysis. *Health Psychology, 18,* 520–531.

McKinnon, W., Weisse, C. S., Reynolds, C. P., Bowles, C. A., & Baum, A. (1989). Chronic stress, leukocyte subpopulations, and humoral response to latent viruses. *Health Psychology, 8,* 389–402.

Mezzetti, M., La Vecchia, C., Decarli, A., Boyle, P., Talamini, R., & Franceschi, S. (1998). Population attributable risk for breast cancer: Diet, nutrition, and physical exercise. *Journal of the National Cancer Institute, 90,* 389–394.

Miller, G., & Cohen, S. (2001). Psychological interventions and the immune system: A meta-analytic review and critique. *Health Psychology, 20,* 47–63.

Mittleman, M. A., Maclure, M., Sherwood, J. B., Mulry, R. P., Tofler, G. H., Jacobs, S. C., Friedman, R., Benson, H., & Muller, J. E. (1995). Triggering of acute myocardial infarction onset by episodes of anger. *Circulation, 92,* 1720–1725.

Must, A., Spadano, M., Coakley, E., Field, A., Colditz, G., & Dietz, W. (1999). The disease burden associated with overweight and obesity. *Journal of the American Medical Association, 282,* 1523–1529.

Nakajima, M., Takeuchi, T., Takeshita, T., & Morimoto, K. (1996). 8-hydroxydeoxyguanosine in human leukocyte DNA and daily health practice factors: Effects of individual alcohol sensitivity. *Environmental Health Perspectives, 104,* 1336–1338.

Naliboff, B., Benton, D., Solomon, G., Morley, J., Fahey, J., Bloom, E., Makinodan, T., & Gilmore, S. (1991). Immunological changes in young and old adults during brief laboratory stress. *Psychosomatic Medicine, 53,* 121–132.

National Institutes of Health (2001). *Expert summary: Global initiative for chronic obstructive lung disease.* NIH Publication no. 2701A. Washington, DC: USDHHS.

Ness, A., & Powles, J. (1997). Fruit and vegetables, and cardiovascular disease: A review. *International Journal of Epidemiology, 26,* 1–13.

Nesse, R. M. (1999). Proximate and evolutionary studies of stress and depression: Synergy at the interface. *Neuroscience and Biobehavioral Reviews, 23,* 895–903.

Nesse, R., & Berridge, K. (1997). Psychoactive drug use in evolutionary perspective. *Science, 278,* 63–66.

Oliver, G., & Detmar, M. (2002). The rediscovery of the lymphatic system: Old and new insights into the development and biological function of the lymphatic vasculature. *Genes and Development, 16,* 773–783.

Peters, C., & O'Brien, E. (1981). The early hominid plant niche: Insight from an analysis of plant exploitation by Homo, Pan and Papio in Eastern and Southern Africa. *Current Anthropology, 22,* 127–146.

Pi-Sunyer, F. X. (1998). NHLBI Obesity Education Initiative Expert Panel on the Identification, Evaluation, and Treatment of Overweight and Obesity in Adults: The evidence report. *Obesity Research, 6,* 51S–209S.

Plaut, M. (1987). Lymphocyte hormone receptors. *Annual Review of Immunology, 5,* 621–669.

Potter, J. D., & Steinmetz, K. (1996). Vegetables, fruit and phytoestrogens as preventive agents. In B. W. Stewart, D. McGregor & P. Kleihues (Eds.), *Principles of chemoprevention* (pp. 61–90). Lyon, France: International Agency for Research on Cancer.

Pryor, W. S. K. (1993). Oxidants in cigarette smoke: Radicals: hydrogen peroxide, peroxynitrate, and peroxynitrite. *Annals of the New York Academy of Sciences, 28,* 12–27.

Ramirez, A. J., Craig, T. K. J., Watson, J. P., Fentiman, I. S., North, W. R. S., & Rubens, R. D. (1989). Stress and relapse of breast cancer. *British Medical Journal, 289,* 291–293.

Reed, D. R., Bachmanov, A. A., Beauchamp, G. K., Tordoff, M. G., & Price, R.A. (1997). Heritable variation in food preferences and their contribution to obesity. *Behavior Genetics, 27,* 373–387.

Ross, R. (1999). Atherosclerosis: An inflammatory disease. *New England Journal of Medicine, 340,* 115–126.

Rozanski, A., Bairey, C. N., Krantz, D. S. Friedman, J., Resser, K. J., Morell, M., Hilton-Chalfen, S., Hestrin, L., Bietendorf, J., & Berman, D .S. (1988). Mental stress and the induction of silent myocardial ischemia in patients with coronary artery disease. *New England Journal of Medicine, 318,* 1005–1012.

Rozanski, A., Blumenthal, J. A., & Kaplan, J. (1999). Impact of psychological factors on the pathogenesis of cardiovascular disease and implications for therapy. *Circulation, 99,* 2192–2217.

Ruse, C. E., & Parker, S. G. (2001). Molecular genetics and age-related disease. *Age and Ageing, 30,* 449–454.

Sabban, E., & Kvetnansk, R. (2001). Stress-triggered activation of gene expression in catecholaminergic systems: Dynamics of transcription events. *Trends in Neurosciences, 24,* 91–98.

Sapolsky, R. M. (1998). *Why zebras don't get ulcers: An updated guide to stress, stress related diseases, and coping.* New York: Freeman.

Sapolsky, R. M., Krey, L., & McEwen, B. S. (1984). Stress down-regulates corticosterone receptors in a site-specific manner in the brain. *Endocrinology, 114,* 287–292.

Schedlowski, M., Falk, A., Rohne, A., Wagner, T. O., Jacobs, R., Tewes, U., & Schmidt, R. E. (1993). Catecholamines induce alterations of distribution and activity of human natural killer cells. *Journal of Clinical Immunology, 13,* 344–351.

Scheier, M. F., & Carver, C. S. (1985). Optimism, coping, and health: Assessment and implications of generalized outcome expectancies. *Health Psychology, 4,* 219–247.

Scheier, M. F., & Carver, C. S. (1992). Effects of optimism on psychological and physical well-being: Theoretical overview and empirical update. *Cognitive Therapy and Research, 16,* 201–228.

Schlesinger, M., & Yodfat, Y. (1991). The impact of stressful life events on natural killer cells. *Stress Medicine, 7,* 53–60.

Schneiderman, N., Antoni, M. H., Saab, P. G., & Ironson, G. (2001). Health psychology: psychosocial and biobehavioral aspects of chronic disease management. *Annual Review of Psychology, 52,* 555–580.

Schooler, T. Y., & Baum, A. (2000). Neuroendocrine influences on the health of diverse populations. In R. M. Eisler & M. Hersen (Eds.), *Handbook of gender, culture and health* (pp. 3–20). London: Erlbaum.

Scully, D., Kremer, J., Meade, M., Graham, R., & Dudgeon, K. (1998). Physical exercise and psychological well being: A critical review. *British Journal of Sports Medicine, 32,* 111–120.

Shannon, A. D., Quin, J. W., & Jones, M. A. (1976). Response of the regional lymphatic system of the sheep to acute stress and adrenaline. *Quarterly Journal of Experimental Physiology and Cognate Medical Sciences, 61,* 169–184.

Simopoulos, A. P. (1999). Evolutionary aspects of omega-3 fatty acids in the food supply. *Prostaglandins, Leukotrienes and Essential Fatty Acids, 60,* 421–429.

Smith, T. W. (1992). Hostility and health: Current status of a psychosomatic hypothesis. *Health Psychology, 11,* 139–150.

Smith, T. W., & Ruiz, J. M. (2002). Psychosocial influences on the development and course of coronary heart disease: Current status and implications for research and practice. *Journal of Consulting and Clinical Psychology, 70*, 548–568.

Smyth, J. (1998). Written emotional expression: Effect sizes, outcome types, and moderating variables. *Journal of Consulting and Clinical Psychology, 66*, 174–184.

Spiegel, D., Bloom, J. R., Kraemer, H. C., & Gottheil, E. (1989). Effect of psychosocial treatment on survival of patients with metastatic breast cancer. *Lancet, 2*, 888–891.

Starkman, M. N., Giordani, B., Berent, S., Schork, A., & Schteingart, D. E. (2001). Elevated cortisol levels in Cushing's disease are associated with cognitive decrements. *Psychosomatic Medicine, 63*, 985–993.

Surwit, R. S., & Schneider, M. S. (1983). Role of stress in the etiology and treatment of diabetes mellitus. *Psychosomatic Medicine, 55*, 380–393.

Surwit, R. S., & Williams, P. G. (1996). Animal models provide insight into psychosomatic factors in diabetes. *Psychosomatic Medicine, 58*, 582–589.

Tajima, F., Kawatani, T., Endo, A., & Kawasaki, H. (1996). Natural killer cell activity and cytokine production as prognostic factors in adult acute leukemia. *Leukemia, 10*, 478–482.

Thune, I., Brenn, T., Lund, E., & Gaard, M. (1997). Physical activity and the risk of breast cancer. *The New England Journal of Medicine, 336*, 1269–1275.

Traub, O., & Berk, B. C. (1998). Laminar shear stress: Mechanisms by which endothelial cells transduce an atheroprotective force. *Arteriosclerosis, Thrombosis, and Vascular Biology, 18*, 677–685.

van Zeeland, A. A., de Groot, A. J. L., Hall, J., & Donato, F. (1999). 8-hydroxydeoxyguanosine in DNA from leukocytes of healthy adults: Relationship with cigarette smoking, environmental tobacco smoke, alcohol and coffee consumption. *Mutation Research, 439*, 249–257.

Wang, T., Delahanty, D., Dougall, A., & Baum, A. (1998). Responses of natural killer cell activity to acute laboratory stressors in healthy men at different times of day. *Health Psychology, 17*, 428–435.

Watkins, L. R., Maier, S. F., & Goehler, L. E. (1995). Immune activation: The role of pro-inflammatory cytokines in inflammation, illness responses and pathological pain states. *Pain, 63*, 289–302.

West, J. B. (Ed.) (1991). *Best and Taylor's physiological basis of medical practice* (12th edn.). Baltimore: Williams & Wilkins.

Whiteside, T., & Herberman, R. (1995). The role of natural killer cells in immune surveillance of cancer. *Current Opinion in Immunology, 7*, 704–710.

Wick, G., Jansen-Durr, P., Berger, P., Blasko, I., & Grubeck-Loebenstein, B. (2000). Diseases of aging. *Vaccine, 18*, 1567–1583.

Willett, W. (1996). Can we prevent cancer by diet today? *Proceedings of the Annual Meeting of the American Association of Cancer Researchers, 37*, 644–645.

Williams, P. (1998). Relationships of heart disease risk factors to exercise quantity and intensity. *Archives of Internal Medicine, 158*, 237–245.

Williams, R. B., Suarez, E. C., Kuhn, C. M., Zimmerman, E. A., & Schanberg, S. M. (1991). Biobehavioral basis of coronary-prone behavior in middle-aged men: Part I. Evidence for chronic SNS activation in type As. *Psychosomatic Medicine, 53*, 517–527.

Wolk, A., Gridley, G., Svensson, M., Nyren, O., McLaughlin, J. K., Fraumeni, J. F., & Adam, H.O. (2001). A prospective study of obesity and cancer risk. *Cancer Causes & Control, 12*, 13–21.

Wood, R. D., Mitchell, M., Sgouros, J., & Lindahl, T. (2001). Human DNA repair genes. *Science, 291*, 1284–1289.

Woods, D., Davis, J., Smith, J., & Nieman, D. (1999). Exercise and cellular innate immune function. *Medicine and Science in Sports and Exercise, 31*, 57–66.

Zakowski, S. G., McAllister, C. G., Deal, M., & Baum, A. (1992). Stress, reactivity and immune function in healthy men. *Health Psychology, 11*, 223–232.

Zimmet, P., Boyko, E. J., Collier, G. R. & de Courten, M. (1999). Etiology of the metabolic syndrome: Potential role of insulin resistance, leptin resistance, and other players. *Annals of the New York Academy of Sciences, 892*, 25–44.

4

Determinants of Health-Related Behaviours: Theoretical and Methodological Issues

STEPHEN SUTTON

INTRODUCTION

The term *health behaviour* (or *health-related behaviour*) is used very broadly in this chapter to mean any behaviour that may affect an individual's physical health or any behaviour that an individual *believes* may affect their physical health.

This chapter focuses on determinants of health behaviours. More specifically, it focuses on what we will refer to as 'cognitive' determinants, as specified by theories of health behaviour or 'social cognition models' as they are sometimes called. After briefly considering some of the more important distinctions and dimensions of health behaviours and the definition and measurement of target behaviours, we provide an extensive discussion of research designs that are used – or could be used – to investigate the cognitive determinants of health behaviours. Then, a classification of theories of health behaviour is presented, followed by a detailed discussion of one particular theoretical approach, the theory of planned behaviour (TPB: Ajzen, 1991, 2002b).

Theories of health behaviour acknowledge that health behaviours may be influenced by numerous biological, psychological, and social factors, but they specify only a limited subset of cognitive determinants that are assumed to be most proximal to the behaviour. For a more complete explanation of particular health behaviours, it is necessary to extend the theories to include other relevant determinants. To this end, we outline a broader theoretical framework, drawing on the 'social ecological framework' (Emmons, 2000; Green, Richard & Potvin, 1996; McLeroy, Bibeau, Steckler & Glanz, 1988; Stokols, 1992, 1996) and ideas from multilevel modelling (Bryk & Raudenbush, 1992; Duncan, Jones & Moon, 1998; Hox, 2002). We conclude by making a number of recommendations to guide future research in this area.

The chapter presents a generic approach to explaining health behaviours, focusing on theoretical and methodological issues. Although a number of different examples of health behaviours are used, we do not attempt to review the determinants of particular health behaviours.

QUESTIONS ADDRESSED IN RESEARCH ON HEALTH BEHAVIOURS

Most health psychological research on health behaviours attempts to explain *between-individual variation* in particular health behaviours using theories of health behaviour. Such research typically addresses questions like: Why do some people engage in regular physical activity while others do not? Why do people differ in the frequency with which they engage in physical activity? Why do some women accept an invitation to go for breast screening while other women do not? Why do some adolescents try smoking while others remain non-smokers? This chapter focuses on determinants of between-individual variation because this is the dominant approach in the field of health behaviour research. However, it is also important to study determinants of *within-individual variation*: why does an individual's behaviour vary over time or across different settings? For example, why does a woman attend for her first breast screen but not for subsequent screens? Why does a smoker smoke more on some days or in some situations than in others?

There are other important questions concerning health behaviours that we do not consider in this chapter. One such question concerns the extent to which health behaviours cluster together (e.g., Røysamb, Rise & Kraft, 1997). For example, do smokers have generally less healthy lifestyles than non-smokers? Are people who attend for one kind of screening test more likely to attend for another kind of screening test?

Health behaviours are extremely diverse. In the next section, some of the more important distinctions and dimensions are briefly discussed (see also Carmody, 1997).

DIMENSIONS OF HEALTH BEHAVIOURS

Positive and Negative Behaviours

A distinction is often made between positive and negative health behaviours. Examples of positive, 'healthy', 'healthful' or 'health-enhancing' health behaviours are taking regular exercise, going for annual health checks, eating at least five portions of fruit and vegetables a day, and using a condom with a new sexual partner. Negative, 'unhealthy', 'risky', 'health-compromising' or 'health-impairing' health behaviours would include, for example, smoking, drinking heavily, driving too fast,

and eating a diet high in saturated fat. In many cases, this is simply a matter of framing. All these behaviours can be thought of as dichotomies that have a positive alternative and a negative alternative, for example going for annual health checks versus not going for annual health checks, or smoking versus not smoking.

Behavioural Stages

Individuals show varying and complex patterns of changes in particular health behaviours over the life course. Take smoking for example. Some adolescents may try a cigarette while others remain never-smokers. Some of those who try smoking may continue to experiment while others never smoke again. Some of those who experiment may become regular smokers whereas others may stop smoking. Some of those who become regular smokers may try to quit while others do not. Some of those who try to quit may succeed while others relapse. Some of those who relapse may make further attempts to quit.

Such a process can be simplified by defining *behavioural stages* such as adoption or initiation, maintenance, cessation and relapse, conceived of as a series of dichotomous dependent variables. Behavioural stages are not the same as the stages specified by stage theories of health behaviour, some of which are defined in terms of non-behavioural variables such as intentions, but can be analysed in similar ways, for example by estimating the transition probabilities: given that an adolescent tries smoking, what is the probability that he or she will become a regular smoker within a specified period of time? The determinants of different stages may differ (Rothman, 2000). For example, the factors that influence whether or not adolescents try smoking may differ from the factors that influence whether or not those who experiment progress to becoming regular smokers.

Health Behaviours versus Illness Behaviours

If a person who has suffered a heart attack takes up regular exercise, perhaps on the advice of his doctor, this could be referred to as an *illness behaviour*, because the person has a medically diagnosed illness or condition. If the same person had started exercising before he had his heart attack, the term *health behaviour* would be more appropriate. Even though the behaviours may be defined in exactly the same way, the determinants of illness behaviours may be different from the determinants of health behaviours. In this chapter, we use the term 'health behaviour' to cover both cases.

Many other types or dimensions may be important, for example 'detection' behaviours versus 'prevention' behaviours (Weinstein, Rothman & Nicolich, 1998), 'public' behaviours (e.g., going jogging) versus 'private' behaviours (e.g., exercising at home), and behaviours that involve the use of health services (e.g., going for a mammogram) versus those that do not (e.g., breast self-examination).

Although we have suggested that different types of health behaviours *may* be influenced by different factors, it is more parsimonious to start from the assumption that all types of health behaviour are influenced by the same limited set of proximal cognitive determinants, that is, that the same theory of health behaviour can be used to explain different behavioural stages, health and illness behaviours, detection and prevention behaviours, and so on.

DEFINING AND MEASURING BEHAVIOUR

In any study of the determinants of health behaviour, it is important to start by defining the behaviour of interest as clearly as possible (Ajzen & Fishbein, 1980; Fishbein et al., 2001). Following Ajzen and Fishbein (1980), behaviours can be defined in terms of four components: action, target, time and context. The action component is a necessary part of the definition of any behaviour. The target component is usually necessary, though not always. Time and context are optional; they enable the definition of behaviour to be as specific as required. For example, consider the definition 'eat breakfast tomorrow'. Here, 'eat' is the action, 'breakfast' is the target (alternative

targets would be 'a bowl of cereal' or 'lunch') and 'tomorrow' is the time component. No context is specified in this example. As an illustration of the importance of context, consider the following definitions:

1 using a condom the next time I have sex
2 using a condom the next time I have sex with my regular partner
3 using a condom the next time I have sex with a new sexual partner.

The first definition omits a potentially important contextual factor, namely type of partner, and is therefore probably too general for most purposes. The other two definitions each specify a context. These may be considered to be quite different behaviours both from a public health viewpoint and from the viewpoint of an individual who has both types of sexual partner.

Such behaviours are often measured as dichotomies: for example, 'Did you use a condom? Yes/No.' This implies that the person has a choice between two mutually exclusive and exhaustive alternatives: performing the behaviour or not performing it. This approach enables the simplest possible application of a given theory of health behaviour: participants' cognitions are assessed with respect to performing the behaviour. Occasionally, their cognitions with respect to *not* performing the behaviour are measured as well, but the usual assumption is that these will be the complement of the first set of cognitions and therefore provide no additional information. For example, if a person states that they are extremely likely to perform a given behaviour, it is assumed that, if asked, they would say that they were extremely unlikely not to perform it. This *complementarity assumption* seems plausible for intentions but questionable in the case of other cognitive variables. For example, a smoker may believe that his chances of developing lung cancer are 'quite high' if he continues to smoke. If we had only this information, we might assume that he would be motivated to quit smoking. However, he may also believe that his chances of developing lung cancer are 'quite high' if he stops smoking (because 'the damage has already been done'). Ideally, then, relevant cognitions should be measured with respect to *both* alternatives (performing and not performing the behaviour). An alternative approach is to phrase measures explicitly in terms of changes or differences (Weinstein, 1993).

In some cases, it is more realistic to define more than two alternatives. For example, in a study of contraceptive use, one could ask: 'The last time you had sex, did you use (a) a condom, (b) the pill, (c) another method of contraception, or (d) no method of contraception?' As an alternative to this multiple-choice format, respondents could be asked a series of separate questions (e.g., 'Did you use a condom? Yes/No', 'Did you use the pill? Yes/No' etc.). In this example, it is possible for respondents to have used more than one method, for example a condom and the pill; the alternatives are not strictly mutually exclusive.

Some behaviours are defined so generally that they are best thought of as *behavioural categories*. Behavioural categories cannot be directly observed. Instead they are inferred from single actions assumed to be instances of the general behavioural category. Ajzen and Fishbein (1980) give the example of dieting. Dieting may be inferred from specific behaviours such as eating two instead of three meals a day, not eating desserts, drinking tea and coffee without adding sugar, taking diet pills, and so on. There are two approaches to assessing behavioural categories. The first is simply to ask respondents questions like, 'Are you currently dieting?' In this case, a definition of 'dieting' should be provided, unless the aim is to explore different interpretations of this term. The second approach is to ask about a number of specific behaviours and use these to create an index of dieting. These approaches have different implications for the measurement of intention and other proximal determinants.

In many situations, we may be interested not in whether or not a behaviour is performed but in the magnitude and/or frequency of a behaviour. For example, in a study of drinking, we could ask people how often they have an alcoholic drink (frequency) and how much they usually drink on such occasions (quantity). Such behavioural criteria pose problems for

theories of health behaviour because they imply multiple alternatives, and it is not practicable to assess relevant cognitions with respect to all possible values of frequency and/or quantity. A common strategy is to convert the behaviour into a dichotomy. For example, one could use the official definition of 'safe' drinking and ask respondents about their cognitions with respect to exceeding the safe drinking limit. For further discussion of the problems created by magnitude and frequency measures, see Courneya (1994; Courneya & McAuley, 1993).

It is also important to distinguish between behaviours and *goals* (Ajzen & Fishbein, 1980, use the term *outcomes*). Losing weight is a goal not a behaviour. Attaining this goal may be influenced in part by behaviours such as eating low-fat foods or jogging 2 miles every day. But goals may be influenced by factors other than the person's behaviour. Losing weight depends on physiological factors such as metabolic rate, as well as on behavioural factors. If the aims are to predict and explain a goal or behavioural outcome, the actions that lead to the goal have to be identified and measured along with other, non-behavioural factors.

Most studies of health behaviours use self-report measures of behaviour. The limitations of self-reports are well known (Johnston, French, Bonetti & Johnston, 2004, Chapter 13 in this volume; Schwarz & Oyserman, 2001; Stone et al., 1999), but in many cases there will be no feasible alternative. Sometimes it may be possible to use 'objective' measures of behaviour, but these usually have limitations too. For example, records of attendance for breast screening may be inaccurate and may miss women who go for screening at other centres; electronic monitoring of tablet use may increase adherence; and biochemical measures of tobacco smoke intake are sensitive only to recent intake. Nevertheless, objective measures of behaviour may be more predictive of relevant health outcomes than are self-report measures. It is conceivable that theories of health behaviour may predict self-reported behaviour quite well but may be less effective in predicting the behavioural measures that are most strongly related to important health outcomes.

PREDICTION VERSUS EXPLANATION

It is important to distinguish between prediction and explanation (Sutton, 1998). A key aim of research on health behaviours is to identify the determinants (causes) of particular health behaviours. Researchers do this by developing theories that identify potentially important determinants of behaviour and specify the causal pathways by which they influence behaviour and by conducting empirical studies that enable the effect sizes to be estimated, usually in the form of regression coefficients. Ideally, we want to obtain *unbiased* and *precise* estimates of the causal effects of the putative determinants of a particular health behaviour in a given target population.

If the aim is prediction rather than explanation, we do not need to concern ourselves with identifying the determinants of behaviour or with specifying causal processes (although a causal model may suggest suitable predictor variables). We are free to choose convenient predictors and weights. Any predictor that 'works' can be included in the regression model. Past behaviour, for instance, is often a strong predictor of future behaviour, even though its theoretical status as a determinant of behaviour is contentious (Sutton, 1994). Similarly, it does not matter if relevant causal variables are omitted from the model.

Prediction can be useful without explanation, particularly when the time interval allows interventions to be applied. For example, it would be useful to be able to predict who is at risk for becoming a problem drinker. Identification of high-risk individuals may enable an early intervention to be made. Thus prediction enables interventions to be targeted to high-risk groups. However, an understanding of the factors that lead some people but not others to develop a drinking problem (explanation) would be even more useful because it would have implications for the nature and content of the intervention programme; it would tell us not only who to target but also what to do to them. Although prediction and explanation are not the same, the first is necessary for the second; models that do not enable us to predict behaviour are unlikely to be useful as explanatory models.

RESEARCH DESIGNS FOR INVESTIGATING COGNITIVE DETERMINANTS OF HEALTH BEHAVIOURS

The most commonly used designs for studying the cognitive determinants of health behaviours are between-individuals cross-sectional studies and prospective studies with two waves of measurement and relatively short follow-up periods of days, weeks or months. We use the relationship between attitude and behaviour to illustrate these designs, where it is hypothesized that attitude influences behaviour and where attitude represents any variable whose values may change over time within an individual and which may be influenced by behaviour (i.e., where there may be *reciprocal causation*); other examples would be self-efficacy, intention, risk perceptions, worry, attributions and illness representations. (See Weinstein, Rothman & Nicolich, 1998, for an illuminating discussion of the use of correlational data to examine the relationship between risk perceptions and behaviour.)

Before discussing between-individuals designs and possible causal models, we consider within-individuals designs, because ultimately we want to draw inferences about within-individual causal processes. Between-individuals designs may or may not be informative about the processes that occur at the within-individual level.

Within-Individuals Designs

Consider a study in which a person's attitude and behaviour with respect to a particular health behaviour are measured on a number of occasions, say once a month over a 12-month period. Figure 4.1 shows one possible relationship between attitude and behaviour. Across occasions, higher levels of attitude are associated with higher levels of behaviour. (For simplicity, we assume that there is no trend in

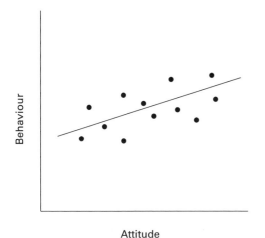

Figure 4.1   *Relationship between attitude and behaviour across 12 occasions for one individual*

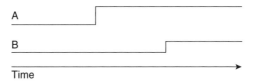

Figure 4.2   *Timeline showing causal relationship between attitude (change) and behaviour (change) for one individual*

behaviour over time, that is, that the individual's behaviour varies across occasions but there is no systematic tendency for behaviour to increase or decrease over time; of course, the analysis could be extended to fit a time trend, if there was reason to expect one.) If we are prepared to make a number of strong assumptions, we can interpret the slope of the regression line as an estimate of the causal effect of attitude on behaviour for this particular individual. We can use the regression line to estimate the likely effect on the person's behaviour if we were to intervene to change their attitude. We can think of such an intervention 'sliding the person up their own regression line'.

Note that at the within-individual level, many variables that may influence attitude and behaviour at the between-individual level are automatically controlled. For example, gender, genetic make-up and childhood experiences are fixed and cannot possibly account for the correlation between an individual's attitude and behaviour over time. Similarly, age changes slowly over the time period in question and personality variables are likely to change very little.

Possible within-individual causal relationships between attitude (or other variables) and behaviour can be represented by timeline

diagrams. Figure 4.2 depicts a simple timeline diagram for one individual, showing one possible causal relationship between attitude and behaviour. The person's attitude is initially stable, then increases by a certain amount, and then remains at this higher level. The increase in attitude is followed after a certain time lag by an increase in behaviour. (Such a lag could be built into the example above by relating attitude at one time point to behaviour at the next time point.) The change in behaviour does not lead to a change in attitude (no reciprocal causation), at least within the time period shown. The main question of interest is how much behaviour change is produced by a unit increase in attitude, holding other relevant variables constant.

Mixed Designs

Now consider a study in which repeated measures of attitude and behaviour are measured in a sample of individuals. This is a *mixed* or two-level design, incorporating both within-individuals and between-individuals components. Given such data, it is possible to estimate both the effect of attitude on behaviour *within* an individual and the effect of attitude on behaviour *between* individuals. An appropriate statistical approach is random-effects or multi-level regression analysis (Bryk & Raudenbush, 1992; Hox, 2002). Figure 4.3a shows one possible pattern of results. For simplicity, only three individuals are shown, with low, medium and high levels of attitude, and we assume that the within-individuals regression lines (shown in bold) have a common slope (it is possible to fit different slopes for different individuals).

The within-individuals slope and the between-individuals slope will not necessarily be equal. In Figure 4.3a, the within-individuals slope is shallower than the between-individuals slope, but other patterns are possible. It is even possible for one slope to be positive (higher attitude going with higher behaviour) and the other to be negative (higher attitude going with lower behaviour), though this would seem implausible in the present case.

Where the two slopes differ, this can be interpreted in causal terms as indicating that an individual's behaviour on a particular occasion is influenced not only by their attitude on that occasion but also by their characteristic level of attitude, as indexed by their mean attitude across occasions. Now we have two different estimates of the causal effect of attitude on behaviour. As outlined above, the within-individuals regression lines can be used to estimate the causal effect of a change in attitude on a particular occasion on behaviour for each individual and hence the likely impact of an attitude-change intervention. By contrast, the between-individuals regression line can be used to estimate the likely effect on a person's behaviour (not just their behaviour on one occasion, but their *characteristic* level of behaviour across occasions) of increasing their *characteristic* level of attitude by a certain amount. Here we are 'sliding the person up the between-individuals regression line' in order to estimate the new level of behaviour corresponding to their new level of attitude.

However, there are two problems with this interpretation. First, it is not clear how we would shift a person's characteristic level of attitude, as opposed to their attitude on a particular occasion. Second, the inference is based on comparing different individuals. What we are saying, in effect, is that if we could increase person 1's characteristic level of attitude so that it was the same as that of person 2, we would expect person 1's behaviour to be the same as person 2's. However, there may be many differences between individuals other than their characteristic level of attitude that may partly explain why one individual has a characteristically high level of behaviour and another person has a characteristically low

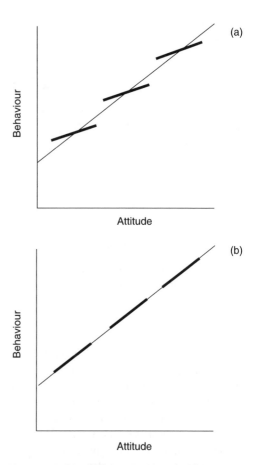

Figure 4.3   *Two different patterns of within-individuals (bold) and between-individuals relationship between attitude and behaviour*

level; for example, differences in childhood experiences, gender, age and personality. Some of these variables may be correlated with attitude level. Thus, the between-individuals slope may give a misleading estimate of the effect of the hypothetical intervention because of uncontrolled differences between individuals. Put simply, we can't turn person 1 into person 2 just by changing their attitude. Of course, it is possible to measure variables that may influence behaviour across individuals and take them into account in the analysis to adjust the between-individuals slope, but it is unlikely that we will be able to anticipate and measure all the important influences.

There will also be relevant causal variables that are uncontrolled in the within-individuals analysis – variables that vary over time, are correlated with attitude over time and that influence an individual's behaviour. Nevertheless, the within-individuals analysis has the advantage of ruling out variables that are stable over time. In sum, where the within-individuals and between-individuals regression slopes differ, there are reasons for believing that the former may give a better estimate of the likely effect of an attitude-change intervention.

Figure 4.3b shows another possible pattern of results from a two-level study. As in Figure 4.3a, the within-individuals regression lines have a common slope but this time they coincide with the between-individuals regression line. This means that we can predict an individual's behaviour on a particular occasion from their attitude on that occasion, but that knowledge of their characteristic level of attitude (or knowing which individual the observation belongs to) does not provide any additional information. Given appropriate assumptions, this can be interpreted in causal terms as follows. Differences between individuals in their behaviour on a particular occasion are influenced by differences in their attitude on that occasion, but differences in their characteristic level of attitude have no additional impact. Or, to put it differently, between-individual differences in behaviour on a particular occasion can be explained in terms of within-individual causal processes without needing to invoke additional, or different, causal processes operating at the between-individual level. In this happy situation, we can make a valid cross-level causal inference from the between-individuals relationship to the within-individuals relationship (or vice versa). See Sutton (2002a) for a detailed example that uses timelines to illustrate this case for the relationship between attitude and intention.

It is possible that attitude and behaviour are relatively stable over time within individuals. If so, we could simply compute the mean level of attitude and the mean level of behaviour for each individual (to give a more reliable estimate of each individual's characteristic levels of attitude and behaviour than would be given by a single measure of attitude and behaviour on one occasion), and then carry out a between-individuals analysis. However, the problems of estimating the likely effect of an attitude-change intervention (assuming that it were possible to change an individual's attitude given its stability over time) would still apply: we would still be inferring within-individual effects from comparisons between individuals. Similar problems arise with variables such as personality that are known to be highly stable.

Within-individuals designs and mixed designs are extremely rare in this field. A number of studies using the TPB have obtained repeated measures of cognitions and behaviour with respect to different target behaviours at the same time point (e.g., Trafimow & Finlay, 1996; Trafimow et al., in press), but only one study to date has obtained a sufficient number of repeated measures of cognitions and behaviour over time with respect to the same target behaviour to allow a within-individuals analysis (Hedeker, Flay & Petraitis, 1996). This study used the theory of reasoned action (TRA; Fishbein & Ajzen, 1975), but the measures of attitude and subjective norm departed widely from Ajzen and Fishbein's (1980) recommendations. Hedeker et al. obtained measures of cognitions and behaviour on four occasions; at least six would be preferable.

We need more studies of social cognition models that use within-individuals designs or mixed designs. However, since the vast majority of studies in this field use between-individuals designs, the remainder of this section focuses on these.

Between-Individuals Designs

Figure 4.4 shows six possible true causal models defined at the between-individual level. (Similar models could be specified at the within-individual level.) In model I, attitude influences behaviour. The small arrow pointing to behaviour represents the aggregate of all other causes of behaviour apart from attitude. This is often referred to as the *error* or *disturbance* term. The disturbance term can be thought of as comprising two components: a systematic component consisting of other

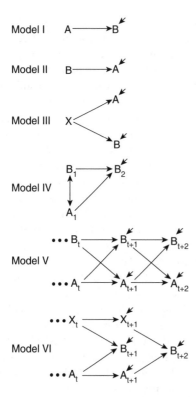

Figure 4.4 *Six possible true models of the relationship between attitude and behaviour*

important causes of behaviour apart from attitude; and a random component consisting of tens, hundreds, or even thousands of minor, independent, and unstable causes of behaviour. The latter causes would be impossible to specify in practice. (An alternative justification for assuming a random component is that 'there is a basic and unpredictable element of randomness in human responses which can be adequately characterized only by the inclusion of a random variable term': Johnston, 1984: 14.) Although, individually, the effects of these 'random shocks' are assumed to be small, in aggregate their effect may be quite large. Conceivably, the majority of the variance in behaviour could be explained by the random component, and only a minority by the major causal factors.

We have assumed no correlation between these other causes and attitude (indicated by the absence of a two-headed arrow between them). This assumption can be restated as saying that all variables that influence behaviour and that either influence attitude or are correlated with attitude because of common causes are specified in the model (or, more simply, that 'all relevant variables are included in the model'). This assumption is necessary in order to be able to interpret the regression coefficient for attitude as an unbiased estimate of the causal effect of attitude on behaviour. Unfortunately, this assumption is arbitrary and untestable (Clogg & Haritou, 1997; Sutton, 2002a).

Model II shows behaviour influencing attitude. In model III, a common cause (or causes), X influences both attitude and behaviour. In this model, attitude does not influence behaviour, and behaviour does not influence attitude. Thus, the correlation between attitude and behaviour is entirely due to X. Of course, the true model may include all these effects: attitude influences behaviour and vice versa (reciprocal causation) and other variables, X influence attitude and behaviour.

Cross-sectional designs

In a cross-sectional design, attitude and behaviour would be measured at the same time point for each of a sample of individuals. (Unlike the mixed design outlined above, we would typically have only a single measure of attitude and behaviour on each individual.) If we assume that model I is the true model, we can regress behaviour on attitude (i.e., conduct a regression analysis in which B is the dependent variable and A is the independent variable) to obtain an estimate of the causal effect of attitude on behaviour, in the form of the regression coefficient. (Note that the standardized coefficient is equal to the correlation in this simple case.) If model I is in fact the true model, and a number of other assumptions hold, then the coefficient will be an unbiased estimate of the true causal effect of attitude on behaviour. Thus, in order to draw causal inferences from cross-sectional data, we have to assume the truth of the hypothesized causal model, and our inference (the estimate of the size of the causal effect) is conditional on this and other strong assumptions. (This is also true of other observational designs: causal inferences are always conditional on the truth of the hypothesized causal model.) Note that the observed correlation between attitude and behaviour in a cross-sectional study can be interpreted as having been generated by causal processes that have occurred *in the past* prior to the time of measurement.

Prospective longitudinal designs

Suppose we measure attitude at time 1 and behaviour at time 2 in a sample of individuals, and regress behaviour on attitude. We refer to this as *design 1*. This appears to be a stronger research design than the cross-sectional design outlined above because the correlation or regression coefficient between attitude and behaviour cannot include a component due to behaviour at time 2 influencing attitude at time 1. The temporal ordering of the measurement of attitude and behaviour rules out this explanation. However, as shown below, the correlation between attitude and behaviour may still be due to behaviour influencing attitude.

In prospective designs, causal lag needs to be considered. The causal lag is the time it takes for a change in attitude to produce a change in behaviour. Ideally, the length of the follow-up period should be approximately equal to the hypothesized length of the causal lag (Finkel, 1995; Sutton, 2002a). If the follow-up period is shorter than the causal lag, a change in attitude that occurs just prior to time 1 will not have produced its effect on behaviour by time 2; thus, the effect of recent changes in attitude will be missed at the later time point. If the follow-up period is too long, a change in attitude that takes place during the follow-up period may produce a change in behaviour within the same period. In both cases, the value of attitude at time 1 and the value of behaviour at time 2 will be mismatched. If the causal lag is very brief (as it may be, for example, in the case of the effect of attitude on intention), a prospective design is not appropriate and a cross-sectional design should be used (though, if feasible, an experimental study would be preferable – see below).

Regardless of the length of the causal lag, if behaviour is extremely stable over the follow-up period (in the sense that individuals show little change over time relative to one another), it makes little difference whether a cross-sectional or a prospective design is used; both should yield similar estimates of the effect of attitude on behaviour. This is likely to be the case, for example, when a quantitative aspect of behaviour such as frequency of exercising is assessed on two occasions over a short period of time (2 weeks, say). Here, the correlation between behaviour at time 1 and behaviour at time 2 is likely to be very high, indicating high stability, and whether the investigator uses behaviour at time 2 or behaviour at time 1 as the dependent variable in the analysis is likely to make little difference to the results.

The observation that behaviour is frequently quite stable (as indexed by a high correlation) over short time periods provides one rationale for extending the prospective design discussed above by including behaviour at time 1. In this design (which we call *design 2*), B_2 is regressed on A_1 and B_1. The assumption here is that the stability of behaviour arises from a causal influence of prior behaviour on future behaviour, that is, both attitude at time 1 and behaviour at time 1 influence behaviour at time 2 (see model IV in Figure 4.4). The two-headed arrow between A_1 and B_1 indicates that the correlation between attitude and behaviour at time 1 is treated as given: the model does not specify how it came about. Unlike a cross-sectional study, which analyses the current correlation between attitude and behaviour in terms of past causal processes, this design focuses on causal processes that are assumed to operate *over the follow-up period*. If model IV is true, then design 2 will give unbiased estimates of the two causal effects (and design 1 will give a biased estimate of the effect of A_1; given positive correlations between A_1 and B_1 and between B_1 and B_2, the effect of A_1 will be overestimated).

In design 2, the coefficient for B_1 is the estimated causal effect of B_1 on B_2, holding A_1 constant. (This is often referred to as the *stability coefficient*.) The coefficient for A_1 is the estimated causal effect of A_1 on B_2, holding B_1 constant.

This coefficient also has an interpretation in terms of behaviour *change*: it estimates the causal effect of A_1 on change in behaviour between time 1 and time 2 ($B_2 - B_1$), holding B_1 constant (Finkel, 1995). This can be shown as follows. The initial model is

$$B_2 = \beta_0 + \beta_1 A_1 + \beta_2 B_1 + \varepsilon$$

where β_0 is the intercept, β_1 and β_2 are the unstandardized coefficients for A_1 and B_1 respectively, and ε is the error term. Subtracting B_1 from both sides gives:

$$B_2 - B_1 = \beta 0 + \beta_1 A_1 + (\beta_2 - 1)B_1 + \varepsilon$$

The coefficient for A_1 is identical in the two equations. Thus, one could estimate β_1 by computing the change score and regressing it on A_1 and B_1. In practice, it is more convenient to regress B_2 on A_1 and B_1.

Model IV in Figure 4.4 can be thought of as being embedded in model V, in which attitude and behaviour influence each other over time. The model assumes that over each time interval, behaviour is influenced by prior behaviour and prior attitude, and attitude is influenced by prior attitude and prior behaviour; in other words, attitude and behaviour have *cross-lagged* effects. If model V (and hence model IV) is true, design 1 will yield a biased estimate of the effect of A_1 on B_2. For example, it can be seen from model V that the correlation between A_{t+1} and B_{t+2} will include a component due to the effects of B_t on A_{t+1} and B_{t+2} (via B_{t+1}). Thus, although design 1 rules out an effect of B_2 on A_1, it does not rule out the possibility that the correlation between A_1 and B_2 is partly or wholly due to the effect of relatively stable behaviour on attitude. Design 1 is of particular interest because it represents, in minimal form, a design that is commonly used to test theories of health behaviour, in which cognitive variables at time 1 are used to predict behaviour at time 2 without controlling for initial behaviour. By contrast, if model V is true, design 2 will yield the appropriate estimate of the causal effect of A_1 on B_2.

An alternative to controlling for prior behaviour statistically is to control for it by *stratification* or *restriction* (Weinstein, Rothman & Nicolich, 1998). If we select people with equivalent behaviour at time 1, there can be no effect of behaviour at time 1 on behaviour at time 2 and we can rule out a causal effect of behaviour on attitude as a possible explanation of the observed correlation between attitude at time 1 and behaviour at time 2. Note that, like design 2, this design focuses on the effect of attitude on behaviour over the follow-up period and can also be interpreted in terms of the effect of initial level of attitude on behaviour *change*.

Design 2 assumes that behaviour is partly determined by prior behaviour. However, it is difficult to explain how past behaviour can *directly* influence future behaviour (Sutton, 1994). More generally, the idea that a variable can directly cause a later version of itself (*autoregression*) is problematic (Allison, 1990; Liker, Augustyniak & Duncan, 1985; Stoolmiller & Bank, 1995). Stoolmiller and Bank give the following example:

> consider a simple experiment designed to study growth of money left in bank accounts. Suppose we deposit a range of sums of money in each of several banks paying a range of interest rates on deposits. In an AR [autoregressive] model with the initial sum of money and the interest rate as predictors of the amount of money at time 2, we would typically find that initial amount was a very strong predictor of money at time 2. But clearly if we ... isolate the money at time 1 away from all suspected causal forces (e.g., in a shoebox under the bed), we will find at time 2, much to our dismay, that the money has failed to grow. Despite the fact that AR effects would be large in the bank example, they are not true direct causal effects. Interest causes money to grow, not initial amount of money ... To discard interest as a predictor of change because it failed to compete with initial amount of money in an AR model would be an error. (1995: 271)

An alternative explanation for the stability of behaviour is that behaviour is stable because its underlying causes are stable. Model VI in Figure 4.4 shows an additional variable X which, like attitude, has a lagged causal effect on behaviour. In this model, there is no direct causal effect of prior behaviour on behaviour.

Behaviour will nevertheless be stable over time to the extent that its causes (A and X) remain stable over time. (Note that, although this model assumes that behaviour is not directly influenced by prior behaviour, it still assumes that X and A have autoregressive effects.)

Assuming model VI is true, the simplest observational design for estimating the effects of A and X on B would be to assess A and X at one time point and B at a later time point and then regress B on A and X, *without* controlling for prior behaviour. This is a version of design 1. If data were available from three time points (X and A measured at time 1; X, A and B measured at time 2; and B measured at time 3), this analysis could be done twice. However, a more sophisticated approach would be to use a *first difference model*, in which difference scores are calculated and change in behaviour is regressed on change in attitude and change in X (Liker et al., 1985; see also Allison, 1990). An advantage of this method is that the effects of unmeasured, stable causes of B are automatically controlled for. For example, suppose behaviour was also influenced by personality variables whose values did not change over the time period in question. If a first difference model were used, omitting such variables from the analysis would not bias the results. This method will work only when the values of A and X change for a substantial portion of individuals over time. If high stability was expected, the investigator could consider introducing an intervention between time 1 and time 2 in order to produce differential changes in A and X across individuals.

Returning to models that assume that behaviour is influenced by prior behaviour, an extension to design 2 is the cross-lagged panel design in which attitude and behaviour are both measured at two time points. As in design 2, B_2 is regressed on A_1 and B_1 but, in addition, B_2 is regressed on A_1 and B_1. If model V in Figure 4.4 is true, such a cross-lagged regression analysis estimates the effect of attitude on behaviour and the effect of behaviour on attitude, assuming that both effects have the same causal lag which is approximately equal to the length of the follow-up period. Note that an alternative analysis using the cross-lagged correlations is

not recommended when the aim is to estimate causal effects (Campbell & Kenny, 1999; Rogosa, 1980). If the cross-lagged regression analysis is done using a structural equation modelling program, an estimate of the residual covariance or correlation between A_2 and B_2 can be obtained. This is the portion of the covariance or correlation between these two variables that cannot be explained by A_1 and B_1. If this residual term is substantial, one interpretation is that there are important variables that influence both attitude and behaviour that have been omitted from the analysis. This would cast doubt on the validity of the estimates of the causal effects in the model (Hertzog & Nesselroade, 1987).

Although we have considered only very simple models in the preceding discussion, many other models are possible. For example, we have assumed that attitude has a lagged effect on behaviour (and vice versa). In some cases, it may be more plausible to postulate 'synchronous' or almost instantaneous causal effects. For example, in the motivational model discussed by Weinstein, Rothman and Nicolich (1998), an increase in precautionary behaviour is assumed to lead promptly to a decrease in perceived risk.

Again, variables such as attitude may act as *predisposing factors* that increase the likelihood that other variables influence behaviour. For example, consider a study in which we select a sample of 12-year-olds who have never smoked, measure their attitude toward smoking, and then use this to predict whether or not they try smoking a cigarette by age 14. Attitude may act as a predisposing factor in the sense that an event such as being offered a cigarette may be more likely to lead to smoking among adolescents who hold a positive attitude.

Health behaviour researchers are recommended to carefully consider possible plausible causal models and to draw timeline and path diagrams to represent them before selecting an appropriate research design and analysis approach.

Experimental Designs

None of the observational designs outlined above can rule out the possibility that an observed correlation between attitude and behaviour is partly or wholly due to omitted variables (as in model III in Figure 4.4). Where possible, health behaviour researchers should consider conducting experimental studies in which the determinant of interest (attitude in this example) is manipulated independently of other potential causes, with random assignment of participants to experimental conditions. In principle, such designs allow strong causal inferences to be drawn. More than one explanatory variable may be manipulated orthogonally in a factorial design. If repeated measures are obtained, experiments can be analysed at the within-individual level as well as at the between-individual or group level.

Of the theories of health behaviour in common use, only protection motivation theory (Rogers & Prentice-Dunn, 1997) has been subjected to extensive experimental testing. In view of the strong assumptions required to draw causal inferences from observational data, health psychology researchers should make much more use of randomized experiments to test predictions from theories of health behaviour. Such experiments should use proper randomization methods rather than arbitrary or alternate assignment of participants to conditions. The huge advantage of randomization is that, if it is done properly, it guarantees that any baseline differences between groups must be due to chance (Shadish, Cook & Campbell, 2002).

Intervention Studies

Such analytic or theory-testing experiments should be distinguished from intervention studies, which may also employ randomization to conditions. In intervention studies, the aim is usually to change a number of potential explanatory variables simultaneously in order to maximize the effect of the intervention on behaviour. Such studies can provide information about the extent to which the intervention effect on behaviour, if one is obtained, is mediated by the hypothesized explanatory variables (Baron & Kenny, 1986; Kenny, Kashy & Bolger, 1998). Mediation analyses are partly experimental and partly observational. In particular, interpretation of the relationship between the hypothesized mediating variable and the dependent variable requires the same assumptions as the analysis of other observational data (Sutton, 2002a).

THEORIES OF HEALTH BEHAVIOUR

Theories of health behaviour can be classified by range of application (general, health-specific, and domain- or behaviour-specific) and formal structure (stage versus non-stage theories) (Sutton, 2003; see Armitage & Conner, 2000, for a related classification scheme). General theories, such as the TPB (Ajzen, 1991, 2002b) and its predecessor the TRA (Fishbein & Ajzen, 1975), are those that, in principle, can be applied to a wide range of behaviours, not simply health-related ones. Health-specific theories like the health belief model (Strecher & Rosenstock, 1997) are specific to health-related behaviours. Behaviour- or domain-specific models have a still narrower range of application. For example, the AIDS risk reduction model (Catania, Kegeles & Coates, 1990) was developed to understand STD-preventive behaviour such as condom use.

Stroebe argues that general models should be preferred for the sake of parsimony: 'it is not very economical to continue to entertain specific theories of health behaviour unless the predictive success of these models is greater than that of general models of behaviour' (2000: 27). If we can use a single theory to explain why some young people use condoms consistently with new sexual partners while others do not, why some people engage in regular exercise more often than others, and why some people recycle their newspapers whereas others throw them away, this is much more useful and economical than developing different theories for each of these three behaviours. The argument, then, is that general theories should be preferred to health- or behaviour-specific theories unless the latter can be shown to be better in some important way. This suggests a strategy of always starting with a general theory and only modifying it if absolutely necessary when applying it to a new behaviour or behavioural domain.

The second important distinction is between stage and non-stage (or *continuum*) theories (Sutton, in press; Weinstein, Rothman & Sutton, 1998). These two types of theories have different formal structures and different implications for intervention. Stage theories assume that behaviour change involves movement through a sequence of discrete stages, that different factors are important at different stages, and therefore that different (*stage-matched*) interventions should be used for people in different stages. The best known stage theory is the transtheoretical model (Prochaska & Velicer, 1997), which has been applied to a wide range of health-related behaviours. The version of the model that has been used most widely in recent years specifies five stages: precontemplation, contemplation, preparation, action, and maintenance. Although the transtheoretical model is the dominant stage theory in the field of health behaviour, it suffers from serious conceptual and measurement problems and cannot be recommended in its present form (Sutton, 2001, in press). Another stage theory that is attracting increasing interest is the precaution adoption process model (Weinstein & Sandman, 1992), which is a health-specific model. Health behaviour researchers who are thinking of using stage theories need to be aware that they are complex and difficult to test (Sutton, 2000, in press; Weinstein, Rothman & Sutton, 1998).

This chapter focuses on continuum or non-stage theories. Each of these theories specifies a small set of proximal cognitive determinants of behaviour. (Note that some theories also include variables that, strictly speaking, cannot be described as cognitive determinants, for example skills and actual behavioural control.) The causal relationships specified by such theories can be represented in the form of a path diagram with behaviour on the far right. Figure 4.5 shows three prototypical representations. The variables *X*, *Y* and *Z* are the hypothesized cognitive determinants; *B* is behaviour. In Figure 4.5a, both *X* and *Y* are assumed to influence behaviour directly. In Figure 4.5b, the effect of *X* and part of the effect of *Y* are mediated by *Z*; *Z* is a *mediator* or *intervening variable* (Baron & Kenny, 1986). Thus, *Y* has direct and indirect effects on behaviour whereas *X* has only an

(a)

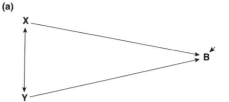

(b)

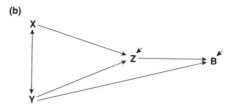

(c)

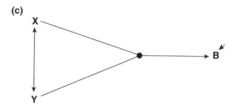

Figure 4.5   *Three prototypical representations of the causal relationships specified by theories of health behaviour (X, Y and Z are explanatory variables; B is behaviour)*

indirect effect. In Figures 4.5a and b, the variables combine *additively*. By contrast, in Figure 4.5c, *X* and *Y* interact to influence behaviour. The effect of *Y* on behaviour depends on the level of *X*, that is, *X moderates* the relationship between *Y* and *B*. (Interactions are symmetric, so, alternatively, *Y* can be regarded as the moderating variable.) Figure 4.5c does not show the nature of the interaction. Where theories of health behaviour specify interactions, they are nearly always of the multiplicative or synergistic type, in which, to put it simply, the effects of two variables together are greater then their sum.

As in the preceding section, the small unlabelled arrows represent the errors or disturbances. Algebraic equations can be used as an alternative to the diagrammatic representation (although, as Pearl, 2000, points out, path diagrams contain more information than equations). Figures 4.5a and c can each be represented by a single equation, but Figure 4.5b requires two equations because there are two endogenous (dependent) variables.

Although theories of health behaviour are sometimes described as 'static' models, they are dynamic in the sense that they specify causal relationships between variables whose values may change over time and may be deliberately changed through interventions. For example, the theory depicted in Figure 4.5b says that, if Y is held constant, a change in X will produce a change in Z, which in turn will produce a change in behaviour. Thus, theories of health *behaviour* are also theories of health *behaviour change*. However, with the exception of Bandura's (1997, 1998) social cognitive theory, the theories do not tell us *how* to change the variables on the far left (the exogenous variables) (Sutton, 2002c).

In Figure 4.5, the exogenous variables X and Y are linked by a two-headed arrow. This indicates that these variables *may* be correlated with each other but that this correlation is not explained by the theory; it is treated as given. The implicit assumption is that the correlation must be due to other variables external to the theory (common causes). If it seems plausible that the correlation is due to one variable influencing the other, then the two-headed arrow should be replaced by a single-headed arrow, thus making one of the exogenous variables endogenous. This apparently minor change can have major implications for estimates of the effect size and for interventions (Sutton, 2002c).

None of the diagrams in Figure 4.5 shows arrows from behaviour back to the explanatory variables. Most theories of health behaviour acknowledge that behaviour may influence cognitions, as well as vice versa, but few theories explicitly incorporate such feedback effects.

Ideally, theories of health behaviour should specify the causal lag for each of the causal relationships in the theory. Causal lag is an important consideration in deciding on an appropriate research design. An alternative approach is to try to estimate the causal lag empirically (Finkel, 1995).

Theories of health behaviour generally assume *linear* (straight-line) relationships. Indeed, none of the social cognition models in common use specifies curvilinear relationships.

All the theories are specified (often implicitly) at the between-individual level and they are nearly always tested at the between-individual level. The main aim of research in this area can be characterized as 'putting numbers on the paths', where these numbers represent unbiased and precise estimates of the causal effects for particular health behaviours in particular target populations in the form of regression coefficients and their standard errors or confidence intervals.

We will not attempt to describe the main theories of health behaviour, even in outline form. The reader is referred to the book by Conner and Norman (1996, in press) for a detailed exposition of the major theories. (See also Sutton, 2002b, and Weinstein, 1993, for comparisons of theories.) The position taken in the present chapter is that there are too many theories of health behaviour and that this is hindering progress in the field. Progress would be more rapid if research efforts were concentrated on a small number of theories. This chapter therefore focuses on one theory, the TPB (Ajzen, 1991, 2002b), which can be argued is a prime candidate for guiding future research on health behaviour, for the following reasons: (1) it is a general theory; (2) the constructs are clearly defined and the causal relationships between the constructs clearly specified; (3) there exist clear recommendations for how the constructs should be operationalized (Ajzen, 2002a); (4) the theory has been widely used to study health behaviours (Ogden, 2003) as well as many other kinds of behaviours; and (5) meta-analyses show that it accounts for a useful amount of variance in intentions and behaviour (but see the later discussion of percentage of variance explained).

Although the next section focuses on the TPB, many of the points made apply equally to other theories of health behaviour.

THE THEORY OF PLANNED BEHAVIOUR

The TPB is shown in Figure 4.6. According to the theory, behaviour is determined by the strength of the person's *intention* to perform

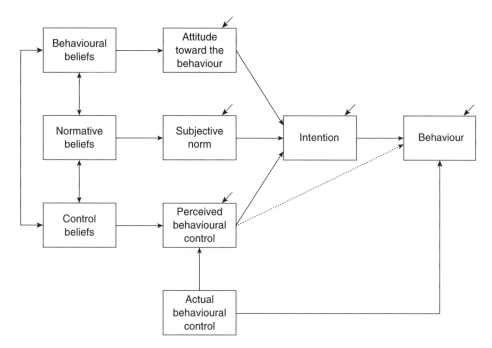

Figure 4.6   *The theory of planned behaviour*

that behaviour and the amount of *actual control* that the person has over performing the behaviour. According to Ajzen (2002b), intention is 'the cognitive representation of a person's readiness to perform a given behavior, and … is considered to be the immediate antecedent of behavior', and actual behavioural control 'refers to the extent to which a person has the skills, resources and other prerequisites needed to perform a given behavior'. Figure 4.6 also shows an arrow from perceived behavioural control to behaviour. *Perceived behavioural control* refers to the person's perceptions of their ability to perform the behaviour. It is similar to Bandura's (1997) construct of self-efficacy; indeed Ajzen (1991) states that the two constructs are synonymous. Perceived behavioural control is assumed to reflect actual behavioural control more or less accurately, as indicated by the arrow from actual to perceived behavioural control in Figure 4.6. To the extent that perceived behavioural control is an accurate reflection of actual behavioural control, it can, together with intention, be used to predict behaviour.

The strength of a person's intention is determined by three factors: their *attitude toward the behaviour*, that is, their overall evaluation of performing the behaviour; their *subjective norm*, that is, the extent to which they think that important others would want them to perform it; and their perceived behavioural control.

Attitude toward the behaviour is determined by the total set of *accessible* (or *salient*) *behavioural beliefs* about the personal consequences of performing the behaviour. Specifically, attitude is determined by $\Sigma b_i e_i$, where b_i is belief strength and e_i is outcome evaluation. Similarly, subjective norm is determined by the total set of accessible *normative beliefs*, that is, beliefs about the views of important others. Specifically, subjective norm is determined by $\Sigma n_j m_j$, where n_j is belief strength and m_j is motivation to comply with the referent in question. Finally, perceived behavioural control is determined by accessible *control beliefs*, that is, beliefs about the presence of factors that may facilitate or impede performance of the behaviour. Specifically, perceived behavioural control is determined by $\sum c_k p_k$, where c_k is belief strength (the perceived likelihood that a given control factor will be present) and p_k is the perceived power of the control factor (the extent to which the control factor will make it easier or more difficult to perform the behaviour).

According to the theory, changing behaviour requires changing these underlying beliefs and/or actual behavioural control (Sutton, 2002c).

The *principle of correspondence* (Ajzen & Fishbein, 1977; Fishbein & Ajzen, 1975) or *compatibility* (as it was renamed by Ajzen, 1988) states that, in order to maximize predictive power, all the variables in the theory should be measured at the same level of specificity or generality. This means that the measures should be matched with respect to the four components of action, target, time and context (see earlier section 'Defining and Measuring Behaviour'). Most researchers who use the TPB recognize the importance of using compatible measures, though the principle is frequently violated in empirical applications of the theory. Researchers who use other theories seem largely unaware of the principle. The rationale given for the principle is a pragmatic one: it improves prediction. Presumably, however, there is also a *theoretical* rationale for the principle, namely that, by measuring the TPB variables at the same level of specificity, we are matching cause and effect (Sutton, 1998).

Although the TPB holds that all behaviours are determined by the same limited set of variables, each behaviour is also substantively unique, in two senses (Fishbein, 2000). First, for a given population or culture, the relative importance of attitude, subjective norm and perceived behavioural control may vary across different behaviours. For example, some behaviours may be influenced mainly by attitude, whereas other behaviours may be influenced mainly by subjective norm. Ogden (2003) points out that many studies using the TPB find no role for one or other of the three putative determinants of intention and therefore that the theory 'cannot be tested'. However, this represents a misunderstanding of the TPB. If at least one of the components is found to predict intention in a given study, this

is consistent with the TPB. Nevertheless, it is a weakness of the theory that it does not specify the conditions under which intention will be mainly influenced by attitude, subjective norm or perceived behavioural control.

The second sense in which each behaviour is substantively unique is that, for a given population or culture, the behavioural, normative and control beliefs that underlie attitude, subjective norm and perceived behavioural control respectively may also differ for different behaviours. In the same way, for a given behaviour, the relative importance of attitude, subjective norm and perceived behavioural control, and the content of the underlying beliefs, may vary across different cultures or populations.

The TPB is a general theory. In principle, it can be applied to any target behaviour without needing to be modified. For example, in applying the theory to a health-related behaviour, there should be no need to add a variable representing risk perceptions. If beliefs about the health risks of the behaviour (or its effect on reducing risk) are salient to a substantial proportion of the target population, this should emerge in an elicitation study that uses open-ended questions to elicit accessible beliefs (Ajzen, 2002a; Ajzen & Fishbein, 1980; for an example of an elicitation study, see Sutton et al., 2003).

Like other theories of health behaviour, the TPB is a *causal model* and should be treated as such. It says, for instance, that if you hold constant a person's subjective norm, perceived behavioural control and actual behavioural control and you change their attitude toward the behaviour, this will lead to a change in their intention (assuming that attitude is a determinant of intention for the behaviour in question in this target group), and this in turn will lead to a change in their probability of performing the behaviour (assuming that the behaviour is at least partly under the person's control).

The TPB is often depicted without actual control in the path diagram and, to date, has always been tested without measuring actual control. In this case, the direct path from perceived behavioural control to behaviour is causally ambiguous (Sutton, 2002a, 2002c). As already pointed out, one rationale for this direct link is that perceived behavioural control can often be used as a substitute for actual control (Ajzen, 1991). Although actual control influences behaviour, it is argued that it is difficult to measure and is less interesting psychologically than perceived control. Perceived control can be used as a proxy for actual control to the extent that people's perceptions of control are accurate. According to this rationale, the direct link between perceived behavioural control and behaviour is not a causal path, and changing perceived behavioural control would not lead to behaviour change directly. (It could lead to behaviour change indirectly, of course, via a change in intention.) In order to change behaviour directly, it is necessary to change actual control.

However, Ajzen suggested a second rationale for the direct link between perceived behavioural control and behaviour: 'holding intention constant, the effort expended to bring a course of behavior to a successful conclusion is likely to increase with perceived behavioral control. For instance, even if two individuals have equally strong intentions to learn to ski, and both try to do so, the person who is confident that he can master this activity is more likely to persevere than is the person who doubts his ability' (1991: 6). Note that this effect is held to be mediated by 'effort' and 'perseverance', neither of which are constructs in the theory.

Putting these two rationales together, this means that if we observe an independent predictive effect of perceived behavioural control on behaviour in an observational study in which actual control is not measured, this may be due partly to a causal effect of perceived behavioural control on behaviour and partly to a correlation induced by actual behavioural control influencing both perceived behavioural control and behaviour (Sutton, 2002a, 2002c). More generally, failing to measure and control for the effects of actual behavioural control will lead to biased estimates of the causal effects of perceived behavioural control and intention on behaviour, unless it can be assumed that perceived control is an accurate reflection of actual control (i.e., that perceived and actual control are perfectly correlated and

this correlation arises from a direct causal effect of actual on perceived control).

Although Figure 4.6 shows an arrow going directly from actual control to perceived control, this is inconsistent with the theory's assumption that the effects of any variable on perceived control must be mediated by control beliefs. The absence of arrows, either one- or two-headed, between actual control and behavioural and normative beliefs respectively can be interpreted as indicating zero correlations and no direct causal influence in either direction. However, to date, Ajzen has not discussed these possible relationships. If actual control were related to one or both of these variables, again this would have implications for the interpretation of regression analyses from which actual control was omitted.

A further complexity concerns the interaction between perceived behavioural control and intention on behaviour that was postulated by Ajzen and Madden (1986). Ajzen (2002b) states it as follows: 'Conceptually, perceived behavioral control is expected to moderate the effect of intention on behavior, such that a favorable intention produces the behavior only when perceived behavioral control is strong.' He also notes that, 'In practice, intentions and perceptions of behavioral control are often found to have main effects on behavior, but no significant interaction' (see also Conner & Armitage, 1998). This interaction derives from an interaction between intention and *actual* control (and so would be predicted to occur only in situations in which perceptions of control are accurate). In particular, intention is expected to have a stronger influence on behaviour, the greater the degree of actual control the person has over the behaviour. As Ajzen (2002b) puts it, 'successful performance of the behavior depends not only on a favorable intention but also on a sufficient level of behavioral control'. For simplicity, this interaction is not shown in Figure 4.6.

Extensions of the TPB

There have been numerous attempts to extend the TPB by adding variables such as anticipated regret, moral norm and self-identity (Conner & Armitage, 1998). For the sake of parsimony and theoretical coherence, candidate variables should be provisionally accepted as official components of the theory only if a number of conditions are satisfied. First, there should be sound *theoretical* reasons for believing that a given candidate variable influences intention or behaviour independently of the existing variables, that is, that the variable has a direct causal effect on intention or behaviour. In some cases, it is possible that the proposed additional variable is already captured by one of the existing variables.

Second, in order to retain the existing structure of the TPB, the proposed new variable should have an expectancy-value basis like attitude, subjective norm and perceived behavioural control; in other words, the new variable should be determined by accessible beliefs that are specific to the target behaviour. This would seem to rule out some variables, for example self-identity. This also means that the expectancy-value basis of *descriptive norm* (the belief that significant others are or are not performing the target behaviour), which Ajzen (2002a) has proposed as a subcomponent of subjective norm in the latest version of the theory, needs to be specified. This requirement, that any additional variable is homologous to the existing variables, also implies that including too many additional variables in the theory would make it unwieldy to use in practice. Furthermore, additional open-ended questions for eliciting accessible beliefs would need to be devised for use in pilot studies. This has not yet been done for descriptive norm (Ajzen, 2002a).

Third, measures of a proposed new variable should be shown to have discriminant validity with respect to measures of the existing components, in other words to be measuring something different from measures of the existing variables.

Finally, the new variable should be shown to predict intention and/or behaviour independently of the existing components in studies in which the latter are well measured in accordance with published recommendations. It is likely that there are many false positive findings in the

literature because the existing components are not always optimally measured. Of course, if the aim is simply to improve the predictive power of the theory rather than to specify additional determinants of intention, only the last of the requirements set out above is relevant.

How Well Does the Theory Perform?

There have been remarkably few experimental tests of the TPB or its predecessor the TRA (Sutton, 2002a). The vast majority of studies have used observational designs. Table 4.1 summarizes the findings from meta-analyses of research using the TPB in terms of the multiple correlation R and its square (which can be interpreted as the proportion of variance explained) for predicting intention and behaviour. Also shown is an effect size index called f^2 that is recommended by Cohen (1988, 1992) for use in power analysis where the statistical test involves multiple correlations.

With the exception of Ajzen (1991), all the meta-analyses explicitly or by implication restricted the analysis of prediction of behaviour to prospective studies in which intention and perceived behavioural control were measured at time 1 and behaviour was measured at time 2, that is, they used a version of what we referred to earlier as design 1. The meta-analyses differed in a number of ways, including the selection criteria for the studies. However, there is not space here to give a detailed comparison and critique of the reviews or to map the degree of overlap between them. Instead we focus on the 'headline' figures to gain an impression of the predictive utility of the theory. The findings for both intention and behaviour show reasonable consistency. For intention, the multiple correlations range from 0.59 to 0.71 (between 35 per cent and 50 per cent of variance explained). Prediction of behaviour was lower, as expected, with the multiple correlation ranging between 0.51 and 0.59 (between 26 per cent and 35 per cent of the variance explained).

Godin and Kok (1996) found differences between different kinds of behaviours with respect to how well the theory predicted

Table 4.1   *Summary of effect sizes[a] from meta-analyses of the theory of planned behaviour*

Meta-analysis	Predicting intention (BI) from AB, SN and PBC				Predicting behaviour from BI and PBC			
	k[b]	R	R^2	f^2	k[b]	R	R^2	f^2
Ajzen (1991)	19	0.71	0.50	1.00	17	0.51	0.26	0.35
Godin & Kok (1996)[c]	76	0.64	0.41	0.69	35	0.58	0.34	0.52
Sheeran & Taylor (1999)[d]	10	0.65	0.42	0.72	–	–	–	–
Albarracín et al. (2001)[d]	23	0.71	0.50	1.00	23	0.53	0.28	0.39
Armitage & Conner (2001)	154	0.63	0.39	0.64	63	0.52	0.27	0.37
Hagger et al. (2002)[e]	49	0.67	0.45	0.82	35	0.52	0.27	0.37
Trafimow et al. (2002):[f]								
PBC as perceived difficulty	11	0.66	0.44	0.79	9	0.59	0.35	0.55
PBC as perceived control	11	0.59	0.35	0.53	9	0.58	0.34	0.52

BI = behavioural intention; AB = atttitude to behaviour; SN = subjective norm; PBC = perceived behavioural control.

[a]Effect sizes are given in terms of the multiple correlation R, R^2, and $f^2 = R^2/(1 - R^2)$. According to Cohen (1988, 1992), an f^2 value of 0.35 is 'large'.

[b]k is the number of datasets.

[c]Restricted to studies of health-related behaviours.

[d]Restricted to studies of condom use.

[e]Restricted to studies of physical activity.

[f]Restricted to studies that included measures of both 'perceived difficulty', defined as 'the extent to which the person believes that performing the behaviour would be easy vs. difficult or the level of confidence about performing the behaviour' (p. 11) and 'perceived control', defined as 'the extent to which the behaviour was perceived to be under or outside one's control or was "up to me"'' (p. 11).

intentions and behaviour. For example, for behaviour, the theory worked better in studies of HIV/AIDS-related behaviours than in studies of 'clinical and screening' behaviours. However, these results were based on small numbers of studies, and possible confounds such as sample characteristics and differences in how the TPB variables were measured were not examined. Godin and Kok's review needs to be updated and extended.

Should we be encouraged or discouraged by these results? The answer depends on the standard of comparison. One possible standard is the ideal maximum of 100 per cent. Clearly, the theory does not perform well by this standard. In practice, however, the maximum percentage of variance that can be explained in a real application is often substantially less than 100; one reason for this will be discussed later in the chapter. There are other more realistic

standards of comparison. Another possible benchmark is provided by the effect sizes that are typically found in the behavioural sciences using a diverse range of outcomes and predictors. According to Cohen's (1988, 1992) operational definitions, the effect sizes in Table 4.1 are 'large' for both intention and behaviour. In evaluating the predictive performance of the TPB, it is important to remember that it is highly parsimonious, at least when direct measures rather than indirect (belief-based) measures of its constructs are used. Thus, although it explains no more than 50 per cent of the variance in intention, on average, it achieves this level of performance with only three predictors. In addition, although percentage of variance explained is widely used as a measure of effect size, it tends to give a rather pessimistic impression (Rosenthal & Rubin, 1979; Sutton, 1998).

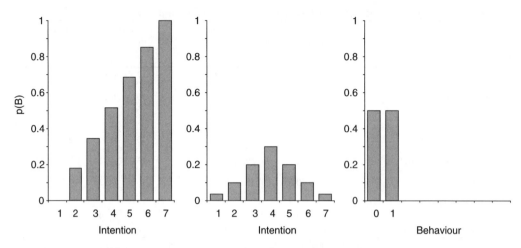

Figure 4.7   *Example showing a perfect linear relationship between a seven-point measure of intention and a dichotomous measure of behaviour and the distributions of the two variables*

Reasons for Poor Prediction

There are a number of important methodological and measurement reasons why theories such as the TPB often have lower predictive power than we would prefer (Sutton, 1998). For example, consider the simple case of predicting behaviour (measured at time 2) from intention (measured at time 1). Intention is often measured using a seven-point semantic differential rating scale. But the measure of behaviour is often a dichotomy, that is people either perform the behaviour or they don't; indeed, this is the classic application of the TPB. However, when predicting a variable with two categories from a variable with seven categories, it is not possible to obtain a perfect correlation or 100 per cent of the variance explained (unless respondents treat the intention measure as if it consisted of only two categories). It is possible to obtain a perfect correlation between the variables only if the distributions match, which means that they have to have an equal number of response categories.

Figure 4.7 shows a hypothetical example. The graph on the far left of the figure shows a *perfect* linear relationship between the seven-point intention measure and the probability of performing the behaviour. So no one who

scores 1 on the intention scale performs the behaviour whereas everyone who scores 7 does so. The middle graph shows the distribution on the intention measure, which is approximately normal, and the graph on the right shows the distribution on the behaviour measure, showing an even split: half the people perform the behaviour and half do not.

In this example, intention explains *less than 20 per cent* of the variance in behaviour. The problem is that the two measures have a different number of response categories and therefore the distributions cannot match. For maximum prediction, we need to make sure that the number of response categories is equal. Note that this problem has nothing to do with the use of dichotomous measures *per se* or with skewed distributions. If we had a dichotomous measure of intention, we could in principle explain 100 per cent of the variance in a dichotomous measure of behaviour. This would be the case even if the distributions were highly skewed. So if we had 100 people in the sample and only one of them performed the behaviour while 99 did not, it would still be possible to explain 100 per cent of the variance in behaviour if the sample were equally skewed on the measure of intention and if the one person who performed the behaviour was also the one person who intended to do so. (This example also shows that the fact that a variable has a small (but non-zero) observed variance cannot on its own explain why it does not correlate highly with other variables.) The same argument would apply if we had a seven-point measure of intention and a five-point measure of behaviour, although the effect would be less dramatic.

There is an important theoretical issue here as well. Theories like the TPB do not explain how intention, which is conceived of as a continuous variable, translates into a binary outcome – performance or non-performance of the behaviour.

Other reasons for poor prediction include random measurement error in the measures of intention and/or behaviour, violation of the principle of compatibility, and lack of stability in intentions (Sutton, 1998). Such measurement factors help to explain both the intention–behaviour 'gap' (Sheeran, 2002) and why theories of health behaviour often do not explain as much variance as we would like them to.

Undue Emphasis on Amount of Variance Explained

Investigators naturally want to maximize the amount of variance explained by a theory and, other things being equal, would usually prefer a model that explains more variance to one that explains less. However, it can be argued that undue emphasis is placed on the total amount of variance explained by theories such as the TPB. First, from the standpoint of assessing the potential of a theory as the basis for interventions, the proportion of variance in behaviour explained by the theory as a whole is less relevant than the proportion explained by the variables on the far left of Figure 4.6. This is because, according to the theory, it is not possible to intervene *directly* to change intention, for example. Interventions have to be applied to the exogenous variables, that is, to the beliefs that are assumed to underlie attitude, subjective norm and perceived behavioural control. It is therefore important to estimate the percentage of variance in behaviour explained by the variables

on the far left, or the *effective variance explained* (Sutton, 2002c). If the effects of the far left variables on behaviour are completely mediated by the other variables in the theory, the effective variance explained will be lower, often much lower, than the variance explained by the theory as a whole.

The effective variance explained can be estimated in a single study simply by regressing behaviour on the variables on the far left, omitting the hypothesized mediating variables from the regression model. Where a primary study or meta-analysis reports the correlations among the exogenous variables and between the exogenous variables and behaviour, the effective variance explained can be computed by entering the correlation matrix into a regression or structural equation modelling program. For example, from Table 3 in Albarracín, Johnson, Fishbein and Muellerleile's (2001) meta-analysis of the TPB applied to condom use, it can be calculated that behavioural beliefs, normative beliefs and perceived behavioural control together explained 13.3 per cent of the variance in condom use, which is substantially lower than the variance explained by intention and perceived behavioural control (Table 4.1). The unique variance explained by each of these components was 2.9 per cent, 1.7 per cent and 1.3 per cent respectively. (A direct measure of perceived behavioural control was used because very few studies assessed control beliefs.)

Why have we apparently lost all this explained variance? One way to look at this is to ask what we gain by including intention in the theory. By adding intention, we gain in terms of explanation, because we have specified a potential mechanism by which attitude, subjective norm and perceived behavioural control (and their underlying beliefs) influence behaviour. We are 'filling in the causal chain'. We also gain in predictive terms, because intention adds to the prediction of behaviour over and above attitude, subjective norm and perceived behavioural control. But this gain in predictive power is not helpful for the purposes of producing behaviour change because of causal dilution. The only way we can change intention, according to the theory, is by changing attitude, subjective norm and perceived behavioural control, and the only way we can change these variables is by changing their underlying beliefs. But behavioural beliefs, for example, may not completely determine attitude; attitude, subjective norm and perceived behavioural control do not completely determine intention; and intention does not completely determine behaviour. Although intention may add to the prediction of behaviour over and above attitude, subjective norm and perceived behavioural control, the additional predictive power provided by intention is useless for the purposes of behaviour change because it arises from *unspecified causes* of intention, as represented by the small arrow pointing to intention in Figure 4.6. Because they are unspecified, they cannot be targeted in an intervention. So we cannot exploit the additional predictive power provided by intention.

The same argument would apply to any theory that specifies a causal chain. Of course, if an exogenous variable has a *direct* effect on behaviour as well as indirect effects, this may offset the dilution effect. An alternative way of gauging the intervention potential of a theory is to use the path-analytic calculus (Heise, 1975; Kenny, 1979) to calculate the total effect of each of the variables on the left-hand side on behaviour, controlling for other relevant variables. Either the standardized or the unstandardized regression coefficients could be used. The total effect can be interpreted as an estimate of the effect on behaviour of increasing the variable on the left by one unit, while holding constant the other variables on the left-hand side.

The example outlined above of effective variance explained should be treated as illustrative only. Because of the way that indirect measures of attitude and subjective norm are computed in applications of the TPB, the analyses involved product terms or multiplicative composites. A problem that affects such analyses is that the correlations between a multiplicative composite and other variables may vary depending on the particular scoring schemes used for its components (Bagozzi, 1984; Evans, 1991; French & Hankins, 2003).

(Although the correlations are difficult to interpret, the multiplicative relationship between, for example, behavioural belief strength and outcome evaluation on attitude can be tested using standard approaches for testing interactions in multiple regression: Aiken & West, 1991; Sutton, 2002c; for an example, see Sutton, McVey & Glanz, 1999).

The second reason for arguing that undue emphasis is placed on the amount of variance explained is that a regression model that explains more variance in behaviour is not necessarily more valid than one that explains less variance. The validity of a regression model depends on the validity of its underlying assumptions, not on the proportion of variance it explains. Sutton (2002a) gives several hypothetical examples, including one in which close to 100 per cent of the variance is explained but the estimates of the causal effects of the predictor variables are seriously biased, and another showing that unbiased estimates of causal effects can be obtained even if the regression model does not explain a large proportion of variance in the criterion.

Is the TPB Too 'Rational'?

Theories like the TPB may be criticized for providing an unrealistically rational explanation of behaviour. However, the term 'rational' has several different meanings. Behaviour as explained by TPB can be regarded as rational in some ways but not in others. On the one hand, the theory holds that a person's behaviour will tend to be consistent with their accessible beliefs. Such consistency can be regarded as rational in one sense of the word. Furthermore, the TPB assumes that beliefs are combined in a systematic way such that a person's attitude towards a given behaviour, for example, is a mathematical function of the belief strengths (subjective probabilities) and outcome evaluations (utilities) of the accessible behavioural beliefs. The function derives from the expected value and expected utility models of 'economic man', which have a long history of use as normative models of decision-making (Edwards, 1954).

On the other hand, people's accessible beliefs may be incomplete and incorrect or influenced by strong emotions. For instance, a person may erroneously believe that a particular health behaviour is doing them good when in fact it is not. Thus, intentions and behaviour may be based on information that is incomplete and incorrect. Furthermore, although some decisions may involve conscious deliberation and careful weighing up of pros and cons, in many cases the processes involved in the formation and modification of beliefs, attitudes and intentions may be largely automatic (Ajzen & Fishbein, 2000; Fishbein & Ajzen, 1975). For example, a person's attitude toward a particular behaviour may be automatically updated when new information about the behaviour is received, and this attitude may be automatically elicited and guide behaviour in relevant situations. (However, although it seems plausible that automatic processes control the formation and change of beliefs, attitudes and intentions, for most health-related behaviours it seems less plausible to suggest that behaviour itself is automatically elicited.)

A BROADER THEORETICAL FRAMEWORK

The TPB, like other social cognition models, does not rule out other causes of behaviour. Many other factors such as socio-demographic, cultural and personality factors may influence behaviour, but these are assumed to be distal factors, in other words to be farther removed from the behaviour than the proximal factors specified by the theory. Thus, the TPB divides the determinants of behaviour into two classes: a small number of proximal determinants, which are specified by the theory (i.e., are internal to the theory); and all other causes, which are left unspecified but which are assumed to be distal and to influence behaviour only via their effects on the proximal determinants. In this sense, the TPB is sometimes said to be *sufficient*.

There are a number of ways in which external factors may impact on the internal variables and on behaviour. First, external factors may influence the beliefs that are assumed to underlie attitude, subjective norm and perceived behavioural control. For instance, people in non-manual occupations may have a *greater number* of accessible beliefs; for example, when asked to list the advantages and disadvantages of performing a given behaviour, people in non-manual occupations may list a greater number of advantages. External factors may also influence the *content* of accessible beliefs. Compared with people in manual occupations, those in non-manual occupations may hold different kinds of accessible behavioural beliefs; for example, beliefs about the health consequences of the behaviour may be more common among people in non-manual occupations. Neither of these effects would necessarily lead to a difference in behaviour between the two groups. Only if the total belief scores differed between the two groups would we expect a difference in behaviour. For instance, if $\sum b_i e_i$ was higher, on average, among people in manual occupations, then, assuming that attitude was an important determinant of intention for the behaviour in question and that the behaviour was under volitional control, we would expect to observe differences in behaviour between the two groups. Differences in one component of the theory may offset differences in another component. For instance, people in manual occupations may be higher on $\sum b_i e_i$ but lower on $\sum sn_j mc_j$; with the result that there is no difference in behaviour between the two groups.

Second, external factors may influence attitude, subjective norm or perceived behavioural control *directly* without influencing the underlying beliefs. Such effects would be inconsistent with the assumptions of the theory. For instance, the theory holds that attitude is completely determined by $\sum b_i e_i$; in the same way, subjective norm and perceived behavioural control are held to be completely determined by normative beliefs and control beliefs respectively.

Third, external factors may influence intention directly without influencing behavioural, normative, or control beliefs, and hence without influencing attitude, subjective norm or perceived behavioural control. Again, such an effect is inconsistent with the assumption that intention is completely determined by attitude, subjective norm and perceived behavioural control. However, if the assumption is relaxed to allow other determinants of intention (e.g., anticipated regret, moral norm), this provides possible pathways by which an external factor could influence intention directly without influencing the official components of the theory.

Fourth, external factors could influence actual control. Figure 4.6 shows actual control influencing perceived behavioural control and behaviour. Thus, there are three distinct pathways by which an external factor could influence behaviour via actual control: (1) from actual control to perceived control to intention to behaviour; (2) from actual control to perceived control then directly to behaviour; and (3) from actual control directly to behaviour.

Fifth, external factors could influence behaviour directly, that is, they could bypass *all* the components of the theory. Conceptually, it is difficult to distinguish this mechanism from the preceding one. Actual control is a nebulous concept that could be thought of as including – or being influenced by – almost every factor that has a systematic influence on behaviour apart from those factors whose effects on behaviour are mediated by the other components of the theory.

Finally, external factors could moderate one or more of the causal relationships in the theory. For example, for a given behaviour, attitude may be a more important determinant of intention among those in manual occupations compared with those in non-manual occupations. Or the size of the causal effect of intention on behaviour may differ for the two groups.

A strategy for guiding future research on the determinants of health behaviour is to continue to use the TPB as a model of the proximal determinants of a given behaviour and to specify external factors that are hypothesized to influence the components of the theory or to influence behaviour directly, that is to develop theories that relate external factors to the theory's components. In effect, this is extending the causal model representing the TPB to the left, specifying the more distal causes of a particular behaviour and the mechanisms by which they influence the components of the theory and behaviour. (The causal model could also be extended to the right by including physiological sequelae of the behaviour and relevant health or disease outcomes, thus 'integrating psychology and epidemiology'; see Hardeman et al., submitted.)

The number of potential external factors or distal causes of a particular behaviour is huge. Other psychological variables such as personality factors may affect health behaviours (Contrada & Goyal, 2004, Chapter 6 in this volume). Variables such as age and sex may influence health behaviours and can be thought of as being on the far left of a complex causal model that has the TPB variables and behaviour on the far right. Health behaviours may also be influenced by biological factors. For example, there may be genetic influences on smoking. Like sex and age, genetic factors will also be located on the far left of the causal model.

All the potential causes of health behaviours mentioned so far are located at the (between-) individual level. However, there are numerous other factors that may influence health behaviours that can be summarized by the label 'social' factors. Several different classifications of such social factors have been proposed by theorists who have contributed to the development of what is known in the fields of health promotion and public health as the 'social ecological framework'. For example, McLeroy and colleagues distinguished the following sets of determinants of health behaviour:

(1) Intrapersonal factors – characteristics of the individual such as knowledge, attitudes, behaviour, self-concept, skills, etc. This includes the developmental history of the individual.

(2) Interpersonal processes and primary groups – formal and informal social network and social support systems, including the family, work group, and friendship networks.

(3) Institutional factors – social institutions with organizational characteristics, and formal (and informal) rules and regulations for operation.

(4) Community factors – relationships among organizations, institutions, and informal networks within defined boundaries.

(5) Public policy – local, state, and national laws and policies. (1988: 355)

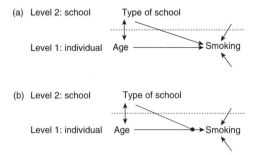

Figure 4.8   *Two-level path diagrams showing*
(a) a main effect of school type and
(b) a cross-level interaction

To many psychologists, the social ecological framework may seem vague and difficult to operationalize. However, multilevel modelling (Bryk & Raudenbush, 1992; Duncan et al., 1998; Hox, 2002) provides a way of operationalizing the framework and of organizing the social causes of health behaviours. From this perspective, the last four items on the above list refer to higher-level units or entities of which the individual is a 'member' and whose characteristics may influence the individual's health-related behaviours either directly or indirectly.

To give a simple concrete example, an adolescent's smoking behaviour may be influenced by the characteristics of the school they attend as well as by individual factors. This is shown in Figure 4.8a. The variables below the dotted line are (between-) individual-level variables including the dependent variable. So, the age of the student (an individual-level variable) is shown as influencing the likelihood that he or she smokes. However, the dependent variable may also be influenced by characteristics of the school, for example whether the school has a strict non-smoking policy, whether it is an independent (fee-paying) or a state school, and the proportion of students who receive free school meals (an index of deprivation). Figure 4.8a shows type of school directly influencing the likelihood that the individual student smokes. Type of school is located above the dotted line to indicate that it is a school-level (level 2) variable. Two error terms are shown in the diagram, one originating from level 2, the other from level 1.

School characteristics may be correlated with individual characteristics. In this example, type of school is shown (by the two-headed arrow) as potentially being correlated with age. In other words, the students who attend one type of school may be older, on average, than those who attend another type of school. The arrow from type of school to smoking is interpreted to mean the causal effect of type of school on smoking, controlling for possible differences in age between different types of school. Older students may be more likely to smoke, and students who attend types of school that cater for older students may be more likely to smoke for this reason. However, the path diagram indicates an *independent* causal effect of type of school on smoking. This can be labelled a *contextual* causal effect, meaning an effect that cannot be accounted for by the *compositional* effect of different types of schools having different kinds of students (in this case, students of different ages). More generally, arrows originating from level 2 indicate contextual causal effects – effects of level 2 variables that cannot be accounted for by the compositional effects of different kinds of individuals being associated with different kinds of level 2 units.

Some causal effects of level 2 variables on the individual-level dependent variable may be mediated by other individual-level variables. To give a simple example, whether or not a school has a strict non-smoking policy may influence an individual student's attitudes to smoking which in turn influences the likelihood that they smoke. Causal pathways may involve more than one variable at level 2 and more than one variable at level 1. One school-level variable may influence another school-level variable which influences one individual-level variable which in turn influences another individual-level variable.

Level 2 variables may also interact with level 1 variables to influence the dependent variable (see Figure 4.8b). For example, the effect of age on smoking may differ in different types of school (e.g., there may be a weaker effect of age on smoking in schools that have a strict non-smoking policy). This is a *cross-level interaction*. Another way of putting this is to say that

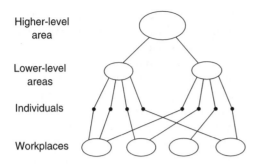

Figure 4.9 *Imperfect hierarchical relationship between individuals and higher-level units*

type of school moderates the effect of age on smoking (or that age moderates the effect of type of school on smoking).

This simple two-level example can be extended to three or more levels. For example, a student's smoking may be influenced by characteristics of the class of which they are a member as well as the school that they attend. Individual, class and school form three hierarchical levels. School-level variables may influence individual-level variables directly or through class-level variables.

However, in general, the levels of factors that may influence an individual's health behaviour do not form a pure hierarchy. For example, individuals' health behaviour may be influenced by characteristics of the neighbourhood in which they live, and, for those who are in work, by characteristics of the workplace. Typically, employees at a given workplace will live in many different neighbourhoods, and the residents of a given neighbourhood will work in many different workplaces. Thus, while both neighbourhood and workplace are at a higher level than the individual, the levels do not form a pure hierarchy (see Figure 4.9). Instead, individuals are nested within a cross-classification of workplaces by neighbourhoods (Rasbash & Browne, 2001). In this example, an individual's health behaviour may be influenced by individual-level variables, workplace-level variables and neighbourhood-level variables, operating additively or interactively. Interactions may be *within-level* (e.g., interactions between two or more workplace-level variables) or *cross-level* (e.g., interactions

between workplace-level and neighbourhood-level variables).

For example, some workplaces may have a non-smoking policy whereas others do not. This variable (has a non-smoking policy, yes/no) is a characteristic of the workplace: it is a workplace-level variable rather than an individual-level variable. Such a higher-level variable may influence the smoking behaviour of employees. In other words, the prevalence of smoking may be lower among employees at workplaces that have a non-smoking policy than it is among employees at workplaces that do not have such a policy, and this difference may be a *consequence* of the presence or absence of such a policy. Thus, a workplace-level variable may influence the behaviour of an individual employee, an example of a cross-level causal effect. There may also be cross-level interactions. For example, the effect of, say, age (an individual-level variable) on the smoking status of the individual may be moderated by characteristics of the workplace: a higher-level variable modifying the causal relationship between two lower-level variables.

Note that there are two kinds of workplace-level variables. The first are characteristics of the workplace that are not derived from the characteristics of the individuals who are employed there, for example, the presence or absence of a non-smoking policy. The second kind is derived by aggregating the characteristics of the individual employees. For example, smoking prevalence among employees at a worksite is a characteristic of the worksite and not of an individual employee, but it is obtained by combining the smoking status (1 = current smoker, 0 = current non-smoker) of all the employees at the worksite.

An individual's cognitions and behaviour may also be influenced by characteristics of the geographical area in which they live. For example, the number of parks and open spaces in an individual's neighbourhood may influence the frequency with which they walk for pleasure. Again, the number of parks and open spaces is a characteristic of a neighbourhood or other geographical area, not of the individual who lives in that area. Geographical areas may form a perfect set of nested levels. For example, in the UK postcode system, sectors are nested within districts, which in turn are nested within areas. There are characteristics attached to each of these levels that may in principle influence the cognitions and behaviour of an individual resident. In general, in a multilevel system, variables at the lowest level (the individual level in this case) may be influenced by variables at a higher level, either directly (i.e., by bypassing intermediate levels) or indirectly (i.e., by influencing variables at intermediate levels). (Of course, cross-level influence may also flow from lower level to higher level, but we are making a simplifying assumption here that only downward influence occurs.)

Thus, the social factors that influence a particular health behaviour at an individual level can be thought of as being located in a complex system of higher levels, some of which may form perfect hierarchies but others of which do not. This framework is individual-level with respect to the dependent variable, that is, the health behaviour of interest, but it is multilevel with respect to the explanatory variables. (It is also possible to define dependent variables at higher levels than the individual. For example, why do some worksites have a non-smoking policy while others do not?)

CONCLUSIONS AND RECOMMENDATIONS

We conclude with a number of recommendations to guide future research in this area. Two important issues are how to manage complexity at both the theoretical and the empirical levels, given multiple theories, multiple causes, multiple behaviours, and multiple target populations, and how to ensure that research findings are cumulative.

First, there are too many theories of health behaviour. More rapid progress would be made in the field if research focused on a smaller number of theories. As mentioned earlier, for the sake of parsimony, general theories are preferable to health-specific or domain-specific theories, although it is acknowledged that a general theory may need to be modified when applied to a particular behaviour. Theories should also be clearly specified with clear definitions of constructs and clear specifications of the causal relationships between them. Health psychology researchers should avoid using theories that are not fully specified. The common practice of 'picking and mixing' components from several different theories (or what Bandura, 1998, calls 'cafeteria style research') should be discouraged. Any study that claims to test or extend a given theory should use a complete version of that theory and should try to make sure that each of its components is measured well. More studies that directly compare two or more different theories would be valuable (Weinstein, 1993); for two examples of empirical comparisons of theories, see Quine, Rutter and Arnold (1998) and Bish, Sutton and Golombok (2000). Some of these aims will be difficult to achieve in practice, though funding initiatives that require researchers to use one or two particular theories would be one possible mechanism.

Second, the field would benefit from greater standardization of measures. This is likely to be facilitated by the creation of a web resource that defines the major theoretical constructs employed in health behaviour research and lists common measures of these constructs, as planned by the US National Cancer Institute's 'Improving Theories' project (see http://cancercontrol.cancer.gov/brp/health_theory_index.html).

Third, more studies are needed that test social cognition models using within-individuals designs in which repeated measures of cognitions and behaviour with respect to the same target behaviour are obtained on a number of occasions. These would allow comparisons between causal effects estimated from within-individuals data and between-individuals data. Where these differ, the former are likely to provide a better estimate of the effects of changing cognitive variables through intervention.

Fourth, wherever possible, predictions from social cognition models should be tested using randomized experiments in which the explanatory variables are manipulated orthogonally and the data are analysed at the within-individual level as well as the between-individual level.

Finally, to properly investigate the effects of what we have called 'social' variables requires multilevel designs in which data are obtained from a sufficient number of units at a higher level than the individual (e.g., neighbourhoods, workplaces, schools) as well as from individuals within units. Ideally, such studies should include a complete implementation of a social cognition model such as the TPB. This would enable mediation analyses to be conducted to examine the extent to which the effects of higher-level variables on behaviour are mediated by cognitive variables. (In the case of the TPB, measurement burden could be reduced by initially using only direct measures of the constructs, that is, by omitting measures of beliefs. If the effects of higher-level variables on behaviour were found to be mediated by the TPB variables measured directly, then subsequent studies could conduct a more fine-grained analysis of mediation using indirect as well as direct measures.)

The data requirements for multilevel studies are formidable (Hox, 2002). For example, in a two-level design, it is recommended that data are obtained from at least 30 higher-level units. Thus such studies are likely to be larger and more expensive than most studies that are conducted in health psychology. In such research, priority should be given to investigating the effects of smaller, more proximal units that are likely to be more meaningful to the individuals who belong to the unit. For instance, the characteristics of a person's neighbourhood are likely to have larger effects on their health behaviour than the characteristics of the region in which they live. Similarly, characteristics of the individual's family or household are likely to have a greater influence than those associated with their network of acquaintances. Where it is difficult to obtain information about higher-level units, one shortcut is to assess social variables at the individual level. For example, instead of objectively measuring the local availability of open spaces where people can walk for pleasure, a study could assess the *perceived* availability of such open spaces. (Where both 'objective' and subjective measures were included, it would be possible to examine the extent to which the effects of objective measures were mediated by their corresponding subjective measures.) Another shortcut is to aggregate variables from the individual level to a higher level. Both the selection of levels (e.g., should we study neighbourhoods or districts?) and the selection of variables to be measured at these levels should be guided by theories that attempt to explain how these variables may influence individuals' cognitions and behaviour. The challenge is for health psychologists to develop and test such theories in collaboration with scientists from other disciplines.

ACKNOWLEDGEMENTS

This chapter is based partly on keynote addresses delivered to the European Health Psychology Society Annual Conference at the University of Leiden, The Netherlands, August 2000, and the 43rd Annual Congress of the German Psychological Association, Humboldt University, Berlin, Germany, September 2002.

REFERENCES

Aiken, L. S., & West, S. G. (1991). *Multiple regression: Testing and interpreting interactions.* Newbury Park, CA: Sage.

Ajzen, I. (1988). Attitudes, personality, and behavior. Buckingham, UK: Open University Press.

Ajzen, I. (1991). The theory of planned behavior. *Organizational Behavior and Human Decision Processes, 50*, 179–211.

Ajzen, I. (2002a). Constructing a TpB questionnaire: Conceptual and methodological considerations. Retrieved from http://www.people.umass.edu/aizen.

Ajzen, I. (2002b). The theory of planned behavior. Retrieved from http://www.people.umass.edu/aizen.

Ajzen, I., & Fishbein, M. (1977). Attitude–behavior relations: A theoretical analysis and review of empirical research. *Psychological Bulletin, 84*, 888–918.

Ajzen, I., & Fishbein, M. (1980). *Understanding attitudes and predicting social behavior.* Englewood Cliffs, NJ: Prentice-Hall.

Ajzen, I., & Fishbein, M. (2000). Attitudes and the attitude–behavior relation: Reasoned and automatic processes. *European Review of Social Psychology, 11*, 1–33.

Ajzen, I., & Madden, T. J. (1986). Prediction of goal-directed behavior: Attitudes, intention, and perceived behavioral control. *Journal of Experimental Social Psychology, 22*, 453–474.

Albarracín, D., Johnson, B. T., Fishbein, M., & Muellerleile, P. A. (2001). Theories of reasoned action and planned behavior as models of condom use: A meta-analysis. *Psychological Bulletin, 127*, 142–161.

Allison, P. D. (1990). Change scores as dependent variables in regression analysis. In C. Clogg (Ed.), *Sociological methodology 1990* (pp. 93–114). Oxford: Blackwell.

Armitage, C. J., & Conner, M. (2000). Social cognition models and health behaviour: A structured review. *Psychology and Health, 15*, 173–189.

Armitage, C. J., & Conner, M. (2001). Efficacy of the theory of planned behaviour: A meta-analytic review. *British Journal of Social Psychology, 40*, 471–499.

Bagozzi, R. P. (1984). Expectancy-value attitude models: An analysis of critical measurement issues. *International Journal of Research in Marketing, 1*, 295–310.

Bandura, A. (1997). *Self-efficacy: The exercise of control.* New York: Freeman.

Bandura, A. (1998). Health promotion from the perspective of social cognitive theory. *Psychology and Health, 13*, 623–649.

Baron, R. M., & Kenny, D. A. (1986). The moderator-mediator variable distinction in social psychological research: Conceptual, strategic, and statistical considerations. *Journal of Personality and Social Psychology, 51*, 1173–1182.

Bish, A., Sutton, S., & Golombok, S. (2000). Predicting uptake of a routine cervical smear test: A comparison of the health belief model and the theory of planned behaviour. *Psychology and Health, 15*, 35–50.

Bryk, A. S., & Raudenbush, S. W. (1992). *Hierarchical linear models.* Newbury Park, CA: Sage.

Campbell, D. T., & Kenny, D. A. (1999). *A primer on regression artifacts.* New York: Guilford .

Carmody, T. P. (1997). Health-related behaviours: Common factors. In A. Baum, S. Newman, J. Weinman, R. West & C. McManus (Eds.), *Cambridge handbook of psychology, health and medicine* (pp. 117–121). Cambridge: Cambridge University Press.

Catania, J. A., Kegeles, S. M., & Coates, T. J. (1990). Towards an understanding of risk behavior: An AIDS risk reduction model (ARRM). *Health Education Quarterly, 17*, 53–72.

Clogg, C. C., & Haritou, A. (1997). The regression method of causal inference and a dilemma confronting this method. In V. R. McKim & S. P. Turner (Eds.), *Causality in crisis? Statistical methods and the search for causal knowledge in the social sciences* (pp. 83–112). Notre Dame, IN: University of Notre Dame Press.

Cohen, J. (1988). *Statistical power analysis for the behavioral sciences* (2nd edn.). Hillsdale, NJ: Erlbaum.

Cohen, J. (1992). A power primer. *Psychological Bulletin, 112*, 155–159.

Conner, M., & Armitage, C. J. (1998). Extending the theory of planned behavior: A review and avenues for further research. *Journal of Applied Social Psychology, 28*, 1429–1464.

Conner, M., & Norman, P. (Eds.) (1996). *Predicting health behaviour: Research and practice with social cognition models.* Buckingham, UK: Open University Press.

Conner, M., & Norman, P. (Eds.) (in press). *Predicting health behaviour: Research and practice with social cognition models* (2nd edn.). Buckingham, UK: Open University Press.

Contrada, R. J., & Goyal, T. M. (2004). Individual differences, health, and illness: The role of emotional traits and generalized expectancies. In S. Sutton, A. Baum & M. Johnston (Eds.), *The Sage handbook of health psychology.* London: Sage.

Courneya, K. S. (1994). Predicting repeated behavior from intention: The issue of scale correspondence. *Journal of Applied Social Psychology, 24*, 580–594.

Courneya, K. S., & McAuley, E. (1993). Predicting physical activity from intention: Conceptual and methodological issues. *Journal of Sport and Exercise Psychology, 15*, 50–62.

Duncan, C., Jones, K., & Moon, G. (1998). Context, composition and heterogeneity: Using multilevel models in health research. *Social Science and Medicine, 46*, 97–117.

Edwards, W. (1954). The theory of decision making. *Psychological Bulletin, 51*, 380–417.

Emmons, K. M. (2000). Health behaviors in a social context. In L. F. Berkman & I. Kawachi (Eds.), *Social epidemiology* (pp. 242–266). New York: Oxford University Press.

Evans, M. G. (1991). The problem of analyzing multiplicative composites: Interactions revisited. *American Psychologist, 46*, 6–15.

Finkel, S. E. (1995). *Causal analysis with panel data.* Thousand Oaks, CA: Sage.

Fishbein, M. (2000). The role of theory in HIV prevention. *AIDS Care, 12*, 273–278.

Fishbein, M., & Ajzen, I. (1975). *Belief, attitude, intention, and behavior: An introduction to theory and research.* Reading, MA: Addison-Wesley.

Fishbein, M., Triandis, H. C., Kanfer, F. H., Becker, M., Middlestadt, S. E., & Eichler, A. (2001). Factors influencing behavior and behavior change. In A. Baum, T. A. Revenson & J. E. Singer (Eds.), *Handbook of health psychology* (pp. 3–17). Mahwah, NJ: Erlbaum.

French, D. P., & Hankins, M. (2003). The expectancy-value muddle in the theory of planned behaviour – and some proposed solutions. *British Journal of Health Psychology, 8*, 37–55.

Godin, G., & Kok, G. (1996). The theory of planned behavior: A review of its applications to health-related behaviors. *American Journal of Health Promotion, 11*, 87–98.

Green, L. W., Richard, L., & Potvin, L. (1996). Ecological foundations of health promotion. *American Journal of Health Promotion, 10*, 270–281.

Hagger, M. S., Chatzisarantis, N. L. D., & Biddle, S. J. H. (2002). A meta-analytic review of the theories of reasoned action and planned behavior in physical activity: Predictive validity and the contribution of additional variables. *Journal of Sport and Exercise Psychology, 24*, 3–32.

Hardeman, W., Sutton, S., Griffin, S., Johnston, M., White, A., Wareham, N. J., & Kinmonth, A. L. Use of causal models in the development of theory-based behaviour change programmes for trial evaluation: Integrating psychology and epidemiology. Paper submitted for publication.

Hedeker, D., Flay, B. R., & Petraitis, J. (1996). Estimating individual influences of behavioral intentions: An application of random-effects modeling to the theory of reasoned action. *Journal of Consulting and Clinical Psychology, 64*, 109–120.

Heise, D. R. (1975). *Causal analysis.* New York: Wiley.

Hertzog, C., & Nesselroade, J. R. (1987). Beyond autoregressive models: Some implications of the trait–state distinction for the structural modeling of developmental change. *Child Development, 58*, 93–109.

Hox, J. (2002). *Multilevel analysis: Techniques and applications.* Mahwah, NJ: Erlbaum.

Johnston, J. (1984). *Econometric methods* (2nd edn.). New York: McGraw-Hill.

Johnston, M., French, D. P., Bonetti, D., & Johnston, D. W. (2004). Assessment and measurement in health psychology. In S. Sutton, A. Baum & M. Johnston (Eds.), *The Sage handbook of health psychology.* London: Sage.

Kenny, D. A. (1979). *Correlation and causality.* New York: Wiley.

Kenny, D. A., Kashy, D. A., & Bolger, N. (1998). Data analysis in social psychology. In D. T. Gilbert, S. T. Fiske & G. Lindzey (Eds.), *The handbook of social psychology* (Vol. 1, 4th edn., pp. 233–265). New York: McGraw-Hill.

Liker, J. K., Augustyniak, S., & Duncan, G. J. (1985). Panel data and models of change: A comparison of first difference and conventional two-wave models. *Social Science Research, 14*, 80–101.

McLeroy, K. R., Bibeau, D., Steckler, A., & Glanz, K. (1988). An ecological perspective on health promotion programs. *Health Education Quarterly, 15*, 351–377.

Ogden, J. (2003). Some problems with social cognition models: A pragmatic and conceptual analysis. *Health Psychology, 22*, 424–428.

Pearl, J. (2000). *Causality: Models, reasoning, and inference.* Cambridge: Cambridge University Press.

Prochaska, J. O., & Velicer, W. F. (1997). The transtheoretical model of health behavior change. *American Journal of Health Promotion, 12*, 38–48.

Quine, L., Rutter, D. R., & Arnold, A. (1998). Predicting and understanding safety helmet use among schoolboy cyclists: A comparison of the theory of planned behaviour and the health belief model. *Psychology and Health, 13*, 251–269.

Rasbash, J., & Browne, W. (2001). Modelling non-hierarchical structures. In A. H. Leyland & H. Goldstein (Eds.), *Multilevel modelling of health statistics* (pp. 93–105). Chichester, UK: Wiley.

Rogers, R. W., & Prentice-Dunn, S. (1997). Protection motivation theory. In D. Gochman (Ed.), *Handbook of health behavior research: Vol.1. Determinants of health behavior: Personal and social* (pp. 113–132). New York: Plenum.

Rogosa, D. R. (1980). A critique of cross-lagged correlation. *Psychological Bulletin, 88*, 245–258.

Rosenthal, R., & Rubin, D. B. (1979). A note on percent variance explained. *Journal of Applied Social Psychology, 9*, 395–396.

Rothman, A. J. (2000). Toward a theory-based analysis of behavioral maintenance. *Health Psychology, 19*, 64–69.

Røysamb, E., Rise, J., & Kraft, P. (1997). On the structure and dimensionality of health-related behaviour in adolescents. *Psychology and Health, 12*, 437–452.

Schwarz, N., & Oyserman, D. (2001). Asking questions about behavior: Cognition, communication, and questionnaire construction. *American Journal of Evaluation, 22,* 127–160.

Shadish, W. R., Cook, T. D., & Campbell, D. T. (2002). *Experimental and quasi-experimental designs for generalized causal inference.* Boston, MA: Houghton Mifflin.

Sheeran, P. (2002). Intention–behavior relations: A conceptual and empirical review. *European Review of Social Psychology, 12,* 1–36.

Sheeran, P., & Taylor, S. (1999). Predicting intentions to use condoms: A meta-analysis and comparison of the theories of reasoned action and planned behavior. *Journal of Applied Social Psychology, 29,* 1624–1675.

Stokols, D. (1992). Establishing and maintaining healthy environments: Toward a social ecology of health promotion. *American Psychologist, 47,* 6–22.

Stokols, D. (1996). Translating social ecological theory into guidelines for community health promotion. *American Journal of Health Promotion, 10,* 282–298.

Stone, A. A., Turkkan, J. S., Bachrach, C. A., Jobe, J. B., Kurtzman, H. S., & Cain, V. S. (Eds.) (1999). *The science of self-report: Implications for research and practice.* Mahwah, NJ: Erlbaum.

Stoolmiller, M., & Bank, L. (1995). Autoregressive effects in structural equation models: We see some problems. In J. M. Gottman (Ed.), *The analysis of change* (pp. 261–276). Mahwah, NJ: Erlbaum.

Strecher, V. J., & Rosenstock, I. M. (1997). The health belief model. In A. Baum, S. Newman, J. Weinman, R. West & C. McManus (Eds.), *Cambridge handbook of psychology, health and medicine* (pp. 113–117). Cambridge: Cambridge University Press.

Stroebe, W. (2000). *Social psychology and health* (2nd edn.). Buckingham, UK: Open University Press.

Sutton, S. (1994). The past predicts the future: Interpreting behaviour–behaviour relationships in social psychological models of health behaviour. In D. R. Rutter & L. Quine (Eds.), *Social psychology and health: European perspectives* (pp. 71–88). Aldershot: Avebury.

Sutton, S. (1998). Predicting and explaining intentions and behaviour: How well are we doing? *Journal of Applied Social Psychology, 28,* 1317–1338.

Sutton, S. (2000). Interpreting cross-sectional data on stages of change. *Psychology and Health, 15,* 163–171.

Sutton, S. (2001). Back to the drawing board? A review of applications of the transtheoretical model to substance use. *Addiction, 96,* 175–186.

Sutton, S. (2002a). Testing attitude–behaviour theories using non-experimental data: An examination of some hidden assumptions. *European Review of Social Psychology, 13,* 293–323.

Sutton, S. (2002b). Psychosocial theories of health behavior. In N. J. Smelser & P. B. Baltes (Eds.), *International encyclopedia of the social and behavioral sciences.* Oxford: Elsevier.

Sutton, S. (2002c). Using social cognition models to develop health behaviour interventions: Problems and assumptions. In D. Rutter & L. Quine (Eds.), *Changing health behaviour: Intervention and research with social cognition models* (pp. 193–208). Buckingham, UK: Open University Press.

Sutton, S. (2003). Using theories of behaviour change to develop and evaluate sexual health interventions. In J. Stephenson, J. Imrie & C. Bonell (Eds.), *Effective sexual health interventions: Issues in experimental evaluation* (pp. 51–66). Oxford: Oxford University Press.

Sutton, S. (in press). Stage theories of health behaviour. In M. Conner & P. Norman (Eds.), *Predicting health behaviour: Research and practice with social cognition models* (2nd edn.). Buckingham, UK: Open University Press.

Sutton, S., French, D. P., Hennings, S. J., Mitchell, J., Wareham, N. J., Griffin, S., Hardeman, W., & Kinmonth, A. L. (2003). Eliciting salient beliefs in research on the theory of planned behaviour: The effect of question wording. *Current Psychology, 22,* 234–251.

Sutton, S., McVey, D., & Glanz, A. (1999). A comparative test of the theory of reasoned action and the theory of planned behavior in the prediction of condom use intentions in a national sample of English young people. *Health Psychology, 18,* 72–81.

Trafimow, D., & Finlay, K. A. (1996). The importance of subjective norm for a minority of people: Between-subjects and within-subjects analyses. *Personality and Social Psychology Bulletin, 22,* 820–828.

Trafimow, D., Sheeran, P., Conner, M., & Finlay, K. A. (2002). Evidence that perceived behavioural control is a multidimensional construct: Perceived control and perceived difficulty. *British Journal of Social Psychology, 41,* 101–121.

Trafimow, D., Sheeran, P., Lombardo, B., Finlay, K. A., Brown, J., & Armitage, C. J. (in press). Affective and cognitive control of persons and behaviors. *British Journal of Social Psychology*.

Weinstein, N. D. (1993). Testing four competing theories of health protective behavior. *Health Psychology, 12*, 324–333.

Weinstein, N. D., Rothman, A. J., & Nicolich, M. (1998). Use of correlational data to examine the effects of risk perceptions on precautionary behavior. *Psychology and Health, 13*, 479–501.

Weinstein, N. D., Rothman, A. J., & Sutton, S. R. (1998). Stage theories of health behavior: Conceptual and methodological issues. *Health Psychology, 17*, 290–299.

Weinstein, N. D., & Sandman, P. M. (1992). A model of the precaution adoption process: Evidence from home radon testing. *Health Psychology, 11*, 170–180.

5

Health-Related Cognitions

KEITH J. PETRIE AND JAMES W. PENNEBAKER

INTRODUCTION

Physical symptoms are very common. If you stop and ask people in the street about recent symptoms you will find most people will have experienced at least one symptom such as headache, cough or fatigue in the past few days. Some people will report a lot more symptoms and many of these individuals will thank you for your interest, sit you down and go through each one in more detail than you may care to hear about. Common sense would suggest that people who seek help for their symptoms are suffering from more severe symptoms than those who don't seek medical attention. However, research shows that this is incorrect. People's interpretation of symptoms and their help-seeking behaviour is determined by a large number of factors aside from physiological activity and symptom severity.

Symptoms and bodily sensations are often difficult to interpret. Is this chest pain indigestion or is it the first sign of a heart attack? Is this mole on my arm something I should be concerned about? Much of the time I seem really tired; should I ask a doctor about this symptom? People have a limited ability to work out what is going on in their bodies. Because of this, they tend to rely on other factors to make judgements about symptoms. Here beliefs and external information can be helpful in deciding

whether a symptom is transitory or serious. The first part of this chapter examines the cognitive factors that influence people to notice and report symptoms and why some individuals tend to consistently report more symptoms than others. Along the way we will also discuss the issues of why some people delay for a long time before seeking medical help while others are quick to visit doctors for minor complaints. In the second part of the chapter we examine individuals' cognitions once they are diagnosed with an illness. In this section we look at personal illness perceptions and how these are assessed. We also examine how illness perceptions are related to managing a chronic illness and whether such perceptions can be successfully changed.

SYMPTOM COMPLAINTS ARE COMMON

Community surveys that ask individuals whether they have recently experienced various symptoms demonstrate, regardless of where the survey is carried out, that physical symptoms are extremely common. In fact, on the basis of these studies it is reasonable to argue that it is more common to experience symptoms than not. Some symptoms like fatigue are extremely common. In general population studies, typically 20 to 40 per cent

Table 5.1   *General population surveys of symptoms*

Symptoms (past 2 weeks)	Glasgow sample, $N = 1,344$ (% reporting)	UK sample, $N = 1,410$ (% reporting)
Tiredness, fatigue	23	16
Sleep disturbance		16
Aching bones, joints and muscles	25	29
Headaches	13	38
Skin problems	15	13
Eye trouble	15	14

of participants report feeling tired or fatigued all the time (Lewis & Wessely, 1992). In primary medical practice samples, the rates are even higher. A recent study, conducted in 1,000 primary practice patients, found 67 per cent of women and 45 per cent of men reported fatigue in the past month (Kroenke, 1998).

Other symptoms also have a high prevalence rate. In large epidemiological surveys, insomnia at least every other day was reported by 21 per cent of women and 29 per cent of men, and 11 per cent of women and 7 per cent of men report daytime sleepiness every or almost every day (Hublin, Kapiro, Heikkila & Koskenvuo, 1996). Thirty-six per cent of primary care patients report headache, 34 per cent insomnia, and 59 per cent joint or limb pain (Kroenke, 1998). The high rates of symptoms are seen in the two epidemiological surveys shown in Table 5.1 conducted in the United Kingdom. These studies show high rates of symptoms such as aching bones, headaches, eye problems and skin problems. Most people only present a very small proportion of physical symptoms to doctors and the vast majority are managed through restricting activity and self-medication (Verbrugge & Ascione, 1987). For about a third of patients presenting with symptoms to their doctor, no medical explanation can be found for their complaint, and for many patients these symptoms are chronic or recur on a regular basis (Kroenke, 2003).

ATTENTION TO SYMPTOMS

The noticing of symptoms is strongly affected by psychological factors. In particular, whether a person will attend to a symptom is influenced by what other external stimuli compete for their attention. The competition for cues hypothesis states that as the number and salience of external cues increase, attention to internal stimuli will decrease and, conversely, as the environment becomes less demanding of attention then focus on internal cues will increase (Pennebaker, 1982; Pennebaker & Lightner, 1980). Most individuals have had the experience that when they have been engrossed in a sporting or other activity they have been unaware of a cut or injury until later.

Research generally supports the competition for cues hypothesis and shows individuals tend to report more symptoms in unstimulating environments than in exciting and interesting ones (Fillingim, Roth & Haley, 1989; Pennebaker, 1982). You can see a demonstration of this for yourself in lectures and movies. People tend to cough more in boring lectures than ones that engage the interest and fascination of the audience. Similarly, moviegoers are more likely to cough in the boring parts of films. Epidemiological evidence is also supportive of the competition for cues hypothesis. Individuals who live alone, who are socially isolated, and who work in the home rather than in paid employment, tend to report more symptoms (Pennebaker, 1982).

COGNITIVE SCHEMATA AND SYMPTOMS

Individuals' beliefs and ideas about illness can also strongly influence the reporting of physical symptoms by guiding the way they pay attention to their body. Cognitive schemata help us organize and make sense of incoming information from our body. There is a strong tendency for individuals to search for information that is consistent with existing schemata and disregard information that does not fit. Individuals also attach more importance to symptoms consistent with a current cognitive schema than other symptoms.

An example of the influence of cognitive schemata is medical students' disease. Here medical students studying a particular illness suddenly believe that they are suffering from the very same illness. For instance, a student studying diabetes may notice that they have been getting more thirsty recently, making more frequent trips to the bathroom during the night, and being more tired than usual. In this case, learning about a disease has changed the way the student interprets symptoms and behaviour so it fits around a diabetes mental schema. A similar process operates when a dinner companion suddenly becomes ill or when someone remarks that you are looking pale and sick. These events may set off a search for body sensations that are consistent with being unwell (Moss-Morris & Petrie, 2001).

A more dramatic application of the role of cognitive schemata influencing symptom reporting is mass psychogenic illness (MPI). In the case of MPI a large number of people suddenly become unwell, often in response to an unusual environmental event such as an odour or seeing an insect. An MPI is characterized by a rapid increase in cases complaining of non-specific symptoms such as headache, cough, abdominal pain and nausea. Symptoms often seem to spread by line of sight rather than direct contact and typically resolve very quickly. For example, an MPI was reported in over 1,000 naval recruits housed in common barracks. All developed at least one new symptom and 375 were evacuated to hospital. There was a belief among recruits that the symptoms were due to an airborne toxin, but air sample testing and laboratory findings failed to support this. Most recruits transported from the scene improved quickly without specific therapy (Struewing & Gray, 1990). Other research has found that MPIs are more common in work settings where workers are involved in stressful work environments and have poor worker–management relationships. Studies have also found that MPIs also often occur in physically demanding work environments

with loud noise, crowding, poor light or high temperatures, which probably create a large range of ambiguous physical sensations (Colligan, Pennebaker & Murphy, 1982).

Both medical students' disease and MPIs illustrate how cognitive schemata can have a powerful effect on individuals noticing and reporting symptoms. Most of the time schemata may work in a more subtle way and without conscious awareness, such as when someone starts yawning at the end of an evening, which immediately sets off others to join in. Or, following the start of medical treatment, when individuals often make a cognitive switch from noticing how ill they feel to noticing symptoms of recovery.

THE INFLUENCE OF PSYCHOLOGICAL DISTRESS

Psychological distress has a close relationship to symptom reporting. The scientific literature uses a number of terms to describe psychological distress such as depression, anxiety and negative affect. Individuals who are high on measures of psychological distress also tend to report more physical symptom complaints in all situations. There is considerable research now showing psychological distress is closely related to symptom reporting but not to organic disease (Costa & McCrae, 1987; Watson & Pennebaker, 1989). Much of the evidence suggests that reports of symptoms and distress are closely interrelated. Some researchers in this area have gone so far as to question whether symptom reports are actually a better measure of emotional distress than health.

Psychological states such as anxiety and depression can make us more aware of physical problems. If someone is feeling anxious, then a new symptom is more likely to be interpreted as a sign of an illness than if it was thought to be a normal response to a stressful situation (Moss-Morris & Petrie, 1999). Distress and bad moods also influence self-reports of health and symptoms. From studies where mood has been manipulated in laboratory settings, we know that people in a positive mood rate themselves as healthier and report fewer symptoms. However, people in sad moods report more symptoms, are more pessimistic that any actions they take would relieve their symptoms, and perceive themselves as more vulnerable to future illness (Salovey, O'Leary, Stretton, Fishkin & Drake, 1991).

Mood is an important influence on the perception of how healthy we see ourselves. This can be illustrated with respect to the immune system. Over the past few years the immune system has gathered increased prominence in public discourse about health and illness. It is seen by the public as the key to avoiding many illnesses including cancer. Many millions of dollars are spent by individuals on products that are marketed as improving their immune system. It is an interesting psychological problem to consider how individuals come to believe their immune system needs upgrading when we do not have direct information on how our immune system is functioning. In fact data suggest that individuals are not at all accurate in perceiving the state of their immune system. In a recent study the perception of immune function was actually unrelated to various immune markers but closely related to mood and, in particular, feelings of fatigue and vigour. The experience of recent physical symptoms, while not having as strong an influence as mood variables, was also important in the perception of immune functioning (Petrie, Booth, Elder & Cameron, 1999). So individuals who are feeling fatigued and who have had recent symptoms are likely to see their immune system as being to blame for their condition.

THE ROLE OF TRAUMA ON SYMPTOM REPORTING

Independent of objective disease, the reports of physical symptoms increase after traumatic experiences. This is seen in studies where large groups of traumatized individuals are followed for weeks, months or years after such traumas as rape (Koss, Koss & Woodruff, 1991), death of spouse (Pennebaker & O'Heeron, 1984), or other trauma (Lehman, Wortman & Williams, 1987). Similarly, studies that have focused on large groups of individuals diagnosed with various somatoform disorders typically report

trauma rates significantly above those of individuals without either somatoform disorders or other problems.

What is it about a trauma that appears to exacerbate symptom reports? One important feature of traumas that is linked to self-reports of health and illness (and even health-related behaviors) is that those traumas that are not openly discussed with others are more problematic than those that are talked about. Across several large-scale surveys, for example, individuals who report having one or more traumas at any point in their lives about which they did not talk reported having higher rates of minor health problems (headaches, upset stomach, racing heart) and well as serious diagnoses (high blood pressure, cancer, ulcers) (see Pennebaker & Susman, 1988). Indeed, these symptom and illness rates were higher than for subjects who had experienced the same types of traumas but who did talk about the events.

One explanation is that traumas are simply biologically stressful and, in some way, result in adverse autonomic and immune function changes that are accurately detected by the perceivers. This is probably true with many cases. However, closer inspection of people suffering from various somatoform disorders indicates that the majority are simply reporting more physical symptoms in the absence of heightened autonomic activity.

Physical symptoms may also serve as a distraction so that people can avoid thinking about emotional problems in their lives. Of all types of information, bodily cues are always available. By focusing on symptoms and sensations, individuals may be able to avoid addressing the overwhelming thoughts of emotional upheavals. A related hypothesis assumes that individuals who actively avoid trying to think about their traumas consistently work to block out trauma-relevant thoughts and emotions.

In reality, aspects of the trauma are continuously processed on both a conscious and an unconscious level. When a dimension of the trauma pops into the individual's thoughts, he or she can suppress the thought fairly quickly. Of prime importance, the brief appearance of the thought together with the work of trying to suppress it results in an emotional and autonomic response. From the individual's perspective, however, the bodily changes associated with the emotional response are not immediately interpretable since trauma-relevant thoughts continue to be suppressed. In other words, the person experiences an emotion without a perceptible eliciting event. Unable to truly define the bodily state as an emotion, the person's only recourse is to label the emotional changes as their components: physical symptoms (Petrie, Booth & Pennebaker, 1998; Wegner, 1994; Wegner, Shortt, Blake & Page, 1990).

Finally, it is important to appreciate that the reporting of symptoms is a social act. By telling others of one's symptoms, the person is seeking help in reducing the symptoms, seeking more information about the causes or consequences of the symptoms, and, in some cases, searching for acknowledgement, attention, or other forms of reward from others. Reporting of symptoms following a stressful event has previously been found to bring stressed families closer together and allow the symptom reporters a way to escape from other stressful situations such as school or work (Minuchin et al., 1975).

DELAY IN SEEKING HELP FOR SYMPTOMS

Many individuals with significant medical symptoms delay before seeking medical help. Symptom delay represents the opposite of the case of the patient who presents to the doctor constantly for minor symptoms. However, often the factors that influence patient delay are different from those that drive high rates of medical attending. Cognitive factors again seem to strongly influence patient delay.

For some medical conditions, such as acute myocardial infarction and breast cancer, delay can have a major impact on prognosis and survival. Patients with breast cancer who wait longer than 3 months before seeing a doctor have a significantly lower rate of survival than those who seek medical help earlier (Raaben & Fossaa, 1996; Richards, Smith, Ramirez, Fentiman & Ruben, 1999). The medical treatment of heart attacks has improved significantly in recent

years with the advent of thrombolytic drugs that can limit the size of the infarct and improve mortality if they are administered in the first few hours. Many patients who die suddenly before reaching hospital with myocardial infarction (MI) do so because of an episode of ventricular fibrillation, which is readily treatable by cardioversion (electric shock). The relationship between delay and mortality in the MI area is not linear but much more potential exists to save lives in the first hour. Unfortunately, there has been little progress in reducing delay time for MI over the past 20 years.

Delay between the start of a symptom and the seeking of medical help is often conceived of in terms of a series of stages with each stage governed by its own set of decisional processes (Andersen & Cacioppo, 1995; Safer, Tharps, Jackson & Leventhal, 1979). The first stage in this process – appraisal delay – is when the individual infers they are ill and need medical help; the second stage is the time between individuals determining they are ill and deciding to seek medical attention; the third stage is acting on this decision and making an appointment; the fourth stage is between the person making an appointment and receiving medical attention, or scheduling delay; and the fifth stage is treatment delay before the patient first starts treatment.

For patients presenting with symptoms of a heart attack, cancer and in many other illnesses, the majority of the total delay period is accounted for by the first stage of symptom appraisal. Some symptoms and symptom patterns are instantly recognized as threats to health from existing knowledge and this prompts earlier help seeking. In myocardial infarction, research has shown that the match between what an individual perceives as the likely symptoms of a heart attack and their own symptoms has a strong relationship with delay time. Figure 5.1a shows the differences between expected and experienced symptoms among MI patients in a recent study (Perry, Petrie, Ellis, Horne & Moss-Morris, 2001), and Figure 5.1b shows the strong association found between the match between expected and experienced symptoms and delay time. Unfortunately many

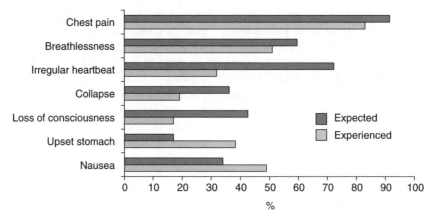

Figure 5.1a   *Differences between expected and experienced symptoms in MI patients*

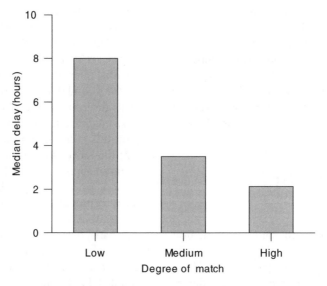

Figure 5.1b   *Match between expected and experienced symptoms of MI and delay time [After Perry, K., Petrie, K.J., Ellis, C.J., Horne, R., & Moss-Morris, R. (2001). Symptom expectations and delay in acute myocardial infarction patients. Heart, 86, 91–92]*

people have an overly dramatic perception of the symptoms experienced during a heart attack. Individuals usually appropriately associate chest pain and breathlessness with a heart attack, but often also expect loss of consciousness and collapse which in fact occur less frequently than less dramatic symptoms such as an upset stomach and nausea.

In the case of breast cancer symptoms, existing knowledge about symptoms also influences delay. Most women see a breast lump as a symptom that needs medical attention, and

research has shown that women who find a lump delay a shorter period of time than those who find other types of breast symptoms such as nipple discharge or a change in shape of the breast (Ramirez et al., 1999). Unfortunately breast symptoms other than a lump also may signal breast cancer but are less associated with the disease by women.

The initial emotional response to the symptom is an important factor for prompting individuals to seek early medical help. In the case of breast symptoms, the emotional activation that

Table 5.2   *Quotes from women asked 'How did you feel on discovering your breast symptom?', with delay times from symptom discovery to medical appointment*

High emotion on symptom discovery
 'I felt sheer panic. I freaked out' (1 day)
 'I was worried – my hands were shaking' (1 day)
 'Scared stiff' (3 days)
 'Scared – I even cried' (1 day)
 'I felt bad – panic and worry' (2 days)
 'I felt a lump – I was about to go to sleep and thought about it all night' (1 day)
 'I was scared, nervous and sweaty' (3 days)

Low emotion on symptom discovery
 'I felt fine' (7 days)
 'I'm not a worrier – sometimes I'm too relaxed' (90 days)
 'Just a little bit worried' (14 days)
 'Just "oh" a lump. I was fairly blasé. I didn't think "Oh my God, I've got a lump"' (7 days)
 'I didn't think anything of it really' (7 days)
 'I wasn't really bothered' (21 days)

follows symptom discovery seems to act as an important motivation for women to see their doctor. Consider the quotes in Table 5.2, which are taken from a study of 85 South Auckland women with self-discovered breast symptoms. These women completed an interview before medical evaluation and diagnosis. Women who expressed high levels of emotional concern following the discovery of a breast symptom tended to seek help earlier, whereas women who were more blasé about the symptom delayed seeing their doctor (Meechan, Collins & Petrie, 2003).

A great deal more psychological research is needed on patient delay. Currently, we only have a sketchy idea about how delay occurs at each stage – particularly the stage where individuals decide they are ill – and how people progress from one stage to another. Emotional factors are clearly important in both encouraging and slowing help-seeking behaviour. However, at present we lack good theoretical models that integrate emotional and cognitive factors to explain delay. There is considerable potential with a better understanding of delay to develop interventions to reduce the mortality and morbidity of a number of medical conditions.

HIGH HEALTH SERVICE USERS

While many people delay before seeking help for important symptoms, another group of patients constantly seek medical care from doctors. This group of patients, who generally do not have significant medical illness, consume an enormous amount of health resources in terms of primary care and specialist appointments, hospital admissions, and laboratory and other investigations (Smith, Monson & Ray, 1986). Psychological factors are important in understanding the development and maintenance of constant medical-care-seeking behaviour and these factors have recently been developed into treatment programmes to reduce the burden of multiple attenders on health care services.

Research has shown that patients who constantly seek medical care tend to have higher levels of psychological distress or anxiety (Banks, Beresford, Morell, Waller & Watkins, 1975). As discussed previously, this factor tends to influence the way these patients make sense of their symptoms. In particular, high health service users tend to be more likely to misattribute benign symptoms to serious medical disease (Sensky, Macleod & Rigby, 1996). Higher levels of anxiety tend to make individuals more introspective and watchful for any unusual symptoms. Sometimes symptoms of anxiety, such as tachycardia, increased sweating and dry mouth, can also be misinterpreted as signs of a physical illness by some patients.

Psychological distress is also related to catastrophizing about symptoms. Catastrophizing is an expectation of a highly exaggerated negative outcome far beyond what normally may be anticipated. Individuals who catastrophize often jump to the worst possible interpretation of any minor symptom – 'this spot must be cancer' – and tend to become more disabled by symptom experiences (Petrie, Moss-Morris & Weinman, 1995). Catastrophizing is also seen in 'cardiac invalidism'. Here patients who have suffered a heart attack or other cardiac event adopt an extremely passive, dependent, and helpless role in the belief that any form of vigorous activity will cause another MI. A hypersensitivity to bodily symptoms means that any symptom such as breathlessness may be misconstrued to indicate overexertion or an impending fatal MI. This pattern often results in a cycle of inactivity and loss of physical condition, which in turn supports these beliefs, as when patients do attempt physical activity they experience symptoms as a result of being unfit. Many patients who develop highly negative illness beliefs overuse medical services, mainly for reassurance about symptoms.

Unfortunately, high health care attenders often fail to be successfully reassured in medical consultations. One of the common expectations of patients attending their general practitioner is to be given an explanation of their symptoms (Williams, Weinman, Dale & Newman, 1995), and for many patients being told that there is no significant illness causing their symptoms is not enough to reduce worry about their symptoms (Channer, James, Papouchado & Rees, 1987). If the symptoms persist or recur it is likely that health concern will again result in further medical visits, as the patient still lacks a satisfactory cognitive model or explanation that enables them to interpret their symptoms as benign. For reassurance to be effective for these patients, the doctor needs to get the patient to outline their views and concerns about their illness. An alternative model of the illness needs to be presented and worries need to be addressed in order for anxiety to be reduced in the long term (Nijher, Weinman, Bass & Chambers, 2001).

MAKING SENSE OF ILLNESS

Once individuals are diagnosed with an illness they generally develop organized beliefs or ideas about their condition. These views are important

as they form the basis for deciding which strategies and behaviours patients will use to manage their illness. Leventhal and his co-workers have developed a self-regulation theory which, simply stated, involves individuals monitoring their efforts and outcomes in managing their illness based on their understanding of the experience (Leventhal, Meyer & Nerenz, 1980; Leventhal, Nerenz & Steele, 1984). This process is conceptualized as a dynamic one, which changes in response to shifts in patients' perceptions of their illness. These illness perceptions or cognitive representations directly influence individuals' emotional response to the illness and their coping behaviour, such as adherence to treatment.

Over recent years considerable research work has been directed at understanding the components that make up patients' perceptions of their illness. Most people already have well developed perceptions of common illnesses, even though they may not have been personally diagnosed with a condition. Illness perceptions can be developed through previous personal experience with the illness, from seeing friends or family who have developed a similar illness or from information acquired through the media. Research has shown that individuals' perceptions of illness are made up of five main cognitive components. Together these components provide a coherent and usually logical internally consistent personal view of their illness.

The first of these components has been called *identity* and comprises the symptoms of the illness and the illness label. Most people have developed ideas about the sort of symptoms that go with common illnesses such as a cold or food poisoning but may have more vague ideas when it comes to other illnesses. However, when diagnosed with a condition people soon develop beliefs about the symptoms that are caused by the illness. The important aspect of the identity component is that the patient's view of the symptoms that are caused by the illness may be quite different from that of the medical staff treating the condition. Often patients may misattribute other commonly occurring symptoms to their diagnosed illness even if no actual relationship exists.

Most patients also develop personal ideas about what caused their illness. This *causal* component is important in some illnesses as it can influence the types of treatments that patients seek out for their condition. For example, if a heart attack patient believes their illness was caused by poor health habits such as smoking and eating fatty foods they are more likely to make changes in these behaviours. On the other hand, if the patient sees their heart attack as caused by stress they may make other changes, such as giving up their job (Weinman, Petrie, Sharpe & Walker, 2000). In other illnesses, causal beliefs can strongly influence the emotional response to illness, particularly if the patient blames him or herself for the illness. Rates of self-blame are high in illnesses such as cancer and sexually transmitted disease as well as other diseases where the aetiology of the condition is unknown. There is some evidence to show that when the patient blames another for their illness this may result in a worse adjustment to the illness, possibly due to unresolved hostility (Taylor, Lichtman & Wood, 1984).

Personal beliefs about the *timeline* of the illness make up a further component of illness perceptions. Illnesses are generally conceptualized as having an acute, chronic or cyclical timeline. As most people only experience short-term acute illnesses during childhood, it is often difficult to conceive of an illness, such as diabetes or arthritis, that lasts for the rest of your life. Perceptions about the timeline of an illness, when they run counter to the natural course of the illness, can cause problems with adherence to treatment. For example, many patients with hypertension believe that their illness is cyclical and that their blood pressure is only high when they are under stress. At other times, when they erroneously believe their blood pressure is not elevated, they often see no need to take medication (Baumann & Leventhal, 1985).

Patients' ideas about how an illness is treated make up the *control-cure* component of illness perceptions. These ideas have a close association with how well patients engage in treatment and rehabilitation programmes for their condition. Patients who believe that it is possible to control their illness seem better adjusted (Helgeson, 1992), more likely to attend rehabilitation programmes (Cooper, Lloyd,

Weinman & Jackson, 1999; Petrie, Weinman, Sharpe & Buckley, 1996) and more likely to comply with treatment (Griva, Myers & Newman, 2000) than patients with lower control-cure beliefs. Other work has looked more intensively into patients' specific beliefs about medication and how this relates to adherence (Horne, 1997). This research has found that high beliefs about the necessity of the medication and low concerns about the negative effects of the treatment independently predict adherence (Horne & Weinman, 1999).

The fifth illness perception component is labelled *consequences* and includes the perceived effect of the illness on the patient's life. This component contains general beliefs about how disabling the illness is likely to be, as well as the impact of the illness on the patient's personal identity, social relationships and finances. Recent work in heart attack patients has shown that illness perceptions measured immediately after admission for a myocardial infarction are related to later disability. Patients who believed their illness would have severe consequences on their life took a longer time to return to work and were more disabled in work around the home, recreational activities and social interaction. Work with patients who have other illnesses has also found patients' beliefs about the personal consequences to be related to important outcomes (see Petrie, Broadbent & Meechan, 2003, for a review).

While the relationships between the various illness perceptions are usually internally consistent, a great deal of variation between patients exists for what seems to be objectively the same illness or injury. Individuals generally hold consistent relationships between the various illness components. Often illnesses seen as having large consequences for the patient's life are also those perceived as having a long timeline and low levels of control or cure. Acute illnesses are generally seen as having low levels of consequences and higher levels of control or cure.

The fascinating aspect of illness perceptions is the wide variability between patients with similar illnesses. For some patients the diagnosis of major illness such as diabetes is a life sentence and the illness is seen as having a great number of symptoms, low levels of control or cure and major consequences on their daily life. For others, the illness is viewed far more benignly. These perceptions have a major impact on the patient's adjustment to the illness. Often major differences can also exist in illness perceptions between the patient and their spouse. Previous research with MI patients has found that when spouses have causal beliefs that the heart attack was caused by poor health habits they are more likely to support and institute changes in the patient's diet and exercise routine (Weinman et al., 2000).

Illness perceptions are increasingly being shown as related to functional outcome in a number of illnesses. For example, in a study of the use of preventer medication in patients with asthma, Horne and Weinman (2002) found that negative perceptions about the consequences of the illness and negative medication beliefs were related to lower levels of adherence to asthma medication. In patients with chronic obstructive pulmonary disease, Morgan, Peck, Buchanan and McHardy (1983) found negative beliefs about treatment and the consequences of the illness were related to 12-minute walking distance more strongly than physiological measures. In patients with chronic fatigue syndrome, illness perceptions have been found to be related to disability and fatigue (Moss-Morris, Petrie & Weinman, 1996). In breast cancer patients undergoing radiation and chemotherapy, illness perceptions have been related to the number of treatment side effects and symptom distress (Buick, 1997).

MEASURING ILLNESS PERCEPTIONS

Patients' cognitive models of their illness are, by their nature, private. Patients may not discuss these beliefs with anyone and are often particularly reluctant to discuss their beliefs about their illness in medical consultations because they fear being seen as stupid or misinformed. In fact, patients are very seldom asked for their own ideas about their illness in medical consultations. When illness perceptions are sought, the patient may be reluctant to discuss their own perceptions of their illness

as they may fear this could put them directly in conflict with their doctor.

Early attempts to measure illness perceptions were conducted by open-ended interviews designed to encourage patients to elaborate their own ideas of their illness. Such interviews have also been successfully used to explore cross-cultural differences in illness perceptions (Kirmayer, Young & Robbins, 1994; Kleinman, Eisenberg & Good, 1978). These semi-structured interviews ask a series of questions about the individual's understanding and beliefs about their illness. The interview may include such questions as: 'What do you believe caused this illness?', 'Why did the illness start when it did?', 'What effects will the illness have on you?', 'What do you think is the best treatment for the illness?', and 'What impact does the illness have on your work and family?'

These open-ended questions provide a rich source of data on both personal and cultural understandings of illness. However, there are difficulties with this approach in terms of the reliability of semi-structured interviews. Often they produce large variations in the quality and quantity of responses, depending on the setting and the relationship the interviewer is able to establish with the patient. Due to the drawbacks of this approach, researchers have recently attempted to develop more systematic and psychometrically sound methods for assessing illness perceptions.

The Illness Perception Questionnaire (IPQ) was the first scale developed to systematically assess each of the five illness representation components (Weinman, Petrie, Moss-Morris & Horne, 1996). This pencil and paper measure contained items designed to tap each of these dimensions but provided the flexibility for users to add items for specific patient groups or contexts. This scale has now been used in a variety of studies to assess illness perceptions (e.g., Horne & Weinman, 2002; Petrie et al., 1996; Scharloo et al., 1998), and it has recently been revised and expanded to include additional subscales assessing the cyclical timeline dimension, illness coherence – or how much the illness makes sense to the patient – and the emotional representation of the illness (Illness Perception Questionnaire–Revised,

IPQ–R: Moss-Morris et al., 2002). This last subscale attempts to measure the emotional reaction of the person to their illness. Leventhal's self-regulatory model proposes that in response to illness and other health threats, people develop parallel cognitive and emotional representations which, in turn, determine problem-based and emotion-focused coping procedures, respectively (Leventhal et al., 1997). Examples of items from the IPQ–R are presented in Table 5.3.

While the IPQ and IPQ–R assess the main dimensions found to underlie patients' beliefs about their illness, in some illnesses they may not accurately identify specific idiosyncratic beliefs that play a role in determining recovery. In the case of MI patients, beliefs about what has actually happened to their heart and how damaged it is are likely to influence their subsequent recovery and return to normal activities. Many MI patients develop erroneous beliefs that hinder their subsequent recovery, such as believing their heart is worn out following their heart attack or that their heart has been damaged to such a degree that any exertion may bring on a further MI or even death (Thompson & Lewin, 2000). It may be difficult to assess patients' beliefs about what has happened to their heart with questionnaires. A recent method to assess patients' illness perceptions has involved the use of patient freehand drawings. Here patients are asked to draw their view of what has happened to their heart following a heart attack.

Patients vary considerably in their drawings in terms of the amount of damage they perceive has occurred to their heart and the location of this damage (see Figure 5.2). Some patients draw considerable amounts of damage on their heart (drawing 6) while others draw only a small amount of damage (7 and 9) or no damage to the heart but a blockage in one or more of the vessels entering the heart (10). Others show both damage and blockages (3 and 5). Some patients see the damage following their heart attack as more central to the heart (1), while others see the damage as more peripheral (4 and 9).

Recent work has shown that patients' drawings of their heart are related to future recovery. While the drawings of damage are to some

Table 5.3 *Examples of items from the IPQ–R subscales*

Timeline acute/chronic
  My illness will last a short time (r)
  My illness is likely to be permanent rather than temporary

Timeline cyclical
  The symptoms of my illness change a great deal from day to day
  I go through cycles in which my illness gets better and worse

Consequences
  My illness is a serious condition
  My illness has major consequences on my life
  My illness does not have much effect on my life (r)

Personal control
  There is a lot which I can do to control my symptoms
  The course of my illness depends on me
  My actions will have no effect on the outcome of my illness (r)

Treatment control
  There is very little that can be done to improve my illness (r)
  My treatment can control my illness
  There is nothing which can help my condition (r)

Illness coherence
  The symptoms of my condition are puzzling to me (r)
  I don't understand my illness (r)
  My illness doesn't make any sense to me (r)

Emotional representations
  I get depressed when I think about my illness
  My illness makes me feel angry
  My illness does not worry me (r)

Causal attributions
Psychological attributions:
  Stress or worry
  My mental attitude, e.g., thinking about life negatively
  Family problems or worries
Risk factors:
  Hereditary – it runs in my family
  Diet or eating habits
  Poor medical care in my past
Accident or chance:
  Chance or bad luck
  Accident or injury

(r) denotes reversed scored items.

degree related to objective medical markers of damage such as peak troponin-T, they seem to bring together in a coherent way how patients think about the effect of their MI. Research shows that the amount of damage drawn on

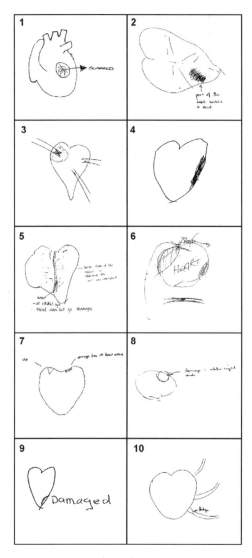

Figure 5.2   *Patient heart drawings*

considerable progress in reducing mortality following the onset of symptoms of acute MI and in the development of medications, the progress in reducing disability in the rehabilitation phase has been disappointing. A significant number of patients do not return to work following their heart attack although they are physically capable of doing so, and vocational disability remains one of the important negative consequences of MI (Shanfield, 1990).

Failure to return to work and normal functioning is often not explained by the severity of the heart attack. It is estimated that in 40–50 per cent of cases, failure to return to work cannot be explained by limitations due to illness (Lewin, 1995). Furthermore, existing cardiac rehabilitation programmes seem to have minimal impact on patients' decisions to return to work (Wenger & Froelicher, 1996). The level of disability following MI in terms of the number of patients who fail to return to work and resume normal functioning represents a significant social and economic cost in terms of lost work hours, increased medical care use, and lowered life satisfaction (Cay, 1995). Some patients following an MI adopt an extremely passive, dependent, and helpless role in the belief that any form of overly vigorous activity will bring on another MI (Riegel, 1993). A hypersensitivity to bodily symptoms means that normal sensations may be misconstrued to indicate overexertion, cardiac damage or an impending fatal MI. This pattern often results in a cycle of inactivity and loss of physical condition, which in turn supports these beliefs and leads to overuse of medical services, mainly for reassurance about symptoms (Maeland & Havik, 1989).

Patients' illness perceptions seem to be important in determining later disability and whether patients will return to a normal working life. Research has shown that MI patients' perceptions of illness, assessed a few days after their MI, have important effects on the rehabilitation phase following discharge from hospital. Studies have found patients' in-hospital expectations of their future work capacity to be a strong predictor of eventual return to work (Maeland & Havik, 1987). Patients who believed that their MI would have more serious long-lasting consequences were found to have

the heart is related to speed of return to work and later perceptions of recovery (Broadbent, Petrie, Ellis, Ying & Gamble, in press).

CHANGING PATIENTS' ILLNESS PERCEPTIONS FOLLOWING MYOCARDIAL INFARCTION

Patient rehabilitation after a heart attack remains an area of concern in the cardiology clinic. While over recent years there has been greater levels of illness-related disability and were slower to return to work (Petrie et al., 1996). Similarly, those patients who had weaker beliefs in the control or cure of their heart condition were less likely to attend cardiac rehabilitation (Cooper et al., 1999; Petrie et al., 1996). In these studies, illness representations were not closely related to medical indicators of MI severity but were more predictive than medical factors of later disability.

These studies raise the question that if patients' illness perceptions can be modified early in their recovery process, can disability be reduced and recovery improved? A recent study attempted to answer this question by comparing whether a cognitive-behavioural intervention designed to alter patients' illness perceptions following a heart attack would improve recovery better than standard care (Petrie, Cameron, Ellis, Buick & Weinman, 2002). A psychologist conducted the three-session intervention while the patient was in hospital. The intervention followed an equivalent structure for all patients but its exact content was personalized according to the patient's responses on the IPQ.

The first session consisted of a brief explanation of the physiology of MI and explored the patient's beliefs about causes of the MI. Attention was given to addressing the common misconception that stress was singularly responsible for the MI, and attempts were made to broaden the patient's causal model by including the importance of other factors such as poor diet, exercise and smoking. By expanding the patient's causal beliefs the session provided more avenues for intervention and future personal control of the illness.

The second session built on the causes identified by the patient and focused on developing an action plan to minimize future risk of another heart attack. This was attempted by focusing on altering risk factors specific to the patient and increasing beliefs about personal control of change in these areas. Highly negative beliefs about the personal consequences of the illness, particularly beliefs about needing to significantly reduce activities over the long term, were challenged and a personalized plan for recovery was developed. This plan included an explicit schedule for exercise (usually regular walking), dietary change and return to work tailored to the patient. The linking of the timeline and consequences beliefs was achieved by explaining that, as patients recovered from the illness, they could expect to return to their work and normal activities.

The patient's action plan was reviewed and symptoms of recovery were discussed in the final session. Normal symptoms of recovery were distinguished from symptoms that may be warning signs of a further heart attack. Concerns that the patient expressed about medication were also explored. The need to take medications consistently and the hazards of relying on symptoms as guides for medications were also discussed in this final session. The normal responses of the spouse and family towards the patient were also discussed in an attempt to reduce dependent behaviour when the patient returns home.

The results of this study showed that intervention induced significant, positive changes in patients' illness beliefs during their time in hospital compared to those assigned to standard care from a rehabilitation nurse. Intervention patients returned to work at a significantly faster rate and had a significantly lower rate of angina symptoms than control patients (Petrie et al., 2002). This study suggests that illness perceptions may be successfully altered by brief cognitive-based interventions and suggests that this approach may be useful in other chronic illnesses to improve adjustment and functioning.

It is clear from the material presented in this chapter that cognitive factors play an important role in symptom perception and the seeking of health care. Cognitive factors influence individuals to delay seeking assistance with symptoms and can also encourage frequent health care attending. Once individuals are diagnosed with an illness or injury, they develop cognitive models to make sense of their symptoms. These models are important in guiding coping strategies and illness-specific behaviours such as adherence to treatment. Illness perceptions can now be assessed by a number of psychometric instruments and new work has opened up the possibility of more innovative assessment approaches, such as the use of patient drawings, to assess patients' beliefs about their illness.

A new area of clinical health psychology is the development of interventions to change illness beliefs in order to improve patient adjustment and outcome. This work and other interventions designed to assess and change cognitive beliefs about symptoms and illness offer considerable opportunity to improve patients' adjustment to illness in the future.

ACKNOWLEDGEMENT

Preparation of this chapter was aided by a grant from the National Institutes of Health (MH59321).

REFERENCES

Andersen, B. L., & Cacioppo, J. T. (1995). Delay in seeking a cancer diagnosis: Delay stages and psychophysiological comparison processes. Special Issue: Social psychology and health. *British Journal of Social Psychology, 34*, 33–52.

Banks, M. H., Beresford, S. A., Morell, D. C., Waller, J. J., & Watkins, C. J. (1975). Factors influencing demand for primary care for women aged 20–44 years. *International Journal of Epidemiology, 43*, 189–195.

Baumann, L. J., & Leventhal, H. (1985). 'I can tell when my blood pressure is up, can't I?' *Health Psychology, 4*, 203–218.

Broadbent, E., Petrie, K. J., Ellis, C. J., Ying, J., & Gamble, G. (in press). A picture of health: Myocardial infarction patients' drawing of their hearts and subsequent disability: A longitudinal study. *Journal of Psychosomatic Research.*

Buick, D. L. (1997). Illness representations and breast cancer: Coping with radiation and chemotherapy. In K. J. Petrie & J. Weinman (Eds.), *Perceptions of health and illness* (pp. 379–410). Amsterdam: Harwood Academic.

Cay, E. L. (1995). Goals of rehabilitation. In D. Jones & R. West (Eds.), *Cardiac rehabilitation.* London: BMJ Books.

Channer, K. S., James, M.A., Papouchado, M., & Rees, J. R. (1987). Failure of a negative exercise test to reassure patients with chest pain. *Quarterly Journal of Medicine, 63*, 315–322.

Colligan, M. J., Pennebaker, J. W., & Murphy, L. R. (1982). *Mass psychogenic illness: A social psychological analysis.* Mahwah, NJ: Erlbaum.

Cooper, A., Lloyd, G., Weinman, J., & Jackson, G. (1999). Why do patients not attend cardiac rehabilitation? Role of intentions and illness beliefs. *Heart and Lung, 82*, 234–236.

Costa, P. T., & McCrae, R. R. (1987). Neuroticism, somatic complaints, and disease: Is the bark worse than the bite? *Journal of Personality, 55*, 299–316.

Fillingim, R. B., Roth, D. L., & Haley, W. E. (1989). The effects of distraction on the perception of exercise-induced symptoms. *Journal of Psychosomatic Research, 33*, 241–248.

Griva, K., Myers, L. B., & Newman, S. (2000). Illness perceptions and self-efficacy beliefs in adolescents and young adults with insulin dependent diabetes mellitus. *Psychology and Health, 15*, 733–750.

Helgeson, V. S. (1992). Moderators of the relation between perceived control and adjustment to chronic illness. *Journal of Personality and Social Psychology, 63*, 656–666.

Horne, R. (1997). Representations of medication and treatment: Advances in theory and measurement. In K. J. Petrie & J. Weinman (Eds.), *Perceptions of health and illness* (pp. 155–188). Amsterdam: Harwood Academic.

Horne, R., & Weinman, J. (1999). Patients' beliefs about prescribed medicines and their role in adherence to treatment in chronic physical illness. *Journal of Psychosomatic Research, 47*, 555–567.

Horne, R., & Weinman, J. (2002). Self-regulation and self-management in asthma: Exploring the role of illness perceptions and treatment beliefs in explaining non-adherence to preventer medication. *Psychology and Health, 17*, 17–32.

Hublin, C., Kapiro, J., Heikkila, K., & Koskenvuo, M. (1996). Daytime sleepiness in an adult Finnish population. *Journal of Internal Medicine, 239*, 417–423.

Kirmayer, L. J., Young, A., & Robbins, J. M. (1994). Symptom attribution in cultural perspective. *Canadian Journal of Psychiatry – Revue Canadienne de Psychiatrie, 39*, 584–595.

Kleinman, A., Eisenberg, E., & Good, B. J. (1978). Culture, illness and care: Clinical lessons from anthropologic and cross-cultural research. *Annals of Internal Medicine, 88*, 251–258.

Koss, M. P., Koss, P. G., & Woodruff, W. J. (1991). Deleterious effects of criminal victimization on women's health and medical utilization. *Archives of Internal Medicine, 151*, 342–347.

Kroenke, K. (1998). Gender differences in the reporting of physical and somatoform symptoms. *Psychosomatic Medicine, 60*, 150–155.

Kroenke, K. (2003). Patients presenting with somatic complaints: Epidemiology, psychiatric comorbidity and management. *International Journal of Methods in Psychiatric Research, 12,* 34–43.

Lehman, D. R., Wortman, C. B., & Williams, A. F. (1987). Long-term effects of losing a spouse or child in a motor vehicle crash. *Journal of Personality and Social Psychology, 52,* 218–231.

Leventhal, H., Benyamini, Y., Brownlee, S., Diefenbach, M., Leventhal, E. A., Patrick-Miller, L., & Robitaille, C. (1997). Illness representations: Theoretical foundations. In K. J. Petrie & J. Weinman (Eds.), *Perceptions of health and illness* (pp. 19–46). Amsterdam: Harwood Academic.

Leventhal, H., Meyer, D., & Nerenz, D. (1980). The common sense representation of illness danger. In S. Rachman (Ed.), *Contributions to medical psychology* (pp. 7–30). New York: Pergamon.

Leventhal, H., Nerenz, D. R., & Steele, D. J. (1984). Illness representations and coping with health threats. In A. Baum & J. Singer (Eds.), *A handbook of psychology and health* (pp. 219–252). Hillsdale, NJ: Erlbaum.

Lewin, R. (1995). Psychological factors in cardiac rehabilitation. In D. Jones & R. West (Eds.), *Cardiac rehabilitation.* London: BMJ Books.

Lewis, G., & Wessely, S. (1992). The epidemiology of fatigue: More questions than answers. *Journal of Epidemiology and Community Health, 46,* 92–97.

Maeland, J. G., & Havik, O. E. (1987). Psychological predictors for return to work after a myocardial infarction. *Journal of Psychosomatic Research, 31,* 471–481.

Maeland, J. G., & Havik, O. E. (1989). Use of health services after a myocardial infarction. *Scandinavian Journal of Social Medicine, 17,* 93–102.

Meechan, G., Collins, J., & Petrie, K. J. (2003). The relationship of symptoms and psychological factors to delay in seeking medical care for breast symptoms. *Preventive Medicine, 36,* 374–378.

Minuchin, S., Baker, L., Rosman, B. L., Liebman, R., Milman, T., & Todd, T. C. (1975). A conceptual model of psychosomatic illness in children: Family organization and family therapy. *Archives of General Psychiatry, 32,* 1031–1038.

Morgan, A. D., Peck, D. F., Buchanan, D. R., & McHardy, G. J. R. (1983). Effect of attitudes and beliefs on tolerance in chronic bronchitis. *British Medical Journal, 286,* 171–173.

Moss–Morris, R., & Petrie, K. J. (1999). Link between psychiatric dysfunction and dizziness. *Lancet, 353,* 515–516.

Moss-Morris, R., & Petrie, K. J. (2001). Redefining medical students' disease to reduce morbidity. *Medical Education, 35,* 724–728.

Moss-Morris, R., Petrie, K. J., & Weinman, J. (1996). Functioning in chronic fatigue syndrome: Do illness perceptions play a regulatory role? *British Journal of Health Psychology, 1,* 15–25.

Moss-Morris, R., Weinman, J., Petrie, K. J., Horne, R., Cameron, L. D., & Buick, D. (2002). The Revised Illness Perception Questionnaire (IPQ–R). *Psychology and Health, 17,* 1–16.

Nijher, G., Weinman, J., Bass, C., & Chambers, J. (2001). Chest pain in people with normal coronary anatomy. *British Medical Journal, 323,* 1319–1320.

Pennebaker, J. W. (1982). *The psychology of physical symptoms.* New York: Springer.

Pennebaker, J. W., & Lightner, J. M. (1980). Competition of internal and external information in an exercise setting. *Journal of Personality and Social Psychology, 39,* 165–174.

Pennebaker, J. W., & O'Heeron, R. C. (1984). Confiding in others and illness rate among spouses of suicide and accidental-death victims. *Journal of Abnormal Psychology, 93,* 473–476.

Pennebaker, J. W., & Susman, J. R. (1988). Disclosure of traumas and psychosomatic processes. *Social Science and Medicine, 26,* 327–332.

Perry, K., Petrie, K. J., Ellis, C. J., Horne, R., & Moss-Morris, R. (2001). Symptom expectations and delay in acute myocardial infarction patients. *Heart, 86,* 91–92.

Petrie, K. J., Booth, R. J., Elder, H., & Cameron, L. D. (1999). Psychological influences on the perception of immune function. *Psychological Medicine, 29,* 391–397.

Petrie, K. J., Booth, R. J., & Pennebaker, J. W. (1998). The immunological effects of thought suppression. *Journal of Personality and Social Psychology, 75,* 1264–1272.

Petrie, K. J., Broadbent, E., & Meechan, G. (2003). Self-regulatory interventions for improving the management of chronic illness. In L. D. Cameron & H. Leventhal (Eds.), *The self-regulation of health and illness behaviour* (pp. 247–277). London: Routledge.

Petrie, K. J., Cameron, L. D., Ellis, C. J., Buick, D. L., & Weinman, J. (2002). Changing illness perceptions following myocardial infarction: An early intervention randomized controlled trial. *Psychosomatic Medicine, 64,* 580–586.

Petrie, K., Moss-Morris, R., & Weinman, J. (1995). The impact of catastrophic beliefs on functioning in chronic fatigue syndrome. *Journal of Psychosomatic Research, 39,* 31–37.

Petrie, K. J., Weinman, J., Sharpe, N., & Buckley, J. (1996). Role of patients' view of their illness in predicting return to work and functioning after myocardial infarction: Longitudinal study. *British Medical Journal, 312,* 1191–1194.

Raaben, N., & Fossaa, S. (1996). Primary invasive breast cancer in Oslo 1980–1989: Incidence and delay. *Acta Oncologia, 35,* 9–15.

Ramirez, A. J., Westcombe, A. M., Burgess, C. C., Sutton, S., Littlejohns, P., & Richards, M. A. (1999). Factors predicting delayed presentation of symptomatic breast cancer: A systematic review. *Lancet, 353,* 1127–1131.

Richards, M. A., Smith, P., Ramirez, A. J., Fentiman, I. S., & Ruben, R. D. (1999). The influence on survival of delay in the presentation and treatment of symptomatic breast cancer. *British Journal of Cancer, 79,* 858–864.

Riegel, B. J. (1993). Contributors to cardiac invalidism after acute myocardial infarction. *Coronary Artery Disease, 4,* 215–220.

Safer, M. A., Tharps, Q. J., Jackson, T. C., & Leventhal, H. (1979). Determinants of three stages of delay in seeking care at a medical clinic. *Medical Care, 17,* 11–29.

Salovey, P., O'Leary, A., Stretton, M. S., Fishkin, S. A., & Drake, C. A. (1991). Influence of mood on judgements about health and illness. In J. P. Forgas (Ed.), *Emotion and social judgements* (pp. 241–262). New York: Pergamon.

Scharloo, M., Kaptein, A. A., Weinman, J., Hazes, J. M., Willems, L. N. A., Bergman, W., & Rooijmans, H. G. M. (1998). Illness perceptions, coping and functioning in patients with rheumatoid arthritis, chronic obstructive pulmonary disease and psoriasis. *Journal of Psychosomatic Research, 44,* 573–585.

Sensky, T., Macleod, A. K., & Rigby, A. F. (1996). Causal attributions about common somatic sensations among frequent general practice attenders. *Psychological Medicine, 26,* 641–646.

Shanfield, S. B. (1990). Return to work after an acute myocardial infarction: A review. *Heart and Lung, 19,* 109–117.

Smith, G. R., Monson, R. A., & Ray, D. C. (1986). Patients with multiple unexplained symptoms: Their characteristics, functional health, and health care utilization. *Archives of Internal Medicine, 146,* 69–72.

Struewing, J. P., & Gray, G. C. (1990). An epidemic of respiratory complaints exacerbated by mass psychogenic illness in a military recruit population. *American Journal of Epidemiology, 132,* 1120–1129.

Taylor, S. E., Lichtman, R. R., & Wood, J. V. (1984). Attributions, beliefs about control, and adjustment to breast cancer. *Journal of Personality and Social Psychology, 46,* 489–502.

Thompson, D. R., & Lewin, R. J. P. (2000). Management of the post-myocardial infarction patient: Rehabilitation and cardiac neurosis. *Heart, 84,* 101–105.

Verbrugge, L. M., & Ascione, F. J. (1987). Exploring the iceberg: Common symptoms and how people care for them. *Medical Care, 25,* 539–569.

Watson, D., & Pennebaker, J. W. (1989). Health complaints, stress, and distress: Exploring the central role of negative affectivity. *Psychological Review, 96,* 234–254.

Wegner, D. M. (1994). Ironic processes of mental control. *Psychological Review, 101,* 34–52.

Wegner, D. M., Shortt, J. W., Blake, A. W., & Page, M. S. (1990). The suppression of exciting thoughts. *Journal of Personality and Social Psychology, 58,* 409–418.

Weinman, J., Petrie, K. J., Moss-Morris, R., & Horne, R. (1996). The Illness Perception Questionnaire: A new method for assessing illness perceptions. *Psychology and Health, 11,* 431–446.

Weinman, J., Petrie, K. J., Sharpe, N., & Walker S. (2000). Causal attributions in patients and spouses following a heart attack and subsequent lifestyle changes. *British Journal of Health Psychology, 5,* 263–273.

Wenger, H. K., & Froelicher, E. S. (1996). *National practice guideline: Cardiac rehabilitation.* Maryland: US Department of Health and Human Services.

Williams, S., Weinman, J., Dale, J., & Newman, S. (1995). Patient expectations: What do primary care patients want from the GP and how far does meeting patient expectations affect patient satisfaction? *Family Practice, 12,* 193–201.

6

Individual Differences, Health and Illness: The Role of Emotional Traits and Generalized Expectancies

RICHARD J. CONTRADA AND TANYA M. GOYAL

INTRODUCTION

Interest in the role of personality in physical health and illness has generated a large volume of speculation, theory, and empirical research. This work has become increasingly sophisticated, both in the types of questions that are asked and in the conceptual and methodological tools being used in the search for answers. We begin this chapter with a discussion of general issues regarding the relationship between personality and physical health. We then review research on a selection of individual difference constructs that have been of particular interest to health researchers, including both emotional dispositions and social-cognitive attributes. We conclude by highlighting some trends and issues that emerge from our review.

PERSONALITY AND HEALTH: CONCEPTUAL FOUNDATIONS

The literature on personality factors in physical health and illness is both large and heterogeneous.

There are three major sources of variation in the nature of this work: how personality is conceptualized, what aspect of physical health/disease is examined, and how the personality–health linkage is explained. Each of these points is discussed below.

Perspectives on Personality

Although something of an oversimplification, it will be useful to consider two contrasting views of personality. One focuses on global dispositions that describe individual differences in psychological activity that are stable across time and context. The other emphasizes more circumscribed personality units related to social-cognitive processes that mediate situational influences on behavior.

Dispositional conceptions of personality

Dispositional approaches have so dominated the personality field that dispositions have at times been equated with personality. Moreover, a particular dispositional construct, the trait, is often discussed as though it were the only way to conceptualize personality dispositions. Going one step further, a single framework – the five-factor (or 'big five') model – has come to dominate thinking about major personality traits (for discussions of these issues, see Pervin, 1994). In the five-factor model (FFM), personality is described in terms of five broad traits, often labeled extroversion, agreeableness, conscientiousness, neuroticism, and openness to experience (Costa & McCrae, 1992).

Trait concepts are defined by their focus on statistical regularities in behavior, where 'behavior' is construed broadly to refer to cognition, affect, and overt action. In many trait approaches, the emphasis is on expression or style, that is, behavior that describes the 'how' of human activity, or a person's characteristic response to the environment. This distinguishes some trait concepts from motives, another class of dispositions, which are usually imbued with the capacity to initiate, guide, and energize behavior. However, there are approaches in which traits are assigned these motivational properties as well. Personality traits can be contrasted with abilities, the latter being defined in terms of maximal rather than typical performance, as judged against some standard for accuracy or correctness. By comparison with expression or style, ability concerns the 'how much' or 'how well' of behavior, rather than the 'how' of behavior.

The statistical aspect of global personality traits takes two major forms: *cross-situational consistency* and *temporal stability*. Cross-situational consistency refers to the tendency for individuals to differ from one another with respect to their average behavioral response across a wide range of contexts and settings. For example, a highly extroverted individual will differ from an extreme introvert in displaying sociable behavior in a variety of situations, including formal and informal gatherings, large groups and small, familiar settings and novel ones. Temporal stability refers to consistency in behavior over time. A person's standing relative to others on FFM traits such as extroversion can be expected to persist over a significant portion of his or her lifetime.

There is a third form of statistical regularity that characterizes some trait concepts. *Hierarchical organization*, which is closely related to factor analysis, refers to evidence suggesting that relatively global traits can be resolved into more narrowly defined attributes, and may themselves be seen as facets of still broader dispositions, sometimes referred to as types. For example, extroversion comprises facets such as gregariousness, assertiveness, activity, excitement-seeking, positive emotions, and warmth. Moving 'up' hierarchically, toward broader personality dimensions, high scores on extroversion have been found to cluster together with low scores on other FFM traits, agreeableness and conscientiousness, forming a more global, 'undercontrolled' personality type.

Social-cognitive process conceptions of personality

The social-cognitive approach takes as its point of departure the processes through which personality interacts with situational factors to influence behavior. Thus, the focus is on the distinctiveness of behavior displayed in different situations rather than on cross-situational consistency. Situational influences are seen as reflecting processes whereby stimuli are discriminated, selected, and interpreted, and cognitive, affective, and behavioral responses are activated. In one social-cognitive model (Mischel & Shoda, 1999), personality is seen as a system of cognitive-affective structures that mediate situational influences. These include encodings, expectancies/beliefs, affects, goals/values, competencies, and plans.

Cognitive-affective structures of interest to social-cognitive models are sometimes referred to as 'middle-level' units because they describe personality at a more circumscribed, less global level of abstraction by comparison with traits such as those of the FFM, and yet are broader than situation-specific thoughts or actions (Cantor & Zirkel, 1990). By comparison with global dispositions, these constructs are generally defined with closer connections to variation in context (both situational and lifespan related), more emphasis on process and change, greater personal relevance, more representation of motivational content, sharper focus on functional aspects of personality, and greater attention to psychological activity that invests everyday life with meaning and purpose. Numerous middle-level units have been proposed, and they have yet to be systematized within a unifying framework comparable to the FFM of traits.

Many of the wide range of middle-level units that have been studied are conceptualized in relation to *goal constructs*. Goals are usually defined as desired or undesired states or directions for change. Several middle-level units are goal constructs that refer to a person's immediate motives and pursuits. For example, life tasks (Cantor & Zirkel, 1990) are defined with reference to goals that are life-stage appropriate within a given culture. For college students in the US, these might involve achieving independence from one's parents and exploring career options. Other middle-level personality units are defined in relation to the *self*. Self constructs have been a part of psychology since its inception (James, 1890). Many refer to cognitive-affective structures that contain a person's mental representations of him/herself. These include self-knowledge (the totality of a person's self-referent beliefs), self-motives (motivational forces that guide processing of self-referent knowledge), and self-evaluation (global self-esteem and comparative 'selves' such as the 'ideal self' involved in self-appraisal) (Baumeister, 1998). Other social-cognitive personality units are not defined as either goal or self constructs *per se*, but are viewed as important determinants of goal-directed activity and as factors that reflect or interact with self-referent structures and processes.

Social-cognitive theory emphasizes a form of statistical structure that differs markedly from the temporal and cross-situational patterns associated with the dispositional approach. The latter assumes that individuals manifest their personalities by responding in a similar manner in diverse settings and contexts. By contrast, social-cognitive models posit that individuals display consistent patterns of behavioral variability across situations. Specifically, Mischel

and Shoda (1999) discussed what they referred to as 'if … then … ' profiles in data gathered at a summer camp, such that a child might consistently show high, intermediate, or low levels of aggressiveness depending upon whether another child or an adult was present, and depending upon the child's or adult's behavior. These patterns were stable over time and across instances of the same psychological situation (e.g., teasing child, punishing adult). Moreover, the 'if … then … ' profiles differentiated among children characterized by the same overall level of aggressiveness. Thus, in a traditional dispositional framework focusing on behavior as averaged across situations, the 'if … then … ' profiles would be ignored as a form of measurement error.

Points of Contact between Personality and Physical Health

Personality may come in contact with physical health in a number of different ways. Of primary interest is the possible role of personality in the development of disease in initially healthy individuals. This idea has been represented in Western medicine throughout its history (McMahon, 1976) and, within psychology, the notion of disease-prone personality characteristics has origins in early psychoanalytic thought (Alexander, 1950). At first, empirical work generated many suggestive associations, but was limited by flawed approaches to measurement and research design.

The cornerstone of evidence to support the role of personality in the initiation and progression of physical disease is a body of work initiated by two cardiologists, Myer Friedman and Ray Rosenman (1959). These investigators developed the concept of coronary-prone behavior, that is, the hypothesis that type A individuals – characterized by excessive achievement striving, competitiveness, time urgency, and hostility – show enhanced risk of coronary heart disease (CHD). Friedman and Rosenman also created tools for measuring type A behavior and conducted research demonstrating that the behavior pattern bears an independent, prospective association with clinical CHD. Although there are unresolved questions about the type A construct, meta-analysis upholds the risk factor status of type A behavior when measured by structured interview (Miller, Turner, Tindale, Posavac & Dugoni, 1991). Moreover, one component of type A, trait hostility, has been identified as the 'toxic' element of the behavior pattern (Miller, Smith, Turner, Guijarro & Hallet, 1996). This work continues to make the most convincing case for a causal role of personality in the development of physical disease.

Documenting a causal role for personality in the initial development of disease is a difficult and costly endeavor (Contrada, Leventhal & O'Leary, 1990). Moreover, it is only one of several important ways that the study of personality may contribute theoretical and practical knowledge about problems of physical health. Once a disease has begun to develop, personality may influence its course and outcome through a variety of processes. Therefore, barring breakthroughs in progress toward more effective biomedical tools for detecting and curing or controlling major chronic disorders such as coronary disease and the cancers, personality will continue to attract attention as a factor in the progression of physical disorders, management of disease, and adaptation to health crises and conditions.

Finally, although it is understandable that researchers have focused on personality as a factor influencing health outcomes, the reverse causal direction has also attracted interest. Physical disease and its treatment may have a profound psychological impact, possibly including effects on personality. The meaning of illness and its actual and perceived effects on self-concept and social functioning have long been of interest to medical anthropologists and sociologists (Charmaz, 1999). Within psychology, acquiring chronic medical conditions and confronting acute health crises have been conceptualized as significant influences on lifespan development and adaptation in the middle-adult years and beyond (Heckhausen & Schulz, 1995). In addition, there are specific medical disorders whose effects on the brain produce marked alterations in emotionality and other personality-related areas of functioning.

Causal Mechanisms

An area of research on personality and health that has seen considerable progress over the past few decades is that concerned with explanatory mechanisms. These fall into two general categories. One involves *pathophysiological processes* whereby personality may influence biological activity that initiates physical disease or influences its progression, course, and/or outcome. These processes are closely related to psychological stress and emotion. The second involves mechanisms that link personality to health/disease through overt behaviors. Among these are *health behaviors* – actions and inactions that increase risk for the development of disease, such as cigarette smoking, unsafe sex, diet, and exercise – and *illness behaviors* – reactions to symptoms and signs of illness, medical diagnosis, and treatment that influence the detection and control of disease, such as delay in care-seeking and nonadherence to medication regimens.

Pathophysiological mechanisms

Discovery of prospective associations linking type A behaviors to CHD stimulated efforts to identify underlying causal mechanisms. Much of this work focused on neuroendocrine and cardiovascular processes. The sympathetic–adrenomedullary system (SAM) and the pituitary–adrenocortical axis (PAC), both of which are activated by psychological stressors, have a number of physiologic and metabolic effects thought to be deleterious to cardiovascular functioning (Manuck, Marsland, Kaplan & Williams, 1995). Chief among these are cardiovascular changes associated with SAM activity, such as elevations in blood pressure and heart rate. These and other biological responses to stressors that may explain associations between psychological factors and physical disease are often referred to as *physiologic reactivity* (Krantz & Manuck, 1984).

Although SAM activation and its cardio-vascular concomitants have been emphasized in the study of personality influences on cardiovascular disease, PAC activity also has been implicated in the development of cardiovascular disease and other physical disorders (Manuck et al., 1995). In addition, stress produces alterations in immunity, some of which involve the influence of SAM and/or PAC activity. Immunologic processes are implicated in the development and progression of various infectious disorders, from the common cold to HIV/AIDS, and may play a role in the etiology of cancers (Cohen & Herbert, 1996). They are also involved in autoimmune diseases in which components of a person's immune system attack his or her own body. Thus, there have been significant advances in the identification of neuroendocrine, cardiovascular, and immunological factors that are plausibly involved in stress-related processes linking personality to physical disease.

Overt behavioral mechanisms

A number of theoretical models have been developed to explain health behaviors and illness behaviors. These models generally incorporate two important sets of factors: (1) recognition of a possible health threat, and (2) identification and execution of action to reduce or eliminate threat (Weinstein, 1993). Recognition of health threats and acquisition and performance of health-protecting actions therefore represent pathways whereby personality may influence the initiation, course, and outcome of physical disorders. Threat recognition requires knowledge about the health consequences of behaviors such as cigarette smoking, unsafe sexual practices, diet, and exercise. This knowledge is acquired in a number of ways, reflecting external inputs such as a person's social network and the media, and internal ones including affective responses, perceptual cues, and neurobiological changes associated with the behavior in question. In individuals experiencing physical symptoms, acute illness, or chronic disease, threat arises from the meanings that are attached to these conditions, which similarly derive from both

external (e.g., interactions with friends and family, doctor–patient communication) and internal (e.g., somatic sensations, medication side-effects) sources. As with pathophysiological mechanisms, these psychological and behavioral processes provide a means of accounting for associations linking a number of personality factors to physical health outcomes.

Psychological stress and self-regulation

The distinction between pathophysiological and health/illness behavior mechanisms is based on the final link in the sequence of events through which personality influences physical health, that is, whether there is a direct mind–body connection or an indirect one involving observable behavior. Although this distinction is useful, there is considerable overlap and interaction between the two sets of disease-promoting processes. For example, cognitive processes such as those that underlie psychological threat are a factor both in the initiation of stress-related biological changes and in the performance of specific health-related actions. Emotional processes also cut across biological and behavioral domains. As a consequence, a given personality factor may influence physical health outcomes through both biological and behavioral pathways. It therefore would be useful to place connections between personality and disease-promoting mechanisms within a larger, more integrative theoretical framework.

One candidate for such a framework is Lazarus's theory of psychological stress and coping (Lazarus & Folkman, 1984), the key conceptual elements of which are *appraisal* and *coping*. Appraisal is a cognitive-evaluative process involved in the perception of threatened or actual harm or loss. *Primary appraisal* focuses on the nature and magnitude of harm or loss, and *secondary appraisal* focuses on available coping options. Coping is cognitive or behavioral activity directed either at modifying the situation that gave rise to threat appraisal, referred to as *problem-focused coping*, or at managing its subjective effects, referred to as *emotion-focused coping*. The appraisal and coping constructs lend themselves most directly to conceptualizing the relationship between personality and biological pathways to physical disease. For example, personality may influence exposure to potentially stressful events or conditions, the appraisal of potential stressors, and/or the enactment and effectiveness of coping responses (Contrada & Guyll, 2001). Through these pathways, personality may activate health-damaging neuroendocrine, autonomic, cardiovascular, and immune processes discussed earlier. The stress-coping framework also extends to health/illness behavior mechanisms. In healthy individuals, disease-promoting behaviors such as nicotine and alcohol use may represent a form of emotion-focused coping. Psychological stress may also influence health-related behaviors such as sleep and diet. And, because symptoms and signs of disease and functional consequences of illness may be viewed as psychological stressors, illness behaviors such as care-seeking and medical compliance may be conceptualized as coping responses generated by the appraisal of health threats.

Another broad framework relevant to the personality–health connection is self-regulation theory (Contrada & Coups, 2003). Although 'self-regulation' has a variety of meanings and refers to a number of different, specific models, these share several common elements. One is the use of concepts drawn from *cybernetics*, the science of communication and control processes in biological and artificial systems (Wiener, 1948). A key example is the *feedback loop*, in which system input is compared to an internal reference, generating corrective action depending upon the degree of discrepancy. Another is the use of *goal constructs*, defined as mental representations of desired or undesired states or directions for change, as the chief type of internal reference (Carver & Scheier, 1999). A third feature of many self-regulation models is a *multilevel perspective* focusing on interactions between phenomena that are otherwise of interest to different scientific disciplines, as where biological processes are altered or controlled psychologically.

The stress-coping and self-regulation perspectives are not mutually exclusive. Each can be used to refer to the same process, as where cognitive appraisal is conceptualized as the perception of a discrepancy between actual and desired (goal) states, and coping is seen as corrective action aimed at reducing or eliminating such a discrepancy. However, self-regulation theory may have wider applicability than stress-coping theory, as it is not restricted to situations that tax or exceed adaptive resources. In addition, its focus on goal constructs provides an explicit linkage to goal-related personality factors, and its multilevel perspective provides a framework for conceptualizing personality's influence on biological processes that affect physical health.

EMOTIONAL PERSONALITY TRAITS AND HEALTH

Emotional characteristics have figured prominently in speculative writings and systematic research on personality and health. Both have emphasized the possibility that personality is linked directly to the etiology and progression of disease, usually via pathophysiologic correlates related to psychological stress and emotion. Such a view characterizes the early formulations of Hippocrates who, in the fourth century BC, discussed temperaments, or emotional dispositions, that in his view were linked to physical health through their associations with body fluids ('humors'). In the time since, the notion that emotional attributes contribute to physical disease appeared in pre-scientific descriptions of cancer-prone personality patterns that featured sadness and depression, and in early psychosomatic formulations such as that implicating anger suppression in essential hypertension.

Below we discuss two sets of emotion-related personality factors. The first, *negative affectivity*, involves individual differences in the tendency to experience negative emotions such as anger, sadness, and anxiety. The second, *emotional expression*, focuses on overt manifestations of negative emotions, rather than on subjective experience. In both cases, we emphasize theory and research implicating these personality factors as risk factors for physical disorders or disease outcomes that presumably operate through pathophysiological mechanisms. Reviews of research linking these dispositions to health behaviors and illness behaviors may be found elsewhere (e.g., Contrada & Guyll, 2001; Smith & Gallo, 2001).

Negative Affectivity

The term 'negative affectivity' is often treated as a synonym for *neuroticism*, one of the FFM traits. It refers to a tendency toward emotional instability and the experience of negative affective states, with facets that include anxiety, angry hostility, and depression (Costa & McCrae, 1992). Although not without its critics, there is considerable agreement regarding the validity of the FFM as a descriptive taxonomy of the broad dimensions of personality, and the existence and utility of the trait neuroticism construct in particular. However, research on individual differences and physical health has only recently come to be influenced by the FFM. In earlier work, emotional characteristics that overlap with negative affectivity, often corresponding to just one of its facets, have been studied in relation to health outcomes.

We begin by discussing health research that involves anger-related personality attributes, much of which is organized around the construct of trait hostility. We then review research linking depressive symptoms to health outcomes, followed by a consideration of work involving trait anxiety. After discussing these specific facets of negative emotionality, we review research more explicitly guided by the broader concept of negative affectivity/neuroticism.

Trait hostility

A linkage between anger-related personality attributes and physical disease may be found in Hippocrates' notions regarding the choleric (fiery, excitable) temperament. The scientific investigation of hostility in relation to physical health received impetus from research

implicating it as the chief health-damaging component of the broader type A behavior pattern (Contrada et al., 1990). In this work, the term 'hostility' has come to have two different but related meanings. In one, it refers to a broad personality attribute involving negative attitudes, easily aroused anger, and aggressive behavior, while in the other, it refers more specifically to cognitive aspects of the broader construct (Smith, 1992). Major tools for assessing hostility differ in their emphasis on different facets of these definitions. Structured interview ratings of 'potential for hostility' are based largely on overt, anger-related responses displayed during a structured interview, including antagonism directed at the interviewer. By contrast, scores on the MMPI-derived, Cook and Medley (1954) hostility scale reflect attitudinal and anger-experience aspects of the broader construct. Although trait hostility overlaps with the angry hostility facet of FFM neuroticism, it is also (inversely) associated with FFM trait agreeableness (e.g., Barefoot, Dodge, Peterson, Dahlstrom & Williams, 1989), whose other facets include trust, altruism, tendermindedness, and compliance (Costa & McCrae, 1992).

A meta-analysis conducted by Miller et al. (1996) indicated that trait hostility is associated with increased risk of coronary heart disease. The evidence was strongest for assessments based on structured interviews. Research examining explanations for these associations has emphasized psychophysiological processes whereby trait hostility provokes heightened neuroendocrine, autonomic, and cardiovascular responses to psychosocial stressors and challenges (Suls & Wan, 1993). This approach is buttressed by findings from a research program utilizing an animal model that more directly implicate behavioral and physiologic responses to psychosocial stressors in the development of coronary atherosclerosis (Manuck et al., 1995). However, there is also evidence to suggest that trait hostility may increase risk for coronary disease and other physical disorders, in part, through its association with health/illness behaviors (for reviews see Contrada, Cather & O'Leary, 1999; Contrada & Guyll, 2001).

Depressive symptoms and major depression

Depressive symptoms include sadness, negative cognitions, anhedonia, and vegetative somatic complaints. Most people experience these states to some degree at one time or another, generating a dimension of individual differences in severity of depressive symptoms. Depressive symptoms are commonly measured using self-report instruments, such as the Beck Depression Inventory (BDI: Beck, Ward, Mendelson, Mock & Erbaugh, 1961), in which respondents are asked to select statements to describe how they have been feeling. Depressive symptomatology may be distinguished from clinical syndromes, such as major depressive disorder and dysthymia, which are diagnosed when symptoms of depression are sufficiently severe and/or prolonged, usually on the basis of a standardized interview (American Psychiatric Association, 1994). Like trait hostility, measures of depressive symptoms appear related to a broad negative affectivity/neuroticism dimension (Watson & Clark, 1992).

Depression has long been implicated as a factor contributing to physical disease. Like anger, sadness is a defining feature of one of Hippocrates' temperaments (melancholic). Further speculation regarding the negative health consequences of depression may be found in the writings of Galen, who, in the second century AD, linked melancholia to the development of breast cancer (Bahnson, 1980). Later, depression came to form part of a pattern of personality traits and coping styles, labeled 'type C', thought to constitute a cancer-prone personality (Contrada et al., 1990).

Reviews of the relevant empirical literature provide evidence of a high rate of co-occurrence between depression and a number of medical disorders (e.g., Stevens, Merikangas & Merikangas, 1995). However, the bases for these associations are unclear and currently the topic of considerable attention. While research findings that document biological correlates of depression are consistent with hypotheses in which depression is involved in the etiology of physical disorders (e.g., Thase & Howland, 1995), there is also reason to suspect that depression is frequently a consequence of illness, and that both depression and physical disease may reflect a common underlying cause. As a result, and in view of methodological limitations of the available empirical investigations (e.g., Fox, 1998), notions regarding the cancer-promoting effects of depressive symptoms and clinical depression must be regarded with caution (Cohen & Herbert, 1996). However, at the same time that confidence has waned regarding the possible causal role of depression in the development of cancer, there has been a sharp increase in attention to the possibility that depression plays an important role in the development and progression of cardiovascular disorders, particularly coronary heart disease (Barefoot & Schroll, 1996; Frasure-Smith, Lesperance & Talajic, 1995).

Trait anxiety

Trait anxiety may be defined as a relatively stable tendency to experience tension, apprehension, and worry. One commonly used measure of trait anxiety is the Spielberger Trait Anxiety Scale (Spielberger, Gorsuch & Lushene, 1970), which comprises statements describing affective, somatic, and behavioral manifestations of anxiety. As with depression, anxiety may be viewed as falling on a continuum ranging from low levels to the presence of a clinical syndrome such as panic disorder or phobia (American Psychiatric Association, 1994). Like trait hostility and depressive symptoms, trait anxiety is a facet of the broader dimension of negative affectivity/neuroticism (Watson & Clark, 1992).

Along with anger and depression, anxiety has appeared in descriptions of disease-prone personality patterns written in both the pre-scientific and scientific eras (Bahnson, 1980). Empirical research examining health consequences of trait anxiety and anxiety disorders includes studies of cardiovascular conditions such as essential hypertension (Jonas, Franks & Ingram, 1997), coronary heart disease (Kubzansky et al., 1997), and sudden cardiac death (Kawachi, Sparrow, Vokonas & Weiss, 1995). Anxiety has also been linked to disease outcomes in cancer patients. However, rather than involving personality assessments obtained prior to diagnosis, this work has more often involved measures reflecting emotional reactions to cancer (e.g., 'anxious preoccupation') (Andrykowski, Brady & Henslee-Downey, 1994). In addition to cardiovascular disorders and cancer, trait anxiety has been examined as a factor contributing to other physical conditions, including asthma, ulcer, arthritis, and headache (Friedman & Booth-Kewley, 1987).

Negative affectivity/neuroticism and the FFM

Neuroticism, along with the other FFM traits, appeared in a number of theoretical and empirical accounts of major personality dimensions during the course of the twentieth century, though often under different labels, such as emotionality, emotional instability, and (low) ego strength or (low) adjustment (John, 1990). In Hans Eysenck's (1967) influential model, neuroticism was one of three broad dimensions of personality structure, the others being extraversion and psychoticism. Eysenck (1967) viewed neuroticism as a biologically based dimension of temperament, explicitly building upon the writings of Hippocrates and Galen. In this model, neuroticism was associated with structures of the limbic system and activity of the autonomic nervous system (Eysenck & Eysenck, 1985). The neurobiological basis of neuroticism continues to be a subject of investigation (Clark & Watson, 1999).

It is interesting to note that considerable interest in negative affectivity/neuroticism has been stimulated by the suggestion that it is responsible for *spurious* associations between psychological factors and illness measures. Watson and Pennebaker (1989) discussed how the tendency of neurotic individuals to experience and report negative emotions may be related to attentional and/or interpretive tendencies that inflate complaints of physical symptoms. This can lead to confounding in research on the health consequences of personality factors that relies on disease measures based either directly (questionnaire) or indirectly (physician's assessments) on the subjects' self-report of physical problems (Costa et al., 1985).

Nonetheless, accumulating evidence indicates that neuroticism also may bear a relationship with actual physical disease (Smith & Gallo, 2001). This includes findings reviewed above in which linkages to objective indicators of physical disorders have been obtained for individual facets of neuroticism reflected in measures of hostility (Miller et al., 1996), anxiety (Jonas et al., 1997), and depressive symptoms (Barefoot & Schroll, 1996; Frasure-Smith et al., 1995). There are also relevant findings based on measures likely to have reflected two or more facets of the broader construct of negative affectivity/neuroticism. For example, Martin et al. (1995) reported an association between psychological maladjustment and all-cause mortality over a 4-year period. More recently, Murberg, Bru and Aarsland (2001) reported that trait neuroticism was associated with enhanced mortality over a 2-year period in a sample of congestive heart failure patients. Caution is in order regarding the interpretation of these and other findings pointing to negative affectivity/neuroticism as a risk factor for physical disease. There are well-conducted studies that have reported no such association, and results obtained for different facets of neuroticism, or for clinical diagnoses as opposed to normal personal variations, are not necessarily comparable (Smith & Gallo, 2001).

Emotional Expression

As with negative emotional experiences, the notion that emotional expression may be related to physical health has appeared in both speculative writings and systematic research. One of the temperaments described by Hippocrates (phlegmatic) was characterized in part by a lack of expressiveness, and early psychosomatic formulations of somatic disorders emphasized the role of defense mechanisms whose hypothesized effects in some cases extended to the modulation of outward emotionality. These and more recent suggestions regarding the role of emotional expression in physical health share a few commonalities, but also differ in a number of ways. Shared features include a focus on negative emotions and the hypothesis that low levels of expression are health-damaging. Differences include variations in the specific negative emotion of interest (e.g., anger versus anxiety) and in the putative basis for low expressiveness (e.g., unconscious repression, conscious suppression, helplessness). In addition to these conceptual distinctions, investigators ostensibly interested in the same construct frequently have taken significantly different measurement approaches. Thus, research on emotional expression has been somewhat lacking in coherence.

Emotional expression and 'type C'

Earlier we alluded to a 'type C', cancer-prone personality characterized in part by sadness/depression and emotional inexpressiveness. In some accounts, low emotionality in cancer patients has been construed as reflecting stoic acceptance or helplessness, and contrasted with the presence of a level of anger considered appropriate and adaptive in patients with such a diagnosis (i.e., 'fighting spirit') (Greer, Morris & Pettingale, 1979). Expressive styles of cancer patients with poor prognoses have also been described as involving low levels of other emotional attributes, such as low neuroticism (Morris, Greer, Pettingale & Watson, 1981), and as containing positive affective features (Derogatis, Abeloff & Melisaratos, 1979). However, it is unclear whether type C represents a unitary phenomenon, and its effects on cancer initiation or progression are unclear (Contrada et al., 1990; Fox, 1998).

Anger expression and cardiovascular disease

The picture that has emerged regarding emotional expressiveness and cardiovascular disease is perhaps somewhat more consistent. Meta-analyses have converged in providing evidence for an association between low levels of anger expression and increased risk of developing elevated blood pressure, a risk factor for coronary heart disease, cerebrovascular disease, and kidney problems (Jorgensen, Johnson, Kolodziej & Schreer, 1996; Suls, Wan & Costa, 1995). However, the magnitude and patterning of this relationship do not support any simple notion of a hypertension-prone personality pattern. Moreover, it is difficult to integrate it with findings noted earlier in which the outward manifestation of anger and hostility was among the most consistent personality predictors of coronary disease (Miller et al., 1996). This inconsistency might be reconciled in terms of differences in the cardiovascular endpoint (high resting blood pressure versus clinical coronary heart disease). Alternatively, it may be that, with regard to anger, both expressiveness and inexpressiveness can be damaging to cardiovascular health.

Repressive coping

A fairly sizeable literature has developed around 'repressive coping', a construct conceptualized in terms of a threat-avoidant orientation that relates to emotional expression. Repressive coping is associated with a measurement strategy that addresses the problem of distinguishing low levels of negative emotional expression from the simple absence of negative emotion. This involves the use of separate instruments to assess individual differences in negative emotionality and threat orientation. Weinberger, Schwartz and Davidson (1979) assessed repressive coping as a combination of low scores on a measure of trait anxiety, the Taylor (1953) Manifest Anxiety Scale (MAS), and high scores on defensiveness, as measured by the Marlowe–Crowne Social Desirability Scale (MCSDS: Crowne & Marlowe, 1964). The other score combinations were taken to reflect truly low-anxious (low MAS, low MCSDS), high-anxious (high MAS, low MCSDS), and defensively high-anxious individuals (high MAS, high MCSDS).

Using this or a related measurement approach, numerous studies have examined emotional response patterning in repressive copers (Krohne, 1996; Weinberger, 1990). This has generated evidence of an association between repressive coping and a pattern of verbal-autonomic dissociation in emotional responding, in which cardiovascular or electro-dermal responses to laboratory stressors are high relative to self-reports of negative affect (e.g., Newton & Contrada, 1992; Weinberger et al., 1979). This implicates lack of emotional expression as a possible determinant of disease-promoting physiological activity. However, evidence of verbal-autonomic dissociation in repressive copers is not entirely consistent, possibly reflecting variations in measurement and statistical analysis. Other research guided by the repressive coping construct has identified individuals with compromised immunological functioning (e.g., Esterling, Antoni, Kumar & Schneiderman, 1993). Moreover, repressive coping has been linked to cancer progression (Jensen, 1987), and an intervention designed to improve prognosis following a myocardial infarction may have had the unintended consequence of *reducing* survival rates among repressive copers (Frasure-Smith et al., 2002), possibly because it was incompatible with a threat-avoidant orientation.

Written emotional expression

A psychological intervention that appears to improve physical wellbeing has generated a body of literature that has implications for research on the health effects of individual differences in emotional expression. It involves the written expression of emotions associated with traumatic experiences. In the original study, Pennebaker and Beall (1986) instructed healthy undergraduates to write either about personally traumatic events, or about neutral topics, on each of four consecutive days. Those in the former condition were encouraged to write about experiences they had not previously discussed. Subjects in the trauma disclosure group showed higher blood pressure levels and reported greater distress, but also made significantly fewer visits to the student health center over the next 6 months. A large number of subsequent studies have sought to replicate this phenomenon. A meta-analysis reported by Smyth (1998) indicated that the health-promoting effects of this written

emotional expression exercise are statistically reliable.

This writing technique has been used to generate measures of individual differences in emotional expression. For example, Pennebaker, Barger and Tiebout (1989) had 33 Holocaust survivors describe their concentration camp experiences. Over the ensuing 14 months, participants whose narratives were rated by judges as disclosing more traumatic events exhibited fewer health problems. Subsequent studies have examined written accounts of trauma for specific linguistic elements thought to reflect processes that account for the health-promoting effects of written emotional expression. Pennebaker and Francis (1996) found that participants whose narratives showed increased use of words hypothesized to reflect insightful thinking, or indicating positive affect, experienced reductions in health center visits. In other studies, individual difference measures derived from the written emotional expressiveness task have been linked to immunity (e.g., Esterling, Antoni, Kumar & Schneiderman, 1990).

SOCIAL-COGNITIVE PERSONALITY TRAITS AND HEALTH

Social-cognitive approaches to personality represent a distinct alternative to the more established trait theories that have dominated the field to date. Of the many personality units that are compatible with the social-cognitive framework, we will focus on three that are of particular relevance to the study of physical health: locus of control, self-efficacy, and optimism/pessimism. Each of these designations actually refers to a family of constructs that differ in a number of respects. We will focus on the most general, or dispositional, versions of each construct, since situation-specific variants are discussed elsewhere in this volume. Our review emphasizes research involving health/illness behaviors, which is reflective of a corresponding emphasis in the literature involving these attributes.

Control-Related Beliefs

A situation is said to be controllable if the probability of a desirable outcome is greater given the performance of some behavioral response than it is if the response is not executed. In research on control and human adaptation, the focus is most often on perceived rather than actual control (Abramson, Garber & Seligman, 1980; Glass & Singer, 1972). In the personality field, individual differences in control-related attributes have been conceptualized in terms of broad traits, such as dominance and autonomy, and in terms of motives, such as need for power. In the area of personality and health, the type A behavior pattern has been construed as a coping style activated by stressors that threaten the person's sense of control (Contrada et al., 1990). Whereas these constructs involve styles, preferences, and motives, social-cognitive theory has formed a basis for conceptualizing control-related personality factors in terms of self-referent beliefs or expectancies.

Locus of control

Locus of control (Rotter, 1966) refers to generalized expectancies about the determinants of the outcomes one experiences. Based on learning history, individuals come to expect that future outcomes will be determined by internal factors, such as their own actions or characteristics, or by external factors, such as chance or luck. As a generalized belief, locus of control is thought to have the greatest influence on behavior in situations for which the individual does not have specific expectancies, for example, those that are novel and/or complex. In Rotter's (1954) social learning theory, behavior is a function of both expectancies and *reinforcement value*, or the subjective importance of the outcome in question. Thus, the effect of locus of control on behavior may be moderated by reinforcement value, such that it is diminished or nonexistent when reinforcement value is low. Its potential relationship to instrumental behavior forms a basis for linkages between locus of control and health/illness-behavior pathways that may influence the development and course of physical disease. In addition, control-related expectancies may interact with cognitive appraisal and coping processes that activate stress-related mechanisms affecting physical health (Folkman, Chesney, Pollack & Coates, 1993).

Rotter's (1966) Internal–External (I–E) Scale measures locus of control by presenting forced choices between internal and external attributions regarding a range of life situations. Locus of control was initially conceptualized as a unidimensional construct, with higher scores on the I–E Scale reflecting external control beliefs and lower scores reflecting internal control beliefs. However, research revealed that internality and externality represent different aspects of control, rather than opposite ends of a continuum. In addition, external expectancies have been shown to involve two distinct factors, powerful others and chance/luck. The I–E Scale was therefore revised to include separate scales for measuring *internality, powerful others externality*, and *chance externality* (Levenson, 1973, 1974).

Research is largely consistent in finding that internality is associated with better health outcomes than externality. For example, external locus of control was found in one study to predict increased mortality in men (though not women) over a 17-year follow-up period (Dalgard & Haheim, 1998). Research suggests that health effects of locus of control reflect processes involving a variety of health/illness behaviors (Wallston & Wallston, 1978). Locus of control also may influence health through stress-related processes. Externality has been linked to greater depressive symptomatology in patients with breast cancer (Gerits & De Brabander, 1999), to significant reductions in immunity among depressed patients (Reynaert et al., 1995), and to increased anxiety in type A individuals (Nowack & Sassenrath, 1980). Despite these and other suggestive findings, interest in the health effects of generalized locus of control has waned as attention has turned to health-specific control expectancies.

Health locus of control

Based on the premise that behaviors in a particular domain would be better predicted by domain-specific beliefs than by generalized beliefs, Wallston, Wallston, Kaplan and Maides (1976) developed the Health Locus of Control (HLC) Scale. The HLC Scale parallels the I–E Scale, assessing the degree to which individuals believe their health is controlled by internal or external factors. Like the I–E Scale, the HLC Scale was subsequently revised to incorporate chance and powerful others subscales as two separate types of externality. This new version, the Multidimensional Health Locus of Control (MHLC) Scale (Wallston, Wallston & DeVellis, 1978), has largely superseded the HLC Scale.

Health locus of control predicts a wide range of health behaviors. Internal health locus of control is positively associated with exercise frequency (Norman, Bennett, Smith & Murphy, 1997), health-promoting dietary behaviors (Callaghan, 1998; Steptoe & Wardle, 2001), and AIDS precautionary behavior (Kelly, St Lawrence, Brasfield & Lemke, 1990). These associations may reflect effects of internality on motivation and intention to engage in health-promoting action (Holt, Clark & Kreuter, 2001). Health locus of control has also been linked to illness behaviors. For example, chance locus of control beliefs have been found to predict delay in seeking care for acute myocardial infarction (O'Carroll, Smith, Grubb, Fox & Masterton, 2001). These and other findings are consistent with the notion that individuals who believe that chance or luck are stronger determinants of their health than their own behavior are less likely to engage in health-protective behavior. External control expectancies do not always promote maladaptive behaviors, however. Powerful other beliefs have been associated with higher rates of medication use in HIV+ men (Evans, Ferrando, Rabkin & Fishman, 2000), and with metabolic indicators of dietary compliance in patients with end-stage renal disease (Schneider, 1992). Findings such as these appear to reflect an interaction between powerful others health locus of control and aspects of the doctor–patient relationship that influence adherence with medical regimens.

Some studies have failed to obtain evidence of associations between health locus of control

and behavior (e.g., Schank & Lawrence, 1993). The fact that much of the empirical work related to locus of control has not taken reinforcement value into account, despite Rotter's emphasis on the joint effects of control and value, may partially account for inconsistent findings (Wallston, 1992). For example, a study of college women receiving brochures containing information about breast self-examination (BSE) reported a significant interaction between health locus of control and health value, such that the greatest improvement in BSE occurred in women with internal control beliefs and high value for health (Quadrel & Lau, 1989). However, other studies have found no effect of health value on the relationship between health locus of control and health behaviors (Norman et al., 1997; Steptoe & Wardle, 2001).

Another strategy for increasing predictive precision has been the use of disease-specific versions of the MHLC Scale. In order to do so without proliferating noncomparable instruments, a generic version of the MHLC Scale was created, called Form C (Wallston, Stein & Smith, 1994), which can be adapted for any disease by simply replacing the word 'condition' in each item with the appropriate word or phrase. Although Form C is based on the MHLC Scale, it represents a relatively situation- specific form of control. Specific forms of perceived control have also been shown to predict health-related behaviors (Ziff, Conrad & Lachman, 1995), health outcomes (Mahler & Kulik, 1990), and adaptation to disease (Moser & Dracup, 1995).

An important issue in the study of control is whether perceptions of control are adaptive in situations that are objectively uncontrollable. Results of several studies suggest that perceived control may not be adaptive in such situations, and can actually be detrimental. For example, control beliefs were unrelated to depressive symptoms in end-stage renal disease patients who had never experienced a failed liver transplant. Among patients who had previously experienced a failed transplant, however, greater perceived disease controllability (by self or powerful others) was associated with greater depressive symptomatology, suggesting that disconfirmed beliefs about control may undermine psychological wellbeing (Christensen, Turner, Smith, Holman & Gregory, 1991). Similarly, greater levels of perceived control over disease course were associated with poorer psychosocial adjustment in rheumatoid arthritis patients with more severe disease, reflecting less objective controllability, although control predicted better adjustment overall (Affleck, Tennen, Pfeiffer & Fifield, 1987). It also has been reported that measures of a related concept, desire for control, were predictive of greater suppression of immunity following exposure to an uncontrollable (noise) stressor (Sieber et al., 1992).

These studies suggest that perceptions of control may only be adaptive when some degree of control is possible. However, other research has demonstrated beneficial effects of perceived control even in situations that lack objective control. An interaction between control and physical functioning has been reported such that high control was more strongly positively associated with adjustment in cancer patients with low physical functioning than in better functioning patients (Thompson, Sobolow-Shubin, Galbraith, Schwankovsky & Cruzen, 1993). Whereas these studies each involve situation-specific perceptions of control, the same issue may be relevant to dispositional forms of control. Is an internal locus of control adaptive when an individual is faced with a situation that cannot be controlled by internal factors? This question, which has yet to be resolved, calls attention to the importance of considering situational factors when studying locus of control.

Beliefs about Efficacy

Efficacy is concerned with agency, or the degree to which the individual is capable of exerting control over outcomes. Although it bears a resemblance to locus of control, the differences are significant. Efficacy expectations form a key component of Bandura's (1977) influential social-cognitive theory, in which they are the strongest determinants of behavior. Efficacy has been conceptualized in terms of situation-specific beliefs as well

as more global dispositions. Numerous constructs have been proposed to capture different aspects of generalized self-efficacy, including mastery, perceived competence, and hope.

Self-efficacy

Bandura defined self-efficacy as 'beliefs in one's capabilities to organize and execute the courses of action required to produce given attainments' (1993: 3). He describes three dimensions of self-efficacy expectancies: *magnitude*, or the level of performance an individual believes he or she is capable of; *strength*, or the degree of confidence an individual has in his or her ability to perform a behavior; and *generality*, or the degree to which the efficacy belief applies to one or more specific behaviors or domains. Bandura proposed that behavioral intent is determined by self-efficacy expectancies along with *outcome expectancies*, the latter representing an individual's belief about the degree to which a given behavior, if performed competently, will lead to a desired outcome. That is, an individual will be most likely to attempt a behavior if he or she believes both that the behavior will have a particular desired effect, and that he or she is capable of performing the behavior. In addition, the degree and persistence of effort put forth in attempting a behavior are believed to be influenced by self-efficacy expectancies.

Self-efficacy is related to internal locus of control in that both concern beliefs about the consequences of behavior. However, an internal locus of control orientation links behaviors to outcomes ('Actions determine outcomes') without necessarily linking the self to effective behavior ('I may or may not be capable of performing the action in question'). Accordingly, it has been suggested that locus of control and reinforcement value moderate efficacy expectancies, and that, to predict actual behavior, three-way interactions among these factors should be considered (Wallston, 2001). Specifically, Wallston suggested that self-efficacy will only be predictive for individuals who highly value their health and hold internal health locus of control beliefs.

Generalized self-efficacy

While self-efficacy as conceptualized by Bandura is strictly situation-specific, it also has been conceptualized as a stable, trait-like disposition. The latter, often referred to as generalized self-efficacy, is defined as a global belief regarding one's ability to perform a wide range of behaviors across a wide range of situations. Bandura does note that the specificity of efficacy beliefs is variable, and that some experiences can foster a sense of efficacy that generalizes beyond the original situation. Indeed, Bandura, Adams, Hardy and Howells (1980) found that changes in self-efficacy beliefs produced by mastery experiences in one situation generalized to other, similar situations. However, this does not necessarily support dispositional constructs such as generalized self-efficacy. Although he has acknowledged that domain-specific efficacy expectancies have some value for predicting behaviors in similar domains, Bandura continues to oppose dispositional or trait-like formulations of self-efficacy, and claims that any predictive value of such measures can be attributed to vagueness in both global efficacy and the outcome being examined (Bandura, 1997).

Sherer et al. (1982), on the other hand, have suggested that experiences with success and failure that are attributed to the self will produce a generalized sense of self-efficacy that operates in subsequent situations, whether related or unrelated to the original situations. To assess individual differences in generalized efficacy expectancies, they developed the Self-Efficacy Scale. Others have also developed measures of generalized self-efficacy (Schwarzer, 1992; Tipton & Worthington, 1984). Although specific and general forms of self-efficacy are moderately correlated, it is unclear whether aggregating specific self-efficacy expectancies for multiple behaviors and/or domains is equivalent to generalized self-efficacy. Indeed, there is evidence that they operate independently of one another (Wang & Richarde, 1988), and it has been suggested that generalized self-efficacy may be a better predictor of behavior in unfamiliar or ambiguous situations,

while situation-specific self-efficacy may be more predictive in situations in which an individual has had prior experience.

A number of other constructs have been proposed to assess generalized efficacy expectancies. 'Mastery' and 'perceived competence' are labels that appear to refer to the same construct and are often used interchangeably. They reflect an individual's self-assessed ability to interact effectively with the environment, and have been measured with instruments such as a perceived competence scale described by Smith, Dobbins and Wallston (1991), and the Pearlin and Schooler (1978) Self-Mastery Scale. In addition, the Perceived Health Competence Scale (Smith, Wallston & Smith, 1995) assesses a mid-level efficacy construct with reference to the domain of physical health. This scale combines measures of behavioral expectancies and outcome expectancies, and, like the MHLC Scale, can be tailored to specific medical conditions.

Generalized efficacy expectancies may be linked to physical health through effects on health behaviors (Waller & Bates, 1992), and may also influence cognitive appraisal and coping processes, thereby buffering the effects of stressors on health-damaging physiological activity (Jerusalem & Schwarzer, 1992). The vast majority of self-efficacy studies have focused on situation-specific efficacy expectancies. However, there is some work examining individual differences in generalized efficacy expectancies in relation to health behavior and adaptation to disease. For example, higher generalized self-efficacy assessed prior to heart surgery has been linked to better quality of life 6 months following surgery (Schwarzer & Schroder, 1997). Generalized self-efficacy also has been found to correlate positively with emotional adjustment and quality of life in patients with epilepsy (Gramstad, Iverson & Engelsen, 2001).

Perceived competence has been shown to predict health-promoting behavior, in some cases even more strongly than health locus of control (Pender, Walker, Sechrist & Frank-Stromborg, 1990). It also has been shown to mediate the effects of social and psychological factors on depression and life satisfaction in patients with rheumatoid arthritis (Smith et al., 1991). Self-mastery has been associated with fewer self-reported health problems and better self-assessed physical health (Marshall, 1991), as well as with better health-related quality of life (Kempen, Jelicic & Ormel, 1997). Mastery and generalized self-efficacy have both predicted lower levels of psychological distress in older adults, and also have partially mediated the effects of chronic medical conditions on distress (Ormel et al., 1997). Finally, perceived coping self-efficacy has been shown to predict better health behaviors (Schwarzer & Renner, 2000) and improved physiological responses to stressors (Bandura, Taylor, Williams, Mefford & Barchas, 1985; Wiedenfeld et al., 1990).

Optimism, Pessimism, Explanatory Style, and Hope

Several constructs have been proposed to conceptualize individual differences in generalized expectancies for positive versus negative outcomes, including dispositional optimism, optimistic explanatory style, and trait hope. Although these constructs are closely related, each has unique features and reflects a somewhat different form or aspect of optimism.

Dispositional optimism

Dispositional optimism refers to a generalized expectation that good things, as opposed to bad, will happen in the future. Of the social-cognitive constructs discussed in this chapter, dispositional optimism is the most general in that it involves expectations about future outcomes without specific regard for how these outcomes come to pass. This contrasts with both locus of control and generalized self-efficacy which, as we have seen, both involve expectations about the causes of outcomes.

Dispositional optimism was introduced by Scheier and Carver (1985) as a component of behavioral self-regulation theory, which conceptualizes goal-directed behavior in terms of a feedback system involving ongoing assessment of goal attainment. Within this framework, when a discrepancy is perceived between a goal and current conditions, expectancies regarding

the prospects for a reduction in the magnitude of the discrepancy are an important determinant of subsequent efforts to attain the goal. Individuals who are optimistic therefore are expected to initiate active, engaged forms of coping in such situations, whereas those who are pessimistic are expected to disengage or to use avoidant forms of coping.

The instrument most commonly used to assess dispositional optimism is the Life Orientation Test (LOT: Scheier & Carver, 1985), a self-report questionnaire. Items inquire about general expectations for positive and negative future events. More recently, a revised version of the LOT was developed (LOT–R: Scheier, Carver & Bridges, 1994). Evidence for the reliability and validity of both versions of the LOT was reviewed by Scheier et al. (1994).

A major criticism of the dispositional optimism construct involves its relationship with neuroticism or negative affectivity. The LOT is moderately correlated with neuroticism, in some cases showing a stronger association than it does with other measures of optimism (Smith, Pope, Rhodewalt & Poulton, 1989). Further, a number of associations between optimism and reports of physical symptoms were substantially reduced or eliminated when neuroticism or negative affectivity were controlled statistically (Robbins, Spence & Clark, 1991; Smith et al., 1989), suggesting that these effects may be attributable to neuroticism rather than optimism. However, studies using other, more objective outcome measures have demonstrated effects of optimism that are independent of neuroticism or negative affectivity (e.g., Scheier et al., 1989, 1999).

Although the LOT was originally believed to measure a single dimension, factor analyses (Marshall, Wortman, Kusulas, Hervig & Vickers, 1992; Robinson-Whelen, Kim, MacCallum & Kiecolt-Glaser, 1997) indicate two related but separable factors, optimism and pessimism, corresponding to positively and negatively worded items. These subscales are typically only moderately correlated, and in addition, have been differentially associated with health outcomes (Lai, 1994; Mahler & Kulik, 2000; Schulz, Bookwala, Knapp, Scheier &

Williamson, 1996). These findings suggest that pessimism may not simply be the absence of optimism, though there is no consistent pattern regarding the differential health effects of optimism and pessimism when measured separately. What is clear is that global expectations for good and bad outcomes are not mutually exclusive. Apparently, a person can be optimistic about certain goals or outcomes, and pessimistic about others, and these expectancies may influence health in different ways.

Dispositional optimism and pessimism have been found to predict a number of physical health outcomes. For example, optimism was associated with a reduced risk of perioperative myocardial infarction, better physical recovery, and lower rates of rehospitalization in patients undergoing heart surgery (Scheier et al., 1989, 1999). In one of the first studies to examine health effects of optimism and pessimism separately, pessimism interacted with age to predict 8-month mortality among younger cancer patients (aged 30–59), but not older cancer patients (aged 60 and over) (Schulz et al., 1996). In contrast, optimism was not related to mortality in this study. Dispositional optimism also appears to be predictive of adaptation to disease. Longitudinal studies have found that optimism predicts lower levels of distress in HIV+ and HIV− gay men (Taylor et al., 1992), and in patients undergoing breast cancer surgery (Carver et al., 1993). Optimists also report better quality of life than pessimists following heart surgery (Scheier et al., 1989).

Potential mechanisms for these associations are thought to involve coping activity. The more active, engaged coping strategies of optimists may modulate psychological and physiologic responses to stressors that influence physical health (Carver et al., 1993; Scheier et al., 1989). In support of this notion, optimism has been associated with lower diastolic blood pressure in healthy adults (Räikkönen, Matthews, Flory, Owens & Gump, 1999), and with lower diastolic blood pressure reactivity to stress (Williams, Riels & Roper, 1990). Behavioral factors represent an additional pathway by which optimism may influence physical health. In patients with heart disease, optimism has been associated with health-promoting behaviors related to diet and exercise (Shepperd, Maroto & Pbert, 1996). Optimism has also been associated with less substance abuse among pregnant women (Park, Moore, Turner & Adler, 1997), and with reduced likelihood of dropout from an alcohol treatment program (Strack, Carver & Blaney, 1987).

Explanatory style

Optimism has also been conceptualized as an explanatory style (Peterson & Seligman, 1984) related to the attributional reformulation of learned helplessness theory (Abramson, Seligman & Teasdale, 1978). When individuals encounter uncontrollable circumstances, they ask why. Their attributions regarding the nature of the causes of events influence expectations about the future and subsequent helplessness. The causes of negative events are evaluated along three dimensions: *internality*, the degree to which a person perceives the cause as involving characteristics of the self; *stability*, the degree to which an individual perceives the cause as remaining constant over time; and *globality*, the degree to which an individual perceives the cause as having influence across different situations. Overall, an individual who tends to attribute negative events to external, unstable, and specific causes is characterized as having an optimistic explanatory style, whereas an individual who tends to attribute negative events to internal, stable, and global causes is characterized as having a pessimistic explanatory style.

There are two major approaches to measuring explanatory style. The first is the Attributional Style Questionnaire (ASQ: Peterson et al., 1982), a self-report instrument that inquires about the perceived causes of six hypothetical negative events. Respondents are asked to imagine that each event has happened, to identify its one major cause, and to rate the cause in terms of internality, stability, and globality. The more recently developed Expanded Attributional Style Questionnaire (EASQ: Peterson & Villanova, 1988) includes 24 negative events, and no longer inquires about positive events. The second major approach to assessing explanatory style is the

Content Analysis of Verbatim Explanation (CAVE) technique (Peterson, Luborsky & Seligman, 1983), which involves content coding of verbal material describing actual events experienced by respondents. Researchers identify good or bad events described in the material, and then identify causal explanations based in part on phrases such as 'because' or 'as a result of'. Causes are then rated for internality, stability, and globality. The reliability and validity of both of these assessment strategies have been reviewed by Peterson and Seligman (1987) and by Peterson, Maier and Seligman (1993).

Individual differences in explanatory style appear related to various indicators of physical health. Longitudinal studies have found that a pessimistic explanatory style predicts self-reported illnesses (Lin & Peterson, 1990; Peterson & Seligman, 1987) and doctor visits (Peterson & Seligman, 1987). Similarly, a 35-year study using the CAVE technique found that individuals with a pessimistic explanatory style experienced poorer physician-assessed physical health over time (Peterson, Seligman & Vaillant, 1988). A pessimistic explanatory style is believed to promote feelings of helplessness and lack of efficacy. These feelings may in turn influence behavioral and physiologic activity through differences in coping strategies, much as is thought to occur with dispositional optimism. With regard to health-damaging mechanisms, a pessimistic explanatory style has been shown to predict poorer immune functioning (Kamen-Siegel, Rodin, Seligman & Dwyer, 1991) as well as decreased likelihood of engaging in adaptive illness behaviors (Lin & Peterson, 1990).

Trait hope

Another construct related to optimism is hope. As conceptualized by Snyder et al. (1991), hope is a generalized, stable disposition consisting of two major components: *agency*, which refers to a sense of determination regarding the successful attainment of past, present, and future goals; and *pathways*, which refers to the perceived availability of plans or strategies for attaining goals. Snyder et al. (1991) compare agency to self-efficacy, whereas the pathways notion bears a similarity to outcome expectancies. Like dispositional optimism, hope is thought to influence the selection and attainment of goals, with goal attainment partially mediated by coping activity. However, the interaction of efficacy expectancies and outcome expectancies distinguishes this construct from others such as dispositional optimism or generalized self-efficacy, which involve only one or the other type of expectancy. Snyder and colleagues assert that the reciprocal relationship between agency and pathways is a more powerful predictor of behavior than either efficacy or outcome expectancies alone.

Trait hope is assessed with the Hope Scale (Snyder et al., 1991), a self-report questionnaire comprising four items that assess general beliefs about agency, and four items that assess general beliefs about pathways. As measured by this scale, trait hope has been shown to be related to but separable from similar constructs such as optimism, self-esteem, and generalized self-efficacy (Magaletta & Oliver, 1999; Snyder et al., 1991). Although this relatively new scale has not yet been investigated extensively with regard to physical health, there is evidence that low trait hope is associated with poorer physical health outcomes. For example, measures of hopelessness have been shown to prospectively predict mortality, as well as incidence of coronary disease and cancer (Anda et al., 1993; Everson et al., 1996).

CONCLUSIONS

Our review is based on only a subset of relevant personality attributes and empirical findings. Nonetheless, it supports the conclusion that personality factors are plausibly involved in the development, course, and outcome of physical disease. It also points to a number of trends and issues in the available literature. Three of these pertain to the nature and breadth of personality units, the linkage between personality and disease-promoting mechanisms, and the potential value of a broad theoretical framework.

Nature and Breadth of Personality Units

Older research and studies seeking to identify factors contributing to the development of disease in healthy individuals have tended to focus on broad, emotion-related personality dispositions. More recent work, particularly that examining health-related behavioral processes, has tended to make use of narrower expectancy constructs. This naturally raises questions about cross-cutting relationships: how relevant are broad emotional constructs to health/illness behaviors, and what is the relationship between individual differences in expectancies and the incidence of slowly developing diseases? Although there is research to address these issues (see Contrada et al., 1990; Smith & Gallo, 2001), these questions do identify gaps in current knowledge. They also point to issues concerning the relationships between broad personality dispositions and more situationally defined personality factors that call for more integrative conceptual models (Contrada et al., 1999).

Pathogenic Mechanisms

Identification of specific causal mechanisms has significantly increased the credibility of the notion that personality and other psychological factors affect physical health. Nonetheless, the case for causal influence is nearly entirely circumstantial. Associations linking personality to physiologic reactivity or to health/illness behaviors have rarely been shown to operate as mediators of change in disease indicators, and even prospective evidence of a personality–mechanism–disease sequence would be correlational and therefore open to third-variable explanations. Ultimately, the issue of causation can only be resolved by demonstrating that experimental

modification of health-damaging personality attributes influences disease-promoting processes and thereby alters physical health.

Theoretical Integration

It follows from the foregoing comments that theoretical progress in the personality–health field will require a more multifactorial approach to personality and greater attention to causal mechanisms. What is also needed is a theoretical framework that can organize, guide, and integrate personality-focused and mechanism-focused research. The leading candidate would seem to be self-regulation theory. Grounded in principles describing the operating characteristics of complex systems, self-regulation theory may provide a suitable basis for elaborating the role of hierarchically organized personality dispositions in processes of adaptation to psychosocial stressors and health threats that influence psychophysiological and behavioral mechanisms culminating in physical disease.

ACKNOWLEDGEMENTS

Preparation of this chapter was supported in part by a grant from the National Institute on Aging (AG16750). Correspondence should be addressed to Richard J. Contrada at the Department of Psychology, Rutgers University, 53 Avenue E, Piscataway, NJ 08854-8040, USA. E-mail: contrada@rci.rutgers.edu.

REFERENCES

Abramson, L. Y., Garber, J., & Seligman, M. E. P. (1980). Learned helplessness in humans: An attributional analysis. In J. Garber and M. E. P. Seligman (Eds.), *Human helplessness* (pp. 3–35). New York: Academic.

Abramson, L. Y., Seligman, M. E. P., & Teasdale, J. D. (1978). Learned helplessness in humans: Critique and reformulation. *Journal of Abnormal Psychology*, *87*, 49–74.

Affleck, G., Tennen, H., Pfeiffer, C., & Fifield, C. (1987). Appraisals of control and predictability in adapting to a chronic disease. *Journal of Personality and Social Psychology, 53*, 273–279.

Alexander, F. (1950). *Psychosomatic medicine.* New York: Norton.

American Psychiatric Association (1994). *Diagnostic and statistical manual of mental disorders* (4th edn.). Washington, DC: American Psychiatric Association.

Anda, R., Williamson, D., Jones, D., Macera, C., Eaker, E., Glassman, A., & Marks, J. (1993). Depressed affect, hopelessness, and the risk of ischemic heart disease in a cohort of U.S. adults. *Epidemiology, 4*, 285–294.

Andrykowski, M. A., Brady, M. J., & Henslee-Downey, P. J. (1994). Psychosocial factors predictive of survival after allogenic bone marrow transplantation for leukemia. *Psychosomatic Medicine, 56*, 432–439.

Bahnson, C. B. (1980). Stress and cancer: The state of the art (Part 1). *Psychosomatics, 21*, 975–981.

Bandura, A. (1977). *Self-efficacy: Towards a unifying theory of behavioral change.* New York: Holt, Rinehart & Winston.

Bandura, A. (1997). *Self-efficacy: The exercise of control.* New York: Freeman.

Bandura, A., Adams, N. E., Hardy, A. B., & Howells, G. N. (1980). Tests of the generality of self-efficacy theory. *Cognitive Therapy and Research, 4*, 39–66.

Bandura, A., Taylor, C. B., Williams, S. L., Mefford, I., & Barchas, J. (1985). Catecholamine secretion as a function of perceived coping self-efficacy. *Journal of Consulting and Clinical Psychology, 53*, 406–414.

Barefoot, J., Dodge, K., Peterson, B., Dahlstrom, G., & Williams, R. (1989). The Cook–Medley Hostility Scale: Item content and ability to predict survival. *Psychosomatic Medicine, 51*, 46–57.

Barefoot, J. C., & Schroll, M. (1996). Symptoms of depression, acute myocardial infarction, and total mortality in a community sample. *Circulation, 93*, 1976–1980.

Baumeister, R. F. (1998). The self. In D. T. Gilbert, S. T. Fiske & G. Lindzey (Eds.), *The handbook of social psychology* (Vol. 2, 4th edn., pp. 680–740). Boston, MA: McGraw-Hill.

Beck, A. T., Ward, C. H., Mendelson, M., Mock, J., & Erbaugh, J. (1961). An inventory for measuring depression. *Archives of General Psychiatry, 4*, 561–571.

Callaghan, P. (1998). Social support and locus of control as correlates of UK nurses' health-related behaviours. *Journal of Advanced Nursing, 28*, 1127–1133.

Cantor, N., & Zirkel, S. (1990). Personality, cognition, and purposive behavior. In L. A. Pervin (Ed.), *Handbook of personality theory and research* (pp. 135–164). New York: Guilford.

Carver, C. S., Pozo, C., Harris, S. D., Noriega, V., Scheier, M. F., Robinson, D. S., Ketcham, A. S., Moffat, F. L., & Clark, K. C. (1993). How coping mediates the effect of optimism on distress: A study of women with early stage breast cancer. *Journal of Personality and Social Psychology, 65*, 375–390.

Carver, C. S., & Scheier, M. F. (1999). Stress, coping, and self-regulatory processes. In L. A. Pervin & O. P. John (Eds.), *Handbook of personality: Theory and research* (2nd edn., pp. 553–575). New York: Guilford.

Charmaz, K. (1999). From the 'sick role' to stories of self: Understanding the self in illness. In R. J. Contrada & R. D. Ashmore (Eds.), *Self, social identity, and physical health: Interdisciplinary explorations* (pp. 209–239). New York: Oxford University Press.

Christensen, A. J., Turner, C. W., Smith, T. W., Holman, J. M., & Gregory, M. C. (1991). Locus of control and depression in end stage renal disease. *Journal of Consulting and Clinical Psychology, 53*, 419–424.

Clark, L. A., & Watson, D. (1999). Temperament: A new paradigm for trait psychology. In L. A. Pervin & O. P. John (Eds.), *Handbook of personality: Theory and research* (2nd edn., pp. 399–423). New York: Guilford.

Cohen, S. B., & Herbert, T. B. (1996). Health psychology: Physiological factors and physical disease from the perspective of human psychoneuroimmunology. *Annual Review of Psychology, 47*, 113–142.

Contrada, R. J., Cather, C., & O'Leary, A. (1999). Personality and health: Dispositions and processes in disease susceptibility and adaptation to illness. In L. A. Pervin & O. P. John (Eds.), *Handbook of personality: Theory and research* (2nd edn., pp. 576–604). New York: Guilford.

Contrada, R. J., & Coups, E. J. (2003). Personality and self-regulation in health and disease: Toward an integrative perspective. In L. D. Cameron & H. Leventhal (Eds.), *The self-regulation of health and illness behaviour* (pp. 66–94). London: Routledge.

Contrada, R. J., & Guyll, M. (2001). On who gets sick and why: The role of personality, stress, and disease. In A. Baum, T. A. Revenson & J. E. Singer

(Eds.), *Handbook of health psychology* (pp. 59–81). Hillsdale, NJ: Erlbaum.

Contrada, R. J., Leventhal, H., & O'Leary, A. (1990). Personality and health. In L. A. Pervin (Ed.), *Handbook of personality theory and research* (pp. 638–669). New York: Guilford.

Cook, W., & Medley, D. (1954). Proposed hostility and pharisaic-virtue scales for the MMPI. *Journal of Applied Psychology, 38*, 414–418.

Costa, P. T., & McCrae, R. R. (1992). Four ways five factors are basic. *Personality and Individual Differences, 13*, 653–665.

Costa, P. T., Zonderman, A. B., Engel, B. T., Baile, W. F., Brimlow, D. L., & Brinker, J. (1985). The relation of chest pain symptoms to angiographic findings of coronary artery stenosis and neuroticism. *Psychosomatic Medicine, 47*, 285–293.

Crowne, D., & Marlowe, D. (1964). *The approval motive: Studies in evaluative dependence.* New York: Wiley.

Dalgard, O. S., & Haheim, L. L. (1998). Psychosocial risk factors and mortality: A prospective study with special focus on social support, social participation, and locus of control in Norway. *Journal of Epidemiology and Community Health, 52*, 476–481.

Derogatis, L. R., Abeloff, M. D., & Melisaratos, N. (1979). Psychological coping mechanisms and survival time in metastatic breast cancer. *Journal of the American Medical Association, 242*, 1504–1508.

Esterling, B. A., Antoni, M. H., Kumar, M., & Schneiderman, N. (1990). Emotional repression, stress disclosure responses, and Epstein–Barr viral capsid antigen titers. *Psychosomatic Medicine, 52*, 397–410.

Esterling, B. A., Antoni, M. H., Kumar, M., & Schneiderman, N. (1993). Defensiveness, trait anxiety, and Epstein–Barr viral capsid antigen antibody titers in healthy college students. *Health Psychology, 12*, 132–139.

Evans, S., Ferrando, S. J., Rabkin, J. G., & Fishman, B. (2000). Health locus of control, distress, and utilization of protease inhibitors among HIV-positive men. *Journal of Psychosomatic Research, 49*, 157–162.

Everson, S. A., Goldberg, D. E., Kaplan, G. A., Cohen, R. D., Pukkala, E., Tuomilehto, J., & Salonen, J. T. (1996). Hopelessness and risk of mortality and incidence of myocardial infarction and cancer. *Psychosomatic Medicine, 58*, 113–121.

Eysenck, H. J. (1967). *The biological basis of personality.* Springfield, IL: Thomas.

Eysenck, H. J., & Eysenck, M. W. (1985). *Personality and individual differences: A natural science approach.* New York: Plenum.

Folkman, S., Chesney, M., Pollack, L., & Coates, T. J. (1993). Stress, control, coping and depressive mood in HIV+ and HIV– gay men in San Francisco. *Journal of Nervous and Mental Disorders, 181*, 409–416.

Fox, B. H. (1998). Psychosocial factors in cancer incidence and prognosis. In J. C. Holland (Ed.), *Psycho-oncology* (pp. 110–124). New York: Oxford University Press.

Frasure-Smith, N., Lesperance, F., Gravel, G., Masson, A., Juneau, M., & Bourassa, M. G. (2002). Long-term survival differences among low-anxious, high-anxious and repressive copers enrolled in the Montreal Heart Attack Readjustment Trial. *Psychosomatic Medicine, 64*, 571–579.

Frasure-Smith, N., Lesperance, F., & Talajic, M. (1995). Depression and 18-month prognosis after myocardial infarction. *Circulation, 91*, 999–1005.

Friedman, H. S., & Booth-Kewley, S. (1987). The 'disease-prone personality': A meta-analytic view of the construct. *American Psychologist, 42*, 539–555.

Friedman, M., & Rosenman, R. H. (1959). Association of a specific overt behavior pattern with increases in blood cholesterol, blood clotting time, incidence of arcus senilis and clinical coronary artery disease. *Journal of the American Medical Association, 169*, 1286–1296.

Gerits, P., & De Brabander, B. (1999). Psychosocial predictors of psychological, neurochemical, and immunological symptoms of acute stress among breast cancer patients. *Psychiatry Research, 85*, 95–103.

Glass, C. C., & Singer, J. E. (1972). *Urban stress.* New York: Academic.

Gramstad, A., Iverson, E., & Engelsen, B. A. (2001). The impact of affectivity dispositions, self-efficacy and locus of control on psychosocial adjustment in patients with epilepsy. *Epilepsy Research, 46*, 53–61.

Greer, S., Morris, T., & Pettingale, K. W. (1979). Psychological response to breast cancer: Effect on outcome. *Lancet, 2*, 785–787.

Heckhausen, J., & Schulz, R. (1995). A life-span theory of control. *Psychological Review, 102*, 284–304.

Holt, C. L., Clark, E. M., & Kreuter, M. W. (2001). Weight locus of control and weight-related attitudes and behaviors in an overweight population. *Addictive Behaviors, 26*, 329–340.

James, W. (1890). *Principles of psychology.* New York: Holt.

Jensen, M. R. (1987). Psychobiological factors predicting the course of breast cancer. *Journal of Personality, 55,* 317–342.

Jerusalem, M., & Schwarzer, R. (1992). Self-efficacy as a resource factor in stress appraisal processes. In R. Schwarzer (Ed.), *Self-efficacy: Thought control of action* (pp. 195–213). Washington, DC: Hemisphere.

John, O. P. (1990). The 'Big Five' factor taxonomy: Dimensions of personality in the natural language and in questionnaires. In L. A. Pervin (Ed.), *Handbook of personality theory and research* (pp. 66–100). New York: Guilford.

Jonas, B. S., Franks, P., & Ingram, D. D. (1997). Are symptoms of anxiety and depression risk factors for hypertension? *Archives of Family Medicine, 6,* 43–49.

Jorgensen, R. S., Johnson, B. T., Kolodziej, M. E., & Schreer, G. E. (1996). Elevated blood pressure and personality: A meta-analytic review. *Psychological Bulletin, 120,* 293–320.

Kamen-Siegel, L., Rodin, J., Seligman, M. E. P., & Dwyer, J. (1991). Explanatory style and cell-mediated immunity in elderly men and women. *Health Psychology, 10,* 229–235.

Kawachi, I., Sparrow, D., Vokonas, P. S., & Weiss, S. T. (1995). Decreased heart rate variability in men with phobic anxiety (data from the Normative Aging Study). *American Journal of Cardiology, 75,* 882–885.

Kelly, J. A., St Lawrence, J. S., Brasfield, I. L., & Lemke, A. (1990). Psychological factors that predict AIDS high-risk versus AIDS precautionary behavior. *Journal of Consulting and Clinical Psychology, 58,* 117–119.

Kempen, G. I. J. M., Jelicic, M., & Ormel, J. (1997). Personality, chronic medical morbidity, and health-related quality of life among older persons. *Health Psychology, 16,* 539–546.

Krantz, D. S., & Manuck, S. B. (1984). Acute psychophysiologic reactivity and risk of cardiovascular disease: A review and methodological critique. *Psychological Bulletin, 96,* 435–464.

Krohne, H. W. (1996). Individual differences in coping. In M. Zeidner & N. S. Endler (Eds.), *Handbook of coping: Theory, research, applications* (pp. 381–409). New York: Wiley.

Kubzansky, L. D., Kawachi, I., Spiro, A., Weiss, S. T., Vokonas, P. S., & Sparrow, D. (1997). Is worrying bad for your heart? A prospective study of worry and coronary heart disease in the Normative Aging Study. *Circulation, 95,* 818–824.

Lai, J. C. L. (1994). Differential predictive power of the positively versus the negatively worded items of the Life Orientation Test. *Psychological Reports, 75,* 1507–1515.

Lazarus, R. S., & Folkman, S. (1984). *Stress, appraisal, and coping.* New York: Springer.

Levenson, H. (1973). Multidimensional locus of control in psychiatric patients. *Journal of Consulting and Clinical Psychology, 41,* 397–404.

Levenson, H. (1974). Activism and powerful others: Distinctions within the concept of internal/external control. *Journal of Personality Assessment, 38,* 377–383.

Lin, E. H., & Peterson, C. (1990). Pessimistic explanatory style and response to illness. *Behavior Research and Therapy, 28,* 243–248.

Magaletta, P. R., & Oliver, J. M. (1999). The hope construct, will, and ways: Their relations with self-efficacy, optimism, and general well-being. *Journal of Clinical Psychology, 55,* 539–551.

Mahler, H. I. M., & Kulik, J. A. (1990). Preferences for health care involvement, perceived control and surgical recovery: A prospective study. *Social Science and Medicine, 31,* 743–751.

Mahler, H. I. M., & Kulik, J. A. (2000). Optimism, pessimism and recovery from coronary bypass surgery: Prediction of affect, pain and functional status. *Psychology, Health and Medicine, 5,* 347–358.

Manuck, S. B., Marsland, A. L., Kaplan, J. R., & Williams, J. K. (1995). The pathogenicity of behavior and its neuroendocrine mediation: An example from coronary artery disease. *Psychosomatic Medicine, 57,* 275–283.

Marshall, G. N. (1991). A multidimensional analysis of internal health locus of control beliefs: Separating the wheat from the chaff? *Journal of Personality and Social Psychology, 61,* 483–491.

Marshall, G. N., Wortman, C. B., Kusulas, J. W., Hervig, L. K., & Vickers, R. R. (1992). Distinguishing optimism from pessimism: Relations to fundamental dimensions of mood and personality. *Journal of Personality and Social Psychology, 62,* 1067–1074.

Martin, L. R., Friedman, H. S., Tucker, J. S., Schwartz, J. E., Criqui, M. H., Wingard, D. L., & Tomlinson-Keasey, C. (1995). An archival prospective study of mental health and longevity. *Health Psychology, 14,* 381–387.

McMahon, C. E. (1976). The role of imagination in the disease process: Pre-Cartesian medical history. *Psychosomatic Medicine, 6,* 179–184.

Miller, T. Q., Smith, T. W., Turner, C. W., Guijarro, M. L., & Hallet, A. J. (1996). A meta-analytic review of research on hostility and physical health. *Psychological Bulletin, 119*, 322–348.

Miller, T. Q., Turner, C. W., Tindale, R. S., Posavac, E. J., & Dugoni, B. L. (1991). Reasons for the trend toward null findings in research on type A behavior. *Psychological Bulletin, 110*, 469–485.

Mischel, W., & Shoda, Y. (1999). Integrating dispositions and processing dynamics within a unified theory of personality: The cognitive-affective personality system. In L. A. Pervin & O. P. John (Eds.), *Handbook of personality: Theory and research* (2nd edn., pp. 197–218). New York: Guilford.

Morris, T., Greer, S., Pettingale, K. W., & Watson, M. (1981). Patterns of expression of anger and their psychological correlates in women with breast cancer. *Journal of Psychosomatic Research, 25*, 111–117.

Moser, D. K. & Dracup, K. (1995). Psychosocial recovery from a cardiac event: The influence of perceived control. *Heart and Lung, 24*, 273–280.

Murberg, T. A., Bru, E., & Aarsland, T. (2001). Personality as predictor of mortality among patients with congestive heart failure: A two-year follow-up study. *Personality and Individual Differences, 30*, 749–757.

Newton, T. L., & Contrada, R. J. (1992). Verbal-autonomic response dissociation in repressive coping: The influence of social context. *Journal of Personality and Social Psychology, 62*, 159–167.

Norman, P., Bennett, P., Smith, C., & Murphy, S. (1997). Health locus of control and leisure-time exercise. *Personality and Individual Differences, 23*, 769–774.

Nowack, K. M., & Sassenrath, J. (1980). Coronary prone behavior, anxiety and locus of control. *Psychological Reports, 47*, 359–364.

O'Carroll, R. E., Smith, K. B., Grubb, N. R., Fox, K. A. A., & Masterton, G. (2001). Psychological factors associated with delay in attending hospital following a myocardial infarction. *Journal of Psychosomatic Research, 51*, 611–614.

Ormel, J., Kempen, G. I. J. M., Penninx, B. W. J. H., Brilman, E. I., Beekman, A. T. F., & van Sonderen, E. (1997). Chronic medical conditions and mental health in older people: Disability and psychosocial resources mediate specific mental health effects. *Psychological Medicine, 27*, 1065–1077.

Park, C. L., Moore, P. J., Turner, R. A., & Adler, N. E. (1997). The roles of constructive thinking and optimism in psychological and behavioral adjustment during pregnancy. *Journal of Personality and Social Psychology, 73*, 584–592.

Pearlin, L. L., & Schooler, C. (1978). The structure of coping. *Journal of Health and Social Behavior, 19*, 2–21.

Pender, N. J., Walker, S. N., Sechrist, K. R., & Frank-Stromborg, M. (1990). Predicting health promoting lifestyles in the workplace. *Nursing Research, 39*, 326–332.

Pennebaker, J. W., Barger, S. D., & Tiebout, J. (1989). Disclosure of trauma and health among Holocaust survivors. *Psychosomatic Medicine, 51*, 577–589.

Pennebaker, J. W., & Beall, S. K. (1986). Confronting a traumatic event: Toward an understanding of inhibition and disease. *Journal of Abnormal Psychology, 95*, 274–281.

Pennebaker, J. W., & Francis, M. E. (1996). Cognitive, emotional, and language processes in disclosure. *Cognition and Emotion, 10*, 601–626.

Pervin, L. A. (1994). A critical analysis of current trait theory. *Psychological Inquiry, 5*, 103–113.

Peterson, C., Luborsky, L., & Seligman, M. E. P. (1983). Attributions and depressive mood shifts: A case study using the symptom-context method. *Journal of Abnormal Psychology, 92*, 96–103.

Peterson, C., Maier, S., & Seligman, M. E. P. (1993). *Learned helplessness: A theory for the age of personal control.* New York: Oxford University Press.

Peterson, C., & Seligman, M. E. P. (1984). Causal explanations as a risk factor for depression: Theory and evidence. *Psychological Review, 91*, 347–374.

Peterson, C., & Seligman, M. E. P. (1987). Explanatory style and illness. *Journal of Personality, 55*, 237–265.

Peterson, C., Seligman, M. E. P., & Vaillant, G. E. (1988). Pessimistic explanatory style is a risk factor for physical illness: A thirty-five-year longitudinal study. *Journal of Personality and Social Psychology, 55*, 23–27.

Peterson, C., Semmel, A., von Bayer, C., Abramson, L. Y., Metalsky, G. I., & Seligman, M. E. P. (1982). The Attributional Style Questionnaire. *Cognitive Therapy and Research, 6*, 287–299.

Peterson, C., & Villanova, P. (1988). An Expanded Attributional Style Questionnaire. *Journal of Abnormal Psychology, 97*, 87–89.

Quadrel, M. J., & Lau, R. R. (1989). Health promotion, health locus of control, and health behavior: Two field experiments. *Journal of Applied Social Psychology, 19*, 1497–1521.

Räikkönen, K., Matthews, K. A., Flory, J. D., Owens, J. F., & Gump, B. B. (1999). Effects of optimism, pessimism, and trait anxiety on ambulatory blood pressure and mood during everyday life.

Journal of Personality and Social Psychology, 76, 104–113.

Reynaert, C., Janne, P., Bosly, A., Staquet, P., Zdanowicz, N., Vause, M., Chatelain, B., & Lejeune, D. (1995). From health locus of control to immune control: Internal locus of control has a buffering effect on natural killer cell activity decrease in major depression. *Acta Psychiatrica Scandinavica, 92,* 294–300.

Robbins, A. S., Spence, J. T., & Clark, H. (1991). Psychological determinants of health and performance: The tangled web of desirable and undesirable characteristics. *Journal of Personality and Social Psychology, 61,* 755–765.

Robinson-Whelen, S., Kim, C., MacCallum, R. C., & Kiecolt-Glaser, J. K. (1997). Distinguishing optimism from pessimism in older adults: Is it more important to be optimistic or not to be pessimistic? *Journal of Personality and Social Psychology, 73,* 1345–1353.

Rotter, J. B. (1954). *Social learning and clinical psychology.* Englewood Cliffs, NJ: Prentice-Hall.

Rotter, J. B. (1966). Generalized expectancies for internal vs. external control of reinforcement. *Psychological Monographs, 80,* 1–28.

Schank, M. J., & Lawrence, D. M. (1993). Young adult women: Lifestyle and health locus of control. *Journal of Advanced Nursing, 18,* 1235–1241.

Scheier, M. F., & Carver, C. S. (1985). Optimism, coping, and health: Assessment and implications of generalized outcome expectancies. *Health Psychology, 4,* 219–247.

Scheier, M. F., Carver, C. S., & Bridges, M. W. (1994). Distinguishing optimism from neuroticism (and trait anxiety, self-mastery, and self-esteem): A reevaluation of the Life Orientation Test. *Journal of Personality and Social Psychology, 67,* 1063–1078.

Scheier, M. F., Matthews, K. A., Owens, J. F., Magovern, G. J., Lefebvre, R. C., Abbott, R. A., & Carver, C. S. (1989). Dispositional optimism and recovery from coronary artery bypass surgery: The beneficial effects on physical and psychological well-being. *Journal of Personality and Social Psychology, 57,* 1024–1040.

Scheier, M. F., Matthews, K. A., Owens, J. F., Schulz, R., Bridges, M. W., Magovern, G. J., & Carver, C. S. (1999). Optimism and rehospitalization after coronary artery bypass graft surgery. *Archives of Internal Medicine, 159,* 829–835.

Schneider, R. A. (1992). Multidimensional health locus of control as partial predictor of serum phosphorus in chronic hemodialysis. *Psychological Reports, 70,* 1171–1174.

Schulz, R., Bookwala, J., Knapp, J. E., Scheier, M., & Williamson, G. M. (1996). Pessimism, age, and cancer mortality. *Psychology and Aging, 11,* 304–309.

Schwarzer, R. (1992). *Self-efficacy: Thought control of action.* Washington, DC: Hemisphere.

Schwarzer, R., & Renner, B. (2000). Social-cognitive predictors of health behavior: Action self-efficacy and coping self-efficacy. *Health Psychology, 19,* 487–495.

Schwarzer, R., & Schroder, K. E. E. (1997). Social and personal coping resources as predictors of quality of life in cardiac patients. *European Review of Applied Psychology, 47,* 131–135.

Shepperd, J., Maroto, J., & Pbert, L. (1996). Dispositional optimism as a predictor of health changes among cardiac patients. *Journal of Personality and Social Psychology, 59,* 517–532.

Sherer, M., Maddux, J. E., Mercandante, B., Prentice-Dunn, S., Jacobs, B., & Rogers, R. W. (1982). The self-efficacy scale: Construction and validation. *Psychological Reports, 51,* 663–671.

Sieber, W. J., Rodin, J., Larson, L., Ortega, S., Cummings, N., Levy, S., Whiteside, T., & Herberman, R. (1992). Modulation of human natural killer cell activity by exposure to uncontrollable stress. *Brain, Behavior, and Immunity, 6,* 141–156.

Smith, C. A., Dobbins, C. J., & Wallston, K. A. (1991). The mediational role of perceived competence in psychological adjustment to rheumatoid arthritis. *Journal of Applied Social Psychology, 21,* 1218–1247.

Smith, M. S., Wallston, K. A., & Smith, C. A. (1995). The development and validation of the Perceived Health Competence Scale. *Health Education Research: Theory and Practice, 10,* 51–64.

Smith, T. W. (1992). Hostility and health: Current status of a psychosomatic hypothesis. *Health Psychology, 11,* 139–150.

Smith, T. W., & Gallo, L. C. (2001). Personality traits as risk factors for physical illness. In A. Baum, T. A. Revenson & J. E. Singer (Eds.), *Handbook of health psychology* (pp. 139–173). Hillsdale, NJ: Erlbaum.

Smith, T. W., Pope, M. K., Rhodewalt, F., & Poulton, J. L. (1989). Optimism, neuroticism, coping, and symptom reports: An alternative interpretation of the Life Orientation Test. *Journal of Personality and Social Psychology, 56,* 640–648.

Smyth, J. M. (1998). Written emotional expression: Effect sizes, outcome types, and moderating variables. *Journal of Consulting and Clinical Psychology*, 66, 174–184.

Snyder, C. R., Harris, C., Anderson, J. R., Holleran, S. A., Irving, L. M., Sigmon, S. T., Yoshinobu, L., Gibb, J., Langelle, C., & Harney, P. (1991). The will and the ways: Development and validation of an individual-differences measure of hope. *Journal of Personality and Social Psychology*, 60, 570–585.

Spielberger, C. D., Gorsuch, R. L., & Lushene, R. E. (1970). *Manual for the state-trait anxiety inventory.* Palo Alto, CA: Consulting Psychologists Press.

Steptoe, A. & Wardle, J. (2001). Locus of control and health behaviour revisited: A multivariate analysis of young adults from 18 countries. *British Journal of Psychology*, 92, 659–672.

Stevens, D. E., Merikangas, K. R., & Merikangas, J. R. (1995). Comorbidity of depression and other medical conditions. In E. E. Beckham & W. R. Leber (Eds.), *Handbook of depression* (2nd edn. pp. 147–199). New York: Guilford.

Strack, S., Carver, C. S., & Blaney, P. H. (1987). Predicting successful completion of an aftercare program following treatment for alcoholism: The role of dispositional optimism. *Journal of Personality and Social Psychology*, 53, 579–584.

Suls, J., & Wan, C. K. (1993). The relationship between trait hostility and cardiovascular reactivity: A quantitative review and analysis. *Psychophysiology*, 30, 615–626.

Suls, J., Wan, C. K., & Costa, P. T. (1995). Relationship of trait anger to resting blood pressure: A meta-analysis. *Health Psychology*, 14, 444–456.

Taylor, J. A. (1953). A personality scale of manifest anxiety. *Journal of Abnormal and Social Psychology*, 48, 285–290.

Taylor, S. E., Kemeny, M. E., Aspinwall, L. G., Schneider, S. G., Rodriguez, R., & Herbert, M. (1992). Optimism, coping, psychological distress, and high-risk sexual behavior among men at risk for acquired immunodeficiency syndrome (AIDS). *Journal of Personality and Social Psychology*, 63, 460–473.

Thase, M. E., & Howland, R. H. (1995). Biological processes in depression: An updated review and integration. In E. E. Beckham & W. R. Leber (Eds.), *Handbook of depression* (2nd edn., pp. 213–279). New York: Guilford.

Thompson, S. C., Sobolow-Shubin, A., Galbraith, M. E., Schwankovsky, L., & Cruzen, D. (1993). Maintaining perceptions of control: Finding perceived control in low-control circumstances. *Journal of Personality and Social Psychology*, 64, 293–304.

Tipton, R. M., & Worthington, E. L. (1984). The measurement of generalized self-efficacy: A study of construct validity. *Journal of Personality Assessment*, 48, 545–548.

Waller, K. V., & Bates, R. C. (1992). Health locus of control and self-efficacy beliefs in a healthy elderly sample. *American Journal of Health Promotion*, 6, 302–309.

Wallston, B. S., & Wallston, K. A. (1978). Locus of control and health: A review of the literature. *Health Education Monographs*, 6, 107–117.

Wallston, B. S., Wallston, K. A., Kaplan, G. D., & Maides, S. A. (1976). Development and validation of the Health Locus of Control (HLC) Scale. *Journal of Consulting and Clinical Psychology*, 44, 580–585.

Wallston, K. A. (1992). Hocus-pocus, the focus isn't strictly on locus: Rotter's social learning theory modified for health. *Cognitive Therapy and Research*, 16, 183–199.

Wallston, K. A. (2001). Conceptualization and operationalization of perceived control. In A. Baum, T. A. Revenson & J. E. Singer (Eds.), *Handbook of health psychology* (pp. 49–58). Mahwah, NJ: Erlbaum.

Wallston, K. A., Stein, M. J., & Smith, C. A. (1994). Form C of the MHLC scales: A condition-specific measure of locus of control. *Journal of Personality Assessment*, 63, 534–553.

Wallston, K. A., Wallston, B. S., & DeVellis, R. (1978). Development of the Multidimensional Health Locus of Control (MHLC) Scales. *Health Education Monographs*, 6, 160–170.

Wang, A. Y., & Richarde, R. S. (1988). Global versus task-specific measures of self-efficacy. *Psychological Record*, 38, 533–541.

Watson, D., & Clark, L. A. (1992). Affects separable and inseparable: On the hierarchical arrangement of negative affects. *Journal of Personality and Social Psychology*, 62, 489–505.

Watson, D., & Pennebaker, J. W. (1989). Health complaints, stress, and distress: Exploring the central role of negative affectivity. *Psychological Review*, 96, 234–254.

Weinberger, D. A. (1990). The construct validity of the repressive coping style. In J. L. Singer (Ed.), *Repression and dissociation* (pp. 337–386). Chicago: University of Chicago Press.

Weinberger, D. A., Schwartz, G. E., & Davidson, R. J. (1979). Low-anxious, high-anxious, and repressive coping styles: Psychosomatic patterns and behavioral and physiologic responses to stress. *Journal of Abnormal Psychology, 88,* 369–380.

Weinstein, N. D. (1993). Testing four competing theories of health-protective behavior. *Health Psychology, 12,* 324–333.

Wiedenfeld, S. A., O'Leary, A., Bandura, A., Brown, S., Levine, S., & Raska, K. (1990). Impact of perceived self-efficacy in coping with stressors on components of the immune system. *Journal of Personality and Social Psychology, 59,* 1082–1094.

Wiener, N. (1948). *Cybernetics; or, control and communication in the animal and the machine.* Cambridge, MA: Technology Press.

Williams, R. D., Riels, A. G., & Roper, K. A. (1990). Optimism and distractibility in cardiovascular reactivity. *Psychological Record, 40,* 451–457.

Ziff, M. A., Conrad, P., & Lachman, M. E. (1995). The relative effects of perceived personal control and responsibility on health and health-related behaviors in young and middle-aged adults. *Health Education Quarterly, 22,* 127–142.

7

Stress, Health and Illness

ANDREW STEPTOE AND SUSAN AYERS

INTRODUCTION

The view that stress can cause illness has been a part of common folklore for a long time. Patients often cite stress as an important cause of their illness, yet some authorities argue that the link between stress and illness is unproved (Jones & Bright, 2001). Although the association between reported stress, illness, and even mortality is well established, conceptual and methodological problems mean it is difficult to establish whether stress is causal, and the precise mechanisms or processes through which stress impacts on health are not well understood. The first part of this chapter examines the concept of stress, the causes of stress, the main theoretical models that have proved useful in health research, and factors that may moderate stress such as characteristics of demands, coping and social support. We illustrate these processes by considering three important sources of stress: work characteristics, caring for disabled or elderly relatives, and low socioeconomic position. The second part of this chapter considers the problems involved in establishing links between stress and health. The pathways through which stress affects illness are illustrated by summarizing research into post-traumatic stress disorder, depression, cardiovascular disease, infectious illnesses, cancer and chronic autoimmune conditions. In the final section of the chapter, we outline approaches to stress management.

THE CONCEPT OF STRESS

Stress has been defined in various ways and used in different disciplines such as engineering, anthropology, sociology, psychology, physiology, and medicine. In science, the concept of stress was initially used in physics where 'stress' is an external force applied to a system, and 'strain' is the change in the system that is due to the applied force. Although there is some debate over the origins of the term 'stress' in biology and psychology, there is no doubt that scientists Walter Cannon and Hans Selye were influential in the study of stress in living organisms: Cannon (1914) with his work on the fight–flight response, and Selye (1956) when he used the term 'stress' to describe the non-specific response of living organisms to noxious stimuli. However, Selye later realized that according to the way the terms 'stress' and 'strain' are used in physics, he should have used the word 'strain' for the phenomenon he described. This may have contributed to early conceptual confusion.

Subsequently, opposing views have emerged about how useful the construct of stress is. Some argue that the concept is so widely misused and poorly defined that it is no longer useful and should be abandoned (e.g., Kasl, 1983). Much medical stress research goes on outside the domain of psychology altogether, and is concerned with the impact of conditions such as extreme atmospheric pressure, blood volume depletion or physical exercise. Most investigators concede that although stress is amorphous, it is an important construct that has the potential to unify different disciplines and help us understand the relationship between mind and body. The term 'stress' is now used in health psychology and behavioural medicine more to describe a field of research and a collection of processes, rather than a single phenomenon.

Stress is a complex and multifaceted construct with many component parts. At a basic level, it is useful to distinguish between *stressors*, which are factors that cause *stress responses*, and *chronic strain*, which is the negative impact of the stress process on the person.

CAUSES OF STRESS

This chapter is primarily concerned with psychosocial stressors, and not physical or physiological challenges such as exercise, pharmacological stimuli, and toxic chemical exposure (a full discussion of these issues can be found in Fink, 2000). Psychosocial stressors are numerous and can be classified in a number of different ways. It is possible, for instance, to distinguish between external objective events such as natural disasters, and internal subjective experiences like role conflict or not achieving one's goals. Then there are interpersonal stressors such as conflict at work, and macrosocial stressors like high unemployment, socioeconomic inequality, and war. Stressors vary on many dimensions, including duration and severity, and these dimensions have also been used to define various categorical systems.

A common distinction is drawn between acute life events such as the death of a relative or job loss, chronic stressors such as family conflict or looking after a disabled relative, and less severe daily hassles. Daily hassles are everyday irritations, like problems travelling to work

or losing things. Further stressor categories such as role strain and traumatic stress (arising from assaults, road traffic accidents, and other acute events) are also sometimes used. One of the advantages of identifying acute life events is that they can be pinpointed in time and are relatively easy to define. This makes it possible to analyse the temporal sequence between life experiences and illness onset, and life event methods have proved especially useful in psychiatric research. As far as physical illness is concerned, chronic stressors are frequently more important, since they elicit long-term disturbances in behavioural and biological processes that contribute to the development of disease.

These categorizations have a number of conceptual and measurement problems. First, the distinction between different categories of stressor is not always clear cut. For example, an apparently acute event, such as divorce, is usually preceded by the chronic stress of a difficult relationship, and can lead to further chronic stressors, such as financial difficulties. There are instances in health research in which the impact of serious life events is mediated through daily hassles. Pillow, Zautra and Sandler (1996) studied the associations between major threats such as death of a spouse, divorce, or having a child with chronic illness, and daily hassles and psychological distress. The impact of divorce on distress was mediated almost entirely through daily hassles, while the association between having a child with a serious illness and distress was independent of hassles.

Second, there are conceptual limitations to many of the categories. For example, whether a stressor is perceived as traumatic varies between individuals, and therefore classifying an event as a 'traumatic stressor' confuses subjective response with the event. Related to this is a third problem, which is that it is difficult to measure stressors without some reference to stress responses. Measures of daily hassles include items such as 'trouble relaxing' and 'not enough personal energy', which are arguably symptoms of strain rather than stressors. Finally, there are instances where non-events, or a lack of stimulation, are stressful.

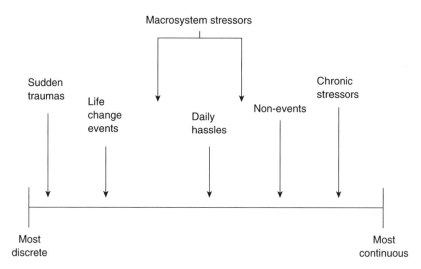

Figure 7.1 *Continuum of stressor types [Reproduced from Wheaton, B. (1996).*
The domains and boundaries of stress concepts. In H. B. Kaplan (Ed.), Psychosocial stress:
Perspectives on structure, theory, life-course, and methods *(pp. 29–70).*
San Diego, CA: Academic]

Wheaton (1996) has proposed a useful taxonomy in which these different types of stressors are placed on a continuum from discrete to continuous events, as shown in Figure 7.1. However, whether a particular event is perceived as stressful varies between individuals, because of the ways in which they appraise and cope with the situation.

COMPONENTS OF THE STRESS RESPONSE

The stress response involves changes in four distinct domains that are loosely integrated, but do not necessarily change in parallel.

Cognitive Effects

Cognitive responses to stress include changes in perception and attention, memory processes, and decision-making. Attentional processes are particularly vulnerable, and failure to notice important but peripheral stimuli under stressful conditions is a common cause of human performance breakdown and accidents among pilots and drivers of cars and trains. Traditionally, the relationship between stress and cognitive performance has been construed as an inverted U, with suboptimal performance at very low or very high levels of stress. This is now known to be an oversimplification, since there is patterning in the deficits in cognitive processes. Different types of challenge have variable effects on speed of processing, attention, and short-term memory. People have the ability to maintain performance under stressful conditions by investing additional effort in carrying out tasks. Breakdown may then only occur after termination of the stressor, with fatigue aftereffects. Stress has manifold effects on memory as well. Memories for stressful events are often incomplete, focusing on small aspects of the situation at the expense of the broader picture. It has been known for many years that retention and recall of emotionally charged material are superior to those for neutral stimuli. Stress can also inhibit recall of important events, as when the person preoccupied with work forgets a family birthday. The corticosteroid responses elicited as part of the stress process play an important role in memory and other cognitive functions (Lupien & McEwen, 1997).

Emotional Effects

The subjective effects of stress involve feelings of distress, anxiety, fear, depression and other emotions. This is the core experience of stress in the everyday sense. Curiously, there is no generally accepted measure of the subjective emotional stress response. This is partly because distress overlaps extensively with other moods, so separate measures of stress would be somewhat redundant. However, this omission does present methodological difficulties, since people vary in their affective responses. Consequently, any particular scale may not capture the subjective experience of all the people exposed to the same stressor.

It has frequently been found that although stressors elicit subjective as well as physiological responses, the two do not correlate well. One study used meta-analytic methods to evaluate the association between cardiovascular and negative emotional responses in nine stress experiments (Feldman et al., 1999). The relationships were positive but small, suggesting that emotional upset does not mediate the other aspects of the stress response, but that the domains respond in parallel.

Behavioural Effects

Behaviour changes are central to stress responses. In animals, common actions are passive behaviours such as freezing and immobility, and active responses like fighting or escaping. Each set of behaviours is underpinned by physiological adjustments supporting the energy demands of the action.

Health psychology is particularly concerned about actions that might compromise wellbeing such as smoking, alcohol consumption, unhealthy food choices, sleep disturbances, physical inactivity, and engaging in risky sexual behaviours. At one extreme, stress contributes directly to major health problems, including alcohol dependence and eating disorders. Acute stressors can cause dramatic and immediate changes. Thus surveys carried out in New York in the aftermath of the attacks on 11 September 2001 showed substantial changes in sleep, physical activity, and alcohol consumption, many of which were still present 4 months later (Ho, Paultre & Mosca, 2002). At the other extreme, the influence of chronic stress can be difficult to disentangle from the many social, cultural and psychological factors that also determine these actions. Detailed accounts of the relationship between stress and behaviour are beyond the scope of this chapter (see Jarvis, 2002; Stewart, 1996).

Physiological Effects

The physiological elements of stress responses are particularly relevant to the development and maintenance of physical illness. These biological processes have been discussed extensively by Henderson and Baum (2004, Chapter 3 in this volume), but there are several points that should be emphasized from the stress perspective. Physiological stress responses encompass many of the principal organ systems and regulatory processes of the body, including glucose metabolism and energy supply, respiration and cardiovascular function, water balance, blood clotting, and immune defences. These multiple components are controlled through activity of the autonomic nervous system and neuroendocrine circuitry. During stressful encounters, the sympathetic branch of the autonomic nervous system is activated in concert with catecholamines (such as epinephrine or adrenaline) released from the medulla of the adrenal glands. Importantly, even short-term (< 30 minute) stressors can trigger gene expression of enzymes regulating catecholamine release that persist for several hours (Sabban & Kvetnansky, 2001). The opposing parasympathetic nervous system may be more prominent under conditions of conservation and behavioural withdrawal. The hypothalamic–pituitary–adrenocortical (HPA) axis is the most important neuroendocrine pathway in stress responses, although other neurotransmitters and hormones are also involved (Chrousos & Gold, 1992). Activation of the HPA leads to the release of corticosteroids (cortisol in humans, corticosterone in rodents) from the adrenal cortex.

Autonomic nervous system and neuroendocrine regulatory processes are interdependent (Sapolsky, Romero & Munck, 2000). In addition, although sympathetic nervous system and HPA activation control many of the peripheral physiological changes observed during stress, the system is complex and involves feedback from the periphery to the central nervous system. For example, corticosteroids have a pronounced inhibitory influence on cellular immune function (Webster, Tonelli & Sternberg, 2002), but products of immune system activation known as cytokines in turn regulate HPA function (Rivest, 2001).

The pattern of physiological stress response depends not only on the behaviours elicited in the situation, but also on time course. Acute stress responses differ from chronic responses in many systems. An example that is relevant to illness is the immune response to stress. Acutely, immune responses include increases in the number of natural killer cells in the circulation, and in natural killer cell activity (Zorrilla et al., 2001). But in chronic stress studies, there are reductions in natural killer cell numbers and cytotoxic activity. Similarly HPA activity varies with the duration of stress exposure, depending on the interplay between central nervous system activation, alterations in receptor density and sensitivity, and changes in peripheral metabolism. This means that interpretation of physiological responses must take the stage and duration of the stress transaction into account.

Another important concept is that risks to health and wellbeing arise from both underactivity and overactivity in physiological stress responses (Dhabhar, 2002). For example, high levels of cortisol may lead to elevated lipids (cholesterol) in the circulation, accumulation of abdominal fat, suppression of some immune processes, decalcification of bone and impaired fertility (Weiner, 1992). Cushing's syndrome involves hypersecretion of cortisol and is an extreme example of these effects; it is characterized by hypertension, insulin resistance, osteoporosis, gonadal dysfunction, and growth retardation, along with depression, irritability and fatigue. But other medical problems are associated with low levels of cortisol, including chronic fatigue syndrome, bronchial asthma, rheumatoid arthritis, and post-traumatic stress disorder (Heim, Ehlert & Hellhammer, 2000). As cortisol suppresses the inflammatory response, low levels of cortisol may also lead to overactivity of the immune system in autoimmune conditions.

Physiological responses are evaluated in human stress research using two principal methods. Acute responses are assessed using mental stress testing, measuring biological reactions to standardized challenges such as problem solving tasks or simulated public speaking. It is carried out in healthy volunteers to understand the impact of stressors on biological processes, and also to evaluate the influence of factors like social support and hostility. Comparisons between groups of patients and controls are conducted to evaluate differences in the regulation of biological stress responses (e.g., Buske-Kirschbaum et al., 1997). Two aspects of the response are important: the magnitude of stress reaction, and the rate of recovery or return to baseline levels after stress. Larger reactions and slower recovery are considered pathogenic in most circumstances.

The second important method is measurement under naturalistic conditions. Blood pressure, heart rate, and haemodynamic indices can be monitored repeatedly or continuously with unobtrusive measures for many hours, while periodic saliva sampling is used to assess cortisol. The cortisol response to waking and levels early in the day are emerging as important markers, with higher values in people experiencing chronic stress in work and other settings (Wüst, Federenko, Hellhammer & Kirschbaum, 2000).

THEORETICAL MODELS OF STRESS

Theoretical models of the stress process have been based on both the components described above, namely stimulus and response models. These will be briefly described before we outline *interactional or transactional models*, which focus on the interaction between the person and environment.

Stimulus-Based Models

The main stimulus-based model of stress is the life change approach, which dominated research in the 1970s and early 1980s. This defined stress as the amount of adjustment or life change with which a person was faced. This approach presumed that any life change would tax resources and is therefore likely to be detrimental to health and wellbeing. Originally, it was characterized by measuring stress using checklists of life events, and an individual's level of stress was determined by the number and type of life events they had experienced over a given period of time. The most widely used measure of life events was the Social Readjustment Rating Scale (Holmes & Rahe, 1967), which listed 43 events that were weighted for average stressfulness on a scale from 1 to 100. Examples of items and the weighting allocated to them are: death of a spouse (100), divorce (73), marriage (50), change in financial state (38), and Christmas (12).

The major advantage of the life change approach has been in its definition of stressful experiences as quasi-objective phenomena. This has made it theoretically possible to distinguish exposure to adverse experiences from the emotional responses they engender, making it possible to discover whether stress exposure precedes illness, even in retrospective studies. However, as a measurement tool, the checklist method has been widely criticized (Turner & Wheaton, 1995). There is the problem of comprehensiveness: it is difficult to develop a practical measure of all life experiences that might be relevant to everyone, so important occurrences for certain individuals may be missed out. Items are open to varied interpretation: a statement like 'change in financial state' is ambiguous, since people may differ in whether they regard a particular change as sufficiently great to be counted. The life change method includes both positive and negative events, but there is strong evidence that negative events are much more important for health. Event scores are often summed, making the assumption that life stress is cumulative, when it is possible that one experience is offset by another. There are also concerns about weighting systems, which give a uniform score for

everyone to a particular event. In addition, the use of checklists to measure life events may be subject to recall biases in terms of both inaccurate recall and mood congruent recall. People with health problems often search for causes of their illness, and therefore identify more life events in the recent past than do comparison groups.

Some of these methodological difficulties have been overcome by the use of interview-based methods such as the Life Events and Difficulties Schedule developed by George Brown (1989). This involves interviewing participants about their life experiences, carefully identifying specific life events and chronic difficulties such as living in crowded conditions, and collecting information about the circumstances surrounding these experiences. In a separate process, a judgement is made about the threat or unpleasantness of the occurrence, taking the circumstances into account but ignoring the person's emotional response. This method has been widely used in psychiatry, and to evaluate stressful experiences related to breast cancer recurrence and other physical health outcomes (Conway, Creed & Symmons, 1994; Graham, Ramirez, Love, Richards & Burgess, 2002). However, the method is more elaborate and time-consuming than administering a life event checklist, so questionnaire measures continue to dominate the assessment of major stressors.

Aside from problems of measurement, the life change approach can be criticized for ignoring psychological processes and moderating variables such as social support and ways of coping. Yet although it does not provide a comprehensive account of the stress process, the concern with trying to assess people's exposure to adverse experiences remains a central issue in health psychology, and is influential in the design of research studies.

Response-Based Approaches to Stress

Response-based models have concentrated on the physiological components of the stress response. Cannon (1914) was the first to detail the response of the autonomic nervous system to stressful stimuli. He labelled this the fight–flight response which prepares the body for fighting or escaping, and argued that the physiological changes were structured around preparing the organism for vigorous physical activity. This accounts for the increased heart rate, increased breathing rate and depth, dilation of the blood vessels supplying the muscles and brain, and constriction of blood vessels supplying skin and viscera.

Selye (1956) expanded on Cannon's work to incorporate the HPA axis, and centred his model of stress on the corticosteroids released by the adrenal cortex. Selye proposed the *general adaptation syndrome* to describe three phases of the physiological stress response. In the first phase, *alarm*, the body activates the fight–flight response to deal with the stressor. In the second phase, *resistance*, the body attempts to restore homeostasis and reach maximum adaptation to the stressor, but may remain in a state of higher arousal than is normal. In the continued presence of the stressor, however, the final phase, *exhaustion*, can occur when physiological resources are overstretched and break down – resulting in disease or death.

Cannon and Selye's approaches are similar in that they both use a homeostatic model of the physiological response to stress where the body attempts to restore equilibrium. In addition, both defined stress as a non-specific physiological response. However, later research has shown that physiological responses are not non-specific, and vary between stressors and individuals. This is true both at the central nervous system level, where stressors are known to differ in their neurochemical 'signature' (Pacak & Palkovits, 2001), and also in terms of peripheral physiological response. A key concept that has emerged over the last 25 years is that there are robust individual differences in the pattern and magnitude of physiological stress responses. For example, one person may display heightened blood pressure responses to a variety of challenges, while another may be more responsive in terms of cortisol. Later, we will develop the argument that individual differences in physiological stress responsivity interact with exposure to environmental challenges to determine vulnerability to physical disease outcomes.

Recent work has also questioned whether the behavioural fight–flight response is universal. Taylor et al. (2000) argue that, although the physiological response to stress may be similar in men and women, the behavioural fight–flight response observable in males is not as strong in females. They propose that female responses to stress are more of a 'tend–befriend' nature. In other words, when females are exposed to threat, their priorities are to protect themselves and nurture offspring, and/or turn to others for support or protection. Taylor et al. suggest these responses may be mediated by neurochemical and neuroendocrine pathways that are specifically activated during stress in females, with a prominent role for the peptide hormone oxytocin, and for endogenous opioid mechanisms. These arguments remain speculative, and the functional significance of oxytocin release during stress remains uncertain. Nevertheless, they do highlight the continued importance of elaborating the pattern of physiological stress response in different conditions in different groups.

The work stimulated by Cannon and Selye has been important in forwarding understanding of biological stress responses. However, this approach has little to say about the environments provoking responses, or the role of protective psychosocial factors, and so provides only a partial account of the stress process.

Interactional and Transactional Approaches to Stress

Interactional and transactional approaches to stress emphasize individual differences in perceived stress and the importance of psychological processes – particularly cognitive appraisal. The interactional approach to stress proposes that the interplay between environmental stimuli and the person is critical in determining stress responses. An example of an interactional approach is the person–environment fit model in occupational psychology, in which stress arises when people are exposed to environments with which they are unfamiliar, or which do not suit their skills and capacity (French, Caplan & Van Harrison, 1982).

The transactional approach goes beyond the interactional by positing that the various factors involved in stress influence each other and act as both independent and dependent variables. The dominant transactional model was developed by Richard Lazarus and his colleagues, who defined stress as 'a particular relationship between the person and the environment that is appraised by the person as taxing or exceeding his or her resources' (Lazarus & Folkman, 1984: 19). Cognitive appraisal is central to this model. Lazarus suggests that when an event occurs, individuals go through three stages of appraisal. The first stage is *primary appraisal*, where the demands of the event on the individual are evaluated. The second stage is *secondary appraisal*, where people evaluate the resources they have available to cope with the demands. Available resources can be environmental (such as economic factors, social factors, the presence of others) or personal (such as previous experience with this type of event, self-efficacy, self-esteem, repertoire of coping strategies). It should be apparent that these resources may also influence primary appraisal. For example, an academic examination will be appraised as less demanding by a student with a thorough knowledge of the subject and plenty of time to revise (good resources to cope). On the other hand, the examination will be appraised as more demanding by a student with little knowledge of the subject and little time to revise (poor resources to cope). Thus primary and secondary appraisal do not necessarily occur in a linear and sequential fashion, but influence each other and may occur in parallel. Recent research suggests that this may vary according to level of demands, and that perceived personal resources are more likely to influence appraisals of stress under low levels of demand (Guillet, Hermand & Mullet, 2002).

As a result of this process, an event can be evaluated as *irrelevant*, that is, not relevant to the individual's wellbeing; *benign-positive*, that is, positive and/or non-threatening; or *stressful*. According to this model, stressful appraisals can be further broken down into those that involve harm or loss, challenge, or threat, although these categories are not mutually exclusive. For example, physical assault can involve appraisals of both immediate harm and future threat of recurrence. These ideas have been incorporated into theories of post-traumatic stress disorder (PTSD), where appraisal of continued threat is thought to be important in the development of the disorder (Ehlers & Clark, 2000). According to the transactional approach, when demands are appraised as exceeding resources, coping strategies are applied in an effort to change the situation, or the response to that situation. The process is iterative, with the situation being reappraised after coping attempts have been made, often leading to further coping efforts.

This model has stimulated a substantial amount of research, much of which supports the role of appraisal in modulating subjective and physiological stress responses. For instance, Lazarus and others have carried out a series of experiments in which people are shown gruesome films, having been randomized to different types of appraisal or cognitive orientation, such as reminding them that the film is acted (denial of reality), or that the film is real but shown for educational purposes (intellectualization). People assigned to denial or intellectualization appraisals have smaller physiological and subjective responses to the film compared with controls (e.g., Steptoe & Vögele, 1986). Non-experimental research also supports a role for appraisal in adaptation to stressors. Pakenham and Rinaldis (2001) found that strong appraisals of challenge, controllability, and weak appraisals of threat were predictive of better psychological adjustment to HIV/AIDS, as measured by depression, global distress, social adjustment, and subjective health status.

However, the model has been criticized on a number of points, many of which question the central role allocated to cognitive appraisal processes (Zajonc, 1984). The difficulty of measuring appraisal as part of a dynamic process means it is hard to distinguish appraisal from cognitive processes that are part of the stress response itself. There are undoubtedly situations where conscious appraisal does not take place and people react quickly to hazards, such as when avoiding accidents. The model has also been criticized for being limited to the psychological level of

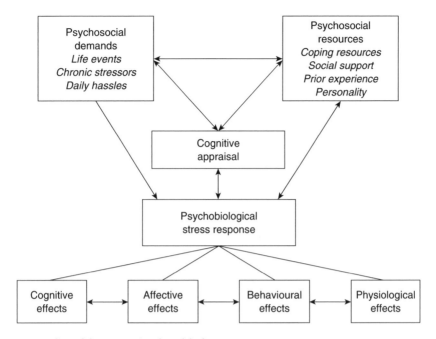

Figure 7.2 *An outline of the transactional model of stress*

analysis, without consideration of physical, social, and cultural influences. It has little to say about the nature of stress responses themselves, and how they interact. Nevertheless, transactional models have greatly increased understanding of individual differences in the stress process, and the role of cognitive factors in integrating experience of the environment with the social and psychological responses that the person brings to bear on the situation.

Figure 7.2 is a simple schematic of a transactional framework that attempts to bring together the factors that are relevant to the stress process. This framework begins with the assumption that stress responses are stimulated by potential or actual threats or challenges to the integrity or survival of the person (Weiner, 1992). Psychosocial stressors may be anticipated, may be real or imaginary, and may involve understimulation as well as overstimulation. The appraisal of these aversive experiences depends in part on the psychosocial resources that the individual brings to bear on the situation. These resources include coping responses, prior experience of similar situations in the past,

and social support, while also being influenced by personality and temperament. The multidimensional stress response arises when adaptive capacity is exceeded. The pattern of stress response varies over time, depending on whether exposure to the threat is acute or chronic, and whether there is habituation or sensitization to the situation. There is also a close interplay between the components of the stress response and the coping process. For example, an increase in cigarette smoking has been frequently observed as part of the stress response (Jarvis, 2002). At the same time, a large proportion of smokers state that smoking helps relieve tension, so smoking is partly a coping response. Smoking may alter the cognitive response to stress by increasing alertness and aiding mental concentration, and so can be viewed as partly adaptive. But smoking also augments physiological stress responses and health risks, and so has maladaptive consequences as well.

It is evident from this framework that stress is a process and not a state, and involves a fully interactive rather than a linear system. A major challenge in health research is teasing out the interplay between these elements.

MODERATORS OF STRESS RESPONSES

Critical Stressor Characteristics

The duration and intensity of stressors are strong determinants of psychobiological stress responses. Over and above these factors, other important characteristics include controllability, predictability, and novelty.

Controllability can be defined as the extent to which actions can be taken by the individual that prevent, terminate, or modify aversive stimulation. Stressors vary greatly in their controllability, from events that are completely beyond personal control (such as the death of a relative in a train crash), to occurrences that are partly down to personal choice (such as injuries during dangerous sports). A wide range of animal and human studies has shown that emotional, behavioural and physiological responses are greater under uncontrollable conditions (Steptoe & Appels, 1989). Uncontrollable stressors elicit greater corticosteroid and catecholamine responses, increase tendencies to gastric lesions, and reduce immune defences. Perceptions of control are also important, and related control constructs such as locus of control and self-efficacy have been extensively examined in stress research (Henderson & Baum, 2004, Chapter 3 in this volume). When people become ill, they often experience a profound reduction in their sense of control over their lives and destiny. Loss of control is also a characteristic of ageing, as people's personal choices are constrained by economic limitations, the loss of social contacts through the death of peers, and the loss of confidence in physical capacity due to disability. However, manipulations of control may have favourable effects. Studies have been carried out with the elderly residents of nursing homes, showing that providing greater choice and autonomy had beneficial effects in terms of cognitive and behavioural function (Langer & Rodin, 1976).

Psychobiological stress responses are more pronounced in unpredictable conditions, even if the duration and intensity of stimulation are the same as those in predictable conditions (Abbott, Schoen & Badia, 1984). For example, Zakowski (1995) found that lymphocyte proliferative responses to mitogens were impaired to a greater extent with unpredictable compared with predictable stressors. The beneficial effects of predictability are associated with the fact that novel and unfamiliar situations enhance stress responses. This was strikingly demonstrated in primate studies by Mason (1975), who found that neuroendocrine responses were as great when animals were placed in the experimental situation for the first time, as they were to any of the 'stressors' subsequently administered. The reduction in stress responses with familiarity may result not only from increased predictability, but also from adaptation in response processes due to habituation and down-regulation of receptor sensitivity. The principle of habituation underpins both behavioural exposure therapy, where repeated exposure results in extinction of physiological and affective responses, and stress inoculation programmes in which people learn to cope in difficult situations through repeated exposure and rehearsal.

Coping Responses

The use of the term 'psychological coping' has changed in health psychology over the past 30 years. In the early literature, coping was taken to describe effective and mature engagement with stressors, and was contrasted with psychological defences such as denial and repression. But within the transactional framework, coping is used to describe the entire repertoire of cognitive and behavioural responses deployed by an individual in an effort to manage stressful situations, whether or not these efforts are successful. The reason for this change is the realization that no particular coping response is always effective; the success of coping depends on the nature of the situation, the time point in the stress process at which adaptation is assessed, and the particular component of the stress response that is being monitored. Coping has several purposes, including the reduction of harmful environmental conditions, the toleration of adverse events, keeping emotional equilibrium, maintaining a positive self-image, and preserving satisfactory social relationships.

A wide range of ways of handling stressors are regarded as coping responses, including problem solving, seeking social support, cognitive reinterpretation or 'restructuring', problem avoidance, wishful thinking, denial, self-criticism, and social withdrawal. Several classification systems have been proposed. Among the most useful is the distinction between problem- and emotion-focused coping. The purpose of problem-focused coping is to manage the situation, and the strategies used may include methods of planning and problem solving, seeking relevant information, escaping or avoiding the situation, or redefining it in a more benign way. Emotion-focused strategies are deployed not to change the stressor but to manage emotional distress, by methods such as seeking emotional social support, denial, cognitive avoidance, distraction, and distancing. Other useful taxonomies distinguish coping responses that involve engagement (problem solving, seeking social support) and those that involve disengagement (problem avoidance, wishful thinking, social withdrawal). Aspinwall and Taylor (1997) have argued that proactive coping, the efforts people make to anticipate or detect potential stressors and act in advance to reduce their impact, are particularly important.

The coping responses mobilized will depend on the nature of threat; coping with the illness of a child is very different from coping with a stressor at work. Individuals also appear to have coping dispositions or preferences for certain types of response. For example, people vary in the extent to which they are vigilant and seek out information about situations, as opposed to being avoidant (Miller, Brody & Summerton, 1988). The combination of these two aspects helps to determine the extent to which different types of coping response are deployed in a particular stress transaction.

Social Support

Social interactions are intimately involved in the stress process. Emotional support can help people come to terms with stressors, while information and advice from friends and family are an important aid to decision-making. At the same time both interpersonal conflict and the absence of social contact (social isolation) are common forms of chronic stress. Research on social relationships and health has stemmed from two traditions (Cohen, Gottlieb & Underwood, 2000). The sociological perspective developed from the work of Durkheim, who argued that migration and industrialization lead to breakdown in family and community ties and social disorganization, as old-established cultural norms and social roles are abandoned. This approach has resulted in a focus on social integration, isolation, and participation in multiple social roles. These can have manifold influences on health through health behaviours, a positive sense of self-worth and wellbeing, and the provision of information and material support. In health psychology, this tradition is embodied in the 'main effect' model of social support, which postulates that social integration is associated with lower mortality and morbidity irrespective of the level of life stress (Berkman & Glass, 2000). The measures used to test these processes usually involve assessments of network size, diversity and reciprocity.

The second tradition views social ties as protective against life stress ('stress-buffering' model), and was stimulated by the work of John Cassel (1976). This argues that the social environment provides several types of support including emotional support, material or practical support, and information or advice, that help mitigate the impact of adverse experiences. From this perspective, social support primarily has beneficial effects on health when people are confronted with stressful demands. For example, a woman with young children whose partner dies will benefit from emotionally supportive people to comfort her and share her distress, material support in terms of finance or help with the children, and informational support in the shape of advice about the future. A substantial amount of evidence supports this perspective, particularly when measures are made of the perceived availability of support, rather than social networks (Cohen & Wills, 1985). Laboratory studies have shown that physiological stress responses are attenuated when tests are carried out in the presence of a supportive individual, and in survey work, low social support has been associated with unfavourable physiological changes such as raised blood pressure and impairment of immune function (Uchino, Cacioppo & Kiecolt-Glaser, 1996).

STRESS AND HEALTH

The influence of stress processes on health and risk of disease is studied from a variety of perspectives, using animal models, epidemiological survey techniques, clinical investigations, and laboratory experiments. There are two broad approaches to studying these effects in humans. The first is to assess the impact of particular categories of potentially stressful conditions, and the second is to investigate the aetiology of specific diseases. We will illustrate the first of these approaches by outlining findings relating to three common forms of stress: work stress, the stress of caring for elderly and dementing relatives, and low socioeconomic position. Other stressors such as marital and family conflict, unemployment, or neighbourhood and community stress could have been selected (Kiecolt-Glaser & Newton, 2001), but the three we have chosen demonstrate the ways in which the different elements outlined in Figure 7.2 combine to create heightened vulnerability in certain individuals. Later in this chapter we will illustrate the second approach by examining the role of stress in specific diseases.

Work Stress

Many aspects of work are potentially stressful, including type of work and work environment (noise, posture, machine pacing, shift work, level of social contact), organizational factors (time pressure, decision-making, career structure, resource problems), and personal factors (role conflict, work–home balance). Two models have emerged in the health field as helpful in investigating these different aspects. The demand/control or job strain model postulates that the two key elements of the work experience are levels of demand, and lack of control over how the work is carried out and how skills are developed and utilized (Karasek & Theorell, 1990). Job strain emerges when high

demands are coupled with low job control. A second model focuses on effort/reward imbalance, and postulates that stress responses arise when the effort resulting from the demands of the job and the personal commitment put into the work are not matched by rewards (money, social esteem, job security, career opportunities) (Siegrist, 1996). Both these conceptualizations of job stress have been related to cardiovascular disease in cross-sectional and prospective studies (Steenland et al., 2000). For instance, in one study 812 employees of a manufacturing company were followed up over 25 years, and cardiovascular deaths were monitored (Kivimaki et al., 2002). The risk of dying from cardiovascular disease in workers who were disease-free at baseline was more than doubled in those experiencing high compared with low job strain, and high compared with low effort/reward imbalance, after controlling statistically for age, occupational status, smoking, physical activity, blood pressure, blood cholesterol level, and body mass. Job strain has also been related to the development of high blood pressure and to increases in cholesterol.

Work stress is associated with other adverse health outcomes as well. Low control at work, high job demands, and low social support at work predict severe emotional distress in prospective studies (Stansfeld, Fuhrer, Shipley & Marmot, 1999). Repetitive jobs such as working as a supermarket cashier elicit muscle tension in the neck and back that contributes to chronic pain (Lundberg, 1999). Minor interpersonal work stressors on a day-to-day basis impair physical wellbeing among women with arthritis (Potter, Smith, Strobel & Zautra, 2002). Work stress is also associated with unhealthy behaviour changes such as smoking and high fat consumption (Matthews & Gump, 2002; Wardle, Steptoe, Oliver & Lipsey, 2000).

Caregiving

Informal caring for dementing, disabled or elderly relatives is increasingly common as people live longer, as medical technology allows more severely handicapped children and adults to survive, and as the provision of residential care services is reduced. The potential sources of stress in caring are great, although caring tasks can also be sources of satisfaction and self-esteem. For example, looking after a dementing relative involves physical demands such as help in eating and washing, and constant surveillance and support, coupled with the emotional loss of observing the deterioration of intellectual function and affective responses in a loved one. These problems are accompanied by fatigue, loss of social contact, financial burdens, and withdrawal from other activities that promote satisfaction. The impact of caregiving varies widely, in part because of differences in the nature of the challenge. Thus some studies have shown that the psychological wellbeing of carers is related not so much to cognitive deterioration in dementing relatives as to behavioural disturbances and emotional withdrawal (Donaldson, Tarrier & Burns, 1997). Adverse effects tend to be more prominent in carers who appraise the health problems of their relative as stressful, who use avoidant coping strategies, and who have low social support (Haley et al., 1996).

Emotional wellbeing is often poor among carers for dementing relatives, and some studies have shown elevated levels of depression (Schulz, O'Brien, Bookwala & Fleissner, 1995). Cellular immune function is impaired, and infectious illness episodes are prolonged (Kiecolt-Glaser, Dura, Speicher, Trask & Glaser, 1991). The rate of wound healing is slowed, and there is some evidence for vaccinations being less successful (Kiecolt-Glaser, Marucha, Malarkey, Mercado & Glaser, 1995). Caregiving is also a risk factor for increased mortality. Schulz and Beach (1999) tracked a large sample of elderly informal carers and non-carers over a 4-year period. After adjusting statistically for age, race, education, stressful life events, sex, and baseline health status, individuals who provided care and who experienced caregiving strain had a 63 per cent higher risk of dying than did non-caregivers.

Socioeconomic Position

There is an inverse relationship between socioeconomic position, whether defined by occupation, income, or educational attainment, and morbidity and mortality from common illnesses throughout the developed world (Adler, Marmot, McEwen & Stewart, 1999). Thus poorer and less educated sectors of society have higher rates of perinatal mortality, childhood accidents, diabetes, coronary heart disease, and many cancers. Some of this difference is not due to stress, but to difference in living and working conditions, exposure to pollutants and hazardous environments, and the direct effects of poverty (Evans & Kantrowitz, 2002). Health behaviours such as smoking, food choice and alcohol consumption make an important contribution. However, it is likely that stress-related factors also play a part. Many forms of chronic stress are more common in lower socioeconomic groups, including low job control, financial strain, neighbourhood living problems and exposure to crime. There is a positive relationship between sense of control and socioeconomic position that contributes to class differences in wellbeing. Protective psychosocial resources may also be limited, with higher rates of social isolation and less active coping (Taylor & Seeman, 1999). In laboratory studies, people in low socioeconomic status positions show more prolonged cardiovascular stress responses, indicating disturbance of homeostatic adaptive mechanisms (Steptoe et al., 2002). Children raised in poverty have higher cortisol and epinephrine excretion than do their more affluent peers (Evans & English, 2002). Thus stress-related psychobiological responses partly mediate socioeconomic inequalities in health.

PROBLEMS IN ESTABLISHING DEFINITIVE LINKS WITH ILLNESS

We have cited a number of instances in which stress and morbidity are associated, but this does not necessarily mean that stress plays a causal role. There are a number of difficulties in establishing a definitive link. First, the diseases in which stress is implicated are typically multifactorial, with a range of genetic, biological, and environmental determinants. It is not a case of a disease being due either to stress or to other

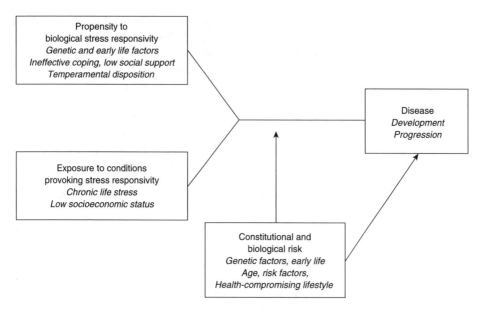

Figure 7.3   *Stress-diathesis model: pathways linking the stress process with disease*

factors, but is one of stress processes contributing to aetiology to a variable extent in different people and different conditions. This can make it difficult to identify an independent role of stress. Much clinical research on stress and health is cross-sectional, so inferences about causality cannot be drawn. Indeed, no single type of scientific investigation is sufficient. Rather, it is necessary to integrate evidence from several sources: animal experiments, prospective epidemiological surveys, clinical investigations, and laboratory experiments.

Second, the impact of stress processes on health is not all mediated through direct biological responses. As noted earlier, behavioural responses also contribute. An elegant example of behavioural mediation comes from studies of the development of high blood pressure in air traffic controllers. Air traffic control is a stressful occupation with persistent high demands and need for rapid decision-making that carries great responsibility. It was established 30 years ago that air traffic controllers have increased risk of hypertension compared with workers in similar environments doing other jobs (Cobb & Rose, 1973). It was supposed that this was due to persistent activation of the sympathetic nervous system. But

DeFrank, Jenkins and Rose (1987) showed that the occurrence of high blood pressure was preceded by marked increases in alcohol consumption, and that this mediated the link between work stress and morbidity.

A third problem in establishing causal links between stress and disease is the wide variation in individual responsivity. How is it that two people have similar life experiences, yet one becomes ill while the other remains healthy? Why do some people contract infectious illness while others experience increased risk of coronary heart diseases when faced with chronic stressors? Some of this variation is due to the interplay of demands and resources outlined in Figure 7.2. But in addition, it is necessary to consider individual vulnerability factors. This has lead to the stress–diathesis model, a version of which is summarized in Figure 7.3. The outcome of the stress process depends on constitutional and biological risk factors that determine whether the individual remains healthy or develops coronary heart disease, experiences musculoskeletal pain, shows exacerbation of autoimmune diseases, or suffers other adverse effects. Some of the factors that contribute to constitutional and biological risk are outlined below.

Genetic Factors

Genetic factors are probably responsible for many of the differences between people in vulnerability to stress responses. They contribute to most of the disorders that are affected by stress, including depression, high blood pressure, coronary heart disease, rheumatoid arthritis, and diabetes. Twin studies indicate that the magnitude of psychophysiological responses is heritable (Hewitt & Turner, 1995). Polymorphisms have been described in processes involved in stress responses. For instance, polymorphisms in alpha- and beta-adrenergic genes affect the magnitude of cardiovascular responses to mental stress (McCaffery, Pogue-Geile, Ferrell, Petro & Manuck, 2002).

Early Life Factors

Early life traumas not only have effects on development, but also influence adult stress responses. Early social isolation in non-human primates leads to increased HPA activation, impaired lymphocyte proliferation to mitogens, and increased norepinephrine turnover in response to stress in adults (Suomi, 1997). Research on depression has shown that the risk of developing the disorder following adverse life events among grown women is increased by severe early trauma such as death of mother while the patient was still a child (Brown & Harris, 1989). Heim, Newport et al. (2000) have reported an intriguing study of depressed and non-depressed women, some of whom had experienced sexual and physical abuse during childhood. Cortisol responses to a standard laboratory stress protocol were heightened in those who were currently depressed and had experienced early abuse, compared with other groups.

Other Factors

Many of the medical conditions studied in health psychology are more common in older adults. As people age, a series of biological changes occur that modify stress responses and reduce the individual's capacity to adapt homeostatically (Seeman & Robbins, 1994). Several other factors also contribute to biological vulnerability including gender, ethnicity, physical fitness, and nutritional status (see Steptoe, 1998).

STRESS AND SPECIFIC HEALTH OUTCOMES

A second approach to studying the link between stress and illness is to study the aetiology of specific illnesses. This section therefore outlines the role of stress in post-traumatic stress disorder, depression, coronary heart disease, infectious illnesses, cancer, and autoimmune conditions.

Post-Traumatic Stress Disorder

Post-traumatic stress disorder (PTSD) is a condition that is defined by exposure to a stressor, and the aetiology of PTSD is assumed to be firmly entrenched in exposure to extreme stress. Post-traumatic stress disorder is formally defined by the *Diagnostic and Statistical Manual* of the American Psychiatric Association, 4th revision (DSM-IV), as a syndrome that develops following an event where a person experiences actual or threatened death/serious injury, or threat to the physical integrity of self or other; and where the person responded with intense fear, helplessness or horror. Symptoms fall into three main clusters that reflect the multidimensional nature of stress responses described earlier: re-experiencing the event through intrusive thoughts, nightmares, or flashbacks (cognitive and affective); avoidance of factors associated with the event and emotional numbing (affective and behavioural); and signs of increased arousal such as hypervigilance and irritability (behavioural and physiological). For a diagnosis of PTSD, symptoms must cause significant distress or impairment and must continue for longer than 1 month. A separate condition known as acute stress disorder (ASD) has also been recognized, although there has been controversy over the validity of the construct (Marshall, Spitzer &

Liebowitz, 1999). For a diagnosis of ASD, symptoms must occur within a month of the traumatic event and the individual must exhibit avoidance as well as symptoms such as numbing/detachment, reduced awareness of surroundings, derealization, depersonalization, and dissociative amnesia.

The traumatic stressors that elicit PTSD can vary greatly, and are not necessarily uncommon events like natural disasters. Symptoms have been observed following events as varied as war, sexual assault, road traffic accidents, diagnosis of cancer, childbirth, myocardial infarction, being the victim of crime, and child abuse. It has also been reported in individuals who have not directly experienced a traumatic stressor but are close to another individual who has been involved in a traumatic event such as assault, homicide, disasters, or the Holocaust (e.g., Baranowsky, Young, Johnson-Douglas, Williams-Keeler & McCarrey, 1998). A national survey in the USA carried out after the 11 September 2001 terrorist attacks showed that 17 per cent of adults living outside New York City had post-traumatic symptoms 2 months after the events, declining to 5.8 per cent 6 months later (Silver, Holman, McIntosh, Poulin & Gil-Rivas, 2002). More controversially, PTSD has even been suggested in people who have not been exposed to an acute, severe stressor either directly or indirectly. Scott and Stradling (1994) detail case studies of PTSD symptoms in people who did not experience an identifiable acute stressor but were in circumstances of chronic duress, such as caring for a terminally ill spouse. Whether this is a justifiable extension of the construct of PTSD is uncertain, since there is a danger that the description is given to responses to any severe aversive experiences.

Thus PTSD illustrates many of the difficulties in understanding stress responses. First, not everyone exposed to a severe stressor develops PTSD. Second, not everyone who has symptoms of PTSD has directly experienced a severe stressor. In addition, many people report positive changes in themselves or their lives following a traumatic event such as increased confidence in their ability to cope and clearer recognition of what is important in

their lives. This has been called 'post-traumatic growth'. Therefore, even with PTSD, a stress–diathesis model needs to be used, where individual vulnerabilities interact with exposure to a stressful event to determine the development of the syndrome. Some of the vulnerability factors that have been associated with PTSD include being female, having a history of trauma or psychological problems, and having additional life events after the trauma. For example, post-traumatic symptoms related to 11 September 2001 were more common in women, in people with a previous history of anxiety and depression, and in those who coped by disengagement, denial and distraction (Silver et al., 2002). Davidson and Foa (1993) propose that the characteristics of the event influence how important individual differences in vulnerability are in determining whether people develop PTSD. Individual differences are not very important following exposure to extreme stressors, since there is a strong likelihood most people will experience symptoms. Individual vulnerability plays a larger part with less extreme stressors, such as being mugged.

Models of PTSD that attempt to explain the pathway between stress exposure and PTSD primarily focus on cognitive processing. A particularly influential model is that of Horowitz (1979, 1986). This model assumes that we have a 'completion tendency' in which important information needs to be processed until reality and cognitive models match through processes of assimilation or accommodation. Horowitz contends that a severe stressor involves massive amounts of internal and external information, most of which cannot be matched with a person's cognitive schemata and so leads to information overload. As the person cannot deal with this information at the time it is happening, it is shunted out of awareness and remains in an unprocessed, active state. Avoidance, denial and numbing are employed as defensive manoeuvres. However, because the information remains active, it will intrude into consciousness in the form of uncontrollable thoughts, flashbacks, and nightmares, until it is properly processed. When the conscious information becomes too distressing the individual will revert to avoidance, denial and numbing. Thus a person oscillates between intrusion and avoidance prior to full integration. Once fully processed, the trauma memory is integrated and is therefore no longer stored in an active state. PTSD may arise when the trauma memory is not properly processed and resolved, and therefore people become trapped in oscillation between intrusions and avoidance.

More recent models of PTSD also focus on cognitive processes during and after the event. Brewin, Dalgleish and Joseph (1996) propose there are two kinds of memory for events: verbally accessible memories and situationally accessible memories. They suggest that trauma memories are situationally accessible and therefore prone to automatic triggering by related stimuli. Ehlers and Clark (2000) focus on appraisal processes that they believe are critical in the development of PTSD, such as mental defeat during the event and negative appraisal of symptoms after the event. However, cognitive models of PTSD can be criticized on similar grounds to the transactional model of stress, in that the focus on appraisal processes ignores the influence of other factors such as additional stressors and social support. Therefore, even with a stress disorder such as PTSD, it is necessary to take individual vulnerability and environmental factors into consideration.

Experiencing trauma may have implications for physical health as well. It has been associated with self-reported health problems, use of medical services, morbidity, and mortality. Studies of female sexual assault victims show they report more somatic symptoms and visit their physicians more often than women who have not experienced sexual assault (e.g., Koss, Koss & Woodruff, 1991). Studies on war veterans indicate that people with PTSD report greater numbers of chronic health problems and perceive their physical health as significantly worse than those without PTSD (Kulka et al., 1990). The mechanisms underlying this link between trauma and physical health are not clear. Like other mental health problems, PTSD may lead to poorer social circumstances, such as unemployment, reduced

financial means and restricted social contact, which in turn may affect physical health. It is also highly comorbid with other psychological disorders. The US National Comorbidity Survey showed that 88 per cent of men and 79 per cent of women with PTSD fulfilled criteria for another psychological disorder – usually major depressive disorder (Kessler, Sonnega, Bromet, Hughes & Nelson, 1995). In addition, the association between trauma and health may be due to physiological responses to trauma. In common with other stress conditions, the responses in people with PTSD include increased sympathetic nervous system reactivity to trauma-related stimuli, and high levels of circulating epinephrine and norepinephrine have been recorded. Yet, paradoxically, people with PTSD show a decreased cortisol response to stress, which suggests that HPA axis function may be altered following exposure to a traumatic event (Yehuda, 1998). The explanation is uncertain, but this hypocortisolism may be due to alterations in peripheral metabolism or to reduced central activation of the HPA axis (Heim et al., 2000).

Depression

Depression is a good example of a stress outcome that is determined by a complex interaction between genetic or biological vulnerability, individual vulnerability (e.g., gender, low self-esteem), social factors (e.g., low socioeconomic status, low levels of support), and environmental factors (e.g., poverty and deprivation). In fact an enduring, if controversial, distinction is made between endogenous and reactive depression. At one extreme, reactive depression is thought to develop as a reaction to stressors. For example, research following the Mount St Helens volcanic eruption found that three mental disorders increased in the year following the disaster. These were PTSD, generalized anxiety disorder, and single-episode depression (Shore, Vollmer & Tatum, 1989). Davidson and Fairbank draw on this to suggest 'the possibility that there exists a subtype of depression following trauma ('posttraumatic depression') ... A person might thus experience such a posttraumatic depressive reaction, without meeting diagnostic criteria for PTSD' (1993: 167). At the other extreme, endogenous depression is due to biological and/or genetic vulnerability, which implies that an individual could develop depression regardless of circumstances and exposure to stress. Psychiatric diagnostic schemes such as DSM-IV concentrate on symptom presentation rather than assumed aetiology, and distinguish between major depressive disorder, minor depression, dysthymic disorder, and bipolar disorder.

Thus depression can differ widely in its presentation and possible aetiology. For unipolar depression, the link between stress and depression is well established. Early research using the life events approach found moderate associations between life events and depression in both community and clinical samples (e.g., Billings & Moos, 1982). Chronic stressors such as poverty and unemployment are also associated with increased risk of depression, but commonly interact with biological vulnerability. For example, Kendler et al. (1995) found that although experiencing a severe stressor was generally predictive of depression, risk was highest in women who both experienced a severe stressor and had a genetic vulnerability to depression (these women were monozygotic twins whose twin had a history of depression).

It would appear that the stress–diathesis approach is most appropriate when considering the aetiology of depression, with the diathesis being in the cognitive domain. A number of models have been put forward, initially by theorists looking at cognitive vulnerability to depression, such as Beck's (1967) theory and hopelessness theory (Abramson, Alloy & Metalsky, 1989). These suggest that early life experiences result in dysfunctional cognitive schemata that can then be activated by stressful life events. Dysfunctional schemata mean that people will appraise and interpret events in a way that is more likely to result in depression. Brown and Harris (1989) have put forward a slightly different stress–diathesis model where the characteristics of the stressor and the psychosocial context in which they occur are considered critical in determining a person's appraisal and response to the event. They propose that depression occurs in response to major life events or chronic strain, but not in response to minor or moderate stressors – however chronic. Brown and Harris also propose that risk of depression is higher if the event involves loss and is salient to a role that is important to the individual. Research has shown that vulnerability to depression is increased by a number of psychological and social factors, for example, social conditions, low levels of support, low self-esteem, and childhood adversity. More recent stress–diathesis approaches have tried to account for gender differences in depression and the emergence of the condition in adolescence (Hankin & Abramson, 2001).

Depression has important implications for physical health. The most obvious is the increased risk of suicide, as it is estimated that between 10 and 15 per cent of people with major depressive disorder are likely to commit suicide (Clark & Fawcett, 1992). Population-based studies also find an association between depressive mood disturbance and suicide and parasuicide (Diekstra, 1990). In addition, many depressed people have altered physiological responses to stress with increased levels of cortisol and corticotropin releasing factor, suggesting dysregulation of the HPA. Longitudinal studies have established that depression is associated with increased mortality due to medical problems or accidents, and is relevant to cardiovascular and other diseases, as detailed below.

Coronary Heart Disease

Coronary heart disease is the physical condition for which there is perhaps the most comprehensive evidence for a causal role of stress (Stansfeld & Marmot, 2002). The underlying problem in coronary heart disease is coronary atherosclerosis, a process involving inflammation of the lining of blood vessels leading to the progressive accumulation of lipid, macrophages and smooth muscle cells in the walls of coronary arteries. This starts early in life and continues for decades without clinical consequences. The disease typically comes to light at an advanced stage with angina pectoris, myocardial infarction, or sudden cardiac death. Stress factors contribute both to the long-term development of coronary atherosclerosis, and to the triggering of cardiac events in patients with established disease.

The influence of stress on long-term aetiology is seen most clearly in animal studies. Research involving cynomolgus macaques has shown in randomized trials that social stress leads to more rapid progression of atherosclerosis (Kaplan et al., 1983). Social stress also provokes disturbances in vascular endothelial function, and the deposition of abdominal fat. At the same time, individual differences are relevant, with greater atherosclerosis in animals that are more stress responsive (Manuck, Kaplan & Clarkson, 1983).

In humans, prospective epidemiological studies have found that stress-related factors predict future coronary heart disease in samples that were originally disease-free. The most consistent evidence is for work characteristics such as low job control, for depressive symptoms, and for social isolation, while the data relating to hostility are also suggestive (Stansfeld & Marmot, 2002).

Laboratory studies have thrown light on the mechanisms that might be involved. Acute mental stress elicits disturbances in vascular endothelial function, an early stage of the atherogenic process that may render the blood vessel walls permeable to lipids and macrophages (Ghiadoni et al., 2000). Stress also elicits increases in blood pressure, mobilizes lipids, and induces a prothrombotic state in clotting mechanisms that predisposes to thrombus formation (von Kanel, Mills, Fainman & Dimsdale, 2001). The combination of heightened stress responsivity and exposure to chronic stress-provoking conditions such as high job demands or low socioeconomic status has been shown to predict accelerated development of atherosclerosis (Everson et al., 1997).

New methods of imaging cardiac function non-invasively have demonstrated that in a proportion of people with heart disease, mental stress can induce transient myocardial ischaemia (Rozanski, Blumenthal & Kaplan, 1999). These abnormalities of cardiac function are typically 'silent', and are not accompanied by chest pain. The implication is that the cardiac function of patients with coronary heart disease is frequently impaired by stress processes without them being aware of it. A number of studies have now shown that patients who show mental stress-induced myocardial ischaemia are at increased risk for future cardiac events (see Strike & Steptoe, 2003). This process may underlie cases in which myocardial infarction appears to have been triggered by emotional stress.

An issue of intense concern over recent years is whether depression in the days following myocardial infarction has adverse effects on prognosis and survival. The data are not all consistent, but a number of studies have shown that even moderate depressive responses are predictive of poor outcome (Ziegelstein, 2001). A counter-view is that depression following acute cardiac events is a product either of the disease process, or of awareness that the outlook for survival is poor. It certainly appears that depressed patients are less adherent to medication and lifestyle advice, and this will contribute to unfavourable outcomes. But there is also the possibility that emotional responses stimulate disturbances in the autonomic control of the heart that increase vulnerability (Carney et al., 2001).

Infectious Illness

Stress does not cause infectious illness. However, it may reduce bodily defences by impairing immune responses and mucosal protection. If an episode of stress-induced impaired immunity coincides with exposure to an infectious agent (such as a bacterium or virus), then illness may be more likely to occur.

The ideal study of this process is a longitudinal investigation in which psychosocial factors are monitored together with measures of bodily defences, exposure to infectious agents, and illness. Research of this type is technically difficult to conduct, and requires a very high level of cooperation from participants. The most convincing evidence to date has come from studies in which infectious agents were administered experimentally. Cohen, Tyrrell and Smith (1991) studied volunteers who agreed to be given a standard dose of common cold virus, and found that the likelihood of infection and clinical illness was positively associated with levels of recent life stress. Later analyses suggested that infection rate was predicted by negative affect and subjectively rated stress, while illness itself was associated with negative life events. These findings have been replicated in other studies that have also shown illness to be more likely in individuals with smaller social networks (Cohen, Doyle, Skoner, Rabin & Gwaltney, 1997). Associations with the production of the cytokine interleukin 6 have also been described.

Naturalistic studies have not been able to document the complete pattern of stress responses leading to reduced immune defences, exposure to infective agents, and subsequent illness. Stressful episodes could raise risk of infectious illness by increasing exposure to infection (if, for example, people become socially more active), or by changes in health behaviours such as smoking and alcohol consumption. However, one longitudinal study of upper respiratory infection has found that the occurrence of illness was predicted by elevations in subjective stress coupled with relatively low immune responses to standardized mental stress (Cohen et al., 2002). An investigation of women with genital herpes showed that those who reported stressful situations lasting more than a week were more likely to suffer a recurrence of the infection, possibly due to the failure of the immune system to keep the latent infection under control (Cohen et al., 1999).

Stress and Cancer

Few topics in the field of psychological factors and health have attracted so much interest as cancer. The fact that immune and neuroendocrine systems contribute to host resistance against some cancers, and that stress can affect these biological responses, provides a functional basis for an influence of stress on cancer. A number of animal studies have shown that the progression of experimentally induced malignancy is affected by behavioural stress. For example, Visintainer, Volpicelli and Seligman (1982) implanted sarcoma tumours in rats that were exposed to inescapable

electric shock, matched escapable shock, or no shock. The likelihood of tumour rejection (reflecting effective body defences) was greater in the escapable and no shock conditions than in the inescapable condition, indicating the benefits of stress controllability.

In humans, a large literature has accumulated concerning the influence of life stress, depression, and coping responses on cancer development and progression. However, the consensus of well-conducted studies is that there are no convincing associations. For example, case-control studies suggest that serious life events or chronic stresses predicted the onset and recurrence of breast cancer, but many of these are methodologically weak, and the association has not been confirmed in prospective designs (Graham et al., 2002; McGee, Williams & Elwood, 1996). Large-scale longitudinal studies of depression have failed to confirm any association with cancer risk, except in as much as depressed people smoke more (Dalton, Boesen, Ross, Schapiro & Johansen, 2002; Kaplan & Reynolds, 1988). The literature relating cancer survival and recurrence with mental attitudes such as helplessness, fighting spirit, positive thinking, avoidance, and fatalism has recently been systemically reviewed (Petticrew, Bell & Hunter, 2002). Little consistent evidence for the impact of these coping responses was found. A general problem in this field has been the use of small samples, inadequate control for confounding factors, and retrospective designs in which psychosocial variables are assessed in patients after diagnosis, or when patients are at least partially aware of their prognosis. It is possible that future studies will delineate a more definite role of the stress process in cancer, but at present the literature is equivocal.

Autoimmune Conditions

There are intimate relationships between stress, disease, and adaptation in autoimmune conditions such as rheumatoid arthritis, type I (insulin-dependent) diabetes, systemic lupus erythematosus, and bronchial asthma. However, in none of these cases is there strong evidence for stress processes being part of the primary aetiology of the condition (Conway et al., 1994; Gonder-Frederick, Cox & Ritterband, 2002; Herrmann, Scholmerich & Straub, 2000). Rather, stress processes aggravate the severity of these chronic disorders and may be involved in episodes of acute exacerbation.

Many aspects of the stress process outlined in this chapter are implicated in autoimmune conditions. Thus personal stressors and negative emotions have been related to disturbances of glycaemic control in diabetes (Lloyd et al., 1999), and to increased airways resistance in bronchial asthma (Ritz & Steptoe, 2000). In a study of women suffering from systemic lupus erythematosus, it was found that changes in functional ability over an 8-month period were predicted by negative life events independently of baseline function and depressive state (Da Costa et al., 1999). Zautra, Hamilton, Potter and Smith (1999) assessed life events weekly in patients with rheumatoid arthritis, patients with osteoarthritis, and healthy controls. Clinical examinations were also carried out, and these indicated that disease activity was worse during high-stress weeks, particularly in the more depressed patients. Sense of helplessness has been related to disability in arthritic conditions, and has been shown to mediate part of the socioeconomic gradient in mortality in patients with rheumatoid arthritis (Callahan, Cordray, Wells & Pincus, 1996).

The links between stress and disease are mediated rather differently in these conditions compared with the other disorders discussed in this chapter. Much of the association is probably mediated through behavioural pathways, specifically self-care behaviours. For example, adherence to medication in asthma, and adherence to advice concerning activity and diet in diabetes, are affected by stress and have a direct impact on clinical outcome. Biologically, autoimmune conditions are different from other diseases in that many are characterized by inflammatory responses that would normally be suppressed by cortisol. Indeed corticosteroids are used in the treatment of arthritis and systemic lupus erythematosus. Likewise in bronchial asthma, bronchoconstriction is stimulated in part by activity of the parasympathetic nervous system, while drugs that activate the sympathetic nervous system are used in treatment. Paradoxically, these patterns would suggest that conventional physiological stress responses (heightened cortisol output and sympathetic activation) would be beneficial for autoimmune conditions rather than deleterious. The mechanisms are not yet understood, but there is evidence that these stress-related responses are reduced in autoimmune conditions (Sternberg, 2001).

STRESS MANAGEMENT

Stress management is a very extensive field of research and practice, and space prohibits a full discussion of methods and outcomes. Instead, we will outline the principles of stress management as they relate to the stress models detailed in Figures 7.2 and 7.3.

It is evident from Figure 7.2 that, theoretically, stress management could address several different stages of the transactional process. First, reduction of stress responses could be achieved by modifying demands, or exposure to potentially stressful conditions. This is not always possible of course, but if a source of stress is modified or removed, then the rest of the process will also be eliminated. Initiatives in the workplace such as job redesign, management of marital conflict, respite support for carers, and anti-bullying programmes are all based on this principle. Second, stress responses can be ameliorated through bolstering psychosocial resources, for example by providing additional social support. Third, stress management can target the cognitive appraisal process, and this underlies many cognitive-behavioural interventions, cognitive restructuring (appraising unalterable stressful conditions more benignly), and assertiveness training. Fourth, stress management can address stress responses directly, through relaxation training, biofeedback, and meditation techniques. Finally, it is likely that the impact of stress responses may be reduced by enhancing the biological resistance factors outlined in Figure 7.3. Hence nutritional interventions and exercise training can also be regarded as relevant to stress management.

Many different interventions fall under the general rubric of stress management. Some are comprehensive, addressing several different elements of the stress process, so the critical ingredient is difficult to define. For instance, the influential Lifestyle Heart Trial, which showed that lifestyle interventions can delay the progression of coronary atherosclerosis in patients with coronary artery disease, involved social support groups, stress management techniques like relaxation and breathing exercises, a prescribed physical exercise programme, smoking cessation and a low-fat vegetarian diet (Ornish et al., 1990). A more recent large-scale randomized trial that demonstrated the benefits of an intervention for the mental health and adaptation of children of divorced parents included group sessions focusing on effective coping, the reduction of negative thoughts about divorce stressors, and improving mother–child relationships (Wolchik et al., 2002). Even a single type of intervention can have markedly variable effects depending on the population involved and the outcomes being assessed.

The fact that a process is implicated in stress responses does not necessarily mean that modifications of it will be beneficial. A controversial example is social support interventions, which have been applied to various problems on the assumption that augmenting the limited social resources of stressed individuals will aid adaptation. There is growing evidence that some types of support interventions may not be helpful, even when applied with the best of intentions. For example, a large study of psychosocial support during high-risk pregnancies in economically deprived women in South America involved visiting women on several occasions, offering them emotional support and health education advice (Villar et al., 1992). This had no effect on reducing the incidence of low birth weight, or on maternal and neonatal health. Helgeson, Cohen, Schulz and Yasko (1999) compared women with breast cancer randomized to educational groups and support groups that focused on feelings and discussion of problems. Positive effects on adjustment and wellbeing emerged for the education groups but not for the peer discussion groups. Indeed, the latter did harm to some patients, who ended up less satisfied with the social support they obtained from their partners. A more recent study of supportive-expressive groups for patients with systemic lupus erythematosus showed no important clinical differences between conditions after 1 year (Dobkin et al., 2002).

Another important issue concerns the expected effects of stress management. These methods are applied in health psychology with two broad aims: improving the emotional wellbeing or quality of life of patients with medical conditions, and modifying disease processes directly. The evidence for beneficial effects is greater for the first than the second of these aims. Thus in patients with cancer, meta-analyses indicate that psychological intervention produces at least short-term improvements in anxiety reduction (Sheard & Maguire, 1999). Studies of patients following myocardial infarction have also shown improvements in psychological wellbeing and quality of life with a range of stress management methods (Linden, Stossel & Maurice, 1996). Impact on physical endpoints has proved more elusive. Convincing evidence has emerged for conditions such as recurrent headache (Holroyd, 2002). But despite the much vaunted effects of supportive-expressive group interventions in breast cancer described by Spiegel, Bloom, Kraemer and Gottheil (1989), more recent and larger studies have generated predominately null results (Andersen, 2002). In an era when medical and surgical treatments are changing rapidly, it is difficult to mount an adequately powered study of stress management in which all possible confounders are precisely monitored. However, attempting to improve quality of life is itself a laudable aim, and should not be ignored in the search for methods of prolonging survival.

REFERENCES

Abbott, B. B., Schoen, L. S., & Badia, P. (1984). Predictable and unpredictable shock: Behavioral measures of aversion and physiological measures of stress. *Psychological Bulletin, 96*, 45–71.

Abramson, L. Y., Alloy, L. B., & Metalsky, G. I. (1989). Hopelessness depression: A theory-based subtype of depression. *Psychological Review, 96,* 358–372.

Adler, N. E., Marmot, M., McEwen, B. S., & Stewart, J. (Eds.) (1999). *Socioeconomic status and health in industrial nations: Social, psychological and biological pathways* (Vol. 896). New York: New York Academy of Sciences.

Andersen, B. L. (2002). Biobehavioral outcomes following psychological interventions for cancer patients. *Journal of Consulting and Clinical Psychology, 70,* 590–610.

Aspinwall, L. G., & Taylor, S. E. (1997). A stitch in time: Self-regulation and proactive coping. *Psychological Bulletin, 121,* 417–436.

Baranowsky, A. B., Young, M., Johnson-Douglas, S., Williams-Keeler, L., & McCarrey, M. (1998). PTSD transmission: A review of secondary traumatization in Holocaust survivor families. *Canadian Psychology, 39,* 247–256.

Beck, A. T. (1967). *Depression: Clinical, experimental, and theoretical aspects.* New York: Harper & Row.

Berkman, L. F., & Glass, T. A. (2000). Social integration, social networks, social support and health. In L. F. Berkman & I. Kawachi (Eds.), *Social epidemiology* (pp. 137–173). New York: Oxford University Press.

Billings, A. G., & Moos, R. H. (1982). Psychosocial theory and research on depression: An integrative framework and review. *Clinical Psychology Review, 2,* 213–237.

Brewin, C., Dalgleish, T., & Joseph, S. (1996). A dual representation theory of posttraumatic stress disorder. *Psychological Review, 103,* 670–686.

Brown, G. W. (1989). Life events and measurement. In G. W. Brown & T. O. Harris (Eds.), *Life events and illness* (pp. 3–45). New York: Guilford.

Brown, G. W., & Harris, T. O. (1989). Depression. In G. W. Brown & T. O. Harris (Eds.), *Life events and illness* (pp. 49–93). New York: Guilford.

Buske-Kirschbaum, A., Jobst, S., Wustmans, A., Kirschbaum, C., Rauh, W., & Hellhammer, D. (1997). Attenuated free cortisol response to psychosocial stress in children with atopic dermatitis. *Psychosomatic Medicine, 59,* 419–426.

Callahan, L. F., Cordray, D. S., Wells, G., & Pincus, T. (1996). Formal education and five-year mortality in rheumatoid arthritis: Mediation by helplessness scale score. *Arthritis Care and Research, 9,* 463–472.

Cannon, W. B. (1914). The interrelations of emotions as suggested by recent physiological researches. *American Journal of Psychology, 25,* 256–282.

Carney, R. M., Blumenthal, J. A., Stein, P. K., Watkins, L., Catellier, D., Berkman, L. F., Czajkowski, S. M., O'Connor, C., Stone, P. H., & Freedland, K. E. (2001). Depression, heart rate variability, and acute myocardial infarction. *Circulation, 104,* 2024–2028.

Cassel, J. (1976). The contribution of the social environment to host resistance. *American Journal of Epidemiology, 104,* 107–123.

Chrousos, G. P., & Gold, P. W. (1992). The concepts of stress and stress system disorders. Overview of physical and behavioral homeostasis. *Journal of the American Medical Association, 267,* 1244–1252.

Clark, D. C., & Fawcett, J. (1992). Review of empirical risk factors for evaluation of the suicidal patient. In B. M. Bongar (Ed.), *Suicide: Guidelines for assessment, management, and treatment* (pp. 16–48). New York: Oxford University Press.

Cobb, S., & Rose, R. M. (1973). Hypertension, peptic ulcer and diabetes in air traffic controllers. *Journal of the American Medical Association, 224,* 489–492.

Cohen, F., Kemeny, M. E., Kearney, K. A., Zegans, L. S., Neuhaus, J. M., & Conant, M. A. (1999). Persistent stress as a predictor of genital herpes recurrence. *Archives of Internal Medicine, 159,* 2430–2436.

Cohen, S., Doyle, W. J., Skoner, D. P., Rabin, B. S., & Gwaltney, J. M. (1997). Social ties and susceptibility to the common cold. *Journal of the American Medical Association, 277,* 1940–1944.

Cohen, S., Gottlieb, B. H., & Underwood, L. G. (2000). Social relationships and health. In S. Cohen, L. G. Underwood & B. H. Gottlieb (Eds.), *Social support measurement and intervention* (pp. 3–25). New York: Oxford University Press.

Cohen, S., Hamrick, N., Rodriguez, M. S., Feldman, P. J., Rabin, B. S., & Manuck, S. B. (2002). Reactivity and vulnerability to stress-associated risk for upper respiratory illness. *Psychosomatic Medicine, 64,* 302–310.

Cohen, S., Tyrrell, D. A. J., & Smith, A. P. (1991). Psychosocial stress and susceptibility to the common cold. *New England Journal of Medicine, 325,* 606–612.

Cohen, S., & Wills, T. A. (1985). Stress, social support, and the buffering hypothesis. *Psychological Bulletin, 98,* 310–357.

Conway, S. C., Creed, F. H., & Symmons, D. P. (1994). Life events and the onset of rheumatoid arthritis. *Journal of Psychosomatic Research, 38,* 837–847.

Da Costa, D., Dobkin, P. L., Pinard, L., Fortin, P. R., Danoff, D. S., Esdaile, J. M., & Clarke, A. E.

(1999). The role of stress in functional disability among women with systemic lupus erythematosus: A prospective study. *Arthritis Care and Research, 12,* 112–119.

Dalton, S. O., Boesen, E. H., Ross, L., Schapiro, I. R., & Johansen, C. (2002). Mind and cancer: Do psychological factors cause cancer? *European Journal of Cancer, 38,* 1313–1323.

Davidson, J. R. T., & Fairbank, J. A. (1993). The epidemiology of posttraumatic stress disorder. In J. R. T. Davidson & E. B. Foa (Eds.), *Posttraumatic stress disorder: DSM-IV and beyond* (pp. 147–169). Washington, DC: American Psychiatric Press.

Davidson, J. R. T., & Foa, E. B. (1993). Epilogue. In J. R. T. Davidson & E. B. Foa (Eds.), *Posttraumatic stress disorder: DSM-IV and beyond* (pp. 229–235). Washington, DC: American Psychiatric Press.

DeFrank, R. S., Jenkins, C. D., & Rose, R. M. (1987). A longitudinal investigation of the relationships among alcohol consumption, psychosocial factors, and blood pressure. *Psychosomatic Medicine, 49,* 236–249.

Dhabhar, F. S. (2002). Stress-induced augmentation of immune function: The role of stress hormones, leukocyte trafficking, and cytokines. *Brain, Behavior and Immunity, 16,* 785–798.

Diekstra, R. F. W. (1990). Suicide, depression, and economic conditions. In D. Lester (Ed.), *Current concepts in suicide.* Philadelphia: Charles.

Dobkin, P. L., Da Costa, D., Joseph, L., Fortin, P. R., Edworthy, S., Barr, S., Ensworth, S., Esdaile, J. M., Beaulieu, A., Zummer, M., Senecal, J. L., Goulet, J. R., Choquette, D., Rich, E., Smith, D., Cividino, A., Gladman, D., St-Pierre, Y., & Clarke, A. E. (2002). Counterbalancing patient demands with evidence: Results from a pan-Canadian randomized clinical trial of brief supportive-expressive group psychotherapy for women with systemic lupus erythematosus. *Annals of Behavioral Medicine, 24,* 88–99.

Donaldson, C., Tarrier, N., & Burns, A. (1997). The impact of the symptoms of dementia on caregivers. *British Journal of Psychiatry, 170,* 62–68.

Ehlers, A., & Clark, D. (2000). A cognitive model of posttraumatic stress disorder. *Behaviour Research and Therapy, 38,* 319–345.

Evans, G. W., & English, K. (2002). The environment of poverty: Multiple stressor exposure, psychophysiological stress, and socioemotional adjustment. *Child Development, 73,* 1238–1248.

Evans, G. W., & Kantrowitz, E. (2002). Socioeconomic status and health: The potential role of environmental risk exposure. *Annual Review of Public Health, 23,* 303–331.

Everson, S. A., Lynch, J. W., Chesney, M. A., Kaplan, G. A., Goldberg, D. E., Shade, S. B., Cohen, R. D., Salonen, R., & Salonen, J. T. (1997). Interaction of workplace demands and cardiovascular reactivity in progression of carotid atherosclerosis: Population based study. *British Medical Journal, 314,* 553–558.

Feldman, P. J., Cohen, S., Lepore, S. J., Matthews, K. A., Kamarck, T. W., & Marsland, A. L. (1999). Negative emotions and acute physiological responses to stress. *Annals of Behavoral Medicine, 21,* 216–222.

Fink, G. (Ed.), (2000). *Encyclopedia of stress* (Vols. 1–3). San Diego, CA: Academic.

French, J. R. P., Caplan, R. D., & Van Harrison, R. (1982). *The mechanisms of job stress and strain.* New York: Wiley.

Ghiadoni, L., Donald, A., Cropley, M., Mullen, M. J., Oakley, G., Taylor, M., O'Connor, G., Betteridge, J., Klein, N., Steptoe, A., & Deanfield, J. E. (2000). Mental stress induces transient endothelial dysfunction in humans. *Circulation, 102,* 2473–2478.

Gonder-Frederick, L. A., Cox, D. J., & Ritterband, L. M. (2002). Diabetes and behavioral medicine: The second decade. *Journal of Consulting and Clinical Psychology, 70,* 611–625.

Graham, J., Ramirez, A., Love, S., Richards, M., & Burgess, C. (2002). Stressful life experiences and risk of relapse of breast cancer: Observational cohort study. *British Medical Journal, 324,* 1420–1422.

Guillet, L., Hermand, D., & Mullet, E. (2002). Cognitive processes involved in the appraisal of stress. *Stress and Health, 18,* 91–102.

Haley, W. E., Roth, D. L., Coleton, M. I., Ford, G. R., West, C. A., Collins, R. P., & Isobe, T. L. (1996). Appraisal, coping, and social support as mediators of well-being in black and white family caregivers of patients with Alzheimer's disease. *Journal of Consulting and Clinical Psychology, 64,* 121–129.

Hankin, B. L., & Abramson, L. Y. (2001). Development of gender differences in depression: An elaborated cognitive vulnerability–transactional stress theory. *Psychological Bulletin, 127,* 773–796.

Heim, C., Ehlert, U., & Hellhammer, D. H. (2000). The potential role of hypocortisolism in the pathophysiology of stress-related bodily disorders. *Psychoneuro-endocrinology, 25,* 1–35.

Heim, C., Newport, D. J., Heit, S., Graham, Y. P., Wilcox, M., Bonsall, R., Miller, A. H., & Nemeroff, C. B. (2000). Pituitary–adrenal and autonomic responses to stress in women after sexual and physical abuse in childhood. *Journal of the American Medical Association, 284,* 592–597.

Helgeson, V. S., Cohen, S., Schulz, R., & Yasko, J. (1999). Education and peer discussion group interventions and adjustment to breast cancer. *Archives of General Psychiatry, 56,* 340–347.

Henderson, B. N., & Baum, A. (2004). Biological mechanisms of health and disease. In S. Sutton, A. Baum & M. Johnston (Eds.), *The Sage handbook of health psychology.* London: Sage.

Herrmann, M., Scholmerich, J., & Straub, R. H. (2000). Stress and rheumatic diseases. *Rheumatic Disorders Clinics of North America, 26,* 737–763.

Hewitt, J. K., & Turner, J. R. (1995). Behavior genetic studies of cardiovascular responses to stress. In J. R. Turner, L. R. Cardon & J. K. Hewitt (Eds.), *Behavior genetic approaches in behavioral medicine* (pp. 87–103). New York: Plenum.

Ho, J. E., Paultre, F., & Mosca, L. (2002). Lifestyle changes in New Yorkers after September 11, 2001. *American Journal of Cardiology, 90,* 680–682.

Holmes, T. H., & Rahe, R. H. (1967). The Social Readjustment Rating Scale. *Journal of Psychosomatic Research, 11,* 213–218.

Holroyd, K. A. (2002). Assessment and psychological management of recurrent headache disorders. *Journal of Consulting and Clinical Psychology, 70,* 656–677.

Horowitz, M. J. (1979). Psychological response to serious life events. In V. Hamilton & D. M. Warburton (Eds.), *Human stress and cognition: An information processing approach* (pp. 235–263). New York: Wiley.

Horowitz, M. J. (1986). *Stress response syndromes.* Northvale, NJ: Aronson.

Jarvis, M. (2002). Smoking and stress. In S. A. Stansfeld & M. G. Marmot (Eds.), *Stress and the heart* (pp. 150–157). London: BMJ Books.

Jones, F., & Bright, J. (2001). *Stress: Myth, theory and research.* Harlow: Pearson Education.

Kaplan, G. A., & Reynolds, P. (1988). Depression and cancer mortality and morbidity: Prospective evidence from the Alameda County study. *Journal of Behavioral Medicine, 11,* 1–13.

Kaplan, J. R., Manuck, S. B., Clarkson, T. B., Lusso, F. M., Taub, D. M., & Miller, E. W. (1983). Social stress and atherosclerosis in normocholesterolemic monkeys. *Science, 220,* 733–735.

Karasek, R. A., & Theorell, T. (1990). *Healthy work.* New York: Basic.

Kasl, S. (1983). Pursuing the link between stressful life experiences and disease: A time for reappraisal. In C. I. Cooper (Ed.), *Stress research* (pp. 79–102). New York: Mentor.

Kendler, K. S., Kessler, R. C., Walters, E. E., MacLean, C., Neale, M. C., Heath, A. C., & Eaves, L. J. (1995). Stressful life events, genetic liability, and onset of an episode of major depression in women. *American Journal of Psychiatry, 152,* 833–842.

Kessler, R., Sonnega, A., Bromet, E., Hughes, M., & Nelson, C. (1995). Post-traumatic stress disorder in the National Comorbidity Survey. *Archives of General Psychiatry, 52,* 1048–1060.

Kiecolt-Glaser, J. K., Dura, J. R., Speicher, C. E., Trask, O. J., & Glaser, R. (1991). Spousal caregivers of dementia victims: Longitudinal changes in immunity and health. *Psychosomatic Medicine, 53,* 345–362.

Kiecolt-Glaser, J. K., Marucha, P. T., Malarkey, W. B., Mercado, A. M., & Glaser, R. (1995). Slowing of wound healing by psychological stress. *Lancet, 346,* 1194–1196.

Kiecolt-Glaser, J. K., & Newton, T. L. (2001). Marriage and health: His and hers. *Psychological Bulletin, 127,* 472–503.

Kivimaki, M., Leino-Arjas, P., Luukkonen, R., Riihimaki, H., Vahtera, J., & Kirjonen, J. (2002). Work stress and risk of cardiovascular mortality: Prospective cohort study of industrial employees. *British Medical Journal, 325,* 857.

Koss, M. P., Koss, P., & Woodruff, W. (1991). Deleterious effects of criminal victimization on women's health and medical utilization. *Archives of Internal Medicine, 151,* 342–357.

Kulka, R. A., Schlenger, W. E., Fairbank, J. A., Hough, R. L., Jordan, B. K., Marmar, C. R., & Weiss, D. S. (1990). *Trauma and the Vietnam war generation.* New York: Brunner/Mazel.

Langer, E. J., & Rodin, J. (1976). The effects of choice and enhanced personal responsibility for the aged: A field experiment in an institutional setting. *Journal of Personality and Social Psychology, 34,* 191–198.

Lazarus, R. S., & Folkman, S. (1984). *Stress, appraisal and coping.* New York: Springer.

Linden, W., Stossel, C., & Maurice, J. (1996). Psychosocial interventions for patients with coronary artery disease: A meta-analysis. *Archives of Internal Medicine, 156,* 745–752.

Lloyd, C. E., Dyer, P. H., Lancashire, R. J., Harris, T., Daniels, J. E., & Barnett, A. H. (1999). Association between stress and glycemic control in adults with type 1 (insulin-dependent) diabetes. *Diabetes Care, 22,* 1278–1283.

Lundberg, U. (1999). Stress responses in low-status jobs and their relationship to health risks: Musculoskeletal disorders. *Annals of the New York Academy of Sciences, 896,* 162–172.

Lupien, S. J., & McEwen, B. S. (1997). The acute effects of corticosteroids on cognition: Integration of animal and human model studies. *Brain Research Reviews, 24*, 1–27.

Manuck, S. B., Kaplan, J. R., & Clarkson, T. B. (1983). Behaviorally induced heart rate reactivity and atherosclerosis in cynomolgus monkeys. *Psychosomatic Medicine, 45*, 95–102.

Marshall, R. D., Spitzer, R., & Liebowitz, M. R. (1999). Review and critique of the new DSM-IV diagnosis of acute stress disorder. *American Journal of Psychiatry, 156*, 1677–1685.

Mason, J. W. (1975). Emotion as reflected in patterns of endocrine integration. In L. Levi (Ed.), *Emotions: Their parameters and measurement* (pp. 143–181). New York: Raven.

Matthews, K. A., & Gump, B. B. (2002). Chronic work stress and marital dissolution increase risk of posttrial mortality in men from the Multiple Risk Factor Intervention Trial. *Archives of Internal Medicine, 162*, 309–315.

McCaffery, J. M., Pogue-Geile, M. F., Ferrell, R. E., Petro, N., & Manuck, S. B. (2002). Variability within alpha- and beta-adrenoreceptor genes as a predictor of cardiovascular function at rest and in response to mental challenge. *Journal of Hypertension, 20*, 1105–1114.

McGee, R., Williams, S., & Elwood, M. (1996). Are life events related to the onset of breast cancer? *Psychological Medicine, 26*, 441–447.

Miller, S. M., Brody, D. S., & Summerton, J. (1988). Styles of coping with threat: Implications for health. *Journal of Personality and Social Psychology, 54*, 142–148.

Ornish, D., Brown, S. E., Scherwitz, L. W., Billings, J. H., Armstrong, W. T., Ports, T. A., McLanahan, S. M., Kirkeeide, R. L., Brand, R. J., & Gould, K. L. (1990). Can lifestyle changes reverse coronary heart disease? The Lifestyle Heart Trial. *Lancet, 336*, 129–133.

Pacak, K., & Palkovits, M. (2001). Stressor specificity of central neuroendocrine responses: Implications for stress-related disorders. *Endocrine Reviews, 22*, 502–548.

Pakenham, K. I., & Rinaldis, M. (2001). The role of illness, resources, appraisal, and coping strategies in adjustment to HIV/AIDS: The direct and buffering effects. *Journal of Behavioral Medicine, 24*, 259–279.

Petticrew, M., Bell, R., & Hunter, D. (2002). Influence of psychological coping on survival and recurrence in people with cancer: Systematic review. *British Medical Journal, 325*, 1066–1069.

Pillow, D. R., Zautra, A. J., & Sandler, I. (1996). Major life events and minor stressors: Identifying mediational links in the stress process. *Journal of Personality and Social Psychology, 70*, 381–394.

Potter, P. T., Smith, B. W., Strobel, K. R., & Zautra, A. J. (2002). Interpersonal workplace stressors and well-being: A multi-wave study of employees with and without arthritis. *Journal of Applied Psychology, 87*, 789–796.

Ritz, T., & Steptoe, A. (2000). Emotion and pulmonary function in asthma: Reactivity in the field and relationship with laboratory induction of emotion. *Psychosomatic Medicine, 62*, 808–815.

Rivest, S. (2001). How circulating cytokines trigger the neural circuits that control the hypothalamic–pituitary–adrenal axis. *Psychoneuroendocrinology, 26*, 761–788.

Rozanski, A., Blumenthal, J. A., & Kaplan, J. (1999). Impact of psychological factors on the pathogenesis of cardiovascular disease and implications for therapy. *Circulation, 99*, 2195–2217.

Sabban, E. L., & Kvetnansky, R. (2001). Stress-triggered activation of gene expression in catecholaminergic systems: Dynamics of transcriptional events. *Trends in Neurosciences, 24*, 91–98.

Sapolsky, R. M., Romero, L. M., & Munck, A. U. (2000). How do glucocorticoids influence stress responses? Integrating permissive, suppressive, stimulatory, and preparative actions. *Endocrine Reviews, 21*, 55–89.

Schulz, R., & Beach, S. R. (1999). Caregiving as a risk factor for mortality: The Caregiver Health Effects Study. *Journal of the American Medical Association, 282*, 2215–2219.

Schulz, R., O'Brien, A. T., Bookwala, J., & Fleissner, K. (1995). Psychiatric and physical morbidity effects of dementia caregiving: Prevalence, correlates, and causes. *Gerontologist, 35*, 771–791.

Scott, M., & Stradling, S. (1994). Post-traumatic stress disorder without the trauma. *British Journal of Clinical Psychology, 33*, 71–74.

Seeman, T. E., & Robbins, R. J. (1994). Aging and hypothalamic–pituitary–adrenal response to challenge in humans. *Endocrine Reviews, 15*, 233–260.

Selye, H. (1956). *The stress of life*. New York: McGraw-Hill.

Sheard, T., & Maguire, P. (1999). The effect of psychological interventions on anxiety and depression in cancer patients: Results of two meta-analyses. *British Journal of Cancer, 80*, 1770–1780.

Shore, J. H., Vollmer, W. M., & Tatum, E. L. (1989). Community patterns of post traumatic stress disorders. *Journal of Nervous and Mental Disease, 177*, 681–685.

Siegrist, J. (1996). Adverse health effects of high-effort/low-reward conditions. *Journal of Occupational Health Psychology, 1*, 27–41.

Silver, R. C., Holman, E. A., McIntosh, D. N., Poulin, M., & Gil-Rivas, V. (2002). Nationwide longitudinal study of psychological responses to September 11. *Journal of the American Medical Association, 288*, 1235–1244.

Spiegel, D., Bloom, J. R., Kraemer, H. C., & Gottheil, E. (1989). Effect of psychosocial treatment on survival of patients with metastatic breast cancer. *Lancet, 2*, 888–891.

Stansfeld, S. A., Fuhrer, R., Shipley, M. J., & Marmot, M. G. (1999). Work characteristics predict psychiatric disorder: Prospective results from the Whitehall II Study. *Occupational and Environmental Medicine, 56*, 302–307.

Stansfeld, S. A., & Marmot, M. G. (Eds.) (2002). *Stress and the heart: Psychosocial pathways to coronary heart disease*. London: BMJ Books.

Steenland, K., Fine, L., Belkic, K., Landsbergis, P., Schnall, P., Baker, D., Theorell, T., Siegrist, J., Peter, R., Karasek, R., Marmot, M., Brisson, C., & Tuchsen, F. (2000). Research findings linking workplace factors to CVD outcomes. *Occupational Medicine, 15*, 7–68.

Steptoe, A. (1998). Psychophysiological bases of disease. In D. W. Johnston & M. Johnston (Eds.), *Health psychology* (pp. 39–78). Oxford: Elsevier.

Steptoe, A., & Appels, A. (Eds.) (1989). *Stress, personal control and health*. Chichester: Wiley.

Steptoe, A., Feldman, P. M., Kunz, S., Owen, N., Willemsen, G., & Marmot, M. (2002). Stress responsivity and socioeconomic status: A mechanism for increased cardiovascular disease risk? *European Heart Journal, 23*, 1757–1763.

Steptoe, A., & Vögele, C. (1986). Are stress responses influenced by cognitive appraisal? An experimental comparison of coping strategies. *British Journal of Psychology, 77*, 243–255.

Sternberg, E. M. (2001). Neuroendocrine regulation of autoimmune/inflammatory disease. *Journal of Endocrinology, 169*, 429–435.

Stewart, S. H. (1996). Alcohol abuse in individuals exposed to trauma: A critical review. *Psychological Bulletin, 120*, 83–112.

Strike, P. C., & Steptoe, A. (2003). Systematic review of mental stress-induced myocardial ischaemia. *European Heart Journal, 24*, 690–703.

Suomi, S. J. (1997). Early determinants of behaviour: Evidence from primate studies. *British Medical Bulletin, 53*, 170–184.

Taylor, S. E., Klein, L. C., Lewis, B. P., Gruenewald, T. L., Gurung, R. A. R., & Updegraff, J. A. (2000). Biobehavioral responses to stress in females: Tend-and-befriend, not fight-or-flight. *Psychological Review, 107*, 411–429.

Taylor, S. E., & Seeman, T. E. (1999). Psychosocial resources and the SES–health relationship. *Annals of the New York Academy of Sciences, 896*, 210–225.

Turner, R. J., & Wheaton, B. (1995). Checklist measurement of stressful life events. In S. Cohen, R. C. Kessler & L. U. Gordon (Eds.), *Measuring stress: A Guide for health and social scientists* (pp. 29–58). New York: Oxford University Press.

Uchino, B. N., Cacioppo, J. T., & Kiecolt-Glaser, J. K. (1996). The relationship between social support and physiological processes: A review with emphasis on underlying mechanisms and implications for health. *Psychological Bulletin, 119*, 488–531.

Villar, J., Farnot, U., Barros, F., Victora, C., Langer, A., & Belizan, J. M. (1992). A randomized trial of psychosocial support during high-risk pregnancies. *New England Journal of Medicine, 327*, 1266–1271.

Visintainer, M. A., Volpicelli, J. R., & Seligman, M. E. (1982). Tumor rejection in rats after inescapable or escapable shock. *Science, 216*, 437–439.

von Kanel, R., Mills, P. J., Fainman, C., & Dimsdale, J. E. (2001). Effects of psychological stress and psychiatric disorders on blood coagulation and fibrinolysis: A biobehavioral pathway to coronary artery disease? *Psychosomatic Medicine, 63*, 531–544.

Wardle, J., Steptoe, A., Oliver, G., & Lipsey, Z. (2000). Stress, dietary restraint and food intake. *Journal of Psychosomatic Research, 48*, 195–202.

Webster, J. I., Tonelli, L., & Sternberg, E. M. (2002). Neuroendocrine regulation of immunity. *Annual Review of Immunology, 20*, 125–163.

Weiner, H. (1992). *Perturbing the organism: The biology of stressful experience*. Chicago: University of Chicago Press.

Wheaton, B. (1996). The domains and boundaries of stress concepts. In H. B. Kaplan (Ed.), *Psychosocial stress: Perspectives on structure, theory, life-course, and methods* (pp. 29–70). San Diego, CA: Academic.

Wolchik, S. A., Sandler, I. N., Millsap, R. E., Plummer, B. A., Greene, S. M., Anderson, E. R., Dawson-McClure, S. R., Hipke, K., & Haine, R. A. (2002). Six-year follow-up of preventive interventions for children of divorce: A randomized controlled trial. *Journal of the American Medical Association, 288*, 1874–1881.

Wüst, S., Federenko, I., Hellhammer, D. H., & Kirschbaum, C. (2000). Genetic factors, perceived chronic stress, and the free cortisol response to awakening. *Psychoneuroendocrinology, 25,* 707–720.

Yehuda, R. (1998) Neuroendocrinology of trauma and posttraumatic stress disorder. In R. Yeduda (Ed.), *Psychological trauma: Review of Psychiatry* (Vol. 17, pp. 97–131). Washington, DC: American Psychiatric Press.

Zajonc, R.B. (1984). On the primacy of affect. *American Psychologist, 39,* 117–123.

Zakowski, S. G. (1995). The effects of stressor predictability on lymphocyte proliferation in humans. *Psychology and Health, 10,* 409–425.

Zautra, A. J., Hamilton, N. A., Potter, P., & Smith, B. (1999). Field research on the relationship between stress and disease activity in rheumatoid arthritis. *Annals of the New York Academy of Sciences, 876,* 397–412.

Ziegelstein, R. C. (2001). Depression in patients recovering from a myocardial infarction. *Journal of the American Medical Association, 286,* 1621–1627.

Zorrilla, E. P., Luborsky, L., McKay, J. R., Rosenthal, R., Houldin, A., Tax, A., McCorkle, R., Seligman, D. A., & Schmidt, K. (2001). The relationship of depression and stressors to immunological assays: A meta-analytic review. *Brain, Behavior, and Immunity, 15,* 199–226.

8

Living with Chronic Illness: A Contextualized, Self-Regulation Approach

HOWARD LEVENTHAL, ETHAN HALM,
CAROL HOROWITZ, ELAINE A. LEVENTHAL
AND GOZDE OZAKINCI

INTRODUCTION

As the number of chronic diseases is legion, each having a different impact on function and quality of life, our chapter must necessarily be limited in scope. The contents of our chapter are as follows. First, we will introduce the idea that people's mental models or representations of a chronic disease are shaped by its biological features. Thus, the content of the representation and its similarity with prior illness representations will determine the degree to which the illness is experienced as stressful. Second, although chronic illness as a stressor is similar in many ways to other life stressors, for example job loss, marital discord, and so on, we suggest a specific way in which it differs quantitatively, if not qualitatively, from other stressors. We then review three frameworks or models for viewing and assessing the effects of chronic illness on the individual's life: (1) the biomedical framework, (2) the stress-coping framework, and (3) a self-regulation framework which describes behavior in the face of

chronic illness from the perspective of the sick individual in his or her social and cultural context. We describe each of these approaches and their strengths and weaknesses. Our review of these frameworks highlights three themes. The first is the close connection between the biomedical framework and the self-regulation analysis of adaptation to chronic illness and their sometimes paradoxical differences. The second is the ongoing assimilation and transformation of stress-coping concepts into the self-regulation framework. The third is the recognition of the gaps in empirical study of the processes involved in understanding how the social and cultural context affects the way in which individuals think about, and cope and learn to live with, chronic illness. A further section comments briefly on two topics of special interest to investigators focused on adaptation to chronic illness: adherence to treatment, and emotional responses to chronic illness. Our analysis will elaborate insights into these topics from the perspective of self-regulation theory.

The concluding section will summarize the themes that we believe are central to the development of theory for understanding adaptations to chronic illnesses and for improving practice for assisting patients with the management of their chronic conditions. One such theme is the transition from acute to chronic self-management or their effective combination, a problem faced by most individuals whose lifetime of illness experience has been with self-limited, acute conditions and who now face the never ending tasks of managing a chronic disease. Both the transition from acute to chronic management, and the alternative of their combination, require reconceptualizing illness and may require changes in self-identity. In this final section we also comment on the importance of using self-regulation theory in the design of clinical trials.

LIFE STRESS, CHRONIC ILLNESS, AND SPECIFIC DISEASES

What Is a Chronic Illness?

Most chronic illnesses share five important biological characteristics: (1) they are systemic, affecting multiple body systems and a wide range of physical and social functions; (2) they are lifespan problems, that is, they develop over many years though most become clinically visible only in late middle age, that is 60 years of age and over; (3) they can be controlled but few can be cured (e.g., Bahls & Fogarty, 2002); (4) many, though not all, have an insidious character, that is, they impinge gradually on an increasingly wide range of life activities; and (5) many are characterized by relatively quiet, tonic phases, punctuated by severe, episodic flares or dramatic onset of complications.

What has been called adult onset, or type II, diabetes is an excellent example of a chronic condition. Although it has begun to appear among teenagers due to the 'epidemic' of obesity, which is especially severe among many Native American populations, type II diabetes typically develops gradually, manifesting itself clinically in the late sixth and the seventh and eighth decades of life (Mokdad et al., 2001). The systemic effects of diabetes impinge upon a wide range of organ systems and impact multiple areas of daily function. Chronic elevation of blood sugar affects the circulatory system and heart, the kidneys, and the sensory-perceptual system (vision and loss of peripheral sensation in the feet leading to ulcers and threat of amputation). These complications intrude on the performance of daily activities ranging from walking to reading. Similarly, pulmonary disease and cancers are systemic with complex and relatively lengthy developmental histories. They typically become symptomatic in late middle to early old age, and affect multiple organ systems. For example, pulmonary disease impacts the cardiovascular system, and cancers, when metastatic, can destroy tissues and function in multiple organ systems. Both the pre-clinical and clinical features of these diseases involve the interaction of lifestyle factors such as diet, inactivity, cigarette smoking, and so on, with physiological processes including gene expression.

Although diabetes and pulmonary disease (e.g., asthma and chronic obstructive pulmonary disease) are chronic, the intensity of their impact varies both across individuals and within the lifetime of any single individual. For example, asthma affects 17 million Americans, the prevalence and number of deaths from asthma having doubled from 1980 to 1996 (Mannino et al., 2002), with costs exceeding $11 billion per year by 1988 (National Heart, Lung, and Blood Institute, 1998; Weiss, Sullivan & Lyttle, 2000). Although asthma affects all races and ethnic groups, it disproportionately affects minority, inner city, and low income populations. Asthmatics experience quiet periods punctuated by attacks of breathlessness. Diabetics, on the other hand, may be experiencing occasional bouts of symptoms due to excessive use of insulin, but their lives can continue in a fairly normal manner until chronic elevation of blood sugar leads to heart attacks, strokes, blindness, kidney failure, and neurological dysfunction, including digestive disorders and painful foot neuropathy that may result in amputation (UK Prospective Diabetes Study (UKPDS) Group, 1998).

As our experiential-perceptual systems are designed to detect changes, it should come as no surprise that diseases that are characterized by severe episodes separated by quiet periods will often be understood and managed as though they are acute conditions. Diseases that are silent at onset may be met with surprise, bewilderment, and fear when diagnosed (e.g., 'I felt fine', 'Didn't know I was sick'). Because the cognitive and emotional systems will focus on episodic flares, self-management will target these acute flares and ignore tonic, or quiescent periods, an outcome that may be inappropriate for effective, long term control (Halm, Sturm, Mora & Leventhal, 2003). Finally, the genetic revolution is introducing new ambiguity respecting the meaning of chronic illness. Testing for genes known to predict clinical disease prior to the appearance of symptoms or physiological dysfunction can raise questions, both for the layperson and clinician, for example when can/should someone be designated as 'sick' (Baron, 1985)?

Biology does not operate in a vacuum; somatic stimuli are interpreted in light of past illness experience, social observation, information from others, and mass media messages that reflect current happenings and cultural beliefs. For example, inappropriate self-management of asthma (using medication only when symptomatic) can reflect the inaccurate perception that asthma is a series of acute attacks separated by periods in which one is completely well. An acute representation of this chronic illness likely reflects prior years of experience with acute colds, headaches and gastrointestinal conditions. Acute representations are often reinforced by family and friends who also are impressed by the episodic flares of chronic conditions and eager to see asymptomatic periods as signs of health and cure. Indeed, there is no inconsistency between the pressure that can be exerted upon an individual by family and friends to seek medical care in order to evaluate, treat and cure symptoms and physical dysfunction (Cameron, Leventhal & Leventhal, 1993; Zola, 1973), and the reluctance of these same others to accept a condition as chronic and as a threat to significant life plans and to life itself. Institutional factors and biomedical themes may also encourage an acute outlook. The emphasis upon cures by means of antibiotics and surgery and the desire to see disease as vanquished when a patient departs the hospital can also reinforce the common-sense view that chronic diseases are little different from acute, curable conditions. In summary, the shift from a mental representation of acute illnesses and the strategies and specific procedures for their management to the mental representations, procedures and strategies for living with chronic conditions poses a major cognitive hurdle for most people, and this shift can be resisted both by the individual and by family and friends and can become a source of considerable emotional distress.

Living with chronic illness does not end with the properties of the disease; formal and informal treatments (Chrisman & Kleinman, 1983) and a wide range of self-care activities (Ory & DeFriese, 1998) are an integral part of the adaptive process. In addition to their impact on the disease and its symptoms, these interventions and lifestyle changes also have mental representations (i.e., identities, expected time frames, expected efficacies). Some procedures, as with the illnesses they treat, may be life threatening, and many are self-administered and lifelong. Practitioners, patients and families and friends are likely to have beliefs about how a procedure produces its effects, for example surgery removes a tumor and repairs a clogged artery, and they are likely to hold expectations as to how effective they are in controlling the disease outcome (Horne, 1997, 2003).

In summary, life with chronic illness is typically a complex affair as the number of such diseases an individual will confront increases with age. Nearly 100 million US citizens are affected by chronic conditions, 41 million have limitations in activities of daily living due to chronic illness, and 12 million are unable to live independently because of them. Individuals over 65 years of age are dealing with an average of 2.2 chronic conditions for which they are taking multiple medications (Hoffman, Rice & Sung, 1996; Rothenberg & Koplan, 1990). In short, much of the 'treatment' for controlling and preventing chronic illnesses requires daily, at-home performance by the patient over a lifetime. The need to perform an ongoing series of minor and major tasks will affect an individual's physical and psychological status and alter the lives of those with whom he or she lives.

Life Stress and Chronic Illness

Investigations of adaptation to chronic illness often follow the same model as that used to study adaptation to other life stressors. Is it reasonable, however, to assume that the same concepts and models can be used to study adaptation to cancer, arthritis, diabetes, asthma and Alzheimer's disease as are used to study adaptation to stressors such as preparing for examinations for medical school (Kiecolt-Glaser et al., 1984), managing job loss (Pearlin, 1989), living within a 10 mile radius of a nuclear accident (Collins, Baum & Singer, 1983), caring for a family member with dementia (Kiecolt-Glaser, Dura, Speicher, Trask & Glaser, 1991), and living in a conflicted marital relationship (Kiecolt-Glaser, Bane, Glaser & Malarkey, 2003)? The underlying notion unifying these studies is that stressors, no matter how diverse they may be, can be described in terms of the extent or intensity of the demand they make upon the individual's adaptive resources (Lazarus & Folkman, 1984) and/or the individual's coping resources or sense of personal efficacy (Bandura, 1977, 1989).

Features differentiating chronic illnesses from other stressors

Many life stressors share properties with one or more chronic illnesses. Some, such as marital conflict, pose prolonged threats to valued life goals, but even these are potentially terminable, and a few, such as combat service, pose threats to life itself. In addition, some, such as nuclear accidents and job loss, may appear with very brief or no prior warning as do many cancers. As both non-illnesses and chronic illnesses require preparation for effective management, make demands on resources and bear a degree of uncertainty regarding future outcomes, they present the conditions for the elicitation of negative affects such as anxiety, fear, and depression (Scherer, 1999a, 1999b).

Chronic illnesses differ, however, in significant ways from other stressors. First, they are universal, and therefore shared. One or more chronic illnesses will strike almost all of us and be with us for the remainder of life; even the most fortunate will have detectable signs of osteoarthritis, arteriosclerosis, and sensory deficits. Second, as they are internal, chronic illnesses undermine the physical and psychological resources necessary for successful adaptation. And as the majority of chronic illnesses appear later in the lifespan, they become clinically evident when resources are on the decline. Thus, the chronically ill individual needs to develop skills for the allocation and replenishment of resources although s/he is in a physically weakened state and under a high level of uncertainty respecting future needs and the future size of his or her pool of physical and mental energy (Leventhal & Crouch, 1997; Leventhal, Rabin, Leventhal & Burns, 2001). In addition to striking when resources are on the decline, chronic conditions do not typically appear alone. As stated earlier, the average 65-year-old will be dealing with 2.2 chronic conditions, each of which presents common and unique problems for management and each of which directly attacks an already diminished pool of personal resources. Thus, because the stressors of chronic illnesses often appear when the individual's social and psychological resources as well as his or her physical resources are declining, they create additional problems for optimization of function (Baltes & Baltes, 1990; Leventhal & Crouch, 1997). Resource allocation is a lifespan problem, and difficulties and/or failures in appropriate allocation may be a cause of aging (Kirkwood & Austad, 2000). Thus, not only are chronic illnesses inescapable and to be lived with for life, but virtually none can be mastered with intense, short term expenditures of energy and relegated to the dim past.

Third, regardless of the age at which they are clinically evident, most chronic illnesses develop over years and decades. Cardiovascular and coronary diseases are an excellent example. Although myocardial infarction, the leading cause of mortality, strikes in the 50s and 60s for men, and in the 60s and 70s for women (Link & Tanner, 2001), the changes preceding their clinical manifestation are evident in the second and third decades of life. Similarly, although most cancers occur later in life – for example, the incidence of breast cancers is highest for women in their early 70s, and virtually 75 per cent of men older than 85 years will have some form of prostate cancer (Gronberg, 2003) – the sequence of cellular changes needed for a cancerous growth may require years or decades prior to the appearance of clinical signs.

Fourth, the actions required to minimize and control the severity of chronic illness may have side effects that are seemingly as disruptive of life and physically invasive and life threatening as the illness itself. For example, the surgical and chemotherapy treatments for breast and colon cancer are debilitating and disruptive of other life activities, and they are often experienced as more threatening than the cancers they are designed to control and hopefully 'cure'. Individuals with coronary disease will benefit if they engage in a level of exercise appropriate for enhancing the vigor and reserve of the cardiovascular system (Curfman, 1993), though excesses in these routines can generate chest pain and the realistic threat of cardiac decompensation and death (Mittleman et al., 1993). Similarly, the diabetic can experience the symptoms of hyperglycemia due to insulin deficit and the opposing symptoms and threat of unconsciousness from hypoglycemia from excessive doses of insulin (Farkas-Hirsch, 1998: 99–120). And the behaviors recommended for the control of cardiovascular disease and diabetes require major lifestyle changes, many of which are difficult to make and require cooperation and lifestyle changes from family members. Finally, quite different self-care procedures may be involved in managing the dramatic episodes and stabilizing the background of chronic illness, and these procedures can work against one another. For example, two-thirds or more of asthmatics do not make use of recommended daily inhaled corticosteroids (Diette et al., 2001), yet many are overly eager to self-medicate with beta agonists in the face of an asthmatic attack (Boulet, 1998; Diette et al., 2001; van Grunsven, 2001). Thus, although the stresses and adaptive demands of chronic illness will be similar to other recurrent stressors, these procedures are often experienced as double-edged swords whose life saving properties are counterbalanced by risk of death.

Fifth, chronic illnesses can generate high and long lasting levels of emotional distress. An array of negative affects, for example depression, anxiety, and pain related distress, can be generated by physiological, functional and psychological paths. At the physiological level, chronic illness can have direct effects on negative affect by depleting neuro-endocrine resources and/or by activating cytokines that generate fatigue and immobility (Swain, 2000). Behavioral dysfunctions leading to disruption of social and economic activities represent a second pathway to depressive affect (Zeiss, Lewinsohn, Rohde & Seeley, 1996). Finally, the features of chronic illness, namely that they are internal, stable and/or worsening, creating essentially uncontrollable dysfunction, overlap with the conditions presumed to underlie depression (Seligman, 1975). Although these three pathways insure an overlap between chronic illness and depression, the resulting psychological morbidity or 'disease related distress' rarely meets the DSM-IV definition of major depressive disorder (Coyne, Benazon, Gaba, Calzone & Weber, 2000; Coyne, Thompson, Klinkman & Nease, 2002; Coyne, Thompson, Palmer, Kagee & Maunsell, 2000).

Finally, chronic illnesses are embedded in a context of both cultural meanings and institutional structures that may include frequent contacts with a variety of specialists, insuring their differentiation from many other life stressors. Most individuals have had multiple contacts with the formal, traditional medical care system prior to the onset of most chronic illnesses, and the medical care system offers a complex set of institutions and roles for dealing with serious, chronic conditions. A lifetime of contacts with medical practitioners for annual or employment physicals, and for treatment for acute injuries and infectious conditions, occasional hospitalization for more serious, short term conditions, and contacts with both medical and life insurers, create a web of interactions and skills that shape how chronic illnesses are viewed, detected, treated and responded to. An equally complex informal system, comprising interpersonal contacts, internet sites and chat rooms (Gustafson et al., 1999, 2000), provides testimonials as to the nature of specific chronic diseases and how to identify and treat them so as to minimize their impact on life (Chrisman & Kleinman, 1983). Television, magazines and newspapers, health food sections in supermarkets and retail establishments and health clubs dedicated to nutrition and exercise, promote specific procedures for preventing, treating and controlling various chronic illnesses, forming retail markets that measure in the tens of billions of dollars (Eisenberg et al., 1998). Chronic illnesses contrast with other life stressors with respect to the variety, level of detail and frequency of contact with contextual factors that affect how we view and cope with them.

Generic versus Disease Specific Features of Chronic illness

The differences between non-illness life stressors and chronic illness might suggest that studies of adaptation to chronic illness can proceed as if chronic illnesses form a homogeneous category. Doing so, however, would ignore important differences among the chronic illnesses. For example, severe asthma and congestive heart failure (CHF) share several of the characteristics ascribed to all chronic conditions as they are part of the self and lifelong, and their severe episodes can be life threatening. They are also, however, very different biologically. The median survival of patients hospitalized for CHF is 1.6 years (MacIntyre et al., 2000). The prognosis is far less grave for individuals with asthma if severe attacks are managed correctly. On the other hand, because both conditions are characterized by quiet periods punctuated by severe attacks, many individuals experience them as episodic rather than chronic and manage them in accord with an episodic model (Halm, Sturm, Mora, & Leventhal, 2003). Generating a conceptual framework to capture, organize and make predictions about these complexities is a central task for behavioral studies.

FRAMEWORKS FOR EXAMINING ADAPTATION TO CHRONIC ILLNESS

The biomedical, stress-coping, and self-regulation frameworks provide different views of the processes involved in adaptation to chronic illnesses.

Investigators have tried to fill the gaps in each of these models by adding concepts from the others; for example, investigators concerned with the theory of clinical practice have expanded the biomedical framework into a biopsychosocial model that is theoretically more rich and necessary for effective clinical practice (Engel, 1977). To avoid repetition, we will present most concepts within the self-regulation framework even though they may have appeared at an earlier time. Thus, the self-regulation framework will serve as a comprehensive model that can incorporate the essential concepts and insights of the biomedical and stress-coping approaches.

THE BIOMEDICAL FRAMEWORK

The traditional biomedical model is focused on the detection and treatment of chronic disease and the understanding of the biological processes underlying disease (Engel, 1977). In its most simple form, the model would predict that the severity of chronic disease is directly related to and responsible for diminutions of physical and psychological function. Decline in physical and psychological function, such as deficits in cognitive function and increases in emotional distress, are directly attributed to the extent of compromise of cardiac muscle and function, the extent of atherosclerotic, arterial constriction and level of blood pressure, the extent of arthritic changes in joints, and elevations in blood sugar level (Leventhal & Burns, 2004). Diagnosis and the identification and description of disease related physiological, structural and mechanical changes are the first, critical steps to treatment, and surgical, prosthetic, and pharmacological treatments are prescribed to control and reverse the disease. Timely and appropriate treatment is critical for favorable prognosis, that is, for the control and in some cases the reversal of these changes and the reduction in the physical and psychological dysfunctions they create. In contemporary medicine, therefore, prognosis is increasingly an issue of treatment rather than an issue of a specific disease (Christakis, 1999), and the elaboration and communication of outcome expectations by physicians to patients is less frequently a topic for medical education.

The above view of biomedicine is clearly stereotypic. It ignores the efforts to transform the biomedical model to a biopsychosocial model. One need not look back more than three decades, however, to find prominent biomedical practitioners claiming that advances in prevention and treatment depend upon biomedical discovery rather than behavioural changes that are impossible to achieve (Thomas, 1977: 39). This outlook is counter to the results of three recent large scale clinical trials conducted in different countries showing that behavioral interventions are effective for the prevention of diabetes among individuals at high risk (Diabetes Prevention Program Research Group, 2002; Pan et al., 1997; Tuomilehto et al., 2001), indeed more effective than medication. In the US trial (Diabetes Prevention Program Research Group, 2002), the lifestyle intervention produced a 58 per cent reduction in transition from high risk, that is abnormal blood sugar management, to levels defined as diabetic, in comparison to 31 per cent for medication. These reductions are in comparison to patients in a standard treatment, control condition.

Although it is noteworthy that behavioral interventions can be sufficient for disease prevention, the strongest pressure to incorporate social and behavioral factors in the biomedical model likely comes from the extent of behavioral involvement in both general and specialized medical treatment for chronic conditions. Internists and cardiologists may diagnose and prescribe diuretics, an ace inhibitor or a beta blocker for hypertension and congestive heart failure, but the use of treatment, that is adherence to medication, is a task to be carried out by the patient in the home and work environments (ACC/AHA Task Force, 1995). It is stating the obvious that adherence is a major issue for lifestyle changes such as diet and exercise, which are important for treatment of cardiac disease and diabetes. Geriatric medicine provides a prime example where success in managing the chronic conditions of the elderly requires managing the behavior of both patient and family (Lough, 1996). Unfortunately, levels

of adherence seldom exceed 50 per cent, and are usually less, although there are exceptions such as chemotherapy treatment for breast cancer. Sackett and Haynes (1976) provided a simple formula for estimating adherence to successful treatment for hypertension: half of hypertensives are diagnosed, half of those diagnosed are in treatment, and half of those in treatment have their blood pressure controlled. And this formula can be applied to treatments for far too many chronic illnesses. Adherence rates for self-management of CHF and asthma differ little from these figures; for example, in a large, national survey only 19 per cent of ambulatory patients with persistent asthma reported using recommended, inhaled corticosteroids (*Glaxo Wellcome*, 1998). In summary, the emphasis and wish for 'magic bullets' completely fails to describe the realities involved in the procedures needed for the prevention of chronic illness, the control of its progression and the maintenance of function following its onset.

Adherence and practitioner–patient communication are two areas in which there has been a conscious introduction of behavioral procedures for medical management (Dunbar-Jacob, Schlenk, Burke & Matthews, 1998). Problems in medication adherence have resulted in the production of combination pharmaceuticals and slow release medications, reducing the number and frequency of use. Pill organizers are prescribed that can be loaded once a week and their simple structure goes far in reducing non-adherence. Virtually all medical practitioners use both letters and phone reminders to insure appointment keeping (McBride & Rimer, 1999). *Monitoring* is seen as critical both for identifying areas for change, for example identifying areas of risk in a patient's diet, and for carrying out prescribed treatments; for example, asthmatics are given peak-flow meters to determine the success and further need for steroids (National Heart, Lung, and Blood Institute, 1997); diabetics have simple devices for testing blood sugar to regulate insulin use (American Diabetes Association, 2001; Cunningham, 2001); and hypertensives are taught to monitor blood pressure changes to assess the adequacy of medication (Chobanian et al., 2003). Internet systems are being developed to increase the 'online' quality of monitoring of diet, blood pressure and blood glucose and to provide the rapid feedback needed to correct indiscretion (Piette, 2002). The National Institutes of Health has convened expert panels and published lengthy documents laying out *action plans* that define 'gold standards' for treatment of chronic illnesses such as asthma (National Heart, Lung, and Blood Institute, 1997). These action plans are filled with detailed instructions on how to perform the specific behaviors needed to reduce pulmonary inflammation and control asthma attacks. Interactive, two-way communication between patient and provider is critical for maintaining effective self-care behaviors (Halm, Wang, Cooperman, Sturm & Leventhal, 2003). Evidence suggests, however, low levels of physician compliance with National Asthma Education and Prevention Program (NAEPP) guidelines for prescribing inhaled corticosteroid therapy, the use of peak-flow meters, and providing action plans (Legorreta et al., 1998). Communication is suboptimal; for example, a typical study showed that only 9 per cent of asthma patients felt that they had been given enough information about their condition and only 27 per cent had been given written instruction about their medication regimen (Partridge, 1995). Conversely, more participatory decision making between physicians and adults with asthma has been associated with more desirable self-management beliefs and behaviors and greater patient satisfaction (Halm, Wang et al., 2003).

Care for patients emerging from surgical treatment for illnesses such as cancer and cardiac disease, and post-stroke treatment, involve complex rehabilitation procedures for restoring physical and psychological function. Metered, daily increases in walking, strength building exercises, diet education (Jolliffe et al., 2000), and so on, and detailed procedures and action plans for skill development and training in self-care, are integral parts of these day, week- and/or month-long procedures. Regimens for the management of such chronic conditions are generally driven by physiological and biomechanical theory and evidence respecting the efficacy of the regimen

for the return of physical function and psychological function (see review by Leventhal et al., 2001). In fact, in one of the most successful behavioral programs, which targeted dietary change to control high blood pressure (Sacks et al., 2001), investigators provided patients with the food for the 'DASH diet' rather than instructing patients how to procure or prepare the diet independently. In other words, the diet was delivered as a prescribed item rather than a lifestyle change.

Numerous studies support the need for and value of behavioral interventions to enhance biological and functional outcomes. As was the case with the successful DASH (Sacks et al., 2001) program, the majority of intervention trials do not present a theoretical rationale for their behavioral components and fail to provide a theoretical or procedural road map for implementing and sustaining the complex self-care behaviors involved in low fat and low sodium diets, daily exercise and the use of devices to monitor expiratory volume and/or blood sugar levels (Leventhal et al., 2001). In many instances, therefore, evidence is lacking as to which specific procedures are essential for generating motivation and skills for initiating and sustaining behavioral changes. It would be remiss to fail to mention that the interventions used in highly developed rehabilitation programs designed to maximize recovery of function following myocardial infarction, stroke and accident related neurological damage have been carefully designed to maximize recovery of function. The focus on the performance of specific behavioral sequences used in these programs, however, is driven more by the physiological and biomechanical details of the recovery process and less by the social and motivational factors involved in patient adherence. For this reason patients may perceive these behavioral programs as excessive and/or unnecessary, leading to suboptimal levels of participation. Regardless of possible deficits in the motivational domain, these intervention programs pose an important lesson for behavioral investigators and practitioners as they make clear that achieving beneficial, functional outcomes requires the systematic application and ongoing monitoring of progress of a series of highly specific actions. As we point out in the following section, the details in this panoply of medically informed interventions form a sharp contrast to the small number of factors examined by investigators using the stress-coping model to understand how coping affects adaptation to chronic illness.

THE STRESS-COPING FRAMEWORK

The stress-coping framework (Lazarus, 1966; Lazarus & Folkman, 1984) has been widely used for the investigation of adaptation to chronic illness. When broadly defined, a number of behavioral models fit within this framework: for example, the health belief model (Janz & Becker, 1984; Rosenstock, 1974), protection motivation theory (Rogers, 1983), and other stress-coping models (Cohen, 1988; Cohen & Herbert, 1996; Cohen & Hoberman, 1983; Moos, 1986; Pearlin, 1989; Pearlin, Menaghan, Lieberman & Mullan, 1981). All of these models propose a three-step process: (1) the appraisal of a threat to health that creates a motive and a goal for action; (2) the selection of a coping response for goal attainment; and (3) the appraisal of the effectiveness of the coping response in moving toward the goal. Thus, all stress-coping models are based upon simple, control system concepts (Miller, Galanter & Pribram, 1960; Powers, 1973). The same is true of self-regulation models which we will describe later.

Although all of these models are built upon a common, three-stage process, they differ in a number of specifics respecting the constructs and processes at each stage, and these differences affect their view of the processes underlying adaptation to chronic illness (Figure 8.1). For example, according to Lazarus (1966), the stress process is initiated by a 'primary appraisal' that involves an evaluation of the demands of the stressor, while Carver and Scheier (1981, 1982) indicate that the appraisal involves the detection of a deviation from a desired standard, a narrower definition of the appraisal process. Neither model specifies the content or degree to which the individual is consciously aware of the details of the appraisal process, that is, it could be focused on highly specific goals or features of the stressful input

as implied in the Carver and Scheier model, or it could involve a much broader interpretation of the stressor and its overall implications for the physical, social and economic wellbeing of the self as stated by Lazarus.

Motivational Stage: Experienced Demand

An important difference among these models is whether the level of threat or demand posed by a stressor is assessed by the participants themselves or by an observer. Early studies of life stress used expert panels to measure the demands of different stressors; participants checked the various stressors they were facing on a pre-existent list and their stress level was based upon an expert panel's rating of the severity of these stressors (Holmes & Masuda, 1974). An important variant of the expert panel method involved scoring the event and the context in which it appeared (Brown & Harris, 1978).

Most stress-coping models, however, relied upon the participant's subjective assessment of the severity of the stressor. The primary appraisal of severity could be conceptualized as the evaluation of the severity or magnitude of the threat and its relevance to the self (Lazarus & Folkman, 1984), as the perception of magnitude × personal vulnerability as conceptualized in utility models (Janz & Becker, 1984; Rogers, 1983), or as the deviation from a desired standard (Carver & Scheier, 1981). The concept of severity is intrinsically ambiguous as the stressor can be highly specific, or, as is the case with many chronic illnesses such as diabetes or breast and colon cancer, the stressor can threaten social relationships, economic security, and the loss of one or more self- identities, or threaten a painful as well as early death (Lazarus, 1964; Leventhal, 1970; Rogers, 1983).

The primary appraisal and/or assessment of the severity of a stressor are complicated by the availability of responses for its control. Subjective judgment of the severity of a stressor and the intensity of the psychological and physiological stress it generates is presumed to depend on the perception that the threat is perceived and/or interpreted as exceeding one's

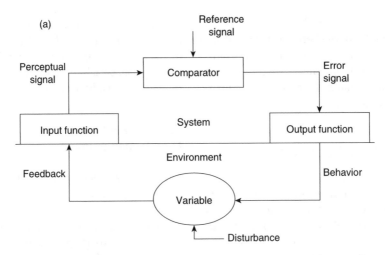

Figure 8.1   (a) Carver and Scheier's (1981) theoretical approach is based upon control system principles in which a stimulus disturbance activates the response system (see Miller et al., 1960). The disturbance could be a novel or an unexpected somatic change, for example a headache, blood in the stool etc., which deviates from the prior, 'normal' status of the body. The behavioral adjustment to close the gap, for example taking an aspirin for the headache or calling the doctor to check on blood in the stool, is taken with the expectation that the response will close the gap (e.g., aspirin will eliminate the headache) or begin to close the gap (e.g., visiting the doctor to determine if the bleeding is due to an acute, non-life-threatening disorder) between the disturbance and the set point. The set points are established by higher order loops, for example normal experience of the body, and generalized expectancies. Their model identifies a small number of higher level psychological variables that affect set points, for example optimism and disengagement (Scheier & Carver, 2003), but it does not specify variables in the somatic domain

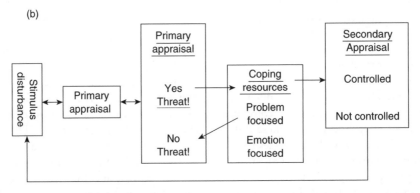

Figure 8.1   (b) The Lazarus stress-coping model is also based on control system principles (Lazarus, 1964; Lazarus & Folkman, 1984; Lazarus & Launier, 1978). The primary appraisal process evaluates whether a stimulus, for example a somatic change or an impending treatment such as surgery for breast cancer, is a threat to one's self and one's goals, and whether the threat is manageable, that is, whether it exceeds available coping resources. This appraisal leads to specific coping responses and the secondary appraisal evaluates whether the response was successful. Leventhal's (1970) early parallel processing model is similar in several respects to both the Carver–Scheier and the Lazarus models. It posits parallel control systems, namely one for the perceived danger and another for the experience of negative affect, that is, fear. The appraisal process in this model is multilevel, some conscious and deliberate, and some automatic and non-conscious (see Leventhal, 1980, 1984)

capacity for successful coping (Lazarus, 1964, 2000; Lazarus & Folkman, 1984). It is unclear whether judgments of severity are independent of the availability of effective coping responses and the 'secondary appraisal' of coping outcomes. A good example of independent assessment of these factors is seen in an early study on the primary appraisal of stressors (economic strain) due to job loss (Pearlin et al., 1981; Pearlin & Schooler, 1978).

Conceptualization and Measurement of Coping

The area in which stress-coping models have been most fully elaborated is in the description of the coping response(s) for controlling the threat. Coping reactions have been classified as problem focused or danger control (e.g., quit smoking, take a screening test to detect a possible cancer), and emotion focused or fear control (e.g., avoid thinking about the threat, think positive thoughts, engage in relaxation, take medication or drink to alleviate anxiety: Carver, Scheier & Weintraub, 1989; Lazarus & Launier, 1978; Leventhal, 1970; see also Endler & Parker, 1990). These factors emerge from analyses of scales such as the 168-item WOC inventory that describe different ways of responding to life threats. These analyses have generated as few as five (Vitaliano, Russo, Carr, Maiuro & Becker, 1985) and as many as eight factors (e.g., Folkman & Lazarus, 1985), four to six of which are focused on the regulation of emotion and one, and on rare occasion two, of which describe confronting with and managing the objective threat (Folkman & Lazarus, 1985; Vitaliano et al., 1985). That problem focused coping is typically identified by a single factor forms a disturbing contrast with the enormous number of procedures that are available and used for the prevention, treatment and control of chronic illnesses. One might question the rationality of using a single category or factor to describe procedures for coping with cardiac disease that are as different as adhering to pharmacological treatment, exercise, and use of herbals and vitamins. Exercise and herbals may be used as complements or as alternatives to medical treatment and this difference is non-trivial. Issues such as the pattern and duration of use are also ignored.

The use of generic scales of this sort is a form of psychological reductionism in which coping responses are treated as personality traits, and fails to examine the how, when, and why an individual chooses a dietary change or exercise, or one of any number of diets or exercise routines, for the prevention or management of cancer, cardiac disease, diabetes or any other chronic or acute illness. The scales also are mute with respect to treatment preferences, for example they are not designed to predict preferences for medication, angioplasty or surgery for the treatment of myocardial infarction, or medication and lifestyle change for the control of diabetes. The scales have also been criticized on methodological grounds, and it has been stated that 'many of the items used in previous coping inventories were ambiguous, at least in terms of the coping concepts … explored. How an item was viewed [by respondents] was based not only on its objective content, but on how the person imagined using it' (Stone, Helder & Schneider, 1988: 197).

Opinions may vary as to the level of specificity required for a theoretically satisfactory assessment of coping. It could be argued that a non-specific concept such as 'problem focused coping' represents the appropriate level of representation for theory, and that concepts respecting a specific type of coping should be represented as implementations of this generic concept. Investigations of personality as a moderator of the stress-coping process suggest, however, that generic factors residing at the level of personal dispositions, for example optimism (Scheier & Carver, 1985), are best conceptualized as second-order or higher level constructs in the stress-coping process. Hierarchical versions of stress-coping models fit better, however, within the self-regulation framework which presents an array of concepts better suited to this conceptual task. The measurement of coping is clearly in this direction (Skinner, Edge, Altman & Sherwood, 2003).

SELF-REGULATION FRAMEWORK

Self-regulation and stress-coping models share a control systems approach in which behavior is regulated by goals, procedures for goal attainment and appraisal of response outcomes. Self-regulation models differ, however, with respect to their conceptual content and dynamics. These models represent the chronically ill individual as a problem solver trying to make sense of her somatic experiences, acting and evaluating the effectiveness of her actions for controlling these changes, and describing how these efforts evolve given her history with illness and her social context. Self-regulation models provide more detailed concepts for describing perceptions of health threats. The threat or target for self-management has a name and symptoms, time frames (time to occurrence, duration, etc.), causes (genes, lifestyles, etc.), consequences and perceived routes for cure and control. Thus, understanding a chronic disease involves more than appraising its magnitude or size in relation to one's coping resources. Second, the self-regulation model is dynamic and process oriented; it proposes specific hypotheses respecting the structure of the information processing system that underlies the individual's experience and behavior and how these experiences and behaviors change and are updated over time. Third, the problem solving approach recognizes the intimate relationship between the physiological and biomechanical events that generate symptoms and the expectations respecting the targets and procedures for disease management.

The self-regulation approach requires, therefore, a detailed understanding of how illness affects experience, moods and function. This is true whether the study is designed to understand the relationship of behavioral factors in response to the illness or an intervention designed to improve illness management. As a consequence, the variables of the self-regulation model will parallel those of the biomedical model, while differing from them in an important way: self-regulation concepts conceptualize illness events from the perspective of the patient, and not that of the medical observer. Because the self-regulation model complements the biomedical model by describing the patient's perceptions and constructions of the illness process, it provides the clinician with a set of concepts for understanding the patient's experience and behavior. Confronting and reducing these discrepancies between these perspectives is a critical factor for trust and long term adherence (Heijmans et al., 2001). Thus, the self-regulation approach makes clear that research, both descriptive and intervention, is fundamentally multidisciplinary.

The self-regulation model is also explicit in identifying the features of the cultural and social context that set limits upon and provide pathways for behavioral management. Because research from this framework calls for concepts that are disease and context specific, investigators will find that generic measuring instruments, such as those used in stress-coping models, often fail to capture the experiences and behavioral strategies that people use in managing chronic health problems. Implementation of the self-regulation framework may require the creation of new instruments to record how individuals manage the day-by-day details of adapting to chronic illness and new approaches to intervention to deal with the changing nature of the disease (Petrie, Broadbent & Meechan, 2003). For example, a chronic condition such as diabetes is not a fixed entity; it is a complex disorder with new features, for example neuropathy leading to loss of sight and loss of feeling in the feet with risk of ulcers and foot amputation, appearing over its natural history (Diabetes Control and Complications Trial Research Group, 1993; Leslie, 1999). Effective self-regulation of diabetes over this life history requires different interpretations of somatic experiences, different goals, different coping skills and different criteria for evaluating response efficacy. The basic design of self-regulation theory makes it a useful platform for the creation of measures and behavior change interventions to deal with the multiple features of chronic disorders as they unfold over the years.

Basic Assumptions

Patient as a common-sense scientist/physician

Consistent with traditional, cognitive models of the behavioral process, self-regulation models treat the individual as a common-sense 'scientist' trying to make sense of her/his world (Kelly, 1955; Mischel, 1973; Rotter, 1954); individuals act as common-sense biologists, physicians and psychologists in their efforts to understand and manage their chronic-illness experience (Cameron & Leventhal, 2003; Leventhal, Meyer & Nerenz, 1980; Nerenz & Leventhal, 1983). The result is an ever changing set of interpretations of experience and the recruitment of varied skills for management. People live with chronic illnesses and manage them over extended time frames in their 'home' environments.

Hierarchical structure

Both self-regulation and stress-coping models share a hierarchical view of the behavioral process. Analogous to other problem solving models such as that for the game of chess, the psychology of the chronically ill person can be described as having a hierarchical structure, the base level of which is the disease label and its symptoms and signs (the chess board and its pieces) and the procedures for their management (the rules governing the movement of the pieces). The ongoing interpretation of symptoms (e.g., of foot pain caused by diabetic neuropathy, the swelling of the feet and breathing difficulties caused by CHP), and appraisals of the efficacy of specific procedures for dealing with these symptoms, generate an increasingly complex representation of the problem, that is the illness and its management. A central proposition of the self-regulation model, one that deserves repetition, is that *patients regulate experiences, symptoms, and functional changes over time*. This functional level, the 'problem space' (Greeno, 1998), is at the heart of the self-regulation process.

Moving up the hierarchy, the problem space is nested in the self-system and both are nested

in the social, cultural and ecological context (Leventhal, Leventhal & Robitaille, 1998; Leventhal, Idler & Leventhal, 1999). Self-system factors, such as one's perceived ability to control disease (self-efficacy or skill at playing the game: Bandura, 1977, 1989), tendencies toward somatization (Barsky, 1992, 2001), emotional responsiveness to symptoms and treatments (Watson & Pennebaker, 1989), and self-assessments of one's health (Idler & Benyamini, 1997), and other self-attributes, generate a sense of vulnerability and perceptions of likely success in preventing and controlling chronic conditions. These self-factors interact with and influence the problem space, that is, they affect the interpretation and representation of the illness, the selection and performance of procedures for illness control, and expectations respecting response outcomes (Carver et al., 1993; Scheier & Carver, 2003).

Social, institutional and cultural factors also act upon the problem space and shape the self-system. For example, the lay referral system plays a major role in how symptoms are interpreted and managed (Chrisman & Kleinman, 1983). As many as 90 per cent of the individuals reporting new symptoms will talk about them to a family member or friend (Cameron et al., 1993), and these contacts will influence whether symptoms are interpreted as serious or not and how they are managed, for example whether they will lead to seeking medical care (Alonzo, 1986; Cameron et al., 1993; Zola, 1973). Finally, broader cultural factors will influence how symptoms are interpreted, causes identified, and treatments judged appropriate and effective (Angel & Thoits, 1987).

Self-Management in the Problem Space

The conceptual additions of self-regulation models to the control system mechanisms that underlie the construction of the problem space lead to the growing divergence of these models from the stress-coping framework. For example, the appraisal process in stress coping models focuses on the balance between the demands of a chronic illness threat and the available resources for threat management. Self-regulation models, by contrast, identify a host of specific procedures or heuristics that are used for the construction of a multifactor representation of the threat, and this representation is critical for goal setting and the identification of resources for threat management and criteria for appraising response outcomes. These domains define the processes involved in the construction of the representation of the illness threat and the variables involved in the appraisal of the balance of threat to resources.

Illness representations: content; interpretive heuristics; prototypes

The representation of a chronic illness consists of more than its label and symptoms; it is an elaborate set of meanings that defines the problem (sets goals) for self-management. Five content domains have been identified for illness representations (Lau, Bernard & Hartman, 1989; Lau & Hartman, 1983; Meyer, Leventhal & Gutmann, 1985; Petrie & Weinman, 1997). These domains establish a framework for action. They point to specific procedures for goal attainment, suggest how these actions achieve their desired effects, set temporal expectations for effectiveness, point to possible 'side effects', and so forth. The ongoing interplay among the representation, the procedures for management, the specific plans for implementing or performing procedures, and the evaluation of post-performance feedback, defines the dynamics of the system (Figure 8.2). These issues have been elaborated as follows.

Content (1) Chronic conditions have names or labels which carry expectations about how they will impact life. Chronic conditions are also identified by their experienced symptoms, signs and changes in function. Labels and concrete experiences together define illness *identity*. Identities, particularly at the symptom level, vary among chronic conditions and among patients with a common condition. (2) Chronic conditions differ with respect to expectations of *control* and actual control;

some are more controllable than others but few are curable with current technology. (3) Chronic illnesses have multiple *time-lines*; there is the perceived time for disease onset, for duration, and for effective treatment. Perceived time-lines can change during the development of a disease and the course of its treatment. (4) Most chronic conditions are perceived to have complex *causes*, including the diathesis of genetic and lifestyle factors (Taylor, Repetti & Seeman, 1997) that are involved in their onset. The individual's age and experience with treatment, whether or not it is successful, will also affect causal beliefs. (5) Each chronic illness has a set of expected and perceived *consequences* with respect to its physical impact and how these physical changes will affect daily function.

Multilevel The factors within these five domains have two levels: they are represented at an experiential level, for example symptoms, felt time, felt and imagined consequences, and so on, and at an abstract level, for example disease label, clock and calendar time (Brownlee, Leventhal & Leventhal, 2000; Leventhal, Diefenbach & Leventhal, 1992; Martin, Lemos & Leventhal, 2001; Martin, Rothrock, Leventhal & Leventhal, 2003) (Figure 8.2). Concrete experiential phenomena, for example pains, rashes, headaches, lumps, secretions, injuries, and functional limitations, are typically the 'disturbances' that bring interpretive processes into play (Martin et al., 2001), activate the procedures for exploring and controlling the disturbance, and function as criteria for evaluating feedback from these actions (Carver & Scheier, 1981, 1999; Scheier & Carver, 2003). The connection of experience to labels, for example the recognition that daily, low levels of fatigue, edema and mild breathlessness are indications of CHF, gives *depth* to the representation of CHF as a chronic condition (Horowitz, Rein & Leventhal, 2004). By connecting these always present symptoms to the label, the individual with CHF is made aware that these symptoms are cues to the possible worsening of her condition and the occurrence of episodes of life threatening decompensation. In the absence of an abstract

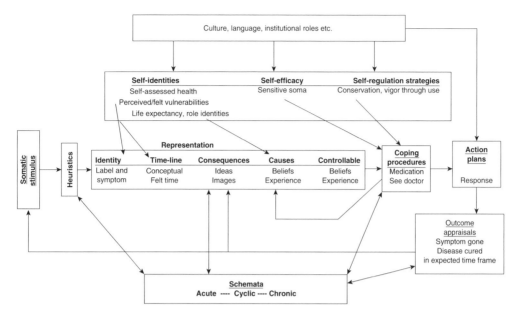

Figure 8.2   *The common-sense model of self–regulation is also based upon control system principles.*
It differs from the other models as it specifies an array of variables involved in the processing of
information and generating responses to control health threats. It specifies a number of heuristics that
are used in interpreting or assigning meaning to somatic changes (e.g., is it a symptom of illness or
stress; illness or aging?). This interpretive process constructs the representation of the health threat.
Representations have attributes in five domains (identity, time-line, consequences, causes, control).
Each attribute is represented at an abstract and an experiential level. The identity of a health
problem consists of a name (asthma) and its symptoms (chest tightness and wheezing). Its conceptual
time-line would be stated as an abstract summary (I have attacks once a month) and its experiential
level as felt time (my last attack feels as if it occurred 6 months ago, and I feel as if another might be
coming on). These attributes, for example symptoms in a time frame, become targets for self-
regulation, and coping procedures are selected to reach these targets, for example using an inhaler to
eliminate the chest tightness and wheezing. The management of the experiential and conceptual
targets can be incompatible with one another: for example, an individual infected with HIV may stop
taking retroviral medication when symptoms clear (concrete goal), leaving himself at risk for
a more serious attack; medication must be used constantly to treat the disease (abstract goal).
Procedures also have representations, for example identities (names and associated symptoms), time-
lines (time for efficacy), and so on, and action plans are formed to insure that procedures are put into
play, for example taking medication for reflux disease with orange juice at breakfast. The above
factors define the 'problem space', that is, the cognitive and affective mental processes involved with
the ongoing management of a health problem.
The problem space resides in a context formed by the self-system and social, institutional and
cultural factors. Perceived attributes of the self can affect the representation of health
problems and the procedures for management. People who perceive their health as poor
rather than excellent may be more likely to interpret symptoms as signs of chronic, life
threatening disease than benign, self-limited conditions. An individual who believes
s/he has a sensitive body will be resistant to using medication and especially resistant if the
medication generates symptoms. Cultural factors affect the self-system and can act directly on
the representation, coping procedures and action plans (e.g., use a chiropractor rather than a
physician for back pain).
The explicit and implicit schemata and scripts for acute, cyclic, and various chronic
conditions (e.g., models for cancer, heart disease, asthma etc.) underlie the processing
system. These schemata affect the heuristics used for interpreting symptoms, the procedures
for management, and set expectations respecting the outcomes of illness
and treatment

label, patients do not monitor these cues and therefore do not develop a time frame for their worsening and do not link them to adverse and dangerous consequences. The abstract level provides the temporal integration of otherwise discrete, concrete experiences.

Heuristics   Although the thermometer, bathroom scales and hot water bottle are found in most households (Konrad, 1998), it appears that the interpretation or self-diagnosis of many if not most somatic changes proceeds with little assistance even from these relatively easy to use technical devices (Stoller, 1998). Somatic events are interpreted, that is self-diagnosed, on the 'fly' using simple, mental rules of thumb, or cognitive heuristics (Figure 8.2). Heuristics such as *symmetry*, or the need to link symptoms to a label, reflect a very basic and highly automatic process; that is, the mind concretizes words and uses words to generalize to concrete experience (Meyer et al., 1985). The *age–illness* heuristic (or question) is involved in decisions as to whether one is dealing with a symptom or sign of illness or an indicator of 'aging' (Kart, 1981; Prohaska, Keller, Leventhal & Leventhal, 1987; Stoller, 1998), and the *stress–illness* heuristic is key to the decision as to whether one is confronting an illness or a temporary stress response (Cameron, Leventhal & Leventhal, 1995). *Locational* heuristics are also common; breathlessness and edema are likely attributed respectively to their location, the lungs and feet, and not to their source, the heart (CHF). Heuristics play a critical role in the decision that an illness is present and its acceptance as chronic.

Heuristics for the appraisal of the severity or risk inherent in symptoms have also been identified. They include the *prevalence* heuristic, that is the perceived severity of a symptom or sign tends to be downgraded if a survey of one's environment reveals that many individuals and not just oneself are at risk for a specific disease (Croyle & Jemmott, 1991); *affective* heuristics, for example anxious and depressed moods increase feelings that one is ill and/or vulnerable to illness (Salovey & Birnbaum, 1989); and *duration* heuristics, that is symptoms that are long lasting are more likely

perceived as threats (Mora, Robitaille, Leventhal, Swigar & Leventhal, 2002).

Temporal change: dynamics   Illness representations are shaped and reshaped by changes in the disease process, by feedback from professional care and self-care, and by social information, for example observation of others (Suls, Martin & Wheeler, 2000; Wood, Taylor & Lichtman, 1985), direct communication from others, media input, and so on. For example, 40 per cent of patients with metastatic breast cancer perceive their illness as acute (like the measles: once cured it doesn't come back) at the first cycle of chemotherapy. The figure drops to 20 per cent by the fourth or fifth cycle (8 to10 weeks) of treatment (Leventhal, Easterling, Coons, Luchterhand & Love, 1986). Temporal perceptions continue to change after the termination of chemotherapy (Rabin, Leventhal & Goodin, submitted). Surprisingly, whether cancer is perceived as acute or chronic is largely independent of the medical judgment of its stage. Self-appraisals of disease status, that is how well one is doing, and emotional distress are influenced by comparisons to other patients. The extent to which a self-appraisal is updated by social comparison depends upon the perceived relevance of the source, that is, the person's health status or where s/he is with respect to the illness, for example just diagnosed, awaiting treatment, post-treatment (Kulik & Mahler, 1997; Leventhal, Hudson & Robitaille, 1997). Experiential information in interaction with self-appraisal heuristics plays an important role in the ongoing effort to 'make sense' of concrete experience.

Procedures for self-regulation

The common sense of self-regulation indicates that the severity and duration of a symptom or dysfunction, and its interpretation or meaning, will affect the choice of procedure: the choice of procedure for managing a chronic or acute health threat is seldom random. For example, a headache, if severe or disruptive, will encourage the use of analgesics: 'Work stress caused my headache and it was cured with aspirin.' If aspirin doesn't work, a stronger analgesic will be considered. If the headache is persistent and accompanied by unusual features, for example dizziness or visual problems, alternative meanings such as a stroke or tumor may be considered, leading to the seeking of expert, medical advice.

Unlike stress-coping models that define and assess one or two generic factors for problem focused 'coping', self-regulation models recognize a vast array of specific actions from which the chronically ill person can choose. These range from traditional medical treatment, for example surgery and prescription medication, through over-the-counter medication and 'natural' substances (herbals), to lifestyle behaviors (exercise, diet), and alternative or complementary treatments (Cassileth, 1998; Eisenberg et al., 1998). A procedure may be selected to control a particular symptom, sign, function, or emotion, or some combination of these events, and it may or may not be perceived to be useful for controlling the underlying disease state. Unlike stress-coping models which focus on broad coping strategies such as problem or emotion focused coping, self-regulation models focus on specific hypotheses respecting how the representation of the threat and that of the procedure affect the selection and maintenance of specific coping procedures.

The illness representation and choice of procedure Far too few studies have examined how the representation of chronic illnesses shapes preferences for particular sets of procedures. Available data make clear, however, the importance of this process. For instance, causal beliefs, such as that immune dysfunction is a cause of cancer, lead many cancer patients to seek 'natural' treatments in addition to their chemotherapy because they are concerned that chemotherapy kills immune cells as well as cancer cells (Cassileth, 1998; Cassileth & Chapman, 1996). The specific symptoms and signs of a disease (identity) can suggest mechanically related treatments. For example, medical texts from the works of ancient Greece and Rome to writings in contemporary indigenous cultures describe the use of suction to the scalp and pressure to the roof of the mouth to 'correct' depressions of infants' fontanelles,

which threaten death (Kay, 1993). These mechanical procedures are useless as the depression is due to dehydration, and death by dehydration is the threat; the cure is adequate doses of liquids (Simons, 1993, comments on the meaning of discrepancies between cultural beliefs and Western medicine).

The treatment representation There is more to the evaluation and selection of a treatment than the perception of its outcome effectiveness, that is, its potency for curing and/or controlling disease. The same five domains are present, that is, beliefs about their identities (symptoms), time-lines for efficacy, consequences (side effects), and causal mode of action. For example, surgery is perceived as a way of cutting out and ridding oneself of a pathogen (cancer) and a way of repairing and returning a vital organ such as the heart to normal function. The mechanical image that makes surgery attractive also makes it threatening: fear of anesthesia; images of the body being cut; fears of death and post-surgical pain and suffering. Kulik and Mahler (1997) showed that patients awaiting cardiovascular surgery were less threatened by the anticipated procedure if they were in rooms with patients who came through bypass surgery rather than with patients also awaiting bypass surgery. Kulik and Mahler's findings contradict the social comparison hypothesis that affiliation with similar others will lower emotional distress (Schachter, 1959), but are consistent with self-regulation theory. Rooming with patients awaiting surgery permits the sharing of fears associated with images of the chest being cut open and the heart assaulted with a scalpel, while rooming with pain-free individuals who have survived is reassuring and distress reducing (Leventhal et al., 1997). The relevance and effects of social comparison are determined by the position of the individual in the sequence from diagnosis, through treatment, to long term adaptation to chronic illness.

Medications also have representations and they may differ depending upon the specific medication under study. The label for a medication can create confusion about its identity and encourage non-adherence to treatment.

For example, asthma patients may resist daily use of inhaled corticosteroids, a treatment for controlling pulmonary inflammation and reducing the frequency and severity of asthma attacks, because the term (identity) 'steroid' raises the specter of risk (consequences) associated with the injection of steroids that are used by athletes (van Grunsven, 2001). Anti-depressants are associated with fears of addiction; 85 per cent of a sample of 2003 respondents favored counseling for treating depression and were opposed to anti-depressant medication; 78 per cent believed these medications addictive (Priest, Vize, Roberts, Roberts & Tylee, 1996). Fear of addiction plays an unfortunate and powerful role in the underprescribing and under use of pain medication in patients suffering from end-stage chronic illness (McCaffery, 1992). Provider and patient concerns about addiction persist despite evidence showing that self-administration of pain medication following surgical treatment does not lead to addiction (Zenz, 1991). Cox and Gonder-Frederick (1992) have identified and assessed fears of insulin and found that these fears are a barrier to effective, long term self-management of diabetes (Cox, Irvine, Gonder-Frederick, Nowacek & Butterfield, 1987). Diabetic patients who are fearful of hypoglycemia attacks undermedicate, have chronically elevated levels of blood sugar (assayed by hemoglobin A1c), and put themselves at risk for complications of kidney failure, blindness, and foot ulceration and amputation. A growing body of data indicates that time-lines, that is both expected and experienced time, affect the use of both pain and anti-depressant medication; people prefer quick to slow remedies (Chapman, 1996; Chapman et al., 2001).

Horne, Weinman and Hankins (1999) have assessed two, higher order medication beliefs that occurred in patients with diverse chronic illnesses and that appear to subsume these specific treatment related fears. The first, the perception that medication is necessary (similar to the concepts of benefits in the health belief model), is strongly related to adherence to medical treatment. The second, that medications pose risks, is related to non-adherence. The belief that medication may be addictive is an important contributor to the belief that medications are risky (Horne, 1997; Horne & Weinman, 1999).

Action plans

Action plans, for example deciding to go for a tetanus shot on a particular day, at a specific time, using a specific mode of transportation, represent a major step toward converting an attitude or intention into performance (Leventhal, Singer & Jones, 1965; Sheeran, 2002). A chronically ill individual may be motivated to act, that is perceive a treatment or self-care behavior as necessary, have specific goals (symptom control) and specific coping procedures in mind, yet fail to act if they have not formed an action plan. Studies conducted over 30 years ago showed that individuals exposed to health warnings took recommended actions, for example tetanus inoculations and reduced cigarette smoking, when the messages combined a health warning with an action plan. Warnings of danger, no matter how strong, had no effects on behavior in the absence of plans, and plans had no effects in the absence of a warning (Leventhal, 1970). Sheeran's (2002) meta-analysis of recent studies clearly reinforces the message: in the absence of action plans, goals, no matter how desirable, typically fail to generate action. Many of these studies, however, involved simple, one-time actions to prevent acute conditions, for example taking flu shots (McCaul, Johnson & Rothman, 2002) or screening (e.g., mammography) for a chronic illness. The efficacy of plans for long term maintenance of behavior is under studied.

Plans appear to be beneficial either because they minimize the demands on memory and need for conscious retrieval by shifting the control of behavior from internal thoughts and intentions to stable external cues, or because they promote rehearsal of the behavior and generate commitments to action (Gollwitzer, 1999). As chronically ill elderly people are most likely dealing with multiple illnesses, minimizing demands at retrieval and reducing the load on working memory may be important for adherence. Relying upon external cues to stimulate action may not be sufficient, however, for appropriate self-management of chronic conditions; plans must not ignore the need for cues to mark the completion of action. It is easy to fail to notice the performance of a repetitive, automated action, for example taking medication daily, and action plans are needed to terminate as well as to stimulate behavior, especially when repetition entails risk.

Important as plans may be, it is clear that 'even the best laid plans can go awry'. Plans can be defeated by undesirable 'side effects' associated with specific procedures such as the worrisome symptoms produced by chronic use of medication. In addition to specifying the where, when and how of action, plans must consider how to integrate a health promotive behavior into the individual's ongoing schedule. This is especially true for individuals whose complex lives and burdensome and unpredictable schedules can disrupt contact with the cues and instruments needed to complete repetitive behaviors. Park and colleagues (1999) found environmental and life task complexity an important predictor and barrier for medication taking for people with rheumatoid arthritis. Motivation and simple action plans were insufficient to conquer hectic and unpredictable environments.

Performance, and performance appraisals

In an ideal world, actions taken to manage disease would provide immediate feedback regarding their efficacy for disease control. Unfortunately, feedback can be surprisingly ambiguous respecting the efficacy of prescribed treatments for many chronic conditions. The ambiguity often resides in the absence of immediate, perceptible change in experience. For example, diuretics may have relatively weak effects on the chronic background symptoms of CHF (swelling of feet, fatigue) relative to their observable impact on urination. As change in these chronic symptoms may be difficult to detect, and these symptoms may not even be seen as related to CHF, perceived benefits and motivation for medication use may be minimal and non-adherence perceived as rational.

Asymptomatic conditions represent a major challenge for adherence: why take anti-hypertension medication when the only symptoms one has are the need to urinate and the diminished sexual function from the prescribed diuretics (Heurtin-Roberts, 1993)? And the elimination of symptoms can be a major barrier to continued use of medication; HIV positive elderly patients see little reason to continue medication once symptoms clear and they believe they are cured (Siegel, Schrimshaw & Dean, 1999).

The target of self-management, for example the chronic disease versus its symptoms, can have important consequences both for the appraisal of control efforts and for emotional adjustment. For example, emotional distress is elevated among arthritic patients the more their actions focus on curing what is an incurable condition. By contrast, emotional distress was reduced among patients whose efforts were focused on the alleviation of symptoms (Affleck, Tennen, Pfeiffer & Fifield, 1987). Self-regulation theory predicts these varied outcomes as they are a consequence of the two-level nature of illness representations, that is, that the identity of a disease involves both abstract knowledge (label) and concrete experience (symptoms).

The time-line concept is another example of the greater specificity and complexity of the self-regulation approach relative to the stress-coping framework. The stress-coping framework conceptualizes outcome appraisals as perceived benefits and/or losses and ignores the temporal expectations associated with these evaluations. Yet only the seriously obtuse clinician will fail to recognize that time is implicit if not explicit in outcome expectancies and treatment appraisals. By contrast, temporal expectations play an important role in Bandura's (1989) conceptualization of agency as a source of motivation for sustaining health promotive behaviors over long time frames.

Coherence in the problem space

When feedback following self-treatment or medical treatment shows movement toward goal attainment, that is that the goals established by the illness representation are being met, the problem solving process (the problem space) is coherent. Coherence insures behavioral stability, until the receipt of disconfirming feedback, but it does not insure positive health outcomes. The hypertensive patient who takes his medication only when symptomatic, for example when he experiences headaches and/or a warm face, because medication reduces these symptoms, is at risk for stroke and myocardial infarction as his representation is biologically invalid; elevations in tonic blood pressure levels are asymptomatic (Meyer et al., 1985). Similarly, the system is coherent for the patient with congestive heart failure who fails to monitor his foot swelling and fatigue but is content with the life saving care he receives at the emergency department after calling 911. Coherence, and a sense of efficacy, can be a basis for adverse health outcomes when they sustain inappropriate, risk inducing health actions. It is important to note that coherence is a system factor, that is, it indicates the consistency among the system components. This definition is different from, but complementary to, that of Antonovsky (1993a), who defines and measures coherence as the possession of a global view of the relationship of the self to one's social and cultural context. Antonovsky (1993b) expects positive association between scores on his scale of coherence and positive health outcomes.

Coherence is at the heart of expertise in self-regulation. Expertise, that is knowing, perceiving and acting to minimize the risk of chronic illnesses such as diabetes, asthma and congestive heart failure, requires the motivation and skill both to monitor and respond to the environment (external and somatic), and to understand that the management of experience differs from the management of disease. The latter often requires the use of procedures that follow the calendar and clock. A self-care expert must also know what gaps exist in the self-regulatory system, that is what it cannot monitor and what it cannot control, and when to seek expert, medical assistance. The effective use of medical practitioners requires bidirectional communication, and many practitioners are unable to understand or communicate with patients whose active self-regulation may deviate from the biomedical perspective. The

consequence is the absence of the shared representations, goals and responsibilities that are important for the management of chronic illnesses. When sharing is present, it can facilitate the formation of a high level of effective self-care (Charmaz, 1999; Leventhal et al., 1999; Zimmerman, Bonner, Evans & Mellins, 1999).

Prototypes

An individual's history with chronic disease gives rise to a memory structure, schema or prototype of the disease process. The facile and swift interpretation that greets the onset of many somatic changes is evidence of prototypes at work (e.g., 'it's just a cold: I'll take some aspirin'; 'it's my migraine'; 'I'm afraid it's my heart: I'll sit down and rest'; 'It's getting bigger. I'm afraid it's a cancer: I'll go see my doctor'). The prototype consists of the illness representation, the procedures for goal attainment, plans for action, and heuristics for evaluating inputs and consequences of action. The prototype's salient features will reflect experiences that are distinctive and compelling, that is symptoms that were unexpected, long lasting, and rapidly changing and physically intense (Mora et al., 2002), and actions that regulate these threatening experiences. The emphasis given to severe, long lasting and rapidly changing events, and the feedback from procedures that terminate these highly stressful experiences, can create biases that introduce deviations between the prototype and the biological processes underlying the chronic condition. The result of this discrepancy will be less than optimal treatment adherence and inappropriate self-management. For example, delay in care seeking can occur when symptoms of a second myocardial infarction differ from the ingrained image of an earlier attack (Wielgosz, Nolan, Earp, Biro & Wielgosz, 1988). These differences can also disrupt long term management.

Context: Self, Social and Cultural

The self-regulation model postulates an ongoing, interactive relationship of contextual factors and the problem space. The representations of a disease and its treatments are affected by beliefs about the self and cultural views of illnesses and treatments (see Leventhal et al., 1999). These relationships are bidirectional: the interpretation of somatic experiences and the outcome of specific procedures for chronic disease management will alter beliefs about the self and will shape cultural beliefs about illness and treatment. This perspective is not fully captured by theoretical analyses which emphasize that contextual person and social factors moderate the perceptions and beliefs involved in the process of adjusting to chronic illness (Christensen, 2000), as the typical moderation view assumes that contextual variables are stable and that influence flows from context to process. Our view is that the variables shape one another, that is, they are involved in a bidirectional constructive process. This does not imply that the amount or rate of change is similar in each direction. In most instances, with the exception perhaps of epidemics (e.g., SARS), influence from the context to the problem space is swifter and more extensive than influence in the other direction.

Self as context

A variety of self-identities can interact with and moderate how representations of specific chronic illnesses will affect behavior. It is obvious, for example, that the emotional distress associated with a chronic illness will be greater if the illness poses a threat to physical and mental functioning and life plans that are central to the self (Ewart, 1991; Hellestrom, 2001; Hooker & Kaus, 1994; Leventhal et al., 1999; Martin et al., 2003). Discrepancies between current levels of symptoms, physical function, and life activities with prior and/or desired levels (Heidrich, Forsthoff & Ward, 1994) are a source of distress and the basis for the development of the representation of the 'ill self' (Cantor, 1990; Cantor & Kihlstrom, 1987; Hellestrom, 2001; Kugelmann, 1999). Discrepancies with the ideal self also can be generated by images of a future, possibly ill self (Hooker, 1992).

A hierarchical model appears to represent how self-identities have been conceptualized and assessed. This view has factors such as self-esteem at the apex; intermediate identities affecting how diseases are represented or how

the self is seen as an agent in a specific domain; and very narrow beliefs at the base, such as response specific self-efficacy, for example believing one is good at monitoring one's heart rate.

Identities interact with representations and procedures

Self-identities such as felt age and self-assessment of health (SAH) are interesting in that they appear to interact specifically with the representation of chronic illnesses, that is, with the meaning of their symptoms and their perceived consequences. For example, age appears to influence perceived vulnerability to risk in different ways throughout the lifespan. The teenager's self-identity is often described as alienated from the adult world and indifferent to future harm, leading to the perception that threats of lung cancer and cardiovascular disease are irrelevant to the self. The net result is failure to accept the relevance of messages to avoid smoking and drug use. Middle-aged women culturally conditioned to perceive heaviness as a sign of good health are unlikely to believe that dieting and weight loss can reduce the risk of diseases such as diabetes; the representations of a healthy self and disease are discrepant (Liburd, Anderson, Edgar & Jack, 1999). And at the upper end of the lifespan, women 70 years of age and older who have children and grandchildren may perceive themselves as no longer at risk for breast cancer and be less motivated to use mammography for early detection. The false sense of security emerges from the representation of breast cancer as a disease that is most likely to strike women in their 40s and 50s, although the incidence of breast cancer is actually highest for women over 70. An individual's report on her health status (SAH), that is, as excellent, very good, good, fair or poor, is a powerful predictor of mortality and is responsive to changes in daily function (Idler & Benyamini, 1997). Although SAH is related to somatic experience, it is difficult to find a consistent relationship between SAH and health relevant behaviors (Mora et al., 2002).

By contrast, self-identities such as self-efficacy (Bandura, 1977, 1989) and self-regulative strategies (Leventhal & Crouch, 1997) have their major impact on the choice and performance of procedures for illness management. Self-efficacy, an indicator of motivation and competence to perform specific behaviors, can be a positive or a negative factor with respect to prevention and adaptation to chronic illness. For example, an elderly patient with adult onset diabetes who is high in self-efficacy is likely to acquire the skills needed to monitor blood sugar levels, adjust his or her diet and insulin use, and maintain good blood sugar regulation over long periods of time (Kavanagh, Gooley & Wilson, 1993; McCaul, Glasgow & Schafer, 1987; Piette, Weinberger & McPhee, 2000; Rubin, Peyrot & Saudek, 1989, 1993). On the other hand, if patients neither perceive diabetes as chronic nor understand its causes (Jayne & Rankin, 2001), for example its link to excessive weight, their self-efficacy may be directed toward behaviors that are ineffective for management of the biological processes underlying the disease. Similarly, patients with CHF may be absolutely confident that they can weigh themselves daily yet fail to do so because they do not see a connection between their states of fatigue and breathlessness and congestive heart failure, and do not see any connection between fluid retention, weight gain and these symptoms (Horowitz et al., in press). The good match between the contextual self and action, that is self-efficacy to weigh oneself, fails to generate action as neither the constant symptoms nor the act of taking one's weight is coherent with CHF and taking diuretics. Many investigators conceptualize and measure self-efficacy as the patient's belief that s/he can achieve a specific outcome, for example 'Can you weigh yourself so you know when to use your water pills to avoid the need for emergency care?' A high score on such a measure is better conceptualized as self-efficacy in CHF management (Bandura, 1989) rather than the ability to take a specific action, that is to stand on a scale and read the weight, the original definition of self-efficacy (Bandura, 1977). When self-efficacy is broadly defined it will assess the coherence of the individual's complete problem solving skills rather than ability to perform any particular aspect of the problem solving process. And when assessed broadly, one cannot identify the specific factors responsible for high or low levels of self-efficacy, making the measure less useful for developing interventions to enhance treatment adherence.

Self-efficacy is only one of a number of beliefs about the self that appear to have a direct effect on strategies for managing chronic illnesses. Generalized approaches to the management of the physical and psychological self, for example self-regulation strategies, will affect the choice and consistent use of procedures for chronic illness management. For example, because they believe that *conserving resources* will insure a longer, disease-free life, individuals 65 years of age and older are quick to visit their primary practitioners to diagnose illness risks and let the practitioner shoulder the burden of illness management (Leventhal, Easterling, Leventhal & Cameron, 1995; Leventhal, Leventhal, Schaefer & Easterling, 1993). The belief that *conservation of resources* is important for a longer, disease-free life does not, however, always lead to effective illness management. Elderly individuals adopting this strategy were less likely to expend the energy needed to find new activities to replace activities that were given up because of the onset or worsening of chronic illness (Duke, Leventhal, Brownlee & Leventhal, 2002). Conservation and disengagement (Scheier & Carver, 2003) appear to be common strategies in the later years of life (Baltes & Baltes, 1990), as is their converse, 'use it or lose it'. Indeed, conservation strategies can be generalized into a lifestyle as seen in cardiac patients who are unfavorably described as cardiac cripples (Aikens, Michael, Levin & Lowry, 1999). A balance between the conservation and exercise of the system are likely critical for sustaining the vigor of the physical self. Finally, as the physical self is the implicit if not the explicit base for all self-identities (Epstein, 1973), it is likely that any strategy designed to enhance the physical self will have significant affective consequences.

Social and cultural context

Social and cultural influences affect all facets of the self-management of chronic illness, from the detection and labeling of symptoms to the decisions to seek medical care, to use alternative practitioners, and to make any lifestyle changes for illness management. The impact of cultural factors is most clearly articulated in anthropological studies of 'folk illnesses', that is, explanatory models of illnesses that differ from the biomedical model of the same disease (Chrisman & Kleinman, 1983; Kleinman, 1988). For example, in many Hispanic communities, gastrointestinal distress (e.g., stomach aches, bloated stomach, cramps, and lack of appetite) are labeled as *empacho*, a disorder 'caused by food getting stuck in the stomach or intestines' (Weller, Pachter, Trotter & Baer, 1993: 121). Lay diagnoses of *empacho* recognize that the symptoms can indicate serious conditions that can lead to death, but do not define it as a bacterial or viral infection. The lay definition encourages treatment with herbal teas, massage, rolling an egg on the stomach, and so on, to dislodge the material 'stuck' in the gastrointestinal tract. Folk models cannot be ignored as they can create barriers to communication between physicians and patients and lead to the use of remedies that, though benign, as in the case of *empacho*, are useless for treating a potentially dangerous disease (Simons, 1993).

People appear to use medical and folk treatments in parallel, which is not problematic as long as the two have no serious interactions (Pachter, 1994: 691). Parallel use is widespread in industrialized, Western culture, where it was labeled initially as 'alternative' medicine and more recently as complementary medicine. The use of complementary medicine is more common among well educated individuals managing life threatening chronic conditions, for example metastatic cancer (Cassileth, Lusk, Strouse & Bodenheimer, 1984; Cassileth, Lusk, Walsh, Doyle & Maier, 1989). The majority of empirical studies on the use of complementary medicine in Western countries report on the prevalence of use in patients with different chronic illnesses (e.g., Eisenberg et al., 1998) and do not examine the mental models driving complementary use. When examined in Western samples, the folk

models that are found appear similar to those reported in less Westernized cultures. Complementary treatments are justified as natural, less risky, and satisfying the need for a spiritual and holistic (Furnham & Forey, 1994) approach to strengthening the body's intrinsic defenses, for example the immune system, without the risk of damaging the body's defenses while killing pathogens (Kaptchuk & Eisenberg, 1998; Moser et al., 1996). Unfortunately, virtually all alternative therapies are of unknown efficacy and are either completely ineffective or less effective than traditional treatments or medically recommended lifestyle changes for prevention and control of chronic disease, for example diet and exercise (e.g., Stampfer, Hu, Manson, Rimm & Willett, 2000).

By nesting the problem space, the representation of illness and procedures for management, in the context of the self and cultural system, the self-regulation model captures the multilevel nature of behavioral controls. This is extremely important on two accounts. First, it makes clear that effective self-management depends upon a coherent relationship among factors across the levels of the problem space, the self and the cultural context (Antonovsky, 1993a). High levels of self-involvement and self-efficacy do not insure effective management of chronic illnesses if the chronically ill individual and/or his or her social network lack a valid representation of the illness and available treatment procedures. Second, the bidirectional arrows between the problem space and these higher order systems indicate that every single feature of the representation, the heuristics for its construction, the procedures and plans for action and the rules for appraising outcomes, are subject to influence from self and cultural systems and will influence the self and cultural system. Moreover, the influence of the context on the problem space can be mediated, that is, social factors can affect management of chronic illness through their effects on the representation of the illness or by acting directly on behaviors through modeling, direct instruction, or coercion (Zola, 1973).

PROTOTYPES, EMOTIONS AND CHRONIC ILLNESS: DEVELOPING THEMES FOR BEHAVIORAL RESEARCH

As our approach to the study of adaptation to chronic illness has focused on theoretical models, it may appear that we have given insufficient attention to the very substantial bodies of empirical work on topics such as emotional distress (i.e., depression) in response to chronic disease, and treatment adherence. As space precludes the traditional review of these areas, a task that is impossible given the size of the literature and the availability of several excellent such reviews, we will focus on theoretically relevant issues in two areas: (1) illness prototypes and the self-management of chronic illnesses, especially models of illness that serve as barriers to effective self-management of CHF, asthma, and diabetes; and (2) emotional distress (anxiety and depression) in response to chronic illness. We also comment briefly on possible effects of testing for early markers of disease vulnerability (e.g., genetic testing) on self-system and preventive behavior.

Illness Prototypes and Self-Management of Chronic Illness: The Non-Adherence Problem

As we stated earlier, non-adherence to treatment and lifestyle options poses major problems for both prevention and control of chronic illnesses. Adherence is more difficult to achieve for long term, complex, lifestyle behaviors, for example diet, exercise and sleep patterns, in contrast to simple, one-time actions such as mammography, fecal occult blood tests and PSA tests for colon and prostate cancer, and annual flu shots. Patients who take more medications, as well as those who believe they are overmedicated, report lower medication adherence, more drug reactions, decreased health related quality of life, and an increase in symptomatology that is compatible with unrecognized side effects of medication (Fincke, Miller & Spiro, 1998). As stated earlier, adherence is adequate, that is sufficient to achieve a clinically measurable effect, for no more than 50 per cent of the individuals

managing one or more chronic conditions (Phillips et al., 2001: 826). Though the level of non-adherence appears to exceed that of adherence, we believe it would be wrong to infer that these data reflect a lack of motivation to avoid and/or control the worsening and more serious side effects of diabetes, asthma, CHF, and other such chronic conditions. People may wish to control and avoid the adverse consequences of serious chronic diseases, but for one reason or another they may forget to act or feel reluctant to act. Their reluctance may stem from a failure to see the logic of treatment and/or concerns about the risks involved in adhering to treatment (Horne, 1997).

Although biologically valid illness representations are only one of many factors influencing adherence, they are potentially of special significance for long term adherence for chronic conditions whose biological base provides rapidly changing and at times inconsistent information about disease status. For example, both asthma and CHF appear to generate episodes of severe and rapidly changing symptoms, encouraging patients to think of themselves as sick and needing treatment only during the episodes; there is no perceived need for treatment during the between-episode, symptom-free, well time. Illnesses such as hypertension and diabetes pose special problems for adherence both because they are asymptomatic (Phillips et al., 2001) and because they may become symptomatic, for example diabetic neuropathy as a cause of foot pain, and become asymptomatic once again (e.g., Chan, 1991; Dyck et al., 1993).

Two decades ago, Bishop (1991) presented data suggesting that illness prototypes underlay the organization generated in the multidimensional scale of disease labels. Prototypes or schemata combine illness representations, coping procedures, and action plans with emotional reactions. Well formed prototypes are comprehensive and coherent structures, relating representations to procedures, plans and anticipations, and interpretations of response produced feedback. The prototypes underlying the behavioral system for chronic illnesses are often less well structured, that is they may be implicit rather than explicit, and incorporate only some of the features found in fully developed schemata. A prototype or mental model may influence behavior for several diseases. We will discuss one prototype that has been identified in clinical practice (Leventhal & Leventhal, in press): the acute/episodic (acute/cyclic) prototype.

The acute/episodic prototype: treatment adherence for CHF and asthma

The illness experience of the great majority of people growing up in industrialized societies consists of months-long disease-free periods, punctuated by episodes of the common cold, gastroenteritis, and non-life-threatening injuries. These conditions are initiated by external pathogens, have relatively rapid onsets, and can be identified by characteristic symptoms such as coughing, sneezing, gastrointestinal bloating and pain; and though disruptive of ongoing activities, they invite procedures such as aspirin for pain control, fluids and rest, and are self- limiting and relatively short lived. This personal, medical history is represented as a mental model that can be characterized as an acute illness schema, a model that plays a role as a 'first line of defense' for separating illness from the self ('I am not "sick", I have a cold': Leventhal et al., 1999).

Although experience with diseases such as adult onset diabetes, myocardial infarction, cancer, and CHF will gradually generate schemata relevant to the chronic features of these illnesses, the chronic schemata are constantly competing with the schema representing the lifetime of acute, self-limited conditions. The blending of the chronic and acute frameworks and the assimilation of symptom and functional changes into this schematic blend will result in a prototype that differs from the chronic biology of the disease. The acute/episodic mental model of disease is common among adults with moderate and severe asthma. In one study of inner city adults with moderate and severe asthma, 53 per cent felt that they only had asthma when they were having asthma symptoms. Patients who held this 'no symptoms, no asthma' health belief

were more likely to have other suboptimal disease and treatment beliefs, less likely to adhere to chronic, daily medications (inhaled steroids), and less likely to perform other self-management behaviors (Halm et al., 2003). This mismatch of schema to biology could be partially responsible for the high rates of death, disability, hospitalization, and emergency department visits of the 10 per cent of asthmatics suffering from severe forms of the disorder and for 54 per cent of the 6.2 billion dollars in annual asthma expenditures (Weiss et al., 2000). The picture for CHF is no less grim: of the nearly 5,000,000 sufferers in the US (American Heart Association, 2002), 75 per cent of the men and 62 per cent of the women will die within 5 years of diagnosis (Ho, Anderson, Kannel, Grossman & Levy, 1993), and it has been, and still is, the most common reason for hospitalization and emergency department visits by persons over 65 years of age in the US.

Unlike acute illnesses which require treatment when symptomatic, self-management activities for asthma and CHF are to be conducted daily whether one is or is not symptomatic, for example peak-flow metering to assess pulmonary function and use of steroid inhalers for asthma, and monitoring edema, weight and the use of diuretics for CHF. Severe exacerbations in each require different treatment (e.g., use of controllers for asthma), and when unsuccessful can lead to hospitalization. Data show that the great majority of patients with CHF do not monitor somatic symptoms or weigh themselves on a daily basis, and the great majority of asthma patients do not use steroids on a daily basis (Chin & Goldman, 1997; Ni et al., 1999). A chronic model is congruent with daily use, that is, the disease is present and to be monitored and treated every day whether one is symptomatic or not. An acute model is inconsistent with this behavioral prescription; illness and treatment are congruent with symptom episodes, not with symptom-free (disease-free) periods. It is important to note that none of these tasks is complex and/or difficult to perform. Asthma patients do use controllers, and do so vigorously and frequently when severely breathless and dysfunctional; indeed, greater use of controllers during crises is associated with more frequent hospitalization. CHF patients in crisis resort to calling for emergency assistance and admission to hospital emergency departments when incapable of breathing and dysfunctional (Chin & Goldman, 1997; Ni et al., 1999). Hence, self-management is episodic and crisis oriented.

Zimmerman and colleagues (1999) have identified four different levels of expertise in self-management of asthma, ranging from those who deal with asthma as a series of crises to individuals who do peak-flow metering, monitor changes in symptoms specific to asthma and use preventive medication (steroid inhalers) on a regular basis. These effective self-managers have fewer episodes of hospitalization, generate less medical costs and put themselves less often at risk for serious complications, including the possibility of death. How do patients make the seemingly linear transition from disorganized (from the medical perspective) to expert self-management? Qualitative interviews with CHF patients suggest it is incorrect to say that inadequate self-care reflects 'failure to develop expert' self management, as individuals who treat their CHF as a series of episodic crises are experts in dialing 911 and heading for the nearest emergency department when in crisis mode (Horowitz, Rein & Leventhal, 2004). This model is non-optimal from the biomedical perspective as it ignores the quiet, symptom-free periods and risks further damage to heart muscle as well as risk of death if an episode proves unmanageable. That severe, rapidly changing symptoms will dominate the patient's mental representations can be predicted from simple, psychophysical rules such as Weber's law; large, rapid changes are highly noticeable and form an excellent fit with the highly available, acute model generated by a lifetime of minor illnesses (Lau et al., 1989). As it takes little time or skill to weigh oneself and use a diuretic, self-regulation for controlling CHF appears to make few demands on self-efficacy. Indeed, it is extremely unlikely that a chronically ill person would think him or herself incapable of performing these tasks. The situation would be similar for the asthmatic; unless he or she challenges the pulmonary system, for example by controlled exposure to a mild allergen or by climbing stairs, it may be difficult to detect the benefits of regular steroid use which would be important experiential evidence to support a chronic model. Thus, although self-efficacy is an important motivator for initiating and sustaining behavior, effective self-regulation requires that self-efficacy be joined with a coherent problem solving structure, that is, an illness representation that is linked to procedures that produce valid feedback for disease control (Horowitz et al., 2004).

Emotional Response to Chronic Illness: Moderators and Pathways

Emotional distress in the context of chronic illness has adverse effects on adherence to treatment, quality of life and the cost of medical care (de Groot, Anderson, Freedland, Clouse & Lustman, 2001; DiMatteo, Lepper & Croghan, 2000). For example, a recent analysis of the annual cost of care for CHF patients found that the median cost per patient for 312 patients who were on anti-depressant medication but had no recorded diagnosis of depression was $11,012 per year, and was $9,550 for 114 patients who were diagnosed as depressive and prescribed anti-depressants, versus $7,474 for 672 patients with CHF with no evidence of depression (Sullivan, Simon, Spertus & Russo, 2002). But, is severe emotional distress a necessary accompaniment of severe, chronic illness? And if not, do self-regulation variables play a role in forming this connection?

Prevalence of emotional distress with severe chronic illness

Although laypersons, clinicians and investigators are prone to expect high levels of emotional distress among individuals with cancer, cardiovascular disease, diabetes, and severe rheumatoid arthritis or osteoarthritis, the expectation that individuals with these illness are more anxious, depressed and angry than well persons matched on various demographic characteristics is not readily supported by empirical data. As Coyne and colleagues have pointed out (Coyne & Schwenk, 1997; Coyne et al., 2000; Palmer & Coyne, 2003), when these comparisons are made there is little or no evidence for increased incidence or prevalence of major depressive disorders and/or severe distress among the severely, chronically ill individuals in comparison to non-chronically ill, matched controls.

Among the problems that appear in assessing the prevalence of distress and/or depression among the physically ill, two stand out. First, investigators may use different criteria for assessing distress, some focusing on major depressive disorders, others on distress or depression as a continuous variable. Second, assessment is complicated by the overlap of the somatic features of depression with the symptoms of physical illness. For example, cancer patients in chemotherapy treatment report fatigue, sleep problems, and so on, symptoms diagnostic of depression, though their responses to non-somatic items of instruments such as the CES–D are no different from those of healthy, non-depressed controls (Bukberg, Penman & Holland, 1984). The Hospital Anxiety and Depression Scale (HADS), which was designed to resolve this problem (Zigmond & Snaith, 1983), excludes items tapping physical symptoms and negative moods; it is, therefore, a measure of anhedonia. If there are multiple forms of depression, for example major depressive disorders, dysthymia, symptomatic depression common in the elderly (Gallo, Anthony & Muthen, 1994), and other forms of depressed affect (Blazer, Hughes & George, 1987; Blazer, 1989), it may not always be appropriate to treat reports or observations of somatic symptoms as a confound of chronic illness. The decision to adopt one or more measures depends, therefore, upon the chronic illness, the definition of distress, and features of the population, for example age, as emotional distress or depression is often manifest by somatic symptoms rather than as negative moods or self-denigrating cognition among elderly patients with multiple chronic illnesses (Gallo, Rabins & Anthony, 1990; Leventhal et al., 1999).

Affect dynamics: time and self-regulation

Although there is little evidence of an increase in major depressive disorders among the chronically ill, they do experience episodes of intense emotional distress. As would be expected by self-regulation models and theories of emotion (Scherer, 1999a), anxiety and depression will be elicited by changes in the individual's illness. Anxiety and fear are more common at the outset of crises, for example when a woman is told she has breast cancer, or the day prior to medical check-up to see if she is cancer free or has a recurrence (Easterling & Leventhal, 1989; Silverman, 1999), and in response to vague, somatic symptoms if she feels vulnerable to cancer (Andrykowski et al., 2002; Easterling & Leventhal, 1989). Similarly, persons with chronic illnesses are likely to have elevated levels of emotional distress and depression when they experience complications, and increased levels of fear and panic at the onset of decompensations of their conditions (Lustman et al., 2000; Musselman, Betan, Larsen & Phillips, 2003). In addition, depression may be more common after prolonged and unsuccessful efforts to moderate the growing dysfunctions associated with an apparently uncontrollable and progressing chronic illness. Differences in the pattern of events surrounding the ongoing efforts by self and others to manage the disease are responsible for the differentiation in emotional experience (Scherer, 1999a).

Counter perhaps to common sense, there are circumstances under which the events surrounding severe and life threatening chronic illness can lead to positive emotional reactions (Antoni et al., 2001). Positive feelings can arise when the illness and its treatment allow the individual to free him or herself of distressing life burdens and when the experience with disease enhances the sense of personal strength and mastery. For example, the contrast formed by successful and pain-free survival from painful surgery and breast cancer, a disease that is perceived as life threatening, can enhance the individual's sense of efficacy, and improve both the individual's interpersonal relationships and their outlook on life (Andrykowski et al., 1996). Although self-regulation theory would predict positive gains when the experience of disease and treatment contrasts with previously held representations, it would also predict that positive affect and personal growth would be unlikely in the face of a chronic condition such as CHF that is both severe and progressively debilitating.

Pathways from chronic illness to affective distress: direct path

Investigators have begun to define the direct and indirect pathways from chronic illness to emotional distress, with depression the most frequently examined outcome. Direct effects occur when depression is elicited by the physiological changes of the disease process. The case for direct effects seems particularly strong for neurological disorders such as Parkinson's disease where disease related reductions in CSF levels of 5-hydroxy indoleacetic acid (5-HIAA), the principal metabolite of serotonin, have been implicated as the cause of the high, 40 per cent on average, prevalence of depression (Cummings, 1992). The variation across studies is also high; Cummings (1992) reports rates of 4 to 70 per cent across 26 studies. Although the variation may be due in part to differences in the criteria for diagnosing depression, it undermines the credibility of the direct effect hypothesis. The case is further undermined as the disruption of motor activity, which is often a mediator connecting depression to illness, is a major consequence of depression. In addition, some chronic illnesses may produce dysregulation of the hypothalamic–pituitary– adrenocortical (HPA) axis and generate pro-inflammatory cytokines that have been implicated in depressive processes. HPA axis dysregulation has been identified in chronic illnesses such as diabetes (Cameron, Kronfol, Greden & Carroll, 1984; Ribeiro, Tandon, Grunhaus & Greden, 1993; Roy, Collier & Roy, 1990). The relationship of depression to diabetes may also be bidirectional, as depression induced elevations in pro-inflammatory cytokines (Maes et al., 1995, 1997) may contribute to the development and maintenance of diabetes (Falcone & Sarvetnick, 1999; Rabinovitch, 1998; Vial & Descotes, 1995), which in turn stimulates HPA axis dysregulation. Direct paths pose a challenge to self-regulation models as the levers for their management are not immediately clear.

Indirect paths: physical and psychological function

The number and complexity of the indirect pathways connecting chronic illness and emotional distress make clear why it is difficult and often naive to attribute the connection to simple, direct paths. Chronic illness and emotional distress can be linked by physical dysfunctions which disrupt social relationships and roles critical to self-identities, and by a variety of psychological processes involved in the representation of the two disorders. For example, although diabetes and depression are differentiated at an abstract level, that is they have different labels, their identities overlap at the experiential level, that is, with the identification and representation of symptoms. Insulin based reduction of blood sugar often generates symptoms of fatigue and anxiety which are common in depression (Gonder-Frederick & Cox, 1991: 229). Further, both diabetes and depression have chronic or stable time-lines, similar consequences, namely disruption of physical function and social relationships (separation from others due to special diet, embarrassment due to medication use, isolation from loss of energy and feelings of stigma and worthlessness) and difficulties of control (neither is easily self-managed). And both can be seen to be caused by deficits in or weaknesses of the self, for example, being unable to regulate diet and engage in other lifestyle behaviors. Thus, the two conditions share factors in each of the five domains of the common-sense representation of illness, that is, in identity, cause, time-line, consequences, and control (Brownlee et al., 2000; Leventhal, Brissette & Leventhal, 2003; Leventhal et al., 1980, 1992).

Numerous cross-sectional and longitudinal studies have confirmed the existence of an indirect path in which chronic illness is connected to depression by illness produced physical dysfunction. Depression in elderly outpatients has been related to both physician ratings of impairment and patient ratings of activity (Williamson & Schulz, 1992b), to functional disability in patients with end-stage renal disease (though only for patients with lower levels of depression: Rodin & Voshart, 1987), and to functional impairment among insulin-dependent diabetics (Littlefield, Rodin, Murray & Craven, 1990) and adult onset diabetics (Lustman, Griffith, Clouse & Cryer, 1986; Lustman, Griffith, Gavard & Clouse, 1992; Moldin et al., 1993). Longitudinal studies have shown that depression among cancer patients is predicted by activity restriction assessed 8 months earlier (Williamson & Schulz, 1995), and to decline in functional status and hospitalization among the elderly (Callahan & Wollinsky, 1995); and depression, anxiety and anger were related to physical disability among patients hospitalized for chronic illness 6 months earlier (Viney & Westbrook, 1991). Indeed, functional impairment is typically a far better predictor of mood than disease status. For example, among cancer patients, performance status and physical disability predicted mood disturbance while the extent of disease and medical measures did not (lung cancer: Cella et al., 1987; other cancers: Bukberg et al., 1984). These factors and activity restriction account for the relationship between pain and depression in the elderly (Walters & Williamson, 1999; Williamson, 2000; Williamson & Schulz, 1992a; 1995; Zeiss et al., 1996).

Only a very few studies, however, assess the hypothesis that functional impairment is the critical mediator of the link between chronic illness and depression by testing whether controlling for function reduces or eliminates the association of illness with depression (e.g., Fitzpatrick, Newman, Archer & Shipley, 1991; Triemstra et al., 1998; Walters & Williamson, 1999; Williamson, 2000; Williamson & Schulz, 1992a, 1995), and very few do so using longitudinal data (e.g., Fitzpatrick et al., 1991; Williamson & Schulz, 1995). A study by Aikens and colleagues is an interesting exception as it found in a sample of diabetics that high levels of physical activity eliminated the association of fluctuations in blood sugar levels with emotional distress over a 2-week period (Aikens, Aikens, Wallander & Hunt, 1997); distress and blood sugar level were associated among diabetics who were physically inactive. Thus, although it is unclear whether disease status

causes distress or vice versa, evidence is good for the moderating role of physical activity.

Psychological factors and indirect paths

The data identifying dysfunction as a mediator of depression raise as many questions as they answer, as illness severity and functional impairment are related only moderately, and higher levels and/or increases in functional impairment have only a moderate effect on elevations in depressed and/or dysfunctional mood. It is clear that disease, function and affective distress are not connected by some sort of mechanical link such that change in one necessarily leads to changes in the other. Cognitive factors are likely playing an important role in creating these links. The perception of the causes, time-lines and eventual consequences of illness and the experience and hopes for treatment play a role in creating the connections of chronic illness to functional impairment and of impairment to increased negative and decreased positive affect. For example, Aikens and colleagues (Aikens et al., 1999; Aikens, Zvolensky & Eifert, 2001) have shown that cardiac patients who interpret chest pain as a threat to life markedly reduce physical activity, a 'self-protective' behavior that avoids the experience of chest pain but increases long term cardiac risk. Similarly, diabetics who are fearful of treatment induced hypoglycemia are non-adherent to prescribed insulin regimens, resulting in elevations of blood sugar, emotional distress, and an increase in risk of diabetic complications (Mollema, Snoek, Ader, Heine & van der Ploeg, 2001; Zambanini, Newson, Maisey & Feher, 1999).

Social factors and self-identities such as optimism and strategies for self-regulation are also involved in connecting disease, function and emotional distress. Scheier and Carver (2003) review a large number of studies consistent with the hypothesis that optimism is a source of motivation that sustains engagement in life tasks and the making of efforts to find replacements for activities that have been relinquished. Consistent with their arguments, a longitudinal study by Duke et al. (2002) found that elderly individuals who replaced activities that had been given up because of chronic illness showed increases in positive affect from the year before to the year after making the replacement. Finding a replacement was negatively related to the self-regulation strategy that the conservation of energy would enhance longevity, and positively related to having social support and personal optimism. The original reduction in activity was due to the severity of the illness and not to social and personal factors. It is unclear whether these outcomes reflect the impact on function of top-down (abstract goals to function), bottom-up, or mid-level factors (self-management strategies: conserve to live longer), or all three. What is clear is that maintenance of function is dependent upon the interpretation of the chronic threat and strategies for self-management, and that maintaining function is inconsistent with depression.

Is it realistic to separate direct and indirect pathways?

Although defining direct and indirect pathways may seem reasonable, the two types of paths may be interrelated by common processes at the physiological level. For example, moderate exercise by older persons, such as walking 2 miles a day, increases life expectancy by 5 five years in healthy, older men (Hakim et al., 1998), maintains strength and physical function (Fiatarone et al., 1994), prevents adverse sequelae of myocardial infarction (death and subsequent heart attacks: Blumenthal et al., 1989), enhances function and reduces morbidity in the final years of life (Fries, 1983), and appears to be as effective as pharmacotherapy and psychotherapy for the treatment of clinically depressed older adults (Moore & Blumenthal, 1998). That exercise has both physical and psychological benefit is consistent with the hypothesis that the bidirectional relationship between physical activity and depression reflects a shared physiological process (reviewed in Leventhal et al., 2001). Thus, the 'indirect' path from disease through disruption

of physical activity to emotional distress and depression may involve the very same mechanisms implicated in the direct paths. Life is complex!

Interventions disrupting the pathways from chronic illness to depression

Interventions that improve physical functioning of chronically ill persons provide the strongest evidence for the hypothesis that function mediates the association of chronic illness with emotional distress. Both stress management training (Antoni et al., 2001) and educational sessions focused on skills to enhance management of disease impact (Helgeson, Cohen, Schulz & Yasko, 1999) have been shown to reduce emotional distress among breast cancer patients. In both cases, lower levels of distress and fewer symptoms of depression were reported by patients in the intervention than in the control arm of a randomized trial. For the past 35 years, Johnson and colleagues have produced the most direct evidence that the representations of illness and treatment can affect function and emotional distress. In an extensive series of studies they have shown that preparatory messages informing patients about the sensory properties (e.g., how it would feel when the instrument contacted the body) of an anticipated, noxious examination (e.g., endoscopy, colposcopy, cast removal etc.), and how to cope and partially control the sensations associated with the procedure, led to substantial reductions in objective indicators (e.g., heart rate) and subjective reports of distress. Monitoring these sensations, interpreting them as limited and benign, and responding to facilitate the examination and control noxious sensations consistently reduced emotional distress (Johnson, 1975; Johnson, Kirchoff & Endress, 1975; Johnson, Lauvier & Nail, 1989; Johnson & Leventhal, 1974). Longitudinal data showed that monitoring and understanding the meaning of somatic sensations enhances long term adaptation to chronic conditions (Suls & Wan, 1989).

Recent experimental data by Petrie, Cameron, Ellis, Buick and Weinman (2002) provides further, albeit somewhat tentative, support for the hypothesis that altering illness representations can enhance function. They tested the effects of altering illness representations on function (returning to work) in a randomized trial of post-MI patients with a relatively small sample of patients. The trial compared standard care with matched contacts for data collection to a three-session intervention that differentiated between symptoms of wound healing and symptoms of heart disease, broadened the range of perceived causes of MI (lifestyle in addition to stress), and cautioned against assuming that inactivity would enhance recovery by conserving resources. The intervention group showed speedier recovery of function, that is return to work for patients who were employed prior to surgery, a trend toward increased participation in rehabilitation (not statistically significant due to lack of power), better understanding of illness at discharge, and less angina and less emotional distress 6 months post-discharge. It is important to distinguish the reduction of distress generated by sensory information which focuses patients on the benign nature of sensory experience from the effects observed when monitoring is operationalized as an individual difference variable (Miller, 1996; Miller, Shoda & Hurley, 1996). The individual difference measure rates individuals who are unable to shift their attention away from noxious cues because they perceive them as threatening and uncontrollable.

In summary, linking of symptoms to labels (depth to the representation), providing alternative views of causation and reasonable time-lines (broadening the representation), and providing information for the performance specific, rehabilitative actions (a coherent self-regulation picture), improved function and reduced reporting of disease symptoms and emotional distress. Although the studies testing such interventions use small samples, the newer studies suggest that theoretically defined interventions can be brief and effective in enhancing function and reducing the negative impact of emotional distress. Coherence, defined as an accurate representation integrated with effective self-management

procedures whose feedback is appraised as effective, plays a critical role in the maintenance of function, that is, activities of daily living, the reduction of emotional distress and the activation of positive emotional reactions.

LOOKING AHEAD

The view of self-regulation here presented has five central features. First, it requires identification of the biomedical features of chronic disease with close attention to the effects of the disease on the individual's subjective experience and physical and cognitive function. There is an intimate connection between biomedical features of chronic disease and self-regulation processes. Second, it recognizes the effects of both the social context and individual history on the interpretation and elaboration of representations of chronic illnesses, the procedures deemed appropriate for their management, and the experiences generated by these procedures. Third, it calls for the identification of the heuristics involved in the interpretation and elaboration of the representation of both the illness and the procedures for management. The representation and heuristics set the goals and questions that are to be answered by expert and self-management procedures. Fourth, an effective self-regulation model is substantive in nature: it does not rely on single constructs to understand behavior or to create interventions to shape behaviors that are effective for disease management. Self-regulation systems viewed in context are complex multivariate systems that can be influenced through multiple routes. The self-system, its strategies and sense of efficacy, are an integral part of self-regulation processes but are not sufficient as explanations for behavioral adaptation to chronic illness or adequate conceptual guides for intervention. Most of the leverage for intervention lies in the factors at work in the 'problem space', or the experiences generated by the performance of specific procedures to reach goals for the regulation of disease and disease related experience. Finally, the heuristics involved in the formation of the five domains of the representations of illness, the procedures for illness management, and the representations and appraisals emerging from the ongoing adaptive process, are the product of the interaction of situational factors (culture, social inputs, biomedical features of disease) with underlying schemata. Schematic templates are prepared to direct attention, behavior, and interpretations of changing experience.

We can envision a number of routes both for the development of self-regulation concepts and for significant contributions to health practices. They are as follows.

Interventions and Causal Analysis

It is relatively easy to imagine a variety of themes to flesh out the self-representation approach to the management of chronic disease. Longitudinal studies examining the effects of theoretically defined interventions are clearly needed. Interventions combined with longitudinal observation provide a useful approach for identifying both direct and indirect 'causal' relationships. Much can be learned by establishing clear starting points for the observation of self-regulation processes and using multivariate procedures to model and compare the unfolding of processes over time in different intervention arms. To be useful, however, interventions must be grounded in theory.

Prototypes: Expert Systems for Patient–Provider Interaction

As we have emphasized throughout, the self-regulation of chronic illness is engaged in by individuals who are embedded in social contexts. The individual with a chronic illness is a patient at the physician's office, a family member, an associate at work, and a member of a church and other civic or informal social groups, whose role performance is impacted in one or more ways by a disease process and how the disease manifests itself in the public arena. Family, colleagues and friends lack the patient's subjective experience but may share with him or her culture-wide stereotypes or observations of other persons with the 'same' chronic disease (Alonzo, 1986). Discrepancies in how

the well and the chronically ill spouse represent a chronic illness, beliefs about its possible cure and severity, can generate emotional distress (Heijmans, de Ridder & Bensing, 1999); their effects on treatment adherence, rehabilitation and efforts at maximizing function and return to pre-illness role functioning have been insufficiently explored (Leventhal, Leventhal & van Nguyen, 1985; Nerenz & Leventhal, 1983).

Discrepancies between patient and provider in the representation of illness and its treatments can be a source of patient dissatisfaction and non-adherence. It is distressing to note that the greatest number of patients (60 per cent) who dropped out of hypertension treatment in the Meyer et al. (1985) study were those who disclosed to their doctors their belief that hypertension was symptomatic. How should information be shared between patients, doctors and family members, and with whom are comparisons most likely to impart valid information in shaping beliefs and preferences for procedures for self-management (Suls et al., 2000)? Can physicians be as expert in the diagnosis and sharing of patient and biomedical models as they are in the diagnosis of disease and its treatment (Leventhal & Leventhal, in press)? Doing so will require time to listen, but the duration and efficacy of listening depend upon the development of models for patient and practitioner interaction, the readiness to identify and make public implicit cognitive structures, and the creation of both micro and treatment systems that allow and indeed encourage these activities (Berwick, 2002).

Emotion and the Management of Chronic Illness

Although the intensity and duration of emotional reactions associated with chronic illness may not rise to the level needed for psychiatric diagnosis, it is clear that emotional distress, particularly depression, may interfere with adherence and disease management. More precise identification of the time in the developmental history and specification of the cognitive and behavioral factors that lead to the differential arousal of fearful versus depressive affect will be one of the challenges for self-regulation theory. Interventions to modify emotional reactions having adverse effects for self-management pose a still greater challenge. This is particularly the case given the ambiguous outcomes seen in prior studies where efforts to ameliorate depression have had negative impact on chronic disease, for example use of pharmacotherapy to alleviate depression and supportive, psychological interventions increasing the risk of mortality for individuals treated for and recovering from myocardial infarction (Friedman et al., in press).

FINAL COMMENT

It is clear that both longitudinal descriptive and intervention studies are needed to enhance our understanding of self-regulation processes and to improve the management of chronic illness. What is less clear, however, is whether current methodologies, particularly the use of linear modeling, whether by means of regression analysis and/or structural equation modeling (SEM), are up to the task. Traditional regression fails because of its focus on prediction over explanation. Path modeling and SEM are at best modest improvements, as they are less than ideal for managing complex interactions or non-linear effects, and are hampered by limitations in the number of variables that can be included in models, and by the conceptual problems in how variables are represented (Borsboom, Mellenbergh & van Heerden, 2003). They also do not depict the moment-by-moment processes involved in the acceptance and/or rejection of information critical for the interpretation of symptoms and the performance of treatment procedures. Whether the addition of approaches under development in the analysis of genetic causation will help is unclear. We firmly believe that interdisciplinary teams combining the skills of cognitive science, social and organizational psychology, medical science and statistical analysis will create decades of exciting and innovative research, important additions to theory, and much needed improvements in clinical practice that will enhance the quality of care for the chronically ill.

REFERENCES

ACC/AHA Task Force (1995). Guidelines for the evaluation and management of heart failure. Report of the American College of Cardiology/American Heart Association Task Force on Practice Guidelines (Committee on Evaluation and Management of Heart Failure). *Journal of the American College of Cardiology, 26*, 1376–1398.

Affleck, G., Tennen, H., Pfeiffer, C., & Fifield, J. (1987). Appraisals of control and predictability in adapting to a chronic disease. *Journal of Personality and Social Psychology, 53*, 273–279.

Aikens, J. E., Michael, E., Levin, T., & Lowry, E. (1999). The role of cardioprotective avoidance beliefs in noncardiac chest pain and associated emergency department utilization. *Journal of Clinical Psychology in Medical Settings, 6*, 317–332.

Aikens, J. E., Michael, E., Levin, T., Myers, T. C., Lowry, E., & McCracken, L. M. (1999). Cardiac exposure history as a determinant of symptoms and emergency department utilization in noncardiac chest pain patients. *Journal of Behavioral Medicine, 22*, 605–617.

Aikens, J. E., Zvolensky, M. J., & Eifert, G. H. (2001). Differential fear of cardiopulmonary sensations in emergency room noncardiac chest pain patients. *Journal of Behavioral Medicine, 24*, 155–167.

Aikens, K. S., Aikens, J. E., Wallander, J. L., & Hunt, S. L. (1997). Daily activity level buffers stress–glycemia associations in older sedentary NIDDM patients. *Journal of Behavioral Medicine, 20*, 371–388.

Alonzo, A. A. (1986). The impact of the family and lay others on care seeking during life threatening episodes of suspected coronary artery disease. *Social Science and Medicine, 22*, 1297–1311.

American Diabetes Association (2001). *Resource Guide. Diabetes Forecast*, 33–110.

American Heart Association (2002). *Heart stroke and statistical update.*

Andrykowski, M. A., Carpenter, J. S., Studts, J. L., Cordova, M. J., Cunningham, L. L. C., Beacham, A., Sloan, D., Kenady, D., & McGrath, P. (2002). Psychological impact of benign breast biopsy: A longitudinal, comparative study. *Health Psychology, 21*, 485–494.

Andrykowski, M. A., Curran, S. L., Studts, J. L., Cunningham, L., Carpenter, J. S., McGrath, P. C., Sloan, D. A., & Kenady, D. E. (1996). Psychosocial adjustment and quality of life in women with breast cancer and benign breast problems: a controlled comparison. *Journal of Clinical Epidemiology*, *49*, 827–834.

Angel, R. J., & Thoits, P. (1987). The impact of culture on the cognitive structure of illness. *Culture, Medicine & Psychiatry*, *11*, 465–494.

Antoni, M. H., Lehman, J. M., Kilbourn, K. M., Boyers, A. E., Culver, J. L., Alferi, S. M., Yount, S. E., McGregor, B. A., Arena, P. L., Harris, S. D., Price, A. A., & Carver, C. S. (2001). Cognitive-behavioral stress management intervention decreases the prevalence of depression and enhances benefit finding among women under treatment for early-stage breast cancer. *Health Psychology*, *20*, 20–32.

Antonovsky, A. (1993a). Complexity, conflict, chaos, coherence, coercion, and civility. *Social Science and Medicine*, *37*, 969–974.

Antonovsky, A. (1993b). The structure and properties of the Sense of Coherence Scale. *Social Science and Medicine*, *36*, 725–733.

Bahls, C., & Fogarty, M. (2002). Reining in a killer disease. Cancer and chronic disease in the same sentence? Researchers hope it's not an oxymoron. *The Scientist*, *16*, 16–18.

Baltes, P. B., & Baltes, M. M. (1990). Psychological perspectives on successful aging: The model of selective optimization with compensation. In P. B. Baltes & M. M. Baltes (Eds.), *Successful aging: Perspectives from the behavioral sciences* (pp. 1–34). New York: Cambridge University Press.

Bandura, A. (1977). Self-efficacy: Toward a unifying theory of behavioral change. *Psychological Review*, *84*, 191–215.

Bandura, A. (1989). Human agency in social cognitive theory. *American Psychologist*, *44*, 1175–1184.

Baron, R. J. (1985). An introduction to medical phenomenology: I can't hear you while I'm listening. *Annals of Internal Medicine*, *103*, 606–611.

Barsky, A. J. (1992). Amplification, somatization, and the somatoform disorders. *Psychosomatics*, *33*, 28–34.

Barsky, A. J. (2001). Clinical practice: The patient with hypochondriasis. *New England Journal of Medicine*, *345*, 1395–1399.

Berwick, D. M. (2002). A user's manual for the IOM's Quality of Chasm Report: Patients' experiences should be the fundamental source of the definition of 'quality'. *Health Affairs*, *21*, 80–90.

Bishop, G. D. (1991). Understanding the understanding of illness: Lay disease representations.

In J. A. Skelton & R. T. Croyle (Eds.), *Mental representations in health and illness* (1st edn., pp. 32–59). New York: Springer.

Blazer, D. G. (1989). Current concepts: Depression in the elderly. *New England Journal of Medicine*, *320*, 164–166.

Blazer, D., Hughes, D. C., & George, L. K. (1987). The epidemiology of depression in an elderly community population. *The Gerontological Society of America*, *27*, 281–287.

Blumenthal, J. A., Emery, C. F., Madden, D. J., George, L. K., Coleman, R. E., Riddle, M. W., McKee, D. C., Reasoner, J., & Williams, R. S. (1989). Cardiovascular and behavioral effects of aerobic exercise training in healthy older men and women. *Journal of Gerontology: Medical Sciences*, *44*, M147–M157.

Borsboom, D., Mellenbergh, G. J., & van Heerden, J. (2003). The theoretical status of latent variables. *Psychological Review*, *110*, 203–219.

Boulet, L. P. (1998). Perception of the role and potential side effects of inhaled corticosteroids among asthmatic patients. *Chest*, *113*, 587–592.

Brown, G. W., & Harris, T. (1978). *Social origins of depression: A study of psychiatric disorder in women*. London: Tavistock.

Brownlee, S., Leventhal, H., & Leventhal, E. A. (2000). Regulation, self-regulation, and construction of the self in the maintenance of physical health. In M. Boekartz, P. R. Pintrich & M. Zeidner (Eds.), *Handbook of self-regulation* (pp. 369–416). San Diego, CA: Academic.

Bukberg, J., Penman, D., & Holland, J. C. (1984). Depression in hospitalized cancer patients. *Psychosomatic Medicine*, *46*, 199–212.

Callahan, C. M., & Wollinsky, F. D. (1995). Hospitalization for major depression among older Americans. *Journals of Gerontology, Series A, Biological Sciences & Medical Sciences*, *50A*(4), M196-M202.

Cameron, L. D., & Leventhal, H. (2003). *The self-regulation of health and illness behaviour*. London: Routledge.

Cameron, L., Leventhal, E. A., & Leventhal, H. (1993). Symptom representations and affect as determinants of care seeking in a community-dwelling, adult sample population. *Health Psychology*, *12*, 171–179.

Cameron, L., Leventhal, E. A., & Leventhal, H. (1995). Seeking medical care in response to symptoms and life stress. *Psychosomatic Medicine*, *57*, 37–47.

Cameron, O. G., Kronfol, Z., Greden, J. F., & Carroll, B. J. (1984). Hypothalamic–pituitary–adrenocortical activity in patients with diabetes mellitus. *Archives of General Psychiatry, 41*, 1090–1095.

Cantor, N. (1990). From thought to behavior: 'Having' and 'Doing' in the study of personality and cognition. *American Psychologist, 45*, 735–750.

Cantor, N., & Kihlstrom, J. F. (1987). *Personality and social intelligence.* Englewood Cliffs, NJ: Prentice-Hall.

Carver, C. S., Pozo, C., Harris, S. D., Noriega, V., Scheier, M. F., Robinson, D. S., Ketcham, A. S., Moffat, F.L. Jr., & Clark, K. C. (1993). How coping mediates the effect of optimism on distress: A study of women with early stage breast cancer. *Journal of Personality and Social Psychology, 65*, 375–390.

Carver, C. S., & Scheier, M. F. (1981). *Attention and self-regulation: A control-theory approach to human behavior.* New York: Springer.

Carver, C. S., & Scheier, M. F. (1982). Control theory: A useful conceptual framework for personality-social, clinical, and health psychology. *Psychological Bulletin, 92*, 111–135.

Carver, C. S., & Scheier, M. F. (1999). Stress, coping, and self-regulatory processes. In L. A. Pervin & O. P. John (Eds.), *Handbook of personality: Theory and research* (2nd edn., pp. 553–575). New York: Guilford.

Carver, C. S., Scheier, M. F., & Weintraub, J. K. (1989). Assessing coping strategies: A theoretically based approach. *Journal of Personality & Social Psychology, 56*, 267–283.

Cassileth, B. R. (1998). *The alternative medicine handbook: The complete reference guide to alternative and complementary therapies.* New York: Norton.

Cassileth, B. R., & Chapman, C. C. (1996). Alternative and complementary cancer therapies. *Cancer, 77*, 1026–1034.

Cassileth, B. R., Lusk, E. J., Strouse, T. B., & Bodenheimer, B. J. (1984). Contemporary unorthodox treatments in cancer medicine. *Annals of Internal Medicine, 101*, 105–112.

Cassileth, B. R., Lusk, E. J., Walsh, W. P., Doyle, B., & Maier, M. (1989). The satisfaction of psychosocial status of patients during treatment for cancer. *Journal of Psychosocial Oncology, 7*, 47–58.

Cella, D. F., Orofiamma, B., Holland, J. C., Silberfarb, P. M., Tross, S., Feldstein, M., Perry, M., Maurer, L. H., Comks, R., & Orav, E. J. (1987). The relationship of psychological distress, extent of disease, and performance status in patients with lung cancer. *Cancer, 60*, 1661–1667.

Chan, A. W. (1991). Chronic pain in patients with diabetes mellitus. *Nursing Times, 87*, 52–53.

Chapman, G. B. (1996). Temporal discounting and utility for health and money. *Journal of Experimental Psychology, 22*, 771–791.

Chapman, G. B., Brewer, N. T., Coups, E. J., Brownlee, S., Leventhal, H., & Leventhal, E. A. (2001). Value for the future and preventive health behavior. *Journal of Experimental Psychology: Applied, 7*, 235–250.

Charmaz, K. (1999). From the 'sick role' to stories of self: Understanding the self in illness. In R. J. Contrada & R. D. Ashmore (Eds.), *Self, social identity, and physical health: Interdisciplinary explorations* (pp. 209–239). New York: Oxford University Press.

Chin, M. H., & Goldman, L. (1997). Factors contributing to the hospitalization of patients with congestive heart failure. *American Journal of Public Health, 87*, 643–648.

Chobanian, A. V., Bakris, G. L., Black, H. R., Cushman, W. C., Green, L. A., Izzo, J. L. Jr., Jones, D. W., Materson, B. J., Oparil, S., Wright, J. T. Jr., & Roccella, E. J. (2003). The Seventh Report of the Joint National Committee on Prevention, Detection, Evaluation, and Treatment of High Blood Pressure: The JNC 7 Report. *Journal of the American Medical Association, 289*, 2560–2571.

Chrisman, N. J., & Kleinman, A. (1983). Popular health care, social networks, and cultural meanings: The orientation of medical anthropology. In D. Mechanic (Ed.), *Handbook of health, health care, and the health professions* (pp. 569–590). New York: Free Press.

Christakis, N. A. (1999). *Death foretold: Prophecy and prognosis in medical care.* Chicago: University of Chicago Press.

Christensen, A. J. (2000). Patient-by-treatment context interaction in chronic disease: A conceptual framework for the study of patient adherence. *Psychosomatic Medicine, 62*, 435–443.

Cohen, S. (1988). Psychosocial models of the role of social support in the etiology of physical disease. *Health Psychology, 7*, 269–297.

Cohen, S., & Herbert, T. B. (1996). Health psychology: Psychological factors and physical disease from the perspective of human psychoneuroimmunology. *Annual Review of Psychology, 47*, 113–142.

Cohen, S., & Hoberman, H. (1983). Positive events and social support as buffers of life change stress. *Journal of Applied Social Psychology, 13*, 99–125.

Collins, D. L., Baum, A., & Singer, J. E. (1983). Coping with chronic stress at Three Mile Island: Psychological and biochemical evidence. *Health Psychology, 2*, 149–166.

Cox, D. J., & Gonder-Frederick, L. (1992). Major developments in behavioral diabetes research. *Journal of Consulting & Clinical Psychology, 60*, 628–638.

Cox, D. J., Irvine, A., Gonder-Frederick, L., Nowacek, G., & Butterfield, J. (1987). Fear of hypoglycemia: Quantification, validation, and utilization. *Diabetes Care, 10*, 617–621.

Coyne, J. C., Benazon, N. R., Gaba, C. G., Calzone, K., & Weber, B. L. (2000). Distress and psychiatric morbidity among women from high-risk breast and ovarian cancer families. *Journal of Consulting and Clinical Psychology, 68*, 864–874.

Coyne, J. C., & Schwenk, T. L. (1997). The relationship of distress to mood disturbance in primary care and psychiatric populations. *Journal of Consulting and Clinical Psychology, 65*, 161–168.

Coyne, J. C., Thompson, R., Klinkman, M. S., & Nease, D. E. J. R. (2002). Emotional disorders in primary care. *Journal of Consulting and Clinical Psychology, 70*, 798–809.

Coyne, J. C., Thompson, R., Palmer, S. C., Kagee, A., & Maunsell, E. (2000). Should we screen for depression? Caveats and potential pitfalls. *Applied and Preventive Psychology, 9*, 101–121.

Croyle, R. T., & Jemmott, J. B. I. (1991). Psychological reactions to risk factor testing. In J. A. Skelton & R. T. Croyle (Eds.), *Mental representations in health and illness* (pp. 85–103). New York: Springer.

Cummings, J. L. (1992). Depression and Parkinson's disease: A review. *American Journal of Psychiatry, 149*, 443–454.

Cunningham, M. A. (2001). Glucose monitoring in type 2 diabetes. *Nursing Clinics of North America, 36*, 361–374.

Curfman, G. D. (1993). The health benefits of exercise: A critical reappraisal. *New England Journal of Medicine, 328*, 574–576.

de Groot, M., Anderson, R., Freedland, K. E., Clouse, R. E., & Lustman, P. J. (2001). Association of depression and diabetes complications: A meta-analysis. *Psychosomatic Medicine, 63*, 619–630.

Diabetes Control and Complications Trial Research Group. (1993). The effect of intensive treatment of diabetes on the development and progression of long-term complications in insulin-dependent diabetes mellitus. *New England Journal of Medicine, 329*, 977–986.

Diabetes Prevention Program Research Group (2002). Reduction in the incidence of type 2 diabetes with lifestyle intervention or metformin. *New England Journal of Medicine, 346*, 393–403.

Diette, G. B., Skinner, E. A., Nguyen, T. T., Markson, L., Clark, B. D., & Wu, A. W. (2001). Comparison of quality of care by specialist and generalist physicians as usual source of asthma care for children. *Pediatrics, 108*, 432–437.

DiMatteo, M. R., Lepper, H. S., & Croghan, T. W. (2000). Depression is a risk factor for noncompliance with medical treatment: Meta-analysis of the effects of anxiety and depression on patient adherence. *Archives of Internal Medicine, 160*, 2101–2107.

Duke, J., Leventhal, H., Brownlee, S., & Leventhal, E. A. (2002). Giving up and replacing activities in response to illness. *Journals of Gerontology Series B, Psychological Sciences & Social Sciences, 4*, 367.

Dunbar-Jacob, J., Schlenk, E. A., Burke, L. E., & Matthews, J. T. (1998). Predictors of patient adherence: Patient characteristics. In S. A. Shumaker, E. B. Schron, J. K. Ockene & W. L. McBee (Eds.), *The handbook of health behavior change* (2nd edn., pp. 491–511). New York: Springer.

Dyck, P. J., Kratz, K. M., Karnes, J. L., Litchy, W. J., Klein, R., Pach, J. M., Wilson, D. M., O'Brien, P. C., Melton, L. J. 3rd, & Service, F. J. (1993). The prevalence by staged severity of various types of diabetic neuropathy, retinopathy, and nephropathy in a population-based cohort: The Rochester Diabetic Neuropathy Study. *Neurology, 43*, 817–824 [erratum appears in *Neurology*, 1993, 43(11), 2345].

Easterling, D. V., & Leventhal, H. (1989). Contribution of concrete cognition to emotion: Neutral symptoms as elicitors of worry about cancer. *Journal of Applied Psychology, 74*, 787–796.

Eisenberg, D. M., Davis, R. B., Ettner, S. L., Appel, S., Wilkey, S., Van Rompay, M., & Kessler, R. C. (1998). Trends in alternative medicine use in the US, 1990–1997: Results of a follow up national survey. *Journal of the American Medical Association, 280*, 1569–1575.

Endler, N. S., & Parker, J. D. (1990). Multidimensional assessment of coping: A critical evaluation. *Journal of Personality and Social Psychology, 58*, 844–854.

Engel, G. L. (1977). The need for a new medical model: A challenge for biomedicine. *Science, 196*, 129–136.

Epstein, S. (1973). The self-concept revisited: Or a theory of a theory. *American Psychologist, 28*, 404–416.

Ewart, C. K. (1991). Social action theory for a public health psychology. *American Psychologist, 46*, 931–946.

Falcone, M., & Sarvetnick, N. (1999). The effect of local production of cytokines in the pathogenesis of insulin-dependent diabetes mellitus. *Clinical Immunology, 90*, 2–9.

Farkas-Hirsch, R. (1998). *Intensive diabetes management* (2nd edn.). Alexandria, VA: American Diabetes Association.

Fiatarone, M. A., O'Neill, E. F., Doyle Ryan, N., Clements, K. M., Solares, G. R., Nelson, M. E., Roberts, S. B., Kehayias, J. J., Kipsitz, L. A., & Evans, W. J. (1994). Exercise training and nutritional supplementation for physical frailty in very elderly people. *New England Journal of Medicine, 330*, 1769–1775.

Fincke, B. G., Miller, D. R., & Spiro, A. 3rd. (1998). The interaction of patient perception of overmedication with drug compliance and side effects. *Journal of General Internal Medicine, 13*, 182–185.

Fitzpatrick, R., Newman, S., Archer, R., & Shipley, M. (1991). Social support, disability and depression: A longitudinal study of rheumatoid arthritis. *Social Science and Medicine, 33*, 605–611.

Folkman, S., & Lazarus, R. S. (1985). If it changes it must be a process: Study of emotion and coping during three stages of a college examination. *Journal of Personality and Social Psychology, 48*, 150–170.

Friedman, M. A., Detweiler-Bedell, J., Leventhal, H., Horne, R., Keitner, G. I., & Miller, I. W. (in press). Combined psychotherapy and pharmacotherapy for the treatment of major depressive disorder. *Clinical Psychology: Science and Practice.*

Fries, J. F. (1983). The compression of morbidity. *Milbank Memorial Fund Quarterly Health and Society, 61*, 397–419.

Furnham, A., & Forey, J. (1994). The attitudes, behaviors and beliefs of patients of conventional vs. complementary (alternative) medicine. *Journal of Clinical Psychology, 50*, 458–469.

Gallo, J. J., Anthony, J. C., & Muthen, B. O. (1994). Age differences in the symptoms of depression: A latent trait analysis. *Journals of Gerontology, 49*, P251–P264.

Gallo, J. J., Rabins, P. V., & Anthony, J. C. (1990). Sadness in older persons: 13-year follow-up of a community sample in Baltimore, Maryland. *Psychological Medicine, 29*, 341–350.

Glaxo Wellcome (1998). *Asthma in America.* Research Triangle Park, NC: Glaxo Wellcome, Inc.

Gollwitzer, P. M. (1999). Implementation intentions: Strong effects of simple plans. *American Psychologist, 54*, 493–503.

Gonder-Frederick, L. A., & Cox, D. J. (1991). Symptom perception, symptom beliefs, and blood glucose discrimination in the self-treatment of insulin-dependent diabetes. In J. A. Skelton & R. T. Croyle (Eds.), *Mental representations in health and illness* (pp. 220–246). New York: Springer.

Greeno, J. G. (1998). The situativity of knowing, learning and research. *American Psychologist, 53*, 5–26.

Gronberg, H. (2003). Prostate cancer epidemiology. *Lancet, 361*, 859–864.

Gustafson, D. H., Hawkins, R., Boberg, E., Pingree, S., Serlin, R. E., Graziano, F., & Chan, C. L. (1999). Impact of a patient centered, computer based health information/support system. *American Journal of Preventive Medicine, 16*, 1–9.

Gustafson, D., Hawkins, R., Pingree, S., McTavish, F., Arora, N., Salmer, J., Stewart, J., Mendenhall, J., Cella, R., Serlin, R., & Apenteko, F. (2000). *Effect of computer support on younger women with breast cancer.* The Center for Health Systems Research and Analysis, University of Wisconsin, Madison.

Hakim, A. A., Petrovitch, H., Burchfiel, C. M., Ross, W. G., Rodriguez, B. L., White, L. R., Katsuhiko, Y., Curb, D., & Abbott, R. D. (1998). Effects of walking on mortality among nonsmoking retired men. *New England Journal of Medicine, 338*, 94–99.

Halm, E. A., Sturm, T., Mora, P., & Leventhal, H. (2003). No symptoms, no asthma: Self-regulation, knowledge, beliefs, and behaviors among inner-city adults. *American Journal of Respiratory and Critical Care Medicine, 167*, A156.

Halm, E. A., Wang, J., Cooperman, A., Sturm, T., & Leventhal, H. (2003). Effects of participatory decision making on self-regulation beliefs, behaviors, and outcomes among inner city asthmatics. *Journal of General Internal Medicine, 18*, 147.

Heidrich, S. M., Forsthoff, C. A., & Ward, S. E. (1994). Psychological adjustment in adults with cancer: The self as mediator. *Health Psychology, 13*, 346–353.

Heijmans, M., de Ridder, D., & Bensing, J. (1999). Dissimilarity in patients' and spouses' representations of chronic illness: Exploration of relations to patient adaptation. *Psychology and Health, 14*, 451–466.

Heijmans, M., Foets, M., Rijken, M., Schreurs, K., De Ridder, D., & Bensing, J. (2001). Stress in chronic disease: Do the perceptions of patients and their general practitioners match? *British Journal of Health Psychology, 6*, 229–242.

Helgeson, V. S., Cohen, S., Schulz, R., & Yasko, J. (1999). Education and peer discussion group interventions and adjustment to breast cancer. *Archives of General Psychiatry, 56*, 340–347.

Hellestrom, C. (2001). Temporal dimensions of the self-concept: Entrapped and possible selves in chronic pain. *Psychology and Health, 16*, 111–124.

Heurtin-Roberts, S. (1993). 'High-pertension': The uses of a chronic folk illness for personal adaptation. *Social Science and Medicine*, *37*, 285–294.

Ho, K. K., Anderson, K. M., Kannel, W. B., Grossman, W., & Levy, D. (1993). Survival after the onset of congestive heart failure in Framingham Heart Study subjects. *Circulation*, *88*, 107–115.

Hoffman, C., Rice, D., & Sung, H. Y. (1996). Persons with chronic conditions: Their prevalence and costs. *Journal of the American Medical Association*, *276*, 1473–1479.

Holmes, T., & Masuda, M. (1974). Life change and illness susceptibility. In B. S. Dohrenwend & B. P. Dohrenwend (Eds.), *Stressful life events*. New York: Wiley.

Hooker, K. (1992). Possible selves and perceived health in older adults and college students. *Journals of Gerontology*, *47*, P85–P95.

Hooker, K., & Kaus, C. R. (1994). Health-related possible selves in young and middle adulthood. *Psychology and Aging*, *9*, 126–133.

Horne, R. (1997). Representation of medication and treatment: Advances in theory and measurement. In K. J. Petrie & J. A. Weinman (Eds.), *Perceptions of health and illness* (pp. 155–188). Amsterdam: Harwood Academic.

Horne, R. (2003). Treatment perceptions and self-regulation. In L. D. Cameron & H. Leventhal (Eds.), *The self-regulation of health and illness behaviour* (pp. 138–154). London: Routledge.

Horne, R., & Weinman, J. (1999). Patients' beliefs about prescribed medicines and their role in adherence to treatment in chronic physical illness. *Journal of Psychosomatic Research*, *47*, 555–567.

Horne, R., Weinman, J., & Hankins, M. (1999). The Beliefs about Medicines Questionnaire: The development and evaluation of a new method for assessing the cognitive representation of medication. *Psychology and Health*, *14*, 1–24.

Horowitz, C. R., Rein, S. B., & Leventhal, H. (2004). A story of maladies, misconceptions, and mishaps: Effective management of heart failure. *Social Science and Medicine*, 58 (3), 631–643.

Idler, E. L., & Benyamini, Y. (1997). Self-rated health and mortality: A review of twenty-seven community studies. *Journal of Health and Social Behavior*, *38*, 21–37.

Janz, N. K., & Becker, M. H. (1984). The health belief model: A decade later. *Health Education Quarterly*, *11*, 1–42.

Jayne, R. L., & Rankin, S. H. (2001). Application of Leventhal's self-regulation model to Chinese immigrants with type 2 diabetes. *Journal of Nursing Scholarship*, *33*, 53–59.

Johnson, J. E. (1975). Stress reduction through sensation information. In I. L. Sarason & C. D. Spielberger (Eds.), *Stress and anxiety* (pp. 361–373). Washington, DC: Hemisphere.

Johnson, J. E., Kirchoff, K. T., & Endress, M. P. (1975). Altering children's distress behavior during orthopedic cast removal. *Nursing Research*, *24*, 404–410.

Johnson, J. E., Lauvier, D. R., & Nail, L. M. (1989). Process of coping with radiation therapy. *Journal of Consulting and Clinical Psychology*, *57*, 258–364.

Johnson, J. E., & Leventhal, H. (1974). Effects of accurate expectations and behavioral instructions on reactions during a noxious medical examination. *Journal of Personality and Social Psychology*, *29*, 710–718.

Jolliffe, J. A., Rees, K., Taylor, R. S., Thompson, D., Oldridge, N., & Ebrahim, S. (2000). Exercise-based rehabilitation for coronary heart disease. *Cochrane Database of Systematic Reviews*, (4), CD001800. [Update in *Cochrane Database Systemative Reviews*, 2001, (1), CD001800, PMID: 11279730].

Kaptchuk, T. J., & Eisenberg, D. M. (1998). The persuasive appeal of alternative medicine. *Annals of Internal Medicine*, *129*, 1061–1065.

Kart, C. (1981). Experiencing symptoms: Attribution and misattribution of illness among the aged. In M. Haug (Ed.), *Elderly patients and their doctors* (pp. 70–78). New York: Springer.

Kavanagh, D. J., Gooley, S., & Wilson, P. H. (1993). Prediction of adherence and control in diabetes. *Journal of Behavioral Medicine*, *16*, 509–522.

Kay, M. (1993). Fallen fontanelle: Culture-bound or cross cultural. *Medical Anthropology*, *15*, 137–156.

Kelly, G. (1955). *The psychology of personal constructs*. New York: Norton.

Kiecolt-Glaser, J. K., Bane, C., Glaser, R., & Malarkey, W. B. (2003). Love, marriage, and divorce: Newlyweds' stress hormones foreshadow relationship changes. *Journal of Consulting and Clinical Psychology*, *71*, 176–188.

Kiecolt-Glaser, J. K., Dura, J. R., Speicher, C. E., Trask, O. J., & Glaser, R. (1991). Spousal caregivers of dementia victims: Longitudinal changes in immunity and health. *Psychosomatic Medicine*, *53*, 345–362.

Kiecolt-Glaser, J. K., Garner, W., Speicher, C., Penn, G. M., Holliday, J., & Glaser, R. (1984). Psychosocial modifiers of immunocompetence in medical students. *Psychosomatic Medicine*, *46*, 7–14.

Kirkwood, T. B., & Austad, S. N. (2000). Why do we age? *Nature*, *408*, 233–238.

Kleinman, A. (1988). *The illness narratives.* New York: Basic.

Konrad, T. R. (1998). The patterns of self care among older adults in western industrialized societies. In M. G. Ory & G. H. DeFriese (Eds.), *Self care in later life research: Program and policy issues* (pp. 24–61). New York: Springer.

Kugelmann, R. (1999). Complaining about chronic pain. *Social Science and Medicine, 49,* 1663–1676.

Kulik, J. A., & Mahler, H. I. M. (1997). Social comparison, affiliation, and coping with acute medical threats. In B. P. Buunk & F. X. Gibbons (Eds.), *Health, coping, and well-being: Perspectives from social comparison theory* (pp. 227–261). Mahwah, NJ: Erlbaum.

Lau, R. R., Bernard, T. M., & Hartman, K. A. (1989). Further explorations of common-sense representations of illness. *Health Psychology, 2,* 167–185.

Lau, R. R., & Hartman, K. A. (1983). Common sense representations of common illnesses. *Health Psychology, 2,* 167–185.

Lazarus, R. S. (1964). A laboratory approach to the dynamics of psychological stress. *American Psychologist, 19,* 400–411.

Lazarus, R. S. (1966). *Psychological stress and the coping process.* New York: McGraw-Hill.

Lazarus, R. S. (2000). Toward better research on stress and coping. *American Psychologist, 55,* 665–673.

Lazarus, R. S., & Folkman, S. (1984). *Stress, appraisal, and coping.* New York: Springer.

Lazarus, R. S., & Launier, R. (1978). Stress related transactions between person and environment. In L. A. Pervin & M. Lewis (Eds.), *Perspectives in interactional psychology* (pp. 287–327). New York: Plenum.

Legorreta, A. P., Christian-Herman, J., O'Connor, R. D., Hasan, M. M., Evans, R., & Leung, K. M. (1998). Compliance with national asthma management guidelines and specialty care: A health maintenance organization experience. *Archives of Internal Medicine, 158,* 457–464.

Leslie, R. D. (1999). United Kingdom Perspective Diabetes Study (UKPDS): What now or so what? *Diabetes Metabolism and Research Review, 15,* 65–71.

Leventhal, E., & Burns, E. A. (2004). The biology of aging. In G. T. Grossberg, J. Sadavoy, L. F. Jarvik & B. Meyers (Eds.), *Comprehensive textbook of geriatric psychiatry,* 3rd edition. New York: Norton.

Leventhal, E. A., & Crouch, M. (1997). Are there differences in perceptions of illness across the lifespan? In K. J. Petrie & J. Weinman (Eds.), *Perceptions of health and illness: Current research and applications* (pp. 77–102). London: Harwood Academic.

Leventhal, E. A., Easterling, D., Leventhal, H., & Cameron, L. (1995). Conservation of energy, uncertainty reduction, and swift utilization of medical care among the elderly: II. *Medical Care, 33,* 988–1000.

Leventhal, E., & Leventhal, H. (in press). Patient–doctor interactions in an aging society: The opportunities for behavioral research. In D. C. Park & L. L. Liu (Eds.), *Social and cognitive perspectives on medical adherence.* Washington, DC: Academic.

Leventhal, E. A., Leventhal, H., & Robitaille, C. (1998). Enhancing self-care research: Exploring the theoretical underpinnings of self-care. In M. G. Ory & G. H. DeFriese (Eds.), *Self-care in later life: Research, program, and policy issues* (pp. 118–141). New York: Springer.

Leventhal, E. A., Leventhal, H., Schaefer, P., & Easterling, D. (1993). Conservation of energy, uncertainty reduction, and swift utilization of medical care among the elderly. *Journals of Gerontology, 48,* P78–P86.

Leventhal, H. (1970). Findings and theory in the study of fear communications. In L. Berkowitz (Ed.), *Advances in experimental social psychology* (Vol. 5, pp. 120–186). New York: Academic.

Leventhal, H. (1980). Toward a comprehensive theory of emotion. *Advances in Experimental Social Psychology, 13,* 139–207.

Leventhal, H. (1984). A perceptual-motor theory of emotion. *Advances in Experimental Social Psychology, 17,* 117–182.

Leventhal, H., Brissette, I., & Leventhal, E. (2003). The common-sense model of self-regulation of health and illness. In C. L. Cameron & H. Leventhal (Eds.), *The self-regulation of health and illness behaviour.* London: Routledge.

Leventhal, H., Diefenbach, M., & Leventhal, E. A. (1992). Illness cognition: Using common sense to understand treatment adherence and affect cognition interactions. *Cognitive Therapy and Research, 16,* 143–163.

Leventhal, H., Easterling, D. V., Coons, H., Luchterhand, C., & Love, R. R. (1986). Adaptation to chemotherapy treatments. In B. Andersen (Ed.), *Women with cancer* (pp. 172–203). New York: Springer.

Leventhal, H., Hudson, S., & Robitaille, C. (1997). Social comparison and health: A process model. In B. Buunk & F. X. Gibbons (Eds.), *Health, coping, and well-being: Perspectives from social comparison theory* (pp. 411–432). Hillsdale, NJ: Erlbaum.

Leventhal, H., Idler, E. L., & Leventhal, E. A. (1999). The impact of chronic illness on the self system.

In R. J. Contrada & R. D. Ashmore (Eds.), *Rutgers series on self and social identity: Self, social identity, and physical health* (Vol. 2, pp. 185–208). New York: Oxford University Press.

Leventhal, H., Leventhal, E. A., & van Nguyen, T. (1985). Reactions of families to illness: Theoretical models and perspectives. In D. Turk & R. Kerns (Eds.), *Health, illness, and families: A life-span perspective* (pp. 108–145). New York: Wiley.

Leventhal, H., Meyer, D., & Nerenz, D. (1980). The common sense representation of illness danger. In S. Rachman (Ed.), *Medical psychology* (Vol. 2, pp. 7–29). New York: Pergamon.

Leventhal, H., Rabin, C., Leventhal, E. A., & Burns, E. (2001). Health/risk behaviors and aging. In R. Birren & W. Schaie (Eds.), *Handbook of the psychology of aging* (5th edn., pp. 186–214). San Diego, CA: Academic.

Leventhal, H., Singer, R., & Jones, S. (1965). Effects of fear and specificity of recommendation upon attitudes and behavior. *Journal of Personality and Social Psychology, 2*, 20–29.

Liburd, L. C., Anderson, L. A., Edgar, T., & Jack, L. J. (1999). Body size and body shape: Perceptions of black women with diabetes. *Diabetes Educator, 25*, 382–388.

Link, N., & Tanner, M. (2001). Coronary artery disease: Part 1. Epidemiology and diagnosis. *Western Journal of Medicine, 174*, 257–261.

Littlefield, C. H., Rodin, G. M., Murray, M. A., & Craven, J. L. (1990). Influence of functional impairment and social support on depressive symptoms in persons with diabetes. *Health Psychology, 9*, 737–749.

Lough, M. A. (1996). Ongoing work of older adults at home after hospitalization. *Journal of Advanced Nursing, 23*, 804–809.

Lustman, P. J., Anderson, R. J., Freedland, K. E., de Groot, M., Carney, R. M., & Clouse, R. E. (2000). Depression and poor glycemic control: A meta-analytic review of the literature. *Diabetes Care, 23*, 934–942.

Lustman, P. J., Griffith, L. S., Clouse, R. E., & Cryer, P. E. (1986). Psychiatric illness in diabetes: Relationship to symptoms and glucose control. *Journal of Nervous and Mental Disease, 174*, 736–742.

Lustman, P. J., Griffith, L. S., Gavard, J. A., & Clouse, R. E. (1992). Depression in adults with diabetes. *Diabetes Care, 15*, 1631–1639.

MacIntyre, K., Capewell, S., Stewart, S., Chalmers, J. W. T., Boyd, J., Finlayson, A., Redpath, A., Pell, J. P., & McMurray, J. J. V. (2000). Evidence of improving prognosis in heart failure: Trends in case

fatality in 66,547 patients hospitalized between 1986 and 1995. *Circulation, 102*, 1126–1131.

Maes, M., Bosmans, E., De Jongh, R., Kenis, G., Vandoolaeghe, E., & Neels, H. (1997). Increased serum IL-6 and IL-1 receptor antagonist concentrations in major depression and treatment resistant depression. *Cytokine, 9*, 853–858.

Maes, M., Meltzer, H. Y., Bosmans, E., Bergmans, R., Vandoolaeghe, E., Ranjan, R., & Desnyder, R. (1995). Increased plasma concentrations of interleukin-6, soluble interleukin-6, soluble interleukin-2 and transferrin receptor in major depression. *Journal of Affective Disorders, 34*, 301–309.

Mannino, D. M., Homa, D. M., Akinbami, L. J., Moorman, J. E., Gwynn, C., & Redd, S. C. (2002). Surveillance for asthma: United States, 1980–1999. *Morbidity and Mortality Weekly Report, Surveillance Summaries, 51*, 1–13.

Martin, R., Lemos, K., & Leventhal, H. (2001). The psychology of physical symptoms and illness behavior. In J. G. Asmundson, S. Taylor & B. J. Cox (Eds.), *Health anxiety* (pp. 22–45). New York: Wiley.

Martin, R., Rothrock, N., Leventhal, H., & Leventhal, E. (2003). Common sense models of illness: Implications for symptom perception and health-related behaviors. In J. Suls & K. Wallston (Eds.), *Social psychological foundations of health and illness*. Malden, MA: Blackwell.

McBride, C. M., & Rimer, B. K. (1999). Using the telephone to improve health behavior and health service delivery. *Patient Education and Counseling, 37*, 3–18.

McCaffery, M. (1992). Pain control: Barriers to the use of available information. World Health Organization Expert Committee on Cancer Pain Relief and Active Supportive Care. *Cancer, 70*(5 Supp.), 1438–1449.

McCaul, K. D., Glasgow, R. E., & Schafer, L. C. (1987). Diabetes regimen behaviors: Predicting adherence. *Medical Care, 25*, 868–881.

McCaul, K. D., Johnson, R. J., & Rothman, A. J. (2002). The effects of framing and action instructions on whether older adults obtain flu shots. *Health Psychology, 21*, 624–628.

Meyer, D., Leventhal, H., & Gutmann, M. (1985). Common-sense models of illness: The example of hypertension. *Health Psychology, 4*, 115–135.

Miller, G. A., Galanter, E., & Pribram, K. H. (1960). *Plans and the structure of behavior*. New York: Holt, Rinehart & Winston.

Miller, S. M. (1996). Monitoring and blunting of threatening information: Cognitive interference and facilitation in the coping process. In I. Sarason, B. Sarason & G. R. Pierce (Eds.), *Cognitive interference: Theories, models and findings* (pp. 175–190). Mahwah, NJ: Erlbaum.

Miller, S. M., Shoda, Y., & Hurley, K. (1996). Applying cognitive-social theory to health-protective behavior: Breast self-examination in cancer screening. *Psychological Bulletin, 119,* 70–94.

Mischel, W. (1973). Toward a cognitive social learning reconceptualization of personality. *Psychological Review, 80,* 252–283.

Mittleman, M. A., Maclure, M., Tofler, G. H., Sherwood, J. B., Goldberg, R. J., & Muller, J. E. (1993). Triggering of acute myocardial infarction by heavy physical exertion: Protection against triggering by regular exertion. Determinants of Myocardial Infarction Onset Study investigators. *New England Journal of Medicine, 329,* 1677–1683.

Mokdad, A. H., Bowman, B. A., Ford, E. S., Vinicor, F., Marks, J. S., & Koplan, J. P. (2001). The continuing epidemics of obesity and diabetes in the US. *Journal of the American Medical Association, 286,* 1195–1200.

Moldin, S. O., Scheftner, W. A., Rice, J. P., Nelson, E., Knesevich, M. A., & Akiskal, H. (1993). Association between major depressive disorder and physical illness. *Psychological Medicine, 23,* 755–761.

Mollema, E. D., Snoek, F. J., Ader, H. J., Heine, R. J., & van der Ploeg, H. M. (2001). Insulin-treated diabetes patients with fear of self-injecting or fear of self-testing: Psychological comorbidity and general well-being. *Journal of Psychosomatic Research, 51,* 665–672.

Moore, K. A., & Blumenthal, J. A. (1998). Exercise training as an alternative treatment for depression among older adults. *Alternative Therapies in Health and Medicine, 4,* 48–56.

Moos, R. H. (1986). *Coping with life crises: An integrated approach.* New York: Plenum.

Mora, P. A., Robitaille, C., Leventhal, H., Swigar, M., & Leventhal, E. A. (2002). Trait negative affect relates to prior-week symptoms, but not to reports of illness episodes, illness symptoms, and care seeking among older persons. *Psychosomatic Medicine, 64,* 436–449.

Moser, G., Tillinger, W., Sachs, G., Maier-Dobersberger, T., Wyatt, J., Vogelsang, H., Lochs, H., & Gangl, A. (1996). Relationship between the use of unconventional therapies and disease-related concerns: A study of patients with inflammatory bowel disease. *Journal of Psychosomatic Research, 40,* 503–509.

Musselman, D. L., Betan, E., Larsen, H., & Phillips, L. S. (2003). Relationship of depression to diabetes types 1 and 2: Epidemiology, biology, and treatment. *Biological Psychiatry, 54,* 317–329.

National Heart, Lung, and Blood Institute (1997). *Expert Panel Report 2: Guidelines for the diagnosis and management of asthma.* Bethesda, MD: National Institutes of Health.

National Heart, Lung, and Blood Institute (1998). *Morbidity and Mortality 1998: Chartbook on cardiovascular, lung, and blood diseases.* Washington, DC.

Nerenz, D. R., & Leventhal, H. (1983). Self-regulation theory in chronic illness. In T. B. L. Bradley (Ed.), *Coping with chronic disease: Research and applications* (pp. 13–37). New York: Academic.

Ni, H., Nauman, D., Burgess, D., Wise, K., Crispell, K., & Hershberger, R. E. (1999). Factors influencing knowledge of and adherence to self-care among patients with heart failure. *Archives of Internal Medicine, 159,* 1613–1619.

Ory, M. G., & DeFriese, G. H. (1998). *Self-care in later life: Research, program, and policy issues.* New York: Springer.

Pachter, L. M. (1994). Culture and clinical care: Folk illness beliefs and behaviors and their implications for health care delivery. *Journal of the American Medical Association, 271,* 690–694.

Palmer, S. C., & Coyne, J. C. (2003). Screening for depression in medical care: Pitfalls, alternatives, and revised priorities. *Journal of Psychosomatic Research, 54,* 279–287.

Pan, X. R., Li, G. W., Hu, Y. H., Wang, J. X., Yang, W. Y., An, Z. X., Hu, Z. X., Lin, J., Xiao, J. Z., Cao, H. B., Liu, P. A., Jiang, X. G., Jiang, Y. Y., Wang, J. P., Zheng, H., Zhang, H., Bennett, P. H., & Howard, B. V. (1997). Effects of diet and exercise in preventing NIDDM in people with impaired glucose tolerance: The Da Qing IGT and Diabetes Study. *Diabetes Care, 20,* 537–544.

Park, D. C., Hertzog, C., Leventhal, H., Morrell, R. W., Leventhal, E., Birchmore, D., Martin, M., & Bennett, J. (1999). Medication adherence in rheumatoid arthritis patients: Older is wiser. *Journal of the American Geriatrics Society, 47,* 172–183.

Partridge, M. R. (1995). Asthma: Lessons from patient education. *Patient Education and Counseling, 26,* 81–86.

Pearlin, L. I. (1989). The sociological study of stress. *Journal of Health and Social Behavior, 30,* 241–256.

Pearlin, L. I., Menaghan, E. G., Lieberman, M. A., & Mullan, J. T. (1981). The stress process. *Journal of Health and Social Behavior, 22,* 337–356.

Pearlin, L. I., & Schooler, C. (1978). The structure of coping. *Journal of Health and Social Behavior, 19,* 2–21.

Petrie, K. J., Broadbent, E., & Meechan, G. (2003). Self-regulatory interventions for improving management of chronic illness. In L. D. Cameron & H. Leventhal (Eds.), *The self-regulation of health and illness behaviour* (pp. 247–277). London: Routledge.

Petrie, K. J., Cameron, L., Ellis, C. J., Buick, D., & Weinman, J. (2002). Changing illness perceptions after myocardial infarction: An early intervention randomized controlled trial. *Psychosomatic Medicine, 64,* 580–586.

Petrie, K. J., & Weinman, J. A. (1997). *Perceptions of health and illness.* Amsterdam: Harwood Academic.

Phillips, L. S., Branch, W. T., Cook, C. B., Doyle, J. P., El-Kebbi, I. M., Gallina, D. L., Miller, C. D., Ziemer, D. C., & Barnes, C. S. (2001). Clinical inertia. *Annals of Internal Medicine, 135,* 825–834.

Piette, J. D. (2002). Enhancing support via interactive technologies. *Current Diabetes Reports, 2,* 160–165.

Piette, J. D., Weinberger, M., & McPhee, S. J. (2000). The effect of automated calls with telephone nurse follow-up on patient-centered outcomes of diabetes care: A randomized, controlled trial. *Medical Care, 38,* 218–230.

Powers, W. T. (1973). *Behavior: The control of perception.* Chicago: Aldine.

Priest, R. G., Vize, C., Roberts, A., Roberts, M., & Tylee, A. (1996). Lay people's attitudes to treatment of depression: Results of opinion poll for Defeat Depression Campaign just before its launch. *British Medical Journal, 313,* 858–859.

Prohaska, T. R., Keller, M. L., Leventhal, E., & Leventhal, H. (1987). The impact of symptoms and aging attributions on emotions and coping. *Health Psychology, 6,* 495–514.

Rabin, C., Leventhal, H., & Goodin, S. (submitted). Conceptualization of disease time-line predicts post-treatment distress in breast cancer patients.

Rabinovitch, A. (1998). An update on cytokines in the pathogenesis of insulin-dependent diabetes mellitus. *Diabetes-Metabolism Reviews, 14,* 129–151.

Ribeiro, S. C., Tandon, R., Grunhaus, L., & Greden, J. F. (1993). The DST as a predictor of outcome in depression: A meta-analysis. *American Journal of Psychiatry, 150,* 1618–1629.

Rodin, R., & Voshart, K. (1987). Depressive symptoms and functional impairment in the medically ill. *General Hospital Psychiatry, 9,* 251–258.

Rogers, R. W. (1983). Cognitive and physiological processes in fear appeals and attitude change: A revised theory of protection motivation. In J. T. Cacioppo & R. E. Petty (Eds.), *Social psychophysiology* (pp. 153–176). New York: Guilford.

Rosenstock, I. M. (1974). Historical origins of the health belief model. *Health Education Monographs, 2,* 1–8.

Rothenberg, R. B., & Koplan, J. P. (1990). Chronic disease in the 1990s. *Annual Review of Public Health, 11,* 267–296.

Rotter, J. B. (1954). *Social learning and clinical psychology.* Englewood Cliffs, NJ: Prentice-Hall.

Roy, M., Collier, B., & Roy, A. (1990). Hypothalamic–pituitary–adrenal axis dysregulation among diabetic outpatients. *Psychiatry Research, 31,* 31–37.

Rubin, R. R., Peyrot, M., & Saudek, C. D. (1989). Effect of diabetes education on self-care, metabolic control, and emotional well-being. *Diabetes Care, 12,* 673–679.

Rubin, R. R., Peyrot, M., & Saudek, C. D. (1993). The effect of a diabetes education program incorporating coping skills training on emotional well being and diabetes self efficacy. *The Diabetes Educator, 19,* 210–214.

Sackett, D., & Haynes, R. B. (1976). *Compliance with therapeutic regimens.* Baltimore, MD: Johns Hopkins University Press.

Sacks, F. M., Svetkey, L. P., Vollmer, W. M., Appel, L. J., Bray, G. A., Harsha, D., Obarzanek, E., Conlin, P. R., Miller, E. R., Simons-Morton, D. G., Karanja, N., & Lin, P.-H. for the DASH-Sodium Collaborative Research Group (2001). Effects on blood pressure of reduced dietary sodium and the Dietary Approaches to Stop Hypertension (DASH) diet. *New England Journal of Medicine, 344,* 3–10.

Salovey, P., & Birnbaum, D. (1989). Influence of mood on health-relevant cognitions. *Journal of Personality and Social Psychology, 57,* 539–551.

Schachter, S. (1959). *The psychology of affiliation.* Stanford, CA: Stanford University Press.

Scheier, M. F., & Carver, C. S. (1985). Optimism, coping, and health: Assessment and implications of generalized outcome expectancies. *Health Psychology, 4,* 219–247.

Scheier, M. F., & Carver, C. S. (2003). Goals and confidence as self-regulatory elements underlying health and illness behavior. In L. D. Cameron & H. Leventhal (Eds.), *The self-regulation of health and illness behavior* (pp. 17–41). London: Routledge.

Scherer, K. R. (1999a). Appraisal theory. In T. Dalgleish & M. J. Power (Eds.), *Handbook of cognition and emotion* (pp. 637–663). Chichester: Wiley.

Scherer, K. R. (1999b). On the sequential nature of appraisal processes: Indirect evidence from a recognition task. *Cognition and Emotion, 13,* 763–793.

Seligman, M. E. (1975). *Helplessness: On depression, development, and death.* San Francisco: Freeman.

Sheeran, P. (2002). Intention–behavior relations: A conceptual and empirical review. *European Review of Social Psychology, 12,* 1–36.

Siegel, K., Schrimshaw, E. W., & Dean, L. (1999). Symptom interpretation: Implications for delay in HIV testing and care among HIV-infected late middle-aged and older adults. *AIDS Care, 11,* 525–535.

Silverman, C. S. (1999). *Psychological adjustment to uncertain outcomes: The threat of cancer recurrence.* Unpublished doctoral dissertation. University of Illinois at Urbana–Champaign, Illinois.

Simons, R. (1993). A simple defense of western biomedical explanatory schemata. *Medical Anthropology, 15,* 201–208.

Skinner, E. A., Edge, K., Altman, J., & Sherwood, H. (2003). Searching for the structure of coping: A review and critique of category systems for classifying ways of coping. *Psychological Bulletin, 129,* 216–269.

Stampfer, M. J., Hu, F. B., Manson, J. E., Rimm, E. B., & Willett, W. C. (2000). Primary prevention of coronary heart disease in women through diet and lifestyle. *New England Journal of Medicine, 343,* 16–22.

Stoller, E. P. (1998). Dynamics and processes of self care in old age. In M. G. Ory & G. H. DeFriese (Eds.), *Self care in later life: Research, program, and policy issues* (pp. 24–61). New York: Springer.

Stone, A. A., Helder, L., & Schneider, M. S. (1988). Coping with stressful life events: Coping dimensions and issues. In L. H. Cohen (Ed.), *Life events and psychological functioning: Theoretical and methodological issues* (pp. 182–210). Beverly Hills, CA: Sage.

Sullivan, M., Simon, G., Spertus, J., & Russo, J. (2002). Depression-related costs in heart failure care. *Archives of Internal Medicine, 162,* 1860–1866.

Suls, J., Martin, R., & Wheeler, L. (2000). Three kinds of opinion comparison: The triadic model. *Personality and Social Psychology Review, 4,* 219–237.

Suls, J., & Wan, C. K. (1989). Effects of sensory and procedural information on coping with stressful medical procedures and pain: A meta-analysis. *Journal of Consulting and Clinical Psychology, 57,* 372–379.

Swain, M. G. (2000). Fatigue in chronic disease. *Clinical Science, 99,* 1–8.

Taylor, S. E., Repetti, R. L., & Seeman, T. (1997). Health psychology: What is an unhealthy environment and how does it get under the skin? *Annual Review of Psychology, 48,* 411–447.

Thomas, L. (1977). On the science and technology of medicine. In J. H. Knowles (Ed.), *Doing better and feeling worse: Health in the United States* (pp. 35–46). The American Academy of Arts and Sciences.

Triemstra, A. H. M., Van der Ploeg, H. M., Smit, C., Briet, E., Ader, H. J., & Rosendaal, F. R. (1998). Well-being of haemophilia patients: A model for direct and indirect effects of medical parameters on the physical and psychosocial functioning. *Social Science and Medicine, 47,* 581–593.

Tuomilehto, J., Lindstrom, J., Eriksson, J. G., Valle, T. T., Hamalainen, H., Ilanne-Parikka, P., Keinanen-Kiukaanniemi, S., Laakso, M., Louheranta, A., Rastas, M., Salminen, V., Aunola, S., Cepaitis, Z., Moltchanov, V., Hakumaki, M., Mannelin, M., Martikkala, V., Sundvall, J., & Uusitupa, M. for the Finnish Diabetes Prevention Study Group (2001). Prevention of type 2 diabetes mellitus by changes in lifestyle among subjects with impaired glucose tolerance. *New England Journal of Medicine, 344,* 1343–1350.

UK Prospective Diabetes Study (UKPDS) Group (1998). Intensive blood glucose control with sulphonylureas or insulin compared with conventional treatment and risk of complications in patients with type 2 diabetes (UKPDS 33). *Lancet, 352,* 837–853.

van Grunsven, P. M. (2001). The magnitude of fear of adverse effects as a reason for nonparticipation in drug treatment: A short review. *Journal of Asthma, 38,* 113–119.

Vial, T., & Descotes, J. (1995). Immune-mediated side-effects of cytokines in humans. *Toxicology, 105,* 31–57.

Viney, L. L., & Westbrook, M. T. (1991). Psychological reactions to chronic illness-related disability as a function of its severity and type. *Journal of Psychosomatic Research, 25,* 513–523.

Vitaliano, P., Russo, J., Carr, J., Maiuro, R. D., & Becker, J. (1985). The Ways of Coping Checklist: Revision and psychometric properties. *Multivariate Behavioral Research, 20,* 3–26.

Walters, A. S., & Williamson, G. M. (1999). The role of activity restriction in the association between pain and depression: A study of pediatric patients with chronic pain. *Children's Health Care, 28,* 33–50.

Watson, D., & Pennebaker, J. W. (1989). Health complaints, stress, and distress: Exploring the central role of negative affectivity. *Psychological Review, 96,* 234–254.

Weiss, K. B., Sullivan, S. D., & Lyttle, C. S. (2000). Trends in the cost of illness for asthma in the United States, 1985–1994. *Journal of Allergy and Clinical Immunology, 106*, 493–499.

Weller, S. C., Pachter, L. M., Trotter, R. T., & Baer, R. D. (1993). *Empacho* in four Latino groups: A study of intra- and inter-cultural variation in beliefs. *Medical Anthropology, 15*, 109–136.

Wielgosz, A. T., Nolan, R. P., Earp, J. A., Biro, E., & Wielgosz, M. B. (1988). Reasons for patients' delay in response to symptoms of acute myocardial infarction. *Canadian Medical Association Journal, 139*, 853–857.

Williamson, G. M. (2000). Extending the activity restriction model of depressed affect: Evidence from a sample of breast cancer patients. *Health Psychology, 19*, 339–347.

Williamson, G. M., & Schulz, R. (1992a). Pain, activity restriction, and symptoms of depression among community-residing elderly adults. *Journal of Gerontology, 47*, 367.

Williamson, G. M., & Schulz, R. (1992b). Physical illness and symptoms of depression among elderly outpatients. *Psychology and Aging, 7*, 343–351.

Williamson, G. M., & Schulz, R. (1995). Activity restriction mediates the association between pain and depressed affect: A study of younger and older adult cancer patients. *Psychology and Aging, 10*, 369–378.

Wood, J. V., Taylor, S. E., & Lichtman, R. R. (1985). Social comparison in adjustment to breast cancer. *Journal of Personality and Social Psychology, 49*, 1169–1183.

Zambanini, A., Newson, R. B., Maisey, M., & Feher, M. D. (1999). Injection related anxiety in insulin-treated diabetes. *Diabetes Research and Clinical Practice, 46*, 239–246.

Zeiss, A. M., Lewinsohn, P. M., Rohde, P., & Seeley, J. R. (1996). Relationship of physical disease and functional impairment to depression in older people. *Psychology and Aging, 11*, 572–581.

Zenz, M. (1991). Morphine myths: Sedation, tolerance, addiction. *Postgraduate Medical Journal, 67*(Suppl. 2), S100–102.

Zigmond, A. S., & Snaith, R. P. (1983). The Hospital Anxiety and Depression Scale. *Acta Psychiatrica Scandinavica, 67*, 361–370.

Zimmerman, B. J., Bonner, S., Evans, D., & Mellins, R. B. (1999). Self regulating childhood asthma: A developmental model of family change. *Health Education and Behavior, 26*, 55–70.

Zola, I. K. (1973). Pathways to the doctor: From person to patient. *Social Science and Medicine, 7*, 677–689.

9

Lifespan, Gender and Cross-Cultural Perspectives in Health Psychology

SIMON MURPHY AND PAUL BENNETT

INTRODUCTION

This chapter focuses on the influence that a number of individual and social contexts have on health, in particular those associated with gender, ethnicity and the family, and how these may differentially affect health at different stages of the lifespan. These factors are intertwined in a complex web of causality; so much so, that an individual's health is likely to be influenced by a variety of related factors. The aim of this chapter is to outline the biological, social and psychological factors that may interact around these social categories.

GENDER AND HEALTH

An average woman's life expectancy in the West is significantly greater than that of men of the same birth cohort. United Kingdom data for 1997, for example, from the World Health Organization (2003) showed that women live 6 years longer than men, with women likely to die at 80 and men at 74 years old. These differences are the result of a number of factors including higher rates of accidents, violence, and adverse work environments among men. A significant portion of this difference is also attributable to the earlier onset of coronary heart disease (CHD) in men than in women. In the USA, for example, nearly three-quarters of those who die of myocardial infarction before the age of 65 years are men (American Heart Association, 1995): men's age-adjusted death rate for heart disease is twice that of women's. Age-adjusted cancer rates are also significantly higher in men than women (Department of Health and Human Services, 1996). Despite the observed differences in mortality, men demonstrate higher self-rated health, contact medical services less frequently and experience less acute illness than women (Reddy, Fleming & Adesso, 1992). By contrast, women have been shown to have higher levels of somatic symptoms and long-standing illnesses than men (Lahelma, Martikainen, Rahkonen & Silventoinen, 1999).

It is, perhaps, cautionary to note that while this pattern of mortality is common among industrialized countries, the pattern of health advantage is often different in industrializing countries. Here, differences in the life expectancy of men and women are smaller and in some cases are reversed, with mortality linked to issues of structural disadvantage and higher rates of infant deaths. Compared with males, females in industrializing countries are more likely to experience higher rates of premature morbidity and mortality due to their more frequent experience of pregnancy, with its associated risks from shorter birth spacing and inadequate health services (Doyal, 2001), and poorer access to health care, education and nutrition (Gray, 1993).

Explanations for Health Differentials

Biological sex differences

Biological models suggest that gender differences in mortality can be explained by underlying physical mechanisms. From this perspective, being born female is seen as conferring a natural biological advantage in terms of longevity. Some have suggested these differences are genetically mediated through immunological differences, with females demonstrating greater resistance to infections (Davey & Halliday, 1994). However, the majority of research has focused on the beneficial effect of oestrogen and sex variation in the stress response. It has been argued that oestrogen delays the onset of CHD by reducing clotting tendency and blood cholesterol levels, whilst testosterone increases platelet aggregation (McGill & Stern, 1979). This would help to explain observed increases in the prevalence of CHD in post-menopausal women (Office for National Statistics, 1996). Apparent gender differences in stress response have been found in studies of reactions to environmental stressors in laboratory settings, in which men typically evidence greater stress hormone, blood pressure, and cholesterol rises in response to stressors than do women (Matthews & Stoney, 1988).

These hormonal differences have also been used to explain the higher levels of risk-taking activities in men. In an investigation of the relationship between testosterone and health-risk behaviours in men, Booth, Johnson and Granger (1999), for example, found that high levels of testosterone increased the likelihood of health-compromising behaviours such as smoking and alcohol misuse. Whether these are innate differences or the result of variation in gender roles and masculine and feminine identity is unclear. Work by Lundberg, de Chateau, Winberg and Frankenhauser (1981) and others, reviewed below, suggests that social and

cultural processes may be implicated. Together, these data suggest that while biological factors may contribute to gender differences in risk for poor health, these may at least in part be driven by social factors, and have both a direct and an indirect influence on health.

Gender roles

The gendered roles that men and women inhabit have been shown to influence disease through environmental risk and stress processes. Research in this area has focused on the impact of paid work on men's health and the influence of work in the home on women's. This dichotomous approach is not without its dangers. As Oakley noted, 'both the official statistics and the social scientists have inflated gender-specific links between men and work and women and the home – so the key processes of the jigsaw to do with women and work and men and the home are missing' (1987: 25). Given this reservation, men have been shown to be more likely to encounter adverse employment conditions than women: although health and safety legislation has improved the working conditions of most workers, there are still environments that carry a significant risk of injury or disability. This is a risk predominantly faced by males, who account for 94 per cent of job-related fatalities (Courtenay, 2000b).

Men seem to exhibit greater stress responses than women in the face of employment demands. Nordstrom, Dwyer, Merz, Shircore and Dwyer (2001), for example, measured the degree of arterial plaque in 467 workers and its association with perceived job strain. In an age-adjusted model, plaque was greatest among men scoring in the highest quintile of work stress: no such association was found among women. Lundberg et al. (1981), however, pointed to the social organization of gender work roles as facilitating particular stress responses. In an examination of gender and employment characteristics they found that women in traditional male occupations and males engaged in traditional female occupations or tasks exhibited the same level of stress hormones as their opposite sex comparison group.

Gender differences have also been found in stress-coping behaviours, with men more likely than women to adopt health-damaging behaviours in response to job strain (Weidner, Boughal, Connor & Pieper, 1997). It has been argued that such behaviours are associated with norms of behaviour, which demonstrate masculine identity. Ames and Janes (1987), for example, found job alienation, job stress, inconsistent social controls and the evolution of a masculine drinking culture to be associated with heavy drinking amongst blue-collar workers. Similarly, Westman, Eden and Shirom (1985) reported that high numbers of work hours and lack of control and support were each positively associated with smoking intensity in men but not women.

In contrast to this, competing demands from home and paid work environments have been shown to impact strongly on women's health. Killien, Habermann and Jarrett (2001), for example, examined employment characteristics and maternal health amongst women returning to work in the year following childbirth. The most consistent predictor of their health status was the level of interference between their work and family lives. These negative effects tend to be greater for female workers with significant responsibilities beyond the workplace. Haynes and Feinleib (1980), for example, found that working women with three or more children were more likely to develop CHD than those with no children, and argued that work strain combined with home demands heightened risk of disease. Risk is increased not only by level of demand but also by the lack of material and social resources required for coping responses. As a consequence, women from lower socio-economic groups may be doubly disadvantaged, as they experience the greatest demands and possess the fewest resources for coping. Artazcoz, Borrell and Benach (2001), for example, found that family demands had the greatest negative impact on the health of female manual workers. For women with children under the age of 15, poor health was associated with a lack of leisure time for physical activity and with sleeping 6 or fewer hours a day. Female manual workers living with adults older than 65 years also evidenced increased likelihood of poor self-reported health status and the presence of a chronic condition.

The gendered effect of work demands is further illustrated by data from Alfredsson, Spetz and Theorell (1985), who compared the risk conferred by work strain and working overtime in a sample of 100,000 men and women. They found that working 10 hours or more overtime decreased risk for MI among men but was associated with a 30 per cent *increased* risk in women. It has been argued that whilst men are able to compensate for increases in work demands by decreasing home demands, the expectations associated with women's roles mean they are unable to engage in a similar process. This hypothesis is supported by Lundberg et al. (1981) who found that female managers' stress hormone levels remained raised following work, while those of male managers typically fell: this effect was particularly marked where the female managers had children. It seems that while men relaxed once at home, women continued their efforts in the home context.

Such findings have led authors such as Weidner et al. (1997) to examine how family members interpret competing demands from within and outside the home and how they allocate resources to deal with them. They found that gender interacted with demand so that when stress originated from within the home, husbands would increase their work in the home. When the demands originated from outside the home, however, husbands' domestic contribution did not change and women contributed more. This has led to a view that issues of social inequality resulting from the gender roles have a more profound effect on women's health than men's. Denton and Walters (1999), analysing Canadian data for example, found that for women, being in a high-income category, having social support and working full-time and caring for a family were more important predictors of good health than for men. Although lifestyle factors did play a part in women's health, with body weight and physical inactivity appearing as predictors, they played more of a part in predicting the health of men, for whom smoking and alcohol consumption emerged as important predictors.

Gender identity

A third factor through which gender may influence health is behaviours that demonstrate masculine and feminine identity. Many of the resources and behaviours available to demonstrate and enact masculinity are largely unhealthy. Men are more likely to smoke cigarettes, and to smoke high-nicotine and high-tar cigarettes, than women. They typically eat less healthily and drink more alcohol than women (Reddy et al., 1992). Powell-Griner, Anderson and Murphy (1997) found more men than women engaged in all but three of 14 non-gender-specific health-risk behaviours including smoking, drinking and driving, not using safety belts, and not attending health screening. Courtenay (2000a) also highlighted higher levels of unhealthy eating, substance misuse, reckless driving, risky sexual activity and violent assault amongst men.

Issues of gender identity have also been shown to influence the negotiation of behaviour through differential power relationships between males and females. Buysee and Van Oost (1997), for example, found that, although young adult women demonstrated more concern regarding safe sex and tried harder to implement safe behaviour than their male counterparts, they faced greater difficulties in behavioural negotiations as a result of gender power relations. While men could implement safe sex practices either without negotiation or by raising the issue at the moment of intercourse, women often had to start negotiating long before the actual encounter in order to be as successful. Gender identity has also been shown to influence the negotiation of health behaviours in relation to family interactions (see later discussion of family).

One of the few health-related behaviours that men engage in more than women is regular exercise (Reddy et al., 1992). This may be because a concern with physical fitness allows men to demonstrate their masculinity and physical power, whereas the discourses surrounding the medicalization of the female body, adolescent physical appearance, the menopause and the stereotypes associated with ageing help to explain lower levels of exercise activity in women (Vertinsky, 1998). Female concern with body image has been used to explain poor dietary practices and it has been argued that the association between thinness and beauty, and the fact that the body represents a realm of control where power may be exerted, may help to explain the incidence of bulimia and anorexia in adolescent females (Banks, 1992; Heaven, 1996). Women have been shown to make more social comparisons around physical appearance than men and to suffer lower self-esteem when these are negative (Freeman, 1987). The importance of body image to feminine identity is perpetuated by the mass media. Andersen and DiDomencio (1992) found women's magazines contained 10 times the amount of coverage of weight loss compared to men's. The narrower range of socially acceptable body shapes for females in our society is illustrated by Furnham and Radley (1989) who found 16-year-olds identifying far fewer female body shapes as attractive in comparison to male body shapes.

Gender has also been shown to be associated with particular forms of stress-coping behaviour, which develop over the lifespan. Groer, Thomas and Shoffner (1992), for example, found increases in stressful life events throughout adolescence and gender-specific changes in coping with them. Utilizing a longitudinal design, they found stressors were greater for females than males at baseline and increased more over the course of the study. Significantly, females showed an increase in passive distraction and males an increase in self-destructive and aggressive coping behaviour over time. Gender socialization may also inhibit males' ability to deal with the negative emotions associated with stress. Robertson, Lin, Woodford, Danos and Hurst (2001), in comparing men who varied on measures of gender role stress (a measure of traditional masculinity), found no differences in physiological arousal in response to stressors, but did find variation in expressed emotions. Those high on traditional masculinity had greater difficulty in expressing emotions than those with low levels of masculinity. This may inhibit opportunities to facilitate social support and impacts directly on immune functioning (Pennebaker, 1997).

Glynn, Christenfeld and Gerin (1999) suggest that there are qualitative differences in the perception of and/or type of social support offered by men and women and that these differentially influence cardiovascular responses to stress. In a laboratory study of the impact of social support during a stressful task, they found that social support provided by women in a stressful situation resulted in reductions in blood pressure and heart rate for both men and women. The social support provided by men resulted in no such changes.

Courtenay (2000b) suggested that men show their masculinity and power not only by engaging in health-risking behaviours, but also by not seeking medical help when ill. According to Courtenay, when men state, 'I haven't been to a doctor in years', refuse to take sick leave from work, insist they need little sleep or assert that their driving is better when they've had something to drink, these attitudes and behaviours reflect both health practices and statements of masculinity. Although Kane (1991) argues that the medicalization of women's reproduction and their increased likelihood of seeking contraception from medical services inflate female consulting rates and their exposure to health screening, Verbrugge and Steiner (1985) suggested that men visit their doctor less frequently than do women, even after excluding reproductive health care visits. When ill, men are significantly less likely to consult a doctor than women: socially disadvantaged men are twice as likely as their female counterpart not to make a consultation (Department of Health and Human Services, 1998). Of interest is that men who score highly on feminine gender role orientation are more likely to report symptoms of illness (Klonoff & Landrine, 1992). Charmaz (1994) also noted several examples of, sometimes quite extreme, behaviours that men engage in to hide potential threats to masculine power. Examples included a wheelchair-bound diabetic man skipping lunch (and risking a coma) rather than embarrass himself by asking for help in the dining area, and a middle-aged man with CHD declining offers of easier jobs to prove he was still capable of strenuous work. Similarly, Jaffe noted the

advice given to a US senator not to 'go public' about his prostate cancer as 'some men might think his willingness to go public with his private struggle as a sign of weakness' (1997: 134). Men's identities are simultaneously supported by women's identities as carers of others (see the section on the family, below).

Issues of gender identity are also reflected in health professionals' understandings of, and responses to, help-seeking behaviours. In some cases, studies have highlighted an awareness of the negative effects that gender identity has on help seeking. Tudiver and Talbot (1999), for example, reported that family physicians attributed low levels of help seeking in men to factors including masculine identity which prevented an admission of vulnerability and structural barriers such as lack of time and role models for male care providers. Gender identity stereotypes have also been shown to influence the level of care and treatment offered. Travis (1988), for example, found that women reporting symptoms of heart disease were less likely to receive adequate treatment than men, as a consequence of physicians viewing it as a male disease, while Bertakis et al. (2001) found that females were more likely to be diagnosed as depressed when reporting the same symptoms as males.

Hunt (2002) argued for an examination of the wider social, political and economic factors that shape and confine the roles and identities available to men and women. Examining the social context highlights influences on the development of gendered norms of behaviour. In one study to do this, Van Etten and Anthony (2001) suggested that current gender differences in the prevalence of illicit drug use result from a greater social acceptance of male drug taking and more opportunities to use illicit drugs, rather than gender differences in cognitions. Women's substance misuse has been shown to be influenced by the politics of drug prescribing. Simoni-Watsila (2000), for example, contended that women are more at risk from prescription drug misuse than men, as they are 48 per cent more likely than men to be prescribed abusable prescription drugs by health services. Wider economic and mass media influences may also play a part in determining gender identity. It has been argued that increases in female smoking can be linked to targeted advertising campaigns by tobacco companies and the growth of positive smoking images aimed at women (Amos, Currie & Elton, 1998).

Together, these data suggest that while bio-logical factors may contribute to some of the differentials in health status between men and women, others are societally mediated. Gender differentials in mortality and morbidity arise, to a significant degree, from the cumulative effects of different social worlds that men and women experience from the moment of their birth.

FAMILIES AND HEALTH

The influence of the family on health and health behaviours is profound. It provides the social context for our experiences of health and illness throughout the lifespan, one in which individuals influence and are recipro-cally influenced by each other (Birch & Davison, 2001). It is within the family that we have the potential to be cared for, care for and support others, impart health information, develop and negotiate health behaviours, and make decisions about and undertake courses of treatment. The family constructs and responds to changes across its lifespan, influ-encing patterns of health and illness as it does so. Key stages in the life of the family can be identified as having differing implications for health. Whilst by no means exhaustive, we highlight a number of these, and in so doing note the importance of social context and social relationships in relation to health and illness. Factors addressed include marriage and social integration, family structure, stress and social support, and health-related behav-iours within the family.

Marriage and Social Integration

Married adults tend to be psychologically and physically healthier, to have better disease survival rates, and to live longer than their unmarried counterparts (Waldron, Hughes & Brooks, 1996). Of course, causal processes may work both ways: whilst marital status influences health, health may also influence marital status, with those individuals who experience poor health being more likely to be single and socially isolated (Joung, 1997).

One explanation for the link between poor health and being single is that those who remain unmarried are more socially isolated and lack social support networks relative to their married counterparts. This not only acts as an explanation but highlights the difficulty of isolating the influence of marriage from the influence of other social ties. In the USA, longevity has been associated with a relatively high number of social ties as a consequence of marriage, as well as contacts with close friends and relatives and membership of social and religious organizations (Berkman & Syme, 1979). These relationships held even after partialling out the impact of other health-compromising behaviours such as smoking, high alcohol intake, and low levels of physical activity. Higher rates of morbidity and mortal-ity amongst those who lack social networks have also been observed (Reynolds & Kaplan, 1990). Results from Europe support these find-ings. Orth-Gomer and Johnsson (1987), fol-lowing a cohort of 17,400 men and women for a period of 6 years, found an increased risk of morbidity associated with social isolation. Men and women scoring in the lowest third on social network measures demonstrated a 50 per cent greater risk for CHD compared to the remaining two-thirds. In addition, Williams et al. (1992), for example, found that patients already diagnosed with CHD who were un-married and without a close friend experi-enced a threefold higher risk of mortality over a 5-year period than those who were socially integrated.

The relationship between marriage/social integration and good health may be less straightforward than it first appears. The posi-tive health outcomes associated with marriage have been shown to be greater for males than females (Waldron et al., 1996), and the study by Orth-Gomer and Johnsson (1987) found that older women who had many social contacts had higher mortality levels than those with medium-sized networks. These findings have led to speculation that the important determinant of health is the quality of social and marital relationships rather than their absolute number (Kiecolt-Glaser & Newton, 2001). Empirical support for this hypothesis was reported by Orth-Gomer and Johnsson (1987), who found that the quality of relationships (in particular the provision of guidance, practical help and a feeling of 'belonging') proved a stronger and more consistent predictor of mortality than the absolute number of contacts.

Marriage provides both practical and emotional support (Berkman & Glass, 2000). These twin roles seem to be particularly important in explaining observed gender differences. Men are more likely to benefit from the practical and social support offered by their partners, but to turn to health-risk behaviours in response to stressful interactions. Women on the other hand are more likely to experience depression and reduced psychological functioning as a result of poor quality relationships (Kiecolt-Glaser & Newton, 2001). Finally, social relationships may exert a normative influence, by either encouraging or discouraging health-risk behaviours such as smoking, excessive eating, and alcohol consumption (Broman, 1993). This type of influence is discussed below in relation to family health behaviours.

Biological mechanisms mediating the impact of ineffective social support systems and health appear to involve both immune and sympathetically mediated processes. Negative social interactions have been associated with elevated stress hormones (Kiecolt-Glaser et al., 1988), increased cardiovascular activity in response to stress (Uchino, Holt, Uno & Flinders, 2001), and depressed immune functioning (Kiecolt-Glaser et al., 1988), while supportive interactions are associated with the opposite effects (Seeman, 2000). The health risks associated with such responses may also be increased when trait hostility is present, particularly among males (Kiecolt-Glaser & Newton, 2001).

Research examining the physiological changes associated with divorce and separation adds to these data. Those experiencing divorce demonstrate poorer immune functioning than those who remain married (Kiecolt-Glaser et al., 1988), although outcome is influenced by gender and whether or not the individual initiated the separation. Buehler (1987), for example, identified different processes of coping and adaptation for initiators and non-initiators. Although both groups shared similar emotional reactions, the timing of the responses differed. Initiators experienced more change and stress in the 6–12 months following divorce, whilst non-initiators reported higher levels of stress 18–24 months post-decree. In general, however, non-initiators have worse immune functioning than initiators (Kiecolt-Glaser et al., 1988). The initial separation phase appears to be more stressful for women than men, regardless of initiator status (Pledge, 1992), perhaps as a result of them facing more structural disadvantage once separated (Arber, 1991).

Family Structure, Stress and Social Support

Structure

Explaining the relationship between family structure and health has proved particularly problematic, given recent trends towards diversity in such structures and difficulties in identifying underlying causative factors. Studies that have assessed the relationship between family structure and health status by, for example, comparing the children of single and dual parents and biological and stepparents, have typically shown that children living with single mothers or non-biological parents are at increased risk for asthma, accidental injuries, and behavioural and emotional problems, and have an increased health vulnerability (Dawson, 1991).

Interpretation of these findings is complicated by the fact that a significant percentage of single mothers are socially and economically deprived relative to their married counterparts. These findings may therefore reflect social disadvantage as much as family structure. Indeed, when McMunn, Nazroo, Marmot, Boreham and Goodman (2001) partialled out the effects of benefits receipt, housing tenure, and maternal education, the differences in psychological morbidity they found between the children of single and married mothers were no longer evident. Data such as these led Sweeting (2001) to argue that the variance in child health explained by family structure alone is extremely small and that the focus of research and any interventions should be on the nature of social interactions rather than the structure in which they occur.

Stress and family support

Living within a supportive family with positive interactions and clear communication has been shown to be associated with low levels of stress, high levels of stress-coping behaviour, good psychological health, active adaptation to acute and chronic illness, and high levels of adherence to treatment (Wamboldt & Wamboldt, 2000). It seems that negative family functioning represents a potential source of stress, while positive interactions have a buffering effect, reducing stress responses by enhancing emotional support and the modelling of coping behaviours amongst family members. Reflecting the reciprocity of family systems, it is also possible that at least some of these data reflect higher levels of stress and poor coping and adaptation leading to the negative family interactions. The lack of longitudinal studies to study this phenomenon makes it difficult to determine the relative influence of these differing causal pathways.

The impact of family environments on the mental and physical health of family members is most apparent during periods of adaptation to change, in particular the arrival of children, psychosocial changes associated with adolescence, and the onset of chronic illness in children. Families appear to have a 'normative lifecycle' (Oppenheimer, 1974), with family stressors increasing when demands exceed family resources. These 'lifecycle squeezes' occur first when young couples attempt to set up home together, then in middle age when supporting older children, and finally in retirement. Parenthood is itself a potential stressor, which can elicit stress-coping behaviours such as smoking and alcohol consumption, particularly in families with poor material circumstances and little social support. Graham (1985), for example, found that working class women with little time to themselves used smoking as a convenient way to relieve high levels of stress and tension by providing 'time out' from the demands of child care. Alcohol consumption may increase for similar reasons, particularly among men (Westman et al., 1985). Gottlieb and Green (1984) highlighted how gender differences in response to family stress differ as a consequence of time constraints and the resources available to cope with the demands of parenting. When faced with increased stress, exercise levels increased among men but not women.

For those with few material resources, increased economic demands associated with bringing up children may negatively impact on behaviour. Backett (1990), for example, found that parents faced with limited resources were neglectful of their own health, sometimes doing without adequate food in order to provide children with a good diet. Families are also required to deal with demands from outside the home environment – in particular the obligations associated with paid employment. These impact more on women than men, especially those in full-time employment and with few resources to help support multiple role demands (Arber, Gilbert & Dale, 1985). Indeed, Waldron et al. (1996), utilizing prospective panel data over a 5-year period, found that the only women to gain any health benefits from marriage were those who were not engaged in paid work outside the home. Data such as these reflect back to the issues of gender roles and identity considered above and show how gender identities interact with family roles and responsibilities to determine health and wellbeing.

Supportive and cohesive family environments, including open communication, seem to help families cope with the stresses associated with adolescence. Wenk, Hardesty, Morgan and Blair (1994), for example, in a longitudinal study, found that high levels of maternal and paternal help and involvement predicted adolescents' wellbeing, including measures of self-esteem, life satisfaction and mental health. Similarly, Jo-Lohman and Jarvis (2000) found that high levels of family cohesion were associated with more adaptive coping strategies and greater psychological health in adolescents.

Family interactions have also been shown to influence coping with acute and chronic illness. Wamboldt and Wamboldt's (2000) summary of the available evidence suggested that negatively expressed emotion within the family was associated with poor outcomes on measures of childhood physical and psychological problems and lower levels of adherence to treatment. More positively, Markson and Fiese (2000) found that the families of children with asthma with well-founded family routines reported lower levels of health anxiety than families without clear routines. Social support from family and friends has also been identified as a key factor in reducing the burden of coping with illness in elderly relatives (e.g., Coen, O'Boyle, Swanwick & Coakley, 1999).

This is not to say that the influence of family interactions is always straightforward. Franks, Campbell and Shields (1992) found that family criticism and high family emotional involvement were both associated with depressive symptoms in the family. By contrast, they also found that high emotional involvement was associated with greater levels of health-protective behaviours, suggesting that high emotional involvement, although impacting negatively on psychological health, can act as a form of social control encouraging individuals to conform to normative family behaviours.

Family Health Behaviours

Normative influences

One approach to understanding family influences on behaviour has focused on the development and communication of attitudinal and behavioural norms, which may be influenced through the communication of information, the modelling of behaviour, and fear of sanctions for non-conformity. Although family norms generally control behaviour, this is not always the case, and individuals within the family may reject such norms, as a result of either personal experience or the influence of factors beyond the family. How these differences are resolved is affected by the family structure, its willingness to accept non-conformity, and its strategies for resolving conflict.

Norms may change as a result of changes in the family structure. One simple example of this is that the presence of children may trigger consideration or initiation of health behaviour change and be implicated in the negotiation of new norms. During pregnancy, approximately one-fifth of women smokers, and particularly those aged below 35 years, stop smoking, while an even greater percentage reduce their alcohol consumption to within the weekly recommended units (Waterson & Murray-Lyon, 1989). Reductions in consumption of alcohol and tobacco have also been observed for fathers, although the percentages are much lower (Waterson, Evans & Murray-Lyon, 1990). Such changes can be motivated by a desire to protect the unborn child and be confined purely to the term of pregnancy, although Hyssaelae, Rautava, Helenius and Sillanpaeae (1995) argued that the arrival of a first child can act as a cue to more sustained parental reductions in alcohol consumption and cessation of smoking. This is most likely to occur when both partners make changes, resulting in new and sustainable family norms. Parenting may lead to changes in adult behaviour: it can also lead to conflicting desires in parents and the adoption of furtive behaviour to avoid children observing health-compromising behaviours such as smoking and poor dietary habits (Backett, 1990).

Changes in parental behaviours may arise out of a desire to act as healthy role models for their children. What evidence there is suggests that they may be successful in this goal. Maguire et al. (2002), for example, found positive correlations between parents' and adolescents' physical activity attitudes and behaviours, although it may well be the case that both parents and children are influenced by other shared social factors. Nevertheless the family environment has been identified as a key influence on the development of food preferences, patterns of food intake, eating styles and the development of activity preferences, particularly during early and middle childhood (Birch & Davison, 2001).

The influence of parents recedes during adolescence, to be replaced by an increasing influence from peers (Beal, Auisello & Perrin, 2001). The interplay between these influences has been explored predominantly in relation to substance misuse. Beal et al. (2001), for example, found that whilst parental modelling and the monitoring and disapproval of health-risk behaviour predicted alcohol use, peer influences were associated with all measured health-risk behaviours, including tobacco and alcohol use, marijuana use and sexual activity. Other studies have focused on how families negotiate the relative influence of peer groups and the developing family throughout the lifespan (Backett & Davison, 1995). Foxcroft, Lowe and May (1994), for example, found that when parents were aware of adolescent drinking, sanctioned its sensible use, and modelled appropriate drinking, their adolescent children engaged in less alcohol misuse.

A number of studies have highlighted how gender socialization influences the modelling and reinforcement of behaviours. Of interest is that women are more influential in the development of protective behaviours in their children and partners than men. Umberson (1992), for example, found that women were more likely to adopt a nurturing and controlling role within families. This was beneficial for male health, as preventive actions were controlled and supported – support that was not reciprocated. Similarly, Rossow (1992) found that the strongest predictor of eldest child's teeth-cleaning behaviour was mother's cleaning behaviour. Behaviour can also be influenced and reinforced by siblings. A strong relationship between the behaviour of elder and younger siblings was explained by equity in the control and reinforcement of behaviour by parents, but also by the modelling of protective behaviour of the eldest sibling. The development of risk behaviours in children has been found to be gender dependent, mirroring their same-sex parent. A 5-year longitudinal study conducted by Wickrama, Conger,

Wallace and Elder (1999) highlighted gender differences in health-risk behaviours. They found an intergenerational transmission of individual behaviours as well as the transmission of a health-risk lifestyle. However, a gender effect showed boys' lifestyle to mirror their fathers', and girls' their mothers'. Whether this transmission occurred through social modelling or the processes discussed below, such findings highlight the need to examine the influence of gender socialization within the family and its cumulative influence across the lifespan.

It is important to recognize that whilst experiences within the family may shape normative behaviours, such experiences are interpreted within an individual's view of the world, including their personal construction of the meaning of health and health risk. In their interviews with people from families with a high risk of CHD, for example, Emslie, Hunt and Watt (2001) found that although individual family members acknowledged that heart problems may run in the family, they differentiated family risk from personal risk by distancing themselves from family members in terms of biological type and by women identifying CHD as a male disease. In addition, individuals saw a family history as legitimizing risk behaviours as there was little they could do to avoid such inherited risk and past behaviours could not now be counteracted. Individuals also focused on CHD as a source of mortality rather than a disabling chronic condition. A common view was that CHD was a sudden and 'quick way to go' rather than a lingering death.

The negotiation of behaviour

Behavioural influence within a family is not necessarily a 'top-down' process. Many behaviours are negotiated within the family system and are shaped through interactions between family members. In such interactions, participants bring their own understandings and expectations of appropriate behaviours. Behaviour is then shaped by the mutual responses of the participants – a process termed 'the negotiated order'. Existing patterns of behaviour are therefore open to modification and change dependent upon the individuals involved and the circumstances they find themselves in. Children have been shown to influence family health behaviours by active negotiation. Mintel (1991), for example, reported that the demands made by children between the ages of 5 and 12 act as significant influences on their parents' dietary purchases. Backett (1990) characterized this process of family interaction as one in which parents negotiate meals comprising both 'bad' (what the children want to eat) and 'good' (what they consider to be healthy) elements.

Many studies have identified the importance of gender in the negotiation of family behaviour. Backett (1990), for example, found gender differences in interactional and situational constraints on opportunities to engage in preventive behaviours. Men were more likely than women to undertake preventive actions such as exercise. These differences frequently did not correspond with desired levels of exercise. Rather, they reflected women's negotiated role within their family, and their affording higher priority to other family commitments than their own participation in regular exercise. Similarly, Young (1999) found that, for women, health-related behaviours were frequently a result of negotiation with other family members based on time–space constraints, rather than the result of individual decision making. Gender roles have also been implicated in family dietary behaviour. Although a majority of women remain the main provider of food within the household, they may exert little control over the choice of foodstuffs. Instead, they frequently find themselves in the role of food negotiator, balancing competing family demands and conflict (Kerr & Charles, 1983). Results from Backett (1990) suggested that negotiation is related not only to gender roles but also to issues of gender identity. Differences emerged relating to the acceptability of health concepts that could be raised in the home and to opportunities to talk about health. Whilst women felt they could raise issues such as diet, exercise and positive health, men felt they could only raise issues related to specific episodes of illness or, in terms of prevention, physical fitness and sport.

This process of negotiation within the family suggests that attempts to facilitate behavioural change should address the family as an interactive system, rather than as a series of isolated individuals. An example is provided by Johnson and Nicklas (1995) whose 'Heart Smart Family' initiative aimed to improve the cardiovascular health of families with children identified as at high risk for CHD, rather than just targeting the children. Their programme involved a 12- to 16-week intervention which focused on increasing awareness of health issues, skills development and problem solving skills. They argued that by involving the whole family system in change, the likelihood of the adoption and maintenance of new behaviours increased. The programme appeared to actually benefit parents more than children. Parents evidenced lowered blood pressures, increased exercise levels, and decreased intake of total fat, saturated fat and sodium intake, whilst children only evidenced a reduction in blood pressure. Similarly, Burke et al. (1999) reported positive changes in a range of health behaviours, self-efficacy, and reductions in perceived barriers to health following a 16-week randomized controlled programme aimed at newly married couples. They suggested that such initiatives can usefully focus on periods in families' lifespan when gender roles and identities are evaluated.

ETHNIC MINORITIES AND HEALTH

In the UK, rates of premature mortality amongst people in ethnic minorities are typically higher than those of the white population. Less information is available on morbidity (Harding & Maxwell, 1997). Similarly, in the USA, blacks have higher age-adjusted mortality rates for a variety of diseases including various cancers, heart disease, liver disease, diabetes and pneumonia (Krieger et al., 1999). They are also more likely to die as a result of violence (Markides, 1983). There is also marked variation within ethnic categories. Epidemiological data from the UK (Balarajan & Raleigh, 1993; Landman & Cruickshank, 2001) shows a 36 per cent higher rate of CHD amongst males from the Indian subcontinent, with rates for those between 20 and 39 years of age being two to three times higher than for whites. In addition, there are higher levels of diabetes among Asians and a greater incidence of obesity amongst South Asians. For Afro-Caribbeans, a particularly high prevalence rate of hypertension and strokes has been observed. For the former, mortality rates four times above the national average for males and seven times greater for females have been recorded. For strokes, males demonstrated a rate of 76 per cent and females a rate of 110 per cent above the national average. In contrast, African Caribbeans and Asians have lower rates of cancer than the national average (Barker & Baker, 1990).

There are difficulties in examining the relationship between ethnicity and health. These include problems in defining and measuring ethnicity, for example whether own country of origin or parents' country of origin should be used and whether classification should be done by an interviewer or the respondent. There is also a danger that in grouping individuals together within ethnic groups, we ignore the diversity of experience and run the risk of pathologizing minority status rather than examining the underlying processes that result in the association between ethnicity and poor health. It has even been argued that including ethnicity as a variable in health research ignores the great variation in, and explanatory power of, language, religion, migration, culture, ancestry, and forms of identity associated with ethnic categories (Nazroo, 1998). These issues should be seen as dynamic and subject to constant change and negotiation. Landman and Cruickshank (2001), for example, in examining ethnicity and dietary risk behaviour, warned against the danger of ignoring generational behavioural differences within ethnic minorities. They highlighted data suggesting that second-generation offspring of former migrants adopt the dietary patterns of their peers, increasing fat and reducing vegetable, fruit and pulse consumption.

Consequently, disentangling the various genetic, social and psychological factors that may contribute to differences in morbidity and mortality between ethnic groups has proved extremely difficult. The high incidence of mental illness among African Caribbeans living in the UK, for example, has variously been explained by theories focusing on genetics, economic deprivation, discrimination and service provision problems (Littlewood & Lipsedge, 1988), whilst in the USA, explanations have focused on interactions between restricted socio-economic mobility, lack of social resources, poor living conditions, racism and the internalization of negative cultural stereotypes (Williams & Williams, 2000). Here we focus on three levels of explanation: normative health behaviours, social disadvantage, and prejudice and discrimination.

Normative Health Behaviours

The frequency and practice of differing health-related behaviours varies across ethnic groups and gender. In the UK, smoking levels are low for women across all ethnic groups, but differ according to ethnic group for males (Waterson & Murray-Lyon, 1989). Alcohol-related morbidity is high amongst African Caribbean men and Asian males of Punjabi origin, while a high dietary fat intake is common among Asians (Clarke, Ahmed, Romaniuk, Marjot & Murray-Lyon, 1990; Fox & Shapiro, 1988). In the USA, whilst black males resemble their white counterparts, black females consume less alcohol and smoke fewer cigarettes than white females (Gottlieb & Green, 1987). These differences in risk behaviours have been used to explain some of the variation in risk for disease across the different ethnic groups.

These findings may be explained by differing cultural norms of behaviour. Gudykunst, Yoon and Nishda (1987), for example, argued that as a result of their socialization, members of non-Western cultures living in the West frequently consider health risks as a concern for other groups in society, and not their own ethnic group. As a consequence they may be less likely to engage in health-protective behaviours than those who feel personally at risk of conditions thought to be present in the majority population. Differing group norms and expectations have powerfully influenced African

Americans' responses to AIDS, which have been influenced by beliefs about their identity, gender role socialization, and attitudes to contraception and homosexuality (Pittman, Solheim & Blanchard, 1992).

Cultural norms may operate as a form of informational social influence, with information communicated and behaviour modelled via social networks. This can affect such things as perceived vulnerability, knowledge and attitudes to prevention and may explain the relationship between CHD risk behaviours and low levels of awareness of cholesterol and dietary risk factors found in South Asian and Indian populations (Lip, Luscombe, McCarry, Malik & Beevers, 1996). In the UK, these subgroup-specific norms may influence behaviours such as smoking, drinking, diet and sexual activity. Best et al. (2001), for example, found white respondents to be more likely to have ever smoked and drunk alcohol and to progress to regular substance use than both black and Asian respondents, who also reported a later onset and the lowest prevalence of smoking and drinking alcohol. Similarly, Dundas, Morgan, Redfern, Lemic-Stojcevic and Wolfe (2001), in a London population, found white respondents were more likely to smoke and have an unhealthy level of alcohol consumption than their African and African Caribbean counterparts, but were less likely to be overweight. It has also been argued that ethnicity may confer different sexual norms. The most common exposure route for HIV infection among whites is through sexual intercourse between men: for blacks it is through heterosexual intercourse, whilst for Asians it is mixture of both (Nazroo, 1997; Rudat, 1994).

Karlsen, Rogers and McCarthy (1998) suggested that familial, religious and peer influences play a part in the development of normative behaviours, and again highlighted the importance of recognizing diversity within ethnic categories. In a survey of inner London schools, they found white school pupils to have the highest levels of tobacco, alcohol and drug use and the highest level of peer influence. Bangladeshis reported the lowest levels of substance use and higher levels of religious and family influence, with Africans and African Caribbeans falling between the two. Other studies have examined the relative influence of families and peers on adolescents' health behaviours. Gittelson, Roche, Alexander and Tassler (2001) provide such an example. Results from their qualitative study suggested that gender interacts with ethnicity to influence levels of conformity to peer and parental norms. They highlighted the level of identification with peer groups and the fear of sanctions for non-conformity to parents as key influences. They found that white females perceived the most permissive parental normative messages around smoking and a high desire to conform to peer smoking behaviour, whereas African American males reported the strictest parental sanctions for smoking.

This is not to say that cultural norms act within a social vacuum. As we noted in our review of gender, it is important to examine the influence of wider social processes on the behaviour of people in ethnic minorities. The mass media may differentially target and influence ethnic groups. Gittelson et al. (1999), for example, found clear differences in patterns of cigarette brand preference between white, African and Native Americans. These patterns corresponded closely with the marketing targeted at each group by tobacco companies. Similarly, Parker, Sussman, Crippens, Elder and Scholl (1998) found that young African Americans avoided tobacco use to distinguish themselves from other ethnic groups, and Latinos used their interactions with those outside their ethnic group as a way of supporting resistance to peer pressure to smoke within their social group.

In drawing attention to cultural explanations of behaviour, there is a danger of victim blaming and stereotyping. Douglas (1995) illustrated this by reference to the UK Department of Health campaign targeted at the reduction in the prevalence of rickets conducted in the 1970s. Campaigns aimed at the white population identified the problem as one of poverty, and messages concentrated on including common foods containing vitamin D in one's diet. The campaign aimed at Asians identified the problem as one of cultural preferences and practices, and its advice focused on changing from traditional diets to British diets. Such an approach views the measurement of ethnicity as unproblematic and neglects structural influences on health.

Social Disadvantage

It could be argued that by focusing on ethnicity we neglect the confounding influence of social disadvantage and exclusion. A significant proportion of people in ethnic minorities occupy relatively low socioeconomic positions, although questions have been raised as to the suitability of traditional indicators for ethnic minority groups in such judgements (Davey Smith, 2002). As a result of this, many people in minority ethnic groups are also more likely to experience environmental stressors such as poverty, poor housing, unemployment and poor working conditions, and to have fewer resources to respond to them than the wider population (Robinson, 1984). African Caribbeans, for example, have been shown to reside in poorer residential areas, to be employed in lower-paid jobs and to experience higher levels of unemployment compared to their white counterparts (Modood et al., 1997). Measures of social disadvantage vary across ethnic groups, with those classified as Bangladeshi and Pakistani facing greatest hardship. Karlsen and Nazroo (2000) found that 80 per cent of Bangladeshi and Pakistani respondents and 40 per cent of African Caribbean and Indian respondents had household incomes below half the national average. These data compared to a 25 per cent prevalence among white respondents.

Studies examining the interaction of socioeconomic status (SES) and ethnicity suggest that social disadvantage plays a significant role in determining poor health among minority ethnic groups. Although some studies have found that including SES as a predictor diminishes the effect of ethnicity on mortality and morbidity (Bassett & Krieger, 1986; Sorlie, Backlund & Keller, 1995), a significant number have found that it negates its influence completely. In the USA, Haan and Kaplan (1985), for example, found no differences in mortality rates between blacks and whites after partialling

out the influence of socioeconomic status. In general, the effect of SES within minority ethnic groups follows that of other social groups, with socially and economically advantaged groups having longer life and better health (Harding & Maxwell, 1997; Davey Smith, Wentworth, Neaton, Stamler & Stamler, 1996). There are exceptions to this rule, however. In the UK there is no gradient of CHD-related mortality for men born in the Caribbean or West or South Africa (Harding & Maxwell, 1997), implicating processes outlined elsewhere in this section. Some authors have argued that ethnic groups are doubly disadvantaged, with skin colour heightening the effect of SES on health. In the USA Klag, Whelton, Coresh, Grim and Kuller (1991), for example, found that African Americans with the lowest SES and darkest skin pigmentation exhibited the highest rates of hypertension. They argued that darker skins were associated with a greater experience of racism, a source of stress which compounds social disadvantage.

Ethnicity also interacts with socioeconomic status as a predictor of health-related behaviours. Lillie-Blanton, Anthony and Schuster (1993) found that higher levels of crack cocaine use amongst African Americans and Hispanics were no longer apparent when comparing ethnic groups that shared similar social environments such as drug availability, socioeconomic status and stress-coping behaviours. Similarly, a study examining the relationship between ethnicity and low levels of self-reported mammography screening behaviour found SES to be the underlying predictor. Women with health care access or health insurance problems were least likely to report attending screening, a consistent relationship across ethnic groups (Qureshi, Thacker, Litaker & Kippes, 2000).

Prejudice and Discrimination

As a consequence of low socioeconomic status, ethnic minorities experience greater exposure to environmental stress and problems in accessing health care (Gottlieb & Green, 1987). Experiences of discrimination and racial harassment and the demands of maintaining or shifting culture provide further environmental stress and reduced access to resources (Kessler & Neighbors, 1986). In addition, as people occupying lower socioeconomic groups have been found to have less future expectancy of quality of life and to lack feelings of self-control, ethnicity may interact with low socioeconomic status to produce a double disadvantage and increased powerlessness in blacks (Sleutjes, 1990). Gilvarry et al. (1999), for example, found that amongst patients with severe mental illness, African Caribbeans reported significantly more negative life events than their white British counterparts and other ethnic minority groups. They were also more likely to attribute negative life events to discrimination. Similarly, Karlsen and Nazroo (2000) found a strong association between perceptions and experiences of racial discrimination and poor health. Respondents reporting verbal abuse had a 50 per cent greater likelihood of reporting poor health compared to those not reporting abuse: those who reported racially motivated assault were twice as likely to assess their health as poor.

One explanation of the relatively high rates of hypertension observed in African Americans is that they are a consequence of exposure to environmental stressors, including racism (Klag et al., 1991). Experiences of racism are associated with habitually stronger emotional and physiological reaction to general stress, which in turn are thought to contribute to the long-term development of hypertension (Brosschot & Thayer, 1998). Laboratory studies seem to support this, with elevated stress responses associated with exposure to racism. Clarke (2000), for example, found that among a sample of African American women, past experiences of racism were positively associated with rises in blood pressure during a task in which participants talked about their views and feelings about animal rights.

Experiences of racism can also be seen to operate at a structural level. When ethnic minorities fall ill, they have been found to experience greater problems in access to health care and poorer quality services. In the UK, ethnic minorities have been shown to experience more difficulty in gaining access to health services such as cancer screening and antenatal care (Doyle, 1991; Narang & Murphy, 1994). These disadvantages help to explain why some ethnic groups have low contact with health services and rely less on physicians and more on their family as the primary source of health information (Grisso, Freeman, Maurin, Garcia-Espana & Berlin, 1999). When structural barriers such as lack of suitable information in an appropriate language are removed, attendance at health screening has been shown to increase (Bell, Branston, Newcombe & Barton, 1999), suggesting that low uptake of this type of health care is a consequence of structural barriers rather than lack of interest among the target group.

Even if ethnic minorities are able to access health care, research, predominantly from the USA, suggests they are likely to receive poorer quality treatments. Black people may be less likely than whites to receive curative surgery for early-stage lung, colon, or breast cancer (Brawley & Freeman, 1999), and less likely to be referred for transplantation or undergo transplantation than whites in chronic renal failure (e.g., Epstein & Ayanian, 2001). These racial and gender differences remained significant after adjustments for patients' preferences, socio-demographic characteristics, the cause of renal failure, and the presence or absence of coexisting illness. Similarly, Mitchell, Ballard, Matchar, Whisnant and Samsa (2000) found that, even after adjusting for demographic factors, comorbidity, ability to pay, and provider characteristics, African American patients with transient ischaemic attacks were significantly less likely to receive non-invasive cerebrovascular testing, cerebral angiography, or carotid endarterectomy. They were also less likely to have a specialist doctor as their attending physician. Other studies have shown that there were variations in doses of analgesics administered in emergency departments, with Hispanics and African Americans substantially undertreated for pain from fractures of long bones, and that postoperative pain was inadequately managed in non-white patients (e.g., Todd, Deaton, D'Adamo & Goe, 2000). Such inequalities provide a substantial explanation of higher mortality rates following disease diagnosis (Friedman et al., 1987; Haan & Kaplan, 1985).

LIFESPAN PERSPECTIVES

We have so far considered both negative and positive influences on health clustered around gender, ethnicity, and the family. This section addresses how these and other influences develop cumulatively across the lifespan. Adopting such a perspective necessitates an assessment of the opportunities for, and constraints on, physical health, psychological well-being, and social functioning, and an examination of the biological, psychological and social contextual variation associated with developmental processes. The importance of a lifespan approach to understanding health and illness was highlighted by Townsend and Davies, who stated that 'any satisfactory explanation (of health) must build essentially on the ideas of the cumulative dispositions and experience of the lifetime and multiple causation' (1988: 104). Despite this, Penny, Bennett and Herbert (1994) noted that here has been surprisingly little recognition within health psychology of the contribution of lifespan psychology.

There is a substantial body of knowledge and theory informing lifespan perspectives on health, from sources as varied as Freud, Piaget, Erikson, and Havighurst. These theories often emphasize the relative importance of internal biological and cognitive changes in the early stages of development, and the increasing influence of external, social, factors on health and behaviour as the individual grows older. Together, these address the relative influence and interaction of biological, psychological and social factors at different stages within the lifespan.

Given the breadth of this chapter it is not possible to cover all the relevant literature. We therefore focus on three areas where health psychologists and others have contributed to our understanding of differences across the lifespan. The first addresses the role of biologically driven cognitive versus social factors on children's perceptions of health and illness. The second section considers the impact of social circumstances on adult health and health behaviour in relation to life events. Finally, we consider whether differing periods within the lifespan leave an individual more vulnerable to illness and other negative events than others. In doing so we raise three key issues:

- the relative influence of individual cognitive development versus social contextual factors in the developing understandings of health and illness
- the interaction of biopsychosocial factors on health and health behaviour, focusing particularly on the moderating influence of age, ethnicity and gender
- the relative and cumulative influence of challenges to health at different stages within the lifespan.

Children's Perceptions of Health and Illness

Many of our health-related beliefs, attitudes and behaviours originate in childhood. Identifying age-related differences in such cognitions and behaviours can facilitate more effective information giving and treatment during episodes of childhood illness, and may enhance health promotion programmes. Two major theoretical stances have been adopted in the study of children's understandings of health and illness. The dominant approach is influenced by the work of Piaget, in which researchers such as Bibace and Walsh (1980) suggest children's understanding of health and illness follows an invariant developmental sequence, mirroring more general and equally sequential cognitive changes. As such, these stress the importance of child rather than adult development, continuity and the influence of internal rather than external factors. This approach has been severely criticized by theorists such as Eiser (1989) who have suggested cognitions and behaviour are more driven by external influences such as children's experiences of health and illness and knowledge acquisition. As such, the microsystem offers the opportunity for change and continues to exert an influence in adulthood.

Bibace and Walsh's (1980) model of children's perceptions of illness causation identified a number of age-related explanations, each associated with Piagetian cognitive developmental stages, although the age ranges identified for each type of thinking are very general and there is considerable variation in the age at which children achieve each stage of illness representation. The first stage of understanding illness occurs between the ages of 5 and 7 years, and is dominated by thoughts of magic or punishment, reflecting pre-operational thinking. Illness is seen as a result of magic or witchcraft, or as a punishment for not obeying parental instructions – a phenomenon known as immanent justice. At this time, there is also the emergence of an understanding that illnesses can be contagious, though the child may overextend this principle to assume that *all* illnesses are contagious. Between the ages of 8 and 10 years, the child begins to consider the mechanisms of disease. He or she can describe the experience of symptoms and explain their cause in terms of external agents or events, through contamination, and that they involve the body as a whole: 'You catch a cold by going out in the wet weather. It stays in your body … and goes up into your chest.' They understand a germ theory of disease causation and begin to realize that not all diseases are contagious. They are also beginning to identify internal processes, focusing on explanations describing how mechanical actions lead to changes in specific internal body parts: 'You catch a cold from germs getting into your lungs and clogging them up. You sneeze to get the germs out.' These beliefs correspond to the concrete-operational stage. By the age of 11 years, the child develops an abstract understanding of disease and realizes that illness can result from the failure of a specific body part, reflecting the Piagetian formal operational stage. By this time, they have a sophisticated understanding of the physiological processes underlying the disease: 'A cold involves symptoms such as … You catch the germs that are all around us. Coughing and running nose are the side effects of the body's fighting them off. It makes mucous to carry away dead germs.' Around the age of 14 years, some children begin to recognize that disease may be a consequence of psychological processes.

Bibace and Walsh's model has been challenged both methodologically and theoretically. Bird and Podmore (1990), for example, noted that there were several aspects of Bibace and Walsh's work that questioned the validity of its findings: in particular, that it was based on children's responses to questions about disease causality that were too short to reliably code.

Other theorists, including Eiser (1989), have argued that children's experiences of illness have more of an influence than stage of cognitive development and that these influences continue into adulthood. Evidence favouring this hypothesis can be found in the findings of Redpath and Rogers (1984), who showed that children experiencing chronic illness had a greater understanding of disease than their healthy peers. A more detailed model of this type was developed by Carey (1985), who suggested that sophisticated explanations are dependent on increased knowledge and a developing understanding of human behaviour and biology. As we develop, our understandings of illness are not constrained at a structural level as Piaget claims; rather the beliefs are logical within our intuitive knowledge of the world. Initially children are 'naive psychologists', with explanations of eating as a behavioural phenomenon ('You eat because your mum tells you it's ready') and illness as a result of human action ('You get ill because you have done something wrong'). As our understanding of underlying biological processes increases we develop as 'naive biologists' ('You eat because you need the food to keep your body healthy' and 'You become ill because of germs'). Relatively unsophisticated explanations in both children and adults are a result of uncertainty and a lack of information, not cognitive structures. Warwick, Aggleton and Homans (1988), for example, in the early days of public information on AIDS, identified three models of causation in young adults: miasmatic ('There's a lot of it about'; 'It's everywhere. You get it from the environment you live in, the people you mix with'); serendipitous ('Whether you fall prey to infection depends on chance or luck'); and endogenous ('Like cancer, it's in everyone from the start, just waiting to be brought out'). This has led to alternative explanations which suggest that children's understandings of illness are better explained by accumulated increases in knowledge than by a qualitative shift from one cognitive stage to another.

Relatively few studies have focused on children's understandings of health (as opposed to illness). Of these, Normandeau, Kalnins, Jutras and Hanigan's (1998) Canadian study of children from a variety of socioeconomic groups and urban and rural locations found multidimensional explanations of health reflecting their everyday experiences. These revolved around three main dimensions frequently found in adult explanations: functionality, adherence to good 'health habits', and mental health. Similarly, Goldman, Whitneysaltiel, Granger and Rodin (1991), questioning 4- and 6-year-olds, found variation in illness representations dependent on type of illness. This variation closely reflected adult representations concerning causation, identity, consequences, probable duration, and whether it was curable (e.g., Nerenz & Leventhal, 1983).

Life Events

A large body of research has assessed the relationship between exposure to life events and physical health, psychological and social functioning, and health-related behaviours. These studies have adopted explanatory frameworks that focus on chronic stressors, acute stressors and stress-coping behaviours.

Chronic stressors

One of the largest sources of health variation in adults is paid employment and its associated occupational class (Arber, 1991). This brings with it a number of factors that impinge on health at this particular life stage. A particularly important factor is the stress-related risk associated with psychosocial environments such as the demands of the job, the latitude the workers have in dealing with these demands, and the support available to them (Karasek & Theorell, 1990). The relative influence of each of these variables may differ across job type and at different career stages – with increased latitude, for example, in later career stages. This importance

of work as a moderator of psychological and physical health is illustrated by Hobson and Delunas (2001), who found that five of the top 10 most frequently reported stressful events in adults were related to work. Work, however, also exerts a less obvious psychological influence on health. Kingsberg (2000), for example, found that the psychological impact of ageing on sexuality and intimate relationships is strongly influenced by sense of identity, self-esteem and self-worth which in turn are derived from occupation or avocation.

Acute stressors

Other theorists have begun to address how the context in which stressful events occur can influence the individual's response to them. Goldberg and Comstock (1980) highlighted the importance of studying different social subgroup responses to life events, as groups, defined for example by ethnicity and gender, are exposed to varying types and levels of events and experience them in different ways (see the earlier sections on gender and health and on ethnic minorities and health).

The psychological impact of adverse life events may differ according to life stage. In a study of people with a chronic illness, for example, Sherbourne, Meredith, Rogers and Ware (1992) found that the impact of stressful life events on health-related quality of life was determined by timing of exposure. Financial events had an immediate negative effect on functioning and wellbeing that persisted over time in the middle-aged. Bereavement, on the other hand, had the most negative impact when it occurred in young adulthood, although its effect was delayed somewhat over time. The importance of the age when the life event is experienced is also suggested by Ensel, Peek, Lin and Lai (1996), who found a prolonged influence for life events on mental health. Using panel data, the influences of stressors over a 15-year period were examined. Distal stressors, some occurring up to 15 years ago, maintained a direct and significant relationship with depressive symptomatology, independent of more proximal stressors. The type of stressor associated with distress varied with age, leading the authors to conclude that the stage of life at which a stressor occurs, rather than its nature, determined its subsequent influence on psychological health.

Coping

One way of coping with adverse negative experiences may involve comparing one's experience in a more positive light than that of others. Heckhausen and Brim (1997), for example, found that a sample of people of all ages experiencing changes in relation to health status, marriage and paid work perceived other people's problems to be more serious than their own. This effect was particularly pronounced amongst older adults. This type of evaluation may help individuals to cognitively restructure their experience, and help them cope emotionally with the experience. Of interest is that it may be particularly important in responding to life events in older age. One explanation for the particularly adverse impact of life events that occur at an inappropriate life stage (such as the death of a parent in adolescence) is that this type of social comparison is not available to the individual. Other theorists have highlighted the importance of issues such as gender, as well as age, in understanding coping responses to life events. Men and women may draw on different resources to cope with life events such as bereavement. In a 1-year follow-up study of men and women who had lost a partner in older age, it was found that, for women, having a best female friend, higher education and perceptions of higher relative health influenced levels of coping. Men, on the other hand, were more likely to share their emotional experiences as time elapsed and to be impeded in their emotional coping by financial stress (van Baarsen & Broese van Groenou, 2001). The reliance of women on family and external social support may make them particularly vulnerable to disruption of such systems (Elliott, 2001). Related to this may be problems associated with the loss of attachment to the extended family as children are more mobile and increasingly move from the family home as they mature. In addition, Simon (1995) suggested that women may react

more strongly to work and family strains than men because of the importance that these roles have for their sense of worth.

Examining health behaviours in the light of life events acknowledges that such behaviours are a response to environmental conditions. In young adulthood, life events, although not associated at that stage with biological risk factors, have been shown to have an association with lifestyle. For example, Twisk, Snel, de Vente, Kemper and van Mechlen (2000) found positive and negative life events and daily uplifts and hassles were related to increases in risk behaviours. Perreira and Sloan (2001), meanwhile, examined the influence of life events on alcohol consumption in a longitudinal study of older adults aged 51 to 61 years. They found that changes in levels of drinking over a 6-year period were associated with key life events. Whilst retirement was associated with an increase in drinking, the onset of chronic conditions and episodes of hospitalization were associated with decreases in consumption. Getting married or divorced facilitated both protective and risky drinking behaviour. These findings suggest that the influence of life events on health behaviours is not necessarily negative. Brennan, Schutte and Moos (1999), in a three-wave panel study of stressors and drinking behaviour amongst late-middle-aged and older men and women, found life stressors did not predict heavier or more frequent drinking. Contrary to expectations, alcohol consumption presages fewer negative life events, health and financial stressors for women and fewer financial stressors for men. For women, health stressors, and for men, financial stressors, predicted reduced alcohol consumption, leading the authors to suggest that there may be a benign feedback cycle where moderate alcohol consumption and life stressors reduce each other. Similarly Andersson and Stanich (1996) found that exposure to negative life events in old age resulted in positive health behaviours. When individuals experienced illness or disease, health practices such as self-care, improved dietary behaviour, increased health-protective behaviour and health information seeking were chosen as positive coping techniques.

Cumulative Disadvantage

One final issue concerns the concept of stability versus change, a central debate within lifespan health psychology. A number of theorists have argued that individuals are not indelibly shaped by their earlier experiences – that change is possible throughout the lifespan. This approach is illustrated by the research discussed above examining exposure to life events such as bereavement, marriage, retirement, chronic and acute illness. In some cases these events can be random and unexpected. Others are likely to occur at particular times in the lifespan and are associated with developmental tasks (Erikson, 1959). Here the timing of experiences is seen as crucial, with normative and ordered events having a different impact on health from those that deviate from commonly shared experiences. For childhood these are conceptualized as critical periods, a time when we are particularly responsive to the presence or absence of experience such as the development of attachments. Among adults, Neugarten (1968) has highlighted the importance of on-time and off-time events. It is suggested that experiences that conform to normative age expectations facilitate adaptation and development, whereas those that are atypical or off-time, such as widowhood early in life, have greater potential for poor health outcomes. Even so, a variety of ways of experiencing and responding to them has been identified. Stress processes, resilience and adaptation to change all play a role in determining health outcomes. Those favouring the concept of stability, however, suggest that early experiences, be they advantageous or disadvantageous, influence subsequent development. We therefore review a final group of studies which examine the cumulative health impact of experiences across the lifespan.

These studies have adopted longitudinal or retrospective designs in order to examine the association between childhood and adulthood experiences and health and illness in later life. They have tended to focus on late-middle-age and old-age populations and use measures associated with SES as predictors and physical, psychological and social measures as dependent variables. Such studies hold that 'social organisation structures life chances so that advantages and disadvantages cluster cross-sectionally and accumulate longitudinally' (Holland, Lee, Blane & Davey Smith, 2000: 1). In this way ongoing psychosocial conditions create pathways to health and illness that operate from the start of life, with timing and duration of exposure as critical features.

Evidence suggests that the earlier and longer the exposure to conditions of social disadvantage the more profound the effect, with individuals experiencing disadvantage as children being more likely to accumulate further disadvantage as they progress through life (Lynch et al., 1994). The relationship between early experience and subsequent physical health is demonstrated by Holland et al. (2000), who found childhood chronic illness and slow growth predicted exposure to subsequent health hazards up to early old age; as childhood height decreased, lifetime exposure to hazards increased. Power (2000) also found that long duration of low family income had a negative effect on children's cognitive development at age 5, school achievement at age 12 and subsequent adult earnings. Overall lifetime exposure measures found that 17.6 per cent of the men with the worst circumstances exhibited poor health at age 33 compared to 4.1 per cent of those with the best circumstances. For women the figures were 19.4 per cent and 3.9 per cent respectively. Similarly, Lynch, Kaplan and Salonen (1997), in a heart disease risk factor study of 2,674 middle-aged Finnish men, found health-risk behaviours and psychosocial dispositions detrimental to health associated with poor childhood conditions and low levels of parental socioeconomic status. They suggest that dietary behaviour and physical activity are determined directly by childhood social environments via the establishment of habitual behaviours early in life. Childhood background was seen to influence smoking behaviour and alcohol consumption indirectly via education level and occupation. Those individuals born to poor parents received the least education and were subsequently engaged in low-paid work with higher job and financial insecurity and more work-related injury. Such occupations were also associated with higher levels of smoking, greater alcohol consumption, more hostility and lack of hope for the future.

It has been suggested that disadvantage across the course of one's life impacts on psychological as well as physical and social health. Using measures of parental education and occupation and attained education and personal income in adulthood, Turrell et al. (2002) found a relationship between socioeconomic position, mobility, cumulative disadvantage across the lifespan and cognitive functioning in a sample of males. Men who remained in a low socioeconomic position scored worst on all cognitive tests, whilst men who rose from disadvantage scored better than those with limited or no upward mobility. Men who experienced downward mobility, on the other hand, had poorer scores than those who remained in their social position. Given the retrospective design of this study, however, it is unclear whether socioeconomic mobility influences cognitive functioning or vice versa.

CONCLUSIONS

No individual can be fully described and understood without knowledge of their gender, age, and social background. The concepts are impossible to isolate, and by doing so one inevitably simplifies reality and fails to acknowledge their often complex interaction. In outlining the individual impact of each of these categories, we have inevitably had to simplify frequently complex systems. It is important to recognize that age, gender, ethnicity, and the family are frequently used labels to identify factors that influence health. They act as signifiers – convenient labels that identify broad categories of risk for advantage and disadvantage. In this chapter, we have attempted to examine the biopsychosocial processes hidden behind these categories. In doing so we have highlighted the importance of examining individual factors within an immediate and wider social context.

For gender, we have seen that health is the outcome of both biological sex differences and the differing social worlds that men and women inhabit. In reviewing the research, it has become apparent that there is great variation in the sources of stress associated with gender roles both inside and outside the home. We have also seen that gender identity impacts greatly on the availability of repertoires of health-related behaviours and their enactment, medical help-seeking behaviour, and the provision of social support. These develop across the lifespan through the process of role socialization and the development of gender identity. It is important to recognize that these processes not only continue through the lifespan, but take place within a dynamic context that encompasses the social, political and economic, which together shape and confine the roles and identities available to men and women.

The influence of gender roles and identity and social and economic conditions can also be found in research that has examined the family. The family can act both as a buffer against sources of stress, such as periods of ill-health, and as a source of models of positive coping behaviour. This may be particularly the case for males. Families may also have a negative effect on health, through family-role-related demands and unhealthy interactions, especially for females. This highlights the need to understand how family roles and responsibilities are negotiated across the lifespan and differ according to societally determined gender-related norms and power relationships (Sweeting, 2001). It is also important to recognize that the family does not exist within a vacuum. It moderates and reflects the influence of the wider social context. By concentrating purely on internal family processes and family structure, there is a danger of ignoring issues of structural advantage and disadvantage that impact on the family, particularly at key points within its lifespan (McMunn et al., 2001).

Perhaps more than any other category, ethnicity highlights the importance of examining the underlying social processes and environmental influences associated with a seemingly 'obvious' single epidemiological indicator. We have seen how behavioural norms are the result of a dynamic interaction involving family, peers, and inter- and intra-group processes

(Gittelson et al., 1999). As with gender and the family, focusing on the single indicator of ethnicity can obscure the multiple impacts of underlying differences in socioeconomic opportunities, social resources, and living conditions on health and behaviour (Brown, 1984). Experiences of discrimination and racial harassment and the demands of maintaining or shifting culture provide further environmental stress and reduced access to resources (Kessler & Neighbors, 1986).

While it is important to recognize that gender, ethnicity, and the family represent axes whereby advantage and disadvantage impact on the individual at any one time, it is equally important to recognize the cumulative effect of these and other influences on health across the lifespan. The nature and distribution of life events and resources differ by age, as does their impact. Events that occur out of the normal developmental pattern, for example, may exert a disproportionate impact on health in comparison to those that occur at more expected life stages. More long-term age-related factors such as social and family context and material resources also contribute to understandings of health and health-related behavioural choices. They have also been implicated in cumulative health advantage and disadvantage via their influence on individual factors, such as health beliefs and expectations, and the normative constraints on behaviour that they impose. Brofenbrenner (1989), for example, proposed a model that pointed to the influence of interacting microsystems such as the family and peers as prime influences on lifespan development. These in turn are influenced by macrosystems such as economics, politics and social status.

This model has its roots in the work of theorists such as Sameroff (1986), who attempted to develop nature/nurture arguments by positing transactional explanations of change, which focus on the constant reciprocal influence between the individual and the environment. Such an approach reflects assumptions associated with the biopsychosocial model of health and frameworks adopted by the World Health Organization (Mendoza, 1990), which identified four interacting factors that determine

health. These are genetic and individual features such as cognitions, the micro-social environment such as family, peers and work, the macrosocial environment such as economics and the media, and the wider physical environment. In this way, biological changes associated with conception, pregnancy, genetic inheritance, physical growth and ageing, puberty and menstruation exert an influence on health. They do so, however, alongside and in interaction with the psychological changes associated with cognitive, moral, personality and identity development and social contextual factors, including relationships with peers, the family, marriage, life events, work demands, the economic environment and social status. Only by adopting such a multilevel perspective can we hope to understand and address the health inequalities associated with gender, ethnicity and the family across the lifespan.

REFERENCES

Alfredsson, L., Spetz, C.-L., & Theorell, T. (1985). Type of occupational and near-future hospitalization for myocardial infarction and some other diagnoses. *International Journal of Epidemiology*, 4, 378–388.

American Heart Association (1995). *Heart and stroke facts: 1995 statistical supplement.* Dallas, TX: American Heart Association.

Ames, G., & Janes, C. (1987). Heavy and problem drinking in an American blue-collar population: Implications for prevention. *Social Science and Medicine*, 25, 949–960.

Amos, A., Currie, C., & Elton, R. (1998). Perceptions of fashion images from youth magazines: Does a cigarette make a difference? *Health Education Research*, 13, 491–501.

Andersen, A., & DiDomencio, L. (1992). Diet vs. shape content of popular male and female magazines: A dose response relationship to the incidence of eating disorders? *International Journal of Eating Disorders*, 11, 283–287.

Andersson, L., & Stanich, J. (1996). Life events and their impact on health attitudes and health behaviour. *Archives of Gerontology and Geriatrics*, 23, 163–177.

Arber, S. (1991). Class, paid employment and family roles: Making sense of structural disadvantage, gender and health status. *Social Science and Medicine, 32,* 425–436.

Arber, S., Gilbert, G., & Dale, A. (1985). Paid employment and women's health: A benefit or a source of role strain? *Sociology of Health and Illness, 7,* 375–400.

Artazcoz, L., Borrell, C., & Benach, J. (2001). Gender inequalities in health among workers: The relation with family demands. *Journal of Epidemiology and Community Health, 555,* 639–647.

Backett, K. (1990). Studying health in families: A qualitative approach. In S. Cunningham, S. Burly & N. McKeganey (Eds.), *Readings in medical sociology* (pp. 57–84). London: Routledge.

Backett, K., & Davison, C. (1995). Lifecourse and lifestyle: The social and cultural location of health behaviours. *Social Science and Medicine, 40,* 629–638.

Balarajan, R., & Raleigh, V. (1993). *Ethnicity and health in England.* London: HMSO.

Banks, C. (1992). Culture in culture-bound syndromes: The case of anorexia nervosa. *Social Science and Medicine, 34,* 95–98.

Barker, R. M., & Baker, M. R. (1990). Incidence of cancer in Bradford Asians. *Journal of Epidemiology and Community Health, 44,* 125–129.

Bassett, M., & Krieger, N. (1986). Social class and black–white differences in breast cancer survival. *American Journal of Public Health, 76,* 1400.

Beal, A., Auisello, J., & Perrin, J. (2001). Social influence on health-risk behaviors among minority middle school students. *The Journal of Adolescent Health, 28,* 474–480.

Bell, T., Branston, L., Newcombe, R., & Barton, G. (1999). Interventions to improve uptake of breast screening in inner city Cardiff general practices with ethnic minority lists. *Ethnicity and Health, 4,* 277–284.

Berkman, L. F., & Glass, T. (2000). Social integration, social networks, social support, and health. In L. F. Berkman & I. Kawachi (Eds.), *Social epidemiology* (pp. 137–173). New York: Oxford University Press.

Berkman, L. F., & Syme, S. L. (1979). Social networks, host resistance, and mortality: A nine-year follow-up study of Alameda County residents. *American Journal of Epidemiology, 109,* 186–204.

Bertakis, K., Helms, L., Callahan, E., Azari, R., Leigh, P., & Robbins, J. (2001). Patient gender differences in the diagnosis of depression in primary care. *Journal of Women's Health and Gender Based Medicine, 10,* 689–698.

Best, D., Rawaf, S., Rowley, J., Floyd, K., Manning, V., & Strang, J. (2001). Ethnicity and gender differences in drinking and smoking among London adolescents. *Ethnicity and Health, 6,* 51–57.

Bibace, R., & Walsh, M. (1980). Development of children's concepts of illness. *Pediatrics, 66,* 912–917.

Birch, L., & Davison, K. (2001). Family environmental factors influencing the developing behavioral controls of food intake and childhood overweight. *Pediatric Clinics of North America, 48,* 893–907.

Bird, J., & Podmore, V. (1990). Children's understanding of health and illness. *Psychology and Health, 4,* 175–185.

Booth, A., Johnson, D., & Granger, D. (1999). Testosterone and men's health. *Journal of Behavioral Medicine, 22,* 1–19.

Brawley, O., & Freeman, H. (1999). Race and outcomes: Is this the end of the beginning for minority health research? *Journal of the National Cancer Institute, 91,* 1908–1909.

Brennan, P., Schutte, K., & Moos, R. (1999). Reciprocal relations between stressors and drinking behaviour: A three-wave panel study of late middle aged and older women and men. *Addiction, 94,* 737–749.

Brofenbrenner, U. (1989). Ecological systems theory. *Annals of Child Development, 6,* 187–249.

Broman, C. (1993). Social relationships and health-related behaviour. *Journal of Behavioral Medicine, 16,* 335–350.

Brosschot, J., & Thayer, J. (1998). Anger inhibition, cardiovascular recovery, and vagal function: A model of the link between hostility and cardiovascular disease. *Annals of Behavioral Medicine, 20,* 326–332.

Brown, C. (1984). *Black and white Britain: The third PSI survey.* London: Policy Studies Institute.

Buehler, C. (1987). Initiator status and the divorce transition. *Journal of Applied Family and Child Studies, 36,* 82–86.

Burke, V., Giangiulio, N., Gilliam, H. F., Beilin, L. J., Houghton, S., & Milligan, R. A. (1999). Health promotion in couples adapting to a shared lifestyle. *Health Education Research, 14,* 269–288.

Buysee, A., & Van Oost, P. (1997). 'Appropriate' male and female safer sex behaviour in heterosexual relationships. *AIDS Care, 9,* 549–561.

Carey, S. (1985). *Conceptual changes in childhood.* Cambridge, MA: MIT Press.

Charmaz, K. (1994). Identity dilemmas of chronically ill men. *Sociological Quarterly, 35,* 269–288.

Clarke, M., Ahmed, N., Romaniuk, H., Marjot, D. H., & Murray-Lyon, I. M. (1990). Ethnic differences in the consequences of alcohol misuse. *Alcohol and Alcoholism, 25,* 9–11.

Clarke, R. (2000). Perceptions of interethnic group racism predict increased vascular reactivity to a laboratory challenge in college women. *Annals of Behavioral Medicine*, 22, 214–222.

Coen, R., O'Boyle, C., Swanwick, G., & Coakley, D. (1999). Measuring the impact on relatives of caring for people with Alzheimer's disease: Quality of life, burden and well-being. *Psychology and Health*, 14, 253–261.

Courtenay, W. H. (2000a). Behavioural factors associated with disease, injury and death among men: Evidence and implications for prevention. *Journal of Men's Studies*, 9, 81–142.

Courtenay, W. H. (2000b). Constructions of masculinity and their influence on men's well-being: A theory of gender and health. *Social Science and Medicine*, 50, 1385–1401.

Davey, B., & Halliday, T. (Eds.) (1994). *Human biology and health: An evolutionary perspective.* Buckingham: Open University Press.

Davey Smith, G. (2002). *Comparative methods for studying socio-economic position and health in different ethnic groups.* Health Variations Programme Newsletter, ESRC.

Davey Smith, G., Wentworth, D., Neaton, J. D., Stamler R., & Stamler, J. (1996). Socio-economic differentials in mortality risk among men screened for the Multiple Risk Factor Intervention Trial: 2. Black men. *American Journal of Public Health*, 86, 497–504.

Dawson, D. (1991). Family structure and children's health and well-being: Data from the National Health Interview Survey on Child Health. *Journal of Marriage and the Family*, 53, 573–584.

Denton, M., & Walters, V. (1999). Gender differences in structural and behavioral determinants of health: An analysis of the social production of health. *Social Science and Medicine*, 48, 1221–1235.

Department of Health and Human Services (1996). *Report of final mortality statistics, 1994. Monthly Vital Statistics Report, 45 (3 Supplement).* Hyattsville, MD: Public Health Service.

Department of Health and Human Services (1998). *Health, United States, 1998: Socio-economic status and health chartbook.* Hyattsville, MD: National Center for Health Statistics.

Douglas, J. (1995). Developing anti-racist health promotion strategies. In R. Bunton, S. Nettles & R. Burrows (Eds.), *The sociology of health promotion* (pp. 70–78). London: Routledge.

Doyal, L. (2001). Sex, gender and health. *British Medical Journal*, 323, 1061–1063.

Doyle, Y. (1991). A survey of the cervical screening service in a London district, including reasons for non-attendance, ethnic responses and views on the quality of the service. *Social Science and Medicine*, 32, 953–957.

Dundas, R., Morgan, M., Redfern, J., Lemic-Stojcevic, N., & Wolfe, C. (2001). Ethnic differences in behavioural risk factors for stroke: Implications for health promotion. *Ethnicity and Health*, 6, 95–103.

Eiser, C. (1989). Children's concepts of illness: Toward an alternative to the 'stage' approach. *Psychology and Health*, 3, 93–101.

Elliott, M. (2001). Gender differences in the causes of depression. *Women and Health*, 33, 163–177.

Emslie, C., Hunt, K., & Watt, G. M. C. (2001). 'I'd rather go with a heart attack than drag on': Lay images of heart disease and the problems they present for primary and secondary prevention. *Coronary Health Care*, 5, 25–32.

Ensel, W., Peek, M., Lin, N., & Lai, G. (1996). Stress in the life course: A life history approach. *Journal of Ageing and Health*, 8, 389–416.

Epstein, A., & Ayanian, J. (2001). Racial disparities in medical care. *The New England Journal of Medicine*, 344, 1471–1473.

Erikson, E. (1959). *Identity and the life cycle: Selected papers.* New York: International Universities Press.

Fox, K. M., & Shapiro, L. M. (1988). Heart disease in Asians in Britain: Commoner than in Europeans, but why? *British Medical Journal*, 297, 311–312.

Foxcroft, D., Lowe, G., & May, C. (1994). Adolescent alcohol use and family influences: Attributive statements by teenage drinkers. *Drug Education, Prevention and Policy*, 1, 63–69.

Franks, P., Campbell, T., & Shields, C. (1992). Social relationships and health: The relative roles of family functioning and social support. *Social Science and Medicine*, 34, 779–788.

Freeman, H. (1987). Structure and content of gender stereotypes: Effects of somatic appearance and trait information. *Psychology of Women Quarterly*, 11, 59–68.

Friedman, S., Sotheran, J., AbdulQuader, A., Primm, B., DesJarlais, C., Kleinman, P., Maugé, C., Goldsmith, D. S., el Sadr, W., & Maslansky, R. (1987). The AIDS epidemic among blacks and Hispanics. *Milbank Quarterly*, 65, 455–499.

Furnham, A., & Radley, S. (1989). Sex differences in the perception of male and female body shapes. *Personality and Individual Differences*, 10, 653–662.

Gilvarry, C., Walsh, E., Samele, C., Hutchinson, G., Mallet, R., Rabe-Hesketh, S., Fahy, T., Van Os, J., & Murray, R. (1999). Life events, ethnicity and perceptions of discrimination in patients with severe mental illness. *Social Psychiatry and Psychiatric Epidemiology, 34,* 600–608.

Gittelson, J., McCormick, L., Allen, P., Grieser, M., Crawford, M., & Davis, S. (1999). Inter-ethnic differences in youth tobacco language and cigarette brand preferences. *Ethnicity and Health, 4,* 285–303.

Gittelson, J., Roche, K., Alexander, C., & Tassler, P. (2001). The social context of smoking among African-American and white adolescents in Baltimore City. *Ethnicity and Health, 6,* 211–225.

Glynn, L., Christenfeld, N., & Gerin, W. (1999). Gender, social support, and cardiovascular responses to stress. *Psychosomatic Medicine, 61,* 234–242.

Goldberg, E., & Comstock, G. (1980). Epidemiology of life events: Frequency in general populations. *American Journal of Epidemiology, 111,* 736–752.

Goldman, S.L., Whitneysaltiel, D., Granger, J., & Rodin, J. (1991). Children's representations of everyday aspects of health and illness. *Journal of Paediatric Psychology, 16,* 747–766.

Gottlieb, N., & Green, L. (1984). Life events, social networks, lifestyle and health. An analysis of the 1979 National Survey of personal health practices and consequences. *Health Education Quarterly, 11,* 91–105.

Gottlieb, N., & Green, L. (1987). Ethnicity and lifestyle health risk: Some possible mechanisms. *American Journal of Health Promotion, 1,* 37–45.

Graham, H. (1985). Providers, negotiators and mediators: Women as the hidden carers. In T. Lewin & V. Olesen (Eds.), *Women, health and healing.* London: Tavistock.

Gray, A. (Ed.), (1993). *World health and disease.* Buckingham: Open University Press.

Grisso, J. A., Freeman, E. W., Maurin, E., Garcia-Espana, B., & Berlin, J. A. (1999). Racial differences in menopause information and the experience of hot flushes. *Journal of General Internal Medicine, 14,* 98–103.

Groer, M., Thomas, S., & Shoffner, D. (1992). Adolescent stress and coping: A longitudinal study. *Research in Nursing and Health, 15,* 209–217.

Gudykunst, W., Yoon, Y., & Nishda, T. (1987). The influence of individualism–collectivism on perceptions of communication in in-group and out-group relationships. *Communication Monographs, 54,* 295–306.

Haan, M. N., & Kaplan, G. A. (1985). The contribution of socio-economic position to minority health. In M. Heckler (Ed.), *Report of the Secretary's Task Force on Black and Minority Health: Crosscutting issues in health and human services* (pp. 41–47). Washington, DC: USDHHS.

Harding, S., & Maxwell, R. (1997). Differences in mortality of migrants. In F. Drever & M. Whitehead (Eds.), *Health inequalities: Decennial supplement* (pp. 108–121). London: HMSO.

Haynes, G., & Feinleib, M. (1980). Women, work, and coronary heart disease: Prospective findings from the Framingham Heart Study. *American Journal of Public Health, 70,* 133–141.

Heaven, P. (1996). *Adolescent health: The role of individual differences.* London: Routledge.

Heckhausen, J., & Brim, O. (1997). Perceived problems for self and others: Self-protection by social downgrading throughout adulthood. *Psychology and Ageing, 12,* 610–619.

Hobson, C., & Delunas, L. (2001). National norms and life events frequencies for the revised Social Readjustment Rating Scale. *International Journal of Stress Management, 8,* 299–314.

Holland, P., Lee, B., Blane, D., & Davey Smith, G. (2000). *Life course influences on health in early old age.* Health Variations Programme Research Findings, Vol. 6, ESRC.

Hunt, K. (2002). A generation apart? Gender related experiences and health in women in early and later life. *Social Science and Medicine, 54,* 663–676.

Hyssaelae, L., Rautava, P., Helenius, H., & Sillanpaeae, M. (1995). Fathers' smoking and use of alcohol: The viewpoint of maternity health care clinics and well baby clinics. *Family Practice, 12,* 22–27.

Jaffe, H. (1997). Dying for dollars. *Men's Health, 12,* 132–137.

Johnson, C. C., & Nicklas, T. A. (1995). Health ahead: The Heart Smart family approach to prevention of cardiovascular disease. *The American Journal of the Medical Sciences, 310,* 127–132.

Jo-Lohman, B., & Jarvis, P. (2000) Adolescent stressors, coping strategies and psychological health studied in the family context. *Journal of Youth and Adolescence, 29,* 15–43.

Joung, I. (1997). The relationship between marital status and health. *Nederlands Tijdschrift Voor Geneeskunde, 141,* 277–282.

Kane, P. (1991). *Women's health: From womb to tomb.* New York: St Martins Press.

Karasek, R., & Theorell, T. (1990). *Stress, productivity and the reconstruction of working life.* New York: Basic.

Karlsen, S., & Nazroo, J. (2000). *The relationship between racism, social class and health among ethnic minority groups.* Health Variations Programme Newsletter, Vol. 5, ESRC.

Karlsen, S., Rogers, A., & McCarthy, M. (1998). Social environment and substance misuse: A study of ethnic variations among inner London adolescents. *Ethnicity and Health, 3*, 265–273.

Kerr, M., & Charles, N. (1983). *Attitudes to the feeding and nutrition of young children: Preliminary report.* York: University of York.

Kessler, R. C., & Neighbors, H. W. (1986). A new perspective on the relationships among race, social class, and psychological distress. *Journal of Health and Social Behavior, 27*, 107–115.

Kiecolt-Glaser, J., Kennedy, S., Malkoff, S., Fisher, L., Speicher, C., & Glaser, R. (1988). Marital discord and immunity in males. *Psychosomatic Medicine, 50*, 213–229.

Kiecolt-Glaser, J., & Newton, T. (2001). Marriage and health: His and hers. *Psychological Bulletin, 127*, 472–503.

Killien, M., Habermann, B., & Jarrett, M. (2001). Influence of employment characteristics on post-partum mothers' health. *Women and Health, 33*, 63–81.

Kingsberg, S. (2000). The psychological impact of ageing on sexuality and relationships. *Journal of Women's Health and Gender Based Medicine, 9*, 33–38.

Klag, M. J., Whelton, P. K., Coresh, J., Grim, C. E., & Kuller, L. H. (1991). The association of skin color with blood pressure in U.S. blacks with low socio-economic status. *Journal of the American Medical Association, 265*, 599–602.

Klonoff, E., & Landrine, H. (1992). Sex roles, occupational roles, and symptom-reporting: A test of competing hypotheses on sex differences. *Journal of Behavioral Medicine, 15*, 355–364.

Krieger, N., Quesenberry, C., Peng, T., Horn-Ross, P., Stewart, S., Brown, S., Swallen, K., Guillermo, T., Suh, D., Alvarez-Martinez, L., & Ward, F. (1999). Social class, race/ethnicity, and incidence of breast, cervix, colon, lung, and prostate cancer among Asian, black, Hispanic, and white residents of the San Francisco Bay Area. *Cancer Causes & Control, 10*, 525–537.

Lahelma, E., Martikainen, P., Rahkonen, O., & Silventoinen, K. (1999). Gender differences in ill health in Finland: Patterns, magnitude and change. *Social Science and Medicine, 48*, 797–813.

Landman, J., & Cruickshank, J. (2001). A review of ethnicity, health and nutrition related diseases in relation to migration in the UK. *Public Health Nutrition, 4* (2B), 647–657.

Lillie-Blanton, M., Anthony, J., & Schuster, C. (1993). Probing the meaning of racial/ethnic differences in crack cocaine. *Journal of the American Medical Association, 269*, 993.

Lip, G., Luscombe, C., McCarry, M., Malik, M., & Beevers, G. (1996). Ethnic differences in public health awareness, health perceptions and physical exercise: Implications for heart disease prevention. *Ethnicity and Health, 1*, 47–53.

Littlewood, R., & Lipsedge, M. (1988). Psychiatric illness among British Afro-Caribbeans. *British Medical Journal, 296*, 950–951.

Lundberg, U., de Chateau, P., Winberg, J., & Frankenhauser, M. (1981). Catecholamine and cortisol excretion patterns in three year old children and their parents. *Journal of Human Stress, 7*, 3–11.

Lynch, J., Kaplan, G., Cohen, R., Krauhanen, J., Wilson, T., Smith, N., & Salonen, J. (1994). Childhood and adult socio-economic status as predictors of mortality in Finland. *Lancet, 343*, 524–527.

Lynch, J., Kaplan, G., & Salonen, J. (1997). Why do poor people behave poorly? Variation in adult health behaviours and psychosocial characteristics by stage of the socio-economic lifecourse. *Social Science and Medicine, 44*, 809–819.

Maguire, M., Hannan, P., Stat, M., Neumark-Sztainer, D., Falkner Cossrow, N., & Story, M. (2002). Parental correlates of physical activity in a racially/ethnically diverse adolescent sample. *Journal of Adolescent Health, 30*, 253–261.

Markides, K. (1983). Mortality among minority populations: A review of recent patterns and trends. *Public Health Reports, 98*, 252–260.

Markson, S., & Fiese, B. (2000). Family rituals as a protective factor for children with asthma. *Journal of Pediatric Psychology, 25*, 471–479.

Matthews, K. A., & Stoney, C. M. (1988). Influences of sex and age on cardiovascular reponses during stress. *Psychosomatic Medicine, 50*, 46–56.

McGill, H., & Stern, M. (1979). Sex and atherosclerosis. *Atheroscleroisis Review, 4*, 157–248.

McMunn, A., Nazroo, J., Marmot, M., Boreham, R., & Goodman, R. (2001). Children's emotional and behavioural well-being and the family environment: Findings from the Health Survey from England. *Social Science and Medicine, 53*, 423–440.

Mendoza, R. (1990). Concept of healthy lifestyles and their determinants. 2nd European Conference on Health Education, Warsaw, 7–9 June.

Mintel (1991). *Children: The influencing factor.* London: Mintel.

Mitchell, J. B., Ballard, D. J., Matchar, D. B., Whisnant, J. P., & Samsa, G. P. (2000). Racial variation in treatment for transient ischemic attacks:

Impact of participation by neurologists. *Health Services Research, 34*, 1413–1428.

Modood, T., Berthoud, R., Lakey, J., Nazroo, J., Smith, P., Virdee, S., & Beishon, S. (Eds.) (1997). *Ethnic Minorities in Britain: Diversity and disadvantage.* London: Policy Studies Institute.

Narang, I., & Murphy S. (1994). An assessment of ante-natal care for Asian women. *British Journal of Midwifery, 2*, 169–174.

Nazroo, J. (1997). *The health of Britain's ethnic minorities: Findings from a national survey.* London: Policy Studies Institute.

Nazroo, J. Y. (1998). *Genetic, cultural or socio-economic vulnerability? Explaining ethnic inequalities in health.* Oxford: Blackwell.

Nerenz, D. R., & Leventhal, H. (1983). Self-regulation theory in chronic illness. In T. G. Burish & L.A. Bradley (Eds.), *Coping with chronic disease* (pp. 13–37). New York: Academic.

Neugarten, B. (Ed.) (1968). *Middle age and ageing.* Chicago: University of Chicago Press.

Nordstrom, C. K., Dwyer, K. M., Merz, C. N. B., Shircore, A., & Dwyer, J. H. (2001). Work-related stress and early atherosclerosis. *Epidemiology, 12*, 180–185.

Normandeau, S., Kalnins, I., Jutras, S., & Hanigan, D. (1998). A description of 5- to 12-year old children's conception of health within the context of their daily life. *Psychology and Health, 13*, 883–896.

Oakley, A. (1987). Gender and generation: The life and times of Adam and Eve. In P. Allat, T. Keil, A. Bryman & B. Bytheway (Eds.), *Women and the lifecycle* (pp. 24–38). London: Macmillan.

Office for National Statistics (1996). *Key health statistics from general practice.* Series SMPS, 60. London: Stationery Office.

Oppenheimer, V. (1974). The lifecycle squeeze. *Demography, 11*, 227–245.

Orth-Gomer, K., & Johnsson, J. V. (1987). Social network interaction and mortality: A six year follow- up study of a random sample of the Swedish population. *Journal of Chronic Diseases, 40*, 949–957.

Parker, V., Sussman, S., Crippens, D., Elder, P., & Scholl, D. (1998). The relation of ethnic identification with cigarette smoking among US urban African American and Latino youth: A pilot study. *Ethnicity and Health, 3*, 135–143.

Pennebaker, J. (1997). *Opening up: The healing power of expressing emotions.* New York: Guilford.

Penny, G., Bennett, P., & Herbert, M. (Eds.) (1994). *Health psychology: A lifespan perspective.* Netherlands: Harwood Academic.

Perreira, K., & Sloan, F. (2001). Life events and alcohol consumption among mature adults: A longitudinal analysis. *Journal of Studies on Alcohol, 62*, 501–508.

Pittman, J., Solheim, C., & Blanchard, D. (1992). Stress as a driver of the allocation of housework. *Journal of Marriage and the Family, 58*, 456–468.

Pledge, D. (1992). Marital separation/divorce: A review of individual responses to a major life stressor. *Journal of Divorce and Remarriage, 17*, 151–181.

Powell-Griner, E., Anderson, J. E., & Murphy, W. (1997). State and sex-specific prevalence of selected characteristics behavioural risk factor surveillance system, 1994 and 1995. *Morbidity and Mortality Weekly Report, Centers for Disease Control, Surveillance Summaries, 46*, 1–31.

Power, C. (2000). *Duration and timing of exposure: Effects of socio-economic environment on adult health.* Health Variations Programme Newsletter, Vol. 5, ESRC.

Qureshi, M., Thacker, H. L., Litaker, D. G., & Kippes, C. (2000). Differences in breast cancer screening rates: An issue of ethnicity or socioeconomics? *Journal of Women's Health and Gender Based Medicine, 9*, 1025–1031.

Reddy, D. M., Fleming, R., & Adesso, V. J. (1992). Gender and health. In S. Maes, H. Leventhal & M. Johnston (Eds.), *International Review of Health Psychology* (Vol. 1, pp. 3–33). Chichester: Wiley.

Redpath, C., & Rogers, C. (1984). Healthy young children's concepts of hospitals, medical personnel, operations and illness. *Journal of Paediatric Psychology, 9*, 13–27.

Reynolds, P., & Kaplan, G. A. (1990). Social connections and risk for cancer: Prospective evidence from the Alameda County Study. *Behavioral Medicine, 16*, 101–110.

Robertson, J., Lin, C., Woodford, J., Danos, K., & Hurst, M. (2001). The (un)emotional male: Physiological, verbal and written correlates of expressiveness. *Journal of Men's Studies, 9*, 393–412.

Robinson, J. (1984). Racial inequality and the probability of occupation-related injury or illness. *Milbank Memorial Fund Quarterly, 62*, 567–590.

Rossow, I. (1992). Intrafamily influences on health behaviour: A study of interdental cleaning behavior. *Journal of Clinical Peridontology, 19*, 774–778.

Rudat, K. (1994). *Black and minority ethnic groups in England: Health and lifestyles.* London: Health Education Authority.

Sameroff, A. (1986). Environmental context of child development. *Journal of Paediatrics, 109*, 192–200.

Seeman, T. (2000). Health promoting effects of friends and family on health outcomes in older adults. *American Journal of Health Promotion, 14,* 362–370.

Sherbourne, C., Meredith, D., Rogers, W., & Ware, J. (1992). Social support and stressful life events: Age differences in their effects on health related quality of life among the chronically ill. *Quality of Life Research, 1,* 235–246.

Simon, R. (1995). Gender, multiple roles, role meanings, and mental health. *Journal of Health and Social Behavior, 36,* 182–194.

Simoni-Watsila, L. (2000). The use of abusable prescription drugs: The role of gender. *Journal of Women's Health and Gender Based Medicine, 9,* 289–297.

Sleutjes, M. (1990). Promoting safer sex among ethnic minority groups: Lifting the real barriers. In M. Paalman (Ed.), *Promoting safer sex: Prevention of sexual transmission of AIDS and other STD* (pp. 154–163). Amsterdam: Swets and Zeitlinger.

Sorlie, P. D., Backlund, E., & Keller, J. B. (1995). US mortality by economic, demographic, and social characteristics: The National Longitudinal Mortality Study. *American Journal of Public Health, 85,* 949–956.

Sweeting, H. (2001). Our family, whose perspective? An investigation of children's family life and health. *Journal of Adolescence, 24,* 229–250.

Todd, K. H., Deaton, C., D'Adamo, A. P., & Goe, L. (2000). Ethnicity and analgesic practice. *Annals of Emergency Medicine, 35,* 11–16.

Townsend, P., & Davies, N. (Eds.) (1988). *Inequalities in health: The Black Report.* London: Penguin.

Travis, C. (1988). *Women and health psychology: Biomedical issues.* Hillsdale, NJ: Erlbaum.

Tudiver, F., & Talbot, Y. (1999). Why don't men seek help? Family physicians' perspectives on help seeking behaviour in men. *Journal of Family Practice, 48,* 47–52.

Turrell, G., Lynch, J. W., Kaplan, G. A., Everson, S. A., Helkala, E.-L., Kauhanen, J., & Salonen, J. K. (2002). Socioeconomic position across the life-course and cognitive function in late middle age. *Journal of Gerontology, 57B,* S43–S51.

Twisk, J., Snel, J., de Vente, W., Kemper, H., & van Mechlen, W. (2000). Positive and negative life events: The relationship with coronary heart disease risk factors in young adults. *Journal of Psychosomatic Research, 49,* 35–42.

Uchino, B., Holt, L., Uno, D., & Flinders, J. (2001). Heterogeneity in the social network of young and older adults: Predictions of mental health and cardiovascular reactivity during acute stress. *Journal of Behavioral Medicine, 24,* 361–382.

Umberson, D. (1992). Gender, marital status and the social control of health behaviour. *Social Science and Medicine, 34,* 907–917.

van Baarsen, B., & Broese van Groenou, M. I. (2001). Partner loss in later life: Gender differences in coping shortly after bereavement. *Journal of Loss and Trauma, 6,* 243–262.

Van Etten, M., & Anthony, J. (2001). Male–female differences in transitions from first drug opportunity to first use: Searching for subgroup variation by age, race, region and urban status. *Journal of Women's Health and Gender Based Medicine, 10,* 797–804.

Verbrugge, L. M., & Steiner, R. P. (1985). Prescribing drugs to men and women. *Health Psychology, 4,* 79–98.

Vertinsky, P. (1998). 'Run, Jane, run': Central tensions in the current debate about enhancing women's health through exercise. *Women and Health, 27,* 81–111.

Waldron, I., Hughes, M., & Brooks, T. (1996). Marriage protection and marriage selection: Prospective evidence for reciprocal effects of marital status and health. *Social Science and Medicine, 43,* 113–123.

Wamboldt, M., & Wamboldt, F. (2000). Role of the family in the onset and outcome of childhood disorders: Selected research findings. *Journal of the American Academy of Child and Adolescent Psychiatry, 39,* 1212–1219.

Warwick, I., Aggleton, P., & Homans, H. (1988). Constructing common sense: Young people's beliefs about AIDS. *Sociology of Health and Illness, 10,* 213–233.

Waterson, E., Evans, C., & Murray-Lyon, I. (1990). Is pregnancy a time of changing smoking and drinking patterns for fathers as well as mothers? An initial investigation. *British Journal of Addiction, 85,* 389–396.

Waterson, E. J., & Murray-Lyon, I. M. (1989). Alcohol, smoking and pregnancy: Some observations on ethnic minorities in the United Kingdom. *British Journal of Addiction, 84,* 323–325.

Weidner, G., Boughal, T., Connor, S., & Pieper, C. (1997). Relationship of job strain to standard coronary risk factors and psychological characteristics in women and men of the Family Heart Study. *Health Psychology, 16,* 239–247.

Wenk, D., Hardesty, C., Morgan, C., & Blair, S. (1994). The influence of parental involvement on the well-being of sons and daughters. *Journal of Marriage and the Family, 56,* 228–234.

Westman, M., Eden, D., & Shirom, A. (1985). Job stress, cigarette smoking and cessation: Conditioning effects of peer support. *Social Science and Medicine, 20,* 637–644.

Wickrama, K., Conger, R., Wallace, L., & Elder, G. (1999). The intergenerational transmission of health-risk behaviors: Adolescent lifestyles and gender moderating effects. *Journal of Health and Social Behavior, 40,* 258–272.

Williams, D., & Williams, M. (2000). Racism and mental health: The African American experience. *Ethnicity and Health, 5,* 243–268.

Williams, R. B., Barefoot, J. C., Califf, R. M., Haney, T. L., Saunders, W. B., Pryor, D. B., Hlatky, M. A., Siegler, I. C., & Mark, D. B. (1992). Prognostic importance of social resources among patients with angiographically documented coronary artery disease. *Journal of the American Medical Association, 267,* 520–524.

World Health Organization (2003). Retrieved from http://www3.who.int/whosis/menu.cfm.

Young, R. (1999). Prioritising family health needs: A time–space analysis of women's health-related behaviours. *Social Science and Medicine, 48,* 797–813.

10

Communicating about Health Threats and Treatments

THERESA M. MARTEAU AND JOHN WEINMAN

INTRODUCTION

Communication between patients and practitioners is a central part of health care. Effective communication is essential, for example, for practitioners to understand the nature of a patient's problem and the patient's perception of this. Explaining how future illness might be averted or current illness treated also requires effective communication. Failure to communicate effectively has numerous adverse effects, including patients not understanding the results of tests they have undergone (Maissi et al., submitted; McBride et al., 2002), false and failed reassurance (Lucock, Morley, White & Peake, 1997; Smith, Shaw & Marteau, 1994), non-adherence (Haynes, McKibbon & Kanani, 1996), and longer lengths of stay in hospital (Johnston & Vogele, 1993). Failed communication also lies at the heart of much litigation (Petticrew, Sowden, Lister-Sharp & Wright, 2000). In addition, it is claimed that good communication skills can avoid 'burnout' in health professionals (Feinmann, 2002). The scale of these problems is large. For example, 20 per cent of mothers taking their children to a paediatric outpatient clinic were not informed clearly about the diagnosis and

nearly 50 per cent were uncertain afterwards as to the course of their child's illness (Korsch & Negrete, 1972). Half of those informed about an enhanced genetic vulnerability to lung cancer were they to continue to smoke failed to understand this (McBride et al., 2002). One-third of those receiving a normal cervical smear test result misinterpreted this as meaning that they had no chance at all of having cervical cancer, as opposed to a low risk of being affected (Maissi et al., submitted).

Problems in communicating between health care professionals and patients have been widely documented over several decades. Ley (1988) produced one of the first systematic attempts based on psychological principles to understand and thereby to address these problems. Ley started from the observation that communication is the aspect of the clinical encounter that engenders least satisfaction. He saw this as stemming from two problems: a failure of patients to understand the information given; and related to this, a failure to recall what had been said.

Failure to understand information was seen as having two main causes. First, information is presented in too difficult a way, using unfamiliar and technical terms or using familiar terms in unfamiliar ways. For example, in screening the term 'positive result' is used to denote one indicating a problem, in contrast with its favourable connotation in the vernacular. The second main cause of misunderstanding is that the information presented clashes with patients' own representations and is interpreted within these. Thus, patients who perceive hypertension as an acute symptomatic condition are less likely to adhere to medical advice to take medication than are those whose perception of the condition coincides with the medical view (Meyer, Leventhal & Guttman, 1985).

Recall of information is affected both by understanding of the information as it is presented and by its amount and complexity (Ley, 1988). Drawing upon findings such as these, Ley developed what he termed a 'cognitive model' depicting the relationships between understanding, memory, satisfaction and compliance. Although disarmingly simple, this model highlights the importance of presenting information in a way that it is understood and recalled. Since this time, research has broadened to consider how the process of communication influences outcome. It has also built upon research on communication in routine consultations to consider communication in specific areas aimed at achieving particular outcomes in different patient groups.

This chapter starts by presenting a summary of some general principles of effective communication focusing on two common media: spoken and written language. The next three sections build upon this, to review the nature of communication problems and their effects in relation to three significant and contrasting areas for health psychology, focusing on (1) healthy individuals, (2) those facing surgery, and (3) those having to engage in longer term adherence to medical treatments.

COMMUNICATING INFORMATION: GENERAL PRINCIPLES

People are not passive recipients of information. They actively process information, trying to make sense of it by drawing upon pre-existing representations or schemata. Such schemata function as a set of expectations that guide the encoding of new information (Hampson, Glasgow & Zeiss, 1994; Leventhal & Diefenbach, 1991). For example, perceptions of the causes of familial adenomatous polyposis, an inherited form of bowel cancer, influence how accurate the results of a genetic test are seen to be (Michie et al., 2002). When genes were seen as the sole cause, those receiving a test result showing they had not inherited the gene were reassured and did not want bowel screening. But when the cancer was seen as caused by many factors, including diet and stress, as well as genes, the genetic test was seen as less accurate at predicting disease onset, with a resultant continued desire for bowel screening, despite a test result showing that they had not inherited the gene for this dominantly inherited predisposition to bowel cancer. Such results highlight the dynamic nature of effective communication requiring eliciting current understanding of a situation and presenting information so that any new information makes sense within an existing schema. Where such schemata will not accommodate some new piece of information or do not exist, the task of the communicator is to present information in order to develop a schema within which the new information will make sense. This approach formed the basis of the first experimental study intervening to alter illness representations to improve outcomes after a heart attack (Petrie, Cameron, Ellis, Buick & Weinman, 2002). The intervention was effective at altering patient representations of a myocardial infarction and reduced the length of time taken to return to work as well as the reporting of symptoms of angina. While further research is needed to determine the most effective ways of eliciting, challenging and changing schemata, such interventions that have much promise in improving patient outcomes depend critically upon basic communication skills.

Communicating with Different Groups

There is good evidence of ethnic and social inequalities in health care and health outcomes (Cooper & Roter, 2002; Department of Health and Social Security, 1980). While much work has focused on access to health care, there is some evidence to show that health care professionals' communication with these groups may contribute to these inequalities (Cooper & Roter, 2002). Thus, ethnic minority patients report less involvement in medical decisions, less partnership with their providers and lower levels of satisfaction with care (Cooper-Patrick et al., 1999; Saha, Komaromy, Koepsell & Bindman, 1999). Patients from lower socio-economic groups are given less information in consultations (Pendleton & Bochner, 1980; Waitzkin, 1985). This stems from them being less verbally active in consultations (Bain, 1977), often mistaken by practitioners as indicating little interest in gaining information. Following a review of this literature, Cooper and Roter (2002) recommend that communication skills training programmes need to be more broadly based to train health care practitioners to communicate in a culturally more sensitive way, and that strategies are needed to empower patients across ethnic and social groups to participate more in their care.

Communicating effectively with those with low levels of literacy and those from minority ethnic groups requires some different considerations from those that govern communication with those who are literate and those from dominant ethnic groups. Those with low levels of literacy, estimated at about 20 per cent of the US and UK populations, derive little benefit from written communication. In inner city hospitals in the US, levels of functional illiteracy are as high as 35 per cent amongst English-speaking patients and 62 per cent in Spanish-speaking patients seeking care (Williams et al., 1995). Their lack of written language skill affects their processing of spoken language, making it less effective than those who can read and write fluently (LeVine et al., 1994). Understanding and comprehension of simple instructions regarding treatment are much improved for this group using pictographs, that is, cartoons depicting instructions. Recall of instructions regarding a range of medical problems was dramatically better when oral instructions were accompanied by pictographs

(Houts et al., 1998; Houts, Witmer, Egeth, Loscalzo & Zabora, 2001). Giving patients tape recordings of their consultations may be particularly useful for this group, as would be videotapes presenting salient information about particular illnesses and their prevention or management. Health practitioners are, however, poor at identifying those with low literacy skills, with patients often keen to disguise this.

Values, customs and beliefs about illness vary across, as well as within, cultural groups. Such variations will affect how information is understood as well as responses to it (Baumann, 2003). Some of the clearest examples of differences in illness beliefs between cultures concern causal beliefs (Landrine & Klonoff, 2001). Cultures characterized as egocentric (mostly Northern European and North American) embrace the dominant medical model of disease, and with it mind–body dualism. By contrast, cultures characterized as sociocentric draw few distinctions between mind and body, religious, spiritual, medical, social and emotional processes. Such differences will affect the effectiveness of communications about illness, treatment and prevention. Thus, informing those who share the beliefs of a sociocentric culture that they can reduce their risks of heart disease by such behaviour changes as increasing levels of physical activity is likely to have little impact when the dominant view of the cause of illness is an imbalance arising out of relationship conflicts, moral transgressions and negative emotions. While it is relatively easy to predict when communications based on an egocentric culture will be ineffective for those subscribing to the values of a sociocentric culture, it is currently unknown how such communications can be made effective. Eliciting and acknowledging existing illness beliefs will be a starting point.

Communication Medium

Information about health care is available from many sources using a variety of media. While there is increasing focus on the use of the internet and interactive media, the two most commonly used media for communicating information in health care are in person and in writing.

Consultation skills

There has been a considerable amount of research over the past 40 years aimed at ascertaining the core communication skills needed for effective face-to-face communication. There is some evidence, for example, that the process of communication influences patient outcomes. Thus, Hall and colleagues' overview of research in this area (Hall, Roter & Katz, 1988) showed that patient satisfaction was higher following consultations in which the health care professional engaged in more social conversation, positive verbal and non-verbal communication and partnership building. Ascertaining the precise relationships between process and different outcomes has, however, proved a difficult task, made more difficult by a paucity of reliable measures of dynamic processes as well as a lack of theoretical models to guide such measurement.

A number of systems have been developed to measure aspects of the doctor–patient relationship (Stewart et al., 1995). A meta-analysis of communication studies found that the many different elements of communication measured in the studies fell into five broad categories: information giving; question asking; partnership building; rapport building; and socioemotional talk (Hall et al., 1988). The links between these and outcomes were reviewed by Stewart (1995). Informativeness was an important factor influencing health outcomes, particularly when accompanied by emotional support, resulting in reduced psychological distress, enhanced symptom resolution and reduced pain. Physicians asking about patients' understanding, concerns and expectations was also important in achieving these outcomes. Using cluster analysis, Roter and colleagues (1997) identified five patterns of relationship in primary care consultations: narrowly biomedical; biomedical (in transition); biopsychosocial; psychosocial; and consumerist. The first two are considered to

reflect a paternalistic model, the third and fourth to reflect variations on patient-centred communication, and the final one to reflect a consumerist model.

Skills that facilitate the effective communication of information include using language that is readily understood, presenting information in a way that takes account of the patient's beliefs, and checking understanding of any information that has been given (Ley, 1988). Video recordings of consultations show that these skills are frequently absent in routine consultations (Braddock, Fihn, Levinson, Jonsen & Pearlman, 1997; Campion, Foulkes, Neighbour & Tate, 2002). Thus, for example, recording of consultations conducted by primary care physicians in the US revealed that in just 2 per cent were direct questions asked of the patient to check understanding (Braddock et al., 1997). Similarly in an analysis of videotaped consultations selected by candidates as part of a qualifying examination for membership of the Royal College of General Practitioners, checking patient understanding was evident in just 20 per cent of the consultations (Campion et al., 2002).

Communication skills can be improved by training (Fallowfield et al., 2002; McGuire, Fairburn & Fletcher, 1986). There is, however, little evidence regarding the effective components of such training. This might be enhanced if a theoretical basis for the type of training is made explicit. For example, based on evidence regarding the acquisition of other types of skills, feedback, preferably based on videos, seems an important component (Hall, 1983). Such a technique may be particularly important in developing communication skills whose quality is difficult to judge and is, therefore, subject to such face saving attribution biases as attributing patient confusion to the patient's inherent incompetence but patient clarity to one's own skills (Miller & Ross, 1975). Bandura's (1997) social cognitive theory is one of the few theoretical models to be applied to describing and changing health care professionals' communication behaviour (Parle, Maguire & Heaven, 1997). Using this model, Maguire and colleagues highlight, for example, the importance of addressing health professionals' negative beliefs about the consequences of giving certain types of information to patients, as well as their self-efficacy in being able to communicate effectively. In addition to using theory to develop effective training, there is an evident need to ensure that such training is an integral part of health professional training. Such training is rarely mandatory. In a study of medical students, confidence in communicating effectively was inversely related to actual skills (Marteau et al., 1991) suggesting that health professionals' ability to judge their own need for training would not ensure a skilled workforce. There is also evidence that those with the most communication skills are those most likely to persist with any training (Michie & Marteau, 1999). Research is needed to ascertain the attitudinal barriers to health professionals embracing more fully the centrality of effective communication skills to their practice, be it as a surgeon, physician or nurse.

Written information

Written information is sometimes used as the sole means of communication, for example when inviting people to participate in population-based screening programmes. More often it is used to supplement orally presented information, acting as a reminder or as a source of additional information, for example, about self-management of chronic conditions. Reviews of written information about a variety of health topics reveal several common problems including the use of inaccurate information, missing information and text that is too complex to be understood by the majority of the intended audience (Coulter, Entwistle & Gilbert, 1999; Ley, 1988; Slaytor & Ward, 1998). Based on research evidence as well as consensus, several checklists have been developed to guide the process of developing written information as well as its content (Coulter et al., 1999; Jadad & Gagliardi, 1998; Silberg, Lundberg & Musacchio, 1997). One of the earliest approaches to improving written information, still used today, is the use of readability

formulae. These most often incorporate estimates of sentence length and vocabulary load (number of syllables per word) to generate an index of the level of education needed to understand the text (Flesch, 1948). Wright (1980) described 'usability' as a helpful heuristic in designing written, factual information. Usable information is designed to take account of readers' fluency and familiarity with the subject matter as well as their cognitive abilities and existing conceptual structures. The order, layout of materials and paragraph structure are also important in contributing to the usability of written information. A checklist generated by Coulter and colleagues (1999) summarizing important steps in developing written information is shown in Table 10.1.

While such checklists are useful in describing the information that is needed, they provide little guidance on the most effective way of presenting it. Some of the evidence relating to this is included in the following sections.

HEALTH RISK INFORMATION

Health risk information comprises, as a minimum, information about the likelihood and nature of an illness or condition that threatens an individual's health. Such information is commonly given as part of health risk assessments or health screening. There is no one best way of presenting risk information. It will depend in part upon the aim of communicating the information. Thus, for example, if the aim is to reassure, likelihood information may be more effective at achieving this if it is presented in the form of an absolute as opposed to a relative risk (Brase, 2002).

Achieving Understanding of Information

Information about the nature of a threat is commonly assumed and thus often not presented in detail. For example, participants in population-based screening programmes are given relatively little information about the

Table 10.1 *Checklist for patient information materials*

The process

1 Involve patients throughout the process
2 Involve a wide range of clinical experts
3 Be specific about the purpose of the information and the target audience
4 Consider the information needs of minority groups
5 Review the clinical research evidence and use systematic reviews wherever possible
6 Plan how the materials can be used within a wider programme promoting shared decision making
7 Consider cost and feasibility of distribution and updating when choosing media
8 Develop a strategy for distribution
9 Evaluate the materials and their use
10 Make arrangements for periodic review and updating
11 Publicize the availability of the information materials

The content

1 Use patients' questions as the starting point
2 Ensure that common concerns and misconceptions are addressed
3 Refer to all relevant treatment or management options
4 Include honest information about benefits and risks
5 Include quantitative information where possible
6 Include checklists and questions to ask the doctor
7 Include sources of further information
8 Use non-alarmist, non-patronizing language in active rather than passive voice
9 Make design structured and concise with good illustrations
10 Be explicit about authorship and sponsorship
11 Include reference to sources and strength of evidence
12 Include the publication date

Source: Coulter, A., Entwistle, V., & Gilbert, D. (1999). Sharing decisions with patients: Is the information good enough? *British Medical Journal, 318*, 318–322.

nature of the condition for which screening is being offered. Such information may be omitted based on a frequently erroneous assumption that familiarity with a term means familiarity with the condition. Thus, for example, while the great majority of people are familiar with diabetes and different types of cancers, there is a tendency to overestimate the severity of all cancers while underestimating the severity of diabetes (Farmer, Levy & Turner, 1999; Gigerenzer, 2002). Understanding the nature of a condition can be important in terms of influencing both representations of its prevention and treatment and, in turn, emotional and behavioural responses (Leventhal et al., 1997).

There have been relatively few studies documenting effective ways of increasing understanding about the nature of an illness. Morgan, Fischhoff, Bostrom and Atman (2002) describe a method of communicating about a threat, based on a mental models

approach to risk communication. This is based on a premise similar to that at the root of Leventhal's self-regulation model, namely that individuals actively process information within the confines of existing schemata. The starting point for communicating about a risk is therefore to elicit lay models using first open-ended interviews followed by confirmatory questionnaires to ascertain the prevalence of salient beliefs and misconceptions.

There are many different ways in which information about the likelihood of a condition can be given. These include the use of verbal descriptors (e.g., high or low risk), numerical expressions of likelihood expressed in language (e.g., absolute and relative risks, expressed as percentages, single event probabilities), or graphically. Such information can be framed positively (e.g., the chances of *not* developing a disease) or negatively (e.g., the chances of developing a disease). There is much debate about the most effective expressions and formats to use. To date, there have been too few comparable studies in clinical contexts for many patterns to emerge (Brun, 1993; Edwards, Elwyn, Covey, Matthews & Pill, 2001; Lipkus & Hollands, 1999). The one dimension of likelihood information where there has been sufficient research for a consensus to begin to emerge concerns the presentation of numerical expressions. Quantitative information is best understood when it is presented using simple frequencies (e.g., 1 in every 100 people) as opposed to single event probabilities (e.g., 0.01) or relative frequencies (percentages, e.g., 1 per cent) (Brase, 2002; Gigerenzer, 2002). In addition, people are better able to compare frequencies when they are presented using the same denominator. Thus, for example, pregnant women were more likely to correctly understand which of two risk estimates was larger when the information was presented as 2.6 versus 8.9 per 1,000 than when it was presented as 1 in 384 versus 1 in 112 (Grimes & Snively, 1999).

Understanding the likelihood of an outcome is, however, different from perceiving personal vulnerability. Thus, for example, smokers may perceive smoking as hazardous but perceive their own risks as lower than those of the average smoker (Weinstein, 1998). In a review of approaches to communicating health risk information, Rothman and Kiviniemi (1999) observe that informing people that particular behaviours can increase the probability of adverse health outcomes generally has little effect on perceptions of personal vulnerability. The authors attribute this in part to a misunderstanding of numerical information and in part to a minimizing or discounting of unfavourable health information. Attempts to overcome these motivational processes in order to motivate behaviour change have generally been unsuccessful (Weinstein & Klein, 1995; Weinstein, Sandman & Roberts, 1991). The relatively weak association between risk perception and behaviour (van der Pligt, 1998) suggests that altering risk perceptions may not be the most effective way of changing behaviour. This then raises the question of what people need to understand about a health threat for its communication to be considered effective. It

may be sufficient for individuals to appreciate that they have some vulnerability to a health threat in order for them to process further relevant information about a threat. The amount of vulnerability experienced may be less important than the fact that some vulnerability is experienced. If risk perceptions reflect fear minimization processes, with little effect on behaviour (Wiebe & Korbel, 2003), it perhaps should not be considered a failure of risk communication that an individual at higher than average risk perceives that they are vulnerable but that their level of vulnerability is lower than average.

Avoiding or Reducing Anxiety

Informing individuals of an increased chance of developing an illness is associated in the short term with raised general levels of anxiety (Shaw, Abrams & Marteau, 1999). After 1 month such anxiety is rarely evident. Anxiety is often an adaptive, initial response to health risk information (Cameron, 2003). It can enhance attention to health threats, elaborate representations and motivate behaviour to reduce threats. It is important, however, that the anxiety and fear generated by health risk information is manageable. A number of cognitive processes have been described which have the effect of minimizing the threat and resultant fear following the provision of health risk information. These include downplaying the seriousness of a problem (Croyle, Sun & Hart, 1997), downplaying the accuracy of the test (Ditto & Lopez, 1992) and unrealistic optimism (Weinstein, 1999). While these defensive processes reduce distress there is too little evidence to judge their impact upon risk reducing behaviour (Wiebe & Korbel, 2003). But while anxiety, particularly in the first few weeks after learning of a health risk, may signal the operation of adaptive processes, it can have adverse effects, particularly when it is excessively high and unabated by time, resulting in anxiety-infused information processing, and a focus upon short-term alleviation of anxiety.

Research effort in this area has focused upon two problems: first, high levels of short-term anxiety, particularly in those informed of increased risks of a cancer; and second, continued concern in those informed that the results of investigations are negative, indicating no problem.

Effective ways of preventing raised anxiety in those informed of an increased risk of disease include presenting information to prevent overestimation of the likelihood of having a significant health problem, a significant predictor of anxiety (Maissi et al., submitted). So, for example, women informed of an abnormal cervical smear test result are significantly less anxious when also informed that such a result is only rarely associated with cancer (Wilkinson, Jones & McBride, 1990). Such effects might be enhanced further by presenting the absolute chances of developing cervical cancer given such a test result. Given the association between perceived seriousness and vulnerability (Hendrickx, Vlek & Oppewal, 1989), interventions aimed at reducing the perceived severity of abnormal cervical smear test results might reduce perceived vulnerability and in turn levels of distress.

Many of those undergoing diagnostic tests, particularly following screening, will have no abnormalities detected. Despite this, some will experience continued concern. While simple reassurance can be very effective in reducing concern (Lucock et al., 1997; Watson, Hall, Langford & Marteau, 2002), it is less so for those with high health anxiety. In a prospective study of patients undergoing gastroscopy which revealed no serious illness, Lucock and colleagues (1997) showed that while oral reassurance from the physician that there was 'nothing seriously wrong' was effective in reducing worry for 24 hours, for those with high health anxiety the worry resurged after this point and was maintained 1 and 12 months later. These results may be explained by findings from a series of experimental analogue studies which suggest that informing someone concerned about their health that they are 'fine' can actually serve to increase their concern (Cioffi, 1994). For information to reassure in the face of uncertainty it needs to be presented in the same frame as the one the patient is using, that is to feature positive information. In one study, students were informed that they were either at low, moderate or high risk of developing a cancer caused by exposure to asbestos. Half of each group then received information about the number of healthy cells they had or the number of mutant cells. Those informed they were at moderate risk (maximum uncertainty) and who received information about the number of healthy cells in their body had least confidence in their health of all six experimental groups. Thus, someone concerned about their health is more likely to be made more concerned by informing them of the chances that they are well as opposed to the chances that they are ill.

In addition to the framing of the information designed to reassure, any explanation is more likely to be accepted and to provide reassurance if it fits with the individual's existing illness schema. This requires eliciting patients' illness schemata alongside their concerns in order that information can be provided that makes sense within that context. So, for example, if someone is presenting with headaches fearing a brain tumour, for which tests reveal no evidence, a reassuring explanation is likely to be one that elicits and maybe alters the existing schema of brain tumours and headaches to allow the one to exist without the other.

False Reassurance

The majority of health risk assessments and many diagnostic test procedures reveal no problems. Such results mean that there is a low chance, but rarely do they mean no chance, of developing or having the tested condition. Erroneously believing that a negative or normal test result means no residual risk may be associated with reinforcement of unhealthy lifestyles (Tymstra & Bieleman, 1987), delay in seeking help when symptoms of disease arise, as well as delay in health professionals responding to such symptoms (Petticrew et al., 2000), poorer adjustment (Hall, Bobrow & Marteau, 2000), and litigation (Petticrew et al., 2000). The challenge is how to present the meaning of a normal test result to avoid false reassurance, that is the belief that low risk means no risk, without inducing anxiety about the residual risk.

Until recently false reassurance was not widely considered a problem. The focus in health risk communication had been firmly upon avoiding disabling levels of anxiety, largely in response to the results of a study reporting the adverse effects upon work attendance of detecting hypertension in a group of steel workers (Haynes, Taylor & Sackett, 1979). The perceived need to avoid high levels of anxiety has probably unwittingly fed into a desire to present health risk assessments in an overly reassuring way. Thus information on test sensitivity (i.e., the proportion of cases a test can detect and, by implication, the proportion it cannot) is most often not given. For example, in an analysis of 58 leaflets describing breast cancer screening, information on the proportion of breast cancers detected by screening was mentioned in just 15 of them (Slaytor & Ward, 1998). In a study of HIV testing, five of 19 counsellors studied incorrectly informed an individual undergoing testing that it was impossible to get a false negative test result (Gigerenzer, Hoffrage & Ebert, 1998).

The few studies conducted to date attempting to avoid or reduce false reassurance show that using the term 'normal' to describe test results encourages false reassurance with as many as 50 per cent believing their results indicate no residual risk (Marteau, Senior & Sasieni, 2001). A range of verbal and numerical expressions to depict residual risk is effective at reducing rates of false reassurance in the short term (Marteau et al., 2000, 2001). While rates of false reassurance can be reduced, as many as 30 per cent in one study continued to be falsely reassured (Marteau et al., 2001), this being more marked in those with lower levels of education who were more likely to be falsely reassured. Further attempts to avoid false reassurance need to focus on this group in particular. There is also a need to understand the emotional and cognitive processes that affect longer-term recall. In one of the few studies assessing recall of the meaning of low risk test results over time, we found that while recall of residual risk was high immediately after testing, with over 90 per cent of participants correctly understanding that their negative test result meant that they had a very low (but not no) risk of being a carrier for cystic fibrosis, 3 years later only 50 per cent correctly recalled this, with over 43 per cent erroneously believing that they had no risk at all (Axworthy, Brock, Bobrow & Marteau, 1996). Such an erosion may reflect the operation of simplifying heuristics (low risk eventually becoming seen as no risk) or the operation of defensive biases, protecting individuals from perceiving themselves at continuing, albeit low levels of risk.

False reassurance is a concept implicit in risk homeostasis or risk compensation theory (Wilde, Robertson & Pless, 2002). This theory is based on two core assumptions. The first assumption is that people are utility maximizers, in that they will behave in the way that maximizes overall benefits. The second assumption is that people have an implicit level of risk that they consider acceptable. By acting to reduce a risk, for example by wearing a seat belt, this decreases their risk below the level they consider acceptable, resulting in behaviour that then increases their risk, for example by driving faster, back to their target level. While the evidence to support the theory and in particular the second premise are contested (McKenna, 2002; Robertson, 2002), it may have some merit as a general explanatory framework in accounting for the failure of many health promoting interventions to reduce risk. Given the well documented use of fear control processes (Croyle et al., 1997), it is plausible that acting to reduce a risk may result in an overestimation of the risk reduction achieved and an underestimation of the risks entailed in unchanged risk enhancing behaviours. Thus, increasing levels of physical activity may result in an overestimation of the risk so reduced, and an underestimation of the risk induced by continuing to smoke or eating a high fat diet.

Risk Information Fails to Result in Behaviour Change

Presenting risk information, including information based on biomarkers, infrequently leads to behaviour change (McClure, 2002).

For example, informing people of a genetic susceptibility to lung cancer does not result in smoking cessation (Audrain et al., 1997; McBride et al., 2002). Dietary change does not follow the provision of information about raised cholesterol (Strychar et al., 1998), nor is activity increased when individuals are informed of their cardiovascular unfitness (Godin, Desharnais, Jobin & Cook, 1987). Such findings reflect in part the limited impact of risk information upon risk perception (Avis, Smith & McKinlay, 1989; Kreuter & Strecher, 1995; Rothman & Kiviniemi, 1999), as well as the limited role that perceived risk plays in motivating behaviour change (van der Pligt, 1998).

The focus of presenting risk information has been upon communicating the likelihood of disease largely to the neglect of other key pieces of information (Rothman & Kiviniemi, 1999; Weinstein, 1999). Recent systematic review evidence shows the importance in motivation to change behaviour in the face of a health threat of not only perceiving the threat as likely, but also perceiving the threat as serious, the recommended behaviour as effective in reducing the risk, and the ability to perform the behaviour as existent (Floyd, Prentice-Dunn & Rogers, 2000; Milne, Sheeran & Orbell, 2000; Witte & Allen, 2000). Much of this research has been conducted using non-clinical samples, often in descriptive studies. The challenge now is to develop effective ways of communicating about these salient dimensions of a risk to motivate behaviour change in clinical populations.

While intention to perform a behaviour is a reliable predictor of actual behaviour, it accounts for between 20 and 30 per cent of the variance (Sheeran, 2002; Sutton, 1998). Many models of health behaviour draw a distinction between intention to engage in a behaviour and the enactment of that intention (Schwarzer, 1992; Sheeran, 2002). It appears that thinking about future behaviour in relation to specific environmental cues of when, where and how to enact a particular behaviour increases the frequency of that behaviour. So, for example, students were more likely to have a tetanus inoculation when the fear message was accompanied by details of where on campus the inoculation could be obtained (Leventhal, Singer & Jones, 1965). More recently action plans have been studied under a new name of implementation intentions (Gollwitzer, 1999). These take the form of individuals writing when, where and how they will enact a particular behaviour. This includes taking vitamin tablets, undergoing exercise, and attending for screening (Sheeran, 2002). While this approach shows much promise, its effectiveness in non-student samples awaits further studies.

Anticipating the negative emotion of regret can also result in people being more likely to engage in behaviour to reduce risks. Thus, those asked to focus on how they would feel were they to experience a related adverse outcome having *not* engaged in a recommended preventive action are more likely to perform the action (Parker, Stradling & Manstead, 1996; Richard, van der Pligt & De Vries, 1995). Anticipated regret has an effect by strengthening the association between intentions and behaviour, thereby reducing the widely acknowledged gap between intentions and behaviour (Abraham & Sheeran, 2003).

THE STRESS OF SURGERY

The Nature of the Problem

There are many situations and contexts in health care where routine communication or communication-based interventions can have important effects on patient wellbeing. This is particularly true for patients coping with medical procedures, which can be painful or distressing. One of these, surgery, has also been found to produce significant adverse emotional effects (Johnston & Wallace, 1990; Kiecolt-Glaser, Page, Marucka, MacCallum & Glaser, 1998), the extent of which will depend on its severity and duration, as well as on psychological factors such as the patient's expectations and coping style and the quality of health care communication.

Recovery from surgery is both multidimensional and variable (Johnston, 1984). There are many indices of recovery, including mood, pain, wound healing and length of hospital stay. Studies that have examined patterns of post-operative recovery provide clear evidence that, whatever recovery index is used, there is considerable variation between patients who have undergone the same surgical procedure. Even for discrete procedures such as minimal access (keyhole) surgery, some patients show rapid return to full function whereas others may take a significantly longer time (McGinn et al., 1995; Schlumpf, Klotz, Wehrli & Herzog, 1994). Moreover, for some quite widely used surgical procedures, some patients may fail to obtain therapeutic benefit. For example, following surgery for a lumbar spinal stenosis, approximately one-third of patients fail to benefit substantially (Turner, Ersek, Hernon & Deyo, 1992). In contrast, there is recent evidence that for another widely used surgical procedure, knee arthroscopy, patients who have undergone 'placebo surgery' show a very similar pattern of post-operative recovery to those patients who have received the full surgical intervention (Mosely et al., 2002).

The determinants of this variability are multifactorial and depend on a range of physical, contextual and psychosocial factors (e.g., Iverson, Daltroy, Fossel & Katz, 1998). One factor, which has been investigated quite extensively, is the pre-operative mood of the patient, particularly their level of state anxiety, which, in turn, may reflect their level of preparedness for the surgery. A large number of studies have investigated the relation between pre-operative mood and post-operative recovery, and the majority have demonstrated a link between the greater anxiety or distress and a range of recovery indicators (see Munafo & Stevenson, 2001, for a review). Early researchers (Janis, 1958) proposed a curvilinear relation between pre-operative distress and recovery but subsequent work indicates that this is more likely to be linear (e.g., Johnston & Carpenter, 1980). Thus patients with higher levels of pre-operative anxiety or distress report more post-operative pain, negative mood and poorer recovery (Munafo & Stevenson, 2001). There is also experimental evidence which has shown that stress slows the speed of wound healing and has implicated the

role of the immune system in this process (Kiecolt-Glaser et al., 1998).

The ways in which pre-operative anxiety influences post-operative recovery are not clearly understood. Some studies (e.g., Kain, Sevarino, Alexander, Pincus & Mayes, 2000) have used path analysis of data collected at multiple time points and have proposed that anxiety has a critical role in the chain of events influencing post-operative pain levels and responses. In contrast, other researchers maintain that the apparent influence of anxiety on recovery is explained by its association with pre-operative function and fatigue. Hence Salmon, Hall and Peerbhoy (2001) propose that while emotional response to surgery partly predicts post-operative recovery, the critical component of emotion is fatigue rather than anxiety.

Patients' emotional responses prior to surgery relate to concerns about the procedure and the outcome (Weinman & Johnston, 1988). Patients have been found to experience emotional reactions, such as fear of surgery and anaesthesia, as well as lack of information about medical details, the roles of different health care professionals and discharge from hospital (Breemhar, van den Borne & Mullen, 1996). To a large part these problems are caused by inadequate information provision which, in turn, may be due to a range of organizational barriers. One large recent study of over 3,000 surgical patients has sought to investigate the difficulties patients have in obtaining information and the ways in which this can affect the patients' evaluation of their experience in hospital (Krupat, Fancey & Cleary, 2000). This study identified four distinct information factors, namely surgical information, recovery information, sensory information and general information, each of which was related to patients' evaluations. They also showed that individual patient factors, such as desire for information and perceived control, were important in moderating and mediating the value and impact of information in determining patients' responses to impending surgery.

Some of these individual difference factors will be considered in more detail later, but the general point to be made here is that lack of patient preparation for surgery and the consequent effects on emotional reactions provide one explanation for the variability in patient recovery. Another potentially influential pre-operative determinant of recovery, which can be influenced by the level of preparation or information provided, is the patient's expectation regarding the surgery. There is a small recent literature on the role of patients' expectations in post-operative recovery and this provides clear evidence that these can influence such factors as pain, functional recovery and satisfaction (Iverson et al., 1998; McCarthy, Lyons, Weinman, Talbot & Purnell, 2003).

This brief overview of pre-operative psychosocial influences on post-operative recovery points to the potential value of different types of communication in preparing patients for surgery. The next section describes a range of approaches to pre-operative psychological preparation and examines the evidence for their efficacy.

Psychological Interventions for Stressful Medical Procedures

Since studies have shown a relation between patients' psychological state and their recovery, it has been recognized that there could be considerable gains from providing a psychological intervention designed to reduce or minimize the psychological impact of a medical procedure. There is a range of interventions that have been used to prepare patients for surgery or other stressful procedures in the hospital setting. In broad terms they can help by providing the patient with information to reduce the uncertainty of the event, or with specific behavioural or cognitive skills to help with some of the discomfort or pain. The main approaches are as follows.

Procedural information

This is probably the most widely used approach and consists of providing information about the various procedures that will take place before and after the operation. It therefore involves the patient being provided with information about what will happen to them at different stages pre- and post-operatively.

Sometimes this information is also accompanied by an explanation of the purpose of each of the procedures that are described. Thus it provides the patient with a realistic set of expectations about the events that will occur and, in doing so, can reduce the uncertainty of the whole process.

Sensory information

This describes what patients are likely to feel, particularly during the immediate post-operative pain period. The function of this information is to provide matter-of-fact or benign interpretations of the sensations so that the patient can recognize them as part of the expected post-operative process. Thus the patient who can recognize post-operative pain as an expected sensation caused by the incision and reflecting the healing process will be far less likely to be distressed than someone who has not been prepared for the pain and who may think of it as a problem or a complication of the surgery.

Contrada, Leventhal and Anderson (1994) have discussed the benefits of sensory and procedural information from the perspective of the self-regulatory model. They propose that the sensory preparation serves to provide a script which describes internal sensations, and that the procedural preparation provides a script of the objective external events involved in surgery. They maintain that it is the availability of the script which reduces uncertainty and worry for the patient. More specifically, sensory information should be particularly helpful since it focuses on potentially threatening sensations (e.g., pain, discomfort) with the aim of ensuring that these are processed as non-threatening or less threatening. However, evidence on the efficacy of both types of preparatory information indicates that procedural information is at least, if not more, effective in producing favourable post-operative outcomes (Johnston & Vogele, 1993: see below).

Behavioural instructions

These typically describe different behaviours that the patient can use to help before, during and after surgery. These include instructions about ways to cough and move in bed that will reduce the likelihood of pain associated with these movements. Other behavioural instructions such as deep breathing and ambulation exercises may also reduce the incidence of pain or complications as well as facilitating recovery.

Modelling

This is based on the use of filmed models who can be seen undergoing the same procedure as the patient. Following Bandura's (1986) social learning theory, modelling or the observation of others completing a difficult or stressful task can serve to increase the individual's sense of self-efficacy for managing the same task. Two main types of model have been investigated: mastery models, who are shown dealing with the task with ease and ability; and coping models, who are shown as having some anticipated concerns but who nevertheless are able to overcome these and cope with the procedure. The coping type of model has been found to be a more effective preparation for children undergoing surgery. For example in a study of children about to be inoculated, Vernon (1974) has compared a group of children who saw a preparatory film which was 'realistic' (the child in the film is seen to experience short-lived, moderate pain and emotion) with a group who saw an 'unrealistic' film (the child shows no pain or emotional expression) and a group who saw no preparatory film. The realistically prepared group were found to experience least pain when receiving their injections. These methods have been more widely used with children than with adults, particularly since it may be more difficult to provide children with sensory or procedural information or behavioural instructions in a helpful way.

Relaxation-based interventions

These can involve a number of different techniques, including deep breathing, progressive muscle relaxation or, less frequently, hypnosis. Relaxation can be used both to provide a general preparation involving anxiety reduction and as a specific skill which can be used

post-operatively for coping with pain and discomfort at times of increased stress or tension.

Cognitive coping procedures

These focus on patients' concerns and fears about the surgery and assist in dealing with them in one of two ways. First, they may make use of coping strategies that the patient has used successfully in the past for coping with stressors, enabling the patient to rehearse and apply these in the surgical context (Langer, Janis & Wolfer, 1975). The second cognitive approach involves coping with negative thoughts by distracting attention from them and by focusing on positive aspects of the surgery and repeating positive self-statements (Ridgeway & Mathews, 1982).

The efficacy of these interventions has been evaluated by examining their effects on a range of post-surgical outcomes, including anxiety, pain and use of pain medication, length of stay in hospital and various indicators of recovery. All the interventions have been found to be successful in improving at least one outcome and the majority have a positive impact on many of the outcomes. The different interventions have been examined and compared systematically in a meta-analysis by Johnston and Vogele (1993). Across the range of outcomes, the largest recovery effects were obtained for pain, negative affect and physiological indices of recovery but there was considerable variation in the magnitude of these effects. Smaller but more consistent advantages of psychological preparation were found on pain medication and length of hospital stay. The interventions that had the most widespread effects on all the outcomes were found to be procedural information provision and behavioural instructions. Relaxation was also found to have beneficial effects on the various outcomes. Whereas Mathews and Ridgeway (1984) had indicated that cognitive coping interventions were most likely to have the greatest efficacy, the meta-analysis results show that their effects appear to be restricted to specific outcomes. Thus cognitive interventions have been shown to have positive effects on negative affect, pain and use of pain medication, and clinical recovery, but do not appear to result in shorter lengths of stay or in improved physiological indices or behavioural recovery. Surprisingly, in view of the importance attached to patient evaluations of health care, only a few studies have examined the effects of these interventions on patient satisfaction but these show quite positive results, indicating that patients view them as acceptable and helpful.

There is now considerable evidence to indicate that different types of psychological preparation can not only reduce the anxiety, stress and pain involved in many medical procedures but also generate considerable related benefits (e.g., less analgesia, better recovery, faster discharge etc.). Although each of the different approaches has been described separately here, they can easily be used in conjunction and often are. What is encouraging from the research and reviews of psychological preparation for surgery is that they show that it is possible to intervene effectively using relatively uncomplicated procedures. Moreover, there is now sufficient information about their efficacy to be confident in recommending that they should be included as routine components of standard medical and nursing care for all patients undergoing surgery.

All the interventions outlined above are relatively brief and can be readily incorporated into routine clinical care, provided that the health care professionals involved are appropriately trained to deliver them. However, there is also evidence that pre-operative patients can gain useful information from fellow patients and that this can also influence post-operative recovery. This evidence comes from an elegant series of studies by Kulik and colleagues (Kulik & Mahler, 1987; Kulik, Mahler & Moore, 1996), who have examined the effects on pre-operative patients of having a roommate who has either undergone or is about to undergo the same operation or a different procedure. Their findings showed the importance of social contact in the recovery of patients following surgery. In their early study, they compared the effects of sharing a room either with a patient who was also about to

undergo cardiac surgery or with one who had already had the same operation. The results showed clear beneficial effects of sharing a room with someone who was recovering from surgery. The patients who had post-surgical roommates were less anxious prior to surgery, engaged in more post-surgical physical activity and were discharged sooner (Kulik & Mahler, 1987). In a more recent variation on this study, they investigated two further variables, namely having a roommate or being on one's own, and having a roommate who was about to undergo or had gone through the same or different type of operation. In addition to replicating their earlier findings respective to the advantage of sharing with a post-surgical patient, they also found that it was advantageous to share with a post-surgical patient who had undergone the same type of surgery and that those who were in rooms on their own had the slowest recovery (Kulik et al., 1996).

From a communications perspective, these results are important for a number of reasons. They serve as a reminder that information from health care professionals is not the only form of communication that can influence the adjustment to and recovery from stressful medical procedures. Important preparatory and other useful information may be communicated verbally and non-verbally from one patient to another, and this can have considerable impact. There is clearly scope for structuring ward environments in order to maximize positive influences of fellow patients on the response to and recovery from surgery.

Pre-Operative Preparation: Is There a Need for More Individually Tailored Approaches?

One of the problems with many of the intervention methods outlined and evaluated above is that they often come as a fixed package, regardless of the level of the pre-operative patient's informational needs or coping style. Surgery is a potential stressor for the patient, and it is known from the broader stress research literature that people cope in a range of ways, which are partly dependent on dispositional factors and partly on their appraisal of the stressor and their own coping capability (Folkman & Lazarus, 1980). One psychological dimension that pervades this research is linked to approach-avoidance, and has been investigated in a number of ways in the study of coping with surgery. Miller and Mangan (1983) have grouped individuals as 'monitors' or 'blunters', according to the extent to which they cope with a stressor in a more vigilant (monitoring) or avoidant (blunting) way, whereas others have used a more general coping style classification (e.g., Krohne, Slangen & Kleemann, 1996; Lazarus & Folkman, 1984). Broadly these studies show that those patients who typically use more avoidant approaches to coping find it most helpful to be given relatively little preparation information, and may react negatively to the provision of more detailed information. Conversely the more vigilant or monitoring copers find more detailed information more helpful in preparing for and recovering from surgery.

Recent overviews of tailored approaches to informational interventions provide further support but raise the practical question of how such tailoring can be incorporated into the routine clinical setting. One obvious approach is to adopt computer-based methods in which the level and type of preparatory information can be determined by the individual patient. These approaches can combine text, images and video sequences to provide different sorts of preparatory information. There are good recent examples of the efficacy of video information for preparing patients for a range of surgical procedures, including cardiac surgery (Roth-Isigkeit et al., 2002) and surgery for osteoarthritis of the knee (Ayral, Gicquere, Duhalde, Boucheny & Dougados, 2002).

ADHERENCE TO TREATMENT

The Nature of the Problem

The failure of many patients to follow recommended treatment or advice is now regarded as a major problem in health care. This is usually referred to as non-compliance or non-adherence, although the latter term tends to be used more widely now. Adherence has been defined as 'the extent to which the patient's behaviour coincides with the clinical prescription' (Sackett & Haynes, 1976). Alternatively, non-adherence has been defined as 'the point below which the desired preventative or desired therapeutic result is unlikely to be achieved' (Gordis, 1976). Problems of adherence have been observed across a wide range of medical recommendations, including pill taking, returning for follow-up appointments, and following behaviour change advice for primary, secondary or tertiary prevention.

Low rates of adherence to recommended treatment are found in most chronic diseases including asthma (Hand, 1998), diabetes (Strychar et al., 1998), heart disease (Rich, Gray, Beckham, Wittenberg & Luther, 1996), cancer (Lilleyman & Lennard, 1996), HIV (Paterson et al., 2000) and kidney disease (Cleary, Matzke, Alexander & Joy, 1995), as well as in psychological treatments such as relaxation training for anxiety-related disorders (Taylor, Agras, Schneider & Allen, 1983). The incidence of non-adherence varies greatly, converging at 30–50 per cent in chronic illness (Haynes et al., 1979; Meichenbaum & Turk, 1987). In the area of primary prevention, it has been found that many participants drop out of lifestyle change programmes designed to improve diet or reduce health risk behaviours (Brownell & Cohen, 1995). Even patients who have experienced major health problems, such as heart attacks, may show low levels of uptake of rehabilitation programmes as well as considerable variation in the adoption of recommended lifestyle change (Petrie, Weinman, Sharpe & Buckley, 1996).

Non-adherence may be categorized in many ways but one useful distinction is between those that are active and those that are passive. Active non-adherence arises when the patient decides not to take the treatment as instructed. From a self-regulatory perspective, the level of treatment adherence may reflect a strategic coping response that is entirely consistent with the patient's view of their problem (Leventhal & Cameron, 1987). Thus, if patients believe that their problem will not last for long, they will be less likely to adhere to their medication over a long period of time than those who perceive their condition as more long-lasting (Meyer et al., 1985). Passive non-adherence may be unintentional when it is caused by barriers such as forgetting, and inability to follow treatment instructions because of a lack of understanding or because of physical problems such as poor eyesight or impaired manual dexterity. Similarly, if the quality of communication is poor and patients receive information that is difficult to understand or recall, as has been outlined above, then this reduces the likelihood that treatment will be adhered to (Ley, 1988).

One of the major problems with all adherence research is the difficulty in obtaining accurate measures. Many different measures have been used to provide both direct and indirect markers of adherence, including tracers of metabolized medications, pill counts, electronically monitored pill bottle tops or inhalers, self-reports and the effects on health or illness outcomes (see Myers & Midence, 1998, for a review). These methods vary in their accuracy and, since none can provide an exact measure, many of the better studies have included multiple measures to provide triangulation and greater reliability. Despite these inherent problems, the evidence of the prevalence of non-adherence is widespread and, if anything, the problems of measurement probably mean that the empirical data represent an underestimation of the true extent of the problem.

The Effects of Low Adherence

Even though there are continuing problems in defining, assessing and explaining variations in adherence behaviours, there are clear reasons why low adherence is a major problem in health care. First, and most obvious, patients who are non-adherent are much less likely to gain benefit from their treatment or advice. The relation between treatment adherence and outcome is a complex one that depends on a number of factors, as has been shown in a recent meta-analysis (DiMatteo, Giordani, Lepper & Croghan, 2002). This examined and

integrated the findings from 63 studies that varied considerably in sample size, patient group and study design. The overall relation between adherence and outcome was found to be positive with an effect size of 0.21, and with the great majority of studies ($n = 51$) showing a significant positive effect. The results indicate that greater adherence reduces the risk of a null or poor treatment outcome by 26 per cent, and that a good treatment outcome is three times more likely to be found in those who have been highly adherent. Although these effects were found to be moderated by the type of disease and treatment, it is notable that the overall effect size is broadly similar to that found in a similar review of patients receiving treatment for coronary heart disease (McDermott, Schmitt & Wallner, 1997) and to that found in a recent meta-analysis of disease management interventions in chronic illness (Weingarten et al., 2002).

In addition to the predicted adherence–outcome relation, there is also evidence now that higher adherence can produce positive effects on outcome by way of indirect factors, such as the patient's expectations. A revealing study by Horwitz et al. (1990) compared the treatment responses of adherent and non-adherent patients to medication for myocardial infarction. This involved a group of patients in a large randomized controlled trial, in which half were randomized to the active treatment (propanalol) and half to the placebo treatment. Unlike the majority of randomized controlled trials, which either ignore or screen out non-adherence, this study made a special effort to assess the adherence of all the participants, who were then categorized as adherent or non-adherent. The comparative advantages found for the adherers on a range of outcomes, including mortality, were very similar for those on the active treatment and the placebo. These findings, which have also been shown in studies with other treatments, indicate that good adherence to any treatment, even when it is a placebo, results in a better outcome, even when factors such as illness severity, comorbidity, and psychosocial differences are taken into account. Thus, for patients, a further disadvantage of low treatment adherence, over and above the obvious lack of any clinical therapeutic effect, is that they are not able to benefit from the considerable non-specific (i.e., placebo) effects which are found with any treatment (Richardson, 1997).

The Determinants of Non-Adherence

From the accumulated research evidence on factors associated with non-adherence, it now seems untenable to accept the idea of a 'non-compliant type' in terms of fixed individual or social characteristics. An early systematic review of 185 studies (Sackett & Haynes, 1976) revealed no clear relationship between race, gender, educational experience, intelligence, marital status, occupational status, income and ethnic or cultural background and adherence behaviours. Moreover, there is little evidence that adherence behaviours can be explained in terms of personality characteristics (Becker, 1979; Bosley, Fosbury & Cochrane, 1995; McKim, Stones & Kozma, 1990). Also the idea that stable socio-demographic or dispositional characteristics are the sole determinants of adherence is discredited by evidence that an individual's levels of adherence may vary over time and between different aspects of the treatment regimen (Cleary et al., 1995; Hilbrands, Hoitsma & Koene, 1995). This limitation also applies to the search for disease and treatment characteristics as antecedents of adherence since there are wide variations in adherence between and within patients with the same disease and treatment (e.g., Cleary et al., 1995; Lilleyman & Lennard, 1996).

One simple explanation for non-adherence is that patients lack basic knowledge about their medication (Cartwright, 1994; Eagleton, Walker & Barber, 1993), but again this does not provide a complete explanation. In a systematic review of the adherence literature Haynes (1976) concluded that, although 12 studies had demonstrated a positive association between knowledge and adherence, there were more that had failed to demonstrate a link. Studies conducted since that time generally indicate that associations between knowledge and adherence are at best small and inconsistent

(Eagleton et al., 1993) and, as will be seen below, information-based interventions do not consistently result in increased levels of adherence (Haynes, Sackett, Taylor, Gibson & Johnson, 1978; Roter, Hall et al., 1998). Patient satisfaction may act as a mediator between information provision, recall and adherence, as would be predicted by Ley's model which was outlined earlier. In a national UK survey of patients' satisfaction with medicines information, over 70 per cent of respondents wanted more information than they were given (Gibbs & George, 1990). Dissatisfaction with the amount of information and explanation provided may also act as a barrier to adherence by making the patient less motivated towards treatment (Hall et al., 1988).

Adherence research has stopped trying to identify stable trait factors which characterize the non-adherent patient and now places a greater emphasis on understanding those patient cognitions which could explain why they decide to take some treatments and not others (Horne, 1998). The application of social cognition models in research indicates that medication non-adherence may arise from a rational decision on the part of the patient and identifies some of the cognitions that are salient to these decisions, particularly for the more active or intentional types of non-adherence. Although there is some variation in the specific type of beliefs that are associated with adherence across studies, the findings show that certain cognitive variables included in the health belief model (HBM: Janz & Becker, 1984) and the theory of planned behaviour (TPB: Ajzen, 1988) appear to predict adherence in certain situations. For example, higher rates of adherence have been found in patients who believe that failure to take the treatment could result in adverse consequences and that they are personally susceptible to these effects (Cummings, Becker, Kirscht & Levin, 1981; Kelly, Mannon & Scott, 1987; Nelson, Stason, Neutra, Soloman & McArdle, 1978). Additionally, adherence decisions may be influenced by a cost–benefit analysis in which the *benefits* of treatment are weighted against the perceived *barriers* (Brownlee-Duffeck et al., 1987; Cummings et al., 1981; Nelson et al., 1978). Other studies based on the TPB have shown that the perceived views of significant others such as family, friends and doctors (*normative beliefs*) may also influence adherence (Cochrane & Gitlin, 1988; Reid & Christensen, 1988). Several studies have demonstrated the value of interventions based on the HBM in facilitating health-related behaviours, such as attending for medical check-ups (Haefner & Kirscht, 1970), or using emergency care facilities in an acute asthma attack (Jones, Jones & Katz, 1987).

A more dynamic cognitive approach which has been used to explain non-adherence is Leventhal's self-regulatory model (Leventhal, Brisette & Leventhal, 2003), which acknowledges the importance of symptom perception in influencing illness representations which, in turn, direct coping responses, including adherence behaviour. Early evidence for this approach is provided by findings from a study of patients with diabetes who used perceived symptoms to indicate their blood glucose levels and to guide self-treatment (Gonder-Frederick & Cox, 1991). However, patients' beliefs about their symptoms, and estimations of their own blood glucose levels, were often erroneous and resulted in poor diabetic control. Further evidence of the role of illness representations in adherence has been found in patients with hypertension (Meyer et al., 1985). Patients who believed that their hypertension was an acute condition were less likely to continue taking anti-hypertensive medication than those who believed it to be a chronic condition. This study also showed that patients' representations of their illness often conflicted with the medical view and provided an insight into the effects of mismatch between the patients' representations and those of their doctor. In a group of 50 patients who had continued in treatment, 80 per cent agreed with the statement that 'people cannot tell when their blood pressure is up'. However, 92 per cent believed that they could tell when their own blood pressure was raised by monitoring symptoms such as tiredness, headache and stress. Patients who believed their anti-hypertensive medication improved symptoms were more likely to adhere, which is consistent with more

recent research on patients' beliefs about the necessity of taking their medication (Horne, 2003: see below).

Illness perceptions have been linked with a range of adherence-related behaviours. These include various self-management behaviours, such as dietary control and blood glucose testing in diabetes, attending rehabilitation and the adoption of various lifestyle changes following myocardial infarction. In studies of non-insulin dependent diabetic patients, Hampson and colleagues have shown that personal models of diabetes are related to dietary self-management and to exercise adherence but not to the more medical aspects of control, such as blood glucose testing and taking medication (Hampson, 1997). Similarly, prospective studies of patients following first-time myocardial infarction (MI) have found that specific illness perceptions are predictive of different post-MI behaviours. Attendance at rehabilitation, which is prescribed for all patients, was predicted by the strength of their belief in the cure/control of their MI (Cooper, Lloyd, Weinman & Jackson, 1999; Petrie et al., 1996) whereas return to work depended more on the extent to which the patient saw their MI as having less serious consequences (Petrie et al., 1996). However, a number of studies have failed to show direct relations between illness perceptions and adherence levels, and have forced researchers to search for more specific cognitive predictors, focusing on beliefs about treatment. There is a small body of earlier work that has examined people's beliefs about medicines and the ways in which these could influence adherence (Britten, 1994; Conrad, 1985; Donovan & Blake, 1992; Morgan & Watkins, 1988). The negative beliefs about medicines identified in these studies appear to be common across several illness and cultural groups and include worries about the possible harmful effects of medicines and about long-term dependence on them.

More systematic recent research by Horne and colleagues (Horne, 2003; Horne, Weinman & Hankins, 1999) indicates that four 'core themes' or factors underlie commonly held beliefs about medicines. Factor analysis of a pool of belief statements revealed two broad factors describing people's beliefs about their prescribed medicines: their perceived necessity for maintaining health (*specific necessity*) and concerns based on beliefs about the potential for dependence or harmful long-term effects and that medication taking is disruptive (*specific concerns*). Two factors were also found to describe people's beliefs about medicines in general. The first relates to the intrinsic properties of medicines and the extent to which they are harmful, addictive substances (*general harm*), and the second comprises views about whether medicines are overused by doctors (*general overuse*).

People's views about the specific medication regimen prescribed for them were more strongly related to adherence reports than were more general views about medicines as a whole. Moreover, an interplay was found between concerns and necessity beliefs, which suggests that people engage in a risk–benefit analysis and consequently attempt to moderate the perceived potential for harm by taking less. Patients with stronger concerns based on beliefs about the potential for long-term effects and dependence reported lower adherence rates, whilst those with stronger beliefs in the necessity of their medication reported greater adherence to medication regimen (Horne, 2003; Horne et al., 1999). This research also showed that, although illness perceptions can explain variance in adherence, they may play a more important role in determining treatment beliefs. For example, in a study of factors influencing adherence to prevention medication, stronger beliefs about the necessity of taking this treatment were found in patients who perceived their asthma as a more chronic condition with more negative consequences (Horne & Weinman, 2002).

Another consistent determinant of adherence behaviour is the affective state of the patient. Negative affect, particularly depression, has been shown in a meta-analysis to be associated with lower levels of adherence to a wide range of treatments (DiMatteo, Lepper & Croghan, 2000). There are a number of ways in which depression could exert an influence on adherence behaviours. The negative cognitions associated with depressive states may well

generalize to patients' beliefs about their illness and treatment. Hence, in those with a physical illness, and who are also depressed, illness may be perceived as less controllable and with more negative consequences. Similarly, medications may also be perceived as having more negative side effects or as less potentially efficacious, as part of the generalized hopelessness experienced in depression (DiMatteo et al., 2000).

Interventions to Improve Adherence

The evidence that low rates of adherence are so widespread in health care at all levels from primary prevention to treatment for chronic conditions has provided the impetus for the development of a wide range of interventions. Many of the earlier attempts were predominantly information-based and sought to improve adherence by increasing patient knowledge and understanding. Although these achieved some small positive effects, they were generally of limited impact since behaviour change is very unlikely to be activated by information provision. Hence a range of other methods has been developed, and these have been described and evaluated in a number of reviews and meta-analyses (e.g., Haynes et al., 1996; Kok, van den Borne & Dolan Mullen, 1997; Macharia, Leon, Rowe, Stephenson & Haynes, 1992; Mullen, Green & Persinger, 1985; Roter, Hall et al., 1998). These studies have varied considerably in the nature of the intervention, the patient group and the study design. Roter, Hall et al. (1998) have grouped these interventions into four broad categories as follows.

Educational

These interventions are primarily concerned with the provision of information to increase the knowledge of the patients about their treatment and/or their illness (e.g., Barth, Campbell, Allen, Jupp & Chisholm, 1991; Gonzalez-Fernandez, Rivera, Torres, Quiles & Jackson, 1990). The information in these interventions has been provided in a number of differing formats (e.g., spoken, written, audiovisual) and has been presented in a range of ways (e.g., one-to-one, groups, by mail or telephone etc.).

Behavioural

These interventions are characterized by their use of basic behavioural principles (e.g., Grady, Goodenow & Borkin, 1988; Tucker, 1989). Thus they have been designed to work by targeting, shaping or reinforcing adherence behaviours to either ensure their adoption or increase their frequency. A range of approaches has been tried including the use of goal setting, financial rewards, contracts, skill building and behavioural modelling. As with the educational approaches described above, the behavioural interventions have been presented in a number of ways and contexts.

Affective

The affectively based methods comprise a range of approaches which attempt to influence by way of appeals to the patient's emotions or by involving their social networks, particularly by using their social supports (Jay, DuRant, Shoffitt, Linder & Litt, 1984; Kellaway & McCrae, 1979). They include the use of various counselling approaches as well as the involvement of other family members to support the patient in their attempts to change and maintain their behaviour. They have been rarely used in isolation and are more commonly part of a broader intervention strategy.

Provider focused

Since it is now recognized that the behaviour of the health care professional in the consultation can have considerable effects on the subsequent affective, behavioural and health outcomes for the patient (Stewart et al., 1995), it is not surprising that approaches have been developed to change clinicians' behaviour in order to improve patient adherence. These typically involve specific training interventions for doctors, nurses or pharmacists to increase adherence through improved communication, usually with clearer information and behavioural instructions (e.g., Berger et al., 1990).

Thus they rely on changing clinicians' behaviour in the first place, using a range of training methods and often with cues or reminders to activate the learned skills at appropriate times.

In many adherence intervention studies these approaches are used in combination to achieve maximum effect, but there have been a reasonably large number of studies that have used either educational or behavioural methods on their own (see Roter, Hall et al., 1998). One other important factor, which needs to be considered in categorizing adherence intervention strategies, is the extent to which they are based on a theory or model of adherence behaviour as well as a theory of behaviour change. For the most part, the interventions have not paid much or any attention to the determinants of non-adherence, and comparatively few take a theoretically based approach to changing adherence behaviour.

These interventions have been evaluated in terms of their effects on a wide range of adherence indicators and related outcomes with mixed success. The Roter, Hall et al. (1998) meta-analysis reveals a mixed pattern of efficacy of the various categories, but the broad picture is moderately optimistic since most types of intervention produce at least weak effects on adherence. No single type of intervention was shown to be clearly stronger than any other type but there is consistent evidence that those which used a range of methods are more effective than those which have a single focus. The overall finding was that the most powerful interventions included a blend of educational, behavioural and affective approaches, a conclusion similar to that found in an earlier review of patient education programmes in chronic illness (Mullen et al., 1985). From a health education perspective it is acknowledged not only that people vary in their preferences for different types of input but also that having a variety of approaches is a good way of increasing and maintaining learner interest (Green, Kreuter, Deeds & Partridge, 1980).

The meta-analysis also showed that evaluating the efficacy of any intervention depended very much on the type of outcome used. Interventions generally had their strongest effects on indirect measures of medication use, such as pill counts or refill records. Also, those studies that used refill records showed bigger effects than those relying on pill count measures, and that intervention effects on appointment making were consistently greater than the effects on appointment keeping. Both of these findings are taken to indicate the levels of commitment reflected in these different types of adherence indicator. Thus, while adherence interventions may have quite strong effects on patients' intentions, a range of other factors will ultimately determine the extent to which intentions are translated into behaviours.

Implications for Communication

As with the approaches described earlier in this chapter, there is increasing evidence that, in order to improve patient adherence, communication needs to be tailored to make it personally salient to the individual patient. Hence effective adherence interventions will not only need to be multidimensional in their focus but also need to take account of patients' pre-existing understanding and beliefs. One example of an intervention that has done this successfully was reported by Petrie et al. (2002), and was described earlier in this chapter.

CONCLUDING COMMENT

The concept of effective communication has now broadened from an earlier focus upon patient satisfaction to one that incorporates engaging patients in their care. Such a broadening reflects a change in the political climate towards a consumerist role for patients. It also reflects the behavioural science evidence presented in this chapter, that to realize the benefits of predictive and therapeutic medicine requires communicating with patients from diverse social and cultural backgrounds to achieve an understanding commensurate with the problem being faced. Achieving such engagement requires specific communication skills to elicit and to work with patient representations as well as a broader appreciation of the patient's social and cultural context. The challenge now is for health psychologists to generate evidence to increase our understanding of how representations of patients from diverse social and cultural groups are most effectively elicited and used in clinical consultations. This will form the basis for evidence-based training of health care professionals.

REFERENCES

Abraham, C., & Sheeran, P. (2003). Acting on intentions: The role of anticipated regret. *British Journal of Social Psychology, 42,* 495–511.

Ajzen, I. (1988). *Attitudes, personality, and behavior.* Buckingham, UK: Open University Press.

Audrain, J., Boyd, N. R., Roth, J., Main, D., Caporaso, N. F., & Lerman, C. (1997). Genetic susceptibility testing in smoking-cessation treatment: One-year outcomes of a randomized trial. *Addictive Behaviors, 22,* 741–751.

Avis, N. E., Smith, K. W., & McKinlay, J. B. (1989). Accuracy of perceptions of heart attack risk: What influences perceptions and can they be changed? *American Journal of Public Health, 79,* 1608–1612.

Axworthy, D., Brock, D. J. H., Bobrow, M., & Marteau, T. M. (1996). Psychological impact of population-based carrier testing for cystic fibrosis: Three year follow-up. *Lancet, 347,* 1443–1446.

Ayral, X., Gicquere, C., Duhalde, A., Boucheny, D., & Dougados, M. (2002). Effects of video information on preoperative anxiety level and tolerability of joint lavage in knee osteoarthritis. *Arthritis and Rheumatism, 47,* 380–382.

Bain, D. J. (1977). Patient knowledge and the content of the consultation in general practice. *Medical Education, 11,* 347–350.

Bandura, A. (1986). *Social foundations of thought and action: A social cognitive theory.* Englewood Cliffs, NJ: Prentice-Hall.

Bandura, A. (1997). *Self-efficacy: The exercise of control.* New York: Freeman.

Barth, R., Campbell, L. V., Allen, S., Jupp, J. J., & Chisholm, D. J. (1991). Intensive education improves knowledge, compliance, and foot problems in type 2 diabetes. *Diabetic Medicine, 8,* 111.

Baumann, L. C. (2003). Culture and illness representation. In L. D. Cameron & H. Leventhal (Eds.), *The self- regulation of health and illness behaviour* (pp. 242–253). London: Routledge.

Becker, M. H. (1979). Understanding patient compliance: The contributions of attitudes and other psychosocial factors. In S. J. Cohen (Ed.), *New directions in patient compliance* (pp. 1–31). Lexington, MA: Lexington Books.

Berger, B. A., Stanton, A. L., Felkey, B. G., Barker, K. N., Keiser, H., Gallelli, J. F., Noel, O. R., & Green, S. B. (1990). Effectiveness of an education program to teach pharmacists to counsel hypertensive patients and influence treatment adherence. *Journal of Pharmaceutical Marketing & Management, 5*, 27–41.

Bosley, C. M., Fosbury, J. A., & Cochrane, G. M. (1995). The psychological factors associated with poor compliance with treatment in asthma. *European Respiratory Journal, 8*, 899–904.

Braddock, C. H., Fihn, S. D., Levinson, W., Jonsen, A. R., & Pearlman, R. A. (1997). How doctors and patients discuss routine clinical decisions: Informed decision making in the outpatient setting. *Journal of General Internal Medicine, 12*, 339–345.

Brase, G. L. (2002). Which statistical formats facilitate what decisions? The perception and influence of different statistical information formats. *Journal of Behavioral Decision Making, 15*, 381–401.

Breemhar, B., van den Borne, H. W., & Mullen, P. D. (1996). Inadequacies of surgical patient education. *Patient Education and Counseling, 28*, 31–44.

Britten, N. (1994). Patients' ideas about medicines: A qualitative study in a general practice population. *British Journal of General Practice, 44*, 465–468.

Brownell, K. D., & Cohen, L. R. (1995). Adherence to dietary regimens: 1. An overview of research. *Behavioral Medicine, 20*, 149–154.

Brownlee-Duffeck, M., Peterson, L., Simonds, J. F., Goldstein, K., Kilo, C., & Hoette, S. (1987). The role of health beliefs in the regimen adherence and metabolic control of adolescents and adults with diabetes mellitus. *Journal of Consulting and Clinical Psychology, 55*, 139–144.

Brun, W. (1993). Risk perception: Main issues, approaches and findings. In G. Wright & P. Ayton (Eds.), *Subjective probability* (pp. 295–320). Chichester: Wiley.

Cameron, L. D. (2003). Anxiety, cognition, and responses to health threats. In L. D. Cameron & H. Leventhal (Eds.), *The self-regulation of health and illness behaviour* (pp. 157–183). London: Routledge.

Campion, P., Foulkes, J., Neighbour, R., & Tate, P. (2002). Patient centredness in the MRCGP video examination: Analysis of large cohort. *British Medical Journal, 325*, 691–692.

Cartwright, A. (1994). The experience of patients and general practitioners. *Journal of the Royal Society of Medicine, 23*(Supp.), 8–10.

Cioffi, D. (1994). When good news is bad news: Medical wellness as a nonevent in undergraduates. *Health Psychology, 13*, 63–72.

Cleary, D. J., Matzke, G. R., Alexander, A. C., & Joy, M. S. (1995). Medication knowledge and compliance among patients receiving long-term dialysis. *American Journal of Health Systems and Pharmacy, 52*, 1895–1900.

Cochrane, S. D., & Gitlin, M. J. (1988). Attitudinal correlates of lithium compliance in bipolar affective disorders. *Journal of Nervous and Mental Disease, 176*, 457–464.

Conrad, P. (1985). The meaning of medications: Another look at compliance. *Social Science and Medicine, 20*, 29–37.

Contrada, R. J., Leventhal, E. A., & Anderson, J. R. (1994). Psychological preparation for surgery: Marshalling individual and social resources to optimise self-regulation. In S. Maes, H. Leventhal & M. Johnston (Eds.), *International review of health psychology* (pp. 219–266). Chichester: Wiley.

Cooper, A., Lloyd, G., Weinman, J., & Jackson, G. (1999). Why patients do not attend cardiac rehabilitation: The role of intentions and illness beliefs. *Heart, 82*, 234–236.

Cooper, L. A., & Roter, D. L. (2002). Patient–provider communication: The effect of race and ethnicity on process and outcomes of health care. In B. D. Smedley, A. Y. Stith & A. R. Nelson (Eds.), *Unequal treatment: Confronting racial and ethnic disparities in health care* (pp. 552–593). Committee on Understanding and Eliminating Racial and Ethnic Disparities in Health Care. Washington, DC: National Academies Press.

Cooper-Patrick, L., Gallo, J. J., Gonzalez, J. J., Thi Vu, H., Powe, N. R., Nelson, C., & Ford, D. E. (1999). Race, gender, and partnership in the patient–physician relationship. *Journal of the American Medical Association, 282*, 583–589.

Coulter, A., Entwistle, V., & Gilbert, D. (1999). Sharing decisions with patients: Is the information good enough? *British Medical Journal, 318*, 318–322.

Croyle, R. T., Sun, Y. -C., & Hart, M. (1997). Processing risk factor information: Defensive biases in health-related judgments and memory. In K. J. Petrie & J. A. Weinman (Eds.), *Perceptions of health and illness* (pp. 267–290). Amsterdam: Harwood Academic.

Cummings, K. M., Becker, M. H., Kirscht, J. P., & Levin, N. W. (1981). Intervention strategies to improve compliance with medical regimens by ambulatory haemodialysis patients. *Journal of Behavioral Medicine*, 4, 111–127.

Department of Health and Social Security (1980). *Inequalities in health: Report of a working group chaired by Sir Douglas Black*. London: DHSS.

DiMatteo, M. R., Giordani, P. J., Lepper, H. S., & Croghan, T. W. (2002). Patient adherence and medical treatment outcomes. *Medical Care*, 40, 794–811.

DiMatteo, M. R., Lepper, H. S., & Croghan, T. W. (2000). Depression is a risk factor for noncompliance with medical treatment: Meta-analysis of the effects of anxiety and depression on patient adherence. *Archives of Internal Medicine*, 160, 2102–2107.

Ditto, P. H., & Lopez, D. F. (1992). Motivated scepticism: The use of differential decision criteria for preferred and nonpreferred conclusions. *Journal of Personality and Social Psychology*, 63, 568–584.

Donovan, J. L., & Blake, D. R. (1992). Patient non-compliance: Deviance or reasoned decision making? *Social Science and Medicine*, 34, 507–513.

Eagleton, J. M., Walker, F. S., & Barber, N. D. (1993). An investigation into patient compliance with hospital discharge medication in a local population. *International Journal of Pharmacy Practice*, July, 107–109.

Edwards, A., Elwyn, G., Covey, J., Matthews, E., & Pill, R. (2001). Presenting risk information: A review of the effects of 'framing' and other manipulations on patient outcomes. *Journal of Health Communication*, 6, 61–62.

Fallowfield, L., Jenkins, V., Farewell, V., Saul, J., Duffy, A., & Eves, R. (2002). Efficacy of a Cancer Research UK communication skills training model for oncologists: A randomised controlled trial. *Lancet*, 359, 650–656.

Farmer, A., Levy, J. C., & Turner, R. C. (1999). Knowledge of risk of developing diabetes mellitus among siblings of type 2 diabetic patients. *Diabetic Medicine*, 16, 233–237.

Feinmann, J. (2002). Brushing up on doctors' communication skills. *Lancet*, 360, 1572.

Flesch, R. (1948). A new readability yardstick. *Journal of Applied Psychology*, 32, 221–233.

Floyd, D. L., Prentice-Dunn, S., & Rogers, R. W. (2000). A meta-analysis of research on protection motivation theory. *Journal of Applied Social Psychology*, 30, 407–429.

Folkman, S., & Lazarus, R. S. (1980). An analysis of coping in a middle-aged community sample. *Journal of Health and Social Behavior*, 21, 219–239.

Gibbs, S. W., & George, C. F. (1990). Communicating information to patients about medicine. Prescription information leaflets: A national survey. *Journal of the Royal Society of Medicine*, 83, 292–297.

Gigerenzer, G. (2002). *Reckoning with risk: Learning to live with uncertainty*. London: Allen Lane, Penguin.

Gigerenzer, G., Hoffrage, U., & Ebert, A. (1998). AIDs counselling for low-risk clients. *AIDS Care*, 10, 197–211.

Godin, G., Desharnais, R., Jobin, J., & Cook, J. (1987). The impact of physical fitness and health-age appraisal upon exercise intentions and behavior. *Journal of Behavioral Medicine*, 10, 241–250.

Gollwitzer, P. M. (1999). Implementation intentions: Strong effects of simple plans. *American Psychologist*, 54, 493–503.

Gonder-Frederick, L. A., & Cox, D. J. (1991). Symptom perception, symptom beliefs and blood glucose discrimination in the self-treatment of insulin dependent diabetes. In J. A. Skelton & R. T. Croyle (Eds.), *Mental representation in health and illness* (pp. 220–246). New York: Springer.

Gonzalez-Fernandez, R. A., Rivera, M., Torres, D., Quiles, J., & Jackson, A. (1990). Usefulness of a systemic hypertension in-hospital education program. *American Journal of Cardiology*, 65, 1384–1386.

Gordis, L. (1976). Methodological issues in the measurement of patient compliance. In D. L. Sackett & R. B. Haynes (Eds.), *Compliance with therapeutic regimens* (pp. 51–66). Baltimore: Johns Hopkins University Press.

Grady, K. E., Goodenow, C., & Borkin, J. R. (1988). The effect of reward on compliance with breast self-examination. *Journal of Behavioral Medicine*, 11, 43.

Green, L. W., Kreuter, M. W., Deeds, S. G., & Partridge, K. B. (1980). *Health education planning: A diagnostic approach*. Palo Alto, CA: Mayfield.

Grimes, D. A., & Snively, G. R. (1999). Patients' understanding of medical risks: Implications for genetic counseling. *Obstetrics and Gynaecology*, 93, 910–914.

Haefner, D. P., & Kirscht, J. P. (1970). Motivational and behavioural effects of modifying health beliefs. *Public Health Reports*, 85, 478–484.

Hall, G. (1983). *Behaviour: An introduction to psychology as a biological science*. London: Academic.

Hall, J. A., Roter, D. L., & Katz, N. R. (1988). Meta-analysis of correlates of provider behavior in medical encounters. *Medical Care*, 26, 657–675.

Hall, S., Bobrow, M., & Marteau, T. M. (2000). Psychological consequences for parents of false negative results on prenatal screening for Down's syndrome: Retrospective interview study. *British Medical Journal, 320,* 407–412.

Hampson, S. E. (1997). Illness representations and the self-management of diabetes. In K. J. Petrie & J. A. Weinman (Eds.), *Perceptions of health and illness* (pp. 323–347). Amsterdam: Harwood Academic.

Hampson, S. E., Glasgow, R. E., & Zeiss, A. M. (1994). Personal models of osteoarthritis and the relation to self-management activities and quality of life. *Journal of Behavioral Medicine, 17,* 143–158.

Hand, C. (1998). Adherence and asthma. In L. Myers & K. Midence (Eds.), *Adherence to treatment in medical conditions* (pp. 383–421). London: Harwood Academic.

Haynes, R. B. (1976). A critical review of the 'determinants' of patient compliance with therapeutic regimens. In D. L. Sackett & R. B. Haynes (Eds.), *Compliance with therapeutic regimens* (pp. 26–39). Baltimore: John Hopkins University Press.

Haynes, R. B., McKibbon, K. A., & Kanani, R. (1996). Systematic review of randomised trials of interventions to assist patients to follow prescriptions for medicines. *Lancet, 348,* 383–386.

Haynes, R. B., Sackett, D. L., Taylor, D. W., Gibson, E. S., & Johnson, A. L. (1978). Increased absenteeism from work after detection and labeling of hypertensive patients. *New England Journal of Medicine, 299,* 741–744.

Haynes, R. B., Taylor, D. W., & Sackett, D. L. (Eds.) (1979). *Compliance in health care.* Baltimore: Johns Hopkins University Press.

Hendrickx, L., Vlek, C., & Oppewal, H. (1989). Relative importance of scenario information and frequency information in the judgment of risk. *Acta Psychologica, 72,* 41–63.

Hilbrands, L. B., Hoitsma, A. J., & Koene, R. (1995). Medication compliance after renal transplantation. *Transplantation, 60,* 914–920.

Horne, R. (1998). Adherence to medication: A review of existing research. In L. Myers & K. Midence (Eds.), *Adherence to treatment in medical conditions* (pp. 285–309). London: Harwood Academic.

Horne, R. (2003). Treatment perceptions and self-regulation. In L. D. Cameron & H. Leventhal (Eds.), *The self- regulation of health and illness behaviour* (pp. 138–153). London: Routledge.

Horne, R., & Weinman, J. (2002). Self-regulation and self-management in asthma: Exploring the role of illness perceptions and treatment beliefs in explaining non-adherence to preventer medication. *Psychology and Health, 17,* 17–32.

Horne, R., Weinman, J., & Hankins, M. (1999). The Beliefs about Medicines Questionnaire (BMQ): The development and evaluation of a new method for assessing the cognitive representation of medication. *Psychology and Health, 14,* 1–24.

Horwitz, R. I., Viscoli, C. M., Berkman, L., Donaldson, R. M., Horwitz, S. M., Murray, C. J., Ransohoff, D. F., & Sindelar, J. (1990). Treatment adherence and risk of death after a myocardial infarction. *Lancet, 336,* 852–855.

Houts, P. S., Bachrach, R., Witmer, J. T., Tringali, C. A., Bucher, J. A., & Localio, R. A. (1998). Using pictographs to enhance recall of spoken medical instructions. *Patient Education and Counseling, 35,* 83–88.

Houts, P. S., Witmer, J. T., Egeth, H. E., Loscalzo, M. J., & Zabora, J. R. (2001). Using pictographs to enhance recall of spoken medical instructions II. *Patient Education and Counseling, 43,* 231–242.

Iverson, M. D., Daltroy, L. H., Fossel, A. H., & Katz, J. N. (1998). The prognostic importance of patient pre-operative expectations of surgery for lumbar spinal stenosis. *Patient Education and Counseling, 34,* 169–178.

Jadad, A. R., & Gagliardi, A. (1998). Rating health information on the internet: Navigating to knowledge or to Babel? *Journal of the American Medical Association, 279,* 611–614.

Janis, I. (1958). *Psychological stress.* New York: Wiley.

Janz, N. K., & Becker, M. H. (1984). The health belief model: A decade later. *Health Education Quarterly, 11,* 1–47.

Jay, M. S., DuRant, R. H., Shoffitt, T., Linder, C. W., & Litt, I. F. (1984). Effect of peer counselors on adolescent compliance in use of oral contraceptives. *Pediatrics, 73,* 126–131.

Johnston, M. (1984). Dimensions of recovery from surgery. *International Review of Applied Psychology, 33,* 505–520.

Johnston, M., & Carpenter, L. (1980). Relationship between pre-operative anxiety and post-operative state. *Psychological Medicine, 10,* 361–367.

Johnston, M., & Vogele, C. (1993). Benefits of psychological preparation for surgery: A meta-analysis. *Annals of Behavioral Medicine, 15,* 245–256.

Johnston, M., & Wallace, L. (Eds.) (1990). *Stress and medical procedures.* Oxford: Oxford University Press.

Jones, P. K., Jones, S. L., & Katz, J. (1987). Improving compliance for asthma patients visiting the emergency department using a health belief model intervention. *Journal of Asthma, 24,* 199–206.

Kain, Z. N., Sevarino, F., Alexander, G. M., Pincus, S., & Mayes, L. C. (2000). Preoperative anxiety and postoperative pain in women undergoing hysterectomy: A repeated-measures design. *Journal of Psychosomatic Research, 49,* 417–422.

Kellaway, G. S., & McCrae, E. (1979). The effect of counselling on compliance-failure in patient drug therapy. *New Zealand Medical Journal, 89,* 161.

Kelly, G. R., Mannon, J. A., & Scott, J. E. (1987). Utility of the health belief model in examining medication compliance among psychiatric outpatients. *Social Science and Medicine, 25,* 1205–1211.

Kiecolt-Glaser, J. K., Page, G. G., Marucka, P. T., MacCallum, R. G., & Glaser, R. (1998). Psychological influence on surgical recovery: Perspective from psychoneuroimmunology. *American Psychologist, 53,* 1209–1218.

Kok, G., van den Borne, B., & Dolan Mullen, P. (1997). Effectiveness of health education and health promotion: Meta-analyses of effect studies and determinants of effectiveness. *Patient Education and Counseling, 30,* 19–27.

Korsch, B. M., & Negrete, V. F. (1972). Doctor–patient communication. *Scientific American, 227,* 66–74.

Kreuter, M. W., & Strecher, V. J. (1995). Changing inaccurate perceptions of health risk: Results from a randomized trial. *Health Psychology, 14,* 56–63.

Krohne, H. W., Slangen, K., & Kleemann, P. P. (1996). Coping variables as predictors of perioperative emotional states and adjustment. *Psychology and Health, 11,* 315–330.

Krupat, E., Fancey, M., & Cleary, P. D. (2000). Information and its impact on satisfaction among surgical patients. *Social Science and Medicine, 51,* 1817–1825.

Kulik, J. A., & Mahler, H. I. (1987). Effects of preoperative room-mate assignment on preoperative anxiety and recovery from coronary by-pass surgery. *Health Psychology, 6,* 525–543.

Kulik, J. A., Mahler, H. I., & Moore, P. J. (1996). Social comparison and affiliation under threat: Effects on recovery from major surgery. *Journal of Personality and Social Psychology, 71,* 967–979.

Landrine, H., & Klonoff, E. A. (2001). Cultural diversity and health psychology. In A. Baum, T. A. Revenson & J. E. Singer (Eds.), *Handbook of health psychology* (pp. 851–891). Mahwah, NJ: Erlbaum.

Langer, E. J., Janis, I. L., & Wolfer, J. A. (1975). Reduction of psychological stress in surgical patients. *Journal of Experimental Social Psychology, 11,* 155–165.

Lazarus, R. S., & Folkman, S. (1984). *Stress, appraisal, and coping.* New York: Springer.

Leventhal, H., Benyamini, Y., Brownlee, S., Diefenbach, M., Leventhal, E. A., Patrick-Miller, L., & Robataille, C. (1997). Illness representations: Theoretical foundations. In K. Petrie & J. Weinman (Eds.), *Perceptions of health and illness* (pp. 19–45). Amsterdam: Harwood Academic.

Leventhal, H., Brisette, I., & Leventhal, E. A. (2003). The common-sense model of self-regulation of health and illness. In L. D. Cameron & H. Leventhal (Eds.), *The self-regulation of health and illness behaviour* (pp. 42–65). London: Routledge.

Leventhal, H., & Cameron, L. D. (1987). Behavioural theories and the problem of compliance. *Patient Education and Compliance, 10,* 117–138.

Leventhal, H., & Diefenbach, M. (1991). The active side of illness cognition. In J. A. Skelton & R. T. Croyle (Eds.), *Mental representation in health and illness* (pp. 247–272). New York: Springer.

Leventhal, H., Singer, R., & Jones, S. (1965). Effects of fear and specificity of recommendation upon attitudes and behavior. *Journal of Personality and Social Psychology, 2,* 20–29.

LeVine, R., Dexter, E., Velasco, P., Levine, S., Joshi, A., Stuebing, K. W., & Tapia-Uribe, F. M. (1994). Maternal literacy and health care in three countries: A preliminary report. *Health Transition Review, 4,* 186–191.

Ley, P. (1988). *Communicating with patients: Improving communication, satisfaction and compliance.* London: Croom Helm.

Lilleyman, J. S., & Lennard, L. (1996). Noncompliance with oral chemotherapy in childhood leukaemia: An overlooked and costly cause of late relapse. *British Medical Journal, 313,* 1219–1220.

Lipkus, I. M., & Hollands, J. G. (1999). The visual communication of risk. *Journal of National Cancer Institute Monographs, 25,* 149–163.

Lucock, M. P., Morley, S., White, C., & Peake, M. D. (1997). Responses of consecutive patients to reassurance after gastroscopy: Results of self administered questionnaire survey. *British Medical Journal, 315,* 572–575.

Macharia, W. M., Leon, G., Rowe, B. H., Stephenson, B. J., & Haynes, R. B. (1992). An overview of interventions to improve compliance with appointment keeping for medical services. *Journal of the American Medical Association, 267,* 1813–1817.

Maissi, E., Marteau, T. M., Hankins, M., Moss, S., Legood, R., & Gray, A. (submitted) The emotional impact of human papillomavirus testing in women with abnormal cervical smear test results. Manuscript submitted for publication.

Marteau, T. M., Humphrey, C., Matoon, G., Kidd, J., Lloyd, M., & Horder, J. (1991). Factors influencing the communication skills of first year clinical medical students. *Medical Education, 25,* 127–134.

Marteau, T. M., Saidi, G., Goodburn, S., Lawton, J., Michie, S., & Bobrow, M. (2000). Numbers or words? A randomised controlled trial of presenting screen negative results to pregnant women. *Prenatal Diagnosis, 20,* 714–718.

Marteau, T. M., Senior, V., & Sasieni, P. (2001). Women's understanding of a 'normal smear test result': Experimental questionnaire based study. *British Medical Journal, 322,* 526–528.

Mathews, A., & Ridgeway, V. (1984). Psychological preparation for surgery. In A. Steptoe & A. Mathews (Eds.), *Health care and human behaviour* (pp. 231–259). London: Academic.

McBride, C. M., Bepler, G., Lipkus, I. M., Lyna, P., Samsa, G., Albright, J., Datta, S., & Rimer, B. K. (2002). Incorporating genetic susceptibility feedback into a smoking cessation program for African-American smokers with low income. *Cancer Epidemiology Biomarkers & Prevention, 11,* 521–528.

McCarthy, S. C., Lyons, A. C., Weinman, J., Talbot, R., & Purnell, D. (2003). Do expectations influence recovery from oral surgery? An illness representation approach. *Psychology and Health, 18,* 109–126.

McClure, J. B. (2002). Are biomarkers useful treatment aids for promoting health behavior change? An empirical review. *American Journal of Preventive Medicine, 22,* 200–207.

McDermott, M. M., Schmitt, B., & Wallner, E. (1997). Impact of medication nonadherence on coronary heart disease outcome: A critical review. *Archives of Internal Medicine, 157,* 1921–1929.

McGinn, F. P., Bell, N., Miles, S., Rew, D., Ozmen, M., Terzi, C., & Uglow, M. (1995). Prospective randomised trial of laparoscopic and 'mini' cholecystectomy. *British Journal of Surgery, 82,* 1374–1377.

McGuire, P., Fairburn, S., & Fletcher, C. (1986). Consultation skills of young doctors: 1. Benefits of feedback training in interviewing as students persist. *British Medical Journal, 292,* 1573–1576.

McKenna, F. P. (2002). Is risk homoeostasis theory successful? Not quite. 28 May 2002. Retrieved from http://bmj.com rapid response to Debate: Wilde, G. J. S., Robertson, L. S., & Pless, I. B. (2002). For and against: Does risk homoeostasis theory have implications for road safety? *British Medical Journal, 324,* 1149–1152.

McKim, W. A., Stones, M. J., & Kozma, A. (1990). Factors predicting medicine use in institutionalized and non-institutionalized elderly. *Canadian Journal on Ageing, 9,* 23–34.

Meichenbaum, D., & Turk, D. C. (1987). *Facilitating treatment adherence: A practitioner guidebook.* New York: Plenum.

Meyer, D., Leventhal, H., & Guttman, M. (1985). Common-sense models of illness: The example of hypertension. *Health Psychology, 4,* 115–135.

Michie, S., & Marteau, T. M. (1999). Non-response bias in prospective studies of patients and health care professionals. *International Journal of Social Research Methodology, 3,* 203–212.

Michie, S., Weinman, J., Miller, J., Collins, V., Halliday, J., & Marteau, T. M. (2002). Predictive genetic testing: High risk expectations in the face of low risk information. *Journal of Behavioral Medicine, 25,* 33–50.

Miller, D. T., & Ross, M. (1975). Self-serving biases in the attribution of causality: Fact or fiction? *Psychological Bulletin, 82,* 213–225.

Miller, S. M., & Mangan, C. E. (1983). Interacting effects of information and coping styles in adapting to gynaecological distress: Should doctor tell all? *Journal of Personality and Social Psychology, 45,* 223–236.

Milne, S., Sheeran, P., & Orbell, S. (2000). Prediction and intervention in health-related behavior: A meta-analytic review of protection motivation theory. *Journal of Applied Social Psychology, 30,* 106–143.

Morgan, M., & Watkins, C. J. (1988). Managing hypertension: Belief and responses to medication among cultural groups. *Sociology of Health and Illness, 10,* 561–578.

Morgan, M. G., Fischhoff, B., Bostrom, A., & Atman, C. J. (2002). *Risk communication: A mental models approach.* Cambridge: Cambridge University Press.

Mosely, J. B., O'Malley, K., Petersen, N. J., Menke, T. J., Brody, B. A., Kuykendall, D. H., Hollingsworth, J. C., Ashton, C. M., & Wray, N. P. (2002). A controlled trial of arthroscopic surgery for osteoarthritis of the knee. *New England Journal of Medicine, 347,* 81–88.

Mullen, P. D., Green, L. W., & Persinger, G. S. (1985). Clinical trials of patient education for chronic conditions: A comparative meta-analysis of intervention types. *Preventive Medicine, 14,* 753–781.

Munafo, R. M., & Stevenson, J. (2001). Anxiety and surgical recovery: Reinterpreting the literature. *Journal of Psychosomatic Research, 51,* 589–596.

Myers, L., & Midence, K. (1998). *Adherence to treatment in medical conditions.* London: Harwood Academic.

Nelson, E. C., Stason, W. B., Neutra, R. R., Soloman, H. S., & McArdle, P. J. (1978). Impact of patient perceptions on compliance with treatment for hypertension. *Medical Care, 16,* 893–906.

Parker, D., Stradling, S. G., & Manstead, A. S. R. (1996). Modifying beliefs and attitudes to exceeding the speed limit: An intervention study based on the theory of planned behavior. *Journal of Applied Social Psychology, 26,* 1–19.

Parle, M., Maguire, P., & Heaven, C. (1997). The development of a training model to improve health professionals' skills, self-efficacy and outcome expectancies when communicating with cancer patients. *Social Science and Medicine, 44,* 231–240.

Paterson, D. L., Swindells, S., Mohr, J., Brester, M., Vergis, E. N., Squier, C., Wagener, M. M., & Singh, N. (2000). Adherence to protease inhibitor therapy and outcomes in patients with HIV infection. *Annals of Internal Medicine, 133,* 21–30.

Pendleton, D., & Bochner, S. (1980). The communication of medical information in general practice consultations as a function of patients' social class. *Social Science and Medicine, 4,* 669–673.

Petrie, K. J., Cameron, L. D., Ellis, C., Buick, D., & Weinman, J. (2002). Changing illness beliefs following MI: Results of an intervention trial. *Psychosomatic Medicine, 64,* 1–7.

Petrie, K. J., Weinman, J., Sharpe, N., & Buckley, J. (1996). Role of patients' view of their illness in predicting return to work and functioning following myocardial infarction. *British Medical Journal, 312,* 1191–1194.

Petticrew, M. P., Sowden, A. J., Lister-Sharp, D., & Wright, K. (2000). False-negative results in screening programmes: Systematic review of impact and implications. *Health Technology Assessment,* 4(5).

Reid, L. D., & Christensen, D. B. (1988). A psychosocial perspective in the explanation of patients' drug-taking behavior. *Social Science and Medicine, 27,* 277–285.

Rich, M. W., Gray, D. B., Beckham, V., Wittenberg, C., & Luther, P. (1996). Effect of a multidisciplinary intervention on medication compliance in elderly patients with congestive heart failure. *American Journal of Medicine, 101,* 270–276.

Richard, R., van der Pligt, J., & De Vries, N. (1995). Anticipated affective relations and prevention of AIDS. *British Journal of Social Psychology, 34,* 9–21.

Richardson, P. (1997). Placebos. In A. Baum, S. Newman, J. Weinman, R. West & C. McManus (Eds.), *Cambridge handbook of psychology, health and medicine* (pp. 237–241). Cambridge: Cambridge University Press.

Ridgeway, V., & Mathews, A. (1982). Psychological preparation for surgery: A comparison of methods. *British Journal of Clinical Psychology, 21,* 243–260.

Robertson, L. S. (2002). In Debate: Wilde, G., Robertson, L., & Pless, B. (2002). Does risk homoeostasis theory have implications for road safety? *British Medical Journal, 324,* 1149–1152.

Roter, D. L., Hall, J. A., Merisca, R., Nordstrom, B., Cretin, D., & Svarsted, B. (1998). Effectiveness of interventions to improve patient compliance: A meta-analysis. *Medical Care, 36,* 1138–1161.

Roter, D. L., Rudd, R. E., & Comings, J. (1998). Patient literacy: A barrier to quality of care. *Journal of General Internal Medicine, 13,* 850–851.

Roter, D. L., Stewart, M., Putnam, S. M., Lipkin, M., Stiles, W., & Inui, T. S. (1997). Communication patterns of primary care physicians. *Journal of the American Medical Association, 277,* 350–356.

Roth-Isigkeit, A., Ocklitz, E., Bruckner, S., Ros, A., Dibbelt, L., Friedrich, H. J., Gehring, H., & Schmucker, P. (2002). Development and evaluation of a video program for presentation prior to elective cardiac surgery. *Acta Anaesthesiologica Scandinavica, 46,* 415–423.

Rothman, A. J., & Kiviniemi, M. T. (1999). Treating people with information: An analysis and review of approaches to communicating health risk information. *Journal of the National Cancer Institute Monographs, 25,* 44–51.

Sackett, D. L., & Haynes, R. B. (1976). *Compliance with therapeutic regimens.* Baltimore: Johns Hopkins University Press.

Saha, S., Komaromy, M., Koepsell, T. D., & Bindman, A. B. (1999). Patient–physician racial concordance and the perceived quality and use of health care. *Archives of Internal Medicine, 159,* 997–1004.

Salmon, P., Hall, G. M., & Peerbhoy, D. (2001). Influence of the emotional response to surgery on functional recovery during 6 months after hip arthroplasty. *Journal of Behavioral Medicine, 24,* 489–502.

Schlumpf, R., Klotz, H. P., Wehrli, H., & Herzog, U. (1994). A nation experience in laparoscopic cholecystectomy: Prospective multicenter analysis of 3,722 cases. *Surgical Endoscopy, 8,* 35–41.

Schwarzer, R. (1992). Self efficacy in the adoption and maintenance of health behaviors: Theoretical approaches and a new model. In R. Schwarzer (Ed.), *Self-efficacy: Thought control of action* (pp. 217–243). Washington, DC: Hemisphere.

Shaw, C., Abrams, K., & Marteau, T. M. (1999). Psychological impact of predicting individuals' risk of illness: A systematic review. *Social Science and Medicine, 49,* 1571–1598.

Sheeran, P. (2002). Intention–behaviour relations: A conceptual and empirical review. *European Review of Social Psychology, 12,* 1–36.

Silberg, W. M., Lundberg, G. D., & Musacchio, R. A. (1997). Assessing, controlling and assuring the quality of medical information on the internet. *Journal of the American Medical Assocation, 277,* 1244–1245.

Slaytor, E. K., & Ward, J. E. (1998). How risks of breast cancer and benefits of screening are communicated to women: Analysis of 58 pamphlets. *British Medical Journal, 317,* 263–264.

Smith, D. K., Shaw, R. W., & Marteau, T. M. (1994). Informed consent to undergo serum screening for Down syndrome: The gap between policy and practice. *British Medical Journal, 309,* 776.

Stewart, M. A. (1995). Effective physician–patient communication and health outcomes: A review. *Canadian Medical Association Journal, 152,* 1423–1433.

Stewart, M., Brown, B. J., Weston, W. W., McWhinney, I. R., McWilliam, C. L., & Freeman, T. R. (Eds.) (1995). *Patient-centered medicine: Transforming the clinical method.* Thousand Oaks, CA: Sage.

Strychar, I. M., Champagne, F., Ghadirian, P., Bonin, A., Jenicek, M., & Lasater, T. M. (1998). Impact of receiving blood cholesterol test results on dietary change. *American Journal of Preventive Medicine, 14,* 103–110.

Sutton, S. (1998). Predicting and explaining intentions and behavior: How well are we doing? *Journal of Applied Social Psychology, 28,* 1317–1338.

Taylor, C. B., Agras, W. S., Schneider, J. A., & Allen, R. A. (1983). Adherence to instructions to practice relaxation exercises. *Journal of Consulting and Clinical Psychology, 51,* 952–953.

Tucker, C. M. (1989). The effects of behavioral interventions with patients, nurses, and family members on dietary noncompliance in chronic hemodialysis patients. *Transplantation Proceedings, 2,* 3985–3988.

Turner, J. K., Ersek, M., Hernon, L., & Deyo, R. (1992). Surgery for lumbar spinal stenosis: Attempted meta-analysis of the literature. *Spine, 17,* 1–8.

Tymstra, T., & Bieleman, B. (1987). The psychosocial impact of mass screening for cardiovascular risk factors. *Family Practice, 4,* 287–290.

van der Pligt, J. (1998). Perceived risk and vulnerability as predictors of precautionary behaviour. *British Journal of Health Psychology, 3,* 1–14.

Vernon, D. T. A. (1974). Modeling and birth order in response to painful stimuli. *Journal of Personality and Social Psychology, 29,* 794–799.

Waitzkin, H. (1985). Information giving in medical care. *Journal of Health and Social Behavior, 26,* 81–101.

Watson, M. S., Hall, S., Langford, K., & Marteau, T. M. (2002). Psychological impact of the detection of soft markers on routine ultrasound scanning: A pilot study investigating the modifying role of information. *Prenatal Diagnosis, 22,* 569–575.

Weingarten, S. R., Henning, J. M., Badamgarav, E., Knight, K., Hasselblad, V., Gano, A., & Ofman, J. J. (2002). Interventions used in disease management programmes for patients with chronic illness: Which ones work? Meta-analysis of published reports. *British Medical Journal, 325,* 925–928.

Weinman, J., & Johnston, M. (1988). Stressful medical procedures: An analysis of the effects of psychological interventions and the stressfulness of the procedures. In S. Maes, C. D. Spielberger, P. B. Defares & I. G. Sarason (Eds.), *Topics in health psychology* (pp. 205–217). Chichester: Wiley.

Weinstein, N. D. (1998). Accuracy of smokers' risk perceptions. *Annals of Behavioral Medicine, 20,* 135–140.

Weinstein, N. D. (1999). What does it mean to understand a risk? Evaluating risk comprehension. *Journal of the National Cancer Institute Monographs, 25,* 15–20.

Weinstein, N. D., & Klein, W. M. (1995). Resistance of personal risk perceptions to debiasing interventions. *Health Psychology, 14,* 132–140.

Weinstein, N. D., Sandman, P. M., & Roberts, N. E. (1991). Perceived susceptibility and self-protective behavior: A field experiment to encourage home radon testing. *Health Psychology, 10,* 25–33.

Wiebe, D. J., & Korbel, C. (2003). Defensive denial, affect, and the self-regulation of health threats. In L. D. Cameron & H. Leventhal (Eds.), *The self-regulation of health and illness behaviour* (pp. 184–203). London: Routledge.

Wilde, G. J. S., Robertson, L. S., & Pless, I. B. (2002). Does risk homoeostasis theory have implications for road safety? *British Medical Journal, 324,* 1149–1152.

Wilkinson, C., Jones, J. M., & McBride, J. (1990). Anxiety caused by abnormal result of cervical smear test: A controlled trial. *British Medical Journal, 300,* 440.

Williams, M. V., Parker, R. M., Baker, D. W., Parikh, N. S., Pitkin, K., Coates, W. C., & Nurss, J. R. (1995). Inadequate functional health literacy among patients at two public hospitals. *Journal of the American Medical Association, 274,* 1677–1682.

Witte, K., & Allen, M. (2000). A meta-analysis of fear appeals: Implications for effective public health campaigns. *Health Education and Behavior, 27,* 591–615.

Wright, P. (1980). Usability: The criterion for designing written information. In P. A. Kolers, M. E. Wrolstad & H. Bouma (Eds.), *Processing of visible language 2* (pp. 183–205). New York: Plenum.

11

Applications in Health Psychology: How Effective Are Interventions?

STAN MAES AND SANDRA N. BOERSMA

INTRODUCTION

As Goethe wrote: 'Knowing is not enough, we must apply. Willing is not enough, we must do.' However, applications imply a body of knowledge, composed of theories or models and/or intervention principles and techniques that can guide these applications. This implies that applications can be approached from both a theoretical and a practical perspective. While a theoretical perspective is more universal and can be a tool as well as an objective, it requires a vast body of research concerning an organized set of hypotheses. In health psychology, these kinds of research findings are frequently absent. There are many successful intervention programs that lack a theoretically sound and effective explanation. Therefore, a chapter on applications should work towards consequences for research and theory development, rather than present a descriptive list of practical successes. As a consequence, the first part of this chapter, which focuses on health promotion, describes research findings in different settings, followed by conclusions and recommendations for future research and theory

building. The second part of this chapter considers psychological interventions in chronic illness. In this case a model of intervention (distinguishing aims, level and channel of intervention) is used as the structure for the description of specific examples of interventions. Likewise recommendations for future research and theory development are given at the end of this section. A general conclusion and discussion section completes the chapter.

HEALTH PROMOTION INITIATIVES

This section provides examples of successful interventions aimed at promoting health behavior, changing risk factors for disease and/or reducing morbidity and mortality at a population level. We have tried to present the state of the art for health promotion in different settings, including media-based health promotion and community-based health promotion, as well as health promotion at school, at the worksite and in health care settings. At the end of this brief review, we have formulated suggestions for future health promotion programs.

Media-Based Health Promotion

Mass media are a very popular and effective mode of communication, which can influence or motivate people to change. However, they are often unsuccessful in producing long-term health behavior changes when utilized alone and without other supporting mechanisms (Tones & Tilford, 1994). Therefore, it is suggested that a combination of several different methodologies be used in order to achieve more enhanced results.

A study by Reid (1985), evaluating the effects of a mass media style campaign on smoking, illustrates its relative ineffectiveness at producing such behavioral change when used on its own. In 1984, the UK sponsored a national No Smoking Day for 2 weeks, in which there was wide newspaper coverage, and radio and television slots devoted to the stopping smoking campaign. As a consequence, public awareness was very high. An evaluation study among 4,000 smokers three months after the campaign revealed that about 11 per cent had tried to stop smoking, but only three out of these 4,000 were successful (following the study) at the time of study. While this is an older initiative, the results are still exemplary for the effectiveness of mass media campaigns.

As a consequence, rather than mass media being used in 'splendid' isolation, they should be designed to support initiatives from health organizations and community groups. More specifically, they can be used to prepare a large population for a health promotion intervention. Such interventions can consist of self-help materials or face-to-face contact. The following study may illustrate the importance of this comprehensive approach. During the late 1980s a televised smoking cessation intervention was broadcast for 20 days on the local Chicago ABC station. Smokers who were interested in quitting received a self-help manual. To prevent relapse within a few weeks without additional intervention, researchers from DePaul University conducted monthly follow-up support groups for a year and provided incentives to the participants. During the two-year follow-up the abstinence rate of this group was much higher (30 per cent) than the

rate of the participants who received no group support (20 per cent) (Jason, 1998). Results from another initiative, the Florida 'Truth' campaign, a teenage led anti-tobacco intervention, support these findings. 'Truth' made use of print and broadcast ads, teenage action groups, school curricula, tobacco sales restrictions and a website. The campaign resulted in increased knowledge of tobacco possession laws in adolescents and in a significant decline in teenage smoking during the first two years of implementation. These results suggest that media that are designed to attract the attention of adolescents may have a significant impact in combination with other methods (Perry, 2000).

In addition, as media reach the masses, heterogeneity of the target population is an important concern. As a consequence, tailoring messages to the needs of different segments of the population may prove to be a more adequate strategy for intervention. Selecting a specific segment of the population may be the easiest way to reach this goal. From this perspective, there is an urgent need to evaluate the differential effectiveness of media-based health promotion campaigns. For example, the COMMIT Program, a campaign which was supported by the Canadian Ministry of Health, failed to show any effect on quitting in heavy smokers, but proved to be successful for moderate smokers (Institute of Medicine, 2002).

Finally, the use of computer technology for intervention development and delivery provides new perspectives on intervention, including the use of internet sites related to health promotion (an example is the Harvard Cancer Risk Index, which provides cancer prevention assessment and feedback: see http://www.yourcancerrisk.harvard.edu); websites set up to support specific intervention programs (as in the Florida 'Truth' campaign); computer-controlled telephone counseling (Friedman, 1998); and tailored interventions using computer-based 'expert systems' programs to match messages to the individuals' information needs (Dijkstra, De Vries, Roijackers & Van Breukelen, 1998; Emmons, 2000). Moreover, a combination of these methods could provide a powerful intervention strategy for health promotion, but to our knowledge there is no published health promotion project that has made use of all these new assets.

Community Health Promotion

The increased awareness that the modification of risk factors and associated lifestyles could influence morbidity and mortality at a population level gave an impetus to community-based health promotion programs. In a first generation of programs there was a concentration on isolated risk factors, such as unhealthy diet, physical inactivity or lack of medication compliance, without documenting whether modification of the risk factor had beneficial effects on morbidity or mortality (Blackburn, 1972). A second generation of programs, which appeared in the 1970s, is characterized by the belief that several risk factors have to be tackled simultaneously in order to influence (cardiovascular) disease outcomes. Examples of these multifactorial trials are the OSLO Study and MRFIT. In both studies large male high-risk populations were selected on the basis of a screening for coronary risk factors (cholesterolemia, hypertension and cigarette smoking). In both cases health education and behavior modification strategies were offered to influence health behaviors that are related to these risk factors (such as smoking, unhealthy diet and lack of medication compliance). The evaluation of the OSLO Study showed impressive results with respect to cholesterol, smoking and consequent cardiovascular morbidity and mortality. The MRFIT Program, on the other hand, was successful in the modification of risk factors but failed to influence cardiovascular endpoints (Van Elderen & Kittel, 1993). Third-generation programs focused primarily on the population at large rather than on selected high-risk groups. However, they were still characterized by a (cardiovascular) disease prevention perspective. Key programs are the Finnish North Karelia Project and the Stanford Three Community and Five City Projects, and more recently the Pennsylvania County Health Improvement, the Pawtucket Heart Health and the Minnesota Heart Health Programs. These

programs have been described extensively elsewhere (Taylor, 2001; Tones & Tilford, 1994), but the most important conclusion is that they have the potential to change risk factors and related health behaviors at a population level. With the exception of the North Karelia Project, however, which produced impressive results, the programs failed to show long-term effects on (cardiovascular) morbidity and mortality. Studies of community programs which were developed in relation to other targets, such as cancer prevention, show comparable results (Hancock et al., 1997). Hancock and colleagues (1997), who reviewed methods and outcomes of six community programs related to cardiovascular disease and seven related to cancer, come to the following conclusions. With regard to the method aspect, they state that while the advantages of community action are potentially high, published evaluation studies do not meet proposed criteria for rigorous evaluation. Although several programs do show effects in terms of behavior change, this cannot be attributed to specific interventions, due to a lack of process evaluation. Finally, due to political pressure, there is not enough investment in the development, pre-testing and evaluation of these programs. With respect to outcomes, they make several observations. First, there is a need for practitioners (and policy makers) to accept that the gains in public health will be small, and that it requires a lot of time before effects in endpoints may appear. Second, the population size must remain manageable (somewhere between 6,000 and 20,000 would be ideal). However, it should be noted that most studies were conducted within far larger communities. Third, interventions should focus not only on the most difficult behavioral targets (e.g., smoking cessation) but also on easier or more accepted targets (e.g., solar protection). Fourth, many studies offered very narrow interventions. More variability and flexibility in approach would be more appropriate. Finally, many programs relied on major external funding. Interventions that use existing community resources will not only increase financial viability, but also enhance community ownership of the problem. The authors suggest that the community should also be involved in the evaluation of the programs.

These last remarks may be vital for future community health promotion programs. Most programs are initiated and financed by external parties, such as for study purposes, and are therefore discontinued at a relatively early stage. O'Loughlin, Renaud, Richard, Sanchez-Gomez and Paradis (1998) investigated the factors related to the perceived sustainability of 189 heart health promotion interventions initiated by a public health department or research initiative and implemented in a variety of organizations in Canada. Overall about 44 per cent of these 189 interventions appeared to be very permanent. Independent correlates of perceived sustainability included: (1) the intervention used no paid staff, (2) the intervention was modified during implementation, (3) there was a good fit between the local provider and the intervention, and (4) there was the presence of a program champion. Consideration of these remarks could importantly increase the effects of community-based health promotion programs.

Health Promotion at School

Schools can be considered as one of the most important settings for health promotion, since young people can be encouraged to adopt healthy lifestyles and avoid the uptake of unhealthy behaviors at an early moment in life. This is important for at least two reasons. The first is that the longer people have adopted an unhealthy lifestyle, the more difficult it is to change it. The second is that some lifestyles may already have irreversible health consequences relatively early in life. Among the many behaviors that have been the focus of school-based health programs, the following have received the most attention: behaviors related to unintentional injury; abuse of tobacco, alcohol and other substances; safe sex in relation both to pregnancy and to sexually transmitted diseases such as HIV; healthy nutrition; and physical exercise.

Health promotion in schools has a long history. During the first stage of school health promotion, the focus was primarily on hygiene, in an effort to prevent infectious diseases from proliferating. Moreover, health promotion was utilized to facilitate an overall healthy lifestyle and increase physical activity. During the second stage in the 1970s, health promotion programs aimed to prevent the development of risk factors, increase safety behaviors, and reduce behaviors related to substance abuse (especially smoking) and obesity. These preventive programs were usually directed at a single behavior problem and were mostly school and instruction based. In the 1980s a third generation of programs provided a shift towards health promotion programs that focused on lifestyle rather than on isolated behaviors.

These programs were accompanied by home-based and mass media approaches and based on psychological models. One of the earliest examples of a third-generation program is the Life Skills Training program, which took a competency enhancing approach to substance abuse prevention. It focused on the development of broad-based coping skills over a period of three years, namely from seventh through ninth grade. During the first year, 15 sessions were offered. Topics covered were: decision making, resisting advertising techniques, stress management, communication skills, social skills and assertiveness. Fifteen reinforcement sessions were offered during the eighth and ninth grades. The program, which was offered by good role models, became widely disseminated and proved to be effective in preventing substance abuse, including problem drinking, cigarette smoking and marihuana use. Assertiveness, self-esteem and negative attitudes towards unhealthy behaviors increased, while social anxiety, external locus of control and susceptibility to social pressure decreased (Botvin et al., 1992). This program showed that a more general intervention approach, focused on various addictive behaviors and based on psychological models, may bring forward broad effects. Many other programs have since profited from these findings.

The Know Your Body program is an example of a more recent skill-based program designed to promote healthy behaviors and prevent risk behaviors from preschool education through grade six (Resnicow, Cross & Wynder, 1993). The program focuses on a wide scope of health issues related to various forms of substance abuse, exercise, nutrition, hygiene, disease and injury prevention, growth and development, social relationships and environmental health. It also includes many extra-curricular activities (e.g., walks and healthy food-tasting parties) and invites the participation of other peers, parents and community members. The program is very flexible as it can be adapted to the schools' needs and resources and can also be integrated in a wide variety of subject areas. The effectiveness of the program was evaluated by means of a quasi-experimental research design and proved to have significant effects on a variety of outcome measures, including blood pressure, smoking and HDL cholesterol, which have been identified as the main risk factors for coronary heart disease. More recent programs such as the Seattle Social Development Project (Hawkins, Catalano, Kosterman, Abbott & Hill, 1999) also highlight the importance of the social environment and the social context in youth and adolescent health promotion initiatives. This multicomponent project consists of continuous interventions from first to sixth grade in 18 urban, public elementary schools. The intervention aimed to increase social bonds between children, family and the school and consisted of: (1) teacher training in classroom management, interactive teaching methods and cooperative learning; (2) social competence training for the children; and (3) parent training to increase skills for promoting school achievement and to prevent substance abuse. At age 18, adolescents who had been exposed to the intervention during the whole primary school period reported less involvement in violence, sexual intercourse and heavy drinking (but not in other forms of substance abuse), as well as a higher commitment to school and better academic achievement, than a comparable control group.

These results show the importance of complementary interventions, which focus on the social context and environment, for interventions directed at health behavior changes at an individual level. Data from the Tobacco Policy Options Program pointed in the same direction. This program aimed at reducing teenage access to tobacco from stores and vending machines by means of a community action team. It resulted in policy changes in the community related to tobacco access. This approach proved to bring about a significant reduction in teenage smoking over the three-year period of intervention (Forster et al., 1998).

As a consequence, the state of the art suggests that comprehensive programs that are based on psychological theory, are supported by out-of-school activities to create a bond with the family and the community, and are offered over a long period, are the most effective (Orlandi & Dalton, 1998).

Health Promotion at the Worksite

The promotion of wellbeing, health and safety at the worksite has a long history which can be characterized in a series of stages (Goldbeck, 1984). During the first stage, interventions focused on the quality of the product and physical aspects of safety. For example, a smoking ban was introduced in the food industry in order to prevent contamination of the products and in the petroleum industry in order to prevent fires and explosions, but not because smoking harms the individual. During the second stage, in the 1960s, there was growing attention to the wellbeing and health of managers. As a consequence, stress management and/or physical fitness programs were offered to this specific group. For the other employees at best only existing safety measures were expanded to promote individual safety. During the third stage in the 1970s, the concept of disease and accident prevention became central: the reduction of recognized risk factors (such as smoking, hypertension, high serum cholesterol or unsafe behaviors) was the focus of a range of interventions that consisted primarily of behavioral advice following screening procedures. During the fourth stage in the 1980s, total 'wellness–health' promotion programs were introduced. These programs recognized the interrelation between these two concepts, and were offered to all employees instead of specific subgroups. Furthermore, health promotion, instead of disease prevention, was the ultimate goal. Two frequently cited examples of such programs are the Johnson and Johnson Live For Life program and the Data Control's Stay Well program. These American programs were designed to improve wellbeing and health by promoting individual behaviors (including, e.g., smoking cessation, weight control, physical exercise, stress management, improved diet and nutrition, reduced alcohol consumption and blood pressure control) and changes in the working environment to support these behaviors (e.g., smoking bans, provision of space and optimal conditions for physical exercise, changes in food and alcohol supplies) (Cataldo & Coates, 1986). The effects of these programs were evaluated by means of quasi-experimental designs. Following one year, the findings indicated more favourable changes in the experimental Johnson and Johnson sites, which were exposed to the Live For Life program, with respect to the percentage of employees above ideal weight, physical exercise, blood pressure, cigarette smoking, and self-reported sick days. At the two-year follow-up, the program had a significant positive impact on exercise, physical fitness, and cigarette smoking. A three-year evaluation period was used to assess the effects of the program on self-reported absenteeism. Results indicated that the impact of the program on absenteeism was restricted to lower-income employees. A health care cost analysis of the Live For Life program indicated that inpatient costs for the experimental groups rose at a significantly lower rate than in the control groups. Evaluation of the Stay Well program showed comparable results (Wilbur, Hartwell & Piserchia, 1986).

Nowadays, a fifth stage can be observed in worksite health promotion (WHP) programs, especially in Europe, Canada and Australia. Besides interventions focusing on lifestyle and health risk of employees, the fifth-stage WHP programs intervene on quality of work aspects, which may be the real cause of problems in the area of wellbeing, health and safety. In this view, the workplace is recognized both as an important target (Wilson, Holman & Hammock, 1996)

and as a determinant of health (Harden, Peersman, Oliver, Mauthner & Oakley, 1999). The improvement of working conditions is assumed to enhance wellness and health. In several countries in Europe, legislative guidelines concerning health and wellness at the worksite have stimulated this development. To give an example, in Norway and Sweden the Work Environment Act emphasizes that work conditions must permit the employee to influence his or her working situation. The work must also be organized to allow the development of competence, social contacts, and the ability to make decisions. In the Netherlands the Dutch Labor Act defines similar healthy work conditions.

One of the first representatives of the fifth stage is the Brabantia Project, named after a Dutch household products manufacturer where the program was implemented and evaluated. The project was evaluated by means of a quasi-experimental pre-test/post-test control group design with repeated measures. Interventions directed at lifestyle and working condition changes were implemented in the experimental site. Two other comparable Brabantia sites formed the control group. The control group received no intervention, but also completed the pre-test and a series of post-tests administered one, two and three years after the pre-test. In addition absenteeism data were gathered during the whole period of intervention. During the first year of intervention, activities were mainly targeted at lifestyles, including physical exercise, healthy nutrition, alcohol and drug consumption, smoking behavior, stress and pain. Interventions directed at working conditions or quality of work were implemented during the second and third years because a longer period of preparation is required for these interventions (Maes, Verhoeven, Kittel & Scholten, 1998). On the basis of a wellness risk assessment, an autonomous group of workers was established for each production unit and given authority over the entire production process, from collection of raw materials to delivery of the product to the sales department. This implied additional tasks for the workers such as initiating work orders, arranging supply and transport of raw materials and finished products, calculating hours spent on tasks, and performing quality checks. In addition to this greater variety of tasks, rotation of tasks became possible. Interventions at the individual level directed at lifestyle changes, which were introduced during the first year of intervention, brought about a favorable change in health risk at the first post-test. However, the initial effect on health risk disappeared at the second post-test, which illustrates the need for continuous and more extensive intervention to produce long-lasting effects on health outcomes. Furthermore, the program had favorable effects on working conditions, including psychological demands, control and ergonomic conditions, as well as on absenteeism.

In conclusion, in contrast to the American fourth-generation WHP programs, the Brabantia Project emphasized the organization and content of work rather than lifestyle. Therefore, it is not surprising that the project had the strongest and most enduring effects on perceived working conditions and absenteeism. The American fourth-generation programs focused more exclusively on a healthy lifestyle and health risk, and therefore tend to score better on health-related variables. It seems that the positive effects that these programs have on outcomes such as absenteeism are achieved through a different pathway. A combination of both approaches may produce superior and more sustainable effects.

Health Promotion in Health Care Settings

From a cost-effectiveness point of view, it is surprising how many existing health care services remain unused as a source of health promotion. In particular, primary health care physicians or nurses and basic health services could play an important role in health promotion. The INSURE/Life Cycle Preventive Health Services Study (Logsdon, Lazaro & Meier, 1989) was one of the first comprehensive trials which demonstrated the possible cost- effectiveness of this approach. The American study was set up in order to determine the possibility and cost of providing preventive health care through

primary health care physicians. The intervention comprised a combination of regular medical check-ups and X-ray examinations with patient education and counseling for behavioral risk factors. The study used a controlled design and involved 5,000 patients, who were seen by 74 physicians from five group practices. Data from a three-year feasibility study revealed that costs were controllable and showed several interesting effects: 17 per cent of the patients who smoked quit smoking as a consequence of the INSURE intervention; 33 per cent of the previous sedentary patients reported to have increased exercise levels one year after their INSURE check-up; 43 per cent of the patients lost weight; 22 per cent of those initially not wearing seat belts reported they were now using them; 53 per cent of the women who did not do breast self-examinations before the intervention now did so; and 35 per cent of the chronic drinkers reported to have decreased their alcohol consumption. The yearly average cost of the INSURE examination was $73 per person and the average utilization by patients was 38 per cent.

However, not all trials were equally successful. Ashenden, Silagy and Weller (1997) published a systematic review on the promotion of lifestyle changes in primary care. This review examined how effective lifestyle advice offered by primary health care physicians influenced patients' behavior related to smoking, alcohol consumption, diet and exercise. The review includes 23 trials for smoking, six for alcohol consumption, 10 for dietary behavior and six for exercise. Two hypotheses were examined: (1) that provision of advice is more effective than no advice; and (2) that intensive advice is more effective than brief advice. For smoking the first hypothesis was supported, but no significant difference was found between intensive and brief advice. Because of the small number of trials on the other three behaviors, only the results for the first hypothesis are reported here. It appears that advice can be effective for alcohol consumption, and that this benefit can be detected at a biochemical level. For dietary behavior, no conclusions could be drawn because of the wide variety of outcome measures used in the different studies. For exercise there is evidence that advice may have an effect on self-reported exercise levels. Notably, all changes were small. The authors conclude: 'that at present there is insufficient evidence to warrant a mass population approach to health checks and lifestyle advice in a general practice setting' (1997: 173). However, even if the effects are small at a population level, the absolute number of people who would change their health behavior might be substantial if an INSURE-like program were to be offered throughout the Western world by all primary health care settings. Indeed, primary health care professionals see large parts of the population on a regular basis and are seen as credible agents of change. However, many of them seem to lack time and/or motivation to engage in health promotion initiatives (Bowler & Gooding, 1995). This is at least partly due to the fact that the main cost of preventive interventions is not covered by (national) health insurances, but also because the role of physicians and nurses as health agents, in the real sense of the word, will require a change in the mentality of the population, the health professionals, and policy makers.

Conclusion and Discussion

Health promotion initiatives in all these settings have proven to be successful in creating health behavior change and/or risk factor reduction and to have the potential to influence morbidity and mortality at a population level. In the beginning, the focus of initiatives was on disease prevention rather than on health promotion. The programs aimed at changing isolated behaviors (e.g., smoking, exercise or diet) that were narrowly linked with proven risk factors for a specific disease. As these programs did not prove to be very successful in influencing disease outcomes and mortality at a population level, a change in strategy followed during recent decades. This development can be described in terms of the following trends. First, program developers realized that unhealthy behaviors do not exist in isolation, but are linked to other behaviors, which constitute a lifestyle. As a consequence, interventions became more comprehensive, focusing for

example on the prevention of substance abuse rather than on smoking (Botvin et al., 1992) or on an even wider variety of behavioral targets (including smoking, weight, physical exercise, use of alcohol, diet and nutrition, and stress), as for example in the Johnson and Johnson Live For Life program (Cataldo & Coates, 1986). Second, program providers were convinced that programs had to be continued over a long period of time in order to have substantial and lasting effects. For example, in contrast to earlier school-based health promotion programs, the Seattle Social Development Project (Hawkins et al., 1999) was offered throughout elementary school from the first to the sixth grade. Third, a related insight concerned the sustainability of programs, which was enhanced by collaboration with the community. A good example of this may be found in the community-capacity building approach of the Stanford Five City Project (Jackson, Altman, Howard-Pitney & Farquhar, 1989). Fourth, many earlier programs were conducted in a social vacuum, focusing on individual health behavior change. Recent successful health promotion programs involve the community to support and complement lifestyle changes. School-based health promotion programs which made use of community action, such as the Seattle Social Development Project (Hawkins et al., 1999) and the Tobacco Policy Options Program (Forster et al., 1998), are good examples of this trend. The Brabantia Project, which focused on changes in the work environment in order to improve quality of work life, next to lifestyle changes, is an example of this social ecological approach at the worksite (Maes et al., 1998). Fifth, there is a trend to combine levels and channels of intervention in order to maximize effects. For example, although media-based health promotion is mostly unsuccessful in bringing about health behavior change, Jason (1998) reports that a combination of a mass media approach with self-help material and support groups proved to substantially cut smoking rates in the target group. The Florida 'Truth' campaign, which made use of broadcasts, teenage action groups, school curricula, tobacco sales restrictions and a website, is another example of a wide scope program which effectively reduced teenage smoking (Perry, 2000).

There are however two other remarks to be made which can further improve future health promotion programs. The first concerns the extent to which these programs are based on sound psychological models for behavior change. While many agree that the use of appropriate theory should be part of the design and evaluation of health promotion initiatives (Green & Tones, 1999), this is not always the practice. On the one hand, there are initiatives which were also set up for research purposes. These initiatives frequently involve psychological expertise and are usually theory based. For example, Botvin and colleagues (1992) developed an effective program for the prevention of teenage substance abuse based on social learning theory. These programs tend however to be smaller and often have problems with sustaining the intervention over time and disseminating them widely in the population (Brunner et al., 1997). On the other hand, there are broader initiatives which involve simultaneous actions in several settings and address large parts of the (general, school, worksite or health care) population. Some of these initiatives have explicit theoretical roots, as for example the North Karelia Project and the Stanford Three Community and Five City Projects (Tones & Tilford, 1994), and are mostly 'demonstration' projects set up by university departments in cooperation with the community. However, policy makers and/or managers at broadcasting centers, schools, worksites or health care institutions usually participate in these larger initiatives. Psychologists are thus seldom at the helm of these initiatives. As a consequence, these programs make use of mass media, and educational or medical (including social epidemiological) expertise, but seldom reflect the psychological knowledge base concerning health behavior change. It should be noted, however, that psychologists have not been very active in cooperating with other experts in this respect (Jason, 1998) and that the diversity of psychological models that can be applied to health promotion constitutes another barrier. The health action model analysis of the psychosocial and environmental

influences on health-related behavior is a good illustration of the diversity of psychological influences on health behavior (change) (Tones & Tilford, 1994). As many health psychologists tend to work only within one or a few paradigms, which are relevant for these influences, psychological knowledge is not very accessible for other professionals, who would like to address the full range of these influences. In other words, psychologists have not put enough effort into the translation and communication of their knowledge base to other professionals. The aforementioned Dutch worksite health promotion program, known as the Brabantia Project, was based on a set of principles for intervention, which can be the start of such a translation effort. The principles are derived from a variety of theoretical perspectives in psychology, including operant conditioning, associative learning, cognitive-behavioral theory, social cognition, social learning, and stage theories, and thus provide a sound basis for an effective and integrative approach to health behavior change (Lee & Owen, 1985; Maes, 1990). Table 11.1 gives a brief description of these principles. The interested reader is referred to Maes and Van Elderen (1998) which describes them in more detail. While these principles may seem elementary, they are frequently violated in existing health promotion initiatives.

A second remark concerns methodological shortcomings. The effectiveness of interventions should be judged in terms of the achievement of prior stated goals. In providing such evidence, evaluation studies frequently suffer from the typical errors known as type I error, type II error, and type III error. Green and Tones (1999) give a good description of the relevance of these methodological requirements for the evaluation of health promotion programs. Type I error occurs when inadequate use of control groups is made in randomized controlled trials. However, for many health promotion initiatives, it is not feasible or even advisable to randomly allocate individuals to experimental and control groups. A more realistic perspective may be to randomize institutions (such as schools, worksites or health care centres), but in some cases, as for

Table 11.1   *Principles of health promotian*

Principle	Description of the principle
1 Behavior change occurs in stages	Behavior change is a dynamic process, characterized by at least three stages: the decision to change, the initial active change and the maintenance and generalization of the new behavior. Different interventions are required for each stage
2 Appropriateness and convenience of settings	Behavioral change programs should be easily accessible, be available to all and free. Environmental changes are thus necessary to support programs
3 Setting realistic goals and shaping the process of change	Small changes are more likely to be effective in producing initial change. The goal of intervention should thus be close to peoples' current behavior and carry them stepwise to other levels
4 Intrinsic value	People are more likely to persist in activities they find enjoyable and interesting. Programs should be attractive and integrate activities that counteract possible reductions in wellbeing, which accompany the change
5 Soundness and specificity of information	Health messages need to be specific and inform people concerning how, when and where to act
6 Variety	Offering many alternative ways to achieve behavior change is more successful
7 Multiple levels	Behavior change should be supported by changes in people's immediate and distant environment, including regulation and legislation
8 Use of social networks	Existing social networks in various settings have an important impact on individuals' lifestyles. Individual behavioral change should thus be complemented by social changes and community action
9 Choice and personal goals	If people make the decision to change themselves, they are more likely to persist in it. Interventions should thus start from personal goals or carefully plan a goal adoption process
10 Independence	Dependence on any particular place or person reduces the individual's capacity to continue the target behavior if the situation alters. People should thus be involved in program development, delivery and dissemination
11 Sustainability of interventions	Maintenance of behavioral change requires continuous intervention. Interventions should thus not occur as single or temporal events, but should be continuous

example in the case of community health promotion programs, it may very difficult to find adequate control groups. In addition, the intervention may be hard to control in the cases where the initiative comes from the community itself and contamination of the control group is also likely to occur. Type II error occurs when the research design fails to tap the actual changes that are caused by the intervention. While this can be due to lack of measurement sensitivity, there are many other

sources that can cause this error. A common problem of many intervention programs is that they are too ambitious in the sense that they set change goals that are hard to achieve, for example changes in morbidity and mortality. These epidemiological changes mostly require a very long time frame, which is preceded by a change in risk factors and health behaviors, which are in turn preceded by determinants of health behavior change like changes in knowledge, context and efficacy beliefs or skills. There are many authors who plead for the formulation of realistic and achievable goals (Hancock et al., 1997). Another problem is that many programs aim for general rather than relative effectiveness. For example, a Canadian anti-smoking campaign, the COMMIT Program, proved to be effective for moderate smokers, but not for heavy smokers (Institute of Medicine, 2002). Finally, another common shortcoming that will cause type II error is that the sample size is too small to demonstrate statistically significant differences (Hancock et al., 1997). Type III error refers to rejection of program effectiveness on the basis of inadequate program design or delivery. To prevent this type of error it is necessary to document and monitor program delivery and implementation. However, this type of information, usually referred to as process evaluation, is seldom available in evaluation studies.

PSYCHOLOGICAL INTERVENTIONS IN CHRONIC ILLNESS

While health promotion initiatives traditionally have a large population focus, psychological interventions in chronic illness focus on smaller, more specific patient groups. Many of the principles that were described at the end of the previous section can also guide the development of psychological interventions for patients with chronic diseases. Nevertheless, most of the existing interventions are more individual or clinical in nature, relying on principles derived from stress management, (cognitive) behavior therapy, rational-emotive therapy, and other clinical intervention paradigms. As a consequence, the theoretical base for many of these interventions is more derivative. In an attempt to structure the variety of interventions offered to patients with chronic diseases, Maes (1993; see also Maes & Van Elderen, 1998) developed a model that makes a distinction between intervention aims, levels and channels. As such three different dimensions are discerned along which an intervention can be located, namely:

(1) intervention aims (restoring or increasing quality of life versus promotion of self-management); (2) intervention level (the patient, a group of patients or the larger physical and social environment of the patient); and (3) intervention channel (direct face-to-face contact between a psychologist and a patient, or indirect interventions through for example trained health professionals). The following sections are based on these three dimensions. All psychological interventions in chronic disease are in principle directed at quality of life, self-management or both, and the intervention aims dimension is considered in terms of these two forms.

Intervention Aims: Quality of Life Interventions

Interventions that focus primarily on quality of life aim at increasing the physical, psychological or social wellbeing of the patient and his or her immediate environment. These interventions are designed to stimulate a process of adaptation to or acceptance of the disease. More specifically, these interventions are aimed at reducing stress, pain, or problems related to the performance of daily activities (including work, leisure and household activities, as well as activities related to social roles within the family). These include physical training programs, stress management programs, and interventions that provide social support.

Various *physical training* programs are offered to different groups of patients, including patients with coronary heart disease (CHD) and chronic respiratory diseases. These programs seem to have effects on quality of life and wellbeing (as, e.g., a reduction of anxiety and depression) as long as patients engage in physical training (Maes, 1992; Van den Broek, 1995). Physical exercise, however, can also have important effects on disease-related outcomes. For example, meta-analyses have indicated beneficial effects on morbidity and mortality of physical exercise for patients suffering from CHD (Maes, 1992), and show that exercise reduces glycosylated hemoglobin (HbA1c) and the risk of complications in diabetic patients (Boule, Haddad, Kenny, Wells & Sigall, 2001).

Stress management programs include intervention techniques such as cognitive restructuring and relaxation, as well as coping skills training and social support interventions. As will be illustrated in this section, more elaborate stress management programs not only improve quality of life but can also affect disease progression and even mortality in patients with cancer, CHD and HIV. An example of a group intervention targeted at enhancing the management of stress is 'the hook'. This technique helps post-myocardial infarction patients to gain control of their emotional reactivity to daily stressors (Powell, 1996). It was part of the Recurrent Coronary Prevention Project, a 4.5-year clinical trial aimed at altering type A behavior, that had impressive beneficial effects on the recurrence of myocardial infarction (Friedmann et al., 1984). This cognitive exercise was especially designed to promote a shift in basic beliefs and attitudes and is a good example of *cognitive restructuring*. The strategy consists of a group discussion around three questions. A simple and straightforward metaphor, that is a hook, was used to allow participants to recognize a stressor as such and to change their cognitions instantly instead of changing the stressor. More specifically, when starting the group session, participants were asked to describe an incident in which they became angered, irritated or impatient. At the first question ('What is behavior modification?'), the general idea of cognitive change was introduced. Participants worked interactively with the therapist to come up with answers and examples. The second question ('What is impatience/irritation?') sensitized participants to the type of stressors, small and unexpected, that are likely to promote the quick response of anger or impatience/irritation. At this point, the metaphor of 'the hook' was introduced to describe these responses. At the third question ('What can we do about it?'), the alternative cognition of labeling a stressor as a hook instead of an unfair situation was used, thus neutralizing its arousal effect. Patients in the trial reported that of all the strategies they were being offered, 'the hook' helped

them most in reducing their irritabilities and anger.

Besides cognitive restructuring, some forms of *relaxation* are often used alone or in combination with other techniques in order to enhance the management of stress and subsequently improve quality of life. Nowadays, there is a wide span of relaxation techniques that can be used either individually or in group programs (Dixhoorn, 1998). Examples are progressive muscle relaxation training, guided imagery, meditation, biofeedback, and breathing techniques such as yoga. Relaxation is widely recognized as an effective intervention strategy for hypertension (Johnston, 1992). An example of a successful intervention program of which this form of stress management is an important ingredient (next to diet, physical exercise and group support) is the Ornish Program for reversing coronary heart disease. This program proved to bring about lifestyle changes in patients with coronary heart disease, paralleled by a reversal of coronary atherosclerosis within one year. Even more regression was noted after four years, resulting in a significant improvement in blood flow to the heart and thus in a reduction in angina complaints, comparable to that achieved after coronary artery bypass grafting or coronary angioplasty. The stress management component is based on hatha yoga and includes stretching, progressive relaxation, breathing techniques, meditation and visualization. Patients practice a combination of these techniques at least 1 hour a day on the basis of an audiocassette with a pre-recorded program (Billings, 2000).

Coping is an important moderator of stress in patients with chronic disease (Maes, Leventhal & De Ridder, 1996). Therefore *coping skills training* may also help patients to adjust to the stresses of illness and treatment. For example, anticipation of hospitalization for surgery and adjustment to limitations afterwards may be difficult, especially for children. In an attempt to reduce the distress that could lead to short-term and long-term behavioral and emotional problems, Zastowny, Kirschenbaum and Meng (1986) developed a coping skills training targeted at the child–parent dyad. The intervention was based on the *stress inoculation theory* (Meichenbaum, 1975). One week prior to hospitalization, both parents and children were shown a videotape in which a frog puppet described his rather positive experiences during hospitalization. Next, they were given a tour of the different units of the hospital. While the children were given an opportunity to play, the intervention focused specifically on the parents. First they were presented with videotaped lectures on the experience of stress and the use of coping skills on a conceptual level. They were explicitly told that deep breathing and physical relaxation could help reduce one aspect of the stress experience. The other aspects of stress could be reduced by going through the four phases of coping, namely: (1) preparing for a stressor; (2) confronting and handling a stressor; (3) coping with feelings at critical moments; and (4) reinforcing oneself for successful coping. Parents were invited to act as 'coping coaches', assisting their children by demonstrating procedures that would help them to reduce their own distress and by working together through a preparatory booklet for high-stress points during the upcoming hospitalization. Finally a videotape was shown to illustrate the desired kind of interaction, and parents were given a handout summarizing their responsibilities as coping coaches. Compared to a group of child–parent dyads who received only information about the positive and stress-reducing effects of spending extra time with their child in the week prior to hospitalization, the coping skills training group showed a reduction of children's self-reported fearfulness and parents' reported distress. Furthermore, there were fewer maladaptive behaviors observed during hospitalization, as well as less problematic behaviours in both the pre-admission week and the second post-discharge week.

Another group of interventions aimed at improving quality of life can be characterized as *social support interventions*. Social support has the potential to buffer stress (Cohen & Wills, 1985). Interventions that aim to increase social support may have important effects on patients' psychological adjustment or quality of life. There is a plethora of literature demonstrating the beneficial effects of patient support or

discussion groups for various groups of chronic patients, including rheumatoid arthritis patients, cancer patients, myocardial infarction patients, and epilepsy patients, among others (Taylor, 2001). However, it seems that not all forms of social sharing with other patients are equally beneficial. For example, patients who were paired up with either a post-operative or a non-surgical patient were shown to experience significantly less anxiety than when they shared a room with another pre-operative patient (Kulik, Moore & Mahler, 1993). Therefore, even more practical and low-cost interventions, such as roommate assignment on the ward, can lead to a reduction of patients' pre-operative anxiety levels by increasing the opportunity for social support.

Some studies show that there is a beneficial effect not only on adjustment but also on recovery and mortality. The study by Spiegel, Bloom, Kraemer and Gottheil (1989) is a well-known example. In this study, which focused on group discussion, metastatic breast cancer patients were randomly assigned to a control group and an intervention group. Weekly group meetings were held during 1 year. These meetings focused on problems that the patients experienced and on ways to improve their social relationships. At the end of the intervention, the patients who received the intervention reported better adjustment than the control group patients. A 10-year follow-up proved that the intervention also increased survival rates. Results of another study (Fawzy et al., 1993) pointed in the same direction. In this study melanoma patients were randomly assigned to a control group and an intervention group that received six weekly 90-minute sessions. The intervention was more comprehensive than the one offered in the Spiegel study. Apart from group discussion, informational support was also provided (education, stress management and coping skills). The intervention proved to reduce psychological distress and to alter immune function at six months, and to increase survival at a six-year follow-up.

Helgeson and Cohen (1996) conducted a literature review on social support and adjustment to cancer. They came to the conclusion that correlational studies suggest that emotional support has the strongest association with better adjustment. However, the effectiveness of peer discussion groups is less convincing, since educational groups providing informational support appear to be at least as effective as peer discussion. In a recent study, researchers from Pittsburgh (Helgeson, Cohen, Schulz & Yasko, 2001) offered psycho-educational intervention, a social support intervention, or a combination of both interventions to three groups of early stage breast cancer patients. A fourth non-intervention group functioned as a control group. Patients who had received the psycho-educational or the combined intervention reported less distress and higher levels of adjustment than those who received the social support intervention or belonged to the control group. Ongoing research (Baum & Andersen, 2001; Helgeson et al., 2001) suggests that these interventions not only have the potential to improve psychological adjustment but also can alter the immune status and disease course.

Effective interventions for enhancing the management of stress in chronic patients seem thus to entail a *combination of different strategies* or components. The already described interventions by Ornish (Billings, 2000) and Helgeson and colleagues (2001) illustrate this point. Another illustration of a comprehensive intervention, targeted at restoring quality of life using a combination of different strategies, is a program designed to reduce anxiety and depression in HIV-seropositive gay men after their first diagnosis (Lutgendorf, Antoni, Schneiderman, Iroson & Fletcher, 1995). Based on those psychological factors that are likely both to facilitate or mediate quality of life in infected individuals and to be accessible to intervention, a 10-week cognitive-behavioral stress management (CBSM) group program was primarily targeted towards enhancing a sense of control, relaxation, effective coping strategies and adequate social support resources. During these 10 weeks, participants met twice a week, and attended one session in which CBSM strategies were taught and one weekly relaxation training. First, the participants were introduced to a cognitively based model of distress and were subsequently taught how to identify their personal and frequently used distortions and how to refute and replace them with more functional appraisals of their HIV status. Second, maladaptive coping strategies like denial and substance use were identified and more direct methods of coping to alleviate distress were introduced, as well as assertiveness training. Finally, the use of social support was emphasized through interaction with the group, and the identification of possible sources of social support and potential problems with social support systems. In the weekly sessions devoted to relaxation training, participants learned progressive muscle relaxation and were requested to practice relaxation at least twice daily at home. Compared to a control group including HIV-seropositive gay men, the men who participated in the program showed no increase in anxiety and depression after receiving the first diagnosis of their infection and reported no decrease in either levels of social support or adaptive coping strategies, in addition to an increase in immunological functioning. Interestingly, the amount of denial used as a coping strategy at the end of the intervention, as well as greater frequency of home practice of relaxation during the 10-week program, predicted better immune functioning one year later. A slightly modified version of the program was also offered to a group of patients with early HIV infection but who were still asymptomatic. Comparable results to the first study were reported. Furthermore, the use of active coping, planning and acceptance of the disease increased and these results were paralleled by immune status changes.

These results show that a psychological intervention with different components aimed at maintaining sufficient levels of life quality, despite challenging circumstances (the onset of a debilitating disease and a shortened but uncertain lifespan with a possible social stigma attached to it), apparently had an impact on psychological wellbeing as well as on the physiological status of the patients.

Thus far, we have focused on interventions that target increases in quality of life. We will now devote attention to interventions that target self-management.

Intervention Aims: Self-Management Interventions

Some intervention programs have a clear focus on self-management in chronic patients. Living with a chronic disease is a difficult task, which frequently requires important lifestyle changes and adherence to medical advice, aimed at stabilizing or slowing down the progression of the disease or reducing undesirable physical consequences and complications. Influencing the progression of the disease or preventing 'things from getting worse' is defined in the literature as secondary prevention. Preventing undesirable consequences and complications, for example accidents in epileptic patients or gangrene in diabetic patients, is seen as tertiary prevention. From a disease management point of view, required behavioral changes may vary from disease to disease, but include changes such as: (1) taking medication or keeping appointments with health care workers for various forms of diagnosis and treatment; (2) changing unhealthy behaviors like smoking and excessive fat, salt, sugar or alcohol intake; (3) adopting healthy habits like physical exercise, taking regular meals, maintaining normal body weight, taking enough sleep, rest or relaxation; and (4) engaging in a variety of self-management behaviors like monitoring blood sugar, taking sanitary measures at home and at work, avoiding working with machines, driving a car or swimming alone, and maintaining regular exercise for arthritic hands and fingers.

Research has repeatedly demonstrated that about half of chronic patients do not adequately follow medical advice. Interventions to assist patients to follow prescriptions for medications can range from instructional pamphlets, workbooks, pill containers and telephone reminders, to counseling and family therapy. Evidence suggests that written information and counseling are effective for short-term treatments. Effective interventions for long-term medication treatment appear to be complex and include various combinations of more convenient care, information, counseling, reminders, self-monitoring, reinforcement, family therapy and other forms of additional supervision or attention. Granted,

these techniques do influence the extent to which patients adhere to medical advice with respect to medication, but the improvements are often not substantial (Haynes, McKibbon & Kanai, 1996). Many health care workers seem to be unfamiliar with the reasons for non-adherence. Research has shown that *adherence* to medical advice is not related to personal characteristics such as age, gender, race, religion, educational level, income or personality characteristics. Non-compliance is also not dependent on objective disease characteristics, such as the severity of the disease or the nature and severity of symptoms. Instead, whether people follow medical advice or not is related to the nature and form of advice and social support, illness perceptions, comprehension of the advice and the treatment plan, and characteristics of the provider–patient relationship (Brannon & Feist, 1997).

In other words, faulty communication by health professionals is one of the most important sources of non-adherence. Unfortunately, faulty communication seems to be the rule rather than the exception. In a study by Phillips (1996) about half of the 320 obstetrics and gynecological patients that were questioned reported that they were dissatisfied with the care they had received. Complaints regarded lack of sensitivity to the patients' conditions, evasion of direct questions, use of medical jargon and lack of information provision. This lack of attention for the patient may however not be a deliberate attitude, but can be attributed to a high workload (care requires time) or a lack of skills training. Remarkably, Williams et al. (1997) reported that only 16 per cent of a sample of young medical doctors affirmed being taught assessment of psychosocial factors. Doctors were also shown to have a different (problem solving) perspective from the patient. A study by Berry, Michas and Gillie (1997) presented 16 categories of information to both doctors and patients, and asked them to rank these from one (not at all important) to five (vital). A rank-order correlation between the doctors' and the patients' rankings showed no correlation (rho = 0.02). While this difference can be explained by the fact that patients and doctors have indeed different perspectives, medical curricula should pay more attention to training in information provision and doctor–patient communication in order to enhance self-management in patients.

It should be noted, however, that it is the patient and not the health professional that is ultimately responsible for adequate management of his or her chronic disease. From this perspective, terms like 'compliance' or 'adherence' are concepts of the past, since they suggest that patients must follow medical advice. Today, the self-management of a chronic disease is a more defendable intervention target. Many types of self-management techniques have been applied in interventions with chronic patients, including self-monitoring, goal-setting, behavioral contracting, shaping the process of change, self-reinforcement, stimulus control, covert control and cognitive restructuring, behavioral assignments and modeling, or observational learning (Bennett, 2000; Taylor, 2001). Self-management programs for chronic patients make use of a combination of these and other techniques such as rational-emotive therapy or training. At present, there are self-management programs for a variety of chronic conditions such as hypertension, coronary heart disease, asthma, diabetes, rheumatic diseases and renal failure. In a meta-analytic review of asthma patient education, Bauman (1993) came to the conclusion that self-management programs produce stronger effects on psychological outcomes, compliance and self-management skills than traditional health education programs, which are characterized by provision of information only. Other meta-analyses of arthritis, cardiac and diabetes education programs came to comparable conclusions (Brown, 1992; Dusseldorp, van Elderen, Maes, Meulman & Kraaij, 1999; Hirano, Laurant & Lorig, 1994; Mullen, Mains & Velez, 1992). This illustrates the need for behavioral expertise in the development and implementation of programs for patients with chronic disease, which goes beyond a traditional instructional approach.

An example of a multicomponent self-management programme is the Arthritis Self-Management Program (ASMP) (Lorig & Holman, 1993). Designed as a community-based program for mild to moderately severe patients, the ASMP is aimed at improving health behaviors and health status by increasing participants' perceptions of arthritis self-efficacy and the use of cognitive-behavioral techniques. The program consisted of six weekly sessions of about two hours, was guided by a manual, and was delivered by pairs of lay leaders, most of whom had arthritis themselves. During the sessions, which were largely interactive, short informational lectures were given, along with group discussion, problem solving, role-plays and mastery experiences. Furthermore, participants were asked to set personal and realistic goals for every forthcoming week in a written contract and report back at the group on their achievements. The receipt of feedback thus enabled participants to monitor their progress, an important element of self-management. In comparison to a group of patients on a waiting list for the program, participants showed improvements in arthritis self-efficacy and health behaviors, and were significantly less depressed and exhibited a more positive mood. One year later, similar effects were reported, together with a decrease in pain and increased visits to the primary care physician.

While this section differentiates between quality of life and self-management interventions, it should be noted that most interventions in chronic patients are *psycho-educational* or a combination of both. The reason for this is probably that both intervention strategies have the potential to produce beneficial effects on comparable outcomes, but by different means, and that a combination of these pathways is thought to produce a stronger effect. For example, the large majority of the 37 studies that were included in a meta-analysis of intervention programs for patients with coronary heart disease (and showed important effects of these programs on health behavior change, risk factor reduction and mortality) offered combined interventions (Dusseldorp et al., 1999). Likewise psycho-educational interventions seem to have more effects on adjustment of cancer patients than emotional support groups (Helgeson & Cohen, 1996).

Intervention Level: The Individual Patient, the Group and the Larger Environment

Psychologists are mostly educated within an intervention paradigm that supports the idea that effective interventions are rather intensive, direct forms of intervention targeted at the psychological problems of *individual patients*. While this approach is certainly valuable in some cases, the disadvantage is that it implies doing a lot for a very small group of patients. More indirect forms of intervention at a group and environmental level are clearly called for, if health psychologists are to make a significant contribution to the care of chronic patients at a population level. In other words, clinical health psychologists must 'go for the numbers' rather than for the most intensive or personally satisfying form of intervention. In line with this reasoning, there is a trend towards development of programs for *groups of patients and their partners*. Most of these interventions are based on cognitive behavior or social learning theory and make use of many of the above mentioned self-management techniques. Such programs exist in several Western countries for patients suffering from diabetes, rheumatic diseases, cancer, chronic respiratory diseases and coronary heart disease (Bauman, 1993; Helgeson & Cohen, 1996; Institute of Medicine, 2002; Lorig & Holman, 1993; Van Elderen, Maes, Seegers, Kragten & Relik-van Wely, 1994).

One such group intervention program is the Dutch 'heart and health' program, which has been developed for patients with coronary heart disease (Van Elderen et al., 1994). The program is offered to groups of about eight patients and their partners during cardiac rehabilitation and consists of eight weekly 2-hour sessions and two follow-up sessions. Each session is devoted to a particular topic, selected on the basis of an assessment of the specific needs of the patient. During each session, patients' questions related to the topic are answered. During the second part of the session patients and partners try, under the supervision of a psychologist, to identify and change irrational beliefs or thoughts, which can obstruct important rehabilitation goals. Apart from positive effects on patient satisfaction, the programme has been shown to have beneficial effects on smoking cessation, changes in diet and use of medical resources (Van Elderen et al., 1994).

Psychologists frequently underestimate the relevance of interventions on an environmental level. Such interventions are sometimes described as *social engineering*, because they are aimed at modifying the home, work or leisure environment of the patient so as to facilitate normal functioning of the patient in everyday life. Psychological expertise at this level is of special importance for some patients, such as those with rheumatic diseases, not only because the screening of these patients' environments requires some psychological expertise, but also because acceptance of environmental changes by patients and their relatives may require psychological guidance (Moos, 1988).

Interventions at the broader environmental level also imply *community-level interventions*. For example, Daniel and colleagues (1999) evaluated a community intervention based on social learning theory, directed at diabetes control. The intervention that was offered to an experimental community included television, radio, and press coverage of program activities, which in turn included physical exercise classes, health events, cooking demonstrations, information provision and diabetes support groups. In comparison to two control communities, the intervention proved to have a beneficial effect on systolic blood pressure, but not on glycated hemoglobin (HbA1c). A combination of face-to-face and community interventions may produce more important and sustainable effects.

What is argued for is thus a combination of various levels of intervention, including individual or group-based interventions, alongside social engineering and community-based interventions. To our knowledge there is no single program that addresses all these levels of intervention, although this would almost certainly enhance program effectiveness.

Intervention Channel: Direct versus Indirect Interventions

Let us now look at the third dimension, namely the intervention channel. Direct face-to-face contact with a patient can be between a patient and a psychologist or between a patient and another health professional. From a psychologist's point of view this latter form of communication is indirect. Other forms of indirect interventions involve the use of volunteers and of printed or audiovisual self-help materials or computer-based communications.

As stated in the previous section, many psychologists prefer direct psychological interventions, which they deliver themselves, rather than indirect interventions. However, such a preference is not defendable from a cost-effectiveness point of view because intensive face-to-face interventions are not the best type of interventions for all patients. Some patients may require less intensive intervention than others. Furthermore, intensive interventions do not necessarily produce superior effects. For example, Lewin, Robertson, Cay, Irving and Campbell (1992) demonstrated that cardiac patients could profit from a manual (The Heart Manual) given to them upon discharge from the hospital by a trained nurse. Together they assess what a good starting level for daily physical exercise would be (a level that even on a 'bad' day the patient would still be able to perform, e.g., walk to the mailbox two blocks away) for the six-week self-help intervention. This program is based on the principles of goal-setting and pacing ('do what you plan, not what you feel like'), cognitive restructuring and relaxation training in order to foster a renewed sense of control, self-efficacy and realism or slight optimism about the future. The manual addresses common misconceptions and stress reactions related to the coronary incident, introduces stress management techniques, and suggests appropriate levels of activity and physical exercise for various stages of recovery. Guided by the structure of the manual, patients are encouraged to do the physical exercises every day both morning and evening, to note down their progress with respect to the physical exercises every evening in a fixed schedule, and to read and fill out quizzes about (mis)perceptions of their disease. They are also encouraged to practice relaxation training by listening to an audiocassette tape at least once a day. Every other week the nurse phones them at home and discusses their progress, motivating them to continue with the program. In the Lewin et al. (1992) study, half of a group of 190

coronary heart disease patients received the manual, while the other half (the control group) did not. Both groups received similar medical and psychosocial care. The experimental group reported less anxiety and depression than the control group, even 1 year after discharge. In addition, patients in the experimental group made significantly fewer visits to their general practitioner and were less frequently readmitted to the hospital than patients in the control group.

Recently, communication with patients also includes *computer-based interaction*. Balas, Jaffrey and Kuperman (1997) reported on the effects of 80 clinical trials that made use of electronic communication with patients, including computerized communication and various forms of computer-based telephone contact (e.g., for counseling, follow-up and reminders). About two-thirds of these studies reported beneficial effects regarding a variety of outcomes related to preventive care, cardiac rehabilitation, diabetes care and management of osteoarthritis.

An example of an intervention program that was delivered indirectly by trained *volunteers* is targeted at improving the quality of life of elderly cancer patients with symptoms of anxiety and/or depression while undergoing chemotherapy (Mantovani et al., 1996). Prior to the delivery of the interventions, these volunteers had received both 40 hours of formal training and 40 hours of supervision in how to provide practical, informational and emotional support to elderly cancer patients. The distressed elderly cancer patients as well as their partners received support for six hours a week, divided into two or three sessions, while still in hospital as well as at home, for the entire period of their cancer treatment. During these sessions, the primary aim was to transmit positive feelings to patients and to assist them emotionally, especially during significant episodes of their medical treatment. Information on the disease and its treatment was also given and patients were assisted in practical matters and invited to participate in recreational activities that could help them to take their minds off worries about their disease. At the same time, patients received psychopharmacological treatment that was progressively reduced or completely withdrawn when symptoms of anxiety and/or depression significantly subsided. The intervention was administered by volunteers and proved to be more effective in improving pain control, functional status, psychological distress and quality of life in general than psychopharmacological treatment alone. Furthermore, social support delivered by volunteers combined with structured psychotherapy proved to be equally effective as the social support alone in terms of the outcome measures mentioned above. Therefore, from a cost/benefit perspective, an inexpensive approach of training volunteers may be preferred with respect to these specific groups of patients. However, it is good to keep in mind that the effectiveness of this intervention in alleviating distress is probably dependent on thorough instruction and close supervision of volunteers.

These results indicate that indirect interventions can have impressive effects. Another advantage is that other *health professionals*, including medical doctors, nurses, physiotherapists and dieticians, are also in a better position to deliver psychological interventions (Swerrison & Foreman, 1991). For example, while there is little doubt that psychosocial care should be offered as a component of cardiac rehabilitation, the results of a European survey showed important differences in the degree of involvement of psychologists in cardiac rehabilitation in different European countries (Maes, 1992). In the Netherlands and Italy, psychologists are key members of most cardiac rehabilitation teams, but their involvement in cardiac rehabilitation is negligible in Sweden, Finland, Denmark, the United Kingdom and Switzerland. This does not necessarily mean that psychosocial care is not offered to cardiac patients in these countries, but rather that other health professionals (e.g., nurses in the UK) play a more central role in its delivery (Maes, 1992). As a consequence, health psychologists need to learn how to assist and *empower others* in the delivery of psychological interventions in order to enhance patients' quality of life and self-management behaviors. Such indirect intervention may involve training of health personnel in psychological intervention and communication skills, and psychological consultation with other health professionals. There

are many examples of effective interventions designed by psychologists but delivered by others, including the Weight Watchers movement. Weight Watchers, originally designed by the American psychologist Stunkard, proved to be an extremely effective weight reduction program offered at a community level by lay persons. Another example can be found in health education and counseling programmes offered to myocardial infarction patients during and after hospitalization. Many of these programmes have been designed by psychologists, although they are typically and effectively delivered by nurses and/or social workers (Van Elderen, Maes & Van den Broek, 1994). In many other contexts, as in the case of terminally ill patients, regular health personnel will be responsible for standard care, while psychologists may play a more distant advisory role.

In short, indirect interventions may vary from developing materials, computer-based programs or self-help courses for patients, through teaching psychological principles and methods to other health professionals, to designing intervention programs and providing advice and training in face-to-face situations to both professionals and lay persons. Some critics of indirect interventions have argued that they imply 'giving psychology away'. As psychologists, we should instead be proud to have so much to give.

Conclusion and Discussion

At the end of this section, the reader may be convinced that psychological interventions have the potential to reduce stress and to increase quality of life in chronic patients via various forms of stress management interventions, including cognitive restructuring, relaxation, coping skills training and social support interventions. On the other hand, there are many intervention programs that are successful in enhancing self-management knowledge and skills in a variety of chronic patient groups, including patients with CHD, cancer, chronic respiratory diseases, arthritis and diabetes. Furthermore, there is evidence that combined interventions can have endocrinological and immunological effects, which can slow down the disease process and thus have the potential to influence morbidity and mortality, especially in the area of CHD, certain types of cancer and HIV. A surprising trend is that the pathways of change become more visible. For example, a meta-analysis of 37 controlled studies on psychological interventions in patients with coronary heart disease showed that these interventions achieved significant reductions in risk factors and related health behavior, as well as in recurrence of MI and in mortality. Studies that had the most effect on blood pressure, smoking and exercise also had the strongest beneficial effects on MI recurrence and mortality. This suggests that a reduction of risk factors and related health behavior can lead to more distant outcomes (Dusseldorp et al., 1999). The studies by Ornish (Billings, 2000) further proved that a reduction of risk-factor-related health behaviors results in a reversal of coronary atherosclerosis. Studies conducted at Miami showed that cognitive-behavioral stress management techniques offered to HIV-seropositive men result not only in enhanced mood but also in a lower production of excretion of stress hormones and testosterone and a 'better' immune function (Baum, 2000). This suggests that interventions that significantly reduce distress in HIV-infected men also have endocrinological and immunological effects. Finally, interventions with breast cancer and melanoma patients have shown effects on the immune system and enhanced survival, even if the results of some studies should be interpreted with care (Baum, 2000). While there is still a long way to go, the biological plausibility of the link between psychological (behavioral and mood) effects and morbidity and mortality is increasing.

Another conclusion concerns the fact that psychological interventions do not address the full scope at which they can be delivered. They are frequently limited to individual and small-group interventions delivered by psychologists. As argued above, this approach should be complemented by community-level interventions and social engineering, and psychologists should be more inclined to train others (including health professionals and volunteers) in the delivery of psychological interventions and to develop self-help materials and computer-based forms of patient education and communication. As Roberts, Towell and Golding (2001) state, psychology should avoid an excessive preoccupation with individualism and build more valid ecological models of human health. The same authors also correctly point at the fact that 'psychologists should be concentrating less on providing justification for their professional role in health care settings and more on working with client groups so that they empower themselves' (2001: 256). Their remark is valid not only for client or patient groups but also for the empowerment and training of other health professionals. Health psychology and medical psychology seem to have become different worlds, but if clinical health psychologists are not prepared to play a major role in the development, training and advice of health professionals, they may seriously endanger the future of their own discipline.

We would like to conclude with two additional remarks. The first concerns the theoretical knowledge base for psychological interventions with chronic patients; the second concerns methodological remarks on evaluation studies of interventions. While the theoretical knowledge base for health psychology is growing, many interventions in patients with chronic diseases do not rely on this knowledge. Among the many examples, research on quality of life in various patient groups is mostly atheoretical, as is research on various forms of rehabilitation, as for example cardiac rehabilitation. Yet, these areas rank among the most researched areas in health psychology, and are frequently cited as successful areas of intervention. The consequence of this is that it is very difficult to understand why some interventions are effective and under which conditions. The lack of a sound knowledge base has many other disadvantages: as not only interventions but also most measuring instruments (e.g., for quality of life) do not reflect well-defined concepts and/or relations in a theoretical framework, it is very difficult to judge whether there is a congruence between the intervention and the way the outcomes are measured, which seriously endangers the validity of the results.

In other words, not only interventions but also measures should be based on sound theory. However, current models of health behavior (change), such as the health belief model, social cognitive theory, the theories of reasoned action and planned behavior, protection motivation theory and the transtheoretical model of change (Norman, Abraham & Conner, 2000), may be too narrow or only partially adequate for the design of interventions in chronic patients. This is because they focus on isolated behaviors, and on the adoption (or initiation) of a new behavior rather than on behavioral maintenance (Rothman, 2000). Moreover, they reduce the influence of the (social) environment on cognitive representations. Likewise, a limitation of the traditional stress-coping models (Lazarus & Folkman, 1984) concerns the underlying assumption that individuals cope in a reactive way with stressful, disease-related or health-related events. By focusing on the way the appraisal of the stressor shapes coping behavior, these models tend to overlook the effects of the individual's life goals on the meaning, the representation of the disease and the selection of coping procedures (Maes et al., 1996). Effective applications may thus need new theoretical frameworks, including behavioral maintenance and self-regulation theory. Furthermore, they should include models that put more emphasis on the influence of the (social) environment on behavior (Brownlee, Leventhal & Leventhal, 2000; Carver & Scheier, 2000; Maes & Gebhardt, 2000; Roberts et al., 2001; Rothman, 2000).

The second remark concerns methodological shortcomings of existing evaluation studies. While a lot of the intervention studies with chronic patients are randomized controlled studies, many of the control groups differ from non-treatment control groups. Most control group patients receive standard care, and it should be noted that standard care has improved substantially over time. For example, in Dutch cardiac rehabilitation settings, it became increasingly difficult to come up with a psychological intervention that would prove to be superior to standard care, since many of these interventions became part of standard care. As a consequence, evaluation studies should offer an adequate description not only of the intervention but also of the so-called standard care, since this can differ substantially from situation to situation, let alone from country to country. The objectives of many evaluative studies are often not well defined or represent a narrow focus on possible outcomes (many studies do not even assess risk factors or physiological outcomes, let alone morbidity and mortality outcomes). In addition, studies should also assess relative effectiveness rather than general effectiveness of a program, and the sample size should be large enough to demonstrate significant effects on risk factors, morbidity and mortality. Finally, process evaluation, which documents and monitors program delivery, should deserve more attention in the future. This would provide information on crucial questions, such as whether the psychologists, health professionals or volunteers who delivered the program were adequately trained and motivated to guarantee that the program was delivered as intended.

In the next part, we formulate some overall conclusions and suggestions for further research.

GENERAL CONCLUSION AND DISCUSSION

In conclusion, there can be little doubt that health psychology interventions can have important contributions to the area of health promotion, disease prevention and adaptation to and management of chronic disease. Psychology provides a useful knowledge base for various health promotion settings, including the community, media-based health promotion, schools, the worksite and health care settings, which proved to be successful in health behavior change, risk factor reduction and/or a reduction in morbidity, mortality and the use of health care resources. However, it seems that only initiatives that combine or link interventions in different settings have the potential to influence all these outcomes. Likewise, there is a lot of evidence demonstrating the effectiveness of quality of life (stress management and social support interventions) and self-management interventions in various chronic disease groups, including for example patients suffering from CHD, HIV, cancer, rheumatoid arthritis and diabetes. Beneficial effects range, depending on the chronic disease, from stress reduction and psychological adaptation to the chronic condition through pain reduction, treatment adherence, and adequate use of medical resources, to risk factor reduction, endocrinological and immunological effects, biological regression or deceleration of the disease process, and a reduction in morbidity and mortality. Also here, a combination of interventions is mostly required to produce (some of) these outcomes, and little is known about the effective components of these 'cocktail' psycho-educational interventions.

A related statement concerns whether many of the existing interventions are applications in the real sense of the word. Applications require, as mentioned in the introduction, a vast body of knowledge to apply, or in other words also a sound theoretical base. Most existing initiatives or programs are not based on such knowledge. It has been argued above that this is mainly because health psychologists are not always at the helm of these initiatives and fail to communicate their knowledge base to others. In addition, we stated that existing models for health behavior (change) (e.g., described by Norman et al., 2000) may also be too narrow for these applications, because they focus on isolated behaviors, concentrate on initiation of the change rather than on maintenance, and reduce the impact of the environment to cognitive representations.

Many methodological remarks have been made in this chapter concerning evaluation of health promotion initiatives and intervention studies with chronic patients. However, one stands out, referring to the fact that many existing evaluation studies seem to search for answers to the wrong question, 'Is this intervention effective or not?' Such a question reflects the quest for the Holy Grail. It implies that there is an effective intervention for all patients under all circumstances or conditions at all times. The question should rather be: 'For which subgroup of individuals is this intervention effective (in comparison to other interventions and a non-intervention), under what conditions, and in which respect?'

The conclusions of both parts of this chapter point at the necessity to develop intervention programs, based on a sound knowledge base, which are offered to large parts of the (healthy or diseased) population for an extended period of time. This requires (1) that decision makers in this area are informed about health psychology knowledge and competencies and (2) that health psychologists are prepared to embark on these initiatives in cooperation with many other professionals. There is an apparent lack of dissemination of health psychology knowledge. As far as we know there are no accessible shortlists of advice or successes that can be sent to these decision makers. The International Academy of Education (a world-wide scientific organization to promote application of educational research findings) tackles this problem for the area of education by publishing small booklets. The booklets, which are widely disseminated all over the world and can be downloaded from the web (www.ibe.unesco.org/publications) thanks to the contribution of the International Bureau of Education, contain about 20 pages with principles, related research findings and advice for applications on topics such as 'teaching', 'tutoring', 'preventing behavior problems', 'preventing HIV/AIDS in schools', 'motivation to learn' and many others. A comparable initiative for health psychology in cooperation with the World Health Organization would help to put health psychology on the decisional map in many countries. Unfortunately, many health psychologists are usually not keen enough to participate in these disseminating initiatives. They frequently prefer to concentrate on the development and/or evaluation of small-scale 'feasible' projects, which mostly focus on single targets. While this may be defendable from a research point of view, in the end these projects should lead to cost-effective initiatives, which can be implemented in our communities.

A related concern regards the fact that the bulk of the existing health promotion research has been conducted in a social vacuum with limited attention to socio-political or regulatory factors. With the exception of social support, the influence of the social context is underrepresented in most health behavior or stress-coping models. Reviews consistently stress the importance of partnership with the community in order to address the social factors in health behaviors, which imply for example collaboration with community groups, social service agencies and health care providers. These forms of collaboration also imply that interventions are based on needs assessment in the community, rather than on experts' opinion or preference (Emmons, 2000). In other words, interventions must be needed. However, for many intervention projects, it is unclear how they relate to the major problems within our health care systems and communities, and as a consequence they run the risk of not being adopted by the community and/or of lacking the funding they might deserve.

This community perspective also implies that more attention should be devoted to subgroups that are traditionally disadvantaged by our health care systems. These include people with a low social economic status (as low income is a predictor of poor health), women (as morbidity is higher in women than in men), the elderly (since they represent a growing part of the population in Western countries with increasing morbidity), and ethnic minority groups (with whom communication through our health care systems frequently fails because of cultural and social barriers) (Taylor, 2001).

Another major concern is that people at risk seem to become an increasing problem group in our health care systems. While health psychology concentrated traditionally on health promotion in healthy populations or interventions in diseased groups, the growth of medical technology and education led to increased identification of groups at risk for developing health problems. Traditionally some health risks attracted the attention of health psychologists, such as for example hypertensives or obese people. Recently, the development of gene technology led to the discovery and communication of new risks, such as those for developing breast cancer, blood diseases, neurological diseases and immune diseases. It is clear that health psychologists can play an important role in the development of screening procedures for such risks, including those in communication or interventions that help people to live with these risks.

This brings us to remarks regarding the interface between psychology and medicine. There is mounting evidence for the biological base of (health) behavior and the biophysiological consequences of a variety of behaviors and psychological conditions, including stress. From this perspective, it is difficult to understand why many psychological interventions in the area of health promotion, disease prevention or treatment of chronic disease have relatively isolated positions within medical care.

Collaborative interventions between psychologists and other health professionals (Taylor, 2001) are required, which will increase not only the relevance of the interventions, but also their implementation in standard health care. To promote communication between various health professions, health psychologists should have a sound biological knowledge base concerning this area of cooperation, and should have opportunities in their education where they learn to communicate with medical professionals. Topics such as screening for risk factors, quality of life, stress, pain management, management of chronic diseases, doctor–patient communication and the use of medical resources are areas where medical and psychological research are frequently conducted from very different perspectives and require closer cooperation. While psychologists frequently point at the medical profession as the main culprit for this lack of cooperation, it may be rather their lack of assertiveness and lack of communication with other health care professionals that are the real causes for this isolated position. There is indeed impressive evidence showing that psychological interventions delivered by non-psychologists can have substantial effects on a variety of health and disease outcomes. The use of new communication technology opens an important new avenue in this respect. On the other hand, efforts must also be directed at the improvement of psychology courses for a variety of health professionals, including for example medical doctors and nurses, since they seem to lack psychological knowledge and skills regarding health promotion, disease prevention and self-management of chronic disease.

REFERENCES

Ashenden, R., Silagy, C., & Weller, D. (1997). A systematic review of the effectiveness of promoting lifestyle change in general practice. *Family Practice, 14,_160–176.*

Balas, E. A., Jaffrey, F., & Kuperman, G. I. (1997). Electronic communication with patients: Evaluation of distance medicine technology. *Journal of the American Medical Association, 278,* 152–159.

Baum, A. (2000). Behavioral and psychosocial interventions to modify pathophysiology and disease course. In B. D. Smedley & S. L. Syme (Eds.), *Promoting health: Intervention strategies from social and behavioral research* (pp. 451–488). Washington, DC: National Academy Press.

Baum, A., & Andersen, B. (Eds.) (2001). *Psychosocial interventions for cancer.* Washington, DC: American Psychological Association.

Bauman, A. (1993). Effects of asthma patient education upon psychological and behavioural outcomes. In S. Maes, H. Leventhal & M. Johnston (Eds.), *International review of health psychology* (Vol. 2, pp. 199–212). Chichester: Wiley.

Bennett, P. D. (2000). *Introduction to clinical health psychology.* Buckingham: Open University Press.

Berry, D. C., Michas, I. C., & Gillie, T. (1997). What do patients know about medicines, and what do doctors want to tell them? A comparative study. *Psychology and Health, 12,* 467–480.

Billings, J. H. (2000). Maintenance of behavior change in cardiorespiratory risk reduction: A clinical perspective from the Ornish program for reversing coronary heart disease. *Health Psychology, 19,* 70–75.

Blackburn, H. (1972). Multifactor preventive trials in coronary heart disease. In G. T. Stuart (Ed.), *Trends in epidemiology* (pp. 212–230). Springfield, IL: Thomas.

Botvin, G. J., Dusenbury, L., Baker, E., James-Ortiz, S., Botvin, E. M., & Kerner, J. (1992). Smoking prevention among urban minority youth: Assessing effects on outcome and mediating variables. *Health Psychology, 11,* 290–299.

Boule, N. G., Haddad, E., Kenny, G. P., Wells, G. A., & Sigall, R. J. (2001). Effects of exercise on glycemic control and body mass in type 2 diabetes mellitus: A meta-analysis of controlled clinical trials. *Journal of the American Medical Association, 286,* 1218–1227.

Bowler, I., & Gooding, S. (1995). Health promotion in primary health care: The situation in England. *Patient Education and Counseling, 25,* 293–299.

Brannon, L., & Feist, J. (1997). *Health psychology: An introduction to behavior and health.* Pacific Grove, CA: Brooks/Cole.

Brown, S. (1992). Meta-analysis of diabetes patient education research: Variations in intervention effects across studies. *Research in Nursing & Health, 15,* 409–419.

Brownlee, S., Leventhal, H., & Leventhal, E. A. (2000). Regulation, self-regulation, and the construction of the self in the maintenance of health. In M. Boekaerts, P. Pintrich & M. Zeidner (Eds.), *Handbook of self-regulation* (pp. 369–416). San Diego, CA: Academic.

Brunner, E., White, I., Thorogood, M., Bristow, A., Curle, D., & Marmot, M. (1997). Can dietary interventions change diet and coronary risk factors? A meta-analysis of randomized controlled trials. *American Journal of Public Health, 87,* 1415–1422.

Carver, C. S., & Scheier, M. F. (2000). On the structure of behavioral self-regulation. In M. Boekaerts, P. Pintrich & M. Zeidner (Eds.), *Handbook of self-regulation* (pp. 41–84). San Diego, CA: Academic.

Cataldo, M. F., & Coates, T. J. (1986). *Health and industry: A behavioral medicine perspective.* New York: Wiley.

Cohen, S., & Wills, T. A. (1985). Stress, social support and the buffering hypothesis. *Psychological Bulletin, 98,* 310–357.

Daniel, M., Green, L. W., Marion, S. A., Ganble, D., Herbert, C. P., Hertzman, C., & Sheps, S. B. (1999). Effectiveness of community-directed diabetes prevention and control in a rural Aboriginal population in British Columbia, Canada. *Social Science and Medicine, 48,* 815–832.

Dijkstra, A., De Vries, H., Roijackers, J., & Van Breukelen, G. (1998). Tailored interventions to communicate stage-matched information to smokers in different motivational stages. *Journal of Consulting and Clinical Psychology, 66,* 549–557.

Dixhoorn, J. J. van (1998). *Ontspanningsinstructie: Principes en oefeningen.* Maarssen: Elsevier/Bunge.

Dusseldorp, E., van Elderen, T., Maes, S., Meulman, J., & Kraaij, V. (1999). A meta-analysis of psychoeducational programs for coronary heart disease. *Health Psychology, 18,* 506–519.

Emmons, K. (2000). Behavioral and social science contributions to the health of adults in the United States. In B. D. Smedley & S. L. Syme (Eds.), *Promoting health: Intervention strategies from social and behavioral research* (pp. 254–321). Washington, DC: National Academy Press/ Institute of Medicine.

Fawzy, F. I., Cousins, N., Fawzy, N. W., Kemeny, M. E., Elashoff, R. & Morton, D. (1993). A structured psychiatric intervention for cancer patients: Changes over time in methods of coping and affective disturbance. *Cancer Intervention*, *47*, 720–725.

Forster, J. L., Wolfson, M., Murray, D. M., Blaine, T. M., Wagenaar, A. C., & Hennrikus, D. J. (1998). The effects of community policies to reduce youth access to tobacco. *American Journal of Public Health*, 88, 1193–1198.

Friedman, R. H. (1998). Automated telephone conversations to assess health behavior and deliver behavioral interventions. *Journal of Medical Systems*, *22*, 95–102.

Friedmann, M., Thoresen, C., Gill, J., Powell, L., Ulmer, D., Thompson, L., Price, V., Rabin, D., Breall, W., Dixon, T., Levy, R., & Bourg, E. (1984). Alteration of type A behavior and reduction in cardiac recurrences in post-myocardial infarction patients. *American Heart Journal*, *108*, 237–248.

Goldbeck, W. B. (1984). Foreword. In M. P. O'Donnell & T. H. Ainsworth (Eds.), *Health promotion in the workplace* (pp. v–vii). New York: Wiley.

Green, J., & Tones, K. (1999). Towards a secure evidence base for health promotion. *Journal of Public Health Medicine*, *21*, 133–139.

Hancock, L., Sanson-Fisher, R., Redman, S., Burton, R., Burton, L., Butler, J., Girgis, A., Gibberd, R., Hensley, M., McClintock, Q., Reid, A., Schofield, M., Tripodi, T., & Walsh, R. (1997). Community action for health promotion: A review of methods and outcomes, 1990–1995. *American Journal of Preventive Medicine*, *13*, 220–239.

Harden, A., Peersman, G., Oliver, S., Mauthner, M., & Oakley, A. (1999). A systematic review of the effectiveness of health promotion interventions in the workplace. *Occupational Medicine*, *49*, 540–548.

Hawkins, J. D., Catalano, R. F., Kosterman, R., Abbott, R., & Hill, K. G. (1999). Preventing adolescent health-risk behaviors by strengthening protection during childhood. *Archives of Pediatrics and Adolescent Medicine*, *153*, 226–234.

Haynes, R. B., McKibbon, K. A., & Kanai, R. (1996). Systematic review of randomised trials of interventions to assist patients to follow prescriptions for medications. *Lancet*, *348*, 383–386.

Helgeson, V. S., & Cohen, S. (1996). Social support and adjustment to cancer: Reconciling descriptive, correlational, and intervention research. *Health Psychology*, *15*, 135–148.

Helgeson, V. S., Cohen, S., Schulz, R., & Yasko, J. (2001). Group support interventions for people with cancer: Benefits and hazards. In A. Baum &

B. Andersen (Eds.), *Psychosocial interventions for cancer* (pp. 269–286). Washington, DC: American Psychological Association.

Hirano, P. C., Laurant, D. D., & Lorig, K. (1994). Arthritis patient education studies 1991: A review of the literature. *Patient Education and Counseling*, *24*, 9–54.

Institute of Medicine (2002). *Speaking of health: Assessing health communication strategies for diverse populations*. Committee on Communication for Behavior Change in the 21st Century. Washington, DC: National Academy Press.

Jackson, C., Altman, D., Howard-Pitney, B., & Farquhar, J. (1989). Evaluating community level health promotion and disease prevention interventions. *New Directions for Program Evaluation*, *43*, 19–32.

Jason, L. A. (1998). Tobacco, drug and HIV preventive media interventions. *American Journal of Community Psychology*, *26*, 151–187.

Johnston, D. W. (1992). The management of stress in the prevention of coronary heart disease. In S. Maes, H. Leventhal & M. Johnston (Eds.), *International Review of Health Psychology* (Vol. 1, pp. 57–83). Chichester: Wiley.

Kulik, J. A., Moore, P. J., & Mahler, H. I. M. (1993). Stress and affiliation: Hospital roommate effects on preoperative anxiety and social interaction. *Health Psychology*, *12*, 118–124.

Lazarus, R. S., & Folkman, S. (1984). *Stress, appraisal and coping*. New York: Springer.

Lee, C., & Owen, N. (1985). Behaviourally-based principles as guidelines for health promotion. *Community Health Studies*, *9*, 131–138.

Lewin, B., Robertson, I. H., Cay, E. L., Irving, J. B., & Campbell, M. (1992). A self-help post MI rehabilitation package: *The Heart Manual*. Effects on psychological adjustment, hospitalisation and GP consultation. *Lancet*, *339*, 1036–1040.

Logsdon, D. N., Lazaro, C. M., & Meier, R. V. (1989). The feasibility of behavioral risk reduction in primary care. *American Journal of Preventive Medicine*, *5*, 249–256.

Lorig, K., & Holman, H. (1993). Arthritis self-management studies: A twelve year review. *Health Education Quarterly*, *20*, 17–28.

Lutgendorf, S., Antoni, M. H., Schneiderman, N., Iroson, G., & Fletcher, M. A. (1995). Psychosocial interventions and quality of life changes across the HIV spectrum. In J. E. Dimsdale & A. Baum (Eds.), *Quality of life in behavioral medicine research* (pp. 205–239). Hillsdale, NJ: Erlbaum.

Maes, S. (1990). Theories and principles of health behaviour change. In P. Drenth, J. Sergeant, &

R. Takens (Eds.), *European Perspectives in Psychology* (Vol. 2, pp. 193–208). Chichester: Wiley.

Maes, S. (1992). Psychosocial aspects of cardiac rehabilitation in Europe. *British Journal of Clinical Psychology*, 31, 473–483.

Maes, S. (1993). Chronische Ziekte [Chronic disease]. In W. T. A. M. Everaerd (Ed.), *Handboek Klinische Psychologie* (pp. 1–31). Houten: Bohn, Stafleu, Van Loghum.

Maes, S., & Gebhardt, W. (2000). Self-regulation and health. In M. Boekaerts, P. Pintrich & M. Zeidner (Eds.), *Handbook of self-regulation* (pp. 343–368). San Diego, CA: Academic.

Maes, S., Leventhal, H., & De Ridder, D. (1996). Coping with chronic disease. In M. Zeidner & N. Endler (Eds.), *Handbook of coping* (pp. 221–251). New York: Wiley.

Maes, S., & Van Elderen, T. (1998). Health psychology and stress. In M. Eysenck (Ed.), *Psychology: An integrated approach* (pp. 591–623). Singapore: Addison Wesley/Longman.

Maes, S., Verhoeven, C., Kittel, F., & Scholten, H. (1998). Effects of a Dutch worksite wellness-health program: The Brabantia Project. *American Journal of Public Health*, 88, 1037–1041.

Mantovani, G., Astara, G., Lampis, B., Bianchi, A., Curelli, L., Orrù, W., Carpiniello, B., Carta, M.G., Sorrentino, M., & Rudas, N. (1996). Impact of psychosocial intervention on the quality of life of elderly cancer patients. *Psycho-Oncology*, 5, 127–135.

Meichenbaum, D. (1975). Self-instructional methods. In F. H. Kanfer & A. P. Goldstein (Eds.), *Helping people change* (pp. 357–392). New York: Pergamon.

Moos, R. H. (1988). Life stressors and coping resources influence health and well-being. *Psychological Assessment*, 4, 133–158.

Mullen, P. D., Mains, D. A., & Velez, R. (1992). A meta-analysis of controlled trials of cardiac patient education. *Patient Education and Counseling*, 19, 143–162.

Norman, P., Abraham, C., & Conner, M. (2000). *Understanding and changing health behaviour: From health beliefs to self-regulation*. Amsterdam: Harwood.

O'Loughlin, J., Renaud, L., Richard, L., Sanchez Gomez, L., & Paradis, G. (1998). Correlates of sustainability of community-based heart health promotion interventions. *Preventive Medicine*, 27, 702–712.

Orlandi, M. A., & Dalton, L. T. (1998). Lifestyle interventions for the young. In S. A. Shumaker (Ed.), *The handbook of health behavior change* (pp. 335–356). New York: Springer.

Perry, C. L. (2000). Preadolescent and adolescent influences on health. In B. D. Smedley & S. L. Syme (Eds.), *Promoting health: Intervention strategies from social and behavioral research* (pp. 217–253). Washington, DC: National Academy Press.

Phillips, D. (1996). Medical professional dominance and client dissatisfaction: A study of doctor–patient interaction and reported dissatisfaction with medical care at four hospitals in Trinidad and Tobago. *Social Science and Medicine*, 42, 1419–1425.

Powell, L. (1996). The hook: A metaphor for gaining control of emotional reactivity. In R. Allan & S. Scheidt (Eds.), *Heart and mind: The practice of cardiac psychology* (pp. 313–327). Washington, DC: American Psychological Association.

Reid, D. (1985). National No Smoking Day. In J. Crofton & M. Wood (Eds.), *Smoking control*. London: Health Education Council.

Resnicow, K., Cross, D., & Wynder, E. (1993). The Know Your Body program: A review of evaluation studies. *Bulletin of the New York Academy of Medicine*, 70, 188–207.

Roberts, R., Towell, T., & Golding, J. (2001). *Foundations of health psychology*. Palgrave: Houndsmill.

Rothman, A. J. (2000). Toward a theory-based analysis of behavioral maintenance. *Health Psychology*, 19 (1/Suppl.), 64–69.

Spiegel, D., Bloom, J. R., Kraemer, H. C., & Gottheil, E. (1989). Effect of psychosocial treatment on survival of patients with metastatic breast cancer. *Lancet*, 334, 888–891.

Swerrison, H., & Foreman, P. (1991). Training health professionals in health psychology. In M. A. Jansen & J. Weinman (Eds.), *The international development of health psychology* (pp. 125–133). Chur: Harwood.

Taylor, S. E. (2001). *Health psychology*. New York: McGraw-Hill.

Tones, K., & Tilford, S. (1994). *Health education: Effectiveness, efficiency and equity*. London: Chapman & Hall.

Van den Broek, A. (1995). *Patient education and chronic obstructive pulmonary disease* (Health Psychology Series no. 1). Leiden: Leiden University.

Van Elderen, T., & Kittel, F. (1993). Community health programmes. In L. Sibilia & S. Borgo (Eds.), *Health psychology in cardiovascular health and disease* (pp. 144–152). Rome: INRC (CNR).

Van Elderen, T., Maes, S., Seegers, G., Kragten, H., & Relik-van Wely, L. (1994). Effects of a post-hospitalization group health education programme for patients with coronary heart disease. *Psychology and Health*, *9*, 317–330.

Van Elderen, T., Maes, S., & Van den Broek, Y. (1994). Effects of a post-hospitalization group health education programme with telephone follow-up during cardiac rehabilitation. *British Journal of Clinical Psychology*, *33*, 367–378.

Wilbur, C. S., Hartwell, T. D., & Piserchia, P. V. (1986). The Johnson & Johnson Live for Life program: Its organization and evaluation plan. In M. F. Cataldo & T. J. Coates (Eds.), *Health and industry: A behavioral medicine perspective* (pp. 338–350). New York: Wiley.

Williams, C., Milton, J., Strickland, P., Ardagh-Walter, N., Knapp, J., Wilson, S., Frigwell, P., Feldman, E., & Sims, A. C. P. (1997). Impact of medical school teaching on preregistration house officers' confidence in assessing and managing common psychological morbidity: Three Center Study. *British Medical Journal*, *315*, 915–918.

Wilson, M. G., Holman, P. B., & Hammock, A. (1996). A comprehensive review of the effects of worksite health promotion on health-related outcomes. *American Journal of Health Promotion*, *10*, 429–435.

Zastowny, T. R., Kirschenbaum, D. S., & Meng, A. L. (1986). Coping skills training for children: Effects on distress before, during and after hospitalization for surgery. *Health Psychology*, *5*, 231–247.

12

Research Methods in Health Psychology

DAVID P. FRENCH, LUCY YARDLEY
AND STEPHEN SUTTON

INTRODUCTION AND PHILOSOPHICAL BACKGROUND

Overview

Research methods is an enormous topic in its own right, with scores of books being dedicated to each of the subsections we cover. Given this, we have necessarily been selective, but have aimed to provide an overview of the main issues of both quantitative and qualitative research methods in a single source, and throughout provide direction to more detailed coverage elsewhere. This first section describes different philosophical approaches taken to research methods, with a view to highlighting where these lead to controversies and debates. The subsequent sections provide an overview of first quantitative research methods, then qualitative research methods. The final section discusses a concrete health services research issue, with the aim of showing how different philosophical viewpoints lead to different research questions, and how particular qualitative and quantitative methods are suitable for answering particular questions.

Philosophical Bases to Research Methods

Many debates about research methods are fundamentally disagreements about the philosophical approaches taken to the investigation of psychological phenomena. Most accounts of research methods tend to avoid these debates, by the use of two main strategies. One strategy is to discuss only what could be considered mainstream or 'scientific', that is, realist/positivist approaches to usually quantitative research methods. The other is to consider alternatives to the 'scientific' approach, where usually qualitative research methods are discussed and defined by the ways in which they differ from the 'mainstream'. Both these approaches have drawbacks. The first approach tends to present quantitative research methods as an uncontested body of statistical truths, whereas there is by no means consensus among statisticians themselves about issues such as definitions of probability and the appropriateness of null hypothesis significance testing (see Gigerenzer et al., 1989). This approach is therefore misleading, implying a false consensus about the appropriateness of a subset of research methods for all research questions. The second strategy for discussing research methods can fall into the trap of emphasizing only the drawbacks of realist/positivist approaches. Furthermore, as the focus is on qualitative alternatives to the 'scientific' approach, it fails to identify where important differences exist within this approach, for example in terms of causality versus prediction. This introductory section therefore aims to provide an overview of the main philosophical approaches to both quantitative and qualitative research methods, with more detailed discussion of how these approaches influence choice of methods contained within later sections.

An Outline of the 'Scientific' Approach to Research

Most quantitative researchers in health psychology broadly agree with a 'scientific' approach to research. This approach will be assumed in the sections on quantitative research methods, and can be characterized in the following way. The central aim of this approach is objectivity: emphasis is placed on precision of observation, thereby eliminating or at least reducing error and bias. Objectivity is also manifested in attempts to discover universal laws or theories, which are as general as possible, and to clearly delineate the circumstances under which laws or theories do not obtain. 'Good' research in this tradition is exemplified by explicit tests of clearly stated theories, with methods designed and reported to allow replication, and results clearly supporting or refuting theoretically derived hypotheses. The gold standard of this approach is usually the randomized experiment, in which highly focused manipulations are targeted at specific psychological 'constructs', with the aim of eliciting an equally specific effect, as predicted by theory (for a different view, see Byrne, 2002).

Realism and Positivism

Although it is possible to characterize a 'scientific' approach to research, there are many differences of opinion covered by this broad heading. Realism and positivism are two such camps of opinion, although as with the broader category of a 'scientific' approach to research, there are many positions within these camps. 'Realism' can be concerned with either or both of psychological constructs and psychological theories (Hacking, 1983: 21–31). Realism about theories asserts that theories ought to be true, or at least attempts should be made for theories to be as close as possible to describing a true state of affairs. Those who disagree with this position argue that theories are at best useful fictions, which should be useful for the purposes of prediction and intervention, but are not to be taken at face value. Realism about constructs asserts that the psychological phenomena described in these theories should be real. The opposing position asserts that any talk of 'beliefs', 'attitudes', or 'intelligence' does not describe things that really exist, but only 'constructs', that is, fictions that we *construct* to help organize description of phenomena. The opposing positions to realism just outlined are often taken by those who hold positivist views. Although the term 'positivism' covers a variety of opinions, there are a number of shared viewpoints (see Hacking, 1983: 41–57). Among the most important of these viewpoints is an emphasis on believing only what can be observed. Thus, positivists tend to judge theories by their ability to predict, as this can be clearly observed, whereas they are sceptical of talk about causation and explanations for observations, unless there is observable evidence for these explanations (Ray, 2000). It is important to note that 'predict' in this sense refers to the prediction of novel phenomena in addition to the more routine use of the term 'prediction' in health psychology to refer to percentage of variance explained. As discussed above, positivists are also sceptical of the reality of psychological constructs and theories, as these cannot be proved, only confirmed or falsified by empirical observation.

Interpretive and Constructivist Approaches

Although 'scientific' approaches to research dominate amongst nearly all quantitative researchers and some qualitative researchers, a number of other viewpoints are apparent amongst the majority of qualitative researchers. The starting point of difference from 'scientific' approaches concerns the possibility of eliminating subjectivity from our knowledge of the world. From a postmodern perspective, science involves the creation of knowledge, rather than its discovery, and consequently knowledge is a function of the concerns of those who are involved in its creation (Fox, 1993). Postmodern critics of the 'scientific' viewpoint argue that as our knowledge of the world is necessarily mediated by our minds and bodies, objective knowledge is impossible to achieve. That is, the way we view the world is not only limited by features of our thoughts and activities, but constructed through these same processes. Given this, the general aim of postmodern approaches to research is to understand subjective experience, such as the different meanings experienced by people in different contexts, and the social processes that lead to people constructing different meanings. Whereas 'scientific' approaches attempt to eliminate context and subjective interpretation of events as sources of bias, postmodern approaches instead take these issues as their central focus. Equally, the aim is not to identify universally applicable theories but to develop insights that are meaningful and useful to particular groups, such as research participants, other people in similar situations and healthcare workers. As with 'scientific' approaches to research, there is a broad range of opinion under the 'postmodern' heading (Guba & Lincoln, 1994). However, a useful distinction

may be made between interpretive researchers who view knowledge as constructed by our thoughts and activities, and social constructivist researchers who view knowledge as constructed by social interaction, culture and specifically language. According to this latter viewpoint, the way we view the world is due in large part to how we habitually talk about it (Gergen, 1985). These issues are discussed in more depth in the later sections on qualitative methods.

THEORIES AND MODELS

Theories, Models and Hypotheses

The terms 'theory' and 'model' are often used interchangeably in health psychology. For example, both the theory of planned behaviour (TPB: Ajzen, 1991) and the health belief model (HBM: Janz & Becker, 1984) are included under the general heading of 'social cognition models' (e.g., Conner & Norman, 1996). A 'model' is sometimes defined as being a schematic, statistical, or mathematical representation of part of a theory (Estes, 1993). However, this use of the term 'model' is not usual in health psychology, and hence will be avoided here. A theory can be thought of as a story about a circumscribed part of the world, which is 'expressed in sentences, diagrams, and models, that is in verbal and pictorial structures' (Harré, 1972). It should not only be consistent with a set of observations, but also attempt to explain why we obtain those observations and not another set. For any well-defined theory, it should be possible to derive predictions about what will happen under a particular set of circumstances. These predictions, derived from a theory, are called hypotheses. The scientific experiment, as classically defined, is an attempt to test one or more hypotheses against a set of observations.

Testing Hypotheses, Not Testing Theories

It is important to note that observations are used to test hypotheses, which are derived from theories, rather than observations being used to test theories. The major implication of this is that if, in one specific study, the data do not accord with a theoretically derived hypothesis, this does not automatically invalidate the theory. In any empirical test of a hypothesis, several additional assumptions are required to infer whether the results are genuinely in conflict with a theory. These additional assumptions are often called auxiliary hypotheses. In health psychology, auxiliary hypotheses typically relate to whether factors such as interventions, outcomes, and process measures were operationalized in accordance with the theory, and that the sample, statistical power and situation were appropriate (see the section below on validity of causal explanations for observed relationships). Thus, in practice, it is highly problematic to claim to have refuted any theory on the basis of one experiment.

Comparing Theories

Any existing set of observations can be accounted for equally well by more than one theory. That is, there is more than one picture or story that can be used to characterize a set of observations, and explain why these observations were obtained. However, if two theories are genuinely different, they should make different predictions about what would happen under at least one new set of circumstances. Thus, different theories may provide different hypotheses about what should be observed under the same conditions. It is under these circumstances that 'critical tests' are possible, whereby two different hypotheses are derived from competing theories. The rationale is that one hypothesis will fit the data better, and the theory from which this hypothesis is derived is supported. An example in health psychology might centre around how the impact of threatening information is affected by participants' levels of efficacy (both response efficacy, the perceived effectiveness of an action to reduce a risk, and self-efficacy, confidence in one's ability to perform that action). Protection motivation theory proposes that high levels of threat with low efficacy would result in a greater intention to protect one's health than low levels of threat with low efficacy (e.g., Rogers, 1985). By

contrast, Witte's (1992) extended parallel processing model would predict the reverse: according to this theory, high threat and low efficacy should result in maximal defensive processing, and hence lower intention to protect health than low threat and low efficacy. These two theories make conflicting predictions, and it is possible for an empirical test to be arranged, such that support for one theory implies a lack of support for the other. A more modest version of the 'critical test' has been termed the 'model comparison approach' (Judd & McClelland, 1989; Judd, McClelland & Culhane, 1985). Here, one compares a series of theoretically derived statistical models, which are related but of increasing complexity, and asks whether each increase in complexity results in a better description of the data. An example from health psychology might be whether the addition of an interaction between threat and efficacy variables results in better prediction of protection motivation than a model containing only main effects (see Rogers, 1985).

Why Do We Need Theories?

Theories serve many purposes, including providing a framework into which observations may be organized, providing guidance on where future research efforts should be directed, and suggesting where and how any health psychology interventions should be targeted. A simple way to highlight the purpose of theories is to consider what would happen if there were no explicit theories. In the absence of explicit theories, one would be left with an aggregation of findings. As these findings would soon become unmanageable in the absence of any organizing principle, implicit theories based on 'common sense' would be employed, or theories would be borrowed from other disciplines (see, e.g., Marteau & Johnston, 1987). It is clear that implicit theories were a driving force behind much earlier psychological research, but proved unsatisfactory. For instance, 'common sense' would suggest that attitudes and behaviour are strongly related, that non-adherence to medication regimens is due to misunderstanding, that arousing fear of consequences of a disease would lead to people taking steps to avoid developing this disease. However, all these empirical propositions have been shown to be wrong, or at least not completely true (see Fishbein & Ajzen, 1975; Leventhal, 1970; Meichenbaum & Turk, 1987). Under these circumstances, 'common sense' implicit theories have little to say about how one should proceed, apart from more of the same; for example, if fear-arousing communications have not led to behaviour change, then more fear should be aroused. Consequently, explicit theories have been developed in an attempt to specify the exact circumstances in which one would expect more precisely defined relationships to obtain. Because they are explicit, these theories have the virtues of being amenable to empirical test, and suggesting where best to target psychological interventions. These theories may subsequently receive little empirical support, but due to their explicit nature, they are open to revision on the basis of subsequent observations.

Theoretical Progress

For those who take a realist or positivist approach to the philosophy of science, theoretical progress is a central concern. For the realist, new theories should be closer to the truth than existing theories; for the positivist, new theories should allow better prediction than existing theories. That is, for the positivist, theories do not have to be literally true, merely more useful than other theories. This point has been well expressed by Box 'all models are wrong, but some are useful' (1979: 201).

The contrast between these two positions can be highlighted by considering the methodology of falsificationism (see, e.g., Newton-Smith, 1981: 44–76). According to Popper (1963), any amount of evidence that is congruent with a theory does not provide evidence of its truth, as this does not preclude the possibility of subsequently finding evidence that is clearly not congruent. More useful, Popper suggested, are tests that can potentially disconfirm a theory, as it is only through empirical tests that theories can be falsified. The upshot of this argument is that

good theories should allow many predictions, with these predictions being open to empirical refutation, rather than *ad hoc* explanations. This approach is a good example of a realist approach to theory development: theories should be true, and one should therefore aim to identify and remove what is not true from theory.

A positivist position is more concerned with the utility of theories, rather than their truth *per se*. Thus, a positivist could consistently believe that a health psychology theory may not be literally true: the proposed constructs may not 'really' exist, and the causal relations proposed may not be causal, but as long as the theory is useful (e.g., in terms of prediction), it is a good theory. For this position, evidence against the reality of the constructs is irrelevant: the theory is being evaluated not on the grounds of its 'truth', but on the grounds of its usefulness. The aim of research is therefore not to falsify the theory, but to increase the novelty and accuracy of prediction, or the utility of application in interventions.

It should be noted that both these positions describe science as a basically gradual process, with broadly true or generally useful theories being increasingly refined, with later theories being similar but more accurate or useful. However, it has been argued that this is not a good description of how science works (Kuhn, 1970). According to Kuhn, this incremental view of science is only a reasonable characterization of 'normal science', that is periods of relative calm. The periods of calm, Kuhn argued, are separated by much more turbulent 'paradigm shifts'. During 'paradigm shifts', shared assumptions that underpin a scientific community's research are questioned and rejected, and different assumptions are instead adopted by that community, allowing 'normal science' to resume, but along different lines from that previously conducted. There has been a great deal of discussion of Kuhn's views (e.g., Newton-Smith, 1981: 102–124), and a continuing debate amongst those adopting a more realist or positivist approach to science.

For constructivists, theories are ways of representing the world that are constrained by language and contemporary sociocultural practices, and that serve sociopolitical functions (Kvale, 1992). Alternative theories are therefore viewed not as more or less accurate depictions of the world, or as better or worse at predicting the future, but rather as the products of different perspectives and values. From this relativist viewpoint, a theory may have pragmatic validity within a particular context, but should not be regarded as having any objective universal timeless truth status (Brown, 1994).

What will hopefully be clear is that a researcher's approach to their work is underpinned by what they believe research should be attempting to achieve. An example of this will be given in the final section of this chapter.

QUANTITATIVE RESEARCH DESIGN

Causality and Prediction

A major issue in considering the appropriateness of a design for a quantitative study is the extent to which it allows inferences to be made about causal relationships. It should be clear from the 'realism and positivism' section above that there are different approaches that can be taken with regard to causality: causality is a complex and controversial issue (see, e.g., Cook & Campbell, 1979; Shadish, Cook & Campbell, 2002). Given this, when reading the following discussion of features of design that enable inference of causality, it should be borne in mind that some researchers use the word 'cause' more literally than others. Researchers with a positivist leaning are more sceptical about the idea that unobservable processes are 'causing' certain events to happen, and more comfortable with discussions of prediction of events by other observable events. Nevertheless, although some quantitative researchers would be uneasy in claiming that they are identifying necessarily *causal* relationships, there is a broad consensus on following the steps outlined below.

Virtually all researchers who conduct quantitative research share an interest in accuracy of prediction. Prediction of individuals likely to perform certain behaviours can be useful in

identifying a target group at which intervention should be aimed. Most researchers would agree with the distinction between those factors that predict behaviour and those that cause behaviour. In many situations, past behaviour is a better predictor of future behaviour than self-efficacy beliefs (e.g., Dzewaltowski, Noble & Shaw, 1990). However, it is unclear in what sense past behaviour can be said to directly cause future behaviour, and certainly past behaviour is of little use as a target for behavioural interventions. As the aim of many health psychologists is to change health-related behaviour, a helpful strategy may therefore be to focus future research on obtaining and evaluating evidence that constructs may 'cause' such behaviour, rather than merely predict it.

Validity of Causal Explanations for Observed Relationships

There are a number of issues to consider when deciding whether it is appropriate to generalize from an observed relationship in a particular sample to a causal relationship that obtains in the wider population. To facilitate understanding of the issues, Shadish et al. (2002) distinguish between four broad classes of validity: statistical conclusion validity, internal validity, construct validity, and external validity. Statistical conclusion validity is demonstrated when inferential statistics are correctly applied, identifying population relationships from a specific sample. To the extent that the results of significance tests are reflections of the true effect in the population, and not chance and/or a lack of power, the inferences drawn from these tests have statistical conclusion validity. Internal validity is demonstrated when the design and conduct of a study are free from systematic error, commonly termed 'bias', which can take many forms. One common type of bias is due to experimenter effects, where the expectations of the experimenter are unintentionally communicated to research participants, thereby influencing their behaviour in the direction of the experimenter's favoured hypothesis.

If both statistical conclusion validity and internal validity are demonstrated, then it is correct to assert a causal relationship between two variables in the form in which the variables were manipulated or measured. However, what has not yet been demonstrated is the extent to which these manipulations or measurements map onto theoretical constructs in the manner in which the researcher intended. That is, if a particular manipulation, for example of 'disease severity', affects only perceptions of severity as intended, and not perceptions of likelihood, then construct validity has been achieved, which permits statements about a specific manipulation to be generalized to the theoretical literature. Similarly, construct validity of measurement is achieved when a measure is assessing only the construct of interest (see Kline, 2000). If construct validity of manipulations or measurements is not achieved, the result is confounding, which occurs when an observed relationship between two variables is assumed to be causal but is due to a third variable for which there are no experimental or statistical controls. A common instance of this is when an intervention to change a specific construct shows an effect, relative to a control group, which may be due not to the intervention actually affecting the construct, but to the increased attention that people in the intervention receive.

External validity is concerned with the extent to which any causal relationships found can be thought of as being general beyond any one particular study: is the causal relationship general to other people, settings, and times? Typical failures of external validity include faulty generalization from student samples to other adult samples (see Sears, 1986), and from Western samples to the rest of the world (e.g., Fletcher & Ward, 1988).

It should be noted that there is a fairly direct correspondence between the distinctions drawn by Shadish et al. (2002), and distinctions drawn in the epidemiological literature (e.g., Hennekens & Buring, 1987). In this literature, for any observed relationship, there are four broad classes of explanation of why that relationship occurs, namely that the relationship is due to: (1) chance, (2) bias, (3) confounding, and/or (4) a causal relationship. Statistical conclusion validity, internal validity,

and construct validity are achieved to the extent that, respectively, chance, bias, and confounding are eliminated as possible explanations for causal relationships. Given the greater sophistication of design in many epidemiological trials, health psychologists wishing to design trials of complex interventions may find accessing the epidemiological literature useful (e.g., Campbell et al., 2000).

Cross-Sectional versus Longitudinal Research Designs

The issue of temporality is particularly important when considering the relative merits of cross-sectional studies compared with longitudinal studies. In cross-sectional studies, a number of variables are measured at one point in time, and the degree of association between selected variables is examined. Although such studies can provide useful estimates of the extent to which variables are associated or not, they are very weak in terms of allowing causality to be inferred. For example, if a cross-sectional study shows that smokers who hold more positive attitudes towards smoking tend to smoke more heavily, no inferences can be derived about whether attitudes are influencing behaviour (Fishbein & Ajzen, 1975) or whether behaviour is influencing attitudes (Bem, 1972).

Longitudinal studies, where variables are measured in the same people on more than one occasion, are stronger in terms of the inferences that they allow. If changes in one variable (e.g., smoking behaviour) tend to follow changes in attitudes (e.g., towards smoking), then this provides some support for the idea that attitudes influence behaviour, rather than vice versa. In practice, inference of causality on the basis of longitudinal data may be more complex, particularly because the causal lag between attitude and behaviour (or behaviour and attitude) may differ from the period between 'waves' of data collection (see Finkel, 1995; Sutton, 2002).

If one is interested in looking at the causal relationship between two variables, such as smoking attitudes and smoking behaviour, it is also stronger to measure both variables at all waves of data collection. If attitudes and behaviour tend to be associated when measured at the same time point, then both of the following will also tend to be true: (1) attitudes measured at an earlier time will be associated with behaviour at a later time, and (2) behaviour measured at an earlier time will be associated with attitudes at a later time. Hence, whichever measure one uses to 'predict' the other measure at a later time point, one should expect to find a relationship, regardless of the direction of causality. However, regression analysis of both measures at both time points allows appropriate statistical controls to be made, thereby permitting less biased estimates to be obtained of the degree to which each construct exerts a causal influence on the other (see Campbell & Kenny, 1999), although confounding is also a possible explanation.

Correlational versus Experimental Designs

Although longitudinal research designs are stronger than cross-sectional designs in terms of permitting inference of causality, they still are liable to suffer from the problem of confounding. That is, although the levels of one variable at an earlier time point may be associated with changes in another variable at a later time point, this association may be due to the causal effect of a third variable. For example, although attitudes toward smoking may be predictive of smoking behaviour, it is entirely plausible that this relationship is due to a third, unmeasured, variable such as socioeconomic status. One solution to this problem is to attempt to identify, measure and statistically control for all potentially important confounding variables. However, there are always practical limits on how many variables may be included in any one study, and furthermore, given that all measurement involves some error, statistically controlling for confounding variables will always involve some error. Longitudinal studies, unlike properly conducted experimental studies, can also suffer bias from the effects of regression to the mean when respondents are selected on a criterion

related to the outcome variable (Yudkin & Stratton, 1996).

Experimental designs, including trials, have a major advantage over correlational designs, whether cross-sectional or longitudinal, which do not involve experimental manipulation, largely due to the consequences of random allocation of respondents to different experimental groups. If this randomization procedure is effective, not only should all known confounding variables be equally distributed within groups, but so also should unknown confounding variables. Furthermore, if confounding from a particular source is thought to be particularly problematic, then the procedure of stratification can ensure that respondents with different levels of this confounding variable are equally distributed throughout all experimental groups. The advantage of eliminating confounding is that, assuming statistical conclusion validity and internal validity, any effects that are found between experimental groups can be attributed fairly unambiguously to the experimental manipulations. Thus, experimental designs permit much stronger inference of cause than non-experimental designs. It should be noted, however, that cause is sometimes reasonably inferred without experimental evidence, a classic example being the lack of *experimental* studies to examine the causal influence of smoking on cancer in humans (see Abelson, 1995: 182–184; Hennekens & Buring, 1987: 39–50).

Single Case Study Designs

Single case study designs are increasingly being used alongside more mainstream designs. The term 'single case study designs' is a misnomer, as is a common alternative 'N = 1 trials', as although these designs focus on the same person over time, they often include many more than one individual (Kazdin, 1982). The use of larger samples in more mainstream designs is due to a focus on establishing the presence of relationships across a population as whole: for example, is a treatment more effective than the control for a particular group of people? Single case studies, by contrast, are more concerned with a thorough evaluation of the effects of a treatment on an individual case.

For example, the aim of a traditional randomized controlled trial may be to examine whether a particular cardiac rehabilitation programme is effective in promoting exercise. Assuming that it is effective for the specified population, there will almost certainly be some heterogeneity of outcome: some people will exercise more, and some will exercise less. Although a large part of this heterogeneity will be due to chance, a further part of it will be due to different people reacting differently to the same programme. The aim of a single case study design would be to establish whether the treatment is effective for particular people. As such, it is much more strongly related to the concerns of clinicians working with individual clients.

Single case study designs are longitudinal, and typically employ multiple crossovers: periods of treatment are alternated with control periods, or periods of an alternative treatment. Success with a particular patient is indicated by more successful outcomes at the end of periods of treatment, and no effect on outcomes, or regression at the end of control periods. There are now examples of the benefits for individual patients of single case study designs, although more comparisons of 'single case' approaches versus a 'one size fits all' approach to treatment are needed (Mahon, Laupacis, Donner & Wood, 1996). It should be noted, however, that a number of prerequisites for single case designs have been identified (Guyatt et al., 1986), not all of which will apply in many clinical or health psychology scenarios (Petterman & Muller, 2001). These criteria are: (1) the condition is stable, (2) the treatment acts quickly, (3) the treatment quickly stops acting when withdrawn, and (4) the treatment does not change the natural course of the disease.

NULL HYPOTHESIS SIGNIFICANCE TESTING

Descriptive and Inferential Statistics

There are two broad aims for calculating statistics: description and inference. Descriptive statistics provide a summary statement about a particular sample, for example their mean height, the weight of the lightest member of the sample, or the variance in their scores on a particular anxiety questionnaire. However, it is usually the case in health psychology that we are less interested in describing a particular sample than in making inferences about the population from which the sample was drawn. As the name suggests, inferential statistics are required here, and these statistical procedures rely on null hypothesis significance testing (NHST).

What Is Null Hypothesis Significance Testing?

In the theories and models section above, it was argued that one function of models was to allow predictions that are empirically testable. NHST is the mechanism by which these predictions are tested. The 'null hypothesis' part of NHST refers to the fact that inferential statistics are based around testing whether there is no association between two variables in the population, for example anxiety and depression, or no population difference on some variable between two groups. The 'alternative hypothesis' is the complement of the null hypothesis: there is some association between two variables, or some difference on a variable between two groups. Note that the alternative hypothesis is true whether there is an absolutely tiny association in the population or an absolutely enormous one. Even when we want to know how much of an association there is between anxiety and depression, statistical tests are concerned with whether there is no association, versus whether there is some association. Furthermore, the tests do not tell us directly about whether this null hypothesis is true or not. Instead, they give us the probability (p-value) of whether the data we have collected are consistent with the null hypothesis. Thus, instead of obtaining the information we really want – the probability that anxiety and depression are associated at a given level – we instead get the probability that our data are consistent with the hypothesis that anxiety and depression are not associated at all.

Accepting and Rejecting Hypotheses

As NHST does not give direct information about the truth or falsity of a particular hypothesis, we instead must infer this from the p-value our statistical test yields. The convention that is almost universally followed is that if the probability of a set of data being consistent with a null hypothesis is less than one in twenty (or $p < 0.05$), our test of this hypothesis is 'statistically significant'. This rather arbitrary cutoff point is the boundary between two contrasting conclusions that are conventionally drawn from a dataset. If the testing is 'significant', that is if the probability of getting a particular pattern of data assuming the null hypothesis is true, is less than one in twenty ($p < 0.05$), then we 'reject' the null hypothesis, and accept the alternative hypothesis. A null hypothesis is rejected when it is true one in twenty times. If, however, the testing is 'non-significant', that is the probability of our data assuming the null hypothesis is true is greater than one in twenty, then we 'fail to reject' the null hypothesis. Note that although NHST gives us information about the probability that our data are consistent with the null hypothesis, the use of the rather arbitrary $p < 0.05$ criterion allows a dichotomous accept/reject decision to be made about the null hypothesis.

Type I and Type II Error

The use of the criterion of a probability of $p < 0.05$ is not completely arbitrary: by definition, when a test yields a 'significant' result, the probability of a particular dataset being consistent with the null hypothesis is less than one in twenty. Thus, we will only reject the null hypothesis on the basis of our data when it is actually true less than one time in twenty. This type of mistake, due to the use of the dichotomous $p < 0.05$ criterion, is called a type I error: the error is in rejecting the null hypothesis when it is, in fact, true. The other main

category of mistake, type II error, is generally more common (see Clark-Carter, 1997). A type II error occurs when we fail to reject the null hypothesis when it is, in fact, false, that is we do not find 'significant' differences whereas differences exist in the population. By definition, the probability of a type I error is set at one chance in twenty. The probability of a type II error is much more variable, and is related to the size of an association or difference (or more generally, an 'effect'), and the number of observations made.

Statistical Power: Sample Size and Effect Size

For any non-zero effect size, such as the degree of association between two variables, the probability of achieving a 'significant' result increases with the number of observations that are included in a dataset. As the number of observations increases, so does the precision of the estimated association: the observed correlation coefficient is more often closer to the 'true' (population) correlation coefficient. Accordingly, if a small sample yields an estimate of a moderate degree of association (e.g., Pearson's $r = + 0.3$), the best guess of the true degree of association is also $r = + 0.3$, but with little confidence: the true degree of association may be much higher or much lower. Thus, if the null hypothesis is true (i.e., population $r = 0.0$), one may still get a sample $r = + 0.3$ by chance alone more often than once in twenty (i.e., $p > 0.05$). However, if a much larger sample yields an observed correlation coefficient of $r = + 0.3$, we may have much more confidence that the 'true' correlation coefficient is around this value: the chances of obtaining a correlation of this size is less than one in twenty (i.e., $p < 0.05$).

The other major determinant of statistical power is effect size: larger differences or associations (or 'effects') in the population are more likely to result in larger effects in a particular sample, and hence to be 'significant'. If two variables are correlated $r = + 0.6$ in the population, then a study is more likely to find a 'significant' association than if the population

$r = +0.3$, all other factors being equivalent. Thus, the two key determinants of observed statistical power are effect size and sample size. When one is conducting sample size calculations, an estimate of effect size is used to calculate the number of respondents needed that will provide type I error rates at (usually) 5 per cent, and type II error rates at (usually) 10 per cent or 20 per cent (Cohen, 1992). Sample size is a feature of a particular study, and therefore not theoretically interesting. Effect size, although estimated from a particular study, is a feature of the population, and so is more theoretically interesting. However, a particular inferential test only tells us whether a test is 'significant' or not: NHST does not distinguish between these causes of statistical significance.

Problems with NHST

Not surprisingly, the fact that NHST does not give us the information we are interested in, i.e. information about the probability of our hypotheses being true, has led to some robust criticism. Paul Meehl has argued that 'the almost universal reliance on merely refuting the null hypothesis … is a terrible mistake, is basically unsound, poor scientific strategy, and one of the worst things that ever happened in the history of psychology' (1978: 817). The main criticism levelled by Meehl is that it is highly unlikely that any estimate of an effect will be correct. Given that we are testing an effect size of zero versus all other effect sizes, it should not be surprising that the null hypothesis is often rejected. Indeed, Cohen (1990, 1994), Tukey (1991) and others have argued that the null hypothesis is almost never literally true, that is that all non-significant NHST is type II error: all a statistically significant effect shows is that there is a sufficiently large sample to detect it. According to Cohen (1994), 'in soft psychology, "everything is related to everything else"'. Meehl (1990) called this non-zero correlation the 'crud factor'. He further claimed that 'the notion that the correlation between arbitrarily paired trait variables will be, while not literally zero, of such minuscule size as to be of no importance, is surely wrong' (1990: 212).

Despite these views it is likely that NHST will be used for some time to come: although an American Psychological Association Task Force including some of these critics recommended the use of confidence intervals and reporting of effect sizes, it did not recommend that NHST no longer be used (Wilkinson & the Task Force on Statistical Inference, 1999).

Confidence Intervals

It has been shown that NHST is concerned with establishing the likelihood that data obtained are inconsistent with an association or difference of zero (or more generally, some pre-specified value). It has also been shown that this likelihood depends on the size of the sample employed in a particular study: everything else being equal, the larger the sample, the more likely a study is to identify a non-zero effect, if such an effect exists in the population. However, we are often less interested in knowing that, for example, a therapy produces a better outcome than no therapy, than in knowing the size of the improvement. As the size of a statistical significance test is highly dependent on sample size, it is problematic to use the degree of significance to infer the size of an effect (Cohen, 1994).

For these reasons, it has become increasingly popular to present results using confidence intervals, in addition to the results of a significance test (e.g., Altman, Machin, Bryant & Gardner, 2000). NHST provides an estimate of the plausibility of a population effect being equal to zero, with 5 per cent chance of error (and therefore 95 per cent confidence). By contrast, confidence intervals estimate the range of values an effect could take, usually with 95 per cent confidence. For example, a t-test provides an estimate of the probability that the observed difference between two sample means is inconsistent with two population means being identical. A 'significant' result means that we can be at least 95 per cent confident that the obtained difference between two sample means is inconsistent with there being no difference between the population means. A confidence interval approach would provide a range of values that the difference between the means might take, with a 95 per cent chance that this range includes the population difference in means. If the 95 per cent confidence interval does not include the value of zero, the result is 'significant' in the NHST sense. Thus, confidence intervals not only subsume an NHST approach, but also have the clear advantage of providing an indication of the size of an effect, and how confident one should be about this effect size estimate, as well as its 'significance'.

QUANTITATIVE DATA ANALYSIS

Selection of Inferential Statistics

Before data collection begins, it is generally recommended that a plan of analysis be constructed, in particular specifying which inferential statistics will be used to test the central null hypothesis. Selection of the appropriate inferential statistics test depends on several factors, which are discussed in detail by many excellent basic (e.g., Howell, 1997) and intermediate textbooks (e.g., Tabachnick & Fidell, 2001). One of the most important of these concerns is the distinction between tests of difference (e.g., *t*-tests, ANOVA) and tests of association (e.g., correlation, regression). In tests of difference, the null hypothesis is that two or more samples are drawn from the same population in terms of a specified variable, whereas in tests of association, the null hypothesis is that two or more variables are not related. This distinction has proven useful in conceptualizing how different inferential tests relate to each other, but it should be emphasized that the distinctions between parametric versions of tests of association and tests of difference are more apparent than real (see Cohen & Cohen, 1983; Miles & Shevlin, 2001; Tabachnick and Fidell, 2001). This is an important point, as all such inferential statistical tests are instances of the general linear model, and therefore with many assumptions and limitations in common, rather than a disparate collection of unrelated techniques.

Parametric versus Non-Parametric Statistical Tests

Non-parametric statistical tests are distinguished from parametric statistical tests on the basis of the assumptions made about the nature of the data tested. Typically, parametric statistical tests require the assumption that the variables involved, or statistical summaries such as differences between means in repeated samples, possess interval or ratio properties (see Johnston, French, Bonetti & Johnston, 2004, Chapter 13 in this volume). By contrast, non-parametric statistical tests do not make these strict requirements, being based on data that are either ordinal or categorical/qualitative, although one should be careful to note that this does not mean non-parametric tests are entirely free of assumptions (see, e.g., Siegel & Castellan, 1988). For many parametric tests, there is a comparable non-parametric version, based on fewer assumptions: for example the Spearman rank correlation coefficient is a non-parametric version of the Pearson product-moment correlation coefficient. However, for more complex multivariate techniques such as regression and factor analysis, there are no comparable non-parametric equivalents. Hence, in choosing an inferential statistical test, on the one hand there are parametric tests, which require more assumptions to be made about the nature of the data to be analysed, but allow more complex forms of analysis. On the other hand, non-parametric tests do not require such strict assumptions, but as a consequence tend to have slightly less statistical power (see Zimmerman & Zumbo, 1993).

Linear Regression: Stepwise versus Hierarchical/Sequential

Linear regression is probably the most common inferential statistical technique used in health psychology. In essence, it is an extension of correlation, which provides an estimate of the extent to which two continuous variables are related, that is how much variance is shared by two variables. For regression, an estimate is derived of how much variance in one specified variable (the dependent variable) is shared with any of a set of other variables (the independent variables). Although there are others (see Tabachnick & Fidell, 2001), the two main approaches to regression analysis are stepwise regression, and hierarchical, sometimes called sequential, regression.

In stepwise regression, the choice of which variables are included in the final regression equation, and which variables are omitted, is decided purely on statistical criteria. This can prove problematic when two independent variables are themselves correlated, which is often the case (Henderson & Denison, 1989). For example, one might want to predict overall quality of life (QoL) using measures of anxiety and depression, which are highly intercorrelated, and which correlate with QoL $r = 0.40$ and $r = 0.39$ respectively. Using a forward stepwise procedure, anxiety would enter the regression equation first, as it shares marginally more variance with QoL than does depression, and all the variance in QoL that is shared by anxiety and depression would be attributed to anxiety. Whether or not depression adds a significant further amount of variance in the next step, and hence would be retained in the final equation, would depend on whether the relationship between depression and QoL is statistically significant, *once the variance shared with anxiety is removed*. In a second sample, measures of anxiety and depression might correlate with QoL 0.40 and 0.41 respectively. In this case, depression would enter first, and the variance in QoL shared with anxiety is attributed to depression. Hence, two virtually identical datasets might easily lead to two entirely different regression equations: the first with anxiety as a sole predictor, the second with depression as a sole predictor. Consequently, if this approach to analysis is adopted, making judgements about replication is far from straightforward.

By contrast, in hierarchical regression, the researcher specifies the order in which variables are considered for entry in the regression equation. Thus, in the example above, (s)he could specify that anxiety is entered first, and then depression second, to see how much

additional variance in QoL depression one can predict once the variance shared with anxiety is removed. In this case, anxiety would be included in the final regression equation to predict QoL on both occasions, with depression unlikely to add much additional variance on either occasion. Assuming researchers follow similar strategies in choosing which variables to enter into regression equations, hierarchical regression should result in fewer instances of failure of replication due to independent variables being correlated. Hierarchical regression also allows researchers to examine issues such as the extent to which psychological variables can predict health outcomes, above and beyond demographic and medical variables. The strength of this approach is that the final regression equation is influenced by researchers' ideas about theory (see Cohen & Cohen, 1983), as well as by statistical criteria.

Moderation and Mediation

The terms *moderator* and *mediator* are sometimes confused but refer to quite different functions of variables in a causal system (Baron & Kenny, 1986). Consider a simple model in which variable X influences variable Y. A third variable Z is said to *moderate* the relationship between X and Y if the size of the relationship varies systematically depending on the level of Z. For example, suppose X is stress, Y is illness and Z is social support. According to the stress-buffering hypothesis (Cohen & Wills, 1985), social support buffers the effect of stress on illness. More specifically, stress is positively related to illness but this relationship is weaker the greater the level of social support. Put another way, stress and social support *interact* to influence illness. Interactions can be tested in a regression framework by incorporating product terms (Aiken & West, 1991; Jaccard, Turrisi & Wan, 1990). In this example, the dependent variable Y would be regressed on X and Z in the first step of a hierarchical regression, followed by the product of X and Z. The approach can be extended to three-way interactions (involving three independent variables), but more complex interactions are rarely considered because they are difficult to interpret, and require very large sample sizes.

A *mediator* or *intervening variable* is a variable in a causal chain that transmits part or all of the causal effect of an antecedent variable on a consequent variable. Consider again the effect of stress X on illness Y. This causal effect may be mediated by unhealthy lifestyle (e.g., eating calorie-rich foods, being physically inactive). In other words, we postulate a causal chain in which stress leads to a more unhealthy lifestyle which in turn results in more physical illness. Thus, stress influences illness indirectly (via unhealthy lifestyle). Mediation can be tested using regression analysis (Kenny, Kashy & Bolger, 1998). The first step is to regress Y on X. If there is a significant effect of X on Y, the next step is to check that Z (unhealthy lifestyle) is a potential mediator of this relationship by regressing Z on X. If the effect of X on Z is significant, the final step is to regress Y on X and Z. Depending on the pattern of findings, it may be concluded that there is no mediation (none of the causal effect of X on Y is transmitted by Z), total mediation (all of the effect is transmitted by Z) or partial mediation (part of the effect is transmitted by Z and part is direct). This is a simple example of *path analysis* (Kenny, 1979). The approach can be extended to more complex models involving multiple mediators and longer causal chains.

ADVANCED QUANTITATIVE DATA ANALYSIS

Exploratory Factor Analysis

Exploratory factor analysis (EFA) describes a group of data analysis techniques that share the common feature of being used to reduce a set of observed variables to a smaller number of latent variables. The most typical application of EFA occurs when it is hypothesized that several questionnaire items are assessing the same underlying construct. As an individual's responses to questionnaire items are clearly observable behaviours, these items are termed

'observed variables'. The psychological constructs that are theoretically manifested in these items cannot be directly observed, only indirectly inferred from the questionnaire responses, and hence are termed 'latent variables' or 'factors'. The process by which one or more factors are identified in a set of observed variables is through an analysis of the degree of association (correlation) between the observed variables.

For example, a factor analysis of a set of questions concerning mood (the latent variables) on the Hospital Anxiety and Depression Scale (HADS: Zigmond & Snaith, 1983) typically yields two latent variables (factors), labelled anxiety and depression. The 'anxiety' questions tend to correlate more highly with each other than they do with the 'depression' questions, and vice versa. The conventional EFA explanation for this is that it is the respondent's particular levels of anxiety and depression that lead them to respond in a manner reflective of this to the questionnaire items assessing anxiety and depression respectively. It is these consistencies within people, supposedly due to their levels of anxiety and depression, which cause the items to correlate: for example, anxious people tend to select responses to the 'anxiety' questions indicating high anxiety, whereas less anxious people select the other responses. EFA is introduced in a number of good books (e.g., Child, 1990; Kline, 1993), and most of the important practical issues are discussed in an excellent recent paper (Fabrigar, Wegener, MacCallum & Strachan, 1999).

Structural Equation Modelling

The most common structural equation modelling (SEM) analyses can be thought of as a combination of EFA and linear regression (e.g., Loehlin, 1998): SEM typically involves linear regression or path analyses (see above), conducted using latent variables rather than observed variables, as is traditionally the case. There are a number of good introductory books on SEM (e.g., Hoyle, 1995; Maruyama, 1997; Schumacker & Lomax, 1996). A good source of references to particular aspects of SEM is available at: http://www.ioa.pdx.edu/newsom/.

There are two major advantages to SEM over the more traditional approaches to regression or path analysis. The first stems from the simultaneous estimation of how reliably the constructs are measured, due to inclusion of latent variables, at the same time as estimation of the degree of relationship between the constructs. In traditional approaches to regression, there is some ambiguity over the reason for a weakly estimated relationship: it could be due to unreliability of measurement of the independent or dependent variable, or these variables could genuinely be weakly related. In SEM approaches, estimates can be derived of how well a set of observed variables load on latent variables. Thus, when the relationship between two latent variables is estimated, it is not biased by insufficient account being taken of poor reliability of measurement, which is essential for some types of analysis, for example cross-lagged panel designs (see Menard, 1991).

The second major advantage of SEM relates to the statistics ('fit indices') it yields, estimating how well a model fits the population from which a particular sample of data is drawn. Thus, SEM not only provides estimates of how well each observed variable is related to each latent variable, and how strongly latent variables are related to each other, but also provides an overall estimate of how good a summary of the population relationships is provided by the model examined. That is, it estimates whether the relationships proposed in a particular SEM model summarize the relationships that obtain in the population from which the sample was drawn. This feature of SEM is particularly useful when one wants to compare a series of models, and critically, how good an estimate is yielded by the inclusion or exclusion of theoretically interesting paths between latent variables.

Multilevel Modelling

Many datasets collected by health psychologists have a hierarchical or clustered structure. For example, patients may be recruited from clinics in several different hospitals or samples of children may be drawn from a number of different schools. In these designs, level 1 units (patients, children) are nested within level 2 units (clinics, schools). Multilevel modelling (also known as hierarchical linear modelling) offers a powerful approach to analysing the data that takes proper account of the hierarchical structure, if two conditions are satisfied (Bryk & Raudenbush, 1992; Goldstein, 1995). These conditions are that variables are measured at both levels, and that there is a sufficient number of units at each level (a minimum of 25 individuals in each of 25 groups, according to Paterson & Goldstein, 1992). This approach also has the advantage of avoiding bias in the type I error rate due to ignoring the hierarchical structure and thereby ignoring non- independence of level 1 units. As in standard regression analysis, the aim is typically to predict and explain a dependent variable measured at level 1, but the predictor set can include variables measured at both levels. For example, in a school-based study in which the aim is to explain variation in self-reported physical activity, the predictors may include gender (a level 1 variable) and type of school (e.g., state versus independent sector – a level 2 variable). Cross-level interactions can also be investigated. For example, the relationship between gender and physical activity may differ for different types of school.

Another situation where multilevel modelling is potentially useful is in repeated-measures designs, where occasions of measurement are the level 1 units and individuals the level 2 units. Unlike repeated-measures ANOVA, different individuals may contribute different numbers of measurements.

In principle, the approach can be extended to three or more levels (e.g., repeated measures nested within pupils nested within schools) but in practice most applications are likely to use only two levels. The method is more suitable for analysing models that include a small number of variables selected on the basis of theory than for exploratory analyses of many variables.

As with SEM, to exploit the advantages of multilevel modelling, health psychologists will need to design their studies with this aim in mind and learn to use specialist software. The most widely used packages are MLwiN and HLM.

COMMON PITFALLS IN QUANTITATIVE RESEARCH

In the quantitative research design section above, four types of validity were described, which must all be demonstrated before one can generalize from the results of a particular study to a more universal causal relationship which obtains with other people, in other settings and at other times (Shadish et al., 2002). If any of these types of validity are not demonstrated, any attempts to infer general relationships from particular studies may be in error. This section describes some of the more common pitfalls that can arise when the four types of validity are not demonstrated.

Failure of Statistical Conclusion Validity: Lack of Power

One way in which statistical conclusion validity can be impaired is when multiple related null hypotheses are tested, resulting in an inflation of type I error to greater than than one chance in twenty (see, e.g., Benjamini & Hochberg, 1995). However, a potentially much more pernicious problem is failing to accept the alternative hypothesis, that is a type II error, due to a lack of statistical power (Wilkinson & the Task Force on Statistical Inference, 1999). As has been discussed above, although the probability of a type I error is conventionally set at the 0.05 level, the probability of a type II error is almost always much more. The probability of a type II error depends largely on the size of the effect the research is seeking to detect, and the sample size employed.

In a classic paper, Cohen (1962) showed that the median power of papers published in the *Journal of Abnormal and Social Psychology* in 1960 was 0.46 for a medium-sized effect. That is, assuming that the size of effects investigated was medium (e.g., $r = 0.3$), the research reviewed had only a 46 per cent chance of finding a statistically significant result, and

therefore a 54 per cent of not finding such a result. More recent research paints an even more gloomy picture: in the *Journal of Abnormal Psychology* in 1984, power to detect a medium effect size was 0.37 (Sedlmeier & Gigerenzer, 1989). Of particular relevance to health psychology, estimates of power for the journal *Health Psychology* in 1997 were 0.34 for small effects, 0.74 for medium effects and 0.92 for large effects (Maddock & Rossi, 2001).

Lack of statistical power in health psychology research will therefore often result in a failure to find a statistically significant result when the null hypothesis is false. Such studies will, on the average, be more difficult to publish, due to the widely observed 'publication bias' against studies that do not obtain statistically significant results: journals tend to publish articles that obtain significant results, in preference to those that do not (Rosenthal, 1979). Aside from the waste of research effort this entails, this 'file drawer problem' also results in a distorted view of a research area, which can create problems for narrative and systematic reviews and meta-analyses (see Egger & Smith, 1998). Smaller studies that obtain significant results are more likely to be published, in comparison with smaller studies that do not obtain significant results, resulting in a misleading impression being obtained of the extent to which variables are associated and which treatments are effective. Research in this 'promising' area persists until a larger study is published, showing that a treatment is not as effective as previously thought, and giving a more accurate impression of the literature. Meta-analysis can minimize this fluctuating view of a research area by providing estimates such as the 'failsafe N', that is the number of studies with non-significant results that have been conducted but not published, necessary to reduce the estimated effect size to a non-significant level (Orwin, 1983).

A possibly more unfortunate consequence of low statistical power arises from researchers attempting to find explanations for inconsistent results based in psychological theory, whereas the true explanation is simply lack of statistical power. It has been argued that people view randomly drawn samples as highly representative of the population, even when samples are small (Tversky & Kahneman, 1971). A corollary of this is that people tend to expect two samples drawn from the same population to be highly similar to one another as well as to the population. Although this is true for large samples, fluctuations in sampling mean that it is not true for small samples. This misplaced confidence in the representativeness of small samples has been termed 'belief in the law of small numbers' (Tversky & Kahneman, 1971). To illustrate their argument, these authors presented a group of psychologists with a series of scenarios concerning the likelihood of obtaining statistically significant results in replication studies, and found systematic overestimates of the likelihood of replication. Of particular concern was the tendency of this psychologist sample not to correctly attribute inconsistency in attaining statistical significance to low statistical power, but instead to search for other reasons for the inconsistent results. More recent work has suggested that these effects are more easily obtained when the questions are framed in terms of sampling distributions than frequency distributions (Sedlmeier & Gigerenzer, 1997, 2000). However, the essential point remains that due to low statistical power, inconsistency in the health psychology literature remains the rule rather than the exception. Therefore, before searching for explanations for inconsistent results based in theoretical elaboration, or in sample or measurement differences, the simplest and often best explanation is likely to be low statistical power (e.g., Hall, French & Marteau, 2003).

Failure of Internal Validity: Missing Data

The failures of statistical conclusion validity just discussed have focused on instances of inadequate statistical reasoning with inferential statistics. Another common failure is where there are biases present in the data upon which inferential statistical tests are conducted. These biases can lead to a lack of internal validity.

One common source of bias is where there are missing data, and more specifically, where the missing data are not randomly distributed across the specified sample. Another common source of bias, low rates of responding, can be thought of as being a special case of missing data: here, entire cases are missing. In the context of poor response rates, the advantages and disadvantages of different methods of collecting survey data have been systematically reviewed (McColl et al., 2001), as has the more circumscribed issue of increasing response rates to postal questionnaires (Edwards et al., 2002).

To deal with the more general problem of missing data, several alternatives have been proposed, each with their particular advantages and disadvantages (see, e.g., Tabachnick & Fidell, 2001: 57–125). The simplest approach is 'case deletion', where each case or construct that contains missing data is deleted. This approach should only be considered where there is a small amount of missing data. Where larger amounts of data are missing, this procedure becomes quite inefficient, resulting in a reduced sample size and hence loss of power (Little & Rubin, 1987). Even when there is a small amount of data missing, the dataset should be scrutinized to ensure that where data are missing, there are no obvious sources of bias. Bias is likely to arise where some subsamples have yielded more missing data than others. Here, some form of imputation of missing values should be considered. The simplest form of imputation occurs when data are missing from a few items in a scale measuring a specific construct, for example anxiety, and the mean value of a sample is substituted for the missing data. Although popular, this practice has little to recommend it, as although it maintains the mean value for the sample, variances and intercorrelations between variables are likely to be distorted (Little & Rubin, 1987). A more defensible imputation is to use the mean of those items for which data are available for each case, to replace the missing data. However, despite its widespread use, there is little evidence of the effects this procedure may have, and as with all procedures for dealing with missing data, caution should be exercised to ensure it does not introduce bias (Allison, 2001). Where constructs are assessed with only single item measures instead of multiple items, the practice of substituting mean values for missing data is likely to lead to even more severe bias. More complex versions of imputation have been developed, based on explicit models of why the data are missing, and should be considered (Schafer & Graham, 2002). In all cases, the following principles should be borne in mind. First, prevention is better than cure, and all feasible steps should be taken to ensure complete data, particularly in piloting materials and procedures. Second, the procedures adopted to replace missing data should be made explicit. Third, researchers should examine the sensitivity of the results obtained to the procedures employed, always bearing in mind that any procedure for treating missing data, including case deletion, may introduce bias.

Failure of Construct Validity: Lack of Manipulation Checks

Having decided that appropriate statistical reasoning has occurred, and that no major sources of bias have influenced this process of reasoning, researchers can then consider how their findings relate to the wider health psychology literature. Problems can arise at this stage when the measures or manipulations used are given a specific label, but where there is a discrepancy between the label assigned and how it is assigned in the rest of the research literature. For instance, a 'threat' manipulation could attempt to influence perceptions of the likelihood of a particular outcome, by presenting information about personal risk on the basis of individualized assessment. An alternative would be to present information about a particular population from whom the research participant could be considered an instance, for example 'a female smoker', or 'a smoker attending colon screening'. Any of these 'threat' manipulations could be presented using numerical information or broader descriptive labels, which could be

framed in a multitude of ways (see Edwards, Elwyn, Covey, Matthews & Pill, 2001; Kuhberger, 1998). A 'threat' manipulation could also describe the presentation of information about the severity of a particular outcome, in isolation or in combination with any or all of the above. Each of these manipulations may have quite different effects. Researchers should therefore be explicit about the nature of their manipulations, and should in addition always employ measures to ensure that their manipulations are having the intended effects, and not plausible alternatives. An intervention designed to alter cognitive beliefs about outcome expectancies may have unforeseen effects on response efficacy or emotion, and vice versa. Similar issues apply to the construct validity of measures as well as manipulations.

Failure of External Validity: Overgeneralization

Having correctly labelled the construct to which their findings relate, researchers must consider the final issue that arises in interpretation, namely how reasonable it is to assert that these findings are general to other people, settings and times. In our view, it is highly optimistic to expect the findings of any one study to be applicable to all humans in all situations at all times. Even highly replicated findings in Western culture have often not been found to hold in other cultures; for example, many findings in attribution theory such as the fundamental attribution error appear not to apply in some other cultures (see Hewstone, 1989). Furthermore, in many areas of health psychology, the success of interventions to change behaviour by altering beliefs will depend critically on the prevalence of particular beliefs, which clearly will vary between groups, and across time. However, in positivist and realist traditions, the extent to which any set of research findings is general and the search for theories that apply in as many contexts as possible are central concerns.

Given the many pitfalls already described, we believe that it is highly problematic to generalize even modestly from the results of a single study. At a bare minimum, one would hope to see a study replicated several times before much confidence is expressed that any set of findings applies generally. More specifically, as study findings may be unique to particular sets of respondents and measures, replication with different populations and different experimental designs would encourage confidence in the generality of findings. In particular, if one is attempting to show that two or more constructs are causally related, a strong case usually requires a demonstration that manipulating one construct results in changes in the other, in a theoretically predicted way. A crucial development in the analysis of the generality of findings has been the widespread implementation of meta-analysis. In addition to estimating the likely size of an effect across studies, with confidence limits, meta-analysis also allows an estimate to be made of the heterogeneity of research findings (Rosenthal & DiMatteo, 2001). Such estimates typically highlight the additional factors that impact on the relationship between psychological constructs than the ones examined, even for well-supported theories such as the TPB (Armitage & Conner, 2001). At the risk of overgeneralizing ourselves, we would advocate that any researchers inclined to generalize from a set of findings consider carefully the range of designs, intervention materials, measures and populations on which these findings are based. Even then, we would recommend that researchers still be cautious in making general statements covering even those areas that the research has included in its scope.

INTRODUCTION TO THE PURPOSES AND PHILOSOPHIES OF QUALITATIVE RESEARCH

Widespread usage of the blanket term 'qualitative methods' tends to give the impression that there is a single philosophy that underpins the wide variety of methods of qualitative data collection and analysis. However, there is actually a range of different approaches to undertaking qualitative research, and the assumptions and aims of these approaches can differ substantially (Marecek, 2003). Before outlining the methods of qualitative research, it is therefore necessary first to consider the objectives and values of the various approaches that may be adopted. Moreover, since the aims and assumptions of each approach differ, there can be no single set of criteria for establishing the validity of qualitative research (Barbour, 2001; Kvale, 1995; Yardley, 2000). Consequently, this section briefly describes the assumptions and aims of some of the principal approaches to qualitative research, and also outlines procedures for demonstrating validity that are appropriate to each of these different approaches.

Realist and Positivist Approaches

Qualitative methods can be used by researchers with realist or positivist assumptions and aims, whose aim is to provide the most accurate analysis they can of objective reality. These researchers may turn to qualitative research in order to explore and describe new phenomena, for which no adequate theories or quantitative measurement tools yet exist. Qualitative methods can also be used to carry out holistic analyses of dynamic phenomena in ecologically valid contexts, if it is suspected that it may not be possible to model all the complex processes and interactions between factors that may be occurring in real-world situations using controlled laboratory settings and quantitative methods.

Realist or positivist qualitative researchers must demonstrate the reliability and objectivity of their data and analyses. At the very least, analyses should be supported by a clear 'paper trail' linking the analyses to the raw data, so that in principle an independent researcher could confirm the links between data and conclusions. A more rigorous demonstration of the reliability of the data can be accomplished by 'triangulation' – comparing the descriptions of phenomena derived from different investigators, data sources or methods of data collection, in order to converge on a verified description (Huberman & Miles, 1994). If qualitative data have been systematically categorized (e.g., by content analysis; see below) then it is possible to calculate the 'inter-rater reliability' of the categories used, that is the degree of correspondence between the categories assigned to the data by two independent raters. In addition, explicitly searching for and analysing 'deviant cases' (instances that seem to contradict or depart from the main interpretation presented) can show that the analysis is not based on a selective sample of data that are consistent with the researcher's argument.

Interpretive Approaches

For some investigators who question whether there can be a single objective psychosocial reality (see the earlier section on interpretive and constructivist approaches), the purpose of qualitative research is to understand and convey key features of *subjective* experiences and perspectives – what life is like from the varied viewpoints of the participants in the research project. Qualitative methods lend themselves to this kind of research because of the opportunity they typically offer participants to express themselves freely in their own ways, and to vividly describe their unique experiences in depth.

Since this approach assumes that the context and perspective of each person will be somewhat different, if triangulation is undertaken then the aim is to provide a rich multilayered understanding of the topic as viewed from different angles, rather than to converge on a single description (Flick, 1992). Moreover, it is assumed that the perspectives of the researchers will themselves inevitably also influence how they interpret the data. Consequently, instead of seeking to develop reliable but rigid coding methods that are relatively independent of individual perspectives, researchers may conduct open discussion of the thinking contributing to the interpretation, both during the analysis and in the final report, in order to promote 'reflexivity', i.e. self-conscious critical awareness of the way in which the analysis may have been influenced by the researchers' perspectives (King, 1996). The validity of the interpretive analysis may also be enhanced by seeking feedback from participants concerning the extent to which the interpretation provides useful insights into their subjective worldview.

Sociocultural Approaches

Constructivist researchers may adopt qualitative methods in order to explore the ways in which psychosocial phenomena are constructed through social interaction, and in particular through language. In this approach, meanings are viewed not as subjective – internal to the individual – but as ceaselessly produced and negotiated through ultimately sociolinguistic activities, such as explaining, defining, excusing, and so on. Consequently, analysis of social interaction, talk and written communication provides the ideal method of examining the processes of meaning construction.

Since all meanings are considered open to reinterpretation in this approach, it is problematic for constructivist authors to make strong claims for the validity of their particular analysis. Instead, the raw data on which an analysis is based may be presented in the report, perhaps including examples of deviant cases, to allow readers to make their own decisions concerning the persuasiveness of the analysis. Alternatively, constructivist researchers may reflexively highlight the limitations of their own interpretation and suggest alternative perspectives (Lincoln & Denzin, 1994).

Sociopolitical Approaches

For researchers who consider that the research process should be a vehicle for immediate positive psychosocial change, qualitative methods are sometimes seen as offering opportunities to empower and engage with people who have personal, practical knowledge of the topic of research to a greater extent than is permitted by methods in which the requirements for scientific control restrict such participants to the role of the passive objects of expert investigation (Greenwood & Levin, 1998). The aims of this approach to research can be to allow relatively disenfranchised people to voice their views, or to enable participants to identify and solve their own problems through collective dialogue, action and reflection. Consequently, the collective judgement of participants concerning how meaningful and useful the research process has been for them is more important than any academic criteria for validity, although additional benefits may be gained by disseminating the results of the research process in order to share and publicize the experiences of the participants (Meyer, 2000).

While the distinction made here between these four approaches serves to illustrate and simplify the different ways in which qualitative research is applied, in practice there are no such clear divisions between approaches, and researchers may adopt various combinations of them. For example, researchers interested in exploring subjective experience may also attend to the sociolinguistic aspects of narrative accounts of such experience, whereas researchers seeking to promote the cause of a disadvantaged group might nonetheless regard it as important to show that their analysis is verifiably grounded in objective empirical data. Moreover, although some qualitative analysis methods are particularly well suited to serving particular purposes, there is no straightforward correspondence between the approach adopted and the methods of data collection and analysis employed; focus groups could be used to determine the attitudes of a group of people, to explore subjective meanings, to study conversational strategies, or to promote group cohesiveness. This gives the researcher considerable freedom to creatively select and modify the methods that best suit the purpose in hand, but also the responsibility of ensuring coherence between the approach adopted and the methods employed.

QUALITATIVE DATA COLLECTION

Interviews and Focus Groups

The most widely used and familiar means of eliciting qualitative data is the semi-structured or depth interview (Wilkinson, Joffe & Yardley, 2004). Whereas structured interviews, like questionnaires, mainly comprise closed questions to which only a limited set of predefined responses can be given ('Is your health good/ fair/poor'?), semi-structured and depth interviews employ open-ended questions that invite interviewees to talk in detail about what is important to them ('How do you feel about your health?'). If interviewees are asked direct or abstract questions ('Why do you think that treatment X is harmful?') they tend to give brief, defensive or socially desirable answers (Hollway & Jefferson, 2000). To allow the interviewee to give extended personal accounts of their views and feelings, a good semi-structured interview schedule consists of a small number of questions that focus on the concrete lifeworld of the interviewee ('Tell me all about the time you tried treatment X'). The key to carrying out a good depth interview is therefore to be a good listener; you should interrupt and guide the interview as little as possible, but encourage the interviewee to continue by using appropriate non-verbal signals (e.g., nodding, intermittent eye contact) and neutral responses ('that's interesting', 'can you tell me more?') that convey non-judgemental attention and empathy.

Focus groups have also become popular as a means of eliciting qualitative data in a collective, group setting (Barbour & Kitzinger, 1999). The views expressed in group discussion may differ in important ways from those expressed in a one-to-one interview. If the focus group consists of people with similar experiences and views then participants may feel more confident and able to express opinions or reveal experiences that they might have concealed in an isolated interview – but it is equally possible that some participants might be inhibited from revealing personal information in a group setting, especially if their views differ from those of dominant members of the group. Moreover, group discussion is a process not simply of expressing but of *formulating* views; through dialogue the participants may arrive at quite different conclusions or positions from those espoused initially by individual members. In both interviews and focus groups it is therefore essential to consider carefully how the relative social status (e.g., gender, age, occupation) and relationships between all the participants and the interviewer may affect what is said.

Observation

Despite the freedom of expression that interviews and focus groups offer participants, both methods involve a meeting and discussion between people and on topics that are initiated and partly controlled by the researcher. While this permits the researcher to raise the issues and speak to the people that are central to the research, if contextual factors are considered important (as they often are in holistic qualitative inquiry) then it may be preferable to obtain data using methods that preserve the context of everyday life, that is by observing or recording naturally occurring events, settings and conversations. These methods can be extremely time-consuming, but have the advantage of gathering vast amounts of rich ecologically valid data. Moreover, some directly observed phenomena cannot be elicited by any method of data collection that relies on self-report, either because they are not consciously registered (e.g., non-verbal behaviour) or because participants are unable or unwilling to provide an accurate self-report, due to cognitive capacity or social motives.

One of the oldest traditions in qualitative research is 'ethnography' or participant observation, which involves immersing oneself in a group setting and observing the group's social activities and interactions in order to build up an understanding of the cultural rules and meanings of the group (Fetterman, 1998; Savage, 2000). Participant observation can pose difficult questions concerning how to obtain informed consent from all those who are observed without influencing the normal flow of daily life, and how to get beyond the assumptions of someone alien to the culture in order to understand the insider's perspective and yet retain sufficient analytical distance to critically evaluate what is observed. An alternative to participant observation is to carry out non-participant observation or audio- or video-recording. In this case, it is necessary to minimize the impact of the recording process on the setting and participants (generally the impact lessens over an extended recording period), and to ensure that the recorder, whether human or technological, will be able to capture the data of interest; for example, that important activity does not take place out of the view of the camera, that conversations are audible, or that the observer has sufficient time to note the events that must be recorded (Ratcliff, 2003).

Additional Considerations When Collecting Qualitative Data

Written and photographic records can also serve useful purposes in qualitative research. Analyses can focus on pre-existing records, such as medical notes or reports on health-related issues in the media. Answers to open-ended questions administered by questionnaire or over the internet can provide qualitative data when it might be difficult to conduct a face-to-face interview, perhaps because respondents are geographically dispersed, or because the topic is so sensitive that anonymity may be preferred by interviewees. Diaries or written reports of thought processes allow participants to record details of their subjective experience in situations that the researcher cannot easily access (e.g., at work, or while participating in an experiment), and may be more accurate than retrospective recall.

Of course, not everyone is able or willing to provide detailed written descriptions of their experiences, and so it is important to be aware that relying on written replies to questions might systematically exclude particular types of people from the sample, such as those who have little spare time, no access to the internet, poor eyesight or manual dexterity, or cannot write easily in English. In qualitative research it is not necessary to obtain a statistically representative sample because the results are not statistically generalized to a wider population. Nonetheless, if the researcher wishes to claim that the findings of the study have theoretical or practical significance beyond the particular setting of the study, it remains important that the sample is clearly defined and contains all those people whose particular situations are considered relevant to the topic investigated. Many researchers therefore use 'purposive' or 'theoretical' sampling to ensure that the relevant range of people is included in the study, using theoretical grounds to decide whether the most relevant factors are demographic or health characteristics, or views, experiences and behaviour. For example, when studying views of a treatment, it might be important to include both people who did and those who did not adhere to the treatment, of different ages, and at different stages of the disease.

METHODS OF QUALITATIVE ANALYSIS

Although the four different approaches to qualitative research described above do not map in a straightforward manner on to procedures for analysis, different types of analysis serve some purposes better than others. Broadly speaking, *thematic analysis* and *content analysis* are useful for systematically identifying, categorizing and describing patterns in qualitative data that are discernible across many respondents. *Phenomenological analysis* and *grounded theory* are well suited to exploring subjective experience and developing new theory. *Discourse analysis* and *narrative analysis* are commonly used to analyse the sociolinguistic construction of identity and meaning. While these three broad headings will be used to organize the brief overview below of some of the most widely used methods of qualitative analysis, there are of course many other methods that could not be covered here: indeed, new methods of analysis are constantly being created and disseminated. Moreover, researchers can adapt and combine these forms of analysis flexibly in the context of their particular objectives; for instance, narrative analysis may be undertaken from a phenomenological or psychoanalytical perspective to explore subjective experience, while content analysis may be employed to identify common, rare or co-occurring forms of discourse for subsequent analysis (Wood & Kroger, 2000).

Thematic Analysis and Content Analysis

Content analysis is a method for categorizing and then counting particular features of a qualitative dataset (Bauer, 2000). Thematic analysis is similar to content analysis, but places less emphasis on development of a reliable quantification of the categories or 'themes' identified, and more emphasis on qualitative analysis of these themes in context (Joffe & Yardley, 2004).

The process of categorizing the qualitative data involves developing and applying codes to label the features of the data that are of interest. Either 'deductive' codes derived from pre-existing theory and research are applied (e.g., previously validated categories of coping strategies), or 'inductive' coding categories are newly created in order to designate emerging patterns or themes identified from examination of the data (Boyatzis, 1998). Developing and applying codes is relatively straightforward if the features of interest are 'manifest' or directly observable characteristics of the data, such as particular words in a written text, particular discursive features in a dialogue (e.g., questions), or particular physical actions in a video sequence. However, it is usually more analytically meaningful to categorize 'latent' characteristics common to a wide range of expressions or actions. For example, latent coding may be used to label as 'coping strategies' all references by interviewees to coping behaviour, which may be described in very different ways, generally without employing the word 'cope' at all.

Considerable effort is required to develop codes for latent characteristics that can be reliably applied. A coding 'manual' (or 'frame') is created that contains the label for each code, its definition, and usually examples of what should and should not be coded with this label. As the codes are applied to the data it may become necessary to split codes that are too heterogeneous, to combine related codes, or to create subcategories of broad categories. To establish the reliability of the coding system (which is essential if strong claims for objectivity are to be made, or numerical analysis undertaken), two people then independently use the manual to apply the codes to a sample of data, and the correspondence between the raters' codes is calculated (ideally using Cohen's [1960] kappa). If the calculated inter-rater reliability is low (i.e., kappa less than 0.60) then it is necessary to discuss and resolve coding disagreements, clarify the definition of the code in the manual, and repeat the test of inter-rater reliability on a new data sample.

Once all the data relevant to the research questions are coded, thematic analysis involves describing the coded themes and exploring their significance by systematically examining the contexts in which they occur and the links between them. In content analysis, numbers can be given to the codes (provided that only one code has been assigned to each data segment), thus transforming the qualitative material into categorical data that can be analysed using appropriate statistical tests to compare groups or test associations.

Phenomenological Analysis and Grounded Theory

Phenomenological analysis has its roots in a longstanding philosophical tradition of inquiry into the nature and content of subjective experience. A good analysis can vividly convey the subjective perspectives of the participants and go beyond existing taken-for-granted understandings to suggest new insights and avenues for inquiry. There is no prescriptive method of analysis, since greater emphasis is placed on producing original, thought-provoking and compelling insights than on following particular methodological procedures. Nonetheless, most phenomenological research involves collecting detailed accounts of an experience, abstracting and describing the key meanings in these accounts, and using these abstracted features as a basis for providing an interpretation of the experience, often relating this to fundamental philosophical and psychosocial theory (Creswell, 1998; Giorgi & Giorgi, 2003; Smith, Jarman & Osborn, 1999).

A more clearly defined set of procedures for developing theoretical interpretations from empirical data is provided by grounded theory (Chamberlain, 1999; Rennie, 1998; Strauss & Corbin, 1990). In grounded theory, data collection and analysis are carried out concurrently, since analysis guides further data collection. An initial dataset can be derived from any relevant sources, and can include any type of qualitative data. Codes or categories to describe these data are first generated by 'open coding', which entails labelling data segments using words and phrases that are closely related to the content, and may actually be based on the words used by participants. The aim is to ground the classifications in a careful inductive description of the data rather than prematurely imposing pre-existing abstract conceptual categories on them. The 'constant comparative method' is central to the process of refining the codes and building a theory of how they are related. Exhaustive comparison between each coded data segment helps the researcher to identify the similarities and differences between each instance of a particular code, relative to other instances of that code and to instances of different codes. The process of theory building is further assisted by persistently questioning the data and interpretations of them, and drawing diagrams of how codes may interrelate. A thorough paper-trail to document the path from data to interpretation is maintained by these codes and diagrams, and by recording 'memos' of the emerging concepts and hypotheses that are shaping the analysis.

Once a tentative understanding of the data has been developed, 'theoretical sampling' is used to identify further participants able to provide data that will be particularly useful for testing, extending and modifying the emerging theory. For example, if it appears that a good relationship with the therapist is an important influence on subsequent adherence to therapy, this can be 'verified' by explicitly sampling people with a poor relationship with their therapist, in order to clarify under what circumstances this does or does not lead to non-adherence. As analysis progresses, the initial grounded categories are subsumed into a smaller set of more abstract 'axial' codes, the properties of these codes and relationships between them are elaborated, and their relationship to existing concepts and theories is considered. When further sampling no longer reveals new ideas or relationships that prompt further revision of the codes or the theory then 'saturation' is said to have occurred, and no further data are required. Finally, an overarching theory or 'core category' is created that integrates the entire set of relationships between the categories into a single coherent interpretation.

Discourse Analysis and Narrative Analysis

Approaches to discourse analysis can be broadly grouped into those that focus on the *process* of how meaning is created in everyday interaction, and those that analyse the socio-cultural context and effects of the *product* or elements of talk, that is the origins and functions of the concepts and linguistic categories dominant in contemporary social usage (Taylor, 2001). Analyses of the product or elements of talk typically draw on poststructuralist and critical theory to examine how social and linguistic structures and practices both construct and are maintained by the categories and meanings that we take for granted. Some analyses focus on concepts or terminology widely used in the public domain; for example, the analyst might consider the way in which the identities and behaviours of particular groups in society may be defined and regulated by notions of 'risk' or of 'disability'. Some analyses are based on published material (e.g., health promotion campaign posters) or on samples of talk or text recorded in daily life (e.g., e-mail exchanges) or elicited in interviews or focus group conversations (Willig, 1999). There are few methodological restrictions or indeed guidelines associated with this kind of discourse analysis. However, in order to undertake a well-informed analysis of the sociocultural origins and implications of discourses it is necessary to be familiar with relevant sociocultural theory and research, much of which may be located in the sociological, anthropological, feminist or philosophical literature.

Analyses of the processes whereby meanings are actively constructed in talk are based on very detailed transcriptions of tape-recorded segments of talk that contain the discursive actions of interest. The analyst identifies the discursive strategies whereby social actions are successfully accomplished by meticulously attending to the immediate effect of each linguistic move on the next turn of the conversation, by making comparisons with segments of dialogue in which the action was *not* successfully accomplished, and by drawing on previous analyses in which similar strategies have been described (Wood & Kroger, 2000).

Narrative analysis focuses on how identity and meaning are constructed by individuals in their accounts of their lives (Murray, 2003). The analysis may examine how elements of the traditional story form are used to give a meaningful structure and coherence to subjective experience, or how the narrative is used to represent the narrator in a particular identity or role. A key feature of narrative analysis is that it preserves the unity and sequencing of what is said, rather than extracting themes or segments. This makes it ideal for understanding the unique and often poetic ways in which individuals can make sense of the complexities and contradictions in their lives.

Practicalities of Carrying Out Qualitative Research

A common misconception about qualitative research is that the research can or even should begin without a clear research objective, and simply 'explore' an ill-defined topic. While qualitative researchers seldom formulate hypotheses as to anticipated findings, and may well alter the focus of their research as their study progresses, a well-designed qualitative research project should commence with relatively precise and realistic objectives concerning the type and scope of the understandings that are to be gained from the research, and the methods by which these will be attained.

It is vital to be aware that qualitative research is *extremely* time-consuming in comparison with survey methods; sufficient time and personnel must therefore be allocated for carrying out in-depth interviewing or observation, detailed transcription, and coding. Although a range of computer programs are now available to assist with analysis, these simply facilitate the process of systematic comparison between coded data segments and do not reduce the time and mental effort that must be devoted to interpreting the data (Gibbs, Friese & Mangabeira, 2002). While the time taken varies according to the method used, as an approximate guide for each participant 1 day should be allowed for arranging and carrying out data collection, and between 2 and 4 days for transcribing and coding the data.

It is also necessary to appreciate that qualitative research can pose particular ethical problems. Although qualitative research is sometimes represented as egalitarian – providing participants with an opportunity to express their viewpoints – participants are seldom given any real control over the analysis that is disseminated, which may contain interpretations and conclusions that participants would not support (Burman, 2001). Moreover, the more intimate relationships that may develop between participant and researcher can actually make it more difficult for participants to resist invitations to reveal personal information that they would rather have not disclosed. An important related consideration is that it can be extremely difficult to preserve anonymity and confidentiality when reproducing accounts of unique personal experiences given by participants from a relatively small, identified population, such as patients with spinal cord injury admitted to a certain hospital in a certain time period.

HEALTH SERVICES RESEARCH

What Is Health Services Research?

There is a variety of definitions of health services research (HSR), but most share the core idea that HSR is concerned with the identification of health care needs, and the study of how health services meet them. One example would

be the need to identify cancers at an early stage, while they are likely to respond better to treatment, and how well population screening services lead to the successful identification and treatment of such cancers in all sections of the population. The other central feature of most definitions of HSR is that it is multidisciplinary: to meet the aims implicit in the definition of HSR given, health psychologists need to work alongside researchers from many disciplines, including the biomedical sciences, epidemiology, economics, and statistics, as well as other health professionals and social scientists. It is also increasingly likely that to answer many applied health care problems, health psychologists will find themselves working with researchers who do not share their philosophical approaches to research. Although this has the undeniable potential to lead to problems between researchers, it also allows for a wider understanding of an applied issue to be obtained, owing to the multiple perspectives that can be taken.

An Example of Applying Qualitative and Quantitative Research

To bring together the material discussed in different parts of the chapter, this section outlines how the four main philosophical approaches described so far each lead to a different research focus, employing both qualitative and quantitative approaches. Although these approaches are discussed separately to help clarify the differences in approach, in practice a researcher may adopt several approaches. For another example of how different philosophical approaches lead to different research questions, see Yardley and Marks (2004).

The topic considered here is the delivery of effective interventions to prevent weight gain in middle life through increasing physical activity, and hence reduce the incidence of obesity. In all Western societies, obesity is an increasing health problem. It is generally agreed that this is not primarily due to a change in diet: the average amount of calories consumed per person appears to be less than 50 years ago. Rather, the increase in obesity appears to be largely due to a marked decrease in physical activity (Prentice & Jebb, 1995). One reaction to this has been to conduct trials to increase physical activity in groups of individuals at particularly high risk, such as the ProActive trial for offspring of people with type II diabetes (Kinmonth et al., 2002).

Positivist approach

This approach was characterized earlier as being less concerned with the reality of theories and constructs, but more focused on their utility in guiding research and intervention. Within health psychology, research using the TPB (Ajzen, 1988, 1991) has maintained a strong focus on prediction (see Armitage & Conner, 2001). A currently vigorous line of research concerns how prediction can be improved by including past behaviour (Ouellette & Wood, 1998), as well as further constructs such as moral norms and anticipated regret (reviewed by Conner & Armitage, 1998).

The causal implications of the TPB have received less attention (Sutton, 2002). Thus, despite the now excellent evidence that TPB constructs are good predictors of intentions to perform a behaviour, and of behaviour itself (Sutton, 1998), the evidence from intervention studies that *changes* in TPB constructs lead to changes in behaviour is still meagre (Hardeman et al., 2002). More to the point, although there are a few instances of successful experimental manipulations based on the TPB, there are even fewer that attempt to test the causal relationships proposed. For example, do attitudes (mediated by intention) influence behaviour more than behaviour influences attitudes? (For an exception see Armitage & Conner, 1999.)

Another issue that does not seem to have arisen in much TPB research concerns the reality of the constructs (see Johnston et al., 2004, Chapter 13 in this volume). It is asserted that attitudes to any behaviour the researcher is interested in can be measured (Ajzen & Fishbein, 1980), but the question of how real these constructs may be has not been investigated. It is far from clear that people possess attitudes towards, for example, eating certain

foods or that they have beliefs concerning how people that are important to them would view them eating these same foods.

By avoiding issues such as the reality of constructs and the causal implications of the theory, much research using the TPB can be considered as a good exemplar of a positivist approach. Thus, an example of a positivist approach to studying low levels of physical activity would be a TPB study that attempts to predict this behaviour from TPB constructs.

Realist approach

By contrast, a realist approach to the same problem would have a different focus. Assuming that the TPB constructs are shown to reliably predict physical activity (as indeed they do: see Blue, 1995; Hagger, Chatzisarantis & Biddle, 2002; Hausenblas, Carron & Mack, 1997), a realist would then be concerned to identify *why* these constructs are predictive. What is the explanation for the observed relationships? That is, what is it about having a positive attitude towards being physically active that leads to an increase in physical activity? Such an explanation is likely to involve descriptions of causal relationships between further theoretical entities. Other issues such as the reality or otherwise of TPB constructs, and the causal ordering of these constructs, would also be of more interest to a realist than a positivist.

However, there are clearly some similarities between the positions labelled 'realist' and 'positivist' here. These labels can be considered as extremes along a continuum of 'scientific', usually quantitative, approaches to health psychology. What these approaches would also share is an interest in attempting to manipulate psychological constructs, such as those in the TPB, to see if a change in levels of physical activity can be brought about. A realist would be more concerned with the reality of constructs, and *why* they are related. Nevertheless, researchers from both realist and positivist perspectives would approach this issue with the reductionist strategy of attempting to identify discrete, atomistic 'constructs', which can be measured and manipulated.

Interpretive approach

The reductionist aims just described would not be shared by a researcher taking an interpretive approach. By contrast, such a researcher would be more interested in eliciting vivid descriptions of subjective experiences, which could help those designing interventions to understand the participants' perspectives on experiences such as participating in an intervention to promote physical activity. Thus, although participants may give reasons for not being physically active, from an interpretive perspective, these reasons are not assumed to provide a causal explanation for their behaviour, since participants may not be aware of or report factors, such as habit or social influence, that actually influence their behaviour. Rather, these reasons provide a valuable insight into the social and personal meanings associated with obesity-related interventions. For example, positivist and realist research might show that low perceived control over eating behaviour was related to intervention outcome. In-depth interpretive qualitative research might complement this finding by shedding light on this experience of helplessness with regard to eating. Moreover, such analysis could identify potentially important differences in the meanings and experiences of subgroups of participants, such as differences associated with gender, socioeconomic status, age or ethnicity. For instance, it might emerge that for those with a lower socioeconomic status, perceived low control over eating healthily is associated with a fatalistic view of human nature and the relative low cost of less healthy food. In contrast, the same predictive variable in those with a higher socioeconomic status might instead be attributed to an occupational and social lifestyle that involved frequent eating out or use of pre-prepared meals to save time.

In summary, the sorts of information that will be yielded by research taking this approach is likely to be accounts of the meanings of different activities for different people's identities and lifestyles, and an understanding of differences in the assumptions and perspectives of researchers and research participants.

Constructivist approach

Researchers adopting a constructivist approach are also likely to use qualitative methods. This might involve examining dialogue in social interactions – for example, to identify ways in which talk is used to construct the idea that increased physical activity is desirable and necessary, and to suppress alternative ways of construing the situation of the obese individual. These processes could be linked to analysis of how questions of social accountability, such as blame and guilt, are managed in interactions related to reducing obesity. Adopting a 'critical' stance, a constructivist might 'deconstruct' the concept of obesity prevention, questioning definitions of 'normal' or 'irresponsible' eating behaviour, or challenging the construction of obesity as the consequence of a failure of control by the individual over eating behaviour, rather than as the consequence of social policies and practices (such as replacement of manual with sedentary work, and the dominance of motorized over pedestrianized ways of life). In summary, aims of critical constructivist analyses might include analysing how power is negotiated in interactions between providers and recipients of interventions, questioning the functions of the discourses and social practices surrounding obesity and its management, and allowing the recipients of interventions to voice their views and reflect upon how these may relate to their own aims and agendas. Like the interpretive approach, this type of analysis can serve the valuable function of revealing the implicit assumptions and aims of the providers of the interventions and how these may differ from those of participants.

Health Services Research: Multidisciplinary and multiple approaches

The example just discussed has hopefully highlighted some of the key characteristics of HSR. The background to the issue of lack of physical activity leading to weight gain in Western populations has been derived from epidemiological studies. The positivist and realist approaches take as their broad aims the prediction and explanation of physical activity, with a view to intervening to promote physical activity. The interpretive approach aims to highlight the personal and social meanings attached to physical activity and participation in a trial to promote physical activity. The constructivist approach aims to investigate the functions of discourses and practices related to physical activity and obesity, on the part of physicians, patients and researchers. These multiple approaches can then be used to inform the desirability and effectiveness of any changes in physical activity likely to be brought about if the intervention was more widely implemented. The evaluation of the intervention would depend on not only these considerations, but also the likely reduction in disease and ill-health, based on epidemiological models of how increases of physical activity are likely to affect prevalence of disease. Economic considerations will also be relevant, balancing the likely individual and population benefits against the costs of any intervention, and specifically against the opportunity costs of benefits that are likely to accrue if the money that could be spent on such an intervention was spent on other health care services.

ACKNOWLEDGEMENTS

David French was funded by a Wellcome Trust Training Fellowship in Health Services Research when this chapter was written (reference number 060634/Z/00/Z).

We are grateful to Jeremy Miles, Toby Prevost, Susan Michie and Martin Cartwright for helpful comments on earlier drafts.

REFERENCES

Abelson, R. P. (1995). *Statistics as principled argument*. Hillsdale, NJ: Erlbaum.

Aiken, L. S., & West, S. G. (1991). *Multiple regression: Testing and interpreting interactions*. Newbury Park, CA: Sage.

Ajzen, I. (1988). *Attitudes, personality and behavior*. Milton Keynes: Open University Press.

Ajzen, I. (1991). The theory of planned behavior. *Organizational Behavior and Human Decision Processes, 50,* 179–211.

Ajzen, I., & Fishbein, M. (1980). *Understanding attitudes and predicting social behavior*. Englewood Cliffs, NJ: Prentice-Hall.

Allison, P. A. (2001). *Missing data*. Thousand Oaks, CA: Sage.

Altman, D. G., Machin, D., Bryant, T. N., & Gardner, M. J. (2000). *Statistics with confidence* (2nd edn.). London: BMJ Books.

Armitage, C. J., & Conner, M. (1999). The theory of planned behaviour: Assessment of predictive validity and 'perceived control'. *British Journal of Social Psychology, 38,* 35–54.

Armitage, C., & Conner, M. (2001). Efficacy of the theory of planned behaviour: A meta-analytic review. *British Journal of Social Psychology, 40,* 471–499.

Barbour, R. S. (2001). Checklists for improving rigour in qualitative research: A case of the tail wagging the dog. *British Medical Journal, 322,* 1115–1117.

Barbour, R. S., & Kitzinger, J. (1999). *Developing focus group research*. London: Sage.

Baron, R. M., & Kenny, D. A. (1986). The moderator– mediator variable distinction in social psychological research: Conceptual, strategic, and statistical considerations. *Journal of Personality and Social Psychology, 51,* 1173–1182.

Bauer, M. W. (2000). Classical content analysis. In M. W. Bauer & G. Gaskell (Eds.), *Qualitative researching with text, image and sound: A practical handbook* (pp. 131–151). London: Sage.

Bem, D. J. (1972). Self-perception theory. In L. Berkowitz (Ed.), *Advances in experimental social psychology* (Vol. 6, pp. 1–62). New York: Academic.

Benjamini, Y., & Hochberg, Y. (1995). Controlling the false discovery rate: A practical and powerful approach to multiple testing. *Journal of the Royal Statistical Society, Series B, 57,* 289–300.

Blue, C. L. (1995). The predictive capacity of the theory of reasoned action and the theory of planned behavior in exercise research: An integrated literature review. *Research in Nursing and Health, 18,* 105–121.

Box, G. E. P. (1979). Robustness in the strategy of (scientific) model building. In R.L. Lawrence & G. N. Wilkinson (Eds.), *Robustness in statistics*. New York: Academic.

Boyatzis, R. E. (1998). *Transforming qualitative information*. London: Sage.

Brown, R. H. (1994). Reconstructing social theory after the postmodern critique. In H. Simons & M. Billig (Eds.), *After postmodernism* (pp. 12–37). Thousand Oaks, CA: Sage.

Bryk, A. S., & Raudenbush, S. W. (1992). *Hierarchical linear models.* Newbury Park, CA: Sage.

Burman, E. (2001). Minding the gap: Positivism, psychology and the politics of qualitative methods. In D. L. Tolman & M. Brydon-Miller (Eds.), *From subjects to subjectivities: A handbook of interpretive and participatory methods* (pp. 259–275). New York: New York University Press.

Byrne, D. (2002). *Interpreting quantitative data.* London: Sage.

Campbell, D. T., & Kenny, D. A. (1999). *A primer on regression artifacts.* New York: Guilford.

Campbell, M., Fitzpatrick, R., Haines, A., Kinmonth, A. L., Sandercock, P., Spiegelhalter, D., & Tyrer, P. (2000). Framework for design and evaluation of complex interventions to improve health. *British Medical Journal, 321,* 694–696.

Chamberlain, K. (1999). Using grounded theory in health research: Practices, premises and potential. In M. Murray & K. Chamberlain (Eds.), *Qualitative health psychology: Theories and methods* (pp. 183–201). London: Sage.

Child, D. (1990). *The essentials of factor analysis* (2nd edn.). New York: Continuum.

Clark-Carter, D. (1997). The account taken of statistical power in research published in the British Journal of Psychology. *British Journal of Psychology, 88,* 71–83.

Cohen, J. (1960). A coefficient of agreement for nominal scales. *Educational and Psychological Measurement, 20,* 37–46.

Cohen, J. (1962). The statistical power of abnormal-social psychological research: A review. *Journal of Abnormal and Social Psychology, 65,* 145–153.

Cohen, J. (1990). Things I have learned (so far). *American Psychologist, 45,* 1304–1312.

Cohen, J. (1992). A power primer. *Psychological Bulletin, 112,* 155–159.

Cohen, J. (1994). The earth is round ($p < .05$). *American Psychologist, 49,* 997–1003.

Cohen, J., & Cohen, P. (1983). *Applied multiple regression/ correlation analysis for the behavioral sciences* (2nd edn.). NJ: Erlbaum.

Cohen, S., & Wills, T. A. (1985). Stress, social support and the buffering hypothesis. *Psychological Bulletin, 98,* 310–357.

Conner, M., & Armitage, C. J. (1998). Extending the theory of planned behavior: A review and avenues for further research. *Journal of Applied Social Psychology, 28,* 1429–1464.

Conner, M., & Norman, P. (1996). *Predicting health behaviour.* Buckingham: Open University Press.

Cook, T. D., & Campbell, D. T. (1979). *Quasi-experimentation: Design and analysis issues for field settings.* Boston, MA: Houghton Mifflin.

Creswell, J. W. (1998). *Qualitative inquiry and research design: Choosing among five traditions.* London: Sage.

Dzewaltowski, D. A., Noble, J. M., & Shaw, J. M. (1990). Physical activity participation: Social cognitive theory versus the theories of reasoned action and planned behavior. *Journal of Sport and Exercise Psychology, 12,* 388–405.

Edwards, A., Elwyn, G., Covey, J., Matthews, E., & Pill, R. (2001). Presenting risk information: a review of the effects of 'framing' and other manipulations on patient outcomes. *Journal of Health Communication, 6,* 61–82.

Edwards, P., Roberts, I., Clarke, M., DiGuiseppi, C., Pratap, S., Wentz, R., & Kwan, I. (2002). Increasing response rates to postal questionnaires: Systematic review. *British Medical Journal, 324,* 1183–1191.

Egger, M., & Smith, G. D. (1998). Bias in location and selection of studies. *British Medical Journal, 316,* 61–66.

Estes, W. K. (1993). Mathematical models in psychology. In G. Keren & C. Lewis (Eds.), *A handbook for data analysis in the behavioral sciences: Methodology issues* (pp. 3–19). Hillsdale, NJ: Erlbaum.

Fabrigar, L. R., Wegener, D.T., MacCallum, R. C., & Strahan, E. J. (1999). Evaluating the use of exploratory factor analysis in psychological research. *Psychological Methods, 4,* 272–299.

Fetterman, D. M. (1998). *Ethnography: Step by step* (2nd edn.). London: Sage.

Finkel, S. E. (1995). *Causal analysis with panel data.* Thousand Oaks, CA: Sage.

Fishbein, M., & Ajzen, I. (1975). *Belief, attitude, intention, and behavior: An introduction to theory and research.* Reading, MA: Addison-Wesley.

Fletcher, G. J. O., & Ward, C. (1988). Attribution theory and processes: A cross-cultural perspective. In M. H. Bond (Ed.), *The cross-cultural challenge to social psychology* (pp. 230–244). Newbury Park, CA: Sage.

Flick, U. (1992). Triangulation revisited: Strategy of validation or alternative. *Journal for the Theory of Social Behaviour, 22,* 175–197.

Fox, N. J. (1993). *Postmodernism, sociology and health.* Milton Keynes: Open University Press.

Gergen, K. J. (1985). The social constructionist movement in modern psychology. *American Psychologist, 40,* 266–275.

Gibbs, G. R., Friese, S., & Mangabeira, W. C. (2002). The use of new technology in qualitative research. *Forum: Qualitative Social Research* (Online journal), *3*(2), 35 paragraphs. Retrieved (11 June 2002) from http://www. qualitative-research.net/fqs/fqs-eng.htm.

Gigerenzer, G., Swijtink, Z., Porter, T., Daston, L., Beatty, J., & Kruger, L. (1989). *The empire of chance: How probability changed science and everyday life.* Cambridge: Cambridge University Press.

Giorgi, A.P., & Giorgi, B. M. (2003). The descriptive phenomenological psychological method. In P. J. Camic, J. E. Rhodes & L. Yardley (Eds.), *Qualitative research in psychology: Expanding perspectives in methodology and design* (pp. 243–273). Washington, DC: American Psychological Association.

Goldstein, H. (1995). *Multilevel statistical models* (2nd edn.). London: Arnold.

Greenwood, D. J., & Levin, M. (1998). *Introduction to action research: Social research for social change.* London: Sage.

Guba, E. G., & Lincoln, Y. S. (1994). Competing paradigms in qualitative research. In N. K. Denzin & Y. S. Lincoln (Eds.), *Handbook of qualitative research* (pp. 105–117). London: Sage.

Guyatt, G., Sackett, D., Taylor, D. W., Chong, J., Roberts, R., & Pugsley, S. (1986). Determining optimal therapy: Randomized trials in individual patients. *New England Journal of Medicine, 314,* 889–892.

Hacking, I. (1983). *Representing and intervening.* Cambridge: Cambridge University Press.

Hagger, M. S., Chatzisarantis, N. L. D., & Biddle, S. J. H. (2002). A meta-analytic review of the theories of reasoned action and planned behavior in physical activity: An examination of predictive validity and the contribution of additional variables. *Journal of Sport and Exercise Psychology, 24,* 3–32.

Hall, S., French, D. P., & Marteau, T. M. (2003). Attributions and adjustment to serious unexpected negative events: A systematic review of the literature. *Journal of Social and Clinical Psychology, 22,* 515–536.

Hardeman, W., Johnston, M., Johnston, D. W., Bonetti, D., Wareham, N. J., & Kinmonth, A. L. (2002). Application of the theory of planned behaviour in behaviour change interventions: A systematic review. *Psychology and Health, 17,* 123–158.

Hausenblas, H. A., Carron, A. V., & Mack, D. E. (1997). Application of the theories of reasoned action and planned behavior to exercise behavior: A meta-analysis. *Journal of Sport and Exercise Psychology, 19,* 36–51.

Harré, R. (1972). *The philosophies of science.* Oxford: Oxford University Press.

Henderson, D. A., & Denison, D. R. (1989). Stepwise regression in social and psychological research. *Psychological Reports, 64,* 251–257.

Hennekens, C. H., & Buring, J. E. (1987). *Epidemiology in medicine.* Philadelphia, PA: Lippincott, Williams & Wilkins.

Hewstone, M. (1989). *Causal attribution: From cognitive processes to collective beliefs.* Oxford: Blackwell.

Hollway, W., & Jefferson, T. (2000). *Doing qualitative research differently.* London: Sage.

Howell, D. C. (1997). *Statistical methods for psychology* (4th edn.). Belmont, CA: Duxbury.

Hoyle, R. H. (Ed.) (1995). *Structural equation modeling: Concepts, issues and applications.* Thousand Oaks, CA: Sage.

Huberman, A. M., & Miles, M. B. (1994). Data management and analysis methods. In N. K. Denzin & Y. S. Lincoln (Eds.), *Handbook of qualitative research* (pp. 428–444). Thousand Oaks, CA: Sage.

Jaccard, J., Turrisi, R., & Wan, C. K. (1990). *Interaction effects in multiple regression.* Newbury Park, CA: Sage.

Janz, N. K., & Becker, M. H. (1984). The health belief model: A decade later. *Health Education Quarterly, 11,* 1–47.

Joffe, H., & Yardley, L. (2004). Content and thematic analysis. In D. Marks & L. Yardley (Eds.), *Research methods for clinical and health psychology* (pp. 56–68). London: Sage.

Johnston, M., French, D. P., Bonetti, D., & Johnston, D. W. (2004). Assessment and measurement in health psychology. In S. Sutton, A. Baum & M. Johnston (Eds.), *The Sage handbook of health psychology.* London: Sage.

Judd, C. M., & McClelland, G. H. (1989). *Data analysis: A model comparison approach.* San Diego, CA: Harcourt Brace Jovanovich.

Judd, C. M., McClelland, G. H., & Culhane, S. E. (1985). Data analysis: Continuing issues in the everyday analysis of psychological data. *Annual Review of Psychology, 46,* 433–465.

Kazdin, A. E. (1982). *Single-case research designs: Methods for clinical and applied settings.* Oxford: Oxford University Press.

Kenny, D. A. (1979). *Correlation and causality.* New York: Wiley-Interscience.

Kenny, D. A., Kashy, D. A., & Bolger, N. (1998). Data analysis in social psychology. In D. T. Gilbert, S. T. Fiske & G. Lindzey (Eds.), *The handbook of social psychology* (Vol. 1, 4th edn., pp. 233–265). New York: McGraw-Hill.

King, E. (1996). The use of self in qualitative research. In J. T. Richardson (Ed.), *Handbook of qualitative research methods for psychology and the social sciences* (pp. 175–188). Leicester: BPS Books.

Kinmonth, A. L., Hardeman, W., French, D., Griffin, S., Wareham, N., & Sutton, S. (2002). The Proactive trial: Development of the intervention. Oral presentation at the Society of Behavioral Medicine Annual Conference, Washington, DC, April.

Kline, P. (1993). *An easy guide to factor analysis.* London: Routledge.

Kline, P. (2000). *The handbook of psychological testing* (2nd edn.). London: Routledge.

Kuhberger, A. (1998). The influence of framing on risky decisions: A meta-analysis. *Organizational Behavior and Human Decision Processes, 75,* 23–55.

Kuhn, T. S. (1970). *The structure of scientific revolutions* (2nd edn.). Chicago, IL: Chicago University Press.

Kvale, S. (Ed.) (1992). *Psychology and postmodernism.* London: Sage.

Kvale, S. (1995). The social construction of validity. *Qualitative Inquiry, 1,* 19–40.

Leventhal, H. (1970). Findings and theory in the study of fear communications. In L. Berkowitz (Ed.), *Advances in experimental social psychology* (Vol. 5, pp. 119–187). New York: Academic.

Lincoln, Y. S., & Denzin, N. K. (1994). The fifth moment. In N. K. Denzin & Y. S. Lincoln (Eds.), *Handbook of qualitative research* (pp. 575–586). Thousand Oaks, CA: Sage.

Little, R. J. A., & Rubin, D. B. (1987). *Statistical analysis with missing data.* New York: Wiley.

Loehlin, J. C. (1998). *Latent variable models: An introduction* (3rd edn.). Hillsdale, NJ: Erlbaum.

Maddock, J. E., & Rossi, J. S. (2001). Statistical power of articles published in three health psychology related journals. *Health Psychology, 20,* 76–78.

Mahon, J., Laupacis, A., Donner, A., & Wood, T. (1996). Randomised study of *n* of 1 trials versus standard practice. *British Medical Journal, 312,* 1069–1074.

Marecek, J. (2003). Dancing through minefields: Towards a qualitative stance in psychology. In P. J. Camic, J. E. Rhodes & L. Yardley (Eds.), *Qualitative research in psychology: Expanding perspectives in methodology and design* (pp. 49–69). Washington, DC: American Psychological Association.

Maruyama, G. M. (1997). *Basics of structural equation modeling.* Beverly Hills, CA: Sage.

Marteau, T. M., & Johnston, M. (1987). Health psychology: The danger of neglecting psychological models. *Bulletin of the British Psychological Society, 40,* 82–85.

McColl, E., Jacoby, A., Thomas, L., Soutter, J., Bamford, C., Steen, N., Thomas, R., Harvey, E., Garratt, A., & Bond, J. (2001). Design and use of questionnaires: A review of best practice applicable to surveys of health service staff and patients. *Health Technology Assessment, 5* (31).

Meehl, P. E. (1978). Theoretical risks and tabular asterisks: Sir Karl, Sir Ronald, and the slow progress of soft psychology. *Journal of Consulting and Clinical Psychology, 46,* 806–834.

Meehl, P. E. (1990). Why summaries of research on psychological theories are often uninterpretable. *Psychological Reports, 66,* 195–244.

Meichenbaum, D., & Turk, D. C. (1987). *Facilitating treatment adherence: A practitioner's guidebook.* New York: Plenum.

Menard, S. (1991). *Longitudinal research.* Thousand Oaks, CA: Sage.

Meyer, J. (2000). Using qualitative methods in health related action research. *British Medical Journal, 320,* 178–181.

Miles, J., & Shevlin, M. (2001). *Applying regression and correlation: A guide for students and researchers.* Thousand Oaks, CA: Sage.

Murray, M. (2003). Narrative psychology and narrative analysis. In P. J. Camic, J. E. Rhodes & L. Yardley (Eds.), *Qualitative research in psychology: Expanding perspectives in methodology and design* (pp. 95–112). Washington, DC: American Psychological Association.

Newton-Smith, W. H. (1981). *The rationality of science.* London: Routledge.

Orwin, R. G. (1983). A fail-safe *N* for effect size. *Journal of Educational Statistics, 8,* 157–159.

Ouellette, J. A., & Wood, W. (1998). Habit and intention in everyday life: The multiple processes by which past behavior predicts future behavior. *Psychological Bulletin, 124,* 54–74.

Paterson, L., & Goldstein, H. (1992). New statistical methods for analyzing social structures: An introduction to multilevel models. *British Educational Research Journal, 17,* 387–393.

Petterman, F., & Muller, J. (2001). *Clinical psychology and single case evidence: A practical approach to treatment planning and evaluation.* New York: Wiley.

Popper, K. R. (1963). *Conjectures and refutations.* London: Routledge & Kegan Paul.

Prentice, A. M., & Jebb, S. A. (1995). Obesity in Britain: Gluttony or sloth? *British Medical Journal, 311,* 437–439.

Ratcliff, D. (2003). Video methods in qualitative research. In P. J. Camic, J. E. Rhodes & L. Yardley (Eds.), *Qualitative research in psychology: Expanding perspectives in methodology and design* (pp. 113–129). Washington, DC: American Psychological Association.

Ray, C. (2000). Logical positivism. In W. H. Newton-Smith (Ed.), *A companion to the philosophy of science* (pp. 243–251). Oxford: Blackwell.

Rennie, D. L. (1998). Grounded theory methodology: The pressing need for a coherent logic of justification. *Theory and Psychology, 8,* 101–119.

Rogers, R. W. (1985). Attitude change and information integration in fear appeals. *Psychological Reports, 56,* 179–182.

Rosenthal, R. (1979). The 'file drawer problem' and tolerance for null results. *Psychological Bulletin, 86,* 638–641.

Rosenthal, R., & DiMatteo, M. R. (2001). Meta-analysis: Recent developments in quantitative methods for literature reviews. *Annual Review of Psychology, 52,* 59–82.

Savage, J. (2000). Ethnography and health care. *British Medical Journal, 321,* 1400–1402.

Schafer, J. L., & Graham, J. W. (2002). Missing data: Our view of the state of the art. *Psychological Methods, 7,* 147–177.

Schumacker, R. E., & Lomax, R. G. (1996). *A beginner's guide to structural equation modeling.* Hillsdale, NJ: Erlbaum.

Sears, D. O. (1986). College sophomores in the laboratory: Influences of a narrow data base on social psychology's view of human nature. *Journal of Personality and Social Psychology, 51,* 515–530.

Sedlmeier, P., & Gigerenzer, G. (1989). Do studies of statistical power have an effect on the power of studies? *Psychological Bulletin, 105,* 309–316.

Sedlmeier, P., & Gigerenzer, G. (1997). Intuitions about sample size: The empirical law of large numbers. *Journal of Behavioral Decision Making, 10,* 33–51.

Sedlmeier, P., & Gigerenzer, G. (2000). Was Bernoulli wrong? On intuitions about sample size. *Journal of Behavioral Decision Making, 13,* 133–139.

Shadish, W. R., Cook, T. D., & Campbell, D. T. (2002). *Experimental and quasi-experimental designs for generalized causal inference.* Boston, MA: Houghton Mifflin.

Siegel, S., & Castellan, N. J. (1988). *Nonparametric statistics* (2nd edn.). Singapore: McGraw-Hill.

Smith, J. A., Jarman, M., & Osborn, M. (1999). Doing interpretative phenomenological analysis. In M. Murray & K. Chamberlain (Eds.), *Qualitative health psychology: Theories and methods* (pp. 218–240). London: Sage.

Strauss, A., & Corbin, J. (1990). *Basics of qualitative research: Grounded theory procedures and techniques.* London: Sage.

Sutton, S. (1998). Predicting and explaining intentions and behavior: How well are we doing? *Journal of Applied Social Psychology, 28,* 1317–1338.

Sutton, S. (2002). Testing attitude–behaviour theories using nonexperimental data: An examination of some hidden assumptions. *European Review of Social Psychology, 13,* 293–323.

Tabachnick, B. G., & Fidell, L. S. (2001). *Using multivariate statistics* (4th edn.). Needham Heights, MA: Allyn & Bacon.

Taylor, S. (2001). Locating and conducting discourse analytic research. In M. Wetherell, S. Taylor & S. Yates (Eds.), *Discourse as data: A guide for analysis* (pp. 5–48). London: Sage.

Tukey, J. W. (1991). The philosophy of multiple comparisons. *Statistical Science, 6,* 100–116.

Tversky, A., & Kahneman, D. (1971). Belief in the law of small numbers. *Psychological Bulletin, 76,* 105–110.

Wilkinson, L. and the Task Force on Statistical Inference (1999). Statistical methods in psychology journals: Guidelines and explanations. *American Psychologist, 54,* 594–604.

Wilkinson, S., Joffe, H., & Yardley, L. (2004). Qualitative data collection. In D. Marks & L. Yardley (Eds.), *Research methods for clinical and health psychology* (pp. 39–55). London: Sage.

Willig, C. (1999). *Applied discourse analysis: Social and psychological interventions.* Buckingham: Open University Press.

Witte, K. (1992). Putting the fear back into fear appeals: The extended parallel processing model. *Communication Monographs, 59,* 329–349.

Wood, L. A., & Kroger, R. O. (2000). *Doing discourse analysis: Methods for studying action in talk and text.* London: Sage.

Yardley, L. (2000). Dilemmas in qualitative health psychology. *Psychology and Health, 15*, 215–228.

Yardley, L., & Marks, D. (2004). Introduction to clinical and health psychology research. In D. Marks & L. Yardley (Eds.), *Research methods for clinical and health psychology* (pp. 1–20). London: Sage.

Yudkin, P. L., & Stratton, I. M. (1996). How to deal with regression to the mean in intervention studies. *Lancet, 347*, 241–243.

Zigmond, A. S., & Snaith, R. P. (1983). The Hospital Anxiety and Depression Scale. *Acta Psychiatrica Scandinavica, 67*, 361–370.

Zimmerman, D. W., & Zumbo, B. D. (1993). The relative power of parametric and nonparametric statistical methods. In G. Keren & C. Lewis (Eds.), *A handbook for data analysis in the behavioral sciences: Methodology issues* (pp. 481–517). Hillsdale, NJ: Erlbaum.

13

Assessment and Measurement in Health Psychology

MARIE JOHNSTON, DAVID P. FRENCH, DEBBIE
BONETTI AND DEREK W. JOHNSTON

INTRODUCTION

Health psychology examines psychological and
behavioural processes in health, illness and
healthcare. Its measures are distinguished by
the nature of the theoretical frameworks and
questions addressed, by the diversity of measurement methods used, and by the context of
the applications. Most measurement issues in
health psychology are similar to those in other
areas of psychology and are characterized by
the problems of assigning numbers in a meaningful way to behaviour and mental states (see
Anastasi & Urbina, 1997, or Johnston, Wright &
Weinman, 1995, for a simple introduction for
non-psychologists).

   This introductory section describes what is
currently being measured, before dealing with
general measurement issues in health psychology. In the following sections, some of the
measures used in the common areas of investigation are presented. We start with the assessment of healthy individuals, followed by
measures used with people who are ill, then
examine the measures adopted with providers
of care, and finally discuss outstanding
measurement issues and challenges.

What Is Currently Being Measured?

In the final quarter of the twentieth century,
there was a massive expansion in the number of
empirical studies in health psychology and in
the range of constructs measured. In order to
be able to describe what is currently measured
in health psychology investigations, we systematically reviewed all primary empirical publications for the year 2001 for the journals of the
three largest English language health psychology organizations: the American Psychological
Association's *Health Psychology* (HP); the
European Health Psychology Society's *Psychology
and Health* (P&H); and the British Psychological Society's *British Journal of Health
Psychology* (BJHP). While these papers can
safely be characterized as health psychology,
they may be a biased sample as they omit
papers published in other psychology journals,
medical journals or interdisciplinary journals in
behavioural medicine, psychosomatic medicine
and social medicine.

   The review is based on a total of 97 papers, 38
from HP, 36 from P&H and 23 from BJHP.
The papers are listed in the Appendix. When
referred to in the text they will be marked*.

Approximately half of the papers (52) described studies of healthy people, 39 studied people who were ill (including 11 investigations of the process of healthcare) and 8 included studies of people giving formal and informal healthcare. This distribution is likely to overestimate studies of healthy people as more studies of illness and healthcare appear in medical and interdisciplinary journals. The measures used are described in the sections dealing with measures in healthy people, ill people and carers.

Theoretical Frameworks and Questions Investigated

Effective measurement depends on clear definition of the constructs to be measured and clarity about the questions being investigated. Constructs are normally defined within a theoretical framework (either explicit or implicit) and this framework will be critical in assessing the validity of measurement. The research questions further constrain the domains and time frames within which psychometric properties such as validity, reliability and sensitivity are evaluated.

Health psychology measurement is undertaken in order to understand behavioural and psychological processes in health, illness[1] and healthcare. The purpose may be research or application, especially in the fields of public health or clinical medicine. Measures are used to address three main theoretically based questions concerning:

- the assessment of psychological and behavioural *indices of the status or amount* of health, illness or healthcare
- the assessment or evaluation of the psychological and behavioural *consequences* of health, illness or healthcare
- the assessment of psychological and behavioural factors as *predictors or explanations* of health, illness or healthcare.

Measurement Approaches

As a result of the types of application, a wide range of measurement strategies or approaches is necessary. Health psychology investigations may include any of the following types of assessment to achieve measurement:

- interview, e.g., demographic information, self-report of behaviour, beliefs or feelings
- questionnaire, e.g., standardized measures of individual differences such as optimism or coping
- observation of behaviour, e.g., performance of self-care
- psychophysiology, e.g., cardiovascular reactivity to stressors
- clinical indices, e.g., pulse rate, temperature, death
- pathophysiological indices, e.g., brain scan, blood cell counts
- information from healthcare records, e.g., attendance at clinics, prescribed medication.

Interviews

Interviews, or interviews incorporating questionnaires, are a common method of collecting data from people who are undergoing healthcare or who are ill. Interviews can help to standardize the presentation of the measurement materials in a way that could not be achieved in routine clinical assessments. They can also motivate and facilitate responses to long questionnaires, while at the same time being sensitive to fatigue especially in people who are ill. Clearly interview techniques can also be a source of both systematic and unsystematic error, if interviewers vary or if an interviewer's behaviour is variable, respectively.

Interviews can result in very diverse kinds of data, which should reflect the philosophical basis of the research being undertaken, and the specific research question (French, Yardley & Sutton, 2004, Chapter 12 in this volume). They may consist wholly or partially of closed precoded questions or they may contain open questions that require later coding or interpretation. Some interviews may reproduce the format of a standardized interview while others use newly designed questions.

Open questions on interviews and on questionnaires require subsequent work by the investigator in order to interpret the data and provide a basis for measurement. Some qualitative methods are used to explore new domains of investigation by examining the predominant themes emerging from responses using a variety of techniques and theoretical frameworks (e.g., Michie, McDonald & Marteau, 1996). These analyses can provide useful insights and may form a basis for the development of hypotheses or of measures that can be satisfactorily validated. However, if evidence of the replicability of the methods and findings is desired, other approaches are necessary to provide even the most basic level of measurement. The minimal level of measurement enables the investigator to classify a response as belonging to a specified category or not. For example, in interviews with patients with motor neurone disease, a question about who was with them when they were told was reliably categorized as 'told alone' or 'with someone present' (Johnston, Earll, Mitchell, Morrison & Wright, 1996). Without at least nominal or categorical measurement it is impossible to establish the reliability, validity, frequency, associations, consequences or causal status of the phenomena investigated.

Normally investigators develop a coding frame from preliminary work with a subset of the data or from a pre-existing theoretically or empirically based framework. For example, the CAVE (Peterson, Buchanan & Seligman, 1995) codes spontaneous utterances in terms of the attributions presented and classifies the material in terms of the respondent's explanatory style, while Pennebaker, Mayne and Francis's (1997) LIWC is a computer program which searches for key words reflecting the individual's attempts to find meaning. A group of four papers using different coding frames to analyse the same interview material (Folkman, 1997; Nolen-Hoeksema, McBride & Larson, 1997; Pennebaker et al., 1997; Stein, Folkman, Trabasso & Richards, 1997) illustrates the diversity of coding approaches that can be applied to spontaneous responses to open questions. This kind of coding frame guides the allocation of a code to the responses. It is then possible to examine the reliability of the coding by comparing coders or the same coder on different occasions or on different

parts of the data. Reliable data can then be investigated using appropriate statistical methods to examine the research questions.

The most widely known example of a completely standardized interview in health psychology is the Structured Interview for the Assessment of Type A Behaviour (Friedman & Rosenman, 1964) where both the content and the style of delivery of the questions are standardized, as is the method of coding responses; both interviewers and coders require training and need to meet an acceptable standard of agreement with benchmark ratings. These ratings depend both on the content and on the style of response. More recently, a modified version of this interview has been used to assess hostility (Haney et al., 1996), and Low et al. (2001*) use a videotaped version of this clinical interview. Where interview responses take a pre-coded closed format, then coding responses is not an issue. Scoring and measurement then depend on the same psychometric issues as apply to questionnaires.

Questionnaires

Questionnaires are widely used in health psychology to assess beliefs, attitudes, knowledge, mood, indices of individual differences, experience of healthcare, health related behaviours, adherence to medical advice, and so on. We have described and evaluated over 50 such measures in a user's portfolio of health psychology measures, which provides a fuller account of the measures and their use (Johnston et al., 1995).

Such easily accessible measures can appear to the novice health psychology investigator as an attractive display of off-the-shelf techniques that can solve many of the problems in research design. However, there are a number of pitfalls. First, the measures vary in the quality of their psychometric properties (for a general discussion, see Kline, 2000). There are measures that have insufficient items to achieve satisfactory reliability, and for some the reliability may not even have been assessed. Internal consistency should be reported and, where appropriate, evidence of test–retest and inter-rater reliability should be provided. Measures should also have demonstrated validity. Validity is normally conceptualized within a theoretical framework that defines the content of the construct being measured, as well as which other constructs it should, and should not, be associated with. A second pitfall for the naive researcher is the use of measures outside the theoretical framework of their development and validity. It can be perplexing when a series of quite different measures all seem to be relevant to the same domain, but this can often be explained in terms of the underlying theoretical framework. For example, many measures assess control cognitions; however, some of these are directly associated with Rotter's (1996) social learning theory, others are related to Bandura's (1977, 1997) social cognitive model, and others arise from attribution theory (Weiner, 1986). Empirically, the measures arising from the different theoretical approaches function as distinct statistical entities (Bonetti et al., 2001*). While this establishes that the measures are discriminable, it does not indicate that they measure the defined theoretical constructs. The investigator should ensure that the measures chosen are compatible with the theory guiding the research. A third pitfall lies in the use of measures with populations for which they were not designed. For example, it may be tempting to use a test validated with adults in work with children or to use assessments shown to be valid with ill people in a study of a healthy community based sample. Clearly it is important that measures are acceptable and applicable to the population being investigated: measures are not validated for once and for all, they are validated for a specific purpose with a specific population.

There are of course even greater hurdles in designing new measures that have no previous development, evaluation or normative data, but this may prove necessary for exploration of new constructs, theoretical approaches or applications. It is helpful if the theoretical formulation guides the development of measures, as was done for the theory of reasoned action (Fishbein & Azjen, 1975) and the theory of planned behaviour (Ajzen, 2002). In the review of 2001 papers, these theoretical frameworks were by far the most commonly used in creating situation or behaviour specific measures,

being used nine times in the 97 papers in assessing health related cognitions. However the content and format of new questionnaires are likely to begin with pilot or exploratory work, often using qualitative methods of data collection (Walker, Grimshaw & Armstrong, 2001*; Schooler, 1998) to identify salient material. For example, in developing a measure of perceived control of recovery from disabling disease, we started with spontaneous comments by patients which were subsequently evaluated using standard reliability analyses and tested for construct validity (Partridge & Johnston, 1989). Issues of measurement and scaling are considered more fully in the final section of this chapter.

Observation of behaviour

Where the construct being measured is behaviour, then ideally observations of behaviour should be undertaken. However this is not always possible and self-report is often used as a proxy measure (e.g., Jones, Abraham et al., 2001*; Seeman, Lusignolo, Albert & Berkman, 2001*). Observations may be made by health professionals, such as the clinical assessments frequently used in studies of preparation for surgery (e.g., Anderson, 1987), by members of the target person's household as in studies of smoking, or by the investigators as in the observation of limitations in the performance of daily activities following illness (e.g., Johnston, Morrison, MacWalter & Partridge, 1999). Some behaviours are systematically and routinely recorded, for example health professional absenteeism (Westman & Etzion, 2001*).

Observations may be limited by the observers' ability to see the full range of the behaviour. Most health professionals will see the patient for quite short periods and even nursing staff are typically limited to 8 or 12 hours per day. Lack of concordance between self-report and the observation of the professional may therefore be due to limitations in their observations as well as the noted problems in self-report. Nurses assess surgical patients as having more emotional problems than the patients report and are less accurate at pinpointing patients' emotional problems than are other patients (Johnston, 1982), perhaps because of the limited interactions they have with patients. Patients and the doctors caring for them may or may not see the stress similarly (Heijmans et al., 2001*). Different health professionals perform different tasks and have very different styles of interaction with patients and this may result in systematic, rather than just random, variations in the assessments made by different professionals (Johnston et al., 1987). Thus the choice of observer may critically affect the results obtained.

Members of the individual's household or social network may also be limited in the observations they can make. Very often they are involved in assessing performance of undesirable, health damaging behaviours such as smoking or consumption of fatty food, or adherence to a recommended medication, diet or exercise regimen. The chosen observer may be unable to ascertain whether the person has participated in the target behaviour when out of sight or may be motivated to present a favourable picture of the friend or relative they are observing. In addition, different observers may adopt different standards based on their experience or beliefs; for example, nurses and physiotherapists made systematically different judgements of patients' activities (Johnston et al., 1987).

Wherever possible, a systematic diary or log of behaviours (e.g., Sears & Stanton, 2001*) is likely to reduce memory biases in responding. The more intrusive practice of ecological momentary assessment (EMA) requires detailed, possibly computerized, logs over extended periods but can result in innovative findings or clarification of results of less intensive observation (Shiffman & Stone, 1998).

When investigators observe behaviour, this is always restricted either in time or in the range of behaviours. For example, assessments of limitations of function typically require the performance of the activity, often in clinical rather than home settings. Thus while observational methods are attractive as an adjunct to self-report methods used in interviews and questionnaires, they too have practical constraints, sources of unreliability and factors that limit their validity.

Direct monitoring and measurement of some behaviours is becoming possible, for example using electronic measures of exercise or mobility (e.g., Tuomisto, Johnston & Schmidt, 1996; Walker, Heslop, Plummer, Essex & Chandler, 1997). Hanson, Stevens and Coast (2001*) use a direct measure of exercise duration in a cycling test. There may be some practical limitations of using the electronic measures, for example faulty equipment, problems with downloading from mobile equipment, and restriction of activities because of wearing the equipment.

Psychophysiological measurement

Many psychological processes implicated in the aetiology, treatment and assessment of disease and disease related processes involve changes in physiological systems in response to psychological stimuli. This is particularly the case if stress, stress reduction or emotion is involved (e.g., Matthews, Gump & Owens, 2001*). The measures used in particular investigations will often reflect the disease under study: so, for example, heart rate and blood pressure are used in studies of heart disease (Krantz & Lundgren, 1998), immune function in relation to HIV (Solano et al., 2001*), gastric measures in studies of gastrointestinal disorders (Turner, 1998) and measures of muscular tension in studies of headache (Martin, 1998). A general review of psychophysiological processes in disease is provided by Steptoe (1998).

The actual use made of psychophysiological techniques obviously depends on the question under investigation. However many studies involve contrasting a period when the subject is relaxed with when they are stressed. The choice of condition for both periods can be critical. Few participants find the psychophysiological laboratory immediately relaxing and it may be difficult to control and standardize the temperature, humidity and sound level. The choice of stressor and control tasks is also critical. The challenging video game that produces an enormous elevation in heart rate and systolic blood pressure in a male teenager may be totally inappropriate in a late middle-aged patient with heart disease where carefully selected role-play may be a more useful task (Ironson et al., 1992). It can also be difficult to find control tasks with similar metabolic requirements to the stressors to ensure that differences due to physical effort are not interpreted as being due to psychological stress.

We outline some of the most commonly used psychophysiological measures below. More complete information on psychophysiological measurement is available in Cacioppo and Tassinary (1990) or Stern, Ray and Quigley (2001). The main bodily systems that are studied in health psychology using psychophysiological methods are the cardiovascular system, the respiratory system, aspects of sweating, the gastrointestinal system, and the skeletomuscular system. Hormonal measures such as adrenaline, noradrenaline and cortisol are also often taken, as are a wide variety of measures of immune function.

Cardiovascular   Cardiovascular measures are among the most widely used psychophysiological measures. This is because of their use in the study of the stress process and also because of the specific relationship between such responses and cardiovascular disease.

Heart rate (HR), the most common cardiovascular measure, is reliably recorded from the electrocardiogram (ECG), a record of the electrical activity of the heart.

Blood pressure (BP) is determined by the amount of blood pumped by the heart (cardiac output) and the resistance of the blood vessels to the passage of blood (peripheral resistance). On each cardiac cycle pressure fluctuates between a maximum value as the blood is ejected (systolic blood pressure, SBP) and a minimal value just before the next heart beat (diastolic blood pressure, DBP). Blood pressure is measured in millimetres of mercury (mmHg). SBP in healthy individuals is approximately 120 mmHg, and DBP 80 mmHg. Blood pressure can rise markedly during psychological stress, and raised blood pressure at rest defines hypertension. There may be both intra- and inter-assessor unreliability in the manual assessment of BP and therefore automatic assessments are better for most purposes.

The more specialist measures of cardiac output and peripheral blood flow are less commonly used. Since there are considerable technical challenges in the direct measurement of *cardiac output*, the most common measurement approaches are indirect, and based on either measuring changes in electrical impedance across the heart or analysing the pulse wave assessed non-invasively from the finger (Imholz, Weiling, Van Montfrans & Wesseling, 1998). *Peripheral resistance* cannot be determined directly, but can be calculated from blood pressure and cardiac output. However flow in specific parts of the vascular system can be measured. The most widely used method is photoelectric plethysmography, which relies on the fact that red blood cells scatter infrared light. When infrared light is passed through the skin or scattered by the blood in skin, variations in light between the light source and a detector can give an indication of blood flow. Such methods are used in some heart rate detectors that do not use the ECG and have been used in the study of abnormalities of blood flow in the temporal artery in headache. More demanding methods based on direct measures of limb volume can provide quantitative measures of peripheral blood flow; see Freedman (1989) for an application in Raynaud's disease.

Respiration   Respiration is studied in its own right in conditions with respiratory symptoms and also because variations in breathing have a profound effect on other bodily systems, such as the cardiovascular system. Respiration rate can usually be determined either from belt-like devices round the chest that produce an electrical signal that varies with chest expansion, or from thermistors placed near a nostril used to detect the difference in temperature between inhaled and exhaled air. However, other measures to indicate different types of breathing, for example in hyperventilation, require the use of several chest movement detectors.

Sweating   Sweating related activity is a useful if rather unfashionable psychophysiological measure. The number of sweat glands open determines variations in the resistance of the body to the passage of a small electric current between two sites. In certain areas of the skin, such as the fingertips, the main cause of sweating is arousal (rather than temperature) and therefore variations in electrodermal measures such as skin conductance provide a very useful measure of arousal. Since sweating is under purely sympathetic control, skin conductance is more readily interpreted than other measures, such as HR, which reflect the balance between the sympathetic and parasympathetic systems.

Gastrointestinal The gastrointestinal system is measured using the electrogastrogram, a record of the electrical signals associated with contractions of the gut.

Musculoskeletal Activity in the musculoskeletal system is recorded using the electromyogram, a record of the electrical impulses produced by contracting muscle fibres. This can give information on small specific muscles such as the frontalis muscle, often studied in relation to headache or larger muscles relating to gross bodily movements.

Stress hormones The stress hormones of adrenaline (epinephrine), noradrenaline (norepinephrine) and cortisol can be measured in blood, urine or saliva. While these measures can be illuminating, the assays involved and their interpretation are a complex matter. Difficulties can arise in the methods of collection of samples, in the storage prior to assay and in the reliability of assays over laboratories, technicians and time.

Immune function measures The use of immunological measures such as various types of immunoglobulin or T lymphocytes is highly attractive in some areas of research such as infection, cancer or HIV (see Steptoe, 1998; Antoni & Schneiderman, 1998). These measures incur the same hazards as do stress hormone assays, but additionally, this is a rapidly advancing field and the choice and interpretation of measures requires current, specialist expertise.

Clinical and pathophysiological indices

In clinical practice, medicine uses many clinical and pathophysiological indices in screening populations, investigating disease and charting recovery. These measures include: routine clinical measures such as temperature or pulse rate; indices of heart disease derived from the ECG or echocardiogram; measures of bacterial infection determined from samples of bodily fluids; simple imaging techniques like the X-ray that have been in use for decades; and complex imaging of the functioning body now possible with techniques such as MRI (magnetic resonance imaging). Much of clinical medicine relies on the patient's report of their symptoms. In many instances treatments are given and terminated and patients are discharged from hospital when they indicate that they are better by their speech or actions. Other sections of this chapter indicate how such symptoms can be measured with much greater reliability and precision than is common in the clinical assessment of symptoms.

If one is investigating or treating a patient with a condition like diabetes, hypertension or asthma, one often wishes to know the severity of the condition, the prognosis or the patient's medical progress. Information on blood sugar, blood pressure or peak respiratory flow may inform treatment or, at the very least, increase communication and rapport between psychologist and client. Of the 39 papers in the 2001 set that dealt with ill people, 16 used explicit measures of disease status. A considerable amount of such information is provided in the chapters in Johnston and Johnston (1998) on specific medical conditions. In addition it is likely that one of the current editions of standard large medical textbooks designed for undergraduate use will provide more than enough information. Difficulties can arise if textbooks use language that is not appropriate to local or national diagnostic and treatment approaches, and locally available patient pamphlets may be equally valuable.

If medical test data are needed for research purposes then the usual concerns over measurement standards apply. It is unwise to assume that clinical measurement is either reliable or valid; for example we have found that repeated measures of height in adults may not achieve high reliability. In overstretched clinical environments clinical testing is often carried out under far from ideal conditions; for example, sphygmomanometers (for measuring blood pressure) may not be serviced or checked for long periods, and standard conditions for the taking of blood or urine samples are not always observed. The information obtained from such tests may be adequate for clinical purposes, such as preliminary screening or monitoring change, but not for research where accurate absolute values are required. It therefore is incumbent on the researcher to ensure that the measures they are using in research are of research quality, with known reliability and validity and adequate to answer the research questions.

Healthcare records

Healthcare records may be used as sources of data on the behaviour of a patient, for example in attending healthcare (Sheeran, Conner & Norman, 2001*), the nature of medical recommendations or treatment (e.g., Orbell, Johnston, Rowley, Davey & Espley, 2001*), the results of clinical assessments, the patient's health or illness status, or the performance of healthcare providers (e.g., absenteeism). Since these data were typically not recorded for the purposes that the health psychology investigator has in mind, they are unlikely to be biased with respect to the question investigated. However, they may have other biases and sources of error and are frequently incomplete and therefore an unreliable source of information. As a result, they are normally used to back up or validate other, more direct methods, rather than as the main source of evidence.

Using multiple measurement

Each method of measurement discussed may be a source of systematic error, due to that particular methodology. It may therefore be useful to use more than one method of measuring key constructs in order either to estimate how much method variance is affecting results or to attempt to control for systematic method variance.

All methods contain biases of one sort or another, such as response styles or sets when responding to questionnaires (see later section). These biases are due to *systematic error* variance that is attributable to the method of measurement, rather than the psychological construct one is interested in measuring. This

systematic error of measurement is additional to *unsystematic error* occurring within each type of measurement. Unsystematic error results in *unreliability*: the more unsystematic error that measurements contain, the less reliable those measurments will be, and the more likely that, as a consequence, the observed degree of association with other variables will be an underestimate. To counter this, the reliability of measurement is routinely estimated, and can be statistically controlled for, if more than one measurement of each construct is taken.

Systematic error variance, on the other hand, can be more problematic. It can lead to a different sort of bias from unsystematic error: if two sets of measurements are obtained in the same way, the observed association between the measured variables will tend to be inflated by the association between the systematic error in the two measures. For example, if one is interested in the degree of association between beliefs about medications and medication adherence, then by using the same method, such as a self-report questionnaire, to assess both constructs, it should be expected that the observed relationship will be overestimated. In this case, both measures may be affected by, for example, social desirability, which inflates the correlations. This does not mean that self-reports of medication adherence are completely invalid: they are correlated with other measures of adherence. To obtain a less biased estimate of the extent to which beliefs and medication adherence are associated, one should use two methods that are unrelated. For instance, biochemical or electronic monitoring measures might be used to assess adherence, if questionnaires are used to assess medication beliefs.

If one is particularly concerned with the problem of systematic error variance, such as social desirability, one can conduct a multitrait multimethod (MTMM) study (see Marsh and Grayson, 1995), where several constructs are assessed using several distinct measurement procedures. The central idea is that different methods are subject to different sources of systematic error variance. Consequently, by measuring two or more constructs using two or more methods, one can assess how much of the observed correlation between two constructs is due to systematic error, i.e. methods effects, and how much is due to the construct variance. Valid construct measurement is achieved when different measures of the same construct correlate more strongly than measures of different constructs using the same procedure. For example, French, Marteau, Senior & Weinman (unpublished) asked respondents what they thought caused myocardial infarction using both an open-ended listing task and a closed questionnaire. They found that when responses to the questionnaire items were factor analysed, they formed apparently sensible factors, but subsequent MTMM analyses showed that these factors appeared to be mainly due to responses to questionnaires sharing systematic error (method) variance rather than any construct variance that was shared with the responses to the listing task.

Measurement Artefacts and Problems

There are a number of well-known sources of measurement and assessment error, including but not limited to fatigue, motivation, test-taking ability, stress, and examiner characteristics. A good overview of these problems is given by Meier (1994: 41–58). It is possible to address many of these sources of error: (1) experimentally, where the artefactual source of variance occurs in each condition and the critical constructs are manipulated: (2) by design, for example by randomizing order or using reverse-scored items; or (3) statistically, by measuring the source of error, and partialling out or making statistical allowance for any variance that can be attributed to them. All three approaches have problems.

Experimental control is difficult to achieve if one wishes to investigate variables that cannot be manipulated, for example demographic or individual difference variables, such as personality and ability. Amongst the most problematic of these individual differences are response sets and response styles. Questionnaire designers frequently attempt to control for response styles in the design of questions, for example using reverse scoring items to overcome acquiescence or extreme responding (e.g., STAI: Spielberger, 1983). However, these methods

simply dampen the effects, giving the biased responder a moderate score, and do not result in valid scores for these individuals. Statistical control may distort findings and there is a limit to how many sources of error can be controlled in any one investigation.

While such considerations apply to all measures, they may prove particularly important where measures involve self-report. These measures are commonly used in health psychology and the sources of error in self-report measures are generally recognized (Abraham & Hampson, 1996; Haaga, 1997). However they may be a particularly serious source of bias if the investigator examines the relationship between two such measures. If both measures are subject to the same form of response set, such as social desirability or negative affectivity, then apparent relationships between constructs might be entirely due to the correlation in the biases in the measures.

Measurement reactivity: how the process of measurement affects what is measured

Most discussions of measurement implicitly conceptualize measurement as a non-reactive process, where more or less reliable and valid 'measures' of participants' mental, behavioural or physiological processes are obtained. Reactivity of measurement, that is the tendency for the process of measurement to alter the phenomena being measured, is recognized in the physical sciences, for example in measuring of temperature or volume, and is clearly an even greater challenge in psychological measurement. Human participants are not simply objects that are measured. Psychological processes are involved in the process of obtaining measurements. People may behave differently when they are observed, they may have psychophysiological responses to the process of measurement, and they may be actively trying to solve the problem of how to complete a questionnaire, respond to an interview or participate in other assessment procedures.

Reactivity to measurement may be of particular importance in health psychology. For example, the process of observing behaviours may increase adherence, lead to exaggerated pain behaviours or reduce the frequency of health damaging behaviours. In psychophysiological assessments, it is widely recognized that heart rate, skin conductance and other measures of sympathetic arousal will be raised by the initial process of measurement and investigators routinely incorporate a period of habituation before using measures obtained. In assessments involving self-presentation or report, the individual may be concerned about the consequences of how they present: for example, minimizing symptoms or health problems may reduce access to treatment, whereas a true presentation may be too challenging for the individual's coping resources.

The following sections describe some common measurement issues resulting from measurement reactivity.

Survey cognition: how respondents tackle questionnaires

Schwarz (1999) describes a number of effects attributable to the response of the individual to the survey or questionnaire context. A number of models of 'survey cognition' have been developed which aim to describe how people approach the task of completing a questionnaire. These models tend to have three core stages (Jobe & Herrmann, 1996): input, mediation, and output, each with different opportunities for error of measurement.

At the *input* stage, respondents interpret what they are being asked in terms of both the norms of everyday speech (see Clark, 1978; Grice, 1975) and the context in which measurements are elicited (Antaki, 1994; Radley & Billig, 1996). There are a number of instances where researchers have interpreted artefacts as real psychological phenomena due to insufficient attention to these processes. One example is the 'actor–observer bias', that is the tendency for a person to attribute causes of their own behaviour to the environment, but others' behaviour to their personality (see Hewstone, 1989). Subsequent research has suggested that this 'bias' is due to different contrasts that are implicit in the questions, namely 'Why did you do X (in particular)?' compared with 'Why did John (in particular) do X?' (Hilton, 1995;

McGill, 1989). At the *mediation* stage, respondents retrieve the information requested and problems can arise due to inaccuracies of recall or estimation strategies, many of which are well discussed in Stone et al. (2000). A more fundamental problem can occur here where survey participants are asked to retrieve information or attitudes that they do not possess. People can give apparently sensible answers to fictitious issues, or issues so obscure they could not reasonably know anything about them. Respondents may fail to give such 'sensible', 'meaningful' responses when a 'don't know' option is available (Schuman & Presser, 1980). At the *output* stage, they map their responses onto the response modes provided. They may respond on the basis of the position of a response alternative, regardless of the label researchers have assigned to it (Diefenbach, Weinstein & O'Reilly, 1993; Schwarz, Hippler, Deutsch & Strack, 1985). Consequently, to interpret responses as simply reflecting literal endorsement of a particular frequency given in the label, for example '2 hours of television' or 'risk of 1 in 100', may be misleading. At this stage, responses will also be affected by the anticipated consequences both for social approval and for self-regulation and management (e.g., cognitive consistency, self-esteem, coping).

Context of measurement

Basic psychology texts discuss general context effects, but additional context is provided in the process of assessment, for example in order effects or the placement of questions within questionnaires. This may result in misleading findings.

A classic measurement context effect, the 'abortion context effect' (Schuman, 1982), was found to be the explanation of an apparent change in attitudes to legal abortion between 1978 and 1979. In 1978, 40 per cent of a large representative sample was in favour, whereas 1 year later, 58 per cent of a similar sample was in favour. The difference between the two results was due not to changes in sampling or in attitudes but to differences in the measurement context of the preceding question. When the context was experimentally manipulated using the 1978 preceding question (which referred to attitudes to abortion when there is a serious defect in the baby), it produced figures similar to the 1978 result, whereas using the 1979 preceding question produced the 1979 result (Krosnick, 1999). Thus the apparent difference in attitudes was attributable to the measurement context.

In a similar manner, earlier questions can create a context that influences mood assessments. Completing questionnaires about health problems appears to induce anxiety (Johnston, 1999, Study 3; Lister, Rode, Farmer & Salkovskis, 2002). When questionnaire order was experimentally manipulated, anxiety was lower if assessed prior to questions about health problems than if it followed such questions. This problem may be overcome by presenting measures of transitory states such as pain or emotion first, rather than embedding them in the measurement context.

The order of items may also affect the apparent reliability of measurement. When theory of reasoned action questions were presented in random order, as opposed to the more normal order prescribed by Ajzen and Fishbein (1980), both Cronbach alphas within constructs and correlations between constructs were reduced (Budd, 1987). It should be noted that subsequent attempts to replicate this finding have been at best only partially successful (Armitage & Conner, 1999; Sheeran & Orbell, 1996).

Habituation to measurement

There is ample evidence that reactivity to measurement reduces with continued measurement in behavioural assessment and in psychophysiological assessment. Observed individuals get used to being observed and return to 'normal' styles of behaviour. Sympathetic arousal or orientation responses habituate with continued measurement. However it is less widely acknowledged that there might be similar effects in self-report methods, that is respondents may respond differently when first exposed to measurement.

Johnston (1999, Study 2) found that respondents gave higher scores on the HADS anxiety scale on the first occasion they completed it. Thus one might expect an artefactual decline in anxiety on a second occasion of measurement. This suggests a methodological explanation for the common observation that anxiety declines over time following an illness event (e.g., in response to risk information, reviewed by Shaw, Abrams & Marteau, 1999), especially if only two measures are obtained. This pattern of results may be at least partly due to a measurement artefact rather than psychological adjustment, as these studies rarely include a pre-illness event baseline measure of anxiety.

Response sets and styles

Lanyon and Goodstein (1982) propose a distinction between *response sets*, the tendency to respond in a way intended to achieve a particular impression (e.g., social desirability), and *response styles*, an unintentional tendency to respond in a particular direction (e.g., response acquiescence, extreme responding, negative affectivity). Social desirability and negative affectivity are of particular importance to health psychology.

Social desirability of responding Social desirability (the tendency to give responses attracting the approval of others) is likely to be important where there are recommended or expected styles of behaviour. For example, social desirability might lead to exaggeration of adherence to medical advice or health protective behaviours but might result in underreporting of health damaging behaviours such as smoking. It is often valuable to assess and make allowance for social desirability by using an instrument such as the Marlow–Crowne Inventory (Crowne & Marlow, 1960) as in Weinberger, Schwartz & Davidson (1979) or in Hanson et al. (2001*), Zakowski, Valdimarsdottir & Bovbjerg (2001*) and Low et al. (2001*).

Negative affectivity A number of personality dimensions have been found to be associated with systematic patterns of responding. Whether this is a problem or not depends on the specific aims of a research investigation. One such dimension that has been found to be particularly problematic is negative affectivity: bias toward a negative view of self, circumstances and events (Watson & Clark, 1984). Negative affectivity appears to influence many self-report measures, especially where the

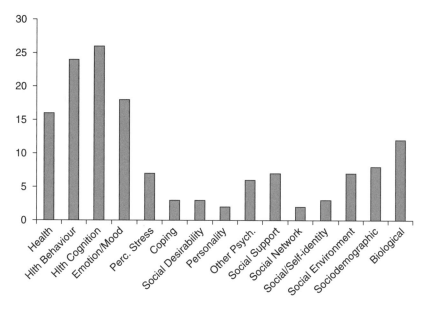

Figure 13.1   *Healthy people: frequency of measurement of constructs in 52 papers*

measures include the possibility of focusing on negative aspects of the situation (Watson & Pennebaker, 1989). Consequently, when the degree of association between two such self-report measures is examined, negative affect is likely to inflate the correlations obtained. For example, correlations between mood and symptom reporting might simply be due to individual differences in negative affectivity colouring perceptions of bodily sensations, regardless of objective health. These problems have been particularly prevalent in studies that have tried to relate retrospective self-reports of hassles and life events to reports of current health (e.g., Dohrenwend, Dohrenwend, Dodson & Shrout, 1984; Schroeder & Costa, 1984). However, Mora, Robitaille, Leventhal, Swigar and Leventhal (2002) suggest that, in other domains, the problem of negative affectivity may have been exaggerated.

MEASURES USED WITH HEALTHY PEOPLE

This section addresses measures used in studying people who have not been selected as being ill or in need of medical care. Typically these are populations of students or community residents and may well contain many people who are ill and may even be receiving care. The two main theoretical questions addressed in these populations has been the understanding of factors influencing health related behaviours, that is behaviours likely to affect health (Conner & Norman, 1998) and identifying psychological and behavioural characteristics predictive of disease, especially heart disease and cancer. A fundamental question that is sometimes addressed explicitly is how to measure health.

Of the 52 papers in our 2001 sample that investigated healthy people, 11 involved children or adolescents, 20 student participants, and 25 other adults. The number of papers in the set of 52 published in 2001 that assess some of the main constructs is shown in Figure 13.1.

Measuring Health

It has proven extremely difficult to measure health (Bowling, 1991). This is hardly surprising given the lack of an agreed definition of health. The complex World Health Organization

(WHO) definition of health that is commonly adopted includes social, psychological and physical aspects (Abelin, Brzezinski & Carstairs, 1986). There is common agreement that health is more than the absence of illness and that it is characterized by the individual's vitality and functional capacity, their mood and outlook, and their participation in activities. Wright (1990) has conceptualized health as three-dimensional: freedom from unpleasant symptoms and sensations; ability to perform conventional roles and duties; and possession of physiological, psychological and social resources.

Of the 16 papers assessing constructs that might be characterized as health, six use measures of symptoms (e.g., Mak & Mueller, 2001*; Seeman et al., 2001*), six are self-report evaluations (Ellickson, Tucker & Klein, 2001*; Vitaliano et al., 2001*), two describe activity levels (Bonetti et al., 2001*; Seeman et al., 2001*), one risk factors (Vitaliano et al., 2001*), three cognitive functioning (e.g., Seeman et al., 2001*), two life satisfaction (Schroeder & Schwarzer, 2001*) and one wellbeing (Eiser, Riazi, Eiser, Hammersley & Tooke, 2001*).

Assessment of absence of symptoms as an index of health has proved problematic as people who would be characterized as healthy are unlikely to be symptom-free. Even number of symptoms presents difficulties as symptom reporting is associated with mood, emotional disorder and negative affectivity. So, for example, many measures of emotional disorder such as the GHQ (Goldberg & Williams, 1988) ask about the experience of somatic symptoms and have found that people with greater emotional disorder report more somatic symptoms. In a similar vein, use of health services may reflect individual patterns of responding to symptoms, rather than indexing health *per se*. Watson and Pennebaker (1989) suggest that there are individual differences in negative affectivity, the tendency to attend to and report negative experiences including sensations that might be interpreted as symptoms (see above). They have developed a measure, the PILL, which assesses the tendency to endorse symptoms that can be used to allow for negative affectivity. Thus measures of symptoms or healthcare usage may be misleading as an index of 'health'.

Simple self-report measures of health, for example ratings on four-point verbal rating scales from excellent to poor, have been found to be predictive of future mortality (Idler, 1992). Even when allowance is made for concurrent illness, people rating their health as 'poor' are more likely to be dead at follow-up than those giving higher ratings. These results suggest that such ratings must have some validity as measures of health. Nevertheless, authors frequently create their own single-item scales rather than using the format with demonstrated validity. The main limitation of the validated items is the lack of sensitivity inherent in such brief scales involving a single item and only four or five response categories.

Measures of general wellbeing such as the Bradburn Affect Balance Scale (Bradburn, 1969) or even measures of satisfaction with life (e.g., Diener, Emmons, Larson & Griffin, 1985; Johansson et al., 2001*; Schroeder & Schwarzer, 2001*) may come closer to the WHO concept of health as they allow the individual to evaluate all aspects of functioning. It is curious to note that the measurement of health related quality of life has mainly been investigated in ill, rather than healthy, populations as discussed below. These measures are rarely evaluated with healthy populations and are therefore likely to be relatively insensitive to variations in their health.

Health may also be characterized as an expectation of continuing absence of illness, either due to engagement in health protective behaviours such as taking exercise, or due to having few risk factors for disease (e.g., Vitaliano et al., 2001*). Risk factors may be genetic as in heart disease or diabetes, physiological (e.g., high blood pressure), or environmental (e.g., living in an area of high air pollution). However, many risk factors are behavioural (e.g., smoking, diet), and these may be assessed along with health protective behaviours as part of the measurement of health.

Activity levels may additionally be measured as evidence of physical fitness (e.g., Bonetti et al., 2001*; Schneider et al., 2001*), while cognitive function measures index 'mental fitness' (e.g., Seeman et al., 2001*; Yang & Spielman, 2001*).

Health related behaviour

Health related behaviour was commonly measured, occurring in 24 of the 52 papers. Most used self-report measures, but four used diary assessments, and one was observed (Hanson et al., 2001*).

Two kinds of health related behaviours can be identified. The first group of behaviours are those that have been *demonstrated* to confer health risk or disease protection. Evidence from epidemiological studies such as the Alameda County Study (Schoenborn, 1993) demonstrate that some behaviours, especially smoking (Doll, Peto, Wheatley, Gray & Sutherland, 1994), increase risk, while others, such as engaging in exercise, appear protective. Clinical and public health interventions are frequently directed at changing behaviour to reduce risk and enhance protective behaviours (e.g., Family Heart Study Group, 1994; Owen & Crawford, 1998; OXCHECK Study Group, 1994). The behavioural assessments found to predict disease end-points in epidemiological studies have demonstrated predictive validity and should be used in order to assess risk in a population. For example, comparison with risk data from the British Regional Heart Study (Shaper, Pocock, Phillips & Walker, 1987) is only valid if questioning about smoking and diet follow the methods used in that study.

The other group of behaviours are the health behaviours that people undertake in the *belief* that they will prevent disease or ensure detection prior to symptoms (Kasl & Cobb, 1966). There is ample evidence that most people report engaging in a number of these behaviours (Amir, 1987; Cox et al., 1987; Harris & Guten, 1979). Several checklists of these behaviours have been published (e.g., Amir, 1987; Prohaska, Leventhal, Leventhal & Keller, 1985), but unlike the risk/protective behaviours, which can be validated against epidemiological findings, there is little evidence of validation of these checklists. Self-reports of behaviour are likely to be subject to bias, especially social desirability bias, as discussed above. Until they are validated against some other measure of health behaviours, their value as assessments of health behaviours is restricted

and their primary value is in assessing the rate of reporting behaviours.

Health Cognitions

A major group of theoretical models have been developed to predict health related behaviours from health relevant social cognitions (see Conner & Norman, 1996, 1998). Models such as the health belief model (HBM), social cognitive theory (SCT), the theory of planned behaviour (TPB) and the transtheoretical model (TTM) propose that a range of health and health behaviour cognitions determine health relevant behaviours. In our 2001 sample, the TPB was the most commonly used model (nine papers), followed by the SCT (five), TTM (three) and HBM (one). Health cognitions include outcome expectancy, perceived severity, perceived vulnerability, health locus of control and health value, while health behaviour relevant cognitions include response efficacy, self-efficacy, behavioural intention, implementation intention and action plans.

In addition to the problems with self-report measures already noted, these models raise some other important measurement issues. The individual may not be aware of their cognitive processes influencing behaviour and therefore may be unable to report them (Bargh & Chartland, 1999). Further, the models vary in the precision of specification of measurement of core constructs, ranging from the prescriptive TPB to the very poorly defined constructs of the HBM. Some constructs have standardized measures that have psychometric validation and published norms.

The best known of these is the Multidimensional Health Locus of Control (MHLC) Scale (Johansson et al., 2001*; Wallston, Wallston & DeVellis, 1978) which assesses three components: internal, powerful others and chance locus of control. While this measure has been criticized for its lack of specific relevance for people who are ill, it continues to be appropriate for healthy populations. Wallston (1992) has proposed that locus of control by itself should not be enough to predict health behaviour and suggests that it should be combined with a new construct, perceived health competence, a construct akin to generalized health self-efficacy (Smith, Wallston & Smith, 1995). The social learning theory from which locus of control derived would suggest that the MHLC should only predict health behaviour in combination with a measure of health value (e.g., Lau, Hartman & Ware, 1986) and there has been criticism of investigations in this area for using the model inappropriately.

This relates to a more general methodological problem in this area of investigation: the selection of variables from models without addressing complete models. The investigator needs to have a clear objective. If the intention is simply to explain as much behaviour as possible, then the investigator is justified in choosing the most likely combination of variables from whichever models seem appropriate. If the primary objective is to test a model then all the constructs of the model, and none from other models, should be assessed. When the objective is to compare models or to enhance a model with external constructs, than it may be appropriate to mix the constructs of more than one model in the same analyses.

If the aim is to test the power or sufficiency of the model to explain behaviour, then only the proximal determinants specified by the model need to be investigated; so, for example, in the TPB (see Conner & Norman, 1998), only behavioural intention and perceived behavioural control would need to be assessed as all other variables act through these two. The investigator may wish to test the additional predictive power of more distal variables, but this goes beyond the testing of the model's predictive power and simply assesses the predictive power of the constructs rather than the model.

Other Measures

Amongst the other measures commonly used, assessments of emotional states or stress are very common. Other psychological variables such as coping and personality were infrequent. More social measures included individual perceptions of social support or social identity (e.g., Schofield, Pattison, Hill & Borland, 2001*), as well as indices of the social network or social environment, e.g., school climate (Novak & Clayton, 2001*), job environment (Matthews et al., 2001*) or job security (Mak & Mueller, 2001*). Sociodemographic variables such as ethnicity and gender were critical for some papers. Of the biological indices, cardiovascular measures were most common, occurring in six papers.

MEASURES USED WITH ILL PEOPLE

Under this heading, measures are considered which have been used with individuals identified by their illness status although they may not be concurrently experiencing illness or receiving healthcare. In addition to their relevance for ill people, such measures share a sensitivity to the respondent's status, for example by being limited in length.

The central issues here are to measure how ill the person is, what the effects of illness are and how individuals respond to and cope with illness and its treatment. The measures used in the 2001 papers are shown in Figure 13.2.

Just as health is measured by psychological and behavioural processes, much of the assessment of illness and recovery from illness lies within this domain. Clinical signs and pathophysiological processes may be available in the assessment of patients with some conditions, e.g., immune function in HIV (Jones, Abraham, Harris, Schulz & Chrispin, 2001*), cardiac status or events in coronary heart disease (e.g., Cochrane, 2001*; van Elderen & Dusseldorp, 2001*), tumour stage or markers in cancer (e.g., Gidron, Magen & Ariad, 2001*) and blood glucose measures in diabetes (Eiser et al. 2001*). However, frequently the clinician assesses disease processes by ascertaining how the patients feel (Helgeson, Cohen, Schulz & Yasko, 2001*; Kendell, Saxby, Farrow & Naisby, 2001*) and what they are doing, for example in arthritis (Orbell et al., 2001*); if patients are recovering well, they describe themselves as feeling better and doing more for themselves. Indeed Kaplan (1990) has argued that these behavioural processes are the most important outcome of illness and healthcare. Measurement of illness

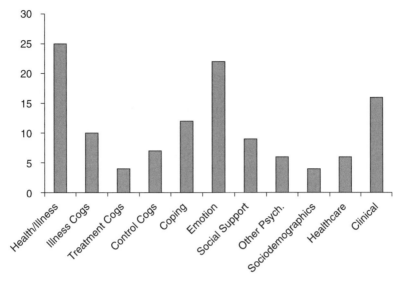

Figure 13.2   *Ill people: frequency of measurement of constructs in 39 papers*

has therefore included the assessment of the psychological and behavioural consequences of the disease processes.

Healthcare is largely a behavioural and interpersonal process. Indices of healthcare assess the use of services by patients, for example attendance at a clinic (e.g., Sheeran et al., 2001*), delay in treatment (Kohlmann, Ring, Carroll, Mohiyeddini & Bennett, 2001*), as well as the performance of those involved in healthcare delivery (e.g., hand hygiene by surgical staff, provision of information by primary care physicians). These behavioural processes are likely to be a major influence on the effectiveness of healthcare as they determine the viability of delivery of biomedical treatments and advice. The importance of the behaviour of patients in adhering to medical recommendations has long been recognized and methods of assessing adherence have been debated and developed (Meichenbaum & Turk, 1987), but the role of health professionals in determining patient outcomes has been less adequately assessed (Marteau & Johnston, 1991).

Measuring Illness

It can be a source of some confusion and frustration to discover that there are no biomedical

indices of 'illness'. While the state seems subjectively recognizable and can be meaningfully replicated in animal studies, there is as yet no measure that reflects it. Animal research suggests that the state of illness may be associated with raised brain cytokines (Dantzer, 1997), but even this research offers little immediate prospect of a useful biomedical measure. The concept of illness, the subjective experience, is contrasted with the concept of disease, the pathophysiological process.

For some diseases, it is possible to obtain a biomedical measure of the disease process such as degree of atherosclerotic occlusion in cardiovascular disease, degree of invasion of cancer cells (Gidron et al., 2001*), loss of CD4 cells in AIDS (Jones, Beach et al., 2001*) or sugar metabolism in diabetes (Macrodimitris & Endler, 2001*). For others such as rheumatoid arthritis there are indices of *current* inflammatory activity. Such measures are included under 'clinical' measures in Figure 13.2.

However, patient 'illness' may not relate directly to the disease process, and for many conditions the main clinical and research assessments depend on patient observation or self-report. So instead of reliable biomedical indices, 'illness' is characterized by the subjective experience and associated behaviours.

The problem of measuring illness and disease is illustrated by Bowling (1995) in her book *Measuring disease*. She includes measures of symptoms, pain, emotional states, disability and quality of life. In Figure 13.2, of the 24 papers assessing illness, nine measure symptoms, three pain, two wellbeing, four health ratings, six activity limitations, four quality of life, plus an additional four using the SF–36. Emotional states are presented separately and were assessed in 22 papers. However, none of these directly measures disease as such and each is influenced by psychological and/or social processes in addition to disease processes. As noted, the experience and report of symptoms may be influenced by individual differences in negative affectivity, but will also be affected by current attention, mood, cognitive and social factors. Since the behavioural, emotional and quality of life consequences of disease are likely to be influenced by different factors, they are each considered separately.

Symptoms and pain

Problems in assessing the subjective experience of *symptoms* have been discussed above for healthy populations. Thus symptom checklists (e.g., Dunnell & Cartwright, 1972; Kendell et al., 2001*) need to be used with caution. In ill populations, disease specific measures of symptoms are included within composite measures such as the Rotterdam Symptom Checklist for cancer (de Haes, van Knippenberg & Neijt, 1990), the Arthritis Impact Measurement Scale (Meenan, Gertman & Mason, 1980) or the symptom checklist used by Schroeder and Schwarzer (2001*) with hypertensive patients. Such measures tend to have good internal consistency, have been developed using factor analytic methods, and demonstrate concurrent and/or predictive validity against other clinical or functional measures.

While *pain* is an important symptom of many conditions and an important motivator in seeking healthcare, it was assessed in only three of the 2001 papers (deBruin, Schaefer, Krohne & Dreyer, 2001*; Miles et al., 2001*; Shnek, Irvine, Stewart & Abbey, 2001*). Like other symptoms it is a subjective experience and therefore difficult to assess and hence to validate measurement. The best known and most widely used measure is the McGill Pain Questionnaire (MPQ: Melzack, 1975), which allows separate evaluation of sensory, affective and evaluative components of pain. It records location, change with time and factors influencing the pain, and provides three main measures of intensity: the number of words chosen, the pain rating index and the present pain intensity rating. A short form of the MPQ has been introduced which correlates well with the full MPQ and demonstrates sensitivity to change (Melzack, 1987). In clinical settings where, due to pain, patients may not have the concentration required for more extensive measures, a variety of single-item numerical and verbal pain rating scales have been used.

Behavioural consequences of disease

The World Health Organization (1980) analysis of the consequences of disease identified three consequences: *impairment* or loss of structure/function, *disability* or loss of performance of activities, and *handicap* or restricted participation in social roles. It was proposed that disability resulted from impairment and that handicap resulted from both impairment and disability. While there has been much debate about this analysis, other (e.g., Nagi, 1991) and more recent World Health Organization (2001) approaches retain the main characterizations of the elements involved.

Disability is defined in terms of behaviour (Johnston, 1996; Johnston, Bonetti & Pollard, 2002) and is measured in terms of behavioural performance or capability. Thus general disability measures assess limitations in the performance of normal functions (e.g., the Barthel Index: includes walking, bladder control, dressing and using stairs: Mahoney & Barthel, 1965), while more specific measures of activities of daily living (ADL) assess the performance of everyday tasks such as self-care, shopping and household tasks (e.g., Katz, Ford, Moskowitz, Jackson & Jaffe, 1963; Lincoln & Edmans, 1990).

There is debate about whether measures should assess what the individual does or what they can do. Clearly limitation in capacity is the construct most closely related to the direct consequence of disease, while limitation in performance may indicate the additional psychological, social and environmental influences. Similar issues arise in other areas of performance psychology where techniques such as dual-task performance have evolved to assess capacity; the argument is that while performance may be maintained despite lower capability, the extra effort involved is assessed by examining the effects on a second task. To date, measures of disability have not taken account of this problem, but there is some evidence that dual-task measures may enhance the measures in this field (Ashburn, Stack, Pickering & Ward, 2001; Bloem, Valkenburg, Slabbekoorn & Willemsen, 2001).

The behavioural consequences may not simply be loss of activities, but may also involve the performance of new activities. The observable behaviours associated with pain have been assessed and they include additional behaviours, as well as loss of activities. Keefe and Block (1982) and Richards, Nepomuceno, Riles and Suer (1982) have developed measures of pain behaviours, for example grimacing, guarding movements, and rubbing, which are assessed by observers. These measures are not necessarily closely related to self-report pain measures and may additionally reflect the individual's response to pain experience.

Emotional consequences of disease

Illness in oneself or in close family or friends is recognized as a significant source of stress in most methods of assessing life events and difficulties, such as the Social Readjustment Rating Scale (Holmes & Rahe, 1967) and the Impact of Events Scale (Horowitz, Wilner & Alvarez, 1979). The emotional consequences can be assessed using any of the available measures of mood such as the STAI (Spielberger, 1983), the Profile of Mood States (POMS: McNair, Lorr & Droppelman, 1992), the CES–D (Radloff, 1977), the Beck Depression Inventory (BDI: Beck, 1996) or the GHQ (Goldberg & Williams, 1988). However there can be confounding where somatic symptoms may be interpreted as emotional symptoms, for example where loss of appetite or slowing

are indices of depression. Zigmond and Snaith (1983) introduced the Hospital Anxiety and Depression Scale (HADS), which they suggested minimized such confounding, by reducing the number of such items. However, the success of this scale compared with other scales has not been assessed and, since it contains items such as 'I feel as if I am slowed down', it may still contain contaminated items (Johnston, Pollard & Hennessey, 2000). Of the 22 papers reporting emotional states, the HADS was used in four, BDI in four, CES–D in three, POMS in two, STAI in two, Impact of Event Scale in two and GHQ in one.

Some measures such as the GAIS and PAIS (Derogatis, 1975, 1986) assess adjustment to illness. Adjustment is frequently addressed as a form of coping or as illness cognitions and is considered below.

Quality of life (QoL)

While the construct of quality of life is widely used in assessing the consequences of disease, there are quite divergent schools of thought regarding definition and measurement. On the one hand it is argued that the measures should assess the quality objectively, while on the other it is proposed that QoL can only be evaluated according to the individual's expectations and values. Measures such as the Quality Adjusted Life Year (QALY: Kind & Rosser, 1988; Rosser & Kind, 1978) or the SF–36 (Jenkinson, Coulter & Wright, 1993) assume a universal value system, and so by assessing the individual's limitations it is possible to give an overall value to QoL. By contrast the Patient Generated Index (PGI: Ruta, Garratt, Leng, Russell & MacDonald, 1994) and the SEIQOL (O'Boyle, McGee & Joyce, 1994) assess the individual's value system as well as the current levels of achievement in valued areas. The values are combined with the levels of achievement to generate an index reflecting quality of life according to the individual's own value system. While the PGI requires the individual to respond in the context of their illness, the SEIQOL is one of the few measures of QoL in current use in health psychology that could be used equally readily with healthy and ill individuals. Measures in other fields such as the Satisfaction with Life Scale

(Diener et al., 1985) do assess QoL without reference to illness and can be used successfully with individuals who are ill.

Some measures have been developed specifically for some diseases, for example the AIMS (Meenan et al., 1980) for arthritis and the Rotterdam Symptom Check List (de Haes et al., 1990) for cancer. The authors argue that a more sensitive and acceptable measure of QoL can be obtained in this way. This reflects the design of disease related QoL measures, depending on assessment of symptoms and limitations in function as a major factor in QoL. Where health related QoL measures assume a value system, this is usually based on assessment of emotional state, symptoms and disability, and the measure offers a method of combining these values. So, for example, the QALY gives values for each combination of distress and disability, and this can be done for individuals with diverse diseases.

It is clear that QoL comes quite close to the WHO concept of handicap/participation restriction or to a combination of disability and handicap. There has been some attempt to measure handicap (e.g., the London Handicap Scale: Harwood, Gompertz & Ebrahim, 1994) and some measures clearly combine disability and handicap, e.g., the Sickness Impact Profile (de Bruin, de Witte, Stevens & Diederiks, 1992) or the Functional Limitations Profile (Patrick & Peach, 1989). It is unlikely that there will be agreement on measurement while there continues to be debate about the constructs to measure. While the construct of QoL would appear to have value as a global measure of health outcome, it may mask the underlying processes as proposed by the World Health Organization (1980) model. The WHO model proposed causal links between impairment, disability and handicap rather than a homogeneous single construct and, further, allows the possibility that factors which may moderate the relationship between impairment and disability may be different from those that moderate the relationship between disability and handicap. Thus, given the current stage of development of theory and measurement, the choice of measure is likely to be determined by whether one is seeking a simple health outcome measure or to understand the processes determining outcomes.

Illness Cognitions

The dominant models of response to illness, including stress and coping (Lazarus & Folkman, 1984), social cognitive (Bandura, 1997) and self-regulation models (Leventhal et al., 1997), agree that individuals develop their own mental representations of the condition and it is these representations that guide the response. Models vary in the cognitions specified and in the level of measurement achieved.

Some address illness simply as a further example of a stressor and consider degree of threat, outcome expectancies, perceived controllability etc. as they would for any stressor. Leventhal and colleagues have attempted to characterize illness cognitions *per se*, and provide the most extensive work on this topic. They have identified five representations commonly occurring in individual representations:

- identity – the label and symptoms associated with the illness
- time-line – the pattern of change over time, especially whether it is acute, chronic or fluctuating
- cause – attributions for the illness
- consequences – the actual and expected consequences
- control/cure – the extent to which the illness can be controlled or cured.

Their work was based initially on open-ended questions and qualitative analyses from which they developed guidelines for interviews (Leventhal & Cameron, 1987; Nerenz, Leventhal, Love & Ringler, 1984). Weinman, Petrie, Moss-Morris and Horne (1996) developed a questionnaire assessing these five components, the Illness Perceptions Questionnaire (IPQ), using psychometric techniques to establish basic properties such as internal reliability of the scales. The scales have demonstrated predictive and construct validity, for example the cognitions predicted subsequent behaviours in patients post-MI as would be expected within the self-regulation model (Petrie, Weinman,

Sharpe & Buckley, 1996). The IPQ has been updated (Moss-Morris et al., 2002) to include greater differentiation of the cognitive representations of illness, but also to incorporate assessment of an additional component of Leventhal's self-regulation model, the emotional representation of illness.

Turk, Rudy and Salovey (1986) used factor analytic methods implying an underlying dimensional structure, and found support for four dimensions: seriousness, personal responsibility, controllability, changeability. While these factors have not proved entirely reproducible in subsequent studies, the degree of overlap between their factors as characterized by the content rather than the labels for the factors, and the components proposed by Leventhal and colleagues, is impressive. Thus their controllability construct matches Leventhal et al.'s control/cure.

Other measures address single constructs that are still compatible with the Leventhal et al. model. For example, Felton, Revenson and Hinrichsen's (1984) measure of Acceptance of Illness appears to examine the consequences of the illness, containing items such as 'My illness makes me a burden on my family and friends' and 'I have a hard time adjusting to the limitations of my illness'. Many measures address the control construct, including Wallston's Form C adaptation of the Health Locus of Control Scales for people with chronic disease (Wallston, Stein & Smith, 1994), and scales for specific groups such as those with diabetes (Bradley, Brewin, Gamsu & Moses, 1984) and those with the prospect of recovery from disabling conditions (Partridge & Johnston, 1989).

These measures assume a dimensional structure, with each of the five types of representation being distributed along a numerical scale. There are other examples of assessments of illness cognitions which start from different premises. Instead of building a representation of the illness from components, it may be useful to examine the prototypes used in evaluating new conditions (Bishop & Converse, 1986). So for example, Lalljee, Lamb and Carnibella (1993) have found seven clusters of illness prototypes. This type of analysis may prove useful in understanding responses to ambiguous sets of symptoms where patterns of response may be different from those where symptoms are more clear-cut.

Healthcare Cognitions

Some of patients' healthcare cognitions are those already considered with reference to health and illness. For example, perceived effectiveness of healthcare may be assessed in social cognition models of health behaviours, and perceived cure and controllability are key elements in illness cognitions. Sheeran et al. (2001*) assessed patients' views of clinic attendance by measuring TPB constructs.

Patients' expectations of healthcare have been investigated in terms of their general preference for managing their own treatment and the information relevant to their condition (Krantz, Baum & Wideman, 1980) as well as preferences for care in a specific consultation with a doctor (Salmon & Quine, 1989). In each case, the scale has been developed using factor analytic procedures and, in both, items referring to provision of information have loaded on different factors from items dealing directly with treatment issues. Thus there is some evidence that distinct elements of patients' preferences for medical care are being investigated.

In addition, attitudes toward a specific treatment (Collins et al., 2001*) or more general measures of attitudes toward physicians (Hulka, Zyzanski, Cassell & Thompson, 1970; Marteau, 1990) and towards medicine (Horne, 1997b) have been assessed.

Healthcare cognitions also include assessments of the stressfulness of receiving healthcare. For example, the Hospital Stress Rating Scale (Volicer & Bohannon, 1975) provides scaled values of the perceived stress associated with a large number of hospital experiences.

An important healthcare cognition is patient satisfaction. A commonly used measure of satisfaction with a medical consultation is the Medical Interview Satisfaction Scale (MISS: Wolf, Putman, James & Stiles, 1978), which assesses affective, behavioural and cognitive aspects of the consultation. Most measures of patient satisfaction have problems of validity and of scaling as responses are skewed towards favourable ratings. Ware and Hays (1988) have found that measures of satisfaction are less skewed and therefore have improved psychometric qualities if respondents are asked to assess the excellence of the medical consultation rather than their satisfaction with the consultation. Only one paper of the 39 reviewed used a measure of patient satisfaction (Wiggs & Stores, 2001*) and this was a measure created by the authors.

Coping with Illness

Coping is defined as what people do to try to control stress and is commonly seen in health psychology as problem-focused, that is directed at reducing the threats and losses of the illness, or emotion-focused, that is directed at reducing the negative emotional consequences. Perhaps the best known measure of coping is the Ways of Coping Questionnaire, developed by Folkman and Lazarus (1980). They used factor analytic procedures to establish the dimensional structure, but later analyses have produced different versions with varying numbers and types of factors.

Many different coping styles have been identified and measured and contrasts are made between avoidant and attention coping, between active and passive coping and between behavioural and cognitive coping. The COPE (Carver, Scheier & Weintraub, 1989) attempts to represent all of these aspects of coping in a multi-dimensional inventory giving scores on 13 conceptually distinct types of coping. Further, the measure can be used to assess coping style, a dispositional measure of habitual ways of coping, or to assess coping strategy, the methods of coping used to address a specific stressor such as a current illness. The disadvantage of the comprehensiveness of the measure is that it is quite long, appears repetitive and can seem burdensome to people who are ill. Carver (1997) has therefore published a shortened version that has proved more acceptable, while retaining the multidimensional features of the measure.

Other measures address specific forms of coping, for example Miller's (1987) measure of monitoring and blunting, or deal with clinical conditions, for example Watson et al.'s (1988) assessment of coping styles employed by people with cancer, Endler, Parker and Summerfield's (1998) measure of Coping with Health Injuries and Problems (Macrodimitris & Endler, 2001*) or the measure of Coping with Surgical Stress used by de Bruin et al. (2001*).

Investigators choosing a measure of coping need to consider the compatibility of the measures with their theoretical perspective, the range of scores available, the acceptability of the measure to their clinical group, and possibly the need to measure not only coping with the illness but also coping with stressful forms of healthcare.

Social Support and Social Environment

Social support was measured in eight studies with an additional study assessing physical contact (Cochrane, 2001*). The social environment of patient care has been investigated, for example by Kulik, Mahler and Moore (1996) studying the effects of sharing with other similar patients and by Honeybun, Johnston and Tookman (1992) examining the effects of seeing other patients die. The wider social environment has been assessed in measures of social deprivation and socioeconomic status (Arnau, Meagher, Norris & Bramson, 2001*; Sheeran et al., 2001*).

Social support has been conceptualized as directly beneficial, with lack of social support being akin to a stressor or as a resource that buffers the effects of stress (Cohen & Wills, 1985). Social support has been found to predict susceptibility to disease, to moderate the effects of stress and to influence health and healthcare outcomes.

Social support has been measured in diverse ways and a major distinction is made between measures of the structure or network available to the individual and the quality or satisfaction with the support available; for example, the Social Support Questionnaire (Sarason, Levine, Basham & Sarason, 1983; Sarason, Sarason, Shearin & Pierce, 1987) gives measures of number and satisfaction with social support. Similarly, there are different types of support with the most common distinction being made between emotional and practical support (e.g., Power, Champion & Aris, 1988), but other forms such as esteem, informational and companionship have also been distinguished (Cohen & Wills, 1985).

Such measures are difficult to validate, but correlations with relevant other self-report measures support the construct validity of the scales.

Other Psychological Measures

Diverse other psychological measures have been used although surprisingly there were no personality measures in the 2001 papers. The only constructs measured more than once were optimism (Antoni et al., 2001*; Shnek et al., 2001*) and self-esteem (Nauta, Hospers & Jansen, 2001*; Vedhara et al., 2001*).

Communications between Patients and Providers

There is ample evidence that the nature and style of communications can determine the outcomes of healthcare (Ley, 1988; Weinman, 1998). Various methods have been developed to describe and characterize the interpersonal communication process, using raters to assess records (audio, video or typed transcripts) of the communication. Roter and Hall's (1989) Interaction Analysis based on the original work by Bales has been used to assess the components of interpersonal communication such as giving information, asking questions, and so on, while Stiles's Verbal Response Mode analysis (Putnam, Stiles, Jacob & James, 1985; Stiles, 1989) identifies eight mutually exclusive modes of responding including disclosure, interpretation, confirmation and reflection. Other rating scale measures have been developed to assess the performance of health professionals against verbal and non-verbal performance criteria used in training (Maguire & Selby, 1989) or to assess the degree to which a doctor is patient- or doctor-centred (Byrne & Long, 1976). In each case, the methods are assessed in terms of inter-rater reliability and the predictive value of the assessments.

Methods of assessing written communications have also been developed (Ley, 1988). A major issue has been the assessment of intelligibility of written information such as leaflets for patients, and some methods, for example the Flesch formula, can readily be applied to text using widely available word-processing software.

An alternative approach is to assess the extent of agreement between healthcare provider and patient (e.g., Heijmans et al., 2001*; McClenahan, Johnston & Densham, 1990).

Uptake and Adherence

When patients do not take up an offer of healthcare or do not adhere to recommended advice or treatment, the process of healthcare is interrupted. While the assessment of uptake *per se* is fairly easy from healthcare records (e.g., Sheeran et al., 2001*), it may be more difficult to ascertain whether a failure of uptake is due to not receiving the invitation, not understanding the invitation, not being able to accept the healthcare offered or refusing the healthcare offered. These different patterns of interrupted healthcare have various causes and may have a variety of effects on health outcomes; for example, Marteau et al. (1992) found different patterns for women refusing tests in pregnancy compared with those who simply omitted to have the test.

Similar contrasts have been drawn between intentional and non-intentional non-adherence to medication regimens, and Horne (1997a) has developed a measure that allows separation of the two types of non-adherence. While self-reports of adherence are widely criticized as being subject to social desirability bias, all other measures of medication adherence have been criticized too. Behavioural observation is limited as no observer can be permanently present, while pill counts can also give erroneous estimates as the patient wishing to appear more compliant can readily dispose of excess pills or manipulate dispensers which record occasions of use.

For adherence to advice on behaviour change, some observational corroboration may be possible, but with the above caveats. For smoking advice, there are physiological indices such as serum cotinine which are less likely to be manipulated, while for dietary advice, measures of weight or serum cholesterol may be relevant. However, none of these measures has a one-to-one relationship with the behaviour and they can therefore be misleading.

In sum, there appears to be no easy accepted solution to the problem of measuring adherence. It may be sufficient to use one measure, probably a self-report measure, for most investigations, but if this is a key variable, then more than one method should be used where possible.

MEASURES USED WITH PROFESSIONAL AND INFORMAL CARERS

People who are ill receive diverse forms of care from paid health and social care professionals and from informal unpaid carers who are frequently family or neighbours or belong to some voluntary structure. In the 97 papers reviewed, three described studies of informal carers and five of health professionals.

Informal Carers

While it would appear to be important to investigate the effects of informal caring on health outcomes for the patient, to date the main focus has been on the effects of caring on the carers. For example, Nijboer, Tempelaar, Triemstra, Sanderman and van den Bos (2001*) examined the effects of caring on caregivers' health, Fang, Manne and Pape (2001*) the mental health of spouses of cancer patients, and Hallarakar, Arefjord, Havik and Maeland (2001*) the mental health and use of health services of wives of MI patients. There is ample evidence that the emotional consequences for people close to the patient may be as great as for the patient, for example following MI. When they are also caregivers it may be appropriate to measure caregiver burden, a combination of the emotional and behavioural burdens of caregivers (Orbell, 1996). Stress is

observed in caregivers not only in self-report measures but also in evidence of impaired immune function (e.g., Kennedy, Kiecolt-Glaser & Glaser, 1988) with resulting vulnerability to disease.

Health Professionals

A major source of variation in healthcare outcomes is due to the health professionals or providers as well as to the patients (Marteau & Johnston, 1991). As health services move toward implementation of evidence based care, the assessment, explanation and modification of their behaviour is likely to be an increasing focus of investigations (Grol, 1992, 1997). Two main areas of behaviour of health professionals have been investigated: their adherence to evidence, guidelines or recommendations and the amount of stress they experience.

Like patient adherence, it can be difficult to measure what cannot be observed and self-report may prove useful. However, some behaviours, such as hand hygiene, are observable and have been investigated. Other behaviours, such as drug dispensing, are likely to be assessable from patient or ward records.

Stress in health professionals has been investigated because of the recognition that working with people who are ill may be stressful and a concern that stressed professionals may be less able to deliver effective healthcare (Payne & Firth-Cozens, 1987). Perceived stress and the emotional impact can be investigated using conventional measures such as the Perceived Stress Scale (Cohen, Kamarck & Mermelstein, 1983) or measures of mood or emotional state. In addition measures of occupational stress have been used, for example the Nursing Stress Index (Cooper & Mitchell, 1990), and the Maslach Burnout Inventory (Maslach, 1982) has been widely used to evaluate disabling levels of stress (e.g., Leiter, Frizzell, Harvie & Churchill, 2001*; Peiro, Gonzalez-Roma, Tordera & Manas, 2001*).

The effects of stress on performance of tasks has been assessed using self-reports of errors or by using cognitive tasks such as reaction time tasks as a proxy for the real task. The prevalence of major errors, for example in drug prescribing, can be investigated from healthcare or medico-legal records (Vincent, Ennis & Audley, 1993).

Providers' healthcare cognitions

Like patients' cognitions, healthcare providers' cognitions have also been investigated using the constructs of social cognition models. For example, their self-efficacy for providing dietary instructions was examined in the context of reducing serum cholesterol (Schucker et al., 1987), and Walker et al., (2001*) investigated prescribing cognitions using the TPB. Investigators have also investigated their views of their working environment in the context of investigations of the stressfulness of caring for patients (Burke & Greenglass, 2001*; Parkes, 1982). Measures of clinicians' attitudes to different patient groups have also been developed; for example, St Lawrence, Kelly, Owen, Hogan and Wilson's (1990) measure of attitudes to AIDS gives an index of favourableness of attitudes and one of willingness to interact with people with HIV/AIDS in a clinical situation.

CHALLENGES IN MEASUREMENT, SCALING AND SCORING

There are a number of important general issues in measurement, scaling and scoring that arise with many of the measures used in health psychology but are perhaps most acute and best recognized in the area of questionnaire design and use. Since questionnaires are the most common form of measurement in health psychology, it is worth considering these issues in more detail.

What Is Measurement?

Michell (1997) has challenged the approach to measurement taken in much of psychology including health psychology. He suggests that (1) it does not meet the standards of measurement required in other sciences and (2) it is not adequate for the statistical methods commonly applied, with the result that apparently clear findings may be due to misleading methods.

The definition of measurement that is most widespread in current psychology textbooks is that of Stevens (see Michell, 1997). According to Stevens, the 'concept measurement is becoming enlarged to include as measurement the assignment of numerals to objects or events according to rule – any rule' (1959: 19). According to this definition, as long as numbers are assigned to observations in a systematic way, measurement is occurring. Consequently, if a set of response options are assigned numbers according to a systematic rule (e.g., 'strongly disagree' = 1, 'disagree' = 2 etc.), psychological measurement is achieved. Nunnally (1978) has argued that these procedures, although not measurement in the sense used in other disciplines, are satisfactory, as they yield 'measurements' that correlate in a meaningful way with other variables, for example measures of 'anxiety' correlate with a variety of other psychological, behavioural and physiological measures.

A different perspective on defining and establishing measurement has been taken by Michell (1997). Michell noted that Stevens's definition of measurement, although widely accepted in psychology, is different from that used in other sciences, notably physics. Michell instead proposed that measurement is 'the estimation or discovery of the ratio of some magnitude of a quantitative attribute to a unit of the same attribute' (1997: 358). This definition differs from that of Stevens, in that according to Michell, measurement involves the *discovery* of properties of the observations, namely that they possess quantitative structure that has a demonstrated relationship to the construct being measured. Quantitative structure has been defined in full in the form of logical axioms (Krantz, Luce, Suppes & Tversky, 1971). Using these axioms, one can test whether a measure achieves quantitative structure and 'the hypothesis that any attribute (be it physical or psychological) is quantitative is a contingent, empirical hypothesis that may, in principle, be false' (Michell, 1997: 359).

A simple empirical test of quantitative structure is whether a sample of participants responds in a way that is consistent with them agreeing on the *order* of a set of psychological stimuli. Thus, if one was testing whether a set of attitude statements possesses quantitative structure, all or nearly all of a set of respondents should see these statements as falling on a single continuum (e.g., from 'pro' to 'anti'), regardless of whether each respondent agrees with any particular statement or not. This is probably true of many of the questionnaire measures in use in health psychology.

A more rigorous test of quantitative structure is that a sample of respondents respond in a way that is consistent with them agreeing on the *size of the intervals* between each of a set of psychological stimuli, for example as in Thurstone scaling. *Conjoint measurement analysis* provides a method of testing whether a group of participants respond in a way consistent with them agreeing on the size of the intervals between stimuli (see Luce & Tukey, 1964; Michell, 1990). A good description of the application of conjoint measurement analysis to attitude measurement is given by Michell (1994).

It is entirely possible that the tests of quantitative structure will not be supported, and according to this view of measurement, it is then not appropriate to try to scale this variable: attaching numbers to response options does not result in meaningful measurements, and parametric statistical analyses are not warranted.

Very few measures of psychological phenomena have been tested to see if they meet the criteria required. There are undoubtedly several good reasons for this (well discussed by Kline, 1998). At least one of these is the positivist approach of many researchers (see French et al., 2004, Chapter 12 in this volume), who are interested in usable measurement instruments, without being concerned about the nature of the measurements obtained. Whatever the reasons, the overwhelming majority of measures currently in use in health psychology are, at least implicitly, still based on Stevens's definition.

Scaling Responses to an Item

Stevens described four types of scaling: (1) categorical, e.g., gender; (2) ordinal, e.g., social class; (3) interval, e.g., Thurstone scaling of functional limitations as in the scaling of items of the SIP (Pollard & Johnston, 2001); and (4) ratio, that is where there is a true zero,

e.g., number of cigarettes smoked. With ratio scaling it is possible to say that someone who smokes 40 cigarettes smokes twice as many as someone smoking 20 cigarettes. By contrast, on an interval scale such as in the SIP items, an individual scoring 80 on ambulation could not be said to be twice as disabled as someone else scoring 40, although one might be able to assert that the difference between 40 and 80 was equivalent to the difference between 80 and 120. On the other hand, on a measure of anxiety such as the STAI, where interval scaling has not been established, one could not say that someone scoring 40 was twice as anxious as someone scoring 20, or that the difference between 20 and 25 was equivalent to the difference between 30 and 35.

Clearly work needs to be done on many health psychology measures before they can be said to meet the requirements of ratio scaling.

Aggregating Items to Form a Score

Many of the questionnaires in use in health psychology are based on summation of item scores. Each measure is made up of a number of constituent items, each of which requires a response. Each response option is assigned a numerical value giving a score for each individual item, and these scores are then summed to yield an overall score. The statistical foundation of summative scales is classical psychometric test theory (for an introduction, see Kline, 2000). According to classical psychometrics, the key features of 'good' measurement instruments are reliability and validity, concepts familiar to the psychology undergraduate (see Johnston et al., 1995). To be valid in terms of correlating with other scales, it should be sufficient for a scale to have ordinal properties: a scale allows respondents to be sorted into more or less the correct order in terms of a specific construct. There is good evidence that the summated rating scale procedure produces measures with these properties (Dawes, 1979).

There are, however, limits to the statistical and mathematical analyses that can be performed with this kind of measure. In particular, a major problem for health psychology is that there are good grounds for doubting that any summated rating scales are valid for indicating the presence or absence of interactions. Since the test of interactions is critical in testing many social cognition models, such as the TPB, this constitutes a significant problem.

For a rating scale to be valid for testing interactions as a dependent variable, it requires genuine interval properties (Levine, 1970). As the procedure for developing summated rating scales usually involves the assumption of equal intervals, there is no reason to believe that the scales produced will have these properties. In addition, there is empirical evidence that summated rating scales may either be insensitive to the presence of interactions, or indicate the presence of artefactual interactions (see French, Gayton, Burton, Thorogood & Marteau, 2002). Equally, when looking for the presence of interactions with summated rating scales as independent variables, problems of interpretation of interactions can arise due to these scales only possessing ordinal properties (see Evans, 1991; French & Hankins, 2003).

In other cases, summation has simply been applied wrongly. For example, each section of the SIP consists of Thurstone scaled items, that is endorsing the item indicates a degree of severity and the items have validated interval scores. Logically, to be consistent with the theoretical basis of the item development, the respondent should simply choose the item that best describes them, but instead the authors have required responses to all items and summed the results. In addition to being theoretically incorrect, the summative scoring leads to empirical anomalies, for example, a wheelchair-bound person with paraplegia scoring fewer limitations of function than someone with arthritic problems who endorses more of the items (Pollard & Johnston, 2001). These difficulties can be overcome using a scoring system that recognizes the inherently hierarchical nature of the items, for example that the person with paraplegia will endorse a much higher item than the highest endorsed by the person with arthritis.

Two alternative approaches to psychometrics and summative ratings are also in use in health psychology. In common with the summated rating scale approach, these measurement strategies involve an attempt to scale people in terms of where they are placed in

relation to a unidimensional construct. First, many clinical measures in use are based on 'clinimetrics' (Fayers & Hand, 2002), which in contrast with psychometrics does not require internal reliability of measures as might be assessed by Cronbach's alpha. In clinimetric scoring, diverse items are aggregated using arbitrary weightings or weightings based on predictive regression equations. Many measures of the severity of conditions use such methods: for example, the Apgar score of foetal distress, the Killip assessment of MI severity, and the APACHE scoring of severity of the patient's condition in intensive care. In each case, the measure has demonstrated validity, usually the capacity to predict survival. Fayers and Hand (2002) argue that such measures offer better sampling of the range of the construct and that internal consistency is unnecessary. However, the measures do not approximate to ratio scaling, even if some of the component items may do so.

The other alternative is item response theory and associated Rasch scaling to achieve psychological measurement with genuine interval properties (for an excellent introduction see Bond & Fox, 2001). This theory recognizes that items may have a hierarchical structure rather than being interchangeable, thus overcoming some of the problems identified with the SIP above. Rasch measurement involves the complementary attempt to calibrate the items in terms of the level of the construct at which they are most sensitive. For example, Rasch measurement applied to disability testing would not only scale respondents in terms of their activity limitations, but also calibrate the items in terms of how difficult these activities are to perform. Using these analyses, Jenkinson, Fitzpatrick, Garratt, Peto and Stewart-Brown (2001) found that, on the SF–36, performing 'vigorous activities' is a more difficult item than 'walking more than a mile' which in turn is more difficult than 'walking 100 yards'. Further health psychology examples of the application of item response theory are several measures of headache impact described by Ware, Bjorner and Kosinski (2000).

It has been argued that this calibration of items allows interval measurement, which results in measures that possess quantitative structure, in the conjoint measurement analysis sense (e.g., Karabatsos, 1998; Perline, Wright & Wainer, 1979; Wright, 1985). The claim that Rasch measurement produces interval measurement seems reasonable, notwithstanding some criticisms of Rasch measurement generally (e.g., Kline, 2000). This allows Rasch measures to be less subject to the problems facing summative rating scales when investigating interactions. However, the tests for quantitative structure in Rasch measurement are less stringent than with conjoint measurement analysis. Thus, the use of procedures such as Rasch measurement may be necessary but not sufficient to achieve genuinely quantitative measurement (see Kline, 1998).

ACKNOWLEDGEMENTS

This chapter is updated and adapted from: Johnston, M., & Johnston, D. W. (1998), Assessment and measurement issues, in *Health psychology*, edited by M. Johnston & D.W. Johnston, in the series *Comprehensive clinical psychology*, Editors in Chief A. Bellack & M. Hersen, Oxford: Elsevier. Some parts of this chapter have been influenced and informed by the work of John Weinman and Stephen Wright in co-authoring *Measures in health psychology: A user's portfolio*, by M. Johnston, S. Wright & J. Weinman, published by NFER-Nelson.

Marie Johnston and Derek Johnston are members of the MRC Health Service Research Collaboration. David French was funded by a Wellcome Trust Training Fellowship in Health Services Research (reference number 060634/Z/00/Z). Debbie Bonetti was funded by an MRC grant.

NOTES

1 The word 'illness' is used to refer to the subjective experience associated with disease processes as we believe it has universal meaning.

In American English, the work 'sickness' would be synonymous, but in other parts of the world this term is confined to illness associated with nausea.

REFERENCES

Abelin, T., Brzezinski, Z. J., & Carstairs, V. D. L. (Eds.) (1986). *Measurement in health promotion and protection*. European Series no. 22. Copenhagen: WHO Regional Office for Europe.

Abraham, C. S., & Hampson, S. E. (Eds.) (1996). Special issue on: Controversy and method in the interpretation of verbal reports in health psychology research. *Psychology and Health, 11* (2).

Ajzen, I. (2002). Constructing a TPB questionnaire: Conceptual and methodological considerations. September. Retrieved from http://wwwunix.oit.umass.edu/~aizen.

Ajzen, I., & Fishbein, M. (1980). *Understanding attitudes and predicting social behavior*. Englewood Cliffs, NJ: Prentice-Hall.

Amir, D. (1987). Preventive behaviour and health status among the elderly. *Psychology and Health, 1*, 353–378.

Anastasi, A., & Urbina, S. (1997) *Psychological testing*. Englewood Cliffs, NJ: Prentice-Hall.

Anderson, E. (1987). Preoperative preparation for cardiac surgery facilitates recovery, reduces psychological distress, and reduces the incidence of acute postoperative hypertension. *Journal of Consulting and Clinical Psychology, 55*, 513–520.

Antaki, C. (1994). *Explaining and arguing: The social organization of accounts*. London: Sage.

Antoni, M. H., & Schneiderman, N. (1998). HIV and AIDS. In D. W. Johnston & M. Johnston (Eds.), *Health psychology* (pp. 237–276). Oxford: Elsevier.

Armitage, C. J., & Conner, M. (1999). Predictive validity of the theory of planned behaviour: The role of questionnaire format and social desirability. *Journal of Community and Applied Social Psychology, 9*, 261–272.

Ashburn, A., Stack, E., Pickering, R. W., & Ward, D. D. (2001). A community-dwelling sample of people with Parkinson's disease: Characteristics of fallers and non-fallers. *Age and Ageing, 30*, 47–52.

Bandura, A. (1977). Self-efficacy: Towards a unifying theory of behavior change. *Psychological Review, 84*, 191–215.

Bandura, A. (1997). *Self-efficacy: The exercise of control*. New York: Freeman.

Bargh, J. A., & Chartland, T. L. (1999). The unbearable automaticity of being. *American Psychologist, 54*, 462–479.

Beck, A. T. (1996). *The Beck Depression Inventory–II (BDI–II)*. San Antonio: Psychological Corporation.

Bishop, G. D., & Converse, S. A. (1986). Illness representations: A prototype approach. *Health Psychology, 5*, 95–114.

Bloem, B. R., Valkenburg, V. V., Slabbekoorn, M., & Willemsen, M. D. (2001). The multiple tasks test: Development and normal strategies. *Gait and Posture, 14*, 191–202.

Bond, T. G., & Fox, C. M. (2001). *Applying the Rasch model: Fundamental measurement in the human sciences*. Mahwah, NJ: Erlbaum.

Bowling, A. (1991). *Measuring health*. Buckingham: Open University Press.

Bowling, A. (1995). *Measuring Disease*. Buckingham: Open University Press.

Bradburn, N. M. (1969). *The structure of psychological well-being*. New York: Aldine.

Bradley, C., Brewin, C. R., Gamsu, D. S., & Moses, J. L. (1984). Development of scales to measure perceived control of diabetes mellitus and diabetes-related health beliefs. *Diabetic Medicine, 1*, 213–218.

Budd, R. J. (1987). Response bias and the theory of reasoned action. *Social Cognition, 5*, 95–107.

Byrne, J. S., & Long, B. E. L. (1976). *Doctors talking to patients*. London: HMSO.

Cacioppo, J. T., & Tassinary, L.G. (Eds.) (1990). *Principles of psychophysiology: Physical, social, and inferential elements*. Cambridge, Cambridge University Press.

Carver, C. S. (1997). You want to measure coping but your protocol's too long: Consider the brief COPE. *International Journal of Behavioral Medicine, 4*, 92–100.

Carver, C. S., Scheier, M. F., & Weintraub, J. K. (1989). Assessing coping strategies: A theoretically-based approach. *Journal of Personality and Social Psychology, 56*, 267–283.

Clark, H. H. (1978). Inferring what is meant. In W. J. M. Levett & G. B. Flures D'Arcais (Eds.), *Studies in the perception of language* (pp. 295–322). London: Wiley.

Cohen, S., Kamarck, T. & Mermelstein, R. (1983). A global measure of perceived stress. *Journal of Health and Social Behaviour, 24*, 385–396.

Cohen, S., & Wills, T. A. (1985). Stress, social support, and the buffering hypothesis. *Psychological Bulletin, 98*, 310–357.

Conner, M., & Norman, P. (Eds.) (1996). *Predicting health behaviour*. Buckingham: Open University Press.

Conner, M., & Norman, P. (1998). Health behavior. In D. W. Johnston & M. Johnston (Eds.), *Health psychology* (pp. 1–38). Oxford: Elsevier.

Cooper, C. L., & Mitchell, S. (1990). Nurses under stress: A reliability and validity study of the NSI. *Stress Medicine, 16*, 21–24.

Cox, B. D., Blaxter, M., Buckle, A. I. J., Fenner, N. P., Golding, J. F., Gore, M., Huppert, F. A., Roth, M., Stark, J., Wadsworth, M., & Whichelow, M. (1987). *The health and lifestyle survey*. London: Health Promotion Research Trust.

Crowne, D. P., & Marlow, D. (1960). A new scale of social desirability independent of psychopathology. *Journal of Consulting Psychology, 24*, 349–354.

Dantzer, R. (1997). Stress and immunity: What have we learned from psychoneuroimmunology? *Acta Physiologica Scandinavia, 161* (Supp.), 43–46.

Dawes, R. M. (1979). The robust beauty of improper linear models in decision making. *American Psychologist, 34*, 571–582.

de Bruin, A. F., de Witte, L. P., Stevens, F., & Diederiks, J. P. M. (1992). Sickness Impact Profile: The state of the art of a generic functional status measure. *Social Science and Medicine, 35*, 1003–1014.

de Haes, J. C. J. M., van Knippenberg, F. C. E., & Neijt, J. P. (1990). Measuring physical and psychological distress in cancer patients: Structure and application of the Rotterdam Symptom Checklist. *British Journal of Cancer, 62*, 1034–1038.

Derogatis, L. R. (1975). *The Global Adjustment to Illness Scale (GAIS)*. Baltimore: Clinical Psychometric Research.

Derogatis, L. R. (1986). The Psychosocial Adjustment to Illness Scale (PAIS). *Journal of Psychosomatic Research, 30*, 77–91.

Diefenbach, M. A., Weinstein, N. D., & O'Reilly, J. (1993). Scales for assessing perceptions of health hazard susceptibility. *Health Education Research, 8*, 181–192.

Diener, E., Emmons, R. A., Larson, R. J., & Griffin, S. (1985). The Satisfaction With Life Scale. *Journal of Personality Assessment, 49*, 71–76.

Dohrenwend, B. S., Dohrenwend, B. P., Dodson, M., & Shrout, P. E. (1984). Symptoms, hassles, social supports, and life events: Problem of confounded measures. *Journal of Abnormal Psychology, 93*, 222–230.

Doll, R., Peto, R., Wheatley, K., Gray, R., & Sutherland, I. (1994). Mortality in relation to smoking: 40 years' observations on male British doctors. *British Medical Journal, 309*, 901–911.

Dunnell, K., & Cartwright, A. (1972). *Medicine takers, prescribers and hoarders*. London: Routledge and Kegan Paul.

Endler, N. S., Parker, J. D. A., & Summerfield, L. J. (1998). Coping with health problems: Developing a reliable and valid multidimensional instrument. *Psychological Assessment, 10*, 195–205.

Evans, M. G. (1991). The problem of analyzing multiplicative composites: Interactions revisited. *American Psychologist, 46*, 6–15.

Family Heart Study Group (1994). Randomised controlled trial evaluating cardiovascular screening and intervention in general practice: Principal results of the British Family Heart Study. *British Medical Journal, 308*, 313–320.

Fayers, P. M., & Hand, D. J. (2002). Causal variables, indicator variables and measurement scales: An example from quality of life. *Journal of the Royal Statistical Society Series A, Statistics in Society, 165*, 233–253.

Felton, B. J., Revenson, T. A., & Hinrichsen, G. A. (1984). Stress and coping in the explanation of psychological adjustment among chronically ill adults. *Social Science and Medicine, 18*, 889–898.

Fishbein, M., & Ajzen, I. (1975). *Belief, attitude, intention and behavior: An introduction to theory and research.* Reading, MA: Addison-Wesley.

Folkman, S. (1997). Introduction to the special section. Use of bereavement narratives to predict well-being in gay men whose partners died of AIDS: Four theoretical perspectives. *Journal of Personality and Social Psychology, 72*, 851–854.

Folkman, S., & Lazarus, R. S. (1980). An analysis of coping in a middle-aged community sample. *Journal of Health and Social Behavior, 21*, 219–239.

Freedman, R. R. (1989). Quantitative measurements of finger blood flow during behavioral treatments for Raynaud's disease. *Psychophysiology, 26*, 437–441.

French, D. P., Gayton, E. L., Burton, J., Thorogood, M., & Marteau, T.M. (2002). Measuring perceptions of synergistic circulatory disease risk due to smoking and the oral contraceptive pill. *Risk Analysis, 22*, 1139–1151.

French, D. P., & Hankins, M. (2003). The expectancy-value muddle in the theory of planned behaviour – and some proposed solutions. *British Journal of Health Psychology, 8*, 37–55.

French, D. P., Marteau, T. M., Senior, V., & Weinman, J. (unpublished). How valid are measures of beliefs about the causes of illness? The case of myocardial infarction.

French, D. P., Yardley, L., & Sutton, S. (2004). Research methods in health psychology. In S. Sutton, A. Baum & M. Johnston (Eds.), *The Sage handbook of health psychology.* London: Sage.

Friedman, M., & Rosenman, R. H. (1964). Procedures for assessment of behavior pattern. *Journal of the American Medical Association, 189*, 15–22.

Goldberg, D., & Williams, P. (1988). *A User's Guide to the General Health Questionnaire.* Windsor: NFER-Nelson.

Grice, H. P. (1975). Logic and conversation. In P. Cole & J. L. Morgan (Eds.), *Syntax and semantics 3: Speech acts* (pp. 95–113). New York: Academic.

Grol, R. (1992). Implementing guidelines in general practice care. *Quality in Health Care, 1*, 184–191.

Grol, R. (1997). Beliefs and evidence in changing clinical practice. *British Medical Journal, 315*, 418–421.

Haaga, D. A. F. (Ed.) (1997). Special section: Measuring cognitive products in research and practice. *Journal of Consulting and Clinical Psychology, 65*, 907–1000.

Haney, T. L., Maynard, K. E., Houseworth, S. J., Scherwitz, L. W., Williams, R. B., & Barefoot, J. C. (1996). Interpersonal hostility assessment: Description and validation against the criterion of coronary artery disease. *Journal of Personality Assessment, 66*, 386–401.

Harris, D. M., & Guten, S. (1979). Health-protective behavior: An exploratory study. *Journal of Health and Social Behavior, 20*, 17–29.

Harwood, R. H., Gompertz, P., & Ebrahim, S. (1994). Handicap one year after a stroke: Validity of a new scale. *Journal of Neurology, Neurosurgery and Psychiatry, 57*, 825–829.

Hewstone, M. (1989). *Causal attribution: From cognitive processes to collective beliefs.* Oxford: Basil Blackwell.

Hilton, D. J. (1995). The social context of reasoning: Conversational inference and rational judgment. *Psychological Bulletin, 118*, 248–271.

Holmes, T. H. & Rahe, R. H. (1967). The Social Readjustment Rating Scale. *Journal of Psychosomatic Research, 11*, 213–218.

Honeybun, J., Johnston, M., & Tookman, A. (1992). The impact of a death on fellow hospice patients. *British Journal of Medical Psychology, 65*, 67–72.

Horne, R. (1997a). *The nature, determinants and effects of medication beliefs in chronic illness.* Unpublished PhD thesis, University of London.

Horne, R. (1997b). Representations of medication and treatment: Advances in theory and measurement. In K. J. Petrie & J. A. Weinman (Eds.), *Perceptions of health and illness* (pp. 155–188). Amsterdam: Harwood.

Horowitz, M., Wilner, N., & Alvarez, W. (1979). Impact of Events Scale: A measure of subjective stress. *Psychological Medicine, 41*, 209–218.

Hulka, B. S., Zyzanski, S. J., Cassell, J. L., & Thompson, S. J. (1970). Scale for the measurement of attitudes towards physicians and primary health care. *Medical Care*, *8*, 429.

Idler, E. L. (1992). Self-assessed health and mortality: A review of studies. In S. Maes, H. Leventhal & M. Johnston (Eds.), *International Review of Health Psychology* (Vol. 1, pp. 33–56). Chichester: Wiley.

Imholz, B. P., Wieling, W., Van Montfrans, G. A., & Wesseling, K. H. (1998). Fifteen years experience with finger arterial pressure monitoring: Assessment of the technology. *Cardiovascular Research*, *38*, 605–616.

Ironson, G., Taylor, C. B., Boltwood, M., Bartzokis, T., Dennis, C., Chesney, M., Spitzer, S., & Segall, G. M. (1992). Effects of anger on left ventricular ejection fraction in coronary artery disease. *American Journal of Cardiology*, *70*, 281–285.

Jenkinson, C., Coulter, A., & Wright, L. (1993). The short form–36 (SF–36) health survey questionnaire: Normative data for adults of working age. *British Medical Journal*, *306*, 1437–1440.

Jenkinson, C., Fitzpatrick, R., Garratt, A., Peto, V., & Stewart-Brown, S. (2001). Can item response theory reduce patient burden when measuring health status in neurological disorders? Results from Rasch analysis of the SF–36 physical functioning scale. *Journal of Neurology, Neurosurgery and Psychiatry*, *71*, 220–224.

Jobe, J. B., & Herrmann, D. J. (1996). Implications of models of survey cognition for memory theory. In D. Herrmann, C. McEvoy, C. Hertzog, P. Hertel & M. K. Johnson (Eds.), *Basic and applied memory research: Volume 2. Practical applications* (pp. 193–205). Mahwah, NJ: Erlbaum.

Johnston, M. (1982). Recognition of patients, worries by nurses and by other patients. *British Journal of Clinical Psychology*, *21*, 255–261.

Johnston, M. (1996). Models of disability. *The Psychologist*, *9*, 205–210.

Johnston, M. (1999). Mood in chronic disease: Questioning the answers. *Current Psychology*, *18*, 71–87.

Johnston, M., Bonetti, D., & Pollard, B. (2002). Disability as behaviour: Models of measurement and explanation. In L. Backman & C. von Hofston (Eds.), *Psychology at the turn of the millennium: Vol. 1. Cognitive, biological and health perspectives* (pp. 319–333).

Johnston, M., Bromley, I., Boothroyd-Brooks, M., Dobbs, W., Ilson, A., & Ridout, K. (1987). Behavioural assessments of physically disabled patients: Agreement between rehabilitation therapists and nurses. *International Journal of Rehabilitation Research*, *10* (Supp. 5), 204–213.

Johnston, M., Earll, L., Mitchell, E., Morrison, V., & Wright, S. (1996). Communicating the diagnosis of motor neurone disease. *Journal of Palliative Medicine*, *10*, 23–34.

Johnston, M., & Johnston, D. W. (1998). Assessment and measurement issues. In D. W. Johnston & M. Johnston (Eds.), *Health psychology* (pp. 113–136). Oxford: Elsevier.

Johnston, M., Morrison, V., Macwalter, R., & Partridge, C. (1999). Perceived control, coping and recovery from disability following stroke. *Psychology and Health*, *14*, 181–192.

Johnston, M., Pollard, B., & Hennessey, P. (2000). Construct validation of the Hospital Anxiety and Depression Scale with clinical populations. *Journal of Psychosomatic Research*, *48*, 579–584.

Johnston, M., Wright, S. & Weinman, J. (1995). *Measures in health psychology: A user's portfolio*. Windsor: NFER- Nelson.

Kaplan, R. M. (1990). Behaviour as the central outcome in health care. *American Psychologist*, *45*, 1211–1220.

Karabatsos, G. (1998). The Rasch model, additive conjoint measurement, and new models of probabilistic measurement theory. *Journal of Applied Measurement*, *2*, 389–423.

Kasl, S. N., & Cobb, S. (1966). Health behavior, illness behavior, and sick role behavior: I. Health and illness behavior. *Archives of Environmental Health*, *12*, 246–266.

Katz, S., Ford, A. B., Moskowitz, R.W., Jackson, B. A., & Jaffe, M. W. (1963). Studies of illness in the aged. The index of ADL: A standardised measure of biological and psychosocial function. *Journal of the American Medical Association*, *185*, 914–919.

Keefe, F. J., & Block, A. R. (1982). Development of an observational method for assessing pain behaviour in chronic low-back pain patients. *Behaviour Therapy*, *13*, 363–375.

Kennedy, S., Kiecolt-Glaser, J. K., & Glaser, R. (1988). Immunological consequences of acute and chronic stressors: Mediating role of interpersonal relationships. *British Journal of Medical Psychology*, *61*, 77–86.

Kind, P., & Rosser, R. (1988). The quantification of health. *European Journal of Social Psychology*, *18*, 63–77.

Kline, P. (1998). *The new psychometrics: Science, psychology and measurement*. London: Routledge.

Kline, P. (2000). *The handbook of psychological testing* (2nd edn.). London: Routledge.

Krantz, D. H., Luce, R. D., Suppes, P., & Tversky, A. (1971). *Foundations of measurement* (Vol. 1). New York: Academic.

Krantz, D. S., Baum, A., & Wideman, M. (1980). Assessment of preferences for self-treatment and information in health care. *Journal of Personality and Social Psychology*, 39, 977–990.

Krantz, D. S., & Lundgren, N. R. (1998). Cardiovascular disorders. In D. W. Johnston & M. Johnston (Eds.), *Health psychology* (pp. 189–216). Oxford: Elsevier.

Krosnick, J. A. (1999). Survey research. *Annual Review of Psychology*, 50, 537–567.

Kulik, J. A., Mahler, H. I. M., & Moore, P.J. (1996). Social comparison and affiliation under threat: Effects of recovery from major surgery. *Journal of Personality and Social Psychology*, 71, 967–979.

Lalljee, M., Lamb, R., & Carnibella, G. (1993). Lay prototypes of illness: Their content and use. *Psychology and Health*, 8, 33–49.

Lanyon, R. I., & Goodstein, L.D. (1982). *Personality assessment* (2nd edn.). New York: Wiley.

Lau, R. R., Hartman, K. A., & Ware, J. E. (1986). Health as a value: Methodological and theoretical considerations. *Health Psychology*, 5, 25–43.

Lazarus, R. S., & Folkman, S. (1984). *Stress, appraisal and coping*. New York: Springer.

Leventhal, H., Benyamini, Y., Brownlee, S., Diefenbach, M., Leventhal, E.A., Patrick-Miller, L., & Robitaille, C. (1997). Illness representations: Theoretical foundations. In K. J. Petrie & J. A. Weinman (Eds.), *Perceptions of health and illness* (pp. 19–46). Amsterdam: Harwood.

Leventhal, H., & Cameron, L. (1987). Behavioural theories and the problem of compliance. *Patient Education and Counseling*, 10, 117–138.

Levine, M. V. (1970). Transformations that render curves parallel. *Journal of Mathematical Psychology*, 7, 410–443.

Ley, P. (1988). *Communicating with patients*. London: Routledge.

Lincoln, N. B., & Edmans, J. A. (1990). A re-validation of the Rivermead ADL Scale for elderly patients with stroke. *Age and Ageing*, 19, 19–24.

Lister, A. M., Rode, S., Farmer, A., & Salkovskis, P. (2002). Does thinking about personal health risk increase anxiety? *Journal of Health Psychology*, 7, 409–414.

Luce, R. D., & Tukey, J. W. (1964). Simultaneous conjoint measurement: A new type of fundamental measurement. *Journal of Mathematical Psychology*, 1, 1–27.

Maguire, P., & Selby, P. (1989). Assessing quality of life in cancer patients. *British Journal of Cancer*, 60, 437.

Mahoney, F. I., & Barthel, D. W. (1965). Functional evaluation: The Barthel Index, *Maryland State Medical Journal*, 14, 61–65.

Marsh, H. W., & Grayson, D. (1995). Multitrait–Multimethod analysis. In T. Husen & T. N. Postlethwaite (Eds.), *The international encyclopedia of education* (2nd edn., pp. 4000–4007). Oxford: Pergamon.

Marteau, T. M. (1990). Attitudes towards doctors and medicine: The preliminary development of a new scale. *Psychology and Health*, 4, 351–356.

Marteau, T., & Johnston, M. (1991). Health professionals: A source of variance in health outcomes. *Psychology and Health*, 5, 47–58.

Marteau, T. M., Johnston, M., Kidd, J., Michie, S., Cook, R., Slack, J., & Shaw, R. W. (1992). Psychological models in predicting uptake of prenatal screening. *Psychology and Health*, 6, 13–22.

Martin, P. R. (1998). Headache. In D. W. Johnston & M. Johnston (Eds.), *Health psychology* (pp. 529–556). Oxford: Elsevier.

Maslach, C. (1982). *Burn-out: The cost of caring*. Englewood Cliffs, NJ: Prentice-Hall.

McClenahan, R., Johnston, M., & Densham, Y. (1990). Misperceptions of comprehension difficulties of stroke patients by doctors, nurses and relatives. *Journal of Neurology, Neuropsychiatry and Psychiatry*, 53, 700–701.

McGill, A. L. (1989). Context effects in judgments of causation. *Journal of Personality and Social Psychology*, 57, 189–200.

McNair, D. M., Lorr, M., & Droppelman, L. F. (1992). *EdITS manual for the Profile of Mood States (POMS)*. San Diego: EdITS/Editorial and Industrial Testing Service.

Meenan, R. F., Gertman, P. M., & Mason, J. R. (1980). Measuring health status in arthritis: The Arthritis Impact Measurement Scales. *Arthritis and Rheumatism*, 23, 146–152.

Meichenbaum, D., & Turk, D. (1987). *Facilitating treatment adherence*. New York: Plenum.

Meier, S. T. (1994). *The chronic crisis in psychological measurement and assessment: A historical survey*. San Diego, CA: Academic.

Melzack, R. (1975). The McGill Pain Questionnaire: Major properties and scoring methods. *Pain*, 1, 277–299.

Melzack, R. (1987). The short-form McGill Pain Questionnaire. *Pain*, 30, 191–197.

Michell, J. (1990). *An introduction to the logic of psychological measurement*. Hillsdale, NJ: Erlbaum.

Michell, J. (1994). Measuring dimensions of belief by unidimensional unfolding. *Journal of Mathematical Psychology*, 38, 244–273.

Michell, J. (1997). Quantitative science and the definition of measurement in psychology. *British Journal of Psychology, 88*, 355–383.

Michie, S., McDonald, V., & Marteau, T. (1996). Understanding responses to predictive genetic testing: A grounded theory approach. *Psychology and Health, 11*, 455–470.

Miller, S. M. (1987). Monitoring and blunting: Validation of a questionnaire to assess styles of information seeking under threat. *Journal of Personality and Social Psychology, 52*, 345–353.

Mora, P.A., Robitaille, C., Leventhal, H., Swigar, M., & Leventhal, E. (2002). Trait negative affect relates to prior-week symptoms, but not to reports of illness episodes, illness symptoms, and care seeking among older persons. *Psychosomatic Medicine, 64*, 436–449.

Moss-Morris, R., Weinman, J., Petrie, J., Horne, R., Cameron, L., & Buick, D. (2002). The revised Illness Perception Questionnaire. *Psychology and Health, 17*, 1–16.

Nagi, S. (1991). Disability concepts revisited: Implications for prevention. In A. Pope & A. Tarlow (Eds.), *Disability in America: Toward a national agenda for prevention* (pp. 309–327). Washington: National Academy Press.

Nerenz, D., Leventhal, H., Love, R. R., & Ringler, K. E. (1984). Psychological aspects of cancer chemotherapy. *International Review of Applied Psychology, 33*, 521–529.

Nolen-Hoeksema, S., McBride, A., & Larson, J. (1997). Rumination and psychological distress among bereaved partners. *Journal of Personality and Social Psychology, 72*, 855–862.

Nunnally, J. O. (1978). *Psychometric theory*. New York: McGraw-Hill.

O'Boyle, C., McGee, H. M., & Joyce, C. R. B. (1994). Quality of life: Assessing the individual. *Advances in Medical Sociology, 5*, 159–180.

Orbell, S. (1996). Informal care in social context: A social psychological analysis of participation, impact and intervention in care of the elderly. *Psychology and Health, 11*, 155–178.

Owen, N., & Crawford, D. (1998). Health promotion: Perspectives on physical activity and weight control. In D. W. Johnston & M. Johnston (Eds.), *Health psychology* (pp. 675–690). Oxford: Elsevier.

OXCHECK Study Group (1994). Effectiveness of health checks conducted by nurses in primary care: Results of the OXCHECK Study. *British Medical Journal, 308*, 308–312.

Parkes, K. R. (1982). Occupational stress among student nurses: A natural experiment. *Journal of Applied Psychology, 67*, 784–796.

Partridge, C., & Johnston, M. (1989). Perceived control of recovery from physical disability: Measurement and prediction. *British Journal of Clinical Psychology, 28*, 53–59.

Patrick, D. L., & Peach, H. (1989) (Eds.), *Disablement in the community*. Oxford: Oxford University Press.

Payne, R., & Firth-Cozens, J. (Eds.) (1987). *Stress in health professionals*. Chichester: Wiley.

Pennebaker, J. W., Mayne, T. J., & Francis, M.E. (1997). Linguistic predictors of adaptive bereavement. *Journal of Personality and Social Psychology, 72*, 863–871.

Perline, R., Wright, D. B., & Wainer, H. (1979). The Rasch model as additive conjoint measurement. *Applied Psychological Measurement, 3*, 237–255.

Peterson, C., Buchanan, G. M., & Seligman, M. E. P. (1995). Explanatory style: History and evolution of the field. In G. M. Buchanan & M. E. P. Seligman (Eds.), *Explanatory style* (pp. 1–20). Hillsdale, NJ: Erlbaum.

Petrie, K. J., Weinman, J. A., Sharpe, N., & Buckley, J. (1996). Role of patients' view of their illness in predicting return to work and functioning after myocardial infarction. *British Medical Journal, 312*, 1191–1194.

Pollard, B., & Johnston, M. (2001). Problems with the Sickness Impact Profile: A theoretically-based analysis and a proposal for a new method of implementation and scoring. *Social Science and Medicine, 52*, 921–934.

Power, M. J., Champion, L. A., & Aris, S. J. (1988). The development of a measure of social support: The Significant Others Scale (SOS). *British Journal of Clinical Psychology, 27*, 349–358.

Prohaska, T. R., Leventhal, E. A., Leventhal, H., & Keller, M. L. (1985). Health practices and illness cognition in young, middle aged, and elderly adults. *Journal of Gerontology, 40*, 569–578.

Putnam, S. M., Stiles, W. B., Jacob, M. C., & James, S. A. (1985). Patient exposition and physician explanation in initial medical interviews and outcomes of clinic visits. *Medical Care, 23*, 74–83.

Radley, A., & Billig, M. (1996). Accounts of health and illness: Dilemmas and representations. *Sociology of Health and Illness, 18*, 220–240.

Radloff, L. (1977). The CES–D Scale: A self-report depression scale for research in the general population. *Applied Psychosocial Measurement, 1*, 385–401.

Richards, J. S., Nepomuceno, C., Riles, M., & Suer, Z. (1982). Assessing pain behaviour: The UAB Pain Behaviour Scale. *Pain, 14*, 393–398.

Rosser, R., & Kind, P. (1978). A scale of valuations of states of illness: Is there a social consensus? *International Journal of Epidemiology, 7*, 347–358.

Roter, D. L., & Hall, J. A. (1989). Studies of doctor–patient interaction. *Annual Review of Public Health, 10,* 163–200.

Rotter, J. B. (1966). Generalized expectancies for internal versus external control of reinforcement. *Psychological Monographs: General and Applied, 80,* 1–28.

Ruta, D. A., Garratt, A. M., Leng, M., Russell, I. T., & MacDonald, L. M. (1994). A new approach to the measurement of quality of life: The Patient-Generated Index. *Medical Care, 32,* 1109–1126.

Salmon, P., & Quine, J. (1989). Patients' intentions in primary care: Measurement and preliminary investigation. *Psychology and Health, 3,* 103–110.

Sarason, I. G., Levine, H. M., Basham, R. B., & Sarason, B. R. (1983). Assessing social support: The Social Support Questionnaire. *Journal of Personality and Social Psychology, 44,* 127–139.

Sarason, I. G., Sarason, B. R., Shearin, E. N., & Pierce, G. R. (1987). A brief measure of social support: Practical and theoretical implications. *Journal of Social and Personal Relationships, 4,* 497–510.

Schoenborn, C. A. (1993). The Alameda Study: 25 years later. In S. Maes, H. Leventhal & M. Johnston (Eds.), *International Review of Health Psychology* (Vol. 2). Chichester: Wiley.

Schooler, N. R. (Ed.) (1998). *Comprehensive clinical psychology: Vol. 3. Research and methods.* Oxford: Elsevier.

Schroeder, D. H., & Costa, P. T. (1984). Influence of life event stress on physical illness: Substantive effects or methodological flaws? *Journal of Personality and Social Psychology, 46,* 853–863.

Schucker, B., Wittes, J., Cutler, J., Cutler, J. A., Bailey, K., Mackintosh, D. R., Gordon, D. J., Haines, C. M., Mattson, M. E., Goor, R. S., & Rifkind, B. M. (1987). Change in physician perspective on cholesterol and heart disease. *Journal of the American Medical Association, 258,* 3521–3526.

Schuman, H. (1982). Artifacts are in the mind of the observer. *The American Sociologist, 17,* 21–28.

Schuman, H., & Presser, S. (1980). Public opinion and public ignorance: The fine line between attitudes and nonattitudes. *American Journal of Sociology, 85,* 1214–1225.

Schwarz, N. (1999). Self-reports: How the questions shape the answers. *American Psychologist, 54,* 93–105.

Schwarz, N., Hippler, H. J., Deutsch, B., & Strack, F. (1985). Response categories: Effects on behavioral reports and comparative judgments. *Public Opinion Quarterly, 59,* 93–97.

Shaper, A. G., Pocock, S. J., Phillips, A. N., & Walker, M. (1987). A scoring system to identify men at high risk of heart attack. *Health Trends, 19,* 37–39.

Shaw, C., Abrams, K., & Marteau, T. M. (1999). Psychological impact of predicting individuals' risks of illness: A systematic review. *Social Science and Medicine, 49,* 1571–1598.

Sheeran, P., & Orbell, S. (1996). How confidently can we infer health beliefs from questionnaire responses? *Psychology and Health, 11,* 273–290.

Shiffman, S. S., & Stone, A. A. (1998). Ecological momentary assessment in health psychology. *Health Psychology, 17,* 3–5.

Smith, M. S., Wallston, K. A., & Smith, C. S. (1995). The development and validation of the Perceived Health Competence Scale. *Health Education Research, 10,* 51–64.

Spielberger, C. D. (1983). *Manual for the State–Trait Anxiety Inventory.* Palo Alto, CA: Consulting Psychologists Press.

St Lawrence, J. S., Kelly, J. A., Owen, A. D., Hogan, I. G., & Wilson, R.A. (1990). Psychologists' attitudes towards AIDS. *Psychology and Health, 4,* 357–365.

Stein, N., Folkman, S., Trabasso, T., & Richards, T. A. (1997). Appraisal and goal processes as predictors of psychological well-being in bereaved caregivers. *Journal of Personality and Social Psychology, 72,* 872–884.

Steptoe, A. (1998). Psychophysiological bases of disease. In D. W. Johnston & M. Johnston (Eds.), *Health psychology* (pp. 39–78). Oxford: Elsevier.

Stern, R. M., Ray, W. J., & Quigley, K. S. (2001). *Psychophysiological recording.* New York: Oxford University Press.

Stevens, S. S. (1959). Measurement, psychophysics and utility. In C.W. Churchman & P. Ratoosh (Eds.), *Measurement: Definitions and theories* (pp. 18–63). New York: Wiley.

Stiles, W. B. (1989). Evaluating medical interview process components: Null correlations with outcomes may be misleading. *Medical Care, 27,* 212–220.

Stone, A. A., Turkkan, J. S., Bachrach, C. A., Jobe, J. B., Kurtzman, H. S., & Cain, V. S. (Eds.) (2000). *The science of self-report: Implications for research and practice.* Mahwah, NJ: Erlbaum.

Tuomisto, M. T., Johnston, D. W., & Schmidt, T. F. H. (1996). The ambulatory measurement of posture, thigh acceleration and muscle tension and their relationship to heart rate. *Psychophysiology, 33,* 409–415.

Turk, D. C., Rudy, T. E., & Salovey, P. (1986). Implicit models of illness. *Journal of Behavioral Medicine, 9,* 453–474.

Turner, S. M. (1998). Functional bowel disorders. In D. W. Johnston & M. Johnston (Eds.), *Health psychology* (pp. 305–320). Oxford: Elsevier.

Vincent, C., Ennis, M., & Audley, R. (1993). *Medical accidents*. Oxford: Oxford University Press.

Volicer, B. J., & Bohannon, M. W. (1975). A hospital stress rating scale. *Nursing Research, 24*, 352–359.

Walker, D. J., Heslop, P. S., Plummer, C. J., Essex, T., & Chandler, S. (1997). A continuous patient activity monitor: Validation and relation to disability. *Physiological Measurement, 18*, 40–49.

Wallston, K. A. (1992). Hocus-pocus, the focus isn't strictly locus: Rotter's social learning theory modified for health. *Cognitive Therapy and Research, 16*, 183–199.

Wallston, K. A., Stein, M. J., & Smith, C. A. (1994). Form C of MHLC Scales: A condition-specific measure of locus of control. *Journal of Personality and Social Assessment, 63*, 534–553.

Wallston, K. A., Wallston, B. S., & Develis, R. (1978). Development of the multidimensional health locus of control (MHLC) scales. *Health Education Monographs, 6*, 161–170.

Ware, J. E., Bjorner, J. B., & Kosinski, M. (2000). Practical implications of item response theory and computerized adaptive testing: A brief summary of ongoing studies of widely used headache impact scales. *Medical Care, 38* (supp. 9), II73–II82.

Ware, J. E., & Hays, R. D. (1988). Methods for measuring patient satisfaction with specific medical encounters. *Medical Care, 26*, 393–402.

Watson, D., & Clark, L. A. (1984). Negative affectivity: The disposition to experience aversive emotional states. *Psychological Bulletin, 96*, 465–490.

Watson, D., & Pennebaker, J. (1989). Health complaints, stress and distress: Exploring the central role of negative affectivity. *Psychological Review, 96*, 234–254.

Watson, M., Greer, S., Young, J., Inayat, G., Burgess, C., & Robertson, B. (1988). Development of a questionnaire measurement of adjustment: The MAC scale. *Psychological Medicine, 18*, 203–209.

Weinberger, D. A., Schwartz, G. E., & Davidson, R. J. (1979). Low-anxious, high-anxious, and repressive coping styles: Psychometric patterns and behavioral and physiological responses to stress. *Journal of Abnormal Psychology, 88*, 369–380.

Weiner, B. (1986). *An attributional theory of motivation and emotion*. New York: Springer.

Weinman, J. (1998). Health care. In D. W. Johnston & M. Johnston (Eds.), *Health psychology* (pp. 79–112). Oxford: Elsevier.

Weinman, J. A., Petrie, K. J., Moss-Morris, K., & Horne, R. (1996). The illness perception questionnaire: A new method for assessing the cognitive representation of illness. *Psychology and Health, 11*, 431–445.

Wolf, M. H., Putman, S. M., James, S. A., & Stiles, W. B. (1978). The medical interview satisfaction scale: Development of a scale to measure patient perceptions of physician behavior. *Journal of Behavioral Medicine, 1*, 391.

World Health Organization (1980). *International classification of impairments, disabilities, and handicaps*. Geneva: World Health Organization.

World Health Organization (2001). *International classification of functioning, disability and health: ICF*. Geneva: World Health Organization.

Wright, D. B. (1985). Additivity in psychological measurement. In E. E. Roskam (Ed.), *Measurement and personality assessment* (pp. 101–112). Amsterdam: Elsevier.

Wright, S. J. (1990). Health status measurement: Review and prospects. In P. Bennett, J. Weinman & P. Spurgeon (Eds.), *Current developments in health psychology* (pp. 93–104). London: Harwood Academic.

Zigmond, A. S., & Snaith, R. P. (1983). The Hospital Anxiety and Depression Scale. *Acta Psychiatrica Scandinavica, 67*, 361–370.

APPENDIX: MEASURES IN HEALTH PSYCHOLOGY JOURNALS, 2001

Authors	Year	Title	Journal	Pages
A. Marsland, S. Cohen, B. Rabin, S. Manuk	(2001)	Associations between stress, trait negative affect, acute immune reactivity and antibody response to hepatitis B injection in healthy young adults	*Health Psychology, 20* (1)	4–11
P. Sheeran, M. Conner, P. Norman	(2001)	Can the theory of planned behaviour explain patterns of health behaviour change?	*Health Psychology, 20* (1)	12–19
M. Antoni, J. Lehman, K. Kilbourn, A. Boyers, J. Culver, S. Alferi, S. Yount, B. McGregor, P. Arena, S. Harris, A. Price, C. Carver	(2001)	Cognitive behavioural stress management intervention decreases the prevalence of depression and enhances benefit finding among women under treatment for early-stage breast cancer	*Health Psychology, 20* (1)	20–32
B. Johansson, J. Grant, R. Plomin, N. Pederson, F. Ahern, S. Berg, and G. McClearn	(2001)	Health locus of control in later life: A study of genetic and environmental influences in twins aged 80 years and older	*Health Psychology, 20* (1)	33–40
S. Alferi, C. Carver, M. Antoni, S. Weiss, R. Duran	(2001)	An exploratory study of social support, distress and life disruption among low-income Hispanic women under treatment for early stage breast cancer	*Health Psychology, 20* (1)	41–46
C. Fang, H. Myers	(2001)	The effects of racial stressors and hostility on cardiovascular reactivity in African American and Caucasian men	*Health Psychology, 20* (1)	64–70
C. Cameron, D. Cella, J. Herndon, A. Kornblith, E. Zuckerman, E. Henderson, R. Weiss, M. Cooper, R. Silver, L. Leone, G. Canellos, B. Peterson, J. Holland	(2001)	Persistent symptoms among survivors of Hodgkins disease: An explanatory model based on classical conditioning	*Health Psychology, 20* (1)	71–75
C. Rabin, S. Ward, H. Leventhal, M. Schmitz	(2001)	Explaining retrospective reports of symptoms in patients undergoing chemotherapy: anxiety, initial symptom experience and posttreatment symptoms	*Health Psychology, 20* (2)	91–98
C. Whalen, L. Jamner, B. Henker, R. Delfino	(2001)	Smoking and moods in adolescents with depressive and aggressive dispositions: Evidence from surveys and electronic diaries	*Health Psychology, 20* (2)	99–111
R. Arnau, M. Meagher, M. Norris, R. Bramson	(2001)	Psychometric evaluation of the Beck Depression Inventory–II with primary care medical patients	*Health Psychology, 20* (2)	112–119
B. Halpern-Felsher, S. Millstein, J. Ellen, N. Adler, J. Tschann, M. Biehl	(2001)	The role of behavioural experience in judging risks	*Health Psychology, 20* (2)	120–126
K. Gorbatenko-Roth, I. Levin, E. Altmaier, B. Doebbeling	(2001)	Accuracy of health-related quality of life assessment: What is the benefit of incorporating patients' preferences for domain functioning?	*Health Psychology, 20* (2)	136–140

APPENDIX: MEASURES IN HEALTH PSYCHOLOGY JOURNALS, 2001

Authors	Year	Title	Journal	Pages
Z. Shnek, J. Irvine, D. Stewart, S. Abbey	(2001)	Psychological factors and depressive symptoms in ischemic heart disease	*Health Psychology*, 20 (2)	141–145
P. Vitaliano, J. Scanlon, J. Zhang, M. Savage, B. Brummett, J. Barefoot, I. Siegler	(2001)	Are the salutogenic effects of social support modified by income? A test of an 'added value' hypothesis	*Health Psychology*, 20 (3)	155–165
M. Cordova, L. Cunningham, C. Carlson, M. Andrykowski	(2001)	Posttraumatic growth following breast cancer: A controlled comparison study	*Health Psychology*, 20 (3)	176–185
P. Ellickson, J. Tucker, D. Klein	(2001)	Sex differences in predictors of adolescent smoking cessation	*Health Psychology*, 20 (3)	186–195
S. Novak, R. Clayton	(2001)	The influence of school environment and self-regulation on transitions between stages of cigarette smoking: A multilevel analysis	*Health Psychology*, 20 (3)	196–207
S. Macrodimitris, N. Endler	(2001)	Coping, control and adjustment in type 2 diabetes	*Health Psychology*, 20 (3)	208–216
K. Tercyak, C. Lerman, B. Peshkin, C. Hughes, D. Main, C. Isaacs, M. Schwartz	(2001)	Effects of coping style and BRCA1 and BRCA2 test results on anxiety among women participating in genetic counseling and testing for breast and ovarian cancer	*Health Psychology*, 20 (3)	217–222
A. Allgower, J Wardle, A. Steptoe	(2001)	Depressive symptoms, social support and personal health behaviours in young men and women	*Health Psychology*, 20 (3)	223–227
T. Seeman, T. Lusignolo, M. Albert, L. Berkman	(2001)	Social relationships, social support, and patterns of cognitive aging in healthy high-functioning older adults: MacArthur Studies of successful aging	*Health Psychology*, 20 (4)	243–255
T. Schneider, P. Salovey, A. Apanovitch, J. Pizarro, D. McCarthy, J. Zullo, A. Rothman	(2001)	The effects of message framing and ethnic targeting on mammography use among low-income women	*Health Psychology*, 20 (4)	256–266
C. Hanson, L. Stevens, J. Coast	(2001)	Exercise duration and mood state: How much is enough to feel better?	*Health Psychology*, 20 (4)	267–275
M. Marvan, S. Cortes-Iniestra	(2001)	Women's beliefs about the prevalence of premenstrual syndrome and biases in recall of premenstrual changes	*Health Psychology*, 20 (4)	276–280
D. Murphy, J. Stein, W. Schlenger, E. Maibach, NIMHM HIV Prevention Trial Group	(2001)	Conceptualizing the multidimensional nature of self-efficacy: Assessment of situational context and level of behavioral challenge to maintain safer sex	*Health Psychology*, 20 (4)	281–290
M. Guyll, K. Matthews, J. Bromberger	(2001)	Discrimination and unfair treatment: Relationship to cardiovascular reactivity among African American and European American women	*Health Psychology*, 20 (5)	315–325

APPENDIX: MEASURES IN HEALTH PSYCHOLOGY JOURNALS, 2001

Authors	Year	Title	Source
S. Sears, A. Stanton	(2001)	Expectancy-value constructs and expectancy violation as predictors of exercise adherence in previously sedentary women	*Health Psychology, 20* (5) 326–333
R. Collins, D. Kanouse, A. Gifford, J. Senterfit, M. Schuster, D. McCaffrey, M. Shapiro, N. Wenger	(2001)	Changes in health-promoting behavior following diagnosis with HIV: Prevalence and correlates in a national probability sample	*Health Psychology, 20* (5) 351–360
D. Britt, L. Cohen, F. Collins, M. Cohen	(2001)	Cigarette smoking and chewing gum: Response to a laboratory-induced stressor	*Health Psychology, 20* (5) 361–368
The National Institute of Mental Health Multisite HIV Prevention Trial Group	(2001)	Social-cognitive theory mediators of behavior change in the National Institute of Mental Health Multisite HIV prevention trial	*Health Psychology, 20* (5) 369–376
L. Chassin, C. Presson, J. Rose, S. Sherman	(2001)	From adolescence to adulthood: Age-related changes in beliefs about cigarette smoking in a Midwestern community sample	*Health Psychology, 20* (5) 377–386
V. Helgeson, S. Cohen, R. Schulz, J. Yasko	(2001)	Long-term effects of educational and peer discussion group interventions on adjustment to breast cancer	*Health Psychology, 20* (5) 387–392
K. Matthews, B. Gump, J. Owens	(2001)	Chronic stress influences cardiovascular and neuroendocrine responses during acute stress and recovery, especially in men	*Health Psychology, 20* (6) 403–410
C. Alonso, C. Coe	(2001)	Disruptions in social relationships accentuate the association between emotional distress and menstrual pain in young women	*Health Psychology, 20* (6) 411–416
D. Jones, S. Beach, R. Forehand, and the Family Health Project Research Group	(2001)	Disease status in African American single mothers with HIV: The role of depressive symptoms	*Health Psychology, 20* (6) 417–423
M. Freeman, E. Hennessy, D. Marzullo	(2001)	Defensive evaluation of antismoking messages among college-age smokers: The role of possible selves	*Health Psychology, 20* (6) 424–433
S. Phipps, R. Steele, K. Hall, L. Leigh	(2001)	Repressive adaptation in children with cancer: A replication and extension	*Health Psychology, 20* (6) 445–451
C. Fang, S. Manne, S. Pape	(2001)	Functional impairment, marital quality and patient psychological distress as predictors of psychological distress among cancer patients' spouses	*Health Psychology, 20* (6) 452–457

APPENDIX: MEASURES IN HEALTH PSYCHOLOGY JOURNALS, 2001

Authors	Year	Title	Journal	Pages
S. Orbell, M. Johnston, D. Rowley, P. Davey, A. Espley	(2001)	Self-efficacy and goal importance in the prediction of physical disability in people following hospitalisation: A prospective study	*British Journal of Health Psychology*, 6 (1)	25–40
K. Kendell, B. Saxby, M. Farrow, C. Naisby	(2001)	Psychological factors associated with short-term recovery from total knee replacement	*British Journal of Health Psychology*, 6 (1)	41–52
P. Sparks, M. Conner, R. James, R. Shepherd, R. Povey	(2001)	Ambivalence about health-related behaviours: An exploration in the domain of food choice	*British Journal of Health Psychology*, 6 (1)	53–68
J. Petrak, A. Doyle, A. Smith, C. Skinner, B. Hedge	(2001)	Factors associated with self-disclosure of HIV serostatus to significant others	*British Journal of Health Psychology*, 6 (1)	69–80
H. Gudmundsdottir, M. Johnston, D. Johnston, J. Foulkes	(2001)	Spontaneous, elicited and cued causal attributions in the year following a first myocardial infarction	*British Journal of Health Psychology*, 6 (1)	81–96
M. Junger, W. Stroebe, A. M. van der Laan	(2001)	Delinquency, health behaviour and health	*British Journal of Health Psychology*, 6 (2)	103–120
A. Dijkstra, H. De Vries	(2001)	Do self-help interventions in health education lead to cognitive changes, and do cognitive changes lead to behavioural change?	*British Journal of Health Psychology*, 6 (2)	121–134
K. Courneya, R. Plotnikoff, S. Hotz, N. Birkett	(2001)	Predicting exercise stage transitions over two consecutive 6-month periods: A test of the theory of planned behaviour in a population-based sample	*British Journal of Health Psychology*, 6 (2)	135–150
S. Zakowski, H. Valdimarsdottir, D. Bovbjerg	(2001)	Emotional expressivity and intrusive cognitions in women with family histories of breast cancer: Application of a cognitive processing model	*British Journal of Health Psychology*, 6 (2)	151–166
P. Heslop, G. Smith, D. Carroll, J. Macleod, F. Hyland, C. Hart	(2001)	Perceived stress and coronary heart disease risk factors: The contribution of socio-economic position	*British Journal of Health Psychology*, 6 (2)	167–178
A. Miles, C. McManus, C. Feinmann, L. Glover, S. Harrison, S. Pearce	(2001)	The factor structure of the BDI in facial pain and other chronic pain patients: A comparison of two models using confirmatory factor analysis	*British Journal of Health Psychology*, 6 (2)	179–196
A. Lohaus, J. Klein-Hessling, C. Vogele, C. Kuhn-Hennighausen	(2001)	Psychophysiological effects of relaxation training in children	*British Journal of Health Psychology*, 6 (3)	197–206
M. Heijmans, M. Foets, M. Rijken, K. Schreurs, D. de Ridder, J. Bensing	(2001)	Stress in chronic disease: Do the perceptions of patients and their general practitioners match?	*British Journal of Health Psychology*, 6 (3)	229–242

APPENDIX: MEASURES IN HEALTH PSYCHOLOGY JOURNALS, 2001

M. Alderfer, D. Wiebe, D. Hartmann	(2001)	Social behaviour and illness information interact to influence the peer acceptance of children with chronic disease	*British Journal of Health Psychology*, 6 (3) 243–256
L. Wiggs, G. Stores	(2001)	Behavioural treatment for sleep problems in children with severe intellectual disabilities and daytime challenging behaviour: Effect on mothers and fathers	*British Journal of Health Psychology*, 6 (3) 257–270
H. Nauta, H. Hospers, A. Jansen	(2001)	One year follow-up effects of two obesity treatments on psychological well-being and weight	*British Journal of Health Psychology*, 6 (3) 271–284
C. Kohlmann, C. Ring, D. Carroll, C. Mohiyeddini, P. Bennett	(2001)	Cardiac coping style, heartbeat detection and the interpretation of cardiac events	*British Journal of Health Psychology*, 6 (3) 285–302
E. Ferguson	(2001)	Personality and coping traits: A joint factor analysis	*British Journal of Health Psychology*, 6 (4) 311–326
L. Quine, D. Rutter, L. Arnold	(2001)	Persuading school-age cyclists to use safety helmets: Effectiveness of an intervention based on the theory of planned behaviour	*British Journal of Health Psychology*, 6 (4) 327–346
A. Walker, J. Grimshaw, E. Armstrong	(2001)	Salient beliefs and intentions to prescribe antibiotics for patients with a sore throat	*British Journal of Health Psychology*, 6 (4) 347–360
K. Umeh, J. Rogan-Gibson	(2001)	Perceptions of threat, benefits and barriers in breast self-examination amongst young asymptomatic women	*British Journal of Health Psychology*, 6 (4) 361–372
S. Roberts, D. Bonnici, A. Mackinnon, M. Worcester	(2001)	Psychometric evaluation of the Hospital Anxiety and Depression Scale (HADS) among female cardiac patients	*British Journal of Health Psychology*, 6 (4) 373–384
N. Cochrane	(2001)	Physical contact experience and coping ability: A study of survivors of myocardial infarction	*British Journal of Health Psychology*, 6 (4) 385–396

APPENDIX: MEASURES IN HEALTH PSYCHOLOGY JOURNALS, 2001

Authors	Year	Title	Source
P. Schofield, P. Pattison, D. Hill, R. Borland	(2001)	The influence of group identification on the adoption of peer group smoking norms	*Psychology & Health, 16* (1) 1–16
K. Martin, M. Leary	(2001)	Self-presentational determinants of health risk behaviour among college freshmen	*Psychology & Health, 16* (1) 17–28
R. Bagozzi, K. Lee, M. Van Loo	(2001)	Decisions to donate bone marrow: The roles of attitudes and subjective norms across cultures	*Psychology & Health, 16* (1) 29–56
J. Eiser, A. Riazi, C. Eiser, S. Hammersley, J. Tooke	(2001)	Predictors of psychological well-being in types 1 and 2 diabetes	*Psychology & Health, 16* (1) 99–110
A. Mak, J. Mueller	(2001)	Negative affectivity, perceived occupational stress and health during organisational restructuring: A follow-up study	*Psychology & Health, 16* (1) 125–137
K. Schroder, R. Schwarzer	(2001)	Do partners' personality resources add to the prediction of patients' coping and quality of life?	*Psychology & Health, 16* (2) 139–160
K. Vedhara, P. Bennett, E. Brooks, L. Gale, K. Munnoch, C. Schreiber-Kounine, C. Fowler, A. Sammon, Z. Rayter, J. Farndon	(2001)	Risk factors for psychological morbidity in women attending a one-stop diagnostic clinic with suspected breast disease	*Psychology & Health, 16* (2) 179–190
F. Jones, C. Abraham, P. Harris, J. Schulz, C. Chrispin	(2001)	From knowledge to action regulation: Modelling the cognitive prerequisites of sun screen use in Australian and UK samples	*Psychology & Health, 16* (2) 191–206
Z. Fekadu, P. Kraft	(2001)	Predicting intended contraception in a sample of Ethiopian female adolescents: The validity of the theory of planned behaviour	*Psychology & Health, 16* (2) 207–222
A. Astrom, J. Rise	(2001)	Young adults' intention to eat healthy food: Extending the theory of planned behaviour	*Psychology & Health, 16* (2) 223–238
M. Fekkes, R. Kamphuis, J. Ottenkamp, E. Verrips, T. Vogels, M. Kamphuis, S. Verloove-Vanhorick	(2001)	Health-related quality of life in young adults with minor congenital heart disease	*Psychology & Health, 16* (2) 239–250
J. deBruin, M. Schaefer, H. Krohne, A. Dreyer	(2001)	Preoperative anxiety, coping and intraoperative adjustment: Are there mediating effects of stress-induced analgesia?	*Psychology & Health, 16* (3) 253–272
Y. Gidron, R. Magen, S. Ariad	(2001)	The relation between hopelessness and psychological and serological outcomes in Israeli women with breast cancer	*Psychology & Health, 16* (3) 289–296

APPENDIX: MEASURES IN HEALTH PSYCHOLOGY JOURNALS, 2001

Authors	Year	Title	Journal
B. Meiser, P. Butow, A. Barratt, M. Gattas, C. Gaff, E. Haan, M. Gleeson, T. Dudding, K. Tucker and the Psychological Impact Collaborative Group	(2001)	Risk perceptions and knowledge of breast cancer genetics in women at increased risk of developing hereditary breast cancer	*Psychology & Health, 16* (3) 297–312
S. Shiloh, N. Eini, Z. Ben-Neria, M. Sagi	(2001)	Framing of prenatal screening test results and women's health–illness orientations as determinants of perceptions of fetal health and approval of amniocentesis	*Psychology & Health, 16* (3) 313–326
T. van Elderen, E. Dusseldorp	(2001)	Lifestyle effects of group health education for patients with coronary heart disease	*Psychology & Health, 16* (3) 327–342
E. Hallaraker, K. Arefjord, O. Havik, J. Maeland	(2001)	Social support and emotional adjustment during and after a severe life event: A study of wives of myocardial infarction patients	*Psychology & Health, 16* (3) 343–356
P. Granqvist, S. Lantto, L. Ortiz, G. Anderson	(2001)	Adult attachment, perceived family support, and problems experienced by tinnitus patients	*Psychology & Health, 16* (3) 357–366
A. Deeks, M. McCabe	(2001)	Menopausal stage and age and perceptions of body image	*Psychology & Health, 16* (3) 367–379
H. Hausenblas, C. Nigg, E. Dannecker, D. Downs, R. Gardner, E. Fallon, B. Focht, M. Loving	(2001)	A missing piece of the transtheoretical model applied to exercise: Development and validation of the Temptation To Not Exercise Scale	*Psychology & Health, 16* (4) 381–390
M. Hagger, N. Chatzisarantis, S. Biddle, S. Orbell	(2001)	Antecedents of children's physical activity intentions and behaviour: Predictive validity and longitudinal effects	*Psychology & Health, 16* (4) 391–408
M. Yzer, F. Siero, B. Buunk	(2001)	Bringing up condom use and using condoms with new sexual partners: Intentional or habitual?	*Psychology & Health, 16* (4) 409–422
G. Godin, C. Gagne, J. Maziade, L. Moreault, D. Beauleau, S. Morel	(2001)	Breast cancer: The intention to have a mammography and a clinical breast examination – application of the theory of planned behaviour	*Psychology & Health, 16* (4) 423–442
P. Bijttebier, T. Vercruysse, H. Vertommen, S. Van Gool, A. Uyttebroeck, P. Brock	(2001)	New evidence on the reliability and validity of the Pediatric Oncology Quality of Life Scale	*Psychology & Health, 16* (4) 461–470
C. Nijboer, R. Tempelaar, M. Triemstra, R. Sanderman, G. van den Bos	(2001)	Dynamics in cancer caregivers' health over time: Gender-specific patterns and determinants	*Psychology & Health, 16* (4) 471–488

APPENDIX: MEASURES IN HEALTH PSYCHOLOGY JOURNALS, 2001

Authors	Year	Title	Source
J. Peiro, V. Gonzalez-Roma, N. Tordera, M. Manas	(2001)	Does role stress predict burnout over time among health care professionals?	*Psychology & Health, 16* (5) 511–526
D. Zapf, C. Seifert, B. Schmutte, H. Mertini, M. Holz	(2001)	Emotion work and job stressors and their effects on burnout	*Psychology & Health, 16* (5) 527–546
M. Leiter, C. Frizzell, P. Harvie, L. Churchill	(2001)	Abusive interactions and burnout: Examining occupation, gender, and the mediating role of the community	*Psychology & Health, 16* (5) 547–564
W. Schaufeli, A. Bakker, K. Hoogduin, C. Schaap, A. Kladler	(2001)	On the clinical validity of the Maslach Burnout Inventory and the Burnout Measure	*Psychology & Health, 16* (5) 565–582
R. Burke, E. Greenglass	(2001)	Hospital restructuring, work–family conflict and psychological burnout among nursing staff	*Psychology & Health, 16* (5) 583–594
M. Westman, D. Etzion	(2001)	The impact of vacation and job stress on burnout and absenteeism	*Psychology & Health, 16* (5) 595–606
D. Bonetti, M. Johnston, J. Rodriguez-Marin, M. Pastor, M. Martin-Aragon, E. Doherty, K. Sheehan	(2001)	Dimensions of perceived control: A factor analysis of three measures and an examination of their relation to activity level and mood in a student and cross-cultural patient sample	*Psychology & Health, 16* (6) 655–674
K. G. Low, G. Casey, A. Megroz, K. Leonard, K. McGuffie, L. Briand	(2001)	Hostility, oral contraceptive use, and cardiovascular reactivity in women	*Psychology & Health, 16* (6) 675–688
L. Solano, F. Montella, S. Salvati, F. Di Sora, F. Murgia, L. Figa-Talamanca, L. Zoppi, F. Lauria, R. Coda, M. Nicotra	(2001)	Expression and processing of emotions: Relationships with CD4 + levels in 42 HIV-positive asymptomatic individuals	*Psychology & Health, 16* (6) 689–698
C. Saetermore, D. Scattone, K. Kim	(2001)	Ethnicity and the stigma of disabilities	*Psychology & Health, 16* (6) 699–714
C. Yang & A. J. Spielman	(2001)	The effect of delayed weekend sleep pattern on sleep and morning functioning	*Psychology & Health, 16* (6) 715–725

14

Professional Issues in Health Psychology

CYNTHIA D. BELAR AND TERESA MCINTYRE

INTRODUCTION

As a field evolves, professional issues surface. This chapter focuses on such issues in the growth and formalization of health psychology as a science and a profession. The order of presentation is not chronological, as in reality, development in each of these areas has been interrelated. The areas addressed include: organizational structures; recognition, standard setting and regulation; interdisciplinary issues; distinctive ethical issues; and related trends.

ORGANIZATIONAL STRUCTURES

Hallmark events in the evolution of any specialty or profession are (1) the emergence of scientific and professional societies devoted to further study and practice in the area, and (2) the publication of new scientific and professional journals specific to the area. As new knowledge develops, members of the discipline gather around mutual interests, develop mechanisms for dissemination of information, and begin teaching this knowledge and its application to new trainees in the discipline. So it has been with health psychology. Although

its conceptual roots can be traced back to Ancient Greece (Belar, McIntyre & Matarazzo, 2003), its formalization as a specialty within psychology has occurred primarily in the last 25 years. Its growth has been marked by the increased number of psychologists involved in the search for new knowledge in health and behavior, and the application of this knowledge to health care services and systems.

Scientific and Professional Societies in Health Psychology

Parallel to the development of health psychology as a science, the first association of health psychology took place in the United States. The Division of Health Psychology, an organization that represented both research and practice interests, was formally installed by the American Psychological Association (APA) in 1978. In 1984, the International Association of Applied Psychology began a Division of Applied Health Psychologists, and in 1986 two new societies were founded continents apart: the European Health Psychology Society and the New Zealand Health Psychology Society. A decade later there was sufficient support to establish an international organization solely focused on health psychology – the International Society of Health Psychology. The Japanese Association of Health Psychology was established in 1998, the same year that the Israel Psychological Association formed a Division of Medical Psychology. In Africa, health psychology has developed mostly in South Africa, although the interchange with European and American psychologists through collaborations with local nongovernmental organizations has fostered the application of psychology to pressing health problems, such as the AIDS epidemic (e.g., Aboud, 2001; Koinange, 2001).

Because of its roots in the biopsychosocial model, health psychologists have historically sought to collaborate with other disciplines in the study of health and behavior. As early as 1942, psychologists, physiologists, and physicians founded the American Psychosomatic Society, whereas in Europe, the Society for Psychosomatic Research (Britain) and the Swiss Society of Psychosomatic Medicine were created in the early 1960s. In the same year that the APA Division of Health Psychology was founded, many of the same psychologists met to establish the interdisciplinary Society of Behavioral Medicine and the Academy of Behavioral Medicine. The International Society of Behavioral Medicine was founded later, in 1990. Many psychologists belong to one or more of the organizations named above, and attend meetings and conferences that promote learning and cross-fertilization of ideas. They also often belong to various disease-oriented or public health and health promotion organizations that are more focused in particular areas of knowledge or expertise. For instance, in Germany, members of several scientific societies (psychology, medicine and dentistry) have founded an organizational network entitled Psychology and Dentistry (PsyDent) which promotes both interdisciplinary and international work in this field.

Specialty Journals

The creation of specialty journals in health psychology has accompanied and sometimes preceded the establishment of scientific and professional societies. These journals have been

Table 14.1 *Journals with a primary focus in health psychology and behavioral medicine*

Annals of Behavioral Medicine
British Journal of Health Psychology
Gedrag & Gezondheid: Tijdschrift voor Psychologie en Gezondheid
Health Psychology
International Journal of Behavioral Medicine
Journal of Behavioral Medicine
Journal of Clinical Psychology in Medical Settings
Journal of Health Psychology
Journal of Health and Social Behavior
Journal of Occupational Health Psychology
Journal of Psychosomatic Research
Psychology and Health
Psychology, Health and Medicine
Psychological Medicine
Psychosocial Oncology
Psychosomatic Medicine
Psychosomatics
Revista de Psicologia de la Salud
Social Science and Medicine
Zeitschrift fur Gesundheitspsychologie

important in establishing the field of health psychology around the world. They disseminate knowledge that supports an 'evidence-based' practice by health psychologists and thus foster the building of the profession. Landmark journals have been *Health Psychology* in the United States (since 1982) and *Psychology and Health* in Europe (since 1985). Health psychologists also subscribe to a number of scientific and professional journals devoted to health and behavior. Table 14.1 provides a sample of journals whose primary focus is health and behavior. In addition, health psychologists often subscribe to journals related to special areas of study or practice, for example *Pain, Fertility and Sterility, Arthritis Care and Research, Preventive Medicine, Developmental and Behavioral Pediatrics, Journal of Dental Research, Headache, American Journal of Medical Genetics, Patient Education and Counseling, Diabetes Care, American Journal of Public Health, AIDS Education and Prevention, Women's Health Issues, Circulation,* and *British Heart Journal,* to name only a few.

A professional issue faced by many health psychologists is their desire to communicate both to their psychology colleagues and to other health disciplines (e.g., to physicians via medical journals, to policymakers via policy publications). This poses dilemmas in decisions regarding the publication of new findings. The academic world of psychology (and often career advancement) values publication in peer-reviewed *psychology* journals, while acceptance of psychological science by other disciplines requires knowledge dissemination in other discipline mainstreams as well. Use in public policy demands availability in yet other venues.

An especially important issue in the dissemination of knowledge for health psychologists around the world has been the 'language barrier', that is, the predominance of English as the language of publication and internationalization. Because of this, the knowledge that is disseminated in well-known periodicals tends to have an Anglo-Saxon and Western bias. Moreover, health psychologists in less developed countries, or countries where English is not as commonly spoken, tend to publish internally, without good access to this knowledge in mainstream health psychology. Winefield (2001) emphasizes that Asian and European cultures have different norms and expectations about health and behavior that challenge this Anglocentrism in our knowledge base.

RECOGNITION, STANDARD-SETTING AND REGULATION

As a new specialty or profession evolves, so does more formal recognition of its knowledge base and the application of this knowledge to societal problems. The knowledge base is taught to others entering the field, and formal education and training programs soon develop. Standards for education and training shortly follow, along with the credentialing of those who apply this knowledge in practice.

Recognition of the Scientific Knowledge Base

In science, when important areas of knowledge are recognized, not only do journals appear as described above, but funding agencies develop special study sections to evaluate applications

from individual investigators and to support the education and training of new researchers in the areas. For example, the Division of Research Grants at the United States National Institutes of Health developed a behavioral medicine study section in 1977. It is also noteworthy that the first chief of the Behavioral Medicine Branch of the National Heart, Lung, and Blood Institute was a psychologist, reflecting the recognition of the importance of psychology's expertise in studying health and behavior relationships.

In the United States, recognition by the federal government also results in increased research funding which in turn increases the knowledge base. A landmark publication in the history of this development was in 1982 by the Institute of Medicine (*Health and behavior: Frontiers of research in the biobehavioral sciences*, 1982). This report documented the scientific basis for the linkage between behavior and health and stimulated a broad range of research and training activities for the next two decades. The most recent Institute of Medicine report (*Health and behavior: The interplay of biological, behavioral, and societal influences*, 2001) not only updates this prior work but examines the implementation of behavioral interventions and makes recommendations for future research, applications and financing.

Internationally, the World Health Organization (WHO) has been a key player in recognizing the role of psychosocial influences in health. WHO's landmark definition of health as 'a state of complete physical, mental and social well-being, and not merely the absence of disease of infirmity' (World Health Organization, 1946) constituted a pivotal shift in conceptualizing health and health care on the basis of the biopsychosocial paradigm. In Europe, the WHO Regional Office published a document in 1984 that clarified the contribution of psychology to the health field. Other WHO documents continued to highlight the role of psychology in disease prevention and health promotion (e.g., Abelin, Brzezinski & Carstairs, 1987; WHOQOL Group, 1993; World Health Organization, 1991).

WHO has also supported interdisciplinary studies involving multiple countries that have contributed important knowledge of epidemiological patterns and associated psychosocial factors. An example is the WHO–MONICA project (World Health Organization, 2000), which tracked heart attack rates, risk factors, and coronary care in pre-defined populations in 37 countries from the mid 1980s to the mid 1990s, including Australia, Canada, China, USA and several European countries. More recently, through a collaboration between members of the European Health Psychology Society and the European Society of Cardiology, a study that involves the adaptation of instruments in 10 languages and 16 countries is being conducted on the quality of life of patients with coronary heart disease (Hevey, 2001). In these collaborations, the expertise of health psychologists is recognized in the choice of instruments and their cross-cultural validation, and there are opportunities for psychologists to counteract the adoption of overly medical models of quality of life research.

Education and Training

Although there are a variety of models of education and training in psychology throughout the world, there appears to be widespread acceptance of core components in the education and training of health psychologists. Frequently identified components include knowledge and skills related to: (1) biological, cognitive-affective, social and psychological bases of health, disease and behavior, and their interrelationships; (2) health and behavior research methods; (3) ethical, legal and professional issues; (4) program development and evaluation (including primary prevention); (5) management and supervision; (6) health care systems and health policy; and (7) interdisciplinary collaboration. An important component of the latter is learning how to collaborate in research and practice, as well as teach other health professionals. For those students who are training for careers in health service provision, broad education and training in evidence-based health psychology assessment, intervention and consultation are recommended in addition to generic clinical skills (Marks et al., 1998; Stone et al., 1987).

Given the breadth of health psychology, no one can be expert in each and every area; thus more focused curricula can be developed for areas such as pediatric psychology, rehabilitation psychology, pain management, primary prevention, and psychosocial oncology. For example, a more focused curriculum for training in primary care has been published by McDaniel, Belar, Schroeder, Hargrove and Freeman (2002). Given that primary care is the *de facto* health care system for mental and addictive disorders, health psychologists in these settings must have comprehensive knowledge and skills related to a wide variety of services.

Despite agreement on the core domains of knowledge and skills for professional health psychologists, the required level of training for practice varies widely around the world. A good example of this diversity can be found among the countries of the European Community (EC). In an attempt to find a minimum length and a basic framework for qualification required for independent practice as a 'health psychologist', the European Federation of Professional Psychologists Association (EFPPA) created a task force in 1992 that produced general training guidelines. This work accompanies the EuroPsych project that proposes a common framework of 6 years for the title of 'psychologist', corresponding to a master's degree with an additional year of supervised practice (Lunt, 2000). Within Europe there are three main patterns: (1) generic preparation with later specialization (e.g., Norway); (2) early specialization (e.g., Portugal, United Kingdom); and (3) mixed mode (e.g., Netherlands). The most common framework favors more generic training with later specialization and the possibility of psychologists getting 'specialist titles' in clinical psychology, health psychology etc. The EuroPsych project takes place within the context of changes in higher education in Europe, following the 1999 Bologna agreement that favors more commonalities in curricula and more possibilities for student and professional mobility.

Formalized doctoral programs in health psychology are most common in the United States and Canada. With respect to education and training for professional practice, APA accreditation in health psychology is not yet available at the doctoral level, although the Council of Health Psychology Training Directors has promulgated criteria for program standards. APA accreditation is currently available for postdoctoral residencies in clinical health psychology. In fact, health psychology is the third most emphasized area in postdoctoral training in the United States (Stewart & Stewart, 1998).

In Europe, health psychology education has increased dramatically in the last 10 years, although a significant number of countries still do not have formal educational opportunities (McIntyre, Maes, Weinman & Marks, 2001). As noted above, the typical model is the master's degree involving generic training with later specialization. In general, doctoral training consists of an independent course of study resulting in a dissertation. In contrast to the US, the model of training is more scientist than scientist-practitioner or practitioner oriented, with the nature of training focusing more on research and coursework and less on consultation and teaching or training.

The master's level model of training for psychology is prevalent throughout the world. In health psychology there are master's programs in New Zealand that prepare for careers in research and health promotion (Stewart, 2001). Postgraduate diplomas with a focus on practice are offered at the University of Auckland, and in Israel at the Tel Aviv University.

Recognition and Regulation of Practitioners

In the United States, regulation of the practice of psychology is at the state level. Although there are some differences in specific regulations across states, licensure for practice in psychology is mostly generic and at the doctoral level. The National Register of Health Service Providers in Psychology is the national mechanism for credentialing those with health service education and training. As in the practice of medicine, the state does not regulate specialty areas of practice; professionals are ethically bound to practice within their areas of competence. Recognition and certification of specialties and specialists in health care are accomplished through nongovernmental groups such as the American Board of Medical Specialties and the American Board of Professional Psychology (ABPP).

In 1991 health psychology was formally recognized by ABPP as a specialty in professional psychology and examinations for board certification of its practitioners commenced. By 1997, the APA, the largest membership organization of psychologists, had formally recognized clinical health psychology as a specialty in professional practice as well. The term 'clinical' had been added in order not to confuse the public as to which psychologists had obtained education and training in patient-related health care services in addition to their training in health psychology research and consultation. The American Board of Clinical Health Psychology, a member board of ABPP, conducts the examination process for psychologists in the United States who wish to pursue board certification in clinical health psychology. At present, board certification among psychologists is not nearly as common as board certification among medical specialists.

Despite the recognition within the profession, it was not until 2001 that the US federal government recognized the importance of psychology as a health profession. Although all other doctoral health professions had identified programs in the Bureau of Health Professions that supported the education and training of its professionals, it was not until the Graduate Psychology Education program was established that formal recognition of psychology as much broader than a mental health profession was achieved.

In Canada, regulations for practice are at the provincial level, although mobility has been facilitated by the development of a set of core competencies for the profession. However, there is no special registration in health psychology.

In Europe, the regulation of practice in psychology varies across countries. For example, licensing and registration procedures exist in England, Holland and Austria, but not in

Portugal, Italy or Romania. Austria was one of the first countries in Europe to regulate the profession of health psychology. Since 1991 there has been a nationally regulated education for health psychologists as well as legal protection for the title 'health psychologist' (Egger & Schoberberger, 1994).

Perhaps the most demanding criteria in terms of professional qualifications in health psychology in Europe can be found in the United Kingdom. For some years the British Psychological Society (BPS) Board of Examiners for Health Psychology has been developing the minimum qualifications and experience required for membership in the BPS Division of Health psychology, which is the major route for chartered health psychologist status. These qualifications include a master's degree in health psychology, 3 years of supervised practice and the submission of a portfolio of work that demonstrates competence in research, consultancy and teaching/ training (Weinman, 1998).

In Finland, a Post-Graduate Specialist Programme in Health Psychology emerged in 1994 as a conjoint effort of three universities and the UKK Institute of Health Promotion Research. The program gives a specialist diploma in health psychology allowing registration as a health psychologist (Nupponen, 1995). Since 1994 all psychologists are registered under a special law, and health psychologists have to be licensed as both psychologists and specialists.

In Greece, there is no formal specialty certification for practice in psychology, although various proposals for specialty regulations are being considered (Macri, 2001). Licensing specific to health psychology is also a current professional issue in New Zealand, where health psychology is estimated to account for approximately half of the expansion in service, teaching and research activities in psychology (Stewart, 2001). Both New Zealand and Australia regulate the general practice of psychology, and have significant activity in the science and practice of health psychology (Oldenburg & Owen, 1991).

According to Andrade and Bueno (2001), Brazil is the country in South America where psychology is most regulated. It has developed along the European model lines, with increasing interest in health psychology becoming apparent. Traditionally, much prevention work in Latin America has been conducted by other health professionals, but psychologists are becoming increasingly involved in designing and implementing behavioral interventions, such as in the area of prevention of sexually transmitted diseases. This is the case in Bolivia and Brazil (Mays & Moscoso, 1995).

Indian psychology has also been dominated by Euro-American theories and models (Prasadarao & Matam Sudhir, 2001). Although it exists in a culture supporting holistic health approaches, psychologists are primarily working in the area of mental health versus broader health arenas. There is no regulation of practice in India, or in Iran, where the focus is also on traditional mental health issues (Ghobari & Bolhari, 2001).

In Russia, licensure for practice is available, but not required (Balachova, Levy, Isurina & Wasserman, 2001). Psychology in Russia is described as a discipline and profession that has been 'interrupted' in its development by governmental policies. A major professional issue is the right of psychologists to provide psychotherapy for mental health problems, with relatively few expanding services to medical-surgical units/ populations.

Psychology is described as in its infancy in Thailand, with most providers at the bachelor's level of education and training and the profession having less status than nursing and physical therapy (Tapanya, 2001). There is no licensure and the medical model dominates, although psychologists have found work serving those with acquired immunodeficiency syndrome. Tapanya warns that if health psychology is not more fully developed in Thailand soon, those services will be dominated by the nursing profession in the future.

In Africa, the regulation of the profession is proportionate to its development, with South Africa being in the lead (Annandale, 1997). In general, the slow development of psychology as a profession in Africa, and of health psychology in particular, has been related to cultural factors, such as the predominance of traditional medicines and healers in the communities, and the difficulty of going outside the family or community for help (Koinange, 2001). However, there is a rapid change in these attitudes given the increase in health epidemics (e.g., HIV/AIDS) and the inefficiency of traditional avenues for solving these problems. Doors are opening to psychosocial interventions in the health domain that are in partnership with traditional resources and have sensitivity and respect for local customs and values. Kenya, Namibia and Nigeria are examples of countries where the profession of health psychology is emerging and the local psychological associations are trying to regulate it (Annandale, 1997; Obot, 1996).

Along with the United States, health psychology is perhaps most formally recognized in Israel. In addition to its divisional status within the national organization, its section in the national journal, and its formal postgraduate program, its practice has been regulated as a separate specialty area since February 2000, when formally recognized by the Ministry of Health (Jacoby, 2001).

INTERDISCIPLINARY COLLABORATION

As noted above, a core feature of health psychology is interdisciplinary collaboration, whether it is for activities in research, teaching, clinical service, consultation, or administration. Technical expertise is not sufficient for success as a psychologist. Moreover, no one discipline is sufficient for comprehensive health care. Health psychologists work with numerous medical specialties as well as epidemiologists, immunologists, sociologists, health service administrators, neuroscientists, dentists, and so on. Although medicine is the dominant profession in health care services, many other disciplines are also integrally involved (e.g., nursing, physical therapy, occupational therapy).

Auerswald (1968) has described the interdisciplinary approach as a 'putting together of heads' or a bringing together of disciplines to resolve a health problem. In the context of interdisciplinary work, professionals can maintain the views of their own discipline, remain bound to their frame of reference, and attempt to convert colleagues to their viewpoints. Seaburn, Lorenz, Gunn, Gawinski and Mauksch (1996) support an *ecological perspective* to interdisciplinary collaboration. This approach invites professionals to focus on the process of interactions and communication among the professionals, the patient and the family, and fosters the bridging of different conceptual frameworks. Another term commonly used is the interprofessional approach for interprofessional health care. We present below some examples of issues that often arise in the process of collaborating with other disciplines.

There is a continual need for education of other groups about psychology and the unique contribution psychology can make in health research and practice. Experience informs us that we should never take others' understanding of our discipline and profession for granted. Teaching is a core activity for all health psychologists, even in nonacademic settings.

Psychologists have been actively involved in the formal education of other professionals. For example, in 1990, over half of behavioral science family medicine educators were psychologists (Mauksch & Heldring, 1995). In practice, health psychologists often need to teach physicians how to prepare the patient for psychological consultation. Mind–body dualism is prevalent in both patients and health care providers, the result of which can be a hostile patient who feels pressured to prove that physical problems are not due to psychological ones. Use of written materials for the physician and for the patient (e.g., explanatory brochures) can facilitate the process. Table 14.2 provides a sample of phrases found useful for referring physicians. Seeing patients side-by-side with physicians and the provision of on-site services are also common and highly recommended. Training health professionals in communication skills with patients and their families, colleagues and superiors is critical to appropriate management of the consultation and to effective referral, with proven benefits to patient satisfaction and adherence (Kaptein, Appels & Orth-Gómer, 2000; Weinman, 2001).

Health psychologists must also have some understanding of the competencies, thinking

Table 14.2 *Phrasing the referral*

Patients may be resistant to the idea of referral to a psychologist. They may respond by thinking (or saying), 'You think X is all in my head', or 'I'm being dumped.' The following approaches are often more palatable to patients:

A referral for pain or stress management, with the acknowledgement that given the particular condition, pain and stress are often associated and worthy of attention.

A referral for preparation for surgery, acknowledging the importance of psychological preparedness and coping.

A referral for symptom management, so that the use of medicines can be reduced to a minimum.

A referral because of interest in the whole patient, with the recognition that all illnesses have psychological components and that other disciplines have skills to offer that have been helpful in similar cases.

A referral with recognition of the stressors that a medical condition has caused the patient, and his or her family.

Source: adapted from p. 105 in Belar, C. D., & Deardorff, W. (1995). *Clinical health psychology in medical settings: A practitioner's guidebook.* Washington, DC: American Psychological Association.

styles, roles, functions, and sociopolitical issues for the other disciplines with which they work. A notable difference between psychologists and physicians has to do with basic training. Physicians are trained in the application of knowledge; they learn to gather facts in a problem-oriented fashion. Psychologists are trained in science as a method to acquire knowledge; they have a more process-oriented approach to dealing with problems. As noted by McDaniel (1995), because of emphases in content, physicians risk 'somatic fixation' while psychologists risk 'psychosocial fixation'. Another difference in paradigm has been noted by Seaburn and colleagues (1996) and pertains to a theory of change. Physicians tend to take greater responsibility for change, assuming what has been labeled a health care provider-centered approach (Grol, de Maesener, Whitfield & Mokkink, 1990), characterized by limited patient responsibility and involvement in the consultation and the treatment. Based on the biopsychosocial model, health psychologists see the role of the patient as an agent of change and an active participant in information gathering and decision-making. Such differences can lead either group to believe that the other is 'off target' and undermine the relationship-building that is critical to the collaborative relationship. Knowing the collaborator's frame of reference and respecting different viewpoints without taking them personally is conducive to effective collaboration even if professionals come from differing paradigms.

Effective communication is a key ingredient in collaboration. Every discipline has its jargon, and cultural differences in content and style of communication may create barriers to collaboration. The style of communication in medical settings is more concrete and instrumental, whereas psychologists tend to value conceptualization of problems and explanations. These differences are reflected in both verbal and written communications between providers. Interdisciplinary work requires communications devoid of 'psychobabble', a frequent complaint about psychological reports. Even more troublesome is physicians' perceived *lack* of communication from psychologists during and after consultations. This has been empirically documented (Meyer, Fink & Carey, 1988) as well as experienced in our professional life. Psychologists need to communicate promptly, succinctly and with information that is relevant to the problem at hand as well as the consultant's future behavior. After the initial consultation, information about initial assessment and treatment plan should be communicated to the referring provider. Unnecessary personal information or clinical observations/hypotheses do not need to be detailed in reports back to referring physicians. The means of communication is becoming more diversified, from face-to-face to electronic communication, with the latter increasingly replacing the 'old' paper charts despite ethical concerns about issues of confidentiality. A clarification of mutual expectations regarding means and frequency of communication will prevent misunderstandings and foster more effective collaboration. In general, both formal and informal rules and regulations of health care systems must be understood. Formal requirements for communications can differ (e.g., in some hospitals only black ink is acceptable) as do customs in care (e.g., referral practices).

Mutual respect and professionalism are also key ingredients in building collaborative relationships. Clinical health psychologists have expertise in interpersonal relationships that can be applied to differentiate between personal and professional issues and to manage conflict effectively. In working with other disciplines, the ability to deal with the occasional disrespect from other professionals is necessary. Moreover, psychologists rarely have the most power in health care settings, and can sometimes feel (or be treated) as 'second-class citizens'. These power differentials need to be skillfully addressed in maintaining a balance between preserving the psychologist's professional identity, and avoiding territoriality and maintaining hierarchical flexibility. It is important not to be overly defensive; with experience it becomes obvious that conflicts occur among specialties within medicine as well. In fact, psychologists often have more prestige with some physicians than another medical specialty.

From their perspective in South Africa, Miller and Swartz (1990) articulate ways in which psychologists might respond when disadvantaged by a hierarchical health care system. Psychologists might: (1) collude in the devaluation of their own expertise; (2) accept medical authority without question; (3) attempt to acquire power using therapeutic skills; and (4) reproduce the power hierarchy by devaluing lower status professionals. These authors call for explicit acknowledgement and confrontation of power differentials in interprofessional work. We have found that staying focused on the task (patient or problem at hand), consistent assertiveness, confrontation as necessary, empathy, a high frustration tolerance, accessibility, and a wealth of good humor are all necessary in interdisciplinary collaboration. In addition, nothing can substitute for

self-direction and the ability to analyze objectively and critically one's interpersonal relationships in the context of work.

It is important to understand the impact on colleagues of stressors associated with different work settings, whether it is a research university where only grant funding is valued, or a burns unit where close, sustained teamwork in the face of often devastating wounds is critical. The fact that health professions are high risk in terms of job stress has been confirmed by stress audits worldwide (e.g., Firth-Cozens & Payne, 1999; McIntyre, McIntyre, Araújo-Soares, Figueiredo & Johnston, 2000). Psychologists with expertise in group dynamics and team functioning are often called upon to provide services to health care workers related to communications, job stress and burnout (Michie, 2001). Stress management interventions have demonstrated positive outcomes in terms of increases in job satisfaction, and reductions in perceived stress, anxiety and other psychological symptoms, as well as improvement in work performance (Michie, Ridout & Johnston, 1996; Reynolds, Taylor & Shapiro, 1993; Tsai & Crockett, 1993). More social, organizational and political approaches to address the wellbeing of health professionals opens an even more vast opportunity for interdisciplinary collaboration.

With an increased emphasis on evidence-based health care there are more needs for research to support clinical and managerial decision-making. Health psychologists can offer expertise in research methodology and design, and their collaboration in biomedical research teams helps to bring the psychosocial component into the research agenda of other scientists (MacLeod & McCullough, 1994). However, health psychologists who collaborate in interdisciplinary research teams also need to be aware of power differentials and other differences in professional conduct which may affect decisions regarding the use of data, distribution of resources, and diffusion of results. A frequent area of professional conflict is authorship. Ethics in psychology requires authorship in proportion to professional contribution. This is not necessarily the same in other disciplines (e.g., a department chair might be listed on all publications emanating from the faculty). Some physicians have been listed as principal investigators on proposals that have been entirely written by psychologists. Psychologists need to promulgate change in such practices; sometimes revisions in hospital by-laws are needed to permit psychologists to be principal investigators.

There are numerous models for collaboration with other professionals. Psychologists use consultation from other disciplines in the course of research or patient care, and they provide consultation to other investigators and service providers. In addition, they participate as members of interdisciplinary research teams and clinical teams (e.g., organ transplant teams, pain clinic teams). Michie (2001: 155) outlines the following areas of contributions health psychologists make in consulting relationships: (1) understanding the contextual nature of health problems; (2) the systematic analysis of problems and potential solutions; (3) the understanding of change processes that enable recommendations about the best ways of achieving the task or goal identified by the consultee; and (4) research skills that enable the evaluation of services, interventions and changes. Michie notes that clinical health psychologists conduct a lot of informal consultancy work but that they need to promote this role by formally contracting for consultations, and carefully evaluating outcomes. The recent initiative of the British Psychological Society in collecting a portfolio of successful case studies of consultancy work is an example of how professional associations can enhance the role of health psychologists as consultants.

ETHICS

Health psychologists do not have a code of ethics that is separate from other psychologists, but they often confront different issues because of the special settings and patient populations encountered in research and practice. In Africa, Asia and South America, the wide variations in the regulation of the profession mirror the heterogeneity of ethical codes. This diversity is equally prevalent in Europe.

However, with the development of the European Community and the directive that allows psychologists qualified in one EC country to practice in another, EFPPA has considered the possibility of developing a meta-code of ethics for member associations (Lunt, 1993). In the United States, the 'Ethical principles of psychologists and code of conduct' (American Psychological Association, 2002) articulates a framework of principles for the development of more specific ethical standards: competence; integrity; professional and scientific responsibility; respect for people's rights and dignity; and concern for others' welfare. We will use these principles to organize our discussion of ethical issues in health psychology.

Competence

As described in Belar and Deardorff (1995), the issues associated with the principle of competence include appropriateness of education and training, recognition of boundaries of competence, and maintenance of current knowledge. Although many senior health psychologists had no formal education or training in the area, there is now an abundance of knowledge disseminated through books, journals and conferences. In addition, there are education and training programs plus opportunities for supervised practice. Although the availability of these opportunities varies worldwide, it behooves any researcher or practitioner to maintain up-to-date knowledge and to seek consultation or supervision when needed.

To facilitate ethical expansion of practice with respect to competence, Belar et al. (2001) proposed a self-assessment model that practitioners could use to gauge readiness to provide professional services in clinical health psychology. A template of questions is provided to promote the practitioner's understanding of his or her shortcomings in knowledge or skill, along with recommendations for self-study. Table 14.3 lists a series of relevant questions.

Competence also requires the ability to work with people of different backgrounds (e.g., age, gender, race, ethnicity, religion,

Table 14.3   *Template for self-assessment of readiness for delivery of services to patients with medical-surgical problems*

1	Do I have knowledge of the *biological bases of health and disease* as related to this problem? How is this related to the biological bases of behavior?
2	Do I have knowledge of the *cognitive-affective bases of health and disease* as related to this problem? How is this related to the cognitive-affective bases of behavior?
3	Do I have knowledge of the *social bases of health and disease* as related to this problem? How is this related to the social bases of behavior?
4	Do I have knowledge of the *developmental and individual bases of health and* disease as related to this problem? How is this related to developmental and individual bases of behavior?
5	Do I have knowledge of the *interactions* among biological, affective, cognitive, social and developmental components (e.g., psychophysiological aspects)? Do I understand the relationships between this problem and the patient and his/her environment (including family, health care system and sociocultural environment)?
6	Do I have knowledge and skills of the *empirically supported clinical assessment* methods for this problem, and how assessment might be affected by information in areas described by questions 1 through 5?
7	Do I have knowledge of, and skill in implementing, the *empirically supported interventions* relevant to this problem? Do I have knowledge of how the proposed psychological intervention might impact physiological processes and vice versa?
8	Do I have knowledge of the roles and functions of *other health care professionals* relevant to this patient's problem? Do I have skills to communicate and collaborate with them?
9	Do I understand the sociopolitical features of the *health care delivery system* that can impact this problem?
10	Do I understand the *health policy issues* relevant to this problem?
11	Am I aware of the *distinctive ethical issues* related to practice with this problem?
12	Am I aware of the *distinctive legal issues* related to practice with this problem?
13	Am I aware of the special *professional issues* associated with practice with this problem?

Source: from p. 137 in Belar, C. D., Brown, R. A., Hersch, L. E., Hornyak, L. M., Rozensky, R. H., Sheridan, E. P., Brown, R. T., & Reed, G. W. (2001). Self-assessment in clinical health psychology: A model for ethical expansion of practice. *Professional Psychology: Research and Practice, 32,* 135–141. Reprinted with permission of the American Psychological Association.

lifestyle, disability, socioeconomic status). In fact the focus on issues of diversity in health, illness and health care meets an important ethical and scientific concern of the discipline itself, that is, the extent of generalizability of psychological processes, constructs, and models across diverse sociodemographic and cultural groups.

In addition to general aspects of multicultural competence, it is essential that health psychologists understand how culture and ethnicity affect health beliefs, including explanatory frameworks and attitudes toward treatment, as well as participation in research. Landrine and Klonoff (2001) highlight the role of culture and ethnicity in US minority health behavior and morbidity (e.g., weight and dieting among Chinese and Japanese Americans; AIDS risk, knowledge of AIDS transmission, and adherence to medical regimens among Mexican Americans; and smoking, alcohol use and hypertension in African Americans). In

our experience, patients in general health care settings represent a wider cross-section of the population than those found in mental health facilities where psychologists have traditionally worked.

Multicultural competence is as important for the conduct of research. Although there is a significant body of knowledge related to ethnicity and health (Landrine & Klonoff, 2001; Roberts, Towell & Golding, 2001), research is plagued by methodological issues, such as the validity of concepts (e.g. ethnicity, acculturation), subject recruitment, measurement issues related to language and meaning, and confounds related to social issues. Moreover, there is a lack of complex models that tease out the relative weight of social, psychological and cultural variables in health processes. Landrine and Klonoff address some of these issues by proposing a tentative theoretical model of variables in minority health, which includes distal predictors of health outcomes (social status), proximal predictors (acculturation, racial discrimination and distrust of whites), and mediating variables (cultural health beliefs and practices, preventive behaviors, acculturative stress, access to health care, and exposure to carcinogens). Ethical research in health psychology requires attention to needs for multicultural competence.

Competence as an ethical issue often surfaces around psychological assessment in health psychology. Health psychologists use multiple assessment approaches including interview, observation, questionnaires, psychometrics, psychophysiological measurement, health status indices and records research. Ethical problems are especially likely to arise around issues of validity of the instruments used for the problems or groups being considered, the appropriateness of their use and the dissemination of results, and the conditions for administration of the measures (McIntyre, 1996). For example, many of the psychometric tools utilized were originally standardized on mental health populations; interpretations based on these norms are often not appropriate for medical-surgical populations and could lead to inaccurate diagnoses. Psychologists need to be aware of the appropriate norms and interpretations for the instruments they utilize.

In addition, it must be recognized that psychometric tools cannot in and of themselves rule out organic disorders. A common request for psychological assessment occurs when physicians are questioning whether the problem is a medical one, having not been able to determine an organic etiology or having had medical treatments fail. Health psychologists who are eager to prove their usefulness in such a context may accept the physician's formulation and prematurely 'psychologize' the problem. From an ethical point of view, psychologists need sufficient competence in a biopsychosocial knowledge base to be able to negotiate the formulation of the problem with their consultee and refer back to the physician for further medical screening when appropriate.

Other ethical issues regarding competent use of psychometric instruments in health psychology are related to their cross-cultural adaptation and validation in other countries. Most psychological instruments have been developed in English-speaking countries, mainly the US. *Ad hoc* translation of instruments from English into another language (often without the consent of the author or test publishers) and the use of translated versions with unsuitable psychometric properties raise ethical questions in terms of competence, scientific and professional responsibility. Awareness of these issues prompted the 1976 establishment of the International Test Commission (ITC) by Swiss psychologist Jean Cardinet and colleagues; this commission now includes most national psychological societies from Europe and North America (Oakland, 2001). In 1999 the ITC approved guidelines for cross-cultural adaptation of psychological instruments.

When working in health care settings, there is also increased risk of inappropriate use of test results by nonpsychologists. It is not uncommon, especially in countries where psychology is less well developed, that other health professionals ask psychologists to do a 'quick training' on test development or test interpretation so as to learn how to evaluate psychopathology or cognitive development during a typical 15 minute medical consultation. Psychologists need to exercise great caution in these situations.

Ethical issues also arise when consultees communicate the results of psychological evaluations to patients. Psychologists need to educate their consultees as to how to communicate results to patients, if they are not delivered by the psychologist him/ herself. To do this, health psychologists must learn how to translate psychological language into terms that are well understood by nonpsychologists and be conservative in divulging unnecessary information both verbally, and in medical charts and psychological reports.

A final issue of competence relates to personal issues of the psychologist. Although all psychologists are expected to recognize personal problems that may impact professional functioning, special issues can arise in situations that challenge one's own sense of body integrity and mortality as well as core values. The mastectomy patient must not be treated with dismay, or the colostomy patient with disgust. The dying patient must not be addressed fearfully. At a minimum a period of acclimation is needed in practice (Belar, 1980). In addition, clinicians can design their own programs to facilitate dealing with these issues. 'Medical libraries are full of pictures and videos that can provide stimuli for desensitization purposes. Colleagues, supervisors, personal therapists, and families are important resources in dealing with personal issues regarding death, dying, and threats to body integrity' (Belar & Deardorff, 1995: 36). In addition, burnout prevention and recognition should be a part of basic training for all health service providers.

Integrity

The promotion of integrity in the science, teaching and practice of psychology is essential. In highlighting the importance of behavior in health, it is important not to overstate the knowledge base with respect to psychological interventions and permanent changes in health status.

Related to integrity is the imposition of values onto the patient. In this context it is important to remember that health, itself, is a value. Health promotion, primary prevention and interventions to promote adherence to treatment regimens impose the value of health on the patient, and may be viewed as paternalistic and disrespectful of patient autonomy. Moreover, a patient's culture may value some presumably unhealthy behaviors. Health behaviors must never be treated in isolation, but rather understood in the context of the biopsychosocial model and individual differences, with consent for services resting solely with the patient. Roberts et al. make an especially cogent comment on the ethics of health promotion: 'Exhorting people to eat healthily, drink sensibly, refrain from smoking and practice safer sex whilst ignoring the functions which particular behaviors have in people's lives or the situation factors (usually social, economic or emotional) which govern them, is at once both a poor method of promoting

health and an arrogant one ... there is a real danger that empirical issues of how people *do behave* can get turned into moral issues of how they *should behave*' (2001: 140–141). The authors go on to point out the core ethical dilemma of balancing individual freedoms and larger social good.

Integrity also requires that psychologists clarify their roles with all those with whom they work. As stated above, health care settings are often confusing to patients, and third-party requests for services can lead to significant misunderstandings regarding issues of confidentiality and whose needs are being met by the service.

Questions of integrity may be even more complex when the health psychologist's client is a group or organization, such as in a consultancy role. For instance, the definition of the problem by a hospital where management is interested in addressing occupational stress in its employees may be at an individual level, with the intervention requested being conceptualized equally at the individual level, such as through a stress management course. However, as Bohle states, 'Interventions of this nature imply that the problem of stress lies primarily with the individual, that the responsibility for change consequently lies primarily with workers, and that organizations are only responsible for assisting individual workers to change ... Since no attempt is made to reduce or remove environmental stressors, interventions can best be seen as attempts to increase workers' tolerance of noxious and stressful organizational, task and role characteristics' (1993: 111). The health psychologist needs to be aware of the implications of such problem definition and intervention strategy chosen. Questions such as who is the client, the formal and informal agendas involved, the people who will be involved in the process of consultation and how the results will be handled, are delicate matters that require professionalism and skillful work on the part of the health psychologist. Preserving professional integrity in the face of political pressures and hidden agendas is a challenge that health psychologists need to negotiate in a manner that is congruent with one's beliefs and the ethical standards of the profession.

Professional and Scientific Responsibility

Responsibility mandates assurance of quality services, which requires quality assessment. Health care systems have developed quality of care indicators to satisfy requirements for accreditation, and there are often peer review systems in place. Of difficulty for health psychologists in these settings is the relevance of these indicators to their practice, and the availability of a qualified reviewer in health psychology. Psychologists often need to apply their own outcome measures to assess their quality of care and service. They can also establish study groups and peer consultation models, mechanisms that have been greatly facilitated by electronic communications. Michie (2001) points out that psychologists need to promote a scientific approach to service evaluation that includes the definition of measurable objectives and clear outcome criteria related to health status of service recipients, staff or patient satisfaction, financial savings or provider adherence to practice guidelines. The evidence gathered by this careful outcome evaluation is in establishing health psychology as a health profession for the twenty-first century and as a key partner in meeting the rapid changes that characterize health and health care.

There is little doubt that in working with patients with medical problems, health psychologists experience increased responsibility for physical health issues. They are often the first to hear of medical complications or failures in adherence in the treatment regimen. They need to refer appropriately, and be aware of signs and symptoms in order to communicate directly with other health care providers.

Another threat to professional responsibility is related to the increased segmentation of health care. Multiple specialists can practice with a narrow focus, and the patient can fall through the cracks. Even within an interdisciplinary team, the sense of shared responsibility for the patient can result in a diffusion of responsibility among health professionals. Informed consent, treatment planning and coordination, follow-up and communication with other professionals can suffer when so many aspects of care occur simultaneously.

Psychologists need to be vigilant regarding communications and follow-up.

Respect of People's Rights and Dignity

As noted before, psychologists need to work competently and in a nonbiased fashion with a diverse population. Awareness of the health beliefs and practices of an individual, a group or a community is essential for intervening in a way that is sensitive to the client's values and frame of reference. In terms of cultural sensitivity, this may mean incorporating into the definition of the health problem the language of the recipient (e.g., *nervos* (nerves) for the Brazilian rather than 'anxiety') and framing the intervention in a way that is consistent with those beliefs (e.g., *acalmar os nervos* (calm the nerves) instead of 'relaxation training') or that integrates traditional medicine and folk medicine (e.g., interest in the patient's folk health practices, *curandeiro,* and acceptance of their complementary or parallel usefulness). Awareness in terms of gender, job status or age requires an additional recognition of the real discrimination that exists in access to health care for certain disadvantaged groups. The social inequalities in health have to be taken into consideration when intervening with these clients as well as with health care providers.

Confidentiality has special challenges in health psychology related to the interdisciplinary nature of practice, the multiple contexts in which sensitive information circulates, and the multiple roles that health psychologists may play (clinical, consulting, educational etc.). When communicating results in a medical chart, the clinician needs to be aware that it may be more widely circulated than a less available psychological record. Discussions with patients in multiple-bed hospital rooms, case discussion in a multidisciplinary team, and communications with the patient's family require the exercise of good clinical judgment; the information reported should be directly relevant to the referral question, treatment or problem at hand. Practitioners should strive to protect confidentiality while informing consumers of associated limits.

Ethical issues also surface regarding patients' rights to information about their health problem and treatment and their understanding of communications with other health care providers. Communications at a level that cannot be understood violate those rights, and preferences of family members and other health professionals as well as cultural differences can present knotty clinical problems in patients asserting these rights.

Concern for Others' Welfare

Concern for others' welfare can conflict with values of confidentiality. For example, confidentiality regarding a patient's HIV infection can conflict with the welfare of an unsuspecting sexual partner. Psychologists working with infectious diseases need to know the level of risk associated with various behaviors. They also need to understand relevant legal standards, consult with colleagues, and document the decision-making process in either maintaining or breaking confidentiality.

Psychologists are also expected to safeguard a consumer of psychological services from exploitation. This requires informed consent and avoidance of conflicts of interest. In addition to informed consent for psychological services, health psychologists also deal with issues of informed consent for services that are provided by other caregivers. They may be requested to assess patient capacity to make rational decisions without coercion. Most often they are involved in assessing patient understanding of information related to an anticipated treatment (e.g., lung transplantation and subsequent needs for lifelong immunosuppressive medication). They may also work with patients to encourage behaviors (e.g., questioning) that enhance informed consent, or help patients deal with feelings of uncertainty that can arise subsequent to informed consent procedures themselves. Once again, understanding of cultural and individual differences is essential to this undertaking.

Conflicting interests can occur in the delivery of health care. For example, a patient may desire to enter a pain rehabilitation program, but the psychologist is hired by the program to screen out inappropriate candidates. Sometimes third parties with other priorities request consultations (e.g., staff want the psychologist to 'talk a patient into treatment' or 'get rid' of the patient by identifying psychopathology; a physician desires to make use of a volunteered kidney; family members want to ensure patient compliance to a medical regimen). Nothing can substitute for clarifying roles and identifying potential conflicts of interest in the informed consent process. Documentation of these issues is also essential.

In research, patients in a psychological study may not understand its relationship to their medical treatment. Special care needs to be taken not to use the physician–patient relationship to coerce patients into participation. It is often necessary to reassure potential participants that ongoing medical treatment will not be jeopardized by their refusal to participate.

TRENDS AND NEW DIRECTIONS

The development of a profession stands on the accumulation of a distinct body of knowledge, organizational structures that support professional development, and the existence of a market base. Despite some skepticism (e.g., Salmon, 1994), it is undeniable that health psychology has established scientific evidence for the role of psychological factors in health, illness and health care, and for the application of this knowledge to improve health status, improve quality of health care, and reduce medical costs. Psychological interventions in the domains of chronic and terminal illnesses, adherence to medical regimens, preparation for medical procedures, psychophysiological disorders, lifestyle change and stress management programs, and prevention programs at school, the workplace and through local communities are some of the classical avenues for the profession of health psychologist. However, with the passage of time, the occurrence of events and the development of knowledge, new areas emerge for both scientific inquiry and professional practice; other areas become more societally relevant and receive increased focus. As the profession changes, new professional issues surface or become more salient. New challenges become new opportunities. Concerns are often never settled, but they must be addressed. Some of the trends that we believe will impact future professional issues in health psychology are as follows:

1 expansion in the area of consultancy, especially to groups, organizations and governments regarding health and behavior, behavior change, and related research methodologies

2 increased emphasis on teaching and training of other health professionals in communication skills, team functioning, patient-centered care, and behavioral/lifestyle interventions

3 expansion in practice with changes in education and training, e.g., medication prescription

4 further subspecialization in practice, with increased tensions related to depth versus breadth in training

5 increased use of human factors engineering in health care system design

6 increased demand for psychological knowledge and expertise in addressing the clinical, ethical and social problems related to new developments and technologies in medicine, such as assisted reproductive technologies, genetics, life-support technologies, informatics

7 increased demands for complex decision-making by providers and patients

8 increased availability of information that promotes consumer choice

9 increased demand for evidence-based practices throughout health care with a concomitant need for behavioral research, e.g., quality of life, as a core aspect of evidence

10 increased emphasis in practice on new groups and problems as the population shifts, as events transpire, and as the profession is more sensitive to issues of diversity (e.g., elderly, poor, minorities, refugees, bisexuals, unemployed)

11 increased focus on global health problems related to war, terrorism and infectious diseases.

The trend toward globalization presents a special challenge to health psychology. As Roberts and colleagues (2001) note, health psychology as a science and profession has been highly Westernized and directed towards resolving health issues in richer countries, often failing to address more global health problems. They state: 'the future of health psychology may be short-lived if the individual and social realms do not stand in closer relation' (2001: 259). This implies moving from an individual/family clinical focus in health psychology to a more global socioeconomic and community focus. Bridging the gap between the Eastern and Western worlds and assuming a global perspective is also a matter of social responsibility for health psychology as a discipline and a profession.

REFERENCES

Abelin, T., Brzezinski, Z., & Carstairs, D. (Eds.) (1987). *Measurement in health promotion and protection.* Copenhagen: World Health Organization.

Aboud, F. (2001). Health psychology program prepares students for international service. *Psychology International, 12,* 4–5.

American Psychological Association (2002). Ethical principles of psychologists and code of conduct. *American Psychologist, 57,* 1060–1073.

Andrade, V., & Bueno, O. (2001). Medical psychology in Brazil. *Journal of Clinical Psychology in Medical Settings, 8,* 9–13.

Annandale, W. (1997). Country profile: Namibia. *Psychology International, 8,* 1–9.

Auerswald, E. (1968). Interdisciplinary versus ecological approach. *Family Process, 7,* 202–215.

Balachova, T., Levy, S., Isurina, G., & Wasserman, L. (2001). Medical psychology in Russia. *Journal of Clinical Psychology in Medical Settings, 8,* 61–68.

Belar, C. D. (1980). Training the clinical psychology student in behavioral medicine. *Professional Psychology: Research and Practice, 11,* 620–627.

Belar, C. D., Brown, R. A., Hersch, L. E., Hornyak, L. M., Rozensky, R. H., Sheridan, E. P., Brown, R. T., & Reed, G. W. (2001). Self-assessment in clinical health psychology: A model for ethical expansion of practice. *Professional Psychology: Research and Practice, 32,* 135–141.

Belar, C. D., & Deardorff, W. (1995). *Clinical health psychology in medical settings: A practitioner's guidebook.* Washington, DC: American Psychological Association.

Belar, C. D., McIntyre, T. M., & Matarazzo, J. D. (2003). Health psychology. In D. K. Freedheim (Ed.), *Handbook of psychology: History of psychology* (Vol. 1, pp. 451–464). New York: Wiley.

Bohle, P. (1993). Work psychology and the management of occupational health and safety: An historical overview. In M. Quinlan (Ed.), *Work and health: The origins, management and regulation of occupational illness* (pp. 92–115). Melbourne: Macmillan Education.

Egger, J., & Schoberberger, R. (1994). Austria. *Newsletter of the European Health Psychology Society, 9,* 5–9.

Firth-Cozens, J., & Payne, R. (Eds.) (1999). *Stress in health professionals: Psychological and organizational causes and interventions.* New York: Wiley.

Ghobari, B., & Bolhari, J. (2001). The current state of medical psychology in Iran. *Journal of Clinical Psychology in Medical Settings, 8,* 39–43.

Grol, R., de Maesener, J., Whitfield, M., & Mokkink, H. (1990). Diseased-centred versus patient-centred attitudes: Comparison of general practitioners in Belgium, Britain and The Netherlands. *Family Practice, 7,* 100–104.

Hevey, D. (2001). Measuring change: Developing health-related quality of life (HRQOL) instruments for use in cardiac populations across Europe. In H. McGee (Chair), *The Potential of Health Psychology in Cardiovascular Diseases Management.* Symposium conducted at the 15th Conference of the European Health Psychology Society, St Andrews, Scotland.

Institute of Medicine (1982). *Health and behavior: Frontiers of research in the biobehavioral sciences.* Washington, DC: National Academy Press.

Institute of Medicine (2001). *Health and behavior: The interplay of biological, behavioral, and societal influences.* Washington, DC: National Academy Press.

Jacoby, R. (2001). Medical psychology in Israel. *Journal of Clinical Psychology in Medical Settings, 8,* 45–50.

Kaptein, A., Appels, A., & Orth-Gómer, K. (Eds.) (2000). *Psychology in medicine.* Houten, The Netherlands: Bohn Stafleu Van Loghum.

Koinange, J. W. (2001). Psychology strides forward in Kenya. *Psychology International, 12,* 1–3.

Landrine, H., & Klonoff, E. (2001). Cultural diversity and health psychology. In A. Baum, T. Revenson & J. Singer (Eds.), *Handbook of health psychology* (pp. 851–891). Mahwah, NJ: Erlbaum.

Lunt, I. (1993). European unification creates tensions within federation of psychologists. *Psychology International, 4,* 1–4.

Lunt, I. (2000). Europsych project funded by the European Union (EU) under Leonardo da Vinci program. *European Psychologist, 5,* 162–164.

MacLeod, S., & McCullough, H. (1994). Social science as a component of medical training. *Social Science and Medicine, 39,* 1367–1373.

Macri, I. (2001). Medical psychology in Greece. *Journal of Clinical Psychology in Medical Settings, 8,* 27–30.

Marks, D., Brucher-Albers, C., Donker, F., Jepsen, Z., Rodriguez-Marin, J., Sidot, S., & Backman, B. (1998). Health Psychology 2000: The development of professional health psychology. European Federation of Professional Psychologists' Associations (EFPA) Task Force on Health Psychology Final Report. *Journal of Health Psychology, 3,* 149–160.

Mauksch, L., & Heldring, M. (1995). Behavioral scientists' views on work environment, roles and teaching. *Family Medicine, 27,* 103–108.

Mays, V., & Moscoso, M. (1995). AIDS pandemic burdens developing world. *Psychology International, 6* (1), 6–7.

McDaniel, S. H. (1995). Collaboration between psychologists and family physicians: Implementing the biopsychosocial model. *Professional Psychology: Research and Practice, 26,* 117–122.

McDaniel, S. H., Belar, C. D., Schroeder, C., Hargrove, D. S., & Freeman, E. L. (2002). A training curriculum for professional psychologists in primary care. *Professional Psychology: Research and Practice, 33,* 65–72.

McIntyre, T. (1996). Ética e avaliação psicológica em Psicologia da Saúde: Algumas questões e reflexões [Ethics and psychological evaluation in health psychology: Some questions and reflections]. In L. Almeida et al. (Eds.), *Avaliação psicológica: Formas e contextos* [Psychological evaluation: Types and contexts] (pp. 671–678). Braga, Portugal: Apport.

McIntyre, T., Maes, S., Weinman, J., & Marks, D. (2001). EHPS Survey on Education and Training in Health Psychology in Europe. In J. Weinman (Chair), *Developing education and training programs in health psychology in Europe: From the present to the future.* Round Table conducted at the 15th Conference of The European Health Psychology Society, St Andrews, Scotland.

McIntyre, T. M., McIntyre, S. E., Araújo-Soares, V., Figueiredo, M., & Johnston, D. (2000). Psychophysiological and psychosocial indicators of the efficacy of a stress management program for health professionals: Phase I. In T. Cox, P. Dewe, K. Nielsen & R. Cox (Eds.), *Occupational health psychology: Europe 2000* (pp. 112–116). Nottingham: European Academy of Occupational Health Psychology Conference Proceedings Series.

Meyer, J. D., Fink, C. M., & Carey, P. F. (1988). Medical views of psychological consultation. *Professional Psychology: Research and Practice, 19,* 356–358.

Michie, S. (2001). Consultancy. In D. W. Johnston & M. Johnston (Eds.), *Health psychology* (pp. 153–170). Oxford: Elsevier.

Michie, S., Ridout, K., & Johnston, M. (1996). Stress in nursing and patient's satisfaction with health care. *British Journal of Nursing, 5,* 1002–1006.

Miller, T., & Swartz, L. (1990) Clinical psychology in general hospital settings: Issues in interprofessional relationships. *Professional Psychology: Research and Practice, 21,* 48–53.

Nupponen, R. (1995). Finnish post-graduate specialist programme in health psychology. *EHPS Newsletter, 10,* 12.

Oakland, T. (2001). Organization profile: International Test Commission. *Psychology International, 12,* 6.

Obot, I. (1996). Country profile: Nigeria. *Psychology International, 7,* 4–5.

Oldenburg, B., & Owen, N. (1991). Health psychology in Australia. In M. A. Jansen & J. Weinman (Eds.), *The international development of health psychology* (pp. 53–61). Chur, Switzerland: Harwood Academic.

Prasadarao, P., & Matam Sudhir, P. (2001) Clinical psychology in India. *Journal of Clinical Psychology in Medical Settings, 8,* 31–38.

Reynolds, S., Taylor, E., & Shapiro, D. (1993). Session impact and outcome in stress management training. *Journal of Community and Applied Social Psychology, 3,* 325–337.

Roberts, R., Towell, T., & Golding, J. (2001). *Foundations of health psychology.* New York: Palgrave.

Salmon, P. (1994). Is health psychology a profession or can it become one? First ask the right questions. *The Psychologist, 7,* 542–544.

Seaburn, D., Lorenz, A., Gunn, J., Gawinski, B., & Mauksch, L. (1996). *Models of collaboration.* New York: Basic.

Stewart, A. E., & Stewart, E. A. (1998). Trends in postdoctoral education: Requirements for licensure and training opportunities. *Professional Psychology: Research and Practice, 29,* 273–283.

Stewart, M. (2001). Medical psychology in New Zealand. *Journal of Clinical Psychology in Medical Settings, 8,* 51–59.

Stone, G. C., Weiss, S. M., Matarazzo, J. D., Miller, N. E., Rodin, J., Belar, C. D., & Follick, M. J. (Eds.) (1987). *Health psychology: A discipline and a profession.* Chicago, IL: University of Chicago Press.

Tapanya, S. (2001). Psychology in medical settings in Thailand. *Journal of Clinical Psychology in Medical Settings, 8,* 69–72.

Tsai, S. L., & Crockett, S. M. (1993). Effects of relaxation training, combining imagery and meditation on the stress level of Chinese nurses working in modern hospitals in Taiwan. *Issues in Mental Health, 14,* 51–66.

Weinman, J. (1998). Development and current status of health psychology in the United Kingdom. In T. McIntyre (Chair), *The state of health psychology in Europe: Education and practice.* Symposium conducted at the 12th Conference of The European Health Psychology Society, Vienna, Austria.

Weinman, J. (2001). Health care. In D. W. Johnston & M. Johnston (Eds.), *Health psychology* (pp. 79–112). Oxford: Elsevier.

WHOQOL Group (1993). *Measuring quality of life: The development of the World Health Organization Quality of Life Instrument (WHOQOL).* Geneva: WHO.

Winefield, H. (2001). Teaching and training other health disciplines. In D. W. Johnston & M. Johnston (Eds.), *Health psychology* (pp. 171–188). Oxford: Elsevier.

World Health Organization (1946). *World Health Organization Constitution.* Geneva: WHO.

World Health Organization (1991). *Supportive environments for health: The Sundsvall statement.* Geneva: WHO.

World Health Organization (2000). Prevention and treatment: Both work, says WHO study on heart disease. Press Release WHO/10, 28 February 2000.

Index

DATE DUE